CASES
IN
CONSTITUTIONAL LAW
Summaries and Critiques

James V. Calvi and Susan Coleman

West Texas A&M University
A Member of The Texas A&M University System

PRENTICE HALL, *Englewood Cliffs, New Jersey 07632*

Library of Congress Cataloging-in-Publication Data

Calvi, James V., (date)
    Cases in constitutional law : summaries and critiques / James
V. Calvi and Susan Coleman.
      p.   cm.
    Includes index.
    ISBN 0-13-177346-1
    1. United States--Constitutional law--Digests.   I. Coleman, Susan
E. II. Title.
KF4547.8.C36   1994
342.73'00264--dc20
[347.3020264]
                                93-26954
                                    CIP

Editor-in-Chief: CHARLYCE JONES OWEN
Editorial/production supervision, interior design, and
  electronic page makeup: ELIZABETH BEST
Copy Editor: ANDREA K. HAMMER
Cover Designer: RAY LUNDGREN GRAPHICS LTD.
Production Coordinator: MARY ANN GLORIANDE
Editorial Assistant: NICOLE SIGNORETTI

To Jerry L. Polinard
with friendship and gratitude–JVC
and
To my family–SC

© 1994 Prentice-Hall, Inc.
A Paramount Communications Company
Englewood Cliffs, New Jersey 07632

Printed in the United States of America

10 9 8 7 6 5 4 3 2 1

ISBN 0-13-177346-1

Prentice-Hall International (UK) Limited, *London*
Prentice-Hall of Australia Pty. Limited, *Sydney*
Prentice-Hall Canada Inc., *Toronto*
Prentice-Hall Hispanoamericana, S.A., *Mexico*
Prentice-Hall of India Private Limited, *New Delhi*
Prentice-Hall of Japan, Inc., *Tokyo*
Simon & Schuster Asia Pte. Ltd., *Singapore*
Editora Prentice-Hall do Brasil, Ltda., *Rio de Janeiro*

CONTENTS

PREFACE, ix

CHAPTER 1—JUDICIAL POWER, 1

INTRODUCTION, 1

The Scope of Judicial Power, 2
Federal Courts and the States, 5
Conclusion, 7

Marbury v. Madison, 7
Ex parte Milligan, 10
Ex parte McCardle, 12
Frothingham v. Mellon and Massachusetts v. Mellon, 14
Chisholm v. Georgia, 16
Fletcher v. Peck, 19
Martin v. Hunter's Lessee, 20
Cohens v. Virginia, 23

CHAPTER 2—FEDERALISM, 26

INTRODUCTION, 26

State Powers under the Constitution, 27
National Powers under the Constitution, 30

Conclusion, 31

   Calder v. Bull, 32
   McCulloch v. Maryland, 33
   The Trustees of Dartmouth College v. Woodward, 36
   Lochner v. New York, 38
   Home Building & Loan Association v. Blaisdell, 40
   West Coast Hotel, Co. v. Parrish, 43
   Munn v. Illinois, 45
   Knox v. Lee and Parker v. Davis: The Legal Tender Cases:, 47
   Missouri v. Holland, 50
   McGrain v. Daugherty, 52
   Adkins v. Children's Hospital, 53
   South Carolina v. Katzenbach, Attorney General, 56

CHAPTER 3—SEPARATION OF POWERS, 59

INTRODUCTION, 59

   Direct Confrontations, 60
   The Scope of Constitutional Powers, 62
   Problems of Encroachment, 63
   Conclusion, 66

   Luther v. Borden, 66
   Mississippi v. Johnson, 68
   Powell v. McCormack, 69
   The Prize Cases, 72
   Korematsu v. United States, 75
   Youngstown Sheet and Tube Co. v. Sawyer, 77
   United States v. Curtiss-Wright Corporation, 80
   United States v. Nixon, 82
   Myers v. United States, 84
   Buckley v. Valeo, 87
   Bowsher v. Synar, 91
   Morrison v. Olson, 94
   Immigration and Naturalization Service v. Chadha, 98

CHAPTER 4—THE COMMERCE POWER, 101

INTRODUCTION, 101

   Federal-State Regulation of Commerce, 102
   The Scope of the Commerce Power, 104
   Conclusion, 107

Gibbons v. Ogden, 107
Cooley v. Board of Wardens of the Port of Philadelphia, 110
Houston, East and West Texas Railway Co. v. United States,
  (The Shreveport Rate Case), 112
Schechter Poultry Corporation v. United States, 114
Southern Pacific Co. v. Arizona, 116
United States v. E. C. Knight Co., 119
Champion v. Ames, 121
Hammer v. Dagenhart, 123
National Labor Relations Board v. Jones & Laughlin Steel
  Corporation, 126
United States v. Darby Lumber Co., 129
Wickard v. Filburn, 131
Heart of Atlanta Motel, Inc., v. United States, 133
National League of Cities v. Usery, 135
Garcia v. San Antonio Mass Transit Authority, 138

CHAPTER 5—THE TAXING POWER, 141

INTRODUCTION, 141

Taxing and Revenue Raising, 142
Taxing and Regulation, 144
Conclusion, 145

Collector v. Day, 146
Pollock v. Farmers' Loan & Trust Company, 147
Frothingham v. Mellon and *Massachusetts v. Mellon, 150*
Flast v. Cohen, 152
McCray v. United States, 155
Bailey v. Drexel Furniture C., 157
J. W. Hampton, Jr., Co. v. United States, 159
United States v. Butler, 161
South Dakota v. Dole, 164

CHAPTER 6—FREEDOM OF RELIGION, 166

INTRODUCTION, 166

The Establishment Clause, 167
The Free Exercise Clause, 169
Conclusion, 171

Mueller v. Allen, 172
Zorach v. Clauson, 173
Engle v. Vitale, 175

Abington School District v. Schempp, 177
Edwards v. Aguillard, 180
West Virginia State Board of Education v. Barnette, 182
Sherbert v. Verner, 184
Wisconsin v. Yoder, 187

CHAPTER 7—FREEDOM OF SPEECH, PRESS, AND ASSOCIATION, 190

INTRODUCTION, 190

Freedom of Speech, 191

Freedom of the Press, 193

Freedom of Association, 195

Conclusion,198

Schenck v. United States, 198
Gitlow v. People of the State of New York, 199
Texas v. Johnson, 201
Near v. State of Minnesota, 203
New York Times Co. v. United States, 206
New York Times Co. v. Sullivan, 209
Roth v. United States, 211
Miller v. California, 213
Paris Adult Theatre I v. Slaton, 216
Whitney v. People of State of California, 218
Dennis v. United States, 220
Pennsylvania v. Nelson, 223
Watkins v. United States, 225
*National Association for the Advancement of Colored People
    v. Alabama, 228*
Barenblatt v. United States, 229

CHAPTER 8—THE RIGHTS OF THE ACCUSED, 233

INTRODUCTION, 233

Search and Seizure, 235

Right to Councel and Self-Incrimination, 236

Cruel and Unusual Punishment, 237

Conclusion, 239

Hurtado v. California, 239
Palko v. Connecticut, 241
Duncan v. Louisiana, 242
Rochin v. California, 244
Adamson v. California, 247
Katz v. United States, 249

Terry v. Ohio, 252
New Jersey v. T. L.O., 254
Mapp v. Ohio, 257
United States v. Leon, 259
Miranda v. Arizona, 262
Powell v. Alabama, 264
Gideon v. Wainwright, 266
Robinson v. California, 268
Gregg v. Georgia, 270
Woodson v. North Carolina, 271
McCleskey v. Kemp, 273
Stanford v. Kentucky, 277

CHAPTER 9—CONSTITUTIONAL RIGHTS, 280

INTRODUCTION, 280

Rights in a Federal System, 280

Racial Discrimination, 282

Gender-Based Discrimination, 284

Political and Economic Discrimination, 285

Privacy and Personal Autonomy, 287

Conclusion, 288

    Barron v. Baltimore, 289
    Dred Scott v. Sandford, 290
    The Slaughterhouse Cases, 294
    The Civil Rights Cases, 297
    Plessy v. Ferguson, 300
    Brown v. Board of Education of Topeka, 302
    Shelley v. Kraemer, 303
    Swann v. Charlotte-Mecklenburg Board of Education, 304
    Regents of the University of California v. Bakke, 306
    City of Richmond, Virginia v. J. A. Croson Co., 309
    Frontiero v. Richardson, 312
    Craig v. Boren, 314
    Johnson v. Transportation Agency, Santa Clara, California, 317
    Baker v. Carr, 319
    Reynolds v. Sims, 322
    Edwards v. California, 325
    Shapiro v. Thompson, 326
    San Antonio Independent School District v. Rodriguez, 329
    Griswold v. Connecticut, 332
    Roe v. Wade, 335
    Webster v. Reproductive Health Services, 339

Bowers v. Hardwick, 343
*Cruzan by Cruzan v. Director, Missouri Department
of Health*, 345
National Treasury Employees Union v. Von Raab, 349

APPENDIX–CONSTITUTION OF THE UNITED STATES, 351

TABLE OF CASES, 363

PREFACE

As college instructors who have taught constitutional and criminal law for many years, we are well aware that students struggle to understand Supreme Court opinions. One problem, especially with the cases from the nineteenth century, is that students find it difficult to understand the archaic language used by some justices. Language and writing styles change and were very different from what students are accustom to today. Another problem is the inability of some students to grasp the subtleties and nuances of an opinion. Even persons who have read these Supreme Court cases several times are amazed to discover new insights upon reading them again. A student reading them for the first time, like one who reads Shakespeare for the first time, needs guidance to receive the full benefit of the decisions. Finally, the process of studying constitutional law is not unlike putting together a jigsaw puzzle: until you have enough pieces put together, it is impossible to see how the cases fit together. It is our desire that this book, especially in the introductory essays, will contribute to the process of piecing together the cases.

We hope that our selection of cases is viewed favorably, although we have never known two constitutional law teachers to reach perfect agreement on the cases that should be covered. We wanted the cases to be ones on which there was a consensus that they were landmark cases or destined to become one. We also hope that our decision to include every dissenting and concurring opinion is met with general approval. Our major goal is to make the covered cases easy for the layperson to understand. Justice Hugo L. Black once remarked that he tried to write his opinions so that ordinary people could understand them. We could do worse than to emulate Justice Black.

The procedure we used to summarize the cases is as follows: First, we provided a background section to furnish the student with information needed to understand the constitutional controversy. Second, we tried to frame a concise question formulating the constitutional question being asked of the court. Third, we summarized the majority plurality, or *seriatim* opinions. Fourth, we summarized all of the concurring and dissenting opinions. Fifth, we explained what we believed to be the significance of the case. Sixth, we provided a series of discussion questions to stimulate critical thinking and further discussion. Finally, we included a list of other related cases to illustrate how the summarized case compares with other Supreme Court decisions handed down before and since.

It is our hope that **CASES IN CONSTITUTIONAL LAW: SUMMARIES AND CRITIQUES** will serve as a learning tool for students struggling to understand constitutional law. We do not intend for our summaries to serve as a substitute for reading the actual case, although we are not naive enough to think that will not happen. Rather, we want this book to be a first step toward understanding the richness of our Constitution as interpreted through Supreme Court decisions. We also hope that this book will appeal to the non-student who merely wishes to know more about our constitutional heritage. As every author must, we shall leave it to our readers to decide if we have succeeded.

We wish to thank the people who helped make this book possible. We thank our families who provided love, understanding, support, and encouragement throughout the project. We wish to thank our colleagues in the Department of History and Political Science at West Texas A&M University for the congenial atmosphere they provide. A special note of thanks goes out to Marilyn Smith and Michael A. Raines of the Department. Marilyn read the page proofs and as any author knows, there comes a time when it is impossible to detect your own mistakes. Michael labored mightily on the Table of Cases checking legal citations and correcting our errors. We also wish to thank the professors for graciously reviewing the manuscript: Paul R. Benson, Jr., *The Citadel*, David S. Calihan, *Longwood College*, and Randall W. Bland, *Southwest Texas State University*. Although we may not have always agreed with their assessments, they perform for institutions an invaluable service, as Justice Holmes observed, of forcing us to question our own principles.

The gracious people at Prentice Hall are deserving of our thanks as well. We wish to thank Charlyce Jones Owen, editor-in-chief, and former political science editor Karen Horton for initially approving the project. We also want to thank Julia Berrisford who helped to rejuvenate the project during a period when it seemed to falter. Our special thanks goes to Nicole Signoretti who inherited us from Karen and Julia and saw us through the final stages. Elizabeth Best served as production editor and did an excellent job in addition to always being there when we needed her. Finally, our copy editor, Andrea K. Hammer, who did a wonderful job of keeping us focused and clarifying our thoughts.

1

JUDICIAL POWER

INTRODUCTION

Article III of the U.S. Constitution states, "The judicial power of the United States shall be vested in one Supreme Court, and in such inferior courts as the Congress may from time to time ordain and establish." Section 2 of the same article declares, "The judicial power shall extend to all cases, in law and equity, arising under this Constitution, the laws of the United States, and treaties made, or which shall be made, under their authority;..." Section 2 continues by defining federal judicial power in terms of specific kinds of cases and parties. For example, admiralty and maritime cases fall within the jurisdiction of the federal courts. In addition, if certain parties, such as a state or foreign ambassador, are involved, federal courts have jurisdiction in the case.

Like many parts of the Constitution, Article III is vague about the scope of judicial power. Therefore, it has been necessary for the Supreme Court to clarify the extent of the judicial power through its interpretation of the Constitution. Although Congress and the president are free to interpret their own powers under the Constitution, their interpretations are subject to judicial review by federal courts. However, the Supreme Court's interpretations of its powers under the Constitution are not subject to review. Unless the Court reverses itself or a constitutional amendment is passed, its interpretation of the Constitution is final. It is only the Court's own sense of self-restraint that limits judicial power.

Cases that define the judicial power fall into two categories. The first category is the scope of judicial power. Because of the vagueness of the judicial article, the federal courts had to establish just what was meant by the "judicial power of the United States."

Note: All cases discussed at length appear in capitals.

The Supreme Court has tended to waver between judicial activism and judicial restraint. Judicial activism asserts that the Court should take an active or positive role in public policy making. Judicial activists maintain that courts have an affirmative duty to intervene whenever the rights of an individual are at stake. Advocates of judicial restraint point out that judges, especially federal judges, are not elected. Public policy should only be made by the elected representatives of the people. Except in those rare cases in which a public policy clearly conflicts with the Constitution, judges should refrain from overruling the people's representatives.

The second category concerns the relationship between federal courts and state courts. In the early years of the United States the federal courts were the newcomers. Local courts had long been established in the colonies, and when the colonies became states, each state organized its own court system. Under the Articles of Confederation each state assumed the status of a sovereign nation. As a result, judges of state courts were used to their own judicial system, which was free from outside control. With the introduction of a national court system, it was unclear to some whether the state courts were to become subordinate to the federal courts or retain their autonomy. The whole question of federal-state court relations was exacerbated by the issue of slavery. Southern states especially feared how the federal judiciary might interpret laws dealing with the regulation of slavery.

The following cases cover how the Supreme Court has confronted these two problems over the years. The scope of judicial review will include cases dealing with the establishment of judicial review and how the Supreme Court has defined its jurisdiction over the years. Next, we will examine the cases in which the Supreme Court established its relation with the courts of the states.

The Scope of Judicial Power

In the American constitutional system any discussion of judicial power must begin with judicial review. Judicial review is often defined as the power of the Supreme Court to invalidate laws of Congress. Judicial review is actually broader than just the power to declare laws unconstitutional. For example, it is frequently forgotten that the Supreme Court upholds as well as voids laws. Judicial review, then, is a positive power that gives legitimacy to the laws of Congress. Also, judicial review is not limited to congressional acts. The Supreme Court may exercise judicial review over the states and its political subdivisions. Finally, judicial review applies to the actions of the president and other members of the executive branch.

Interestingly, the Constitution does not mention judicial review. There has been much speculation on why the framers of the Constitution failed to make judicial review an explicit grant of power. Some constitutional scholars contend that the framers took judicial review for granted and believed it was unnecessary to confer the power expressly. Whether true or not, from the beginning the Supreme Court presupposed the power of judicial review. For example, in *Hylton v. United States* (1796), the Supreme Court was asked to rule on the constitutionality of a tax on carriages. Although the Court found the tax to be constitutional, it was implied that it could have ruled otherwise. That is, implicit in *Hylton* was the understanding that judicial power includes the power to invalidate legislation.

MARBURY V. MADISON (1803) is, of course, the usual starting point for the discussion of judicial review. *MARBURY* is the first case in which the Supreme Court used judicial review to invalidate a law of Congress. The law in question was § 13 of the Judiciary Act of 1789. Section 13 empowered the Supreme Court to issue, as an original action, a writ of *mandamus* to government officials. On orders from President Jefferson, Secretary of State James Madison refused to hand over some judicial commissions to Jefferson's political opponents. William Marbury, one of those designated judges, applied to the Supreme Court for the writ of *mandamus* as permitted under § 13. President Jefferson let it be known that he had no intention of turning over the commissions no matter what the Court ruled.

MARBURY V. MADISON was a master stroke of political ingenuity. Chief Justice John Marshall, himself a political opponent of Jefferson, had a dilemma. If he ruled in Marbury's favor the ruling would be ignored by Jefferson. If he ruled for Madison, he would have to concede victory to Jefferson. Marshall chose to do neither. Instead, he ruled that § 13 unconstitutionally added to the original jurisdiction of the Supreme Court. The Constitution gives the Supreme Court original jurisdiction only in cases involving states and foreign ambassadors. Section 13, in effect, created a third category of original actions: writs of *mandamus*. Marshall argued that because the Court's original jurisdiction was fixed by the Constitution, it could only be enlarged or diminished by amending the Constitution. Because Congress had not amended the Constitution but merely passed an ordinary statute, § 13 was unconstitutional.

MARBURY V. MADISON may be viewed as the height of judicial activism. In it Chief Justice Marshall asserted that "It is, emphatically, the province and duty of the judicial department to say what the law is." In doing so, Marshall placed the Congress and president on notice that the Court alone was to be the final arbiter of meaning of the Constitution. The federal courts were to have the last word on the true meaning of the Constitution. However, after asserting the power of judicial review the Court wisely refrained from using it against Congress for another fifty-four years until the ill-fated decision in *DRED SCOTT V. SANDFORD* (1857).

The Supreme Court's assertion of the power of judicial review should not be construed to imply that the Court is irresponsible in defining its judicial power. Over the years the Court has astutely known when to exercise and when to refrain from exercising its judicial power. The Court has formulated several doctrines on which it relies to avoid situations that may prove difficult. In *LUTHER V. BORDEN* (1848), for example, the Court devised the political question doctrine. This doctrine, later elaborated on in *BAKER V. CARR* (1962), holds that courts will not exercise judicial power in cases that involve political questions. A political question is one better left to a political branch of government to resolve. The political question doctrine is designed to prevent situations that might bring the Court into direct confrontation with Congress or the president.

The political question doctrine notwithstanding, conflict with Congress has been unavoidable. During the Civil War, for instance, Congress passed the Habeas Corpus Act of 1863. This law authorized President Lincoln to suspend the writ of *habeas corpus*. The suspension of *habeas corpus* meant that a civilian could be tried by a military tribunal. Lambdin Milligan was charged with treason, found guilty by a military tribunal, and sentenced to be hanged. Milligan was tried by a military tribunal, although the regular civil courts of Indiana were in operation. In *EX PARTE MILLIGAN* (1866), the Supreme Court ruled that a civilian may not be tried by a military court when the regular civil courts are functioning. The *MILLIGAN* decision angered radical members of Congress who wished to deal harshly with southern sympathizers.

Three years after *MILLIGAN*, the Supreme Court faced another crisis with Congress. After the war, Congress passed the Reconstruction Acts. Among other things, the Acts gave the military commanders in charge of the defeated South almost dictatorial powers. William McCardle, like Milligan, was a civilian who was arrested and charged by a military commission. McCardle sought a writ of *habeas corpus* under a 1867 law of Congress. Fearing that McCardle's case would give the Supreme Court the opportunity to declare the Reconstruction Acts unconstitutional, Congress repealed the 1867 *habeas corpus* law. The Supreme Court then held oral arguments to decide whether, in light of the repeal of the 1867 act, the Court still had jurisdiction. In not one of its finer moments, the Supreme Court backed down and ruled it no longer had jurisdiction in McCardle's case.

Over the years the Supreme Court has developed several other doctrines to avoid exercising its judicial power. For example, in *Muskrat v. United States* (1911), the Court refused to take jurisdiction in a lawsuit that was not a real case or controversy. In *Muskrat*, Congress initiated a "friendly lawsuit" in an attempt to induce the Court to validate a law some questioned as unconstitutional. In *FROTHINGHAM V. MELLON* (1923), the doctrine of standing was used. Mrs. Frothingham disapproved of the use of federal taxes to fund a program to reduce infant deaths. The Maternity Act of 1921 set up a federal grant-in-aid program to assist the states in preventing infant deaths. Mrs. Frothingham argued that Congress lacked the power to set up such a program and that, as a taxpayer, she had standing to challenge the law. The Supreme Court, however, denied her standing thus virtually eliminating so-called taxpayers' suits. The Court held that a person's status solely as a taxpayer was insufficient to challenge an act of Congress. In a companion case, *MASSACHUSETTS V. MELLON* (1923), the Court dismissed a similar challenge to the Maternity Act by Massachusetts. The state challenged the grant-in-aid program as an infringement on states' rights. The Supreme Court rejected the state's argument and held that any infringement on the sovereignty of Massachusetts could be avoided by the simple expedient of not participating in the program.

Two other doctrines of judicial restraint are ripeness and mootness. The Supreme Court will not hear a case that is not "ripe for review." This doctrine says that the Court will not hear a case in advance of the need to decide it. Mootness, conversely, is a situation in which the Court's intervention is unnecessary because a conflict has resolved itself. Mootness also allows the Supreme Court to postpone a decision in a particularly controversial area. For example, in *DeFunis v. Odegaard* (1974), the Court skirted the thorny issue of the constitutionality of affirmative action programs. DeFunis was denied admission to law school even though lesser-qualified minority students had been admitted. The lower court had ordered DeFunis admitted pending the final outcome of an appeal. By the time the case reached the U.S. Supreme Court, DeFunis was in his last quarter of law school and ready to graduate. Consequently, the Court held that the case had been rendered moot.

The Supreme Court is generally accused of judicial activism by opponents of its decisions. When the Court ruled that segregated public schools were unconstitutional in

BROWN V. BOARD OF EDUCATION (1954), opponents of school desegregation accused the Court of judicial activism. Police officers opposed to the *MIRANDA V. ARIZONA* (1966) decision made similar charges. More recently in *Missouri v. Jenkins* (1990), the Supreme Court upheld, at least in principle, the power of a federal district court to order a local school district to raise its property taxes to fund a court-ordered desegregation plan. A person's position on judicial activism and judicial restraint often depends on whether he or she agrees with the kinds of decisions the Court is making. Liberals call for judicial restraint when the Court is in a conservative mode, and conservatives call for restraint when the Court is making liberal decisions. The debate brings to mind the old adage, "One's position on goring oxen depends on whose ox is being gored."

Federal Courts and the States

The second category of cases concerning the federal judicial power deals with the relationship of the federal courts to the states. As previously noted, the states acted as independent and sovereign nations under the Articles of Confederation. States believed that they possessed all the attributes of sovereignty and had become accustomed to their autonomy. When the Union was formed after the ratification of the Constitution, the legal status of the states changed. The states had agreed to surrender some traditional rights of sovereignty. The power to conduct foreign relations, for example, was given to the national government. Some states found it more difficult to adjust to the new order. Southern states were especially sensitive about issues of states' rights.

The question of state sovereignty arose almost immediately over the issue of sovereign immunity. Sovereign immunity is the doctrine that the sovereign (here, the state) may not be sued without its consent. As sovereign states under the Articles, the states assumed they still possessed sovereign immunity. Indeed, the issue had been raised during the ratification campaign, and assurances were given by Alexander Hamilton and others that sovereign immunity remained intact.

Although a state could refuse to give its consent to be sued in its own courts, the question arose whether it was immune from a suit in federal court. The Supreme Court addressed the question in *CHISHOLM V. GEORGIA* (1793). Chisholm, a citizen of South Carolina, was the executor of the estate of Robert Farquahr. At the time of his death, Georgia owed Farquahr some money for supplies purchased by the state during the Revolution. Unable to sue Georgia in her own courts, Chisholm filed suit in a federal court in Georgia. The state's officials were so outraged, they refused even to appear before the Supreme Court. They maintained that the state could not be sued, even in a federal court, without its consent. Unfortunately, the Supreme Court ruled otherwise. In a series of *seriatim* (individual) opinions, the majority ruled that the judicial power of the United States does extend to cases involving a state and a citizen of another state. Georgia had argued in the lower court that the provision in Article III applied only to cases in which the state was the plaintiff in the case, not the defendant. The Supreme Court found no basis for such an interpretation in its reading of the Constitution.

CHISHOLM so outraged public opinion that a movement to overturn the decision began immediately. Georgia was not the only state plagued by an inability to pay its revolutionary war debts. The Eleventh Amendment was soon added. It made clear that the judicial power of the United States did not extend to suits against a state by a citizen of another state. Despite the widespread condemnation of *CHISHOLM*, the Court's prestige was already such that a constitutional amendment was required to reverse its decision.

Having established its power to invalidate federal laws in *MARBURY V. MADISON*, few doubted the Supreme Court would extend judicial review to state laws. *FLETCHER V. PECK* (1810) arose in connection with the Yazoo land scandal. Members of the Georgia Legislature had accepted bribes to sell millions of acres of public lands for a fraction of their value. When the scandal became public, outraged voters ousted those responsible from office. The newly elected legislature proceeded to rescind the sale on the grounds it was tainted by bribery. Meanwhile, however, the land had been purchased by innocent parties not involved in the scheme. They had purchased the land in good faith and were in danger of losing it.

The Supreme Court ruled that the law that rescinded the original sale was unconstitutional. The Constitution forbids states to impair the obligations of contracts. Although tainted with corruption, the sale of the land by the legislature was legal. The subsequent sales of the land to innocent third parties were valid contracts as well. To void these sales impaired the obligation of contracts.

The last two cases in this section pertain to the relationship of state courts to federal courts. The Virginia Court of Appeals, led by a man named Spencer Roane, resented the idea that the U.S. Supreme Court could review its decisions. Roane's position was that Virginia judges were every bit as qualified to interpret the Constitution as federal judges. Also, as a slave state, Virginia did not relish the idea that judges beyond the state's control could invalidate Virginia's laws regarding slavery. In *MARTIN V. HUNTER'S LESSEE* (1816), the issue of the supremacy of the federal courts came before the Supreme Court. The dispute was over some prime Virginia land that the state had confiscated from a British Loyalist during the Revolution. The state's confiscation law, however, conflicted with the terms of a treaty the United States had signed with Great Britain after the war. When the Supreme Court upheld the treaty over the Virginia law, the Virginia Court of Appeals refused to accept the Court's jurisdiction. Instead, the Virginia Court of Appeals held that § 25 of the Judiciary Act of 1789 was unconstitutional. Section 25 empowered the Supreme Court to review the decisions of a state's highest court when a federal question was involved. The Supreme Court, in an opinion by Justice Joseph Story, again reversed the Virginia ruling and held that § 25 was constitutional.

Five years later the issue of reviewability of state court decisions came up again in *COHENS V. VIRGINIA* (1821). Congress passed a law creating a lottery, and the Cohen brothers sold tickets in Virginia violating a state law. The Cohens were prosecuted and fined $100. They appealed on the grounds that the law of Congress establishing the lottery superseded the Virginia law. The Virginia Court of Appeals rejected this argument and sustained their convictions. When the Cohens appealed to the U.S. Supreme Court, the Virginia Court of Appeals again denied the Supreme Court's right to review its decisions. The decision, this time written by Chief Justice John Marshall, reaffirmed *MARTIN*. Chief Justice Marshall argued that if the Supreme Court were unable to review the decisions of state courts, the Constitution would have as many different meanings as there are states. There can be only one definitive interpretation of the Constitution. The Supreme Court, which represents the government of all the American people, is the only court empowered to make that interpretation.

Conclusion

The judicial power, like the Constitution itself, has evolved over nearly two hundred years. The Constitution left unanswered many questions about the scope of the judicial power and the relationship between federal and state courts. Through the cases covered in this section and others, the Supreme Court has defined the role of the federal courts in our constitutional system. Just as important, the Court has made it possible for the federal courts and fifty state court systems to coexist in relative harmony. As much as anything else, this coexistence has defined the essence of America's federal form of government.

MARBURY V. MADISON
1 Cranch 137 (1803)

BACKGROUND The election of 1800 saw John Adams's Federalist party lose control of the Presidency and both Houses of Congress to the Jeffersonians. In those days the new President did not take office until the following March 4 so Adams and the "lame duck" Federalist party still held power for several months after the election. In an attempt to hold onto power, the lame duck Congress passed a law creating forty-two new federal judgeships. President Adams quickly nominated Federalists to these judgeships, and the Senate quickly confirmed the nominations. The outgoing Secretary of State, John Marshall, failed to see that all of the commissions were delivered to the new judges before he left office on March 4. When President Jefferson took office he ordered his Secretary of State, James Madison, not to deliver the commissions because of the blatant way the Federalists tried to "pack" the federal judiciary. William Marbury, nominated to be a justice of the peace in the city of Washington, was one of those who did not receive his commission. After several unsuccessful attempts to secure the commission, Marbury brought suit against Madison. Section 13 of the Judiciary Act of 1789 authorized the Supreme Court to issue a writ of *mandamus* to persons holding office under the authority of the United States. A writ of *mandamus* is a court order commanding an official to do something that is required by law and over which the official has no discretion. Marbury brought this *original action* before the Supreme Court under § 13. The case was highly controversial and highly partisan in nature. The Federalists had blatantly packed the federal judiciary with its members. Jefferson withheld the commissions for partisan reasons. The stage was set for a historic decision.

CONSTITUTIONAL ISSUES

(1)   Whether Marbury has a legal right to the commission? YES

(2)   Whether the laws of the United States provide Marbury with a legal remedy? YES

(3)   Whether the remedy of a writ of *mandamus* was issued *by the Supreme Court*? NO

MAJORITY OPINION   Chief Justice John Marshall delivers the opinion of the Court. Because the case raises three questions, Marshall divides the opinion into three parts. The first question is whether Marbury has a legal right to the commission he demands. Marshall answers the first question by analyzing the appointment process. The first part of the process is the nomination of the person by the President, an act that is entirely at the President's discretion. The second part is the appointment that is also a voluntary act by the President but one that can only be done with the advice and consent of the Senate. The third part is the commission. Once Senate approval is achieved, the President signs the commission, and it is sent to the secretary of state who affixes the Great Seal of the United States on it. Marshall argues that in the case of a judicial appointment there must be a point where the President's power to remove the appointed person ends. Marshall argues that once the President's signature is written, he may no longer remove a judicial appointee at will. At that point the secretary of state is not an agent of the President bound to do the President's will, but becomes a minister bound by law to affix the seal and to deliver the commissions. Thus, when President Adams signed the commissions and the seal was affixed, the secretary of state's duty was to do what was required by law. Marshall concludes that Marbury, having been nominated by the President and confirmed by the Senate in accordance with the Constitution, does have a right to the commission he demands.

The second question posed by Chief Justice Marshall is whether the laws of the United States provide Marbury with a remedy when his rights have been violated. Marshall states that the government of the United States could hardly be called a government of laws, not men, unless it provided a legal remedy for the violation of rights. In this case, however, the issue is whether Madison's refusal to deliver the commission is an act reviewable by a court of law. Marshall acknowledges that in certain circumstances the secretary of state acts on behalf of the President. If the acts of the secretary are discretionary, they are not reviewable by a court. If, however, the law requires the secretary to do certain things, then his failure to do what the law requires is reviewable. Marshall concludes that the delivery of Marbury's commission is required by law and therefore is reviewable by a court. Marshall then turns his attention to whether or not the writ of *mandamus* is the appropriate legal remedy in this case. After a brief discussion of the nature of the writ, Marshall rules that it is the appropriate remedy. Thus, Marshall answers the second question by stating that the law does provide Marbury with a legal remedy, and the writ of *mandamus* is it.

Finally, Marshall turns to the crucial third question, which is whether the Supreme Court may issue the writ of *mandamus* to Madison. Marshall says that § 13 authorizes the Court to issue writs of *mandamus* to persons holding office under the authority of the United States, which Madison surely is. Therefore, if the Court does not have the power to issue the writ it must be because § 13 is unconstitutional. The Constitution, Marshall notes, divides the Court's jurisdiction into two categories: original and appellate. The Court's original jurisdiction is limited by the Constitution to cases involving foreign representatives and cases in which a state is a party. What § 13 does is create a third category of original jurisdiction: jurisdiction to issue writs of *mandamus* to persons holding office under the authority of the United States. This, Marshall asserts, Congress may not do. The framers intended to limit the Court's original jurisdiction to just two kinds of cases and therefore intended the remainder of the Court's jurisdiction to be appellate. The only way the Supreme Court can possibly have jurisdiction over this case is under its appellate jurisdiction. Insofar as § 13 adds to the Court's original jurisdiction by authorizing it to issue writs of *mandamus*, § 13 is unconstitutional.

Marshall uses the rest of the opinion to explain why § 13 is unconstitutional. The purpose of a written constitution is to put limits on governmental power. If Congress is free to increase the original jurisdiction of the Court when the Constitution limits the Court's original jurisdiction, Marshall asks: What good is a written constitution? Either the Constitution is the supreme law, unchangeable by ordinary laws, or the Constitution is an absurd attempt to limit the power of Congress. Next, Marshall asks if judges must enforce a law even if it appears to be contrary to the Constitution. Marshall states, "It is emphatically the province and duty of the judicial department to say what the law is." The nature of judicial duty is to decide which law should prevail if two laws conflict. Judges are not required to close their eyes to laws that conflict with the Constitution. Suppose, Marshall asks, Congress passed a bill of attainder or an *ex post facto* law. Should courts enforce the law even though the Constitution expressly forbids passing such laws? To Marshall the answer is clear. Judges take an oath to uphold the Constitution, and it would be a mockery to ignore their judicial duty. Finally, Marshall notes that only laws of Congress "made in pursuance" of the Constitution are the supreme law of the land. Thus, laws repugnant to the Constitution are null and void. Because § 13 is unconstitutional, the Supreme Court has no jurisdiction to issue the writ of *mandamus* requested by Marbury.

SIGNIFICANCE OF THE CASE   *Marbury v. Madison* is significant on several levels. First, it established for the judiciary the power of judicial review, the power to determine if laws passed by legislative bodies are constitutional. Judicial review gives the courts the power to have the final word on most issues of public policy. If the Supreme Court, for example, declares prayer in school unconstitutional, only the Court itself or a constitutional amendment can overturn that decision. *Marbury* is also significant because of its partisan overtones. Both sides were guilty of "playing politics" with the federal courts: the Federalists for packing the courts and the Jeffersonians for withholding the commissions from their rightful owners. *Marbury* is significant because it gave the Federalist-dominated judiciary the power to invalidate the laws passed by the Jeffersonians in Congress. Although judicial review was not used again to strike down a federal law until the *Dred Scott* decision, the threat of its use was always present. Finally, Marshall was able to save the Court's reputation. President Jefferson had made it clear that he would not turn over the commissions even if ordered to do so by the Supreme Court. For a president to refuse to obey a Supreme Court decision today is virtually unthinkable, but Jefferson was enormously popular and the Court at that time was not. By not ordering Madison to deliver the commissions, Marshall saved the Court the humiliation of being defied by Jefferson.

QUESTIONS FOR DISCUSSION

(1)   Who do you think won in *Marbury v. Madison*? Why?

(2)   Because John Marshall had been Secretary of State under Adams, was it improper for him to rule in this case? Why?

(3)   What would you have ruled if you were in Marshall's position?

(4)   What, exactly, did the Court really rule in *Marbury v. Madison*?

RELATED CASES   *Hylton v. United States*, 3 Dallas 171 (1796); *DRED SCOTT V. SANDFORD*, 19 Howard 393 (1857); *Cooper v. Aaron*, 358 U.S. 1 (1958); and *UNITED STATES V. NIXON*, 418 U.S. 683 (1974).

EX PARTE MILLIGAN
4 Wallace 2 (1866)

BACKGROUND   Under the Habeas Corpus Act of 1863 the President was authorized to suspend the writ of *habeas corpus,* which President Lincoln did on September 15, 1863. Lambdin Milligan was arrested in October 1864, brought before a military commission, tried for treason, and sentenced to be hanged. Milligan, a civilian, applied to the Circuit Court of the United States for Indiana for a writ of *habeas corpus.* Milligan's petition stated that he was not nor ever had been in the military, that he had been a citizen of Indiana for the past twenty years, that the civil courts of Indiana were still in operation, and that he should either be brought before a civil court or discharged from custody altogether. The circuit court, composed of only two judges, was evenly divided and therefore certified three questions to the Supreme Court. The first was whether, on the facts stated, a writ of *habeas corpus* should be issued. The second asked whether Milligan should be discharged from custody of the military, and the third asked whether the military commission had jurisdiction legally to try and sentence Milligan.

CONSTITUTIONAL ISSUE

Whether a civilian may be tried by a military commission while civil courts are open and operating? NO

MAJORITY OPINION   Justice David Davis delivers the opinion of the Court. Justice Davis first turns to the question of whether the circuit court had the authority to certify the three questions to the Supreme Court. After a lengthy discussion, Justice Davis concludes that it did have such authority. Justice Davis then discusses the Habeas Corpus Act of 1863 under which the action was brought. Under the Act either the secretary of state or the secretary of war was obligated to submit a list of persons arrested without benefit of *habeas corpus* to a circuit court judge. If a grand jury convened and then adjourned without indicting a person, he was to be discharged within twenty days of its adjournment. Milligan had not been indicted nor discharged. Justice Davis notes that even though the writ of *habeas corpus* had been suspended, other rights, such as trial by jury, were not and could not be suspended by Congress. Davis states that it is the birthright of every American to be tried according to law. There is, he claims, no more dangerous doctrine than the one that asserts provisions of the Constitution may be suspended during times of crisis.

Justice Davis then turns to the source of the military commission's authority. The commission did not share part of the judicial power because it was not established by Congress under Article III of the Constitution. It could not receive its authority from the President because he is also controlled by the law. Finally, Justice Davis rejects the "laws and usages of war" as a source of the commission's authority because they may never be applied to civilians when the civil courts are open and their process unobstructed. Justice Davis then boldly asserts that "Congress could grant no such power."

Justice Davis discusses the use of martial law as a justification for Milligan's arrest. Although acknowledging martial law as a possible source of authority, he notes that no hostile armies were actually in Indiana at the time. For martial law to be imposed, the threat of invasion must be actual and present, not merely threatened. Martial law, he declares, is incompatible with civil liberty and may never exist when civil courts are open. Justice Davis is puzzled why Milligan was not taken to the circuit court. The penalty for treason on conviction would have been the same, and the government had no reason to believe that Milligan would not have been punished if convicted.

Justice Davis concludes his opinion by answering the first two certified questions in the affirmative, but answering the third one in the negative. That is, the answer to the questions whether the writ should be issued and Milligan should be discharged from military custody is yes. The question whether the military commission had jurisdiction legally to try and sentence Milligan is no. Almost as an afterthought, Justice Davis discusses whether Milligan could be considered a prisoner of war. Despite the obvious response that Milligan had been a citizen of Indiana for the past twenty years, he could not plead the rights of war. If he is not entitled to the immunities of a prisoner of war, it is difficult to see how he can be subject to the penalties of one.

OTHER OPINIONS Chief Justice Salmon P. Chase writes an opinion joined by Justices James M. Wayne, Noah H. Swayne, and Samuel F. Miller, in which they concurred in part and dissented in part. The chief justice agrees that the three certified questions are answered correctly. His objection is that the majority opinion goes further than it should by asserting that it is not within the power of Congress to authorize the military commission that tried Milligan. Chase agrees that Congress did not authorize the commission but that is not to say that Congress could not authorize it as the majority asserts. Chief Justice Chase believes that under its power to make rules and regulations for the army and navy, and under its power to declare war, Congress, under certain conditions, may authorize the trial of civilians by military authorities even when civil courts are operating. When peace prevails, the laws of peace must govern. But, in times of public danger, it is for Congress to determine which states are in such imminent danger to justify military trials of civilians. Chase notes that Indiana was under a constant threat of invasion and that bad men, like Milligan, were conspiring against the government. Happily, Chase notes, the civil judges in Indiana remained loyal to the government, but it might have been otherwise. Chief Justice Chase is also concerned about the civil liability of the officers who arrested and sentenced Milligan. Their actions were in obedience to superior officers acting under the authority of President Lincoln. In conclusion, the chief justice restates his belief that Congress may establish, under its powers to make rules for the military and to declare war, military commissions to try civilians even when civil courts are open. Because Congress did not do so in this case, the chief justice agrees that the writ of *habeas corpus* must be issued.

SIGNIFICANCE OF THE CASE *Ex parte Milligan* deals with one of the most difficult issues in a constitutional government. It asks the classic question: Do the ends justify the means? It also raises the question whether a crisis enlarges or increases constitutional power. In *Milligan* the entire Court is in agreement that Milligan was illegally arrested and tried. The minority justices maintain that Congress could have authorized the military commission that tried Milligan. Even more disturbing is the minority's assertion that the war power supersedes other constitutional limits on Congressional power. In other words, along with *habeas corpus* Congress, under this interpretation, could suspend the right to a trial by jury, the right to counsel, the protection against self-incrimination, or any other constitutional guarantee. Although the minority view does not prevail, it is easy to see why Justice Davis said that, "No doctrine, involving more pernicious consequences, was ever invented by the wit of man."

QUESTIONS FOR DISCUSSION

(1) Why do you think the military was reluctant to have Milligan tried before a civilian court?

(2) Do you agree with the majority that Congress may never authorize the trial of civilians by military courts while civil courts are open? Why or why not?

(3) Should Congress be permitted to suspend constitutional guarantees during times of great crisis?

(4) From what you can tell from the facts in this case, did the threat of invasion justify the actions taken against Milligan? Why or why not?

RELATED CASES   *EX PARTE McCARDLE*, 7 Wallace 506 (1869); *Hirabayashi v. United States*, 320 U.S. 81 (1943); *KOREMATSU V. UNITED STATES*, 323 U.S. 214 (1944); and *YOUNGSTOWN SHEET AND TUBE CO. V. UNITED STATES*, 343 U.S. 579 (1952).

EX PARTE McCARDLE
7 Wallace 506 (1869)

BACKGROUND   William McCardle was a newspaper editor in Mississippi after the Civil War. He was arrested by military authorities under the Reconstruction Acts and was charged with disturbing the peace, inciting to insurrection, and spreading libel. McCardle believed that as a civilian he was not subject to arrest and trial by the military. He sought a writ of *habeas corpus* from the U.S. Circuit Court for the Southern District of Mississippi. The circuit court issued the writ but after a hearing ruled that McCardle's arrest was lawful. McCardle then appealed to the Supreme Court. For technical reasons the government argued that the Supreme Court lacked jurisdiction in the case. However, in February 1868 the Court ruled that a law passed by Congress on February 5, 1867, did give the Court jurisdiction according to its interpretation. The Court then set a date for hearing the merits of McCardle's case. Before that could happen, however, on March 27, 1868, Congress repealed the part of the February 5, 1867, law that had given the Supreme Court jurisdiction over McCardle's case. Now the question arose whether the Court still had jurisdiction.

McCardle argued that the removal of jurisdiction did not apply to cases already pending before the Court, whereas the government argued that the Court now lacked jurisdiction to hear McCardle's case on the merits.

CONSTITUTIONAL ISSUE

Whether a law that withdraws previously held appellate jurisdiction from the Supreme Court applies to cases pending before the Court? YES

MAJORITY OPINION Chief Justice Salmon P. Chase delivers the opinion of the Court. After going over the chronological facts in the case, Chief Justice Chase discusses the question of jurisdiction. Because the Act of March 27, 1868 (passed over President Andrew Johnson's veto), allegedly repealed the Court's jurisdiction over *habeas corpus* cases on appeal from circuit courts, the issue of jurisdiction must be settled before any discussion of the legality of McCardle's arrest. The chief justice then discusses the nature of the Court's appellate jurisdiction. The Constitution grants the Court appellate jurisdiction but allows Congress to make exceptions to it. Congress, in 1789, enacted a law that "granted" appellate power to the Court. Since then, Chase notes, most laws have been positive grants of appellate jurisdiction rather than exceptions to it. In other words, instead of telling the Court what appellate jurisdiction it does not have, Congress tends to tell the Court what appellate power it does have. However, Chase argues, that does not mean Congress may not expressly remove a portion of the Court's appellate jurisdiction. The Act of March 27 plainly removes the Court's jurisdiction in *habeas corpus* cases that come from circuit courts. The effect of the law, Chase asserts, is the same as if the jurisdiction had never existed. Chase quotes a legal scholar, writing, "when an Act of the Legislature is repealed, it must be considered, except to transactions past and closed, as if it never existed." Chase concludes the opinion by observing that not all of the Court's *habeas corpus* jurisdiction has been removed but only in those cases that come from circuit courts.

SIGNIFICANCE OF THE CASE The significance of *McCardle* cannot be understood without some additional background. McCardle was a *civilian* who was going to be tried by a *military* commission under the Reconstruction Acts. McCardle was trying to get his case before the Supreme Court so that he could challenge the constitutionality of those Acts. Congress, fearing that the Supreme Court might rule the Acts unconstitutional, passed the Act of March 27 to prevent McCardle from bringing the issue of constitutionality before the Court. The Court cooperated by ruling it lacked jurisdiction in the case.

McCardle set a dangerous precedent in the opinion of many constitutional scholars. It allows Congress to prevent the Court from ruling on controversial issues by removing the Court's appellate jurisdiction. Since most of the major issues that the Court hears come to it under its appellate jurisdiction, this could have a serious impact on our constitutional system. For example, opponents of the segregation, reapportionment, school prayer, and abortion decisions have tried to have Congress remove the Court's appellate jurisdiction in these cases. So far these "Court-curbing" attempts have failed, but *McCardle* serves as a reminder that it can be done under certain circumstances.

QUESTIONS FOR DISCUSSION

(1)   Why do you think McCardle wasn't tried in a civilian court in the first place?

(2)   Do you think the Supreme Court made the correct decision in this case? Why or why not?

(3)   Did McCardle receive justice? Why or why not?

(4)   Does having the Supreme Court hear your case mean you will receive justice? Why or why not?

RELATED CASES *EX PARTE MILLIGAN*, 4 Wallace 2 (1866); and *Ex parte Endo*, 323 U.S. 283 (1944).

FROTHINGHAM V. MELLON
and
MASSACHUSETTS V. MELLON
262 U.S. 447 (1923)

BACKGROUND In 1921 Congress passed the Maternity Act, which was a forerunner of modern federal grant-in-aid programs. The Act provided an initial appropriation and annual appropriations over a five-year period that was to be apportioned among the states. The purpose of the Act was to encourage states to develop their own programs to find ways to reduce infant and maternal deaths by providing financial assistance. The Act created guidelines with which the states had to comply and a federal bureau to ensure compliance with the Act's provisions. Participation was voluntary on the part of the states.

The Commonwealth of Massachusetts filed suit under the Supreme Court's original jurisdiction to enjoin the Secretary of the Treasury, Andrew Mellon, from enforcing the law. Massachusetts alleged that the appropriations provided for by the Act were for concerns that were of a local, not national, character. The state also alleged that the Act forced the states to surrender a portion of their sovereignty, that the burden of paying for the Act fell largely on the industrial states, like Massachusetts, and that Congress was attempting to exercise a power reserved to the states by the Tenth Amendment.

Mrs. Frothingham, a taxpayer, challenged the constitutionality of the Act on the grounds that it takes her property under the guise of taxation without due process of law in violation of the Fifth Amendment. The Supreme Court, without ruling on the constitutionality of the Act, focused on whether the Court had jurisdiction in the cases.

CONSTITUTIONAL ISSUES

(1)   Whether the Maternity Act of 1921 usurps powers reserved to the states under the Tenth Amendment? NO

(2)   Whether a federal taxpayer, based solely on her status as a taxpayer, has standing to challenge the constitutionality of an Act of Congress? NO

MAJORITY OPINION Justice George Sutherland delivers the opinion of the Court. Justice Sutherland separates the two cases and disposes of the state's claim first. Massachusetts argues that the Act usurps powers reserved to the states by the Tenth Amendment. However, the Maternity Act imposes no obligation on the state because participation is voluntary. Justice Sutherland notes that Article III of the Constitution does give the Court jurisdiction in cases in which a state is a party, but only in cases that involve a true controversy. The Court is not obligated to hear a case that fails to raise a real controversy merely because a state is a party. A real controversy means that the plaintiff has suffered some injury, but Massachusetts has not been injured. The state makes a general complaint that its sovereignty has been usurped by the Act. Sutherland notes that the state may frustrate this attempt to usurp its power by refusing to participate in the program. Sutherland also points out that it is the inhabitants of Massachusetts as federal taxpayers who finance the program, not the state. The question, Sutherland asserts, is essentially a political one that the Court normally will not adjudicate. Nor may Massachusetts file suit on behalf of its citizens. Although the Court refuses to say a state may never intervene to protect its citizens, this is not a case in which it may. A state may not institute judicial proceedings to protect its citizens from the operation of a federal law.

Justice Sutherland then turns to Mrs. Frothingham's claim and acknowledges that the Court has never ruled on the right of a taxpayer to challenge a federal appropriation. Although the Court has upheld the right of a municipal taxpayer to enjoin the illegal use of public monies by a city, the situation of a federal taxpayer is different. The interest of the municipal taxpayer is direct and immediate, whereas the interest of the federal taxpayer is remote, minute, and indeterminate. The federal tax burden is shared with millions of other taxpayers, and each taxpayer's individual share is small. Justice Sutherland also alludes to the mischief that would result if every taxpayer had standing to challenge every use of public funds. Justice Sutherland concludes his opinion by observing that the Court has no general power to rule on the constitutionality of acts of Congress. It may only do so in cases that raise controversies in which a party has sustained a direct injury as the result of the enforcement of a law. To assume jurisdiction over these cases would give the Court a power over Congress the Constitution never intended the Court to have.

SIGNIFICANCE OF THE CASE *Frothingham* virtually closed the door on so-called taxpayer's suits. If allowed, a taxpayer's suit would permit the average citizen to challenge the constitutionality of a law based merely on his or her status as a taxpayer. Because almost every law is opposed by someone, virtually every appropriation law passed by Congress could be challenged and subjected to judicial review. This would elevate the Supreme Court to the status of a "superlegislature" and give the Court the last word in the spending of public money. The framers of the Constitution obviously did not intend for that to happen. Still, it is frustrating for citizens to be unable to challenge what they consider to be unconstitutional uses of public money. The Court modified the *Frothingham* decision somewhat in *Flast v. Cohen*, but overcoming the barrier created by *Frothingham* is formidable. *Massachusetts v. Mellon* is significant because it paved the way for expansion of the federal grant-in-aid concept. Such programs have significantly changed the character of our federal form of government. *Massachusetts v. Mellon* should also be recognized as an example of the discredited doctrine of interposition. Interposition was a pre–Civil War doctrine that held that a state may interpose its authority between its citizens and the national government. Southern states invoked the doctrine to protect slave owners from the threat of real or imagined congressional antislavery legislation.

QUESTIONS FOR DISCUSSION

(1)   Should a taxpayer, as a taxpayer, be allowed to challenge the constitutionality of acts of Congress? Why or why not?

(2)   Do taxpayer's suits conflict with the ideal of representative government? Why or why not?

(3)   What possible harms could result from taxpayer's suits?

RELATED CASES   *FLAST V. COHEN*, 392 U.S. 83 (1968); *United States v. Richardson*, 418 U.S. 166 (1974); *Schlesinger v. Reservists' Committee to Stop the War*, 418 U.S. 208 (1974); and *Allen v. Wright*, 468 U.S. 737 (1984).

CHISHOLM V. GEORGIA
2 Dallas 419 (1793)

BACKGROUND   After the American Revolution, many states, including Georgia, found themselves unable to pay the debts they had incurred during the war. As a result, they faced the embarrassing prospect of being sued by their creditors. However, the states invoked a doctrine known as sovereign immunity, which holds that the sovereign (in this case, the state itself) may not be sued without its consent. Under the English common law, the king, the ultimate dispenser of justice, could not be sued in his own courts, and the states claimed to be the heirs of that privilege. Although the doctrine saved a state from being sued in its own courts, the question arose whether a state could be sued in a federal court. Article III of the Constitution extends the judicial power of the United States to controversies "between a State and Citizens of another State." In the present case, Chisholm, acting as executor of the estate of a deceased creditor, sued Georgia for money owed to the estate. As a citizen of South Carolina, Chisholm had filed the suit in federal court. Georgia refused to answer the suit by claiming sovereign immunity. Georgia's position was that the clause, "between a State and Citizens of another State" referred only to cases in which the state was the plaintiff and was not intended to cover cases in which a state might be the defendant. The rest of the states followed the *Chisholm* case with great concern because the outcome would affect every debtor state. After giving Georgia every opportunity to respond to the suit, the Supreme Court, in a 4–1 decision, ruled against Georgia. The justices during this period wrote separate (*seriatim*) opinions, and each is summarized individually below. In addition, there were only five justices on the Supreme Court during this period.

CONSTITUTIONAL ISSUE

Whether a citizen of another state may sue a state in a federal court? YES

SERIATIM OPINIONS   Justice James Iredell writes the first opinion, and he takes the position that the Supreme Court has no jurisdiction over a state because there is no way for the Court to enforce a judgment against a state. Iredell rejects the argument made by Chisholm's lawyer, Edmund Randolph, that courts may employ any judicial power "necessary for the exercise of their respective jurisdictions." In other words, according to Randolph, courts may exercise any power necessary to enforce decisions in cases falling within their jurisdiction. Iredell rejects that position and claims that because Congress has passed no law giving the Court enforcement power, the Court has no authority to act. Finally, Iredell asserts that there are no principles at common law that would allow the Court to enforce a judgment against Georgia.

Justice John Blair believes that Georgia may be sued in a federal court by a citizen of another state. Blair asserts that states joined the Union on the adoption of the Constitution by the people of the state. In doing so, a state submits itself to the authority of the Constitution that clearly gives federal courts jurisdiction in controversies between a state and citizens of other states. Blair addresses the argument that a state may be the plaintiff but not a defendant in such cases. First, he gives no significance to the fact that in the clause in question the word "State" appears first. Second, the Constitution gives jurisdiction to federal courts in "Controversies between two or more States." Under such circumstances it would be impossible for a state not to be a defendant. Third, federal jurisdiction extends to cases involving a state and a foreign nation. Georgia's interpretation would allow her to sue a foreign nation but not allow her to be sued in turn. This would allow a state, by denying justice to a foreign nation, to embroil the other states in its controversies. Finally, Blair argues that by adopting the Constitution, Georgia, in effect, has given up her right of sovereign immunity. He concludes by suggesting that Georgia be given another chance to answer the suit and if she continues to refuse that a default judgment be entered against her.

Justice James Wilson's opinion centers on three definitions of sovereignty. The first meaning of "sovereign" requires the presence of a "subject," and because the Constitution speaks only of citizens, not subjects, Wilson dismisses its relevance. He also dismisses the second meaning that a state is free from any outside interference. The people of Georgia, he asserts, are not dependent on the state; rather, the state is dependent on the people. Therefore, a state can never be sovereign. Finally, Wilson rejects the feudal concept of sovereignty, which holds that all property ultimately belongs to the state. Wilson concludes his opinion by stating that the people of Georgia, as sovereign, intended to bind the state to the authority of the United States and did so by ratifying the Constitution. He points out that the states are limited by the Constitution in several ways such as being forbidden to impair the obligation of contracts. He agrees with Justice Blair that the clause giving the Supreme Court jurisdiction in controversies between two or more states supports the argument that states can be defendants in lawsuits.

The fourth opinion is by Justice William Cushing. Justice Cushing, like his colleagues in the majority, concludes that the Court has jurisdiction in the case. Like Blair, Cushing addresses the question of a suit between a state and a foreign nation. He states that it does not make sense for the Constitution to give a state the right to sue a foreign nation while denying a foreign nation the right to sue a state. Cushing also noted that there are numerous limitations on the sovereignty of states in the Constitution. Finally, Cushing concludes that although states do not enjoy sovereign immunity, the national government does. He notes that the language governing the jurisdiction of the Court over cases in which the United States is a party is different from the language that confers jurisdiction over cases involving states.

The final opinion is that of Chief Justice John Jay. The chief justice makes observations similar to those of his colleagues about the nature of sovereignty, the language of the Constitution, and the relationship of the states to the national sovereignty. He also notes that if the framers of the Constitution had intended to deny the citizens of other states the right to sue a state in federal courts "it would have been easy to have found words to express it." Chief Justice Jay concludes his opinion by addressing the issue raised by Justice Cushing concerning the immunity of the national government from suits. The significant difference, according to the chief justice, is that although the Court has the assistance of the legislative and executive branches of the national government to enforce judgments against the states, "in cases of actions against the United States, there is no power which the courts can call to their aid."

SIGNIFICANCE OF THE CASE *Chisholm v. Georgia* is significant for several reasons. First, the Court acknowledged for the first time that the creation of the Union had somehow transformed the nature of the states. By joining the Union, the states had surrendered some of the traditional attributes of sovereignty. Second, *Chisholm* foreshadowed the problem of states' rights, which would eventually lead to the Civil War. When the people of the South sought to withdraw their sovereignty from the United States only the use of force by the North prevented the dissolution of the Union. Third, *Chisholm* raised fundamental questions about the entire concept of sovereign immunity that are still relevant. Questions about the wisdom of permitting the states to be sued are still being debated today. Finally, almost immediately after *Chisholm* was decided a constitutional amendment was introduced in Congress to reverse the decision. The Eleventh Amendment reads, "The judicial power of the United States shall not be construed to extend to any suit in law or equity, commenced or prosecuted against one of the United States by Citizens of another State, or by Citizens or Subjects of any Foreign State." Some scholars maintain this is evidence of the Court's prestige even this early in our nation's history.

QUESTIONS FOR DISCUSSION

(1) Why does the doctrine of sovereign immunity exist?

(2) Do you think that suits against states should be limited to citizens of another state? Why or why not?

(3) Should a citizen of a state be allowed to sue his own state? Why or why not?

(4) Does it make any sense to you to exempt states from lawsuits like the one involved in *Chisholm*?

(5) Should a state be allowed to renege on its debts?

RELATED CASES *COHENS V. VIRGINIA*, 6 Wheaton 264 (1821); and *Texas v. White*, 7 Wallace 700 (1869).

FLETCHER V. PECK
6 Cranch 87 (1810)

BACKGROUND In 1795, the Georgia Legislature authorized the sale of more than thirty million acres of public land to four private land companies, and the governor executed the deeds in fee simple to the company stockholders as tenants in common. The companies sold the land, and further resales were made by the initial purchasers. In 1796, the legislature revoked the Act amid a great public hue and outcry because most of the legislators had been involved in the land companies and profited personally from the deals. Fletcher purchased a tract of the Georgia land in the interim and filed suit against Peck who sold him the land claiming that Peck could not convey good title because of the revocation of the 1795 Act. Peck responded that he and all others past the first grantees were purchasers in due course and were protected. The suit was filed in federal court because Peck was a Massachusetts resident, and Fletcher was a New Hampshire resident.

CONSTITUTIONAL ISSUES

(1) Whether the legislative act revoking the original sale of the land constitutes a violation of the Contract Clause? YES

(2) Whether individuals may look to the national Constitution for protection of private economic and proprietary interests against derogation by state governments? YES

MAJORITY OPINION Chief Justice John Marshall writes the opinion of the Court. The legislature of Georgia had the constitutional power to dispose of its land, and the grant is tantamount to an executed contract. Both parties are bound by the terms of the contract, and repeal of the Act cannot divest those rights just as a private grantor could not, acting on his own, repeal a deed. The law is well settled that conveyances may be set aside if fraud is involved but only between the parties, but "the rights of third persons, who are purchasers without notice, for a valuable consideration," as here, are protected.

In addition, "it would be indecent in the extreme, upon a private contract between two individuals, to enter into an inquiry respecting the corruption of the sovereign power of the state." It is the role of the Court, however, to protect residents and their property from "violent acts which might grow out of the feelings of the moment...effects of those sudden and strong passions to which men are exposed"—a phenomenon that the framers wished to guard against in creating a federal system with an independent judiciary. Georgia "cannot be viewed as a single, unconnected power" but is a member of the American Union, which has a constitution that imposes limits on the legislatures of several states. "[T]he state of Georgia was restrained, either by general principles, which are common to our free institutions, or by the particular provisions of the constitution of the United States" from passing a law that impaired the rights under this contract.

OTHER OPINIONS Justice William Johnson also enters an opinion. Once the legislature conveyed title to the land, it gave up all control over it, and it vested in the individual. However, the intent of the language in Article I, § 10 that forbids states to impair the obligations of contracts is not clear. States properly legislate on various aspects of contracts such as prescribing the method of authentication or setting the time limits for filing lawsuits on contracts. To interpret this clause as a "restriction of the state powers in favor of private rights is certainly going very far beyond the obvious and necessary import of the words."

SIGNIFICANCE OF THE CASE In *Fletcher v. Peck*, the Court early indicated that it would act to protect the economic interests of individuals against action of state government. Chief Justice Marshall's statement that Georgia is restrained either by "general principles, which are common to our free institutions, or by the particular provisions of the constitution" left it unclear as to whether the Court was deciding the case on the basis of natural law or the explicit restrictions in the Constitution. This paved the way for the use of natural law or implied limitations on governmental power in other cases as well. It also portended the Court's later laissez-faire approach to economic regulation.

QUESTIONS FOR DISCUSSION

(1)   In light of the recent discussions concerning justices looking only to the original intent of the Constitution, what arguments would you make regarding natural law and certain rights existing beyond the written pages of the Constitution?

(2)   What factors would you consider as a justice in balancing the economic interests of the parties and the role of the state in regulating contract contents?

(3)   Because the legislators were acting as agents of the public, do you feel that the Court should have intervened to protect the public in light of the fraud involved here? Why? Are the citizens of Georgia left without effective recourse?

RELATED CASES   *Calder v. Bull*, 3 Dallas 386 (1798); *THE TRUSTEES OF DART-MOUTH COLLEGE V. WOODWARD*, 4 Wheaton 518 (1819); *Charles River Bridge v. Warren Bridge*, 11 Peters 420 (1837); *LOCHNER V. NEW YORK*, 198 U.S. 45 (1905); and *WEST COAST HOTEL COMPANY V. PARRISH*, 300 U.S. 379 (1937).

MARTIN V. HUNTER'S LESSEE
1 Wheaton 304 (1816)

BACKGROUND This case involves title to land that once belonged to Thomas Lord Fairfax. When Lord Fairfax died in 1781 he bequeathed his estates in northern Virginia to his nephew, Denny Martin, a British subject who had never become an American citizen. In 1779 Virginia passed a law that forbade aliens like Martin from inheriting property in the state. The Virginia law was designed to wrest control of valuable land from British subjects who had remained loyal to the Crown during the Revolution. Consequently, Virginia claimed that title to the land had reverted to the state. In 1789, David Hunter was granted title to the land by Virginia, but Denny Martin was still physically in possession of it. Hunter initiated a suit of ejectment seeking to remove Martin from the property. Two U.S. treaties, the Treaty of Paris of 1783, which ended the revolutionary war, and Jay's Treaty of 1794, sought to protect the property rights of British subjects in the United States. Because of those treaties, the Virginia trial court ruled in favor of Martin. However, the Virginia Court of Appeals reversed in favor of Hunter. Section 25 of the Judiciary Act of 1789 permitted Martin to appeal his case to the United States Supreme Court. In 1813, in *Fairfax's Devisee v. Hunter's Lessee*, the Supreme Court reversed the Virginia Court of Appeals and reinstated the original trial court's ruling in favor of Martin. The Virginia Court of Appeals refused to recognize the validity of the Supreme Court's ruling and unanimously declared that the appellate jurisdiction of the Supreme Court did not extend to the Virginia Court of Appeals, that § 25 of the Judiciary Act of 1789, which gave the Supreme Court jurisdiction, was unconstitutional, and that the writ of error issued by the Supreme Court to the Virginia Court of Appeals in *Fairfax's Devisee v. Hunter's Lessee* was invalid. The present case, *Martin v. Hunter's Lessee*, is concerned chiefly with the Supreme Court's right to review the decisions of a state supreme court.

CONSTITUTIONAL ISSUE

Whether the Supreme Court has the power to review the decisions of a state's highest court of appeal? YES

MAJORITY OPINION Justice Joseph Story delivers the opinion of the Court. Justice Story begins his opinion with a discussion of the nature of the federal union. He asserts that the people, not the states, created the union and that the people could bestow any power they wished on the national government including the power of the Supreme Court to review the decisions of state supreme courts. Justice Story then proceeds to discuss the judicial power of the United States. He notes that Article III extends the judicial power of the United States to all cases arising under the Constitution, U.S. laws, and U.S. treaties. Therefore, any case that falls within that definition comes under the jurisdiction of federal courts regardless of the court from which it comes. In other words, it is the nature of the case, not the nature of the court, that determines federal jurisdiction.

Virginia's position is that the Supreme Court's appellate jurisdiction is limited to hearing appeals from inferior federal courts but not from the highest courts of the states. Otherwise, the state's highest court would be considered inferior to the Supreme Court, and this is an affront to the state's sovereignty. Story refutes Virginia's argument in several ways. First, if Congress had failed to establish inferior federal courts, cases involving federal questions would never come to the Supreme Court under its appellate jurisdiction. That is, without inferior federal courts, under Virginia's interpretation, the Supreme Court would be limited to hearing cases arising under its original jurisdiction. That, Story insists, would defeat the purposes of the framers in giving any appellate jurisdiction to the Supreme Court. Therefore, realizing that Congress might not create inferior federal courts, the framers must have intended the Supreme Court to have appellate jurisdiction over cases in state courts that arise under the Constitution, a federal statute, or a U.S. treaty. Second, Article VI states that the Constitution and U.S. laws and treaties are "the supreme law of the Land; and the Judges in every State shall be bound thereby." Story believes that this clause is proof the framers knew that some federal issues would begin in state courts. Finally, Supreme Court review of state court decisions can hardly be an affront to state sovereignty. The Constitution places numerous limits on the state's sovereignty. For example, states are forbidden to coin money or pass *ex post facto* laws. Congress may make exceptions to a state's election laws. If the Court itself has the authority to review the actions of state legislatures and state governors, why should the state's judiciary be exempt?

In the next section of the opinion, Justice Story makes a logical case for upholding Supreme Court review of state supreme courts. The framers, he asserts, were concerned that state jealousies could cause state courts to be biased in some controversies. In the interest of justice, an appeal to a neutral national court seemed advisable. The framers also believed that the courts of the nation should make the final decision in cases involving foreign diplomats and the national sovereignty. Story argues that the need for uniform interpretation of the Constitution is another consideration. Judges of equal learning in different states might arrive at different interpretations of the law. According to Story, this would result in the law having different meanings in different states causing great mischief. Finally, Story notes that because the plaintiff gets to decide in which court his suit is filed, he might select a state court likely to be favorable to his claim. It would be unfair to the defendant if he were unable to appeal an unfavorable decision of a state court to the Supreme Court.

Justice Story concludes the opinion by reasserting the constitutionality of § 25 of the Judiciary Act of 1789 and by reasserting the Court's previous decision in *Fairfax's Devisee*. The Court reverses the Virginia Court of Appeals and reaffirms the verdict of the Virginia trial court, which had ruled in favor of Denny Martin.

OTHER OPINIONS   Justice William Johnson writes an opinion in which he agreed with the holding of the Court but not with all of its reasoning.

SIGNIFICANCE OF THE CASE   This case represents a milestone in the struggle to establish the supremacy of the federal courts in cases that raise a federal question. A case that raises a federal question is one that involves the interpretation of the Constitution itself, a federal statute, or, in the *Martin* case, a U.S. treaty. Although not every case involves a federal question, in those that do *Martin* makes it clear that the Supreme Court is the final authority. *Martin* illustrates some of the dangers inherent in the Virginia Court of Appeals position. In this case, Denny Martin, a resident alien, was challenging the validity of a state law that he alleged violated the terms of two treaties with Great Britain. The Virginia Court of Appeals upheld the validity of the state law in *Fairfax's Devisee*. Here, then, a state court was upholding a state law alleged to be in violation of U.S. treaties. Without an appeal to a federal court, Martin would have seen his property confiscated by the state.

Of the arguments Justice Story makes in defense of his position, the most compelling is that of uniformity. If the Supreme Court were unable to review and correct the decisions of state courts when they interpret federal law, there would be no "supreme law of the land." Instead, there would be fifty interpretations of the Constitution that Story foresaw as having disastrous consequences for the country.

QUESTIONS FOR DISCUSSION

(1)   Do you think it was fair for Virginia to forbid aliens to inherit property in the state? Why or why not?

(2)   What is the real issue in this case? Is it who has title to the land or is it something else? Explain.

(3)   What importance does *Martin v. Hunter's Lessee* hold for us today?

(4)   What does this case tell you about our federal form of government and our judicial system?

(5)   What do you suppose would have happened if Virginia's position would have prevailed?

RELATED CASES   *MARBURY V. MADISON*, 1 Cranch 137 (1803); *FLETCHER V. PECK*, 6 Cranch 87 (1810); and *COHENS V. VIRGINIA*, 6 Wheaton 264 (1821).

COHENS V. VIRGINIA
6 Wheaton 264 (1821)

BACKGROUND   In 1812 Congress passed a law authorizing the sale of lottery tickets to raise revenue for the financing of civic improvements in the District of Columbia. P. J. and M. J. Cohen were prosecuted for selling some of the lottery tickets in Virginia in violation of a state law banning such sales. The Cohens offered as their defense the thesis that the congressional law authorizing the sale of the tickets took precedence over the state law. The Virginia courts upheld the state law, and the Cohens were fined $100. They appealed their convictions to the Supreme Court, which granted the writ of error under § 25 of the Judiciary Act of 1789. Virginia denied that the Supreme Court had jurisdiction on the grounds that a state was a defendant in the case, that no writ of error lay from the Supreme Court to a state court, and that the Judiciary Act did not give jurisdiction in the case. Virginia's position was that because no federal law had been declared unconstitutional, the judgment of the Virginia court was final.

CONSTITUTIONAL ISSUE

Whether the decision of a state court in a case where a federal law has been cited as a bar to prosecution under a state criminal law is reviewable by the Supreme Court under § 25 of the Judiciary Act of 1789? YES

MAJORITY OPINION   Chief Justice John Marshall delivers the opinion of the Court. The chief justice divides the opinion into three parts with each part addressing one of Virginia's objections to the Court's assumption of jurisdiction. Virginia's first objection is that a state, as a sovereign entity, cannot have its judicial decisions reviewed by the Supreme Court. Marshall answers by examining the jurisdiction of federal courts. The Constitution gives federal courts jurisdiction when certain parties, such as foreign ambassadors, are involved regardless of the nature of the case. Likewise, the Constitution gives federal courts jurisdiction in all cases arising under the Constitution, the laws of the United States, or its treaties regardless of the parties involved. Because the Constitution makes no exception to this rule, where the interpretation of a federal law is involved, the fact that a state is a party to the case is irrelevant. The people of the United States formed the Union, and it was their right to give the national government any power they deemed appropriate. Among those powers is the power of the federal courts to hear all cases arising under the Constitution, laws, and treaties of the United States. It would have been strange, Marshall notes, if the framers of the Constitution had failed to give to the federal courts the power to enforce the laws of the nation. He points out that fear of state prejudices and the experience of the national government (which had to rely on the state courts to enforce national laws) under the Articles of Confederation led the framers to give federal courts their jurisdiction. Marshall also notes that allowing the judgments of state courts to be final would result in many different interpretations of the same federal law. The need for a single, uniform interpretation of the law makes review by the Supreme Court the only logical solution.

Marshall then dismisses the Eleventh Amendment (which prohibits a citizen of one state from suing a state in federal court) as a bar against the Court's jurisdiction. The Eleventh Amendment, he observes, was added to the Constitution to protect states from being sued by their creditors in federal courts. But this is a criminal case and not a suit against a state for money damages. At any rate, the Amendment bars suits "commenced" against a state. However, a suit that is commenced in one court and then appealed to a higher court is merely a continuation of that same suit. It was Virginia that commenced the suit by prosecuting the Cohens, and the Supreme Court's review is just a continuation of that suit.

In the second part of the opinion, Marshall addresses the issue of whether the Supreme Court can issue a writ of error to a state court. Virginia would like to limit the Supreme Court's appellate jurisdiction to cases appealed from lower federal courts only. Marshall repeats many of his earlier arguments noting the supremacy of the national government, the necessity of uniform interpretations, and the mischief that would result from multiple interpretations of the same law. Finally, Marshall states that the third objection (that the Virginia court's ruling is sufficient to settle the case) is really just a restatement of the first two. He notes that Congress, in passing a law, could either intend for the law to have effect only in the District of Columbia or to have effect in the nation at large. However, the correct interpretation depends on the wording of the individual statute. It is for the federal courts, he declares, to make that determination.

After holding that the Supreme Court does indeed have jurisdiction to review the Cohens' convictions, Marshall proceeds to uphold the ruling of the Virginia court. There is no evidence, he states, to indicate that Congress intended for the sale of the lottery tickets to occur outside the District. Because the purpose of the law was local improvements, without an express authorization to sell tickets outside the District, the Court must assume Congress intended the ticket sales to be local. Therefore, the Court affirmed the convictions of the Cohens.

SIGNIFICANCE OF THE CASE   In some respects *Cohens* hardly seems worthy of constitutional notice. The $100 fine for the illegal sale of a few lottery tickets seems inconsequential. But, *Cohens* is significant because it firmly established the Supreme Court's authority to review the decision of the state's highest court in cases involving federal questions. Although *Martin v. Hunter's Lessee* raised essentially the same issue, there are differences. In *Martin* the Court invalidated a state law in conflict with a U.S. treaty, but the state itself was not a party to the case. Nor did *Martin* involve the review of a state criminal law. Finally, *Cohens* definitively answers the question whether the Eleventh Amendment bars Supreme Court review of cases in which a state is a party. The

Supreme Court held that any state law challenged in a state court as violative of federal law is reviewable by the Court.

QUESTIONS FOR DISCUSSION

(1) Why do you think Virginia was so unwilling to have the decisions of its state courts reviewed by the Supreme Court?

(2) Because the Supreme Court affirms the Cohens' convictions, was it really necessary for the Supreme Court to review their case? Why or why not?

(3) If Congress had authorized the sale of the lottery tickets outside the District of Columbia, would such a law, in your opinion, be constitutional? Why or why not?

(4) Do you think the Cohens commenced a suit against the state of Virginia within the meaning of the Eleventh Amendment? Why or why not?

RELATED CASES *CHISHOLM V. GEORGIA*, 2 Dallas 419 (1793); *FLETCHER V. PECK*, 6 Cranch 87 (1810); and *MARTIN V. HUNTER'S LESSEE*, 1 Wheaton 304 (1816).

2

FEDERALISM

INTRODUCTION

In some respects, federalism is a peculiar form of government. The old adage, "Necessity is the mother of invention" certainly applies to federalism. The framers of the Constitution were familiar with the basic forms of government. Under Great Britain, the colonies had experienced a unitary type of government. Although they enjoyed a great deal of autonomy, the colonies were not allowed to forget that they were colonies. When the British government decided to assert greater control over the colonies after the French and Indian War, the framers learned of the drawbacks of unitary government. Parliament was too remote to understand the problems and needs of colonies separated by three thousand miles of ocean.

The experience of the colonies, now states, under the Articles of Confederation was not much happier than their colonial experience. It was true that as sovereign states they enjoyed complete autonomy and independence. While colonies they had faced a common enemy in Great Britain and had suppressed their differences. However, once the Revolution ended, differences among the states began to surface. The institution of slavery was already beginning to divide North and South. Trade and currency problems also caused friction. The national government was one in name only as Shays's Rebellion had shown. Most thoughtful observers realized that the nation was in danger of splintering into thirteen separate nations.

The framers who met in Philadelphia in May 1787 faced a dilemma. Some states had been in existence for more than one hundred years. It was inconceivable to expect them to surrender their governmental powers to an omnipotent central government.

Conversely, it was clear that the national government would have to be strengthened if the United States were to survive. The solution the framers created is what we now call a federal form of government. The states would surrender some governmental powers to the national government. Other governmental powers were to be exercised, as they had always been, by the individual states. Thus, federalism can be defined as a division of governmental powers between a central government and the states. The necessity of reconciling existing states and the need for a strong national government resulted in the invention of American federalism.

The genius of the framers was to formulate federalism and set it in motion. For all their wisdom, however, the framers could not foresee every contingency. What the framers created was a blueprint for American government, the mere shadow of what would come later. It was for future generations of Americans to define federalism more fully. It was the fate of one generation to define federalism by means of a civil war. Each generation leaves its mark on federalism and passes it on to the next.

Federalism has been a learning process. It has been, as suggested, an evolutionary process. Federalism is like a marriage in which both partners are uncertain as the union begins. Adjustments have to be made. Compromises have to be negotiated. Accommodations have to be worked out. Finally, the partners become comfortable with each other, and a lasting relationship develops. But, like a marriage that stage of comfort is not reached without conflict.

In the cases that follow we will trace the events that have been instrumental in the shaping of federalism. In the next section we examine cases that focus on the states as they define their roles and powers under the Constitution. In the following section we look at how Congress has viewed its powers under the Constitution. The key to understanding this process is to appreciate that when the nation embarked on this journey it had only a vague idea where it was headed. There were so many questions the Constitution failed to answer. There were even more questions yet to be raised. Throughout the journey the Supreme Court has helped mark out the course. Sometimes wisely and sometimes not, the Court has guided our federalism for more than two hundred years. History will judge if the course has been the right one.

State Powers under the Constitution

It was impossible, as we have seen, to have predicted all the consequences of the division of powers between the national government and the states. For example, the states never dreamed that by ratifying the Constitution they had forfeited their right of sovereign immunity. But, in *CHISHOLM V. GEORGIA* (1793) the Supreme Court ruled that a citizen of another state could sue Georgia in a federal court. *CHISHOLM* was reversed almost immediately with the passage of the Eleventh Amendment. However, it illustrates the uncertainty caused by the new order created by the Constitution. As new controversies arose, different clauses of the Constitution had to be interpreted for the first time. The early decisions of the Supreme Court were especially important because they set the precedents on which later decisions were based. The Court was writing on a clean slate, and many of its early decisions remain the law of the land.

CALDER V. BULL (1798) provides an excellent example of how an early decision has affected constitutional interpretation. *CALDER* involved a dispute over a will. Under Connecticut law, Bull, the loser in the dispute, had eighteen months to appeal the case. Bull failed to file a timely appeal but later prevailed on the state legislature to change the law so that he could appeal the decision. Bull then did so and was eventually successful in getting the earlier decision in favor of Calder reversed. Calder cried "foul!" and appealed to the U.S. Supreme Court. Calder argued that states may not pass *ex post facto* laws, which was exactly what Connecticut had done. The Supreme Court disagreed. It held that historically only criminal laws were considered *ex post facto* laws. Laws that changed the rules of evidence in a criminal case, increased the penalty for a crime, or punished an act that was not unlawful when performed were cited as examples of *ex post facto* laws. The Court's holding in *CALDER* is essentially the approach to *ex post facto* laws that is used today.

During the process of breathing life into the phrases of the Constitution the Supreme Court sometimes restrains the hand of the state. In *McCULLOCH V. MARYLAND* (1819) the Court decided whether a state could tax an instrument of the national government. As independent states under the Articles of Confederation, states were unaccustomed to having their taxing power questioned. However, Chief Justice John Marshall, writing for the majority, held that a state could not use its taxing power to interfere with the Second Bank of the United States. If permitted to tax at its discretion, a state could undermine the operation of the national government.

A clause in the Constitution that has generated a considerable amount of litigation is Article I, § 10. Article I, § 10 prohibits states from impairing the obligation of contracts. An early test of the Contract Clause involved the state of Georgia. The state's corrupt legislature had sold millions of acres of public lands for pennies an acre. Members of the legislature had been bribed to approve the sale. When the Yazoo Land Scandal, as it was known, became public, irate voters threw out the rascals responsible and elected a new legislature. The new legislature then passed a law rescinding the original sale of the land. Meanwhile, however, the land had been sold to third parties who had no role in the corruption. In *FLETCHER V. PECK* (1810), the Supreme Court ruled on the constitutionality of the rescinding law. The Court held that the original sale of the land, although tainted with bribery, was legal. The Court held that contracts had been entered into and executed. By invalidating the rescinding law the Court for the first time struck down a state law as unconstitutional.

The Contract Clause was also prominent in *THE TRUSTEES OF DARTMOUTH COLLEGE V. WOODWARD* (1819). In that case the state of New Hampshire sought to change the terms of the College's charter. Dartmouth's original charter had been a royal one granted before the Revolution in 1769. New Hampshire argued that as heir to British sovereignty, it could alter the terms of the charter. If New Hampshire had remained an independent nation, it undoubtedly could have altered the charter. However, when New Hampshire entered the Union it agreed to abide by the terms of the Constitution. The Supreme Court held that the original charter was a contract and was therefore protected by Article I, § 10. The *DARTMOUTH COLLEGE* case is significant because it gave corporations the legal protection against state interference that later became vital to the rise of capitalism.

The Contract Clause has undergone an interesting transformation. The Supreme Court moved from a position of merely protecting contracts from state impairment to elevating the right of contract to a sacred status. The Court not only protected contracts but also protected the freedom to enter contracts. In the process, the Court used the Contract Clause to limit state police power. *LOCHNER V. NEW YORK* (1905) is illustrative. The New York Legislature enacted a law limiting the number of hours a baker could work in a day to ten. The state passed the law as a health measure to protect bakers from the effects of breathing flour dust. The Supreme Court held that the law interfered with the right of employer and employee alike to negotiate their own terms of employment.

LOCHNER is one of the most criticized cases in constitutional history. The Court's reliance on "freedom of contract," a phrase that does not even appear in the Constitution, is cited as the essence of substantive due process. Substantive due process is the charge that the justices inject their personal social and economic views into the Constitution. The dissent of Justice Oliver Wendell Holmes, Jr., in *LOCHNER* is the classic condemnation of substantive due process. Substantive due process has been largely discredited for economic issues. In *Williamson v. Lee Optical* (1955) the Court made it clear that, at least in economic cases, it would not question the motives or second guess legislative bodies.

Another major test of the Contract Clause occurred during the Great Depression. Minnesota enacted the Minnesota Mortgage Moratorium Act, which extended the period of redemption for mortgages. The period of redemption is the time a person who has defaulted on a mortgage is allowed to redeem the mortgaged property. The law, in effect, gave borrowers more time to raise the money and to avoid foreclosure on their property. The Court upheld the Act in *HOME BUILDING AND LOAN ASSOCIATION V. BLAISDELL* (1934). Chief Justice Charles Evans Hughes held that the emergency caused by the Great Depression merely triggered an otherwise legitimate use of the police power. The dissenters in *BLAISDELL* argued that the very purpose of the Contract Clause was to prevent state legislatures from canceling debts. The Contract Clause was designed to prevent laws like the Minnesota Mortgage Moratorium Act.

As noted, *LOCHNER* used freedom of contract to prevent use of the police power to regulate working conditions. The national government was precluded from regulating working conditions under the Commerce Clause. This, however, began to change. In *WEST COAST HOTEL CO. V. PARRISH* (1937), the Court again addressed the issue of state minimum wage laws. The state of Washington enacted a minimum wage law that applied to women and minors employed in the state. A similar law passed by Congress to regulate wages in the District of Columbia had been invalidated by the Court in *ADKINS V. CHILDREN'S HOSPITAL* (1923). Because the two laws were virtually identical, the Court agreed to reconsider *ADKINS*. With Chief Justice Hughes again writing for the majority, the Court held that freedom of contract is not absolute. Hughes maintained that freedom of contract is subject to reasonable use of the state's police power. Chief Justice Hughes noted that employees are not equal to employers when negotiating terms of employment. Often employees must either accept the terms offered or remain jobless. Given the harsh economic conditions then in existence, the state's minimum wage law was not an unreasonable exercise of the police power.

One final case worthy of note concerning use of the police power is *MUNN V. ILLINOIS* (1877). Illinois had amended its state constitution to empower its legislature to regulate the rates grain elevators could charge for storage. Munn, a grain elevator owner, challenged the constitutionality of the practice. The Supreme Court held that under some circumstances private property becomes "affected with a public interest." When that occurs, the state may regulate the use of even privately-owned property. *MUNN* was critical to legitimizing use of the police power for regulating business. Today, restaurants, hotels, insurance companies, barber shops, and countless other businesses are regulated by the state. When an individual opens his or her private property to the public, the right to resist reasonable regulation in the public interest is forfeited.

National Powers under the Constitution

The powers of the national government have been a major focus of Supreme Court decisions since the ratification of the Constitution. Consequently, it would be impossible to cover all the powers of the national government in a single essay. In addition, the powers to regulate interstate commerce, to tax, and to protect constitutional rights are covered in other chapters of this book. In this section, we will examine cases that do not fit neatly into other categories of congressional powers. But, as we shall see, these powers are just as important to constitutional development in the United States.

The power to coin money is essential to all governments. During the Confederation states used paper money to ease the burden of debtors much to the chagrin of creditors. State legislatures were viewed as too willing to succumb to popular pressure to devalue money. For these reasons, the framers decided to vest Congress with the power to coin money and to regulate its value. In addition, Article I, § 10 forbade states to make anything but gold or silver legal tender. Section 10 also forbids states to impair the obligation of contracts. State actions that devalued currency were seen as impairing the obligations of contracts.

Neither of the prohibitions of Article I, § 10 apply to the national government. During the Civil War Congress passed the Legal Tender Acts. These Acts permitted the national government to issue paper money as legal tender. (Legal tender has to be accepted for the payment of debts.) Although initially held unconstitutional in *Hepburn v. Griswold* (1870), the Supreme Court reversed itself and upheld the Acts in *THE LEGAL TENDER CASES* (1871). Modern Americans, accustomed to paper money, find it difficult to understand the reluctance of nineteenth-century Americans to accept paper money as legal tender.

The Constitution declares that treaties, along with the Constitution itself and federal laws, are the supreme law of the land. The scope of the treaty power was tested in *MISSOURI V. HOLLAND* (1920). The question arose whether a treaty empowers Congress to enact legislation it would otherwise be forbidden to enact. Under the Migratory Bird Treaty Congress passed the Migratory Bird Treaty Act. The Act prohibited the killing, capturing, or selling of certain species of birds. Missouri claimed that the power to regulate wildlife within the state was a reserved power of the state under the Tenth Amendment. The opinion, written by Justice Oliver Wendell Holmes, Jr., upholding the constitutionality of the Act created quite an uproar. Critics of the opinion argued Congress could exercise virtually any power reserved to the states merely by entering into a treaty with a foreign country and enacting legislation under the treaty. Although the fears voiced by critics of *HOLLAND* are largely unfounded, there is no doubt the decision broadened the scope of Congress's treaty power.

Congress also exercises a misunderstood but important power to govern the District of Columbia. The Constitution says that Congress may "exercise exclusive Legislation in all Cases whatsoever over such District (not exceeding ten Miles square) as may...become the Seat of the Government of the United States." Pursuant to this power, Congress created a Minimum Wage Board to determine the wages of women and minors working in the District. The law was challenged as a violation of the Due Process Clause of the Fifth Amendment. The conservative Supreme Court of that era held that the law violated the "liberty of contract" protected by the Amendment. As noted earlier in this section, the Supreme Court reversed itself in *WEST COAST HOTEL CO. V. PARRISH* (1937).

A key feature of American constitutionalism is the doctrine of separation of powers. Although described as "separate" the powers of the three branches of the national government often overlap. A case that evolved from the famous Teapot Dome Scandal, *McGRAIN V. DAUGHERTY* (1927) raised the issue whether Congress possessed the power to subpoena. The subpoena power is usually associated with the judiciary. A related power, the contempt power, is also considered within the judicial power. The Supreme Court was asked to decide if Congress could compel witnesses to appear before it and find them in contempt if they failed to answer congressional inquiries. The Court held that the power to legislate involves the power to investigate. The power to investigate, in turn, involves the power to compel witnesses to appear and to testify. The Supreme Court did hold in *WATKINS V. UNITED STATES* (1957) that Congress may not abuse the power and expose people to congressional questioning just for the sake of exposure.

One final often neglected area of constitutional power involves enabling sections of constitutional amendments. Enabling sections perform a function similar to the Necessary and Proper Clause. For example, § 2 of the Fifteenth Amendment declares "The Congress shall have the power to enforce this article by appropriate legislation." In 1965 Congress passed the Voting Rights Act. Among its provisions were some that suspended state-mandated qualifying tests for voting, such as a literacy test. The law also provided for federal registrars to enter a state and to register Negro voters who had been prevented from registering in the past. Finally, the law provided for federal poll watchers to monitor state elections. South Carolina challenged the law in *SOUTH CAROLINA V. KATZENBACH* (1966). South Carolina argued that the law was an invasion of state powers under the Tenth Amendment. The Supreme Court upheld the Act, thereby allowing federal intervention in states where a pattern of racial discrimination in voting existed. The Court's decision signaled a willingness to permit Congress to use its powers to the fullest to end racial discrimination.

Conclusion

Federalism may not be the most exciting topic of American government. Still, federalism has aroused the passions of Americans unlike few other issues. The proper balance between the power of the national government and the states is a never-ending debate. As described at the beginning of this essay, federalism has been like a marriage.

Sometimes the road has been rocky, and sometimes it has been smooth. However, to the students of federalism—those who truly seek to understand it—the study of the federal union has never been dull.

CALDER V. BULL
3 Dallas 386 (1798)

BACKGROUND This Connecticut case involves a dispute over a will between Calder and Bull. The Court of Probate for Hartford initially ruled in favor of Calder. Under Connecticut law, Bull had 18 months in which to appeal the decision but apparently he decided not to do so. Later, Bull changed his mind and prevailed on the Connecticut Legislature to pass a law ordering a new trial in the case. At the new trial the property that had been awarded to Calder was given to Bull. Ultimately, Calder appealed to the U.S. Supreme Court on the grounds that the act of the Connecticut Legislature constituted the passing of an *ex post facto* law in violation of Article I, § 9 of the U.S. Constitution. The Justices at that time wrote separate (*seriatim*) opinions, so there was no majority opinion even though the decision was unanimous.

CONSTITUTIONAL ISSUE

Whether the Connecticut law in this case constitutes an *ex post facto* law in violation of Article I, § 9 of the Constitution? NO

SERIATIM OPINIONS Justice Samuel Chase writes the first opinion. Justice Chase argues that *ex post facto* laws were meant to apply only to criminal laws and not to all retrospective laws. He cites examples of the historical use of *ex post facto* laws. One is a law that punishes a citizen for an act that is, when done, not unlawful. Another is a law that increases the penalty for a crime and applies it retroactively. A third is a law that changes the rules of evidence; for example, a law that reduces the number of eyewitnesses needed in treason cases from two to one. Chase argues that every *ex post facto* law by nature is retrospective but that not every retrospective law is an *ex post facto* law. Chase cites provisions from the state constitutions of Massachusetts, Maryland, and North Carolina to support his view that only criminal laws could be *ex post facto* laws. Interestingly, Chase foreshadows the *Marbury v. Madison* case. He states that without giving an opinion whether the Court has jurisdiction to void an act of Congress contrary to the Constitution, he has no doubt that the Court lacks jurisdiction to determine if a state law violates a state constitution.

Justice William Paterson delivers the next opinion. Justice Paterson focuses on whether the law that required the new trial was a legislative or judicial act. Historically, the Connecticut Legislature possessed the power to order new trials. Although in 1762 the legislature granted the same power to the courts, it retained the power for itself and had used it twice since 1762. If the law was a judicial act, Paterson asserts, then the matter is settled as far as he is concerned. However, if the law was a legislative act, the question of an *ex post facto* law remains. Paterson, like Chase, adopts the view that *ex post facto* laws apply to criminal acts only. Paterson adds the Delaware constitution to Chase's list of state constitutions that limit *ex post facto* laws to criminal law.

Justice James Iredell, in his opinion, also notes the Connecticut Legislature's history of granting new trials. But even assuming the law is a legislative act, Iredell agrees with the other justices that *ex post facto* laws are for criminal cases only. Iredell cites historical evidence to show that *ex post facto* laws were used by the winning faction in power struggles to punish members of the losing faction and that this was the evil the prohibition was designed to prevent.

SIGNIFICANCE OF THE CASE *Calder v. Bull* clarified, as Justice Chase explained, the difference between an *ex post facto* law and a retrospective law. Laws often alter the rights, privileges, and status of persons when they are changed, but not every change is an *ex post facto* law within the meaning of the Constitution. By limiting the prohibition against *ex post facto* laws to criminal matters, the Court allowed the states more flexibility to enact changes in their existing laws. In other words, laws already enacted were not "carved in stone" never subject to change. Although it may be desirable for laws always to be prospective, *Calder* makes it clear they are not required to be. *Calder* also foreshadows the *Marbury v. Madison* case. Although the Court upholds the Connecticut law challenged in this case, the justices hint that eventually the Court will have to decide if it has the power to invalidate a law contrary to the Constitution.

QUESTIONS FOR DISCUSSION

(1)   Do you think what the Connecticut Legislature did was fair? Why or why not?

(2)   Do you agree that *ex post facto* laws should be limited to criminal matters only? Why or why not?

(3)   Try to think of some other noncriminal situations in which retrospective laws would be unfair.

RELATED CASES *MARBURY V. MADISON*, 1 Cranch 137 (1803); and *FLETCHER V. PECK*, 6 Cranch 87 (1810).

McCULLOCH V. MARYLAND
4 Wheaton 316 (1819)

BACKGROUND   In 1791 Congress created the First Bank of the United States and gave it a twenty-year charter. The Bank was unpopular in some of the states, and so when its charter expired in 1811 Congress did not renew it. By 1815 even critics of the Bank realized it had been a mistake to abolish it, so President James Madison asked Congress to charter the Second Bank of the United States, which it did. The Maryland Legislature, in retaliation, passed a law imposing a $15,000 tax on any bank in the state that had not been chartered by the state. In lieu of the flat tax, the Bank could pay a tax stamp on each $5, $10, or $20 bank note up to a $1000 note. James McCulloch, the cashier of the Baltimore branch of the Bank, was fined $100 for passing an unstamped bank note. The Maryland courts upheld McCulloch's conviction, and he appealed to the Supreme Court. Maryland argued that the power to incorporate a bank was reserved to the states, and that the Bank was unconstitutional but that if the Bank was constitutional, Maryland was free to tax it.

CONSTITUTIONAL ISSUES

(1)   Whether Congress has the power to incorporate a bank? YES

(2)   Whether a state may tax an instrumentality of the national government? NO

MAJORITY OPINION   Chief Justice John Marshall delivers the opinion of the Court. At the outset the chief justice gives some of the history of the Bank, noting that it was created by the First Congress, which had among its members some of the framers of the Constitution. Although the Bank was controversial, even its opponents were persuaded that it was necessary, prompting Congress to establish the Second Bank. Marshall then turns to the issue of the Bank's constitutionality.

One of Maryland's arguments centers around the subordination of the national government to the states. Maryland claims that the powers of the national government emanate from the states. Marshall disagrees, arguing that the national government derives its authority from the people. Although it is true that the national government's powers are limited, the national government is supreme within its sphere. Next, Marshall concedes that the power to incorporate a bank is not among the enumerated powers of Congress. However, he argues that the Constitution was intended to outline the powers of government. The details or means for implementing those powers were to be left to the discretion of Congress. Among the enumerated powers of Congress are the powers to lay and collect taxes, to coin money, and to borrow money. Congress, Marshall insists, must be free to choose the most appropriate means for implementing these powers. Marshall cites the Necessary and Proper Clause in Article I, § 8 as the constitutional basis for incorporating the Bank.

After ruling that the Necessary and Proper Clause provides the authority for the creation of the Bank, Marshall proceeds to rebut Maryland's interpretation of that Clause. First, Maryland argued that the Clause was merely designed to give Congress the authority to pass laws. Marshall answers by noting that such an interpretation would make the Clause redundant because Article I gives Congress "all legislative power," which implies the power to make laws. Second, Maryland would have the Court interpret the word "necessary" to mean "essential," "indispensable," or "absolutely necessary." Marshall prefers to interpret "necessary" to mean "appropriate" or "convenient." He notes that the framers knew how to qualify terms. For example, in Article I, § 10 a state is forbidden from laying imposts or duties on imports or exports "except what may be absolutely necessary for executing its laws." Finally, Marshall points out that the Necessary and Proper Clause appears in the part of the Constitution that enlarges the powers of Congress as opposed to passages, such as Article I, § 9, which limit congressional power.

After upholding the constitutionality of the Bank, Marshall turns to the question of the tax. Marshall notes that a state's power to tax is not absolute. The Constitution, as shown, limits taxes on imports and exports to those absolutely necessary for executing the state's inspection laws. This limitation being acknowledged, Marshall asserts that any use of the taxing power incompatible with the spirit of the Constitution is also forbidden. The power to create the Bank involves the power to preserve it. The power to destroy the Bank by laying excessive taxes on its operation is incompatible with the power to preserve. Maryland has confidence that the states will not abuse this power. Marshall answers that the people of the state can control their representatives' abuse of the taxing power through the ballot, but the people of the whole nation have no way to control a state that abuses its power to tax a national operation. Marshall, who asserts the supremacy of the national government, claims that because the power to tax involves the power to destroy, the power to tax cannot be exercised by the people of a single state over the government of the whole people of the United States. This would allow the people of a single state to frustrate the will of the people of the nation. Marshall then argues that the national government may tax state banks. Again, he argues that the national government reflects the will of all of the people and that national laws must be uniform. Marshall concludes the opinion by declaring the Maryland tax unconstitutional. However, he narrows the ruling to taxes placed on the operation of the Bank and states that the ruling does not necessarily apply to property taxes or other taxes of a general nature.

SIGNIFICANCE OF THE CASE *McCulloch v. Maryland* ranks with *Marbury v. Madison* as one of the most important decisions in our constitutional history because it serves as the basis for the doctrine of implied powers. This means that if whatever Congress wants to do can be logically implied from one of its enumerated powers, it will be constitutional. The importance of this cannot be exaggerated. Marshall says that if the end is legitimate and within the power of Congress, then any appropriate means to reach the legitimate end is constitutional. Marshall's ruling permits each new generation of Americans to adopt for itself the most appropriate solutions to its problems. *McCulloch* forms the basis of the idea of the "living" constitution, which can be adapted to fit the needs of the people in the future as it has met their needs in the past. *McCulloch* paved the way for the expansion of the power of the national government and served as a response to those who wanted a strict or limited interpretation of the powers of the national government.

QUESTIONS FOR DISCUSSION

(1) What does Marshall mean when he writes that "the power to tax involves the power to destroy"?

(2) Try to imagine some of the consequences if Maryland's position would have carried the day. What are some of the dangers in Maryland's position?

(3) Try to think of some other laws that have been passed by Congress and determine which of the enumerated powers Congress relied on in passing the law.

(4) Do you agree with Maryland's position that the creation of a bank is not absolutely necessary to execute Congress's power to coin money? Why or why not?

RELATED CASES *McCRAY V. UNITED STATES*, 195 U.S. 27 (1904); *HAMMER V. DAGENHART*, 247 U.S. 251 (1918); and *HEART OF ATLANTA MOTEL, INC. V. UNITED STATES*, 379 U.S. 241 (1964).

THE TRUSTEES OF DARTMOUTH COLLEGE V. WOODWARD
4 Wheaton 518 (1819)

BACKGROUND In 1754, Rev. Eleazar Wheelock created, at his own expense and on his own property, a school for the instruction of Indians in the Christian religion. The success of the school lead Dr. Wheelock and his agent, Rev. Nathaniel Whitaker, to solicit funds in this country and in England, and to expand the goal to provide education for both Indians and English youth. To that end, they selected trustees, including the Earl of Dartmouth, who received a charter from George III in 1769 establishing Dartmouth College as a body corporate. In 1816, the New Hampshire Legislature passed laws adding additional trustees, altering the method of selection of trustees to *ex officio* members and those appointed by elected officials, and changing the name of the institution to Dartmouth University. The trustees under the original charter filed suit to recover the corporate property held by the new trustees under the legislation. The New Hampshire courts found for the defendants.

CONSTITUTIONAL ISSUE

Whether the national government may act to sustain private agreements against state action?
YES

MAJORITY OPINION Chief Justice John Marshall writes the opinion for the Court. This case involves the balance of power between a state and the national government and arises under Article I, § 10 of the Constitution, which bars states from passing laws that impair the "Obligation of Contracts." The established policy of the Court is to defer to state legislative enactments whenever possible if it can do so without abdicating its own responsibility to enforce constitutional provisions and protections.

The first issue is whether the charter given to the original trustees is a contract that is protected by the Constitution. Two types of contracts—public and private—are recognized in law; the former relates to the public compact between the government and its citizens and the conduct of internal government, whereas the latter refers to organizations chartered for carrying out business or charitable activities. The framers of the Constitution did not intend "to restrain the states in the regulation of the civil institutions, adopted for internal government," but Dartmouth College is a private eleemosynary institution—founded by a private individual and funded with private donations, not government monies.

May the act of incorporation convert a private institution to a public one that is outside the scope of Article I, § 10? A corporation is "an artificial being, invisible, intangible, and existing only in contemplation of the law," able to manage its own affairs. The object of the donor's bounty was not explicitly the "particular interests of New Hampshire" where the college was located due to fortuitous gifts of land but instead the object was to educate youths. Obtaining a charter and incorporating does not automatically change the character of the institution from private to public.

The Crown was bound by the terms of the contract, and so too are the people of New Hampshire on whom the powers and duties of the king devolved. The changes made by the legislature were substantial and conflicted with the provision of the U.S. Constitution against impairment of contract.

OTHER OPINIONS   Justice William Johnson concurs in the opinion of Chief Justice Marshall. Justice Henry Livingston concurs with Chief Justice Marshall and the opinions of Justice Washington and Justice Story. Justice Gabriel Duval dissents but does not enter an opinion.

Justice Bushrod Washington writes a concurring opinion. The Supreme Court has limited jurisdiction over state legislative acts, but here there is an allegation of violation of an explicit constitutional provision. The essential elements of a contract are the parties, consent, and an obligation to either carry out some act or refrain from some act. Both executed and executory contracts are within the constitutional protection against impairment of contracts. The charter in the instant case is a contract as legally defined. The assent of the parties is essential to a valid contract, and alterations, however minimal, change that contract. The New Hampshire legislation is a substantial alteration to the contract in violation of that principle and cannot stand.

Justice Joseph Story also concurs in the decision. Dartmouth College is not a public corporation because it does not exist only for public purposes such as towns, cities, parishes, and counties. The mere fact that an entity provides benefits to the general public as an object of its bounty does not transform it into a public organization such that the government controls its operations. The government may not arbitrarily alter the terms of the contract unless it specifically reserves that right in the articles of incorporation; in the instant case, the Crown did not make such a reservation. This is a valid contract, and the

> only authority remaining to the government is judicial, to ascertain the validity of the grant, to enforce its proper uses, to suppress frauds, and, if the uses are charitable, to secure their regular administration through the means of equitable tribunals, in cases where there would otherwise be a failure of justice.

The validity of the contract is not affected in the change of government from the monarchy to the newly organized United States.

SIGNIFICANCE OF THE CASE   *Dartmouth College v. Woodward* is noteworthy on several levels. First, the case was decided early in our history when the boundaries between the state and national governments were still being defined. State legislation about a very controversial issue fell to the dictates of the national Constitution. Second, the Supreme Court's position as arbiter of the meaning of the Constitution is strengthened. Third, contracts were given constitutional protection that portended their almost sacrosanct nature in later court decisions.

QUESTIONS FOR DISCUSSION

(1)   Are there points at which government should be able to alter or abrogate contracts? What boundaries would you set?

(2)   Assume that a United States contractor has received a defense contract from a foreign nation because of a bribe offered to the leaders of that country. Should our government cancel that contract because that is an illegal practice in this country? Why?

(3)   Regarding consumer transactions, when should government intervene, and when should the free market be allowed to function? Consider, for example, sales in the area of tobacco, legal pharmaceuticals, pesticides, or other products that harm the environment.

RELATED CASES   *FLETCHER V. PECK*, 6 Cranch 87 (1810); *LOCHNER V. NEW YORK*, 198 U.S. 45 (1905); *HOME BUILDING & LOAN ASSOCIATION V. BLAISDELL*, 290 U.S. 398 (1934); *WEST COAST HOTEL COMPANY V. PARRISH*, 300 U.S. 379 (1937); and *Allied Structural Steel v. Spannaus*, 438 U.S. 234 (1978).

LOCHNER V. NEW YORK
198 U.S 45 (1905)

BACKGROUND   An 1897 New York law made it a misdemeanor for a bakery owner to employ bakers for more than ten hours a day or sixty hours a week. Although enacted as a labor law, another purpose of the law was to protect the health of bakery workers. The maximum hour provision was included in a statute that had, among other things, provisions requiring proper ventilation and washroom facilities in bakeries. Joseph Lochner was twice convicted for violating the law and on the second conviction was fined $50. Lochner challenged the law as a violation of the liberty of contract protected by the Due Process Clause of the Fourteenth Amendment. New York defended its statute as a valid exercise of the state's police power.

CONSTITUTIONAL ISSUE

Whether a state law that prohibits an employer from allowing a bakery worker to work more than ten hours a day or sixty hours a week is a violation of the liberty of contract guaranteed by the Due Process Clause of the Fourteenth Amendment? YES

MAJORITY OPINION   Justice Rufus Peckham delivers the opinion of the Court. Justice Peckham approaches the New York law in a very straightforward manner. The case, he claims, involves the right of the individual to contract for his labor and the right of the state to exercise its police power. The law, Peckham asserts, interferes with the worker's right to contract with his employer for more than ten hours of work per day and the right of the employer to hire a worker who is willing to work for more than ten hours per day. Justice Peckham concedes that the Court has upheld infringements on the freedom to contract in other contexts. For example, in *Holden v. Hardy*, the Court upheld a Utah law that limited to eight the number of hours a miner could work in one day. However, the Court believed that the dangerous work involved in mining justified the interference with workers' and employers' right to contract. In addition, the Utah law waived the limit of hours in times of emergency that the New York law did not.

After conceding that the state's police power may sometimes limit freedom of contract, Justice Peckham argues that there must be some limit to the exercise of the state's police power, otherwise states would have unbounded power, and the Fourteenth Amendment would be meaningless. The test to be applied, he says, is whether the law is a "fair, reasonable, and appropriate" use of the police power. Justice Peckham obviously does not think the New York law meets the test. First, Peckham states that there is no reason to assume that individual bakers are unable to protect their own interests when contracting out their labor. Second, because the law cannot be meant to protect public health, it was obviously meant to protect the health of bakers. However, there is no evidence that bakers need any special protection from the state. Some occupations pose greater health risks than bakery work, and some pose less. Third, even if there are some respiratory diseases associated with bakery work, it takes more than the mere risk of unhealthiness to justify interfering with the right of contract. Fourth, Justice Peckham is concerned about the scope of such an exercise of the police power should the New York law be sustained. For example, the state could regulate the hours of bank clerks on the grounds that, working indoors, they receive inadequate sunlight that is unhealthy. Finally, Justice Peckham rejects the argument that shorter workdays will result in cleaner bakers, which in turn will result in a cleaner product for consumers. He calls such a justification "flimsy" and certainly not sufficient to overcome freedom of contract. He says that in such cases the Court is free to examine the legislature's hidden motives. This law, Peckham asserts, is not a health law but an attempt to regulate the hours of labor between a master and his employees.

OTHER OPINIONS Justice Oliver Wendell Holmes, Jr. dissents. Holmes views the dispute as one over economic differences of opinion. He does not believe the Court should allow its economic views to be the basis for invalidating a law enacted by the representatives of the people. He notes that many laws interfere with the freedom of individuals. For example, laws that impose compulsory school attendance, compulsory vaccinations, prohibit lotteries, and regulate monopolies interfere with someone's freedom, yet are seen as valid exercises of the state's police power. Holmes believes that the New York Legislature has the power to enact this law regardless of the opinion of the Court about its ultimate wisdom.

Justice John Marshall Harlan I, joined by Justice Edward White and Justice William Day, also writes a lengthy dissent. Justice Harlan argues that in previous cases, such as *Allgeyer v. Louisiana*, the Court has conceded that the right to contract is not absolute and may be regulated if a certain activity is contrary to the public policy of a state. Although the state's police power may not be used for oppressive or unjust legislation, states enjoy great discretion in its use. The Court, Justice Harlan argues, should never invalidate an exercise of the state's police power unless it is beyond question an excessive use of that power. If there is any doubt about a statute's validity, the Court should resolve the doubt in favor of the state. Justice Harlan believes that the New York law is a valid means to a proper end. Despite the allegation that the law really regulates hours, the state has ample evidence to support it as a health measure. Bakers, according to Harlan, do arduous work in extreme heat often working late at night. In addition, the inhalation of flour dust inflames the lungs and causes a person's eyes to water. Finally, Justice Harlan argues that the proper length of the working day varies greatly among the industrialized nations indicating widespread disagreement. Therefore, it should be state legislatures, not the courts, that decide the issue.

SIGNIFICANCE OF THE CASE *Lochner* is often cited as the classic example of a majority of justices rather blatantly injecting their personal economic views into the Court's decision. The *Lochner* Court very clearly favored *laissez-faire* capitalism. It is rather ironic that Justice Peckham's opinion seemed more concerned about the right of a worker to work twelve or fourteen hours a day if he wished than the rights of the employer. The *Lochner* Court assumed that the worker and employer enter into a contractual arrangement as equals free to negotiate to their own advantage. In reality, to secure employment, workers must often accept whatever terms are imposed by the employer. The *Lochner* Court was subjected to severe criticism from social critics who saw the decision as a setback in the movement to use state laws to secure social and economic justice for workers.

QUESTIONS FOR DISCUSSION

(1) Is it reasonable to assume, as the Court did, that an individual bakery worker can protect his own interests regarding the number of hours in an employment situation? Why or why not?

(2) Do you believe the state has a right to limit your right to work as many hours per day as you wish? Why or why not?

(3) Do you think a court is better qualified than a state legislature to decide what is a "fair, reasonable, and appropriate" use of the state's police power? Why?

RELATED CASES *Mugler v. Kansas*, 123 U.S. 623 (1887); *Allgeyer v. Louisiana*, 165 U.S. 578 (1897); *Holden v. Hardy*, 169 U.S. 366 (1898); *ADKINS V. CHILDREN'S HOSPITAL*, 261 U.S. 525 (1923); and *WEST COAST HOTEL CO. V. PARRISH*, 300 U.S. 379 (1937).

HOME BUILDING & LOAN ASSOCIATION V. BLAISDELL
290 U.S. 398 (1934)

BACKGROUND During the Great Depression the Minnesota Mortgage Moratorium Act extended the period of redemption on mortgages during the effective dates of the Act, April 18, 1933, to May 1, 1935. The period of redemption is the time period in which a mortgagor who has defaulted on his mortgage may redeem the mortgaged property. The Blaisdells, husband and wife, borrowed $3,800.00 from the Home Building & Loan Association to purchase a fourteen-room house in Minneapolis. The Blaisdells defaulted on the loan, and the Association foreclosed and sold the property to itself for $3,700.95, the amount of the mortgage debt. The original purchase price was $4,056.39, but the current market value was estimated to be at $6,000.00. Under the terms of the Minnesota Mortgage Moratorium Act, the Blaisdells requested and received a sixteen-day extension, until May 18, 1933. They then applied to a state district court for another extension, which the court granted until May 1, 1935, when the Act was due to expire. The state court ordered the Blaisdells to pay the Association $40 per month during the period of redemption to cover taxes, insurance, and interest on the property. The sum of $40 was the rental value of the property as determined by the state court. The Association maintained that the Minnesota Mortgage Moratorium Act was enacted in violation of Article I, § 10 of the Constitution, which forbids a state from impairing the obligation of contracts. The Minnesota supreme court upheld the Act on the grounds that it was an emergency measure authorized under the state's police power.

CONSTITUTIONAL ISSUE

Whether a state law that extends the period of redemption on mortgages violates the Impairment of the Obligation of Contracts Clause? NO

MAJORITY OPINION Chief Justice Charles Evans Hughes delivers the opinion of the Court. The chief justice concedes that but for the interference of the Act, the Association would have been able to take legal possession of the property on May 2, 1933. He points out, however, that the Act does not reduce the Blaisdells' indebtedness and that aside from the period of redemption, all of the other conditions of the contract are unaltered. The Blaisdells must pay rent equal to the fair market value of the house. The Association still owns the house even though it is not free to dispose of it during the period of redemption. The factors that the Court must consider, according to the chief justice, are the relation of emergency power to constitutional power, the historical setting of the Contract Clause, the jurisprudence of the Contract Clause, and the principles of construction.

Chief Justice Hughes asserts that "emergency does not create power," but that emergency may furnish the occasion for the use of power. Hughes cites Congress's war power as an example. The war power is not created by the emergency of war but is given to meet the emergency. Some powers in the Constitution are so specific that emergency may never justify exceptions. For example, emergency would never allow states to coin money. However, general grants of power, the commerce power, for example, are open to construction and the Contract Clause is in that category. The chief justice admits that after the Revolution there was a tendency for state legislatures to pass laws for the benefit of debtors at the expense of creditors. But, he says, the prohibition against the impairment of the obligation of contracts was not meant to be absolute. Chief Justice Marshall said in *Sturges v. Crowninshield* that the remedies contained in contracts could "be modified as the wisdom of the nation shall direct." Chief Justice Waite believed that modification of remedies for debtors was a question of reasonableness for the legislative body to decide.

The chief justice then turns to the specific question of the impairment of the obligation of contract raised by this case. He states that the obligation of contract is impaired if a law invalidates, releases, or extinguishes a legal obligation. But, the Contract Clause presupposes the maintenance of a government capable of enforcing contracts because without government, contracts are meaningless. The Clause does not prevent a state from exercising its police powers to promote the public good. The state's police powers, the chief justice asserts, are superior to any rights secured by a contract. It cannot be maintained that the Contract Clause would prevent limited and temporary interpositions in the event of a great calamity, such as a fire or an earthquake. In this case, Minnesota, as much of the rest of the nation, was suffering from severe economic hardship. The chief justice compares the current situation to one in New York in which the Court upheld limits on contracts during a critical housing shortage. The chief justice rejects the notion that the Constitution's meaning is frozen to the interpretations or understanding of the framers. Quoting Chief Justice Marshall, Hughes says we must remember that it is a "constitution we are expounding."

Chief Justice Hughes concludes by making the following points. First, the emergency provided the proper occasion for Minnesota to use its police powers to protect vital community interests. Second, the means adopted by the Minnesota Legislature were appropriate to achieve the legitimate ends of protecting those community interests. Third, the conditions of the Act, such as the payment of rent to the Association, were reasonable. And fourth, the measure was a temporary one.

OTHER OPINIONS   Justice George Sutherland writes a dissent in which he was joined by Justices James C. McReynolds, Pierce Butler, and Willis Van Devanter. Justice Sutherland is upset with what he sees as an assault on the sanctity of contract. However, he is even more disturbed with the majority's position that the Constitution can mean one thing at one time and something entirely different at another. Because a constitutional provision may be inconvenient in an emergency does not mean it is any less binding. The purpose of the Constitution is to remove the fundamentals of government, such as the protection of contracts, from the "varying moods of public opinion."

Justice Sutherland then examines both the contemporary and historical accounts of the meaning of the Contract Clause. Using the writings of the framers and accounts of the state-ratifying conventions, Sutherland shows that the Contract Clause clearly was placed in the Constitution to prevent the laws relieving debtors that state legislatures passed after the Revolution. The histories of the period also indicate that the overriding motive for the Contract Clause was to protect the rights of creditors from state laws that sought to ease debtors' economic distress. Sutherland also predicts the dire consequences that result when such laws cause people to lose faith in government and the economic system.

Justice Sutherland then examines the case law that involves interpretation of the Contract Clause. In previous economic depressions, notably in 1837 and again in 1893, state legislatures passed laws that the Court struck down under the Clause. Time and again, Sutherland maintains, the grounds on which the Minnesota law rests have been rejected by the Court. The issue, he states, is not whether the emergency gives rise to an occasion to use an existing power but whether emergency allows the relaxation of a restriction imposed by the Constitution.

Justice Sutherland's opinion concludes with two final points. Previous cases in which the police power had been used to impair the obligation of contract were cases in which something once legal had been made illegal. For example, after Prohibition contracts to buy or sell liquor became invalid. The second point is the burden this Act places on the Association. The value of the property might fall, or the Association may need to sell the land to meet its financial obligations. Sutherland concludes by observing that if constitutional principles cannot be "upheld when they pinch as well as when they comfort, they may as well be abandoned."

SIGNIFICANCE OF THE CASE   In a sense Justice Sutherland is correct when he asserts at the beginning of his dissent that the Minnesota law itself is trivial in importance. The real issue is the age-old debate whether the Constitution is a "living" document or the embodiment of immutable fundamental principles that may not be changed to keep up with the times. The issue is not insignificant because it touches the heart of democratic theory and the very purpose of constitutional government. The Minnesota Legislature was obviously responding to a pressing concern of many people. People, like the Blaisdells, were losing their homes and the money they had invested in them. Legislative bodies, designed to reflect the views of majorities, tend to do what is popular or expedient. Constitutions are designed to protect the rights of minorities, in this case the Association's, from the "tyranny of the majority." Therein lies the classic dilemma. If the Constitution is to be a "living" document adaptable to the needs of the present generation, it must be flexible enough to respond to emergencies. If, conversely, it is the embodiment of "self-evident truths," it must remain true to its first principles. As *Blaisdell* illustrates, it is not an easy dilemma to resolve.

QUESTIONS FOR DISCUSSION

(1) How would you have voted in this case if you had been a member of the Supreme Court?

(2) Put yourself in the position of the Association. Is this a case of changing the rules in the middle of the game?

(3) Assume that the overriding purpose of government is to secure "the greatest good for the greatest number." Can this be used to justify the Minnesota Mortgage Moratorium Act? Why or why not?

(4) Discuss the effect on society if government fails to enforce contracts.

RELATED CASES *Sturges v. Crowninshield*, 4 Wheaton 122 (1819); *Ogden v. Saunders*, 12 Wheaton 213 (1827); *Charles River Bridge Co. v. Warren Bridge*, 11 Peters 420 (1837); *Bronson v. Kinzie*, 1 Howard 311 (1843); *EX PARTE MILLIGAN*, 4 Wallace 2 (1866); and *Edwards v. Kearzey*, 6 Otto 595 (1877).

WEST COAST HOTEL CO. V. PARRISH
300 U.S. 379 (1937)

BACKGROUND In 1913 the state of Washington passed a law creating the Industrial Welfare Commission. The Commission was required to ascertain wages and conditions of labor for women and minors, and after public hearings set the minimum wage to be paid for a particular occupation or industry. The West Coast Hotel Company employed a chambermaid, Elsie Parrish, at a wage that was less than the minimum wage set by law. Parrish brought suit against the hotel to recover the difference between the actual wages she received and the state's minimum wage. Parrish lost at the trial court level, but the Washington supreme court reversed and upheld the validity of the minimum wage law. The hotel then appealed to the U.S. Supreme Court. Although the state's attorney tried to distinguish Washington's law from the one held invalid in *Adkins v. Children's Hospital*, the essential features of the two laws were identical.

CONSTITUTIONAL ISSUE

Whether a state law that sets minimum wages for women deprives both workers and employers of "liberty of contract" protected by the Due Process Clause of the Fourteenth Amendment? NO

MAJORITY OPINION   Chief Justice Charles Evans Hughes delivers the opinion of the Court. Chief Justice Hughes makes it clear at the outset that the Washington law in this case and the congressional law held invalid in *Adkins* are identical. He states that in light of the fact that several states have adopted similar minimum wage laws, that economic conditions have changed, and that the law appears to be reasonable, the Court will reconsider *Adkins*.

Chief Justice Hughes states that the opponents of the law claim it violates freedom of contract. But the Constitution does not even mention freedom of contract; instead it speaks of "liberty." Liberty, the chief justice notes, has never been considered absolute but subject to reasonable regulation by the state in the exercise of its police power. The chief justice then points out that state laws regulating the maximum number of hours for women have been upheld as reasonable restrictions on freedom of contract. Next, the chief justice observes that employers and employees do not stand on equal footing when entering into an employment contract and that the state may intervene to protect the worker's interest. This is especially true in the case of women. Hughes cites examples of cases in which the Court has upheld different treatment for women even where a similar law affecting men would be unconstitutional.

Chief Justice Hughes continues by asserting that the establishment of a minimum wage law for women is not beyond the state's broad protective powers. Insofar as *Adkins* held otherwise, it was a departure from previous cases that limited freedom of contract in employment. The chief justice takes judicial notice of the economic conditions created by the Great Depression and the large number of people receiving public relief. He notes, "The community is not bound to provide what is in effect a subsidy for unconscionable employers." It is also no argument that the law does not apply to men. The Court has often held that an exercise of legislative power does not have to be as broad as it could be. The failure to include men does not render the law discriminatory. Finally, the chief justice declares *Adkins* to be overruled.

OTHER OPINIONS   Justice George Sutherland, joined by Justices Willis Van Devanter, James C. McReynolds, and Pierce Butler, dissents. Justice Sutherland is critical of the majority for allowing current economic conditions to influence their decision. The power of the states under the Constitution does not vary with changing economic conditions. If the Constitution prohibits the enactment of reasonable legislation, the remedy, he maintains, is to amend the Constitution. On the merits, Sutherland maintains that the Washington statute is identical to the one held invalid in *Adkins*, and he believes *Adkins* should be followed. According to his view, freedom of contract is the rule, and any exception to it should be made only under extraordinary circumstances. Sutherland asserts that there is a difference between laws setting maximum work hours and minimum wages. He quotes the *Adkins* opinion on the one-sided nature of the law. For example, no guarantee is made to the employer that he will receive a fair day's work for his money. Wages, Sutherland says, should be determined on an individual basis. He denies that women are in need of any special protection calling them the political equals of men. Finally, he warns that the power to set a minimum wage can also set a maximum wage.

SIGNIFICANCE OF THE CASE *West Coast Hotel Co., v. Parrish* is often viewed as another defeat for the forces of *laissez-faire* economic policy. Conservatives argue that market forces, not state legislatures, should determine minimum wages. They also criticize minimum wage laws as excessive governmental interference in business affairs. Finally, conservatives argue that minimum wage laws actually hurt some workers by pricing their labor out of the market. Liberals respond by maintaining that minimum wage laws are necessary to protect workers from exploitation by employers who want only the cheapest labor they can find. They also point out that most labor costs are passed on to the consumer anyway. Finally, they point out that a minimum wage is necessary to keep the working poor off public welfare. Despite the rhetoric, it is clear that *West Coast Hotel Co.* eliminated a major barrier to the use of the state's police power as a means of regulating labor-management relations.

QUESTIONS FOR DISCUSSION

(1) Do you think it was appropriate for the majority to consider the existing economic conditions in making their decision? Why or why not?

(2) Do you think Justice Sutherland's suggestion of amending the Constitution to allow minimum wage laws is a practical solution?

(3) Are both sides guilty of injecting their economic viewpoint into their decision? How?

(4) Do you think it is possible for any judge to decide a case like *West Coast Hotel Co.* without injecting his or her economic views?

(5) What is your position on minimum wage laws?

RELATED CASES *MUNN V. ILLINOIS*, 4 Otto 113 (1877); *Holden v. Hardy*, 169 U.S. 366 (1898); *LOCHNER V. NEW YORK*, 198 U.S. 45 (1905); *Muller v. Oregon*, 208 U.S. 412 (1908); *Bunting v. Oregon*, 243 U.S. 426 (1917); and *ADKINS V. CHILDREN'S HOSPITAL*, 261 U.S. 525 (1923).

MUNN V. ILLINOIS
4 Otto 113 (1877)

BACKGROUND In 1871 the Illinois Legislature passed a law setting up a commission to set the maximum rates that grain elevators could charge for storage. This law was enacted under the Illinois Constitution and was intended to protect farmers from unreasonable rates charged by the owners of the elevators. In Chicago, nine companies controlled thirty-one grain elevators, a situation the Court called a "virtual monopoly." Munn, an elevator owner, challenged the law on two grounds: First, the law was a regulation of interstate commerce, a power that belongs to the Congress exclusively. Second, the law denies the owners their property without due process of law in violation of the Fourteenth Amendment. The Court's majority opinion emphasized the due process issue.

CONSTITUTIONAL ISSUE

Whether a state law regulating maximum rates for grain elevators is a taking of property without due process of law in violation of the Fourteenth Amendment? NO

MAJORITY OPINION   Chief Justice Morrison R. Waite delivers the opinion of the Court. The chief justice begins the opinion by outlining in detail the extensive operation of the grain elevators in Chicago. Although he concedes that the operation is interstate in character, Chief Justice Waite addresses the due process question first. Waite notes that states possess the police power, which is the power to regulate the behavior of people. In addition, the police power allows the state to regulate private property for the good of the public. This is especially true for private property that has been affected with a public interest. Waite points out that in the 1820s Congress enacted laws to regulate hackney carriers (cabs), chimney sweepers, and even laws that regulated the weight of loaves of bread. Although each activity involved private property, each had become affected with the public interest. Waite declares that when a person devotes his property to a use in which the public has an interest, that person must submit to control by the public for the common good. Waite has no trouble concluding that the operation of the grain elevators, like the preceding examples, has been affected with the public interest. The chief justice says that it is irrelevant that the grain elevators were in existence before the regulations went into effect. Waite disagrees with Munn's contention that the determination of what constitutes a "reasonable rate" is a judicial, not legislative, question. Waite notes that it is customary in common law countries for the legislature to set such rates. If this power is subject to abuse, it is for the people to correct through the ballot box and not for the courts to correct. Finally, although this activity is indeed interstate commerce, Congress has taken no action. The states may exercise power that affects matters outside their jurisdiction until Congress does act.

OTHER OPINIONS   Justice Stephen J. Field delivers the only dissenting opinion, which was joined by Justice William Strong. Justice Field begins his opinion by asserting that a legislative act or even a constitutional provision declaring grain elevators "public warehouses" does not necessarily make them so. If that were the case, the legislature could regulate any use of private property merely by declaring it to be "affected with a public interest." Field believes that the Court misinterpreted the opinions of Sir Matthew Hale, an eminent English judge, which the majority opinion quoted at length. Hale meant that private property became affected with a public interest only if the owner dedicated its use to the public use or if the owner received some special privilege from the government. In this case, the grain elevator owners have done neither. Field also disputes the majority's view that Munn has not been denied his property because he retains ownership and possession of it. Field argues that limiting the denial of property to title and possession is too narrow an interpretation of the Due Process Clause. Munn has been denied the use and fruits of his property as well. If the state sets the rates so low that Munn cannot operate the warehouses profitably and must therefore cease operations, he has been denied his property without due process of law in Field's view. Field concedes that the state can, under its police power, make all kinds of regulations governing the use of private property. However, these regulations have always been justified on the grounds that a person may not use private property in such a way as to cause injury or to endanger other persons. Regulations, such as the removal of garbage or the requirement of fire exits, are health and safety regulations that are necessary to protect individuals and the general public. Finally, Field argues that the analogy of states setting interest (usury) rates is inappropriate. At one time the charging of interest on money was totally forbidden. In agreeing to allow the charging of interest, Parliament did so only on the condition that it could set the maximum rate, a power retained by state legislatures. Here a previously illegal activity (loaning money) was made legal on the condition that the legislature could set the maximum rate. Operating a grain elevator, Field asserts, is not an illegal activity so the comparison is invalid.

SIGNIFICANCE OF THE CASE The legislation challenged in *Munn v. Illinois* represented a triumph for the Grange movement in the United States. The Granges were farm organizations that protested the practices of monopolies like the railroads and grain elevators. The Supreme Court, in upholding the Illinois legislation, gave its approval to state attempts to regulate the abuses of monopolies. *Munn* was a departure from the generally conservative positions the Court took during this period. Ordinarily, the Court could be depended on to side with the business or property interests. Indeed, after *Munn* the Court does rely more on the doctrine of substantive due process. Substantive due process held that the Court was free to strike down state or federal laws that interfered with a person's liberty or property. The Court's later emphasis on property rights over human rights eventually made it more difficult for progressive legislation like that involved in *Munn* to pass constitutional scrutiny.

QUESTIONS FOR DISCUSSION

(1) In what way is the operation of a grain elevator "affected with a public interest"? Explain.

(2) Do you agree with Justice Field that under the majority's ruling virtually any business can be construed as being "affected with a public interest"?

(3) Can you think of any current privately-owned businesses that might be "affected with a public interest"?

(4) What if, instead of fixing rates, the state had given the grain operators a subsidy? Would that affect the outcome in Fields' opinion? Should it? Why?

RELATED CASES *LOCHNER V. NEW YORK*, 198 U.S. 45 (1905); *ADKINS V. CHILDREN'S HOSPITAL*, 261 U.S. 525 (1923); and *Nebbia v. New York*, 291 U.S. 502 (1934).

LEGAL TENDER CASES
KNOX V. LEE **and** *PARKER V. DAVIS*
12 Wallace 457 (1871)

BACKGROUND On February 25, 1862, Congress passed the Legal Tender Acts, which permitted the government to make paper money legal tender for the payment of debts. Previously only money made with either gold or silver had been used as legal tender. The nation's involvement in the Civil War created pressing financial needs that justified the use of paper money.

The Legal Tender Acts were initially challenged in *Hepburn v. Griswold* and declared unconstitutional in a 5–3 decision. The eight-member Court ruled that the government could not require paper money to be used to pay debts under contracts made before the passage of the Acts. Subsequently, Justice Robert C. Grier, one of the *Hepburn* majority, left the Court, and Congress increased the Court's membership from eight to nine. President Ulysses S. Grant, who favored the Acts, nominated two new justices who were thought to favor the Acts. The Grant appointees and the three *Hepburn* dissenters combined to overrule *Hepburn*, 5–4.

CONSTITUTIONAL ISSUE

Whether Congress can constitutionally make paper money legal tender for all contracts made both before and after the passage of the Legal Tender Acts? YES

MAJORITY OPINION   Justice William Strong delivers the opinion of the Court. Justice Strong asserts at the start that if Congress has the power to enact the Legal Tender Acts, it is irrelevant whether the treasury notes are used to pay debts contracted before or after the passage of the Acts. The focus of the inquiry, then, must be on whether the Constitution permits Congress to pass the Acts. Justice Strong makes several points in defense of Congress's authority to do so. First, he asserts that because of *McCulloch v. Maryland* it has been recognized that Congress may pass all laws necessary and proper to implement its delegated powers. There is little doubt that Congress possesses unenumerated powers, that are derived from its delegated powers. The Bill of Rights was added to the Constitution out of fear that Congress might exercise certain unenumerated powers, a fact that proves the framers foresaw their use by Congress. As long as the means chosen by Congress are appropriate to achieve a constitutionally-legitimate end, those means are constitutional. It is for the Congress, not the Court, to choose among the alternative means to achieve a legitimate end.

A second point made by Justice Strong is that the Court has traditionally allowed Congress wide discretion in the use of its implied powers. A nation, Strong maintains, must be free to choose all means not prohibited by the Constitution that are necessary for its self-preservation. Justice Strong notes the critical situation that existed at the time the Acts were passed and asserts that there can be little doubt the Acts affected the outcome of the war. Third, the implied powers of Congress can be deduced from more than one of the delegated powers. In this case, the power to coin money and the war power combine to serve as the basis of the Acts. Finally, before the Acts can be declared unconstitutional it must be shown that they violate the Necessary and Proper Clause in some way. Strong concludes that the Acts are a legitimate means to a legitimate end.

In the remainder of the opinion, Justice Strong rebuts some of the arguments made by the dissenters. Strong denies that the coinage of money requires the use of money with a metal content. He asserts that the power to coin money is the power to regulate currency. Although states are prohibited from using anything but gold or silver as legal tender, Congress has no such prohibition. Nor do the Acts impair the obligation of contracts. Again, that prohibition applies to the states, not Congress. Strong notes that Congress's power to pass bankruptcy laws by its very nature impairs the obligation of contracts. In any case, a contract calling for payment of a debt in money means only what the government provides as money. Finally, the Acts, if they violate the Due Process Clause of the Fifth Amendment at all, do so only indirectly. Use of the war power, for example, may reduce the value of a person's property, but such an effect is indirect.

OTHER OPINIONS   Justice Joseph P. Bradley writes the only concurring opinion. Bradley notes that during the Revolution states issued bills of credit to help pay for the war. All that the national government is doing is demanding that the public accept its credit. Such an inconvenience, if it is one, is no different from other inconveniences the government imposes through its power to conscript and to confiscate. The fact that the Acts depreciate the value of debts does not render them invalid.

Chief Justice Salmon P. Chase writes the first dissent. The chief justice does not deny the purpose of the Necessary and Proper Clause but does claim that it is being incorrectly applied in this case. Chase, President Lincoln's secretary of the treasury when the Acts were passed, candidly admits that he was wrong in supporting the Acts. In his judgment, the Acts were not necessary for the successful prosecution of the war. Chase also disputes the majority's assertion that the power to make paper money is analogous to the war power. The latter is a direct power, whereas the former is merely an implied power. Chase also challenges the assertion that bankruptcy laws impair the obligation of contract.

Justice Nathan Clifford writes the second dissent. Justice Clifford asserts that the power to coin money is limited to setting the weight and quality of gold and silver coins. The framers, aware of the problems of paper money during the era of the Articles of Confederation, intended only precious metals to be used as money. He notes that during the more than seventy years of constitutional history, Congress had never required the use of paper money.

Justice Stephen Field writes the final dissent. Justice Field believes that Congress is forcing people to loan money to the government interest free. The government's right to borrow is the same as anyone else's and cannot violate the rights of third parties. Justice Field states that the value of the notes rose and fell as Northern victories and defeats occurred. This indicates that the notes had no value other than people's faith in the government's ability to repay them. Field, with the other dissenters, shows historically that the framers intended to bar the use of paper money unbacked by gold or silver.

SIGNIFICANCE OF THE CASE   The Legal Tender Cases vividly illustrate the political nature of the Supreme Court. The addition of the two Grant appointees changed a minority opinion into a majority one without a single justice from the *Hepburn* decision changing his mind. It is also clear that necessity was an important factor in the decision. In 1862 the war was going badly for the North, and money was needed. In addition, the paper money had been in circulation for nine years, and a ruling of unconstitutionality would have brought economic chaos. Finally, the case illustrates again the importance of the Necessary and Proper Clause in our constitutional system.

QUESTIONS FOR DISCUSSION

(1)   Why was the use of paper money so controversial?

(2)   Do you agree with the dissenters that "coining" money implies the use of precious metals? Why or why not?

(3)   Is the passage of the Legal Tender Acts a situation in which the ends justify the means?

(4)   Is it unseemly for the Court to reverse itself so soon after *Hepburn*? Why or why not?

RELATED CASES   *McCULLOCH V. MARYLAND*, 4 Wheaton 316 (1819); *United States v. Marigold*, 9 Howard 557 (1850); *Veazie Bank v. Fenno*, 8 Wallace 533 (1869); *Hepburn v. Griswold*, 8 Wallace 603 (1870); and the *Gold Clause Cases*, 294 U.S. 240 (1935).

MISSOURI V. HOLLAND
252 U.S. 416 (1920)

BACKGROUND   On December 8, 1916, the United States and Great Britain entered into a treaty designed to protect certain endangered species of birds that migrate between Canada and the United States. On July 3, 1918, Congress enacted the Migratory Bird Treaty Act prohibiting the killing, capturing, or selling of any species of bird listed in the treaty. The Act also permitted the secretary of agriculture to make regulations compatible with the terms of the treaty. Such regulations were proclaimed on July 31 and October 25, 1918. The state of Missouri brought a suit in equity seeking to prevent Holland, a U.S. game warden, from attempting to enforce the Act. Missouri claimed that the Migratory Bird Treaty Act was an unconstitutional interference with rights reserved to the states under the Tenth Amendment. Missouri noted that an earlier act of Congress that had attempted by itself to regulate migratory birds was held invalid by lower federal courts in two separate cases.

CONSTITUTIONAL ISSUE

Whether Congress may enact legislation in pursuance of a treaty that it is not free to enact under its other constitutional powers? YES

MAJORITY OPINION   Justice Oliver Wendell Holmes, Jr. delivers the opinion of the Court. Justice Holmes says it is not sufficient to refer to the Tenth Amendment alone because Article II, § 2 gives the United States the power to make treaties, and Article VI declares that treaties, along with the Constitution and laws of the United States, are the supreme law of the land. Therefore, if the treaty is valid, the Migratory Bird Treaty Act is also valid under Article I, § 8 as a "necessary and proper means" to execute the powers of the national government.

The first contention, according to Holmes, is that a treaty cannot be valid if it infringes the Constitution. The second contention is that the treaty power being so limited, an act of Congress made in pursuance of a treaty cannot accomplish what could not be done in the absence of the treaty. In other words, if congressional regulations of migratory birds violate states' rights, the same regulations made pursuant to a treaty also violate states' rights.

Justice Holmes states that whether the two lower federal court decisions were decided correctly is not important because that is not the test of the treaty power. Acts of Congress are the supreme law of the land when they are made in pursuance of the Constitution, but treaties become the supreme law of the land when made under the authority of the United States. That does not mean that the treaty power is unlimited, but that it requires a different kind of analysis. Turning to the treaty in question, there are no words in the Constitution to prohibit the regulation of migratory birds. Therefore, if regulation of the birds is forbidden it must be "by some invisible radiation from the general terms of the Tenth Amendment." Missouri claims title to the birds, and Holmes acknowledges that the state may regulate the killing and selling of the birds. However, title to possession rests "upon a slender reed." Wild birds cannot be in possession of anyone. Yesterday they had not arrived in the state and in a week they may be a thousand miles away. It is no argument that the birds are temporarily in the state, and the federal laws must be carried out in the state. That, says Holmes, is true of most federal laws: They must be carried out within the boundaries of a state. Valid treaties are binding everywhere within the dominion of the United States.

Justice Holmes concludes the opinion by asserting that the treaty involves a national interest that can only be protected by national action in conjunction with another power. Finally, without such a treaty there soon would be no birds for any powers to deal with. The Court finds both the treaty and the act to be valid.

OTHER OPINIONS No other opinions were filed, but Justices Willis Van Devanter and Mahlon Pitney register their dissent.

SIGNIFICANCE OF THE CASE *Missouri v. Holland* was considered to be yet another blow to the doctrine of states' rights. The case held that Congress could exercise additional powers, not specifically delegated to it by the Constitution, by employing the indirect method of the treaty power. States' rights advocates feared that the national government would bestow great new powers on itself by this "back door" approach. The already formidable powers of Congress, however, make this fear unfounded. For example, it seems unlikely that today Congress would have difficulty enacting legislation regulating migratory birds under its commerce power.

QUESTIONS FOR DISCUSSION

(1)   How valid do you think Missouri's claim to possession of the birds really is?

(2)   How could Congress use the treaty power to enlarge its powers?

(3)   What limits, if any, do you see to the use of the treaty power of Congress?

(4)   Would it be possible for Congress to enact an *ex post facto* law, although expressly forbidden by the Constitution, pursuant to a treaty with another nation? Why or why not?

(5)   Explain the difference between a law made "pursuant to the Constitution" and a treaty made "under the authority of the United States."

RELATED CASES *DeGeofroy v. Riggs*, 133 U.S. 258 (1890); and *Reid v. Covert*, 354 U.S. 1 (1957).

McGRAIN V. DAUGHERTY
273 U.S. 135 (1927)

BACKGROUND Harry Daugherty, Attorney General of the United States from 1921 to 1924, was the subject of a Senate inquiry for his failure to prosecute Albert Fall and other key figures in the Teapot Dome Scandal as well as for allegedly not prosecuting violators of the Sherman Anti-Trust Act and the Clayton Act. In the course of the investigation, subpoenas were twice issued and served on Mally S. Daugherty, Harry's brother and bank president, to appear before the Senate Committee. Daugherty failed to appear either time. The Senate then passed a resolution authorizing the issuance of a warrant for Daugherty to be taken into custody by the sergeant at arms and held until such time as he testified. Daugherty was duly arrested by the sergeant's deputy and successfully filed a writ of *habeas corpus* in the federal district court. The deputy was allowed to appeal to the Supreme Court directly.

CONSTITUTIONAL ISSUE

Whether Congress has the power, through its own processes, to compel an individual to appear before it and to give information regarding the matter under investigation? YES

MAJORITY OPINION Justice Willis Van Devanter writes the Court's opinion. The Constitution does not expressly give Congress the power to conduct inquiries; however, the power to gather information is a necessary and accepted extension of the power to legislate. Parliament, early sessions of Congress attended by the writers of the Constitution, and state legislatures have all historically gathered information through the use of committee investigations, and all provided procedures for compelling testimony from reluctant witnesses.

The power of such investigative committees is restricted to matters over which it has jurisdiction. As stated in *Kilbourn v. Thompson*, Congress and its committees do not possess a "general power of making inquiry into the private affairs of the citizen." Witnesses may rightfully and constitutionally refuse to answer questions when the committee is exceeding its bounds or the questions are not pertinent to the matter under inquiry. Congressional investigative power is limited to matters over which it may legislate, and the exercise of that power is subject to review by the courts, although the courts will defer to Congress and initially assume that the inquiry has a legitimate purpose.

When properly exercising its authority, Congress does have the power to compel testimony from recalcitrant witnesses with such process as was employed against Daugherty. This is a necessary auxiliary to the power to investigate, because without it, Congress would be powerless in the face of witnesses who are unwilling to testify or who choose to ignore the request to appear and provide needed information. The possibility of incarceration or criminal proceedings acts as an initiative to encourage people to provide the information that Congress is seeking. The procedures chosen by Congress to compel testimony are also subject to court review to determine their constitutionality. Here, the process met constitutional standards even though

Daugherty challenged it on the technical grounds that it was directed to the sergeant at arms and not the deputy who actually served the warrant and that it was not sworn (the Court found that the oaths of the officeholders who issued the warrant covered that element).

SIGNIFICANCE OF THE CASE   The Court, in *McGrain v. Daugherty*, recognizes the authority of Congress to conduct investigations and even to compel testimony from reluctant witnesses; however, the Court emphasizes the very limited nature of that power. First, the investigations must be related to matters on which Congress may legislate; there is no general power of inquiry vested in Congress. Second, those called before the committee may refuse to answer questions that are not related to the subject matter or that deal with topics beyond the scope of the committee's authority. Third, the process used to compel the testimony must meet constitutional standards. Fourth, the entire matter of congressional investigations from consideration of the constitutionality of the power itself through the exercise of such power is subject to judicial review by the courts.

QUESTIONS FOR DISCUSSION

(1)   Why does the Court emphasize the limited nature of congressional inquiry?
(2)   What are the implications in terms of separation of powers of this case?
(3)   Is this an example of judicial activism or judicial restraint? Why?

RELATED CASES   *Kilbourn v. Thompson*, 13 Otto 168 (1881); *In re Chapman*, 166 U.S. 661 (1897); *Sinclair v. United States*, 279 U.S. 263 (1929); *WATKINS V. UNITED STATES*, 354 U.S. 178 (1957); and *BARENBLATT V. UNITED STATES*, 360 U.S. 109 (1959).

ADKINS V. CHILDREN'S HOSPITAL
261 U.S. 525 (1923)

BACKGROUND   Congress passed a law in 1918 to create the Minimum Wage Board of the District of Columbia. This Board was authorized to investigate and ascertain the wages of women and minors working in various occupations in the District. After holding public hearings, the Board was authorized to set minimum wages to be paid to women and minors. The minimum wage was justified as a means of protecting the health and morals of women and children. Employers who paid less than the minimum wage set by the Board were subject to misdemeanor charges resulting in a fine and imprisonment. Children's Hospital employed several women at less than the minimum wage. The Hospital sought an injunction to restrain the Board from enforcing the minimum wage order on the grounds that the act of Congress violated the Due Process Clause of the Fifth Amendment. In a companion case, *Adkins v. Lyons*, Ms. Lyons was dismissed from her job as a hotel elevator operator because her employer refused to pay the minimum wage set by the Board. She also sought to enjoin the Board from enforcing the Act as a violation of her Fifth Amendment right to enter into employment contracts.

CONSTITUTIONAL ISSUE

Whether a law permitting the Minimum Wage Board to set minimum wages for women and children in the District of Columbia violates the "liberty of contract" implicit in the Due Process Clause of the Fifth Amendment? YES

MAJORITY OPINION Justice George Sutherland delivers the opinion of the Court. Justice Sutherland begins his opinion by noting that the Court's review of the constitutionality of an act of Congress is very serious and should not be taken lightly. Nevertheless, it is sometimes the duty of the Court to strike down laws contrary to the Constitution. Justice Sutherland asserts that the Court has clearly established that freedom of contract is guaranteed as one of the liberties protected by the Due Process Clause of the Fifth Amendment, and he cites *Lochner v. New York* as an example. In *Lochner*, the Court ruled that a New York law regulating the number of hours a baker could work interfered with the baker's right to enter into agreements with his employer. Although Sutherland concedes that freedom of contract is not absolute, only exceptional circumstances can justify a limitation on the right to make contracts.

Next, Sutherland does a survey of the exceptions the Court has made to freedom of contract. In *Munn v. Illinois* the Court ruled that a state could set rates on businesses that have been "impressed with a public interest." The Court has also upheld laws that prescribe the character, methods, and times for payment of wages. However, it is legislation that regulates the hours of labor on which the Board and Congress rely most heavily to justify setting minimum wages. In *Holden v. Hardy*, the Court upheld a Utah law limiting the number of hours men could work in mines. Other laws limiting hours were upheld because they were temporary or emergency measures, or because they regulated a business impressed with a public interest. In *Muller v. Oregon*, the Court upheld a law limiting women to working ten hours a day even though a similar law (in *Lochner*) for bakers was struck down. The Act of 1918 does not fall into any of these categories according to Sutherland but is merely a "price-fixing" law.

Sutherland finds several other reasons why the Act of 1918 is defective. In setting the minimum wage for an occupation the Board is to consider the "health and morals" of women and children. But the law fails to consider the situation of each individual. One woman may live alone, whereas another may live with her family. It is also doubtful whether receiving a minimum wage has anything to do with protecting a woman's morals. Under the Board's policies a woman employed where food is served earns $16.50 a week, whereas a woman employed in a printing shop earns only $15.50 a week. Why, Sutherland wonders, does a woman working in a printing shop need less money to protect her morals? Nor does the Board take into consideration the needs of the employer who may need the employee but is unable to pay her the minimum wage set by the Board. Finally, Justice Sutherland notes that if the police power allows Congress or the states to set minimum wages, then it must also allow them to set maximum wages. Sutherland argues that this law creates a bad precedent. The Supreme Court's decision upheld the lower courts' ruling that the Act of 1918 is unconstitutional.

OTHER OPINIONS There are two dissenting opinions: one by Chief Justice William Howard Taft and one by Justice Oliver Wendell Holmes, Jr. Chief Justice Taft indicates that the law allowing the Board to set minimum wages for women rests on the assumption that employees are not "equals" with employers but "are prone to accept pretty much anything that is offered." Taft believes that employees are often at the mercy of "the harsh and greedy employer." He states that although the law may cause hardships in individual cases (for example, Ms. Lyons's), Congress concluded that the law would benefit the general class of employees. Taft sees no difference in laws that regulate wages from those that regulated hours, which, with the exception of *Lochner*, the Court previously had upheld. The worker's salary is determined by the number of hours multiplied by the hourly wage rate. The regulation of either will increase or decrease the worker's salary. Taft also fails to see how setting a minimum wage differs from requiring workers to be paid in cash, forbidding employers to pay sailors in advance or fixing the time intervals in which workers must be paid, laws that the Court has upheld.

Justice Holmes begins his opinion with the statement that he thinks the law is absolutely within the power of Congress to enact. Holmes notes that "freedom of contract" as contained in the "liberty" guaranteed by the Due Process Clause is merely "an example of doing what you want to do." But practically every law prohibits people from doing things they would like to do. Holmes then cites several examples of laws that interfere with freedom of contract. Usury laws that regulate interest rates, laws prohibiting fraud, and Sunday closing laws are but three examples of the many that interfere with one's freedom of contract. Holmes concludes his opinion by noting that the statute does not force anyone to pay anything. Nor does it force the employer to pay a wage he cannot afford or pay an employee unless the work has been done. In Holmes's view the minimum wage is a lawful means to a lawful end.

SIGNIFICANCE OF THE CASE *Adkins* is a classic example of what is known as substantive due process of law. The Court has often been accused of inventing or creating new rights through its interpretation of the Constitution, and "freedom of contract" is a prime example. The phrase, "freedom of contract," does not appear anywhere in the Constitution. The Fifth Amendment does state that no person shall "be deprived of life, liberty, or property, without due process of law." The pre–*Adkins* Court had already firmly established that "liberty" included the freedom to enter into contractual agreements. *Adkins* is also interesting because of the Court's attitude toward women. In *Muller* the Court apparently felt that women needed special legislation to protect them from working long hours. Justice Sutherland believed that women were just as capable as men of protecting themselves from exploitation by employers. *Adkins* was short-lived as a precedent. In 1937 the Court reversed the decision in *West Coast Hotel Co. v. Parrish*.

QUESTIONS FOR DISCUSSION

(1) Do you agree or disagree with Chief Justice Taft that workers are prone to accept pretty much anything that is offered? Why?

(2) Do you see any difference in regulating the hours but not the wages of women workers?

(3) Is it the proper role of government to regulate workers' hours and wages, or should the "free-market system" be allowed to reign? Why?

(4) Do you think that women require special legislation to protect their rights as employees? Why?

RELATED CASES *TRUSTESS OF DARTMOUTH COLLEGE V. WOODWARD*, 4 Wheaton 518 (1819); *MUNN V. ILLINOIS*, 94 U.S. 113 (1877); *Holden v. Hardy*, 169 U.S. 366 (1898); *LOCHNER V. NEW YORK*, 198 U.S. 45 (1905); *Muller v. Oregon*, 208 U.S. 412 (1908); *Bunting v. Oregon*, 243 U.S. 426 (1917); *Adkins v. Lyons*, 261 U.S. 525 (1923); and *WEST COAST HOTEL CO. V. PARRISH*, 300 U.S. 379 (1937).

SOUTH CAROLINA V. KATZENBACH, ATTORNEY GENERAL
383 U.S. 301 (1966)

BACKGROUND South Carolina, invoking the Supreme Court's original jurisdiction, filed suit in the Supreme Court challenging portions of the Voting Rights Act of 1965 and seeking an injunction against their enforcement by Attorney General Katzenbach. The Act applied only to those states or political subdivisions where the attorney general determined that a voting "test or device" such as a literacy, educational, character, or voucher requirement as defined by the Act was used and where the director of the census determined that less than 50 percent of the voting-age residents were registered to vote or had voted in the 1964 presidential election. Neither official's findings were to be subject to court review. Once the provisions of the Act had been triggered by these findings, the use of voting tests was suspended, all changes in election laws or rules were to be reviewed by the U.S. attorney general, federal examiners were allowed to register voters, and federal poll watchers were to monitor elections. Coverage under the Act could only be terminated by a declaratory judgment of a three-member District of Columbia District Court stating that no discriminatory voting tests or devices had been used for the preceding five years. South Carolina brought suit challenging the constitutionality of these provisions.

CONSTITUTIONAL ISSUE

Whether Congress in passing such encompassing legislation has exercised its power under the Fifteenth Amendment in an appropriate manner with relation to the states and their reserved powers of setting voter standards and determining their own election laws? YES

MAJORITY OPINION Chief Justice Earl Warren writes the majority opinion of the Court. He characterizes the Voting Rights Act as an attempt to "banish the blight of racial discrimination in voting...an insidious and pervasive evil which had been perpetuated in certain parts of our country through unremitting and ingenious defiance of the Constitution." He reviews the history of voting rights from the adoption of the Fifteenth Amendment to the present and notes that, despite repeated legislative and judicial efforts to prevent it, racial discrimination in voting still exists. The failure of the prior approaches including case-by-case litigation justifies the use of the bolder and broader remedies crafted by Congress in enforcing its constitutional responsibilities of seeing that no citizen was denied the right to vote "on account of race, color, or previous condition of servitude."

In balancing the constitutionality of congressional action under the Fifteenth Amendment against the reserved powers of the states, the Court adopts the "rational means" test first promulgated by Chief Justice Marshall in *McCulloch v. Maryland*.

Let the end be legitimate, let it be within the scope of the constitution, and all means which are appropriate, which are plainly adapted to that end, which are not prohibited, but consist with the letter or spirit of the constitution, are constitutional.

It is within Congress's power to fashion rational means or remedies to effectuate the constitutional provisions, and the states can not rely on their reserved powers to circumvent a federally protected right. The remedies here are legitimate responses to an ongoing, widespread problem where previous attempts have not alleviated it. That the provisions do not apply to the entire nation but instead are limited to certain troublesome areas does not violate the doctrine of equality of states that applied only to the admission of states to the Union. All states using the voting tests or devices were included under the act so that all were treated equally in that regard. The Court determines that the statutory scheme enacted by Congress is "rational" and meets constitutional standards.

South Carolina also complained that the only court that could lift the coverage was located in the District of Columbia, a distant forum, but the Court briefly disposes of that argument by pointing out other laws that require that suits be filed in the district's courts. Likewise, the burden of proof that South Carolina challenged as being impossible to meet is dealt with handily; the Court responds that the information relating to conduct of voting officials is "peculiarly within the knowledge of the States themselves," and much of the matter could be resolved through filing affidavits. The Court also rejects both the state's claims that it was a "person" within the meaning of the Due Process Clause of the Fifth Amendment, and that it had standing to claim a violation of the Bill of Attainder Clause and violation of separation of powers by adjudicating guilt through legislation because they exist "only as protections for individual persons and private groups, those who are peculiarly vulnerable to nonjudicial determinations of guilt" and not for states.

OTHER OPINIONS Justice Hugo Black writes an opinion concurring in part and dissenting in part. He agrees with the majority that Congress had the authority to suspend a state literacy test and to authorize the appointment of federal examiners to register qualified voters. He concurs in supporting the formula, which triggered the Act's enforcement but for different reasons, "Congress...has merely exercised its hitherto unquestioned and undisputed power to decide when, where, and upon what conditions its laws shall go into effect." He dissents from the majority regarding the Act's requirement that the states cannot amend their voting laws without approval of the attorney general or the District Court for the District of Columbia in the two cases involving states. Second, he views the requirement of federal approval for amending state constitutions or state laws as an abuse of federal power and unconstitutional because of two constitutional provisions—the one insuring each state a republican form of government and the Reserved Power Clause. Congress should not have the right to veto any prospective state law because then states would be "helpless to function as effective governments." For Black, the power to challenge an already enacted law—a case or controversy—is far different from the power to prevent a state from passing a law.

SIGNIFICANCE OF THE CASE *South Carolina v. Katzenbach* is noted for its impact in two areas—voting rights and legislative powers. In the civil rights arena, the Voting Rights Act is thought by many to be the most effective piece of civil rights legislation ever passed. It has been subsequently renewed and was extended for twenty-five years in 1982. The Court's ratification of the Act permitted the registration of many new voters, which resulted in shifting of control away from the traditionally dominant groups to the newly empowered voters in many communities. Upholding the provisions of the Act markedly affected the dynamics and the complexion of American elections.

The legislative powers vested in Congress arise from several sources including the enumerated powers, the Necessary and Proper Clause, inherent powers, and the amendments. In *Katzenbach*, Congress's use of its amendment-enforcing powers was being challenged, and the Court employed the tried-and-true test of "rational means" found in *McCulloch v. Maryland* as the measure of constitutionality. In similar cases, especially those involving enforcement of the Civil Rights Amendments (Thirteenth, Fourteenth, and Fifteenth Amendments), the Court would follow this precedent and follow the same standard.

QUESTIONS FOR DISCUSSION

(1)   If you were in Congress, would you have voted for this Act? What reasons would you have given your constituents for your position?

(2)   Do you agree that Congress improperly invaded an area that fell within the traditional reserved powers of the states regarding voting and election laws? Why or why not?

(3)   As a member of the Court, would you have followed the same line of reasoning, or would you have preferred to cast the opinion in terms of voting being a fundamental aspect of democracy? Why?

RELATED CASES   *McCULLOCH V. MARYLAND*, 4 Wheaton 316 (1819); *City of Richmond v. United States*, 422 U.S. 358 (1975); *City of Mobile v. Bolden*, 446 U.S. 55 (1980); and *Thornburg v. Gingles*, 478 U.S. 30 (1986).

3

SEPARATION OF POWERS

INTRODUCTION

The doctrine of separation of powers is considered fundamental to the American Constitution. Strangely, however, the term "separation of powers" does not appear in the text of the Constitution. Like other constitutional concepts, such as federalism and checks and balances, separation of powers is said to be woven into the fabric of the Constitution. Although not explicitly provided for in the Constitution, few would doubt the importance of separation of powers as a constitutional doctrine. It is also clear that the Supreme Court regards separation of powers as something more than a discredited doctrine of a bygone era.

Separation of powers holds that the framers placed *primary* responsibility for certain governmental functions in the hands of three separate and distinct branches of government. Congress exercises the legislative power, the president exercises the executive power, and the federal courts exercise the judicial power. Although each branch has primary responsibility for a given function, the other two branches were given some responsibilities as well. For example, the federal courts possess the judicial power, but federal judges are nominated by the president and confirmed by the Senate. Congress controls the number of federal judgeships and may make exceptions to the appellate jurisdiction of federal courts. Similarly, Congress must confirm the president's nominees for cabinet offices, ambassadorships, and other high-ranking executive positions. Through its legislative and budgetary powers, Congress exercises great influence over the structure, programs, and personnel of the executive branch.

Besides giving each branch a role to play in the operation of the other two, the framers incorporated a system of checks and balances into the Constitution. Each branch was armed with weapons to protect itself from possible encroachments from the others. Should Congress pass a law seeking to exercise powers that rightfully belong to the president, the latter could protect his constitutional prerogatives by exercising his veto. The Supreme Court, through its power of judicial review, could declare a law unconstitutional if it infringes on the Court's power. Congress may impeach the president or federal judges.

The disputes that have occurred in our constitutional history sometimes set one branch against another. At other times, third parties bring lawsuits accusing one branch of attempting to exercise powers reserved to another under the Constitution. Whatever the source, conflicts over separation of powers invariably come before the Supreme Court for resolution. Though the Court may itself be embroiled in the controversy, the Court must resolve the conflict. As Chief Justice John Marshall said in *MARBURY V. MADISON* (1803), "It is, emphatically, the province and duty of the judicial department to say what the law is." It is a measure of the Court's integrity and the respect with which it is held that Americans entrust the Court with the final resolution of separation of powers conflicts.

In this introduction, we examine some major cases involving separation of powers. The cases fall into three basic categories, none of which is discrete. The first category concerns cases that had the potential for bringing the Supreme Court into direct confrontation with either the president or Congress, or both. The second category involves challenges to the powers of a branch of government. In these cases the Court is called on to define the scope of a power of another branch. The last category concerns charges that one branch has encroached on the powers of another. The issue is whether one branch of government is attempting to exercise powers reserved to another under the Constitution.

Direct Confrontations

While recognizing its duty to resolve constitutional disputes, the Supreme Court, nevertheless, seeks to avoid direct confrontations with the political branches. Characterized by Alexander Hamilton as the "least dangerous branch," the Court is well aware of its own vulnerability. The Court has been remarkably skillful at identifying and avoiding potential pitfalls that might lead to confrontation. This is not to say that the Supreme Court will always back down from the political branches. In *MARBURY V. MADISON* (1803), the Court appeared to retreat in the face of President Thomas Jefferson's refusal to turn over Marbury's judicial commission. In reality, the Court put the president and his party in Congress on notice that they would decide the final meaning of the Constitution. Similarly, in *UNITED STATES V. NIXON* (1974), former President Richard Nixon hinted that he might not comply with an order from the Court to surrender the Watergate Tapes unless the ruling was "definitive." The Court's 8–0 ruling sent the president a strong message about the political risks of noncompliance.

On other occasions the Supreme Court has recognized that "discretion is the better part of valor." An excellent example of this is the Court's ruling in *LUTHER V. BORDEN* (1849). In *LUTHER* the Court was faced with a seemingly simple case of trespass. In the early 1840s two rival factions in Rhode Island were competing for political power. Luther

Martin, supporting the faction out of power, sought to have the government in control of the state declared unconstitutional. Luther argued that Rhode Island did not have a "republican form of government" within the meaning of Article IV of the Constitution.

On the surface, the possibility for a confrontation between the Supreme Court and either the president or Congress seemed remote. But Chief Justice Roger B. Taney foresaw a problem. In this controversy the president had already made a commitment to Rhode Island's governor to send federal troops to help in putting down the rebellion. A Supreme Court decision in favor of the rebel faction could result in a clash with the president. Chief Justice Taney was also concerned that Congress might refuse to seat House and Senate members from Rhode Island elected by the rebel faction. Taney ruled that the dispute raised a "political question" and therefore should be resolved by the political branches of government.

MISSISSIPPI V. JOHNSON (1867) was another case in which the Supreme Court avoided a possible conflict with a coequal branch. After the Civil War Congress passed the Reconstruction Acts, which dealt harshly with the defeated South. The state of Mississippi brought an original suit in the Supreme Court to enjoin President Andrew Johnson from enforcing the Acts in Mississippi. The Supreme Court, led by Chief Justice Salmon Chase, refused to issue an injunction against the president. The Court held that the enforcement of the law was discretionary on the president's part and that it could not interfere with his discretionary powers. What is more important, the Court would be unable to enforce its ruling against the president if he should decide to disregard it. Finally, Chief Justice Chase foresaw a situation in which the Court might be caught in the middle of a power struggle between the president and Congress over the enforcement of the Acts. Given the highly charged political climate that eventually led to Johnson's impeachment, the Court's caution was prudent.

MISSISSIPPI V. JOHNSON did not end the Court's post–Civil War problems with Congress. In *EX PARTE McCARDLE* (1867), the Court acquiesced in Congress's attempt to curb its appellate jurisdiction. At issue were the same Reconstruction Acts challenged in *JOHNSON*. McCardle, a civilian, was tried by a military tribunal and was seeking a writ of *habeas corpus* to overturn his conviction. Congress, fearing that the Court might declare the Acts unconstitutional, withdrew the Court's appellate jurisdiction in certain *habeas corpus* cases including McCardle's. The Court backed down and ruled that Congress had the power to make exceptions to its appellate jurisdiction and therefore its action was constitutional. Two years later, in *EX PARTE MILLIGAN* (1869), the Court ruled that Milligan, also a civilian, could not be tried by a military tribunal when the state's civil courts were still in operation.

A more recent case that raised the question of the existence of a "political question" is *POWELL V. McCORMACK* (1969). After a select committee found evidence of illegal acts on his part, Congressman Adam Clayton Powell was either expelled or excluded (a point in controversy) from the House of Representatives. Powell argued that he was excluded from the House. The difference is important because Powell argued a person could only be excluded from the House if he or she failed to meet the constitutional requirements of age, residency, and citizenship that he met. Powell maintained that his exclusion was unconstitutional, and he sought a declaratory judgment from a district court. The district court dismissed for want of jurisdiction, and the court of appeals affirmed. The Supreme Court had to decide if the power to expel/exclude a member of Congress is a political question or a justiciable question. The Court's analysis led it to conclude that Powell had been excluded from the House and that his exclusion was unconstitutional. *POWELL V. McCORMACK* is significant because the Supreme Court did not retreat in the face of a controversy that clearly could have put the Court in conflict with Congress.

The Scope of Constitutional Powers

A more delicate problem of judicial review is when the Supreme Court is called on to define the powers of a coequal branch of government. Each branch of the national government is free to make an initial determination of its own powers under the Constitution. For example, because the president's powers as commander-in-chief are ill defined, presidents have had to make decisions about the scope of their military powers. When the initial decision is challenged, it is the duty of the Supreme Court to decide if the president has stayed within his or her constitutional authority. In this section we examine cases in which the Supreme Court has been asked to rule on the constitutionality of acts of Congress or actions of the president.

As noted previously, a particularly sensitive area is the president's power as commander-in-chief. During the Civil War, the Supreme Court was asked to rule on President Lincoln's authority in *THE PRIZE CASES* (1863). At the outbreak of the war, President Lincoln ordered a naval blockade of Southern ports. Several foreign-owned ships attempting to run the blockade were seized and their cargoes confiscated. The ships' owners challenged the seizures because Congress had not officially declared war, and therefore the president's action was illegal. The Supreme Court upheld the president's contention that his action was based on his power as commander-in-chief and not on a declaration of war by Congress.

Both the powers of the president and Congress were challenged at the start of World War II. In 1942, President Franklin Roosevelt issued an executive order empowering military commanders to ban certain persons from designated military areas. This order and a law passed by Congress in March 1942 served as the legal basis for the relocation of more than one hundred thousand Japanese-American citizens living on the West Coast of the United States. In *KOREMATSU V. UNITED STATES* (1944), the Supreme Court upheld the relocation policy as a valid exercise of the war power. As in *EX PARTE McCARDLE*, the Court was reluctant to challenge the authority of the president and Congress during a time of grave national crisis.

Although World War II is often characterized as a "popular" war, the conflict in Korea was not so popular. At the height of the Korean War a strike in the steel industry posed a threat to national security. When negotiations failed to avert a strike, President Harry Truman ordered his secretary of commerce, Charles Sawyer, to seize the steel companies and to keep them operating. Less than two months later, in *YOUNGSTOWN SHEET AND TUBE CO. V. SAWYER* (1952), the Supreme Court held the president's action unconstitutional. Justice Hugo Black, writing for the Court, rejected the president's claim of an inherent power as commander-in-chief to seize private property during wartime. Only Congress, Black ruled, could authorize such an exercise of power.

During the Vietnam era several attempts were made to have the Supreme Court declare the war unconstitutional. The Court denied *certiorari* in *Mitchell v. United States* (1966), *Mora v. McNamara (1967)*, and *Massachusetts v. Laird* (1970). Although the war in Vietnam had become unpopular by the early 1970s, the Court was unwilling to be drawn into the politics of that conflict. Except for the *YOUNGSTOWN* case, the Court has afforded the president and Congress wide latitude in the conduct of the nation's wars.

Two final cases in this section depict the Supreme Court's duty to interpret the powers of its coequal branches. In *UNITED STATES V. CURTISS-WRIGHT CORP.* (1936), the Court had the opportunity to expound on the president's foreign relations powers. Congress had authorized President Franklin Roosevelt to prohibit the sale of military weapons to countries engaged in war. Despite a presidential proclamation banning the sale of weapons to Bolivia and Paraguay, the Curtiss-Wright Corporation sold fifteen machine guns to Bolivia. The company challenged the law and the president's proclamation as an unconstitutional delegation of power from Congress to the president. The Supreme Court drew a distinction between excessive delegation in foreign affairs versus domestic affairs. The Court conceded that Congress's delegation would have been excessive in domestic affairs. However, the Congress is granted greater latitude to delegate authority to the president in foreign affairs. *CURTISS-WRIGHT* is often cited for its sweeping grant of power to the president in matters of foreign policy.

Perhaps the most historic declaration of the scope of presidential power is *UNITED STATES V. NIXON* (1974). The famous Watergate scandal set President Richard Nixon on a collision course with both Congress and the judiciary over the Watergate tapes. President Nixon refused to turn over the tapes to the special Watergate prosecutor on the grounds of executive privilege. When the case reached the Supreme Court the justices were asked to define the scope of the doctrine of executive privilege. Chief Justice Warren Burger, himself a Nixon appointee to the Court, sought to preserve the general right of a president to withhold information from Congress. However, the chief justice ruled for a unanimous Court that executive privilege could not be interpreted to permit the president to withhold information needed for a criminal investigation. The Court also rejected President Nixon's assertion that the president alone decides when executive privilege may be invoked. The Court's decision resulted in the president's resignation a few weeks later in August 1974.

Problems of Encroachment

As explained earlier in this essay, the system of checks and balances was placed in the Constitution so that each branch could protect itself from encroachments from the other two branches. Problems of encroachment occur when one branch seeks to exercise powers reserved to another. As with other separation-of-power issues, it is the duty of the Supreme Court to decide when an encroachment has occurred. Frequently disputes over encroachments are due to the ambiguity of the Constitution's wording. Many provisions of the Constitution are vague enough to permit more than one interpretation. Therefore, the Court must clarify the meaning of the Constitution through its power of judicial review.

The president's power to appoint and remove members of the executive branch illustrates how ambiguous the Constitution can be. The Appointments Clause authorizes the president to appoint executive officials with the consent of the Senate. Unfortunately, the Constitution is silent on the removal of executive officials. Initially, it was assumed that the president alone could remove his subordinates. However, in 1867 as a result of its feud with President Andrew Johnson, Congress passed a law over Johnson's veto prohibiting the president from removing members of his cabinet without Senate approval. After Johnson left the presidency, an uneasy truce left the issue unresolved.

In 1926 the matter of presidential removal surfaced again in *MYERS V. UNITED STATES*. President Woodrow Wilson demanded the resignation of Myers, who was a first-class postmaster in Portland, Oregon. An 1876 law required the consent of the Senate to remove a first-class postmaster. After his firing, Myers sued the government for the remainder of his salary. Chief Justice William Howard Taft, himself a former president, ruled for the Court that the 1876 law was unconstitutional. Chief Justice Taft, relying on the records of the First Congress, ruled that Congress had encroached on a prerogative of the president.

MYERS appeared to have settled the issue until nine years later when the question arose again in *Humphrey's Executor v. United States* (1935). Humphrey was asked by President Franklin D. Roosevelt to resign as chair of the Federal Trade Commission. Roosevelt's reasons had nothing to do with Humphrey's performance on the FTC. The president simply wanted someone whose policy views were similar to his and had a general desire to put a person of his own choosing in the position. Like Myers, Humphrey sued for the salary he would have received if he had been allowed to finish his term on the FTC. When the case reached the Supreme Court, Humphrey's case was distinguished from Myers's. The Court held that Myers's position was a "purely executive" one whose occupant was removable at will by the president. Humphrey, conversely, was a member of the FTC, which possessed quasi-legislative and quasi-judicial functions. Congress had created agencies like the FTC to be free of presidential control. To that end, members of the FTC were given fixed terms of office and could only be removed for cause. The only legal grounds for removal of a member of the FTC were specified in the Federal Communications Act. The Supreme Court reaffirmed *Humphrey's Executor* in 1958 in *Wiener v. United States*.

MYERS, *Humphrey's Executor*, and *Wiener* involved attempts by the Congress to control the president's removal of his subordinates. The next three cases pertain to attempts by Congress to control the initial appointment of officials. The central issue is whether Congress can place the appointment of certain officials in the hands of persons other than the president. *BUCKLEY V. VALEO* (1976) challenged the constitutionality of the Federal Campaign Act. A key provision of the Act was the creation of the Federal Election Commission. Under the Act two members of the Commission were appointed by the Speaker of the House, two were appointed by the president *pro tempore* of the Senate, and two were appointed by the president. The clerk of the House and the secretary of the Senate were *ex officio* members. The Supreme Court, in a *per curiam* opinion, held that the Appointments Clause had been violated. Inferior officers may only be appointed by the president, heads of executive departments, or the judiciary subject to Senate approval. The Court held that the Commission had to be reconstituted in a way that did not violate the Constitution.

In *BOWSHER V. SYNAR* (1986) the issue was whether an official named by Congress could exercise "executive" power. The Gramm-Rudman-Hollings Act created a scheme for reducing the nation's deficit over a period of years. Under the Act, the comptroller general played a key role in the deficit reduction process. The comptroller general is nominated by the president from a list of three names submitted by the Speaker of the House and the president *pro tempore* of the Senate. The comptroller is removable by a joint resolution of Congress. In an opinion written by Chief Justice Warren Burger, the Court held that the comptroller general is a legislative agent and that the functions assigned under the Act were essentially executive functions. The chief justice found the provisions to be a violation of separation of powers and voided the sections of the Act pertaining to the responsibilities of the comptroller general.

MORRISON V. OLSON (1988) is the third case in which the Supreme Court was asked to rule on the Appointments Clause. In the aftermath of the Watergate scandal Congress passed the Ethics in Government Act. This Act provides for the appointment of independent counsel or "special prosecutors" to investigate allegations of wrongdoing and corruption among officials at the highest levels of government. Olson, an assistant attorney general in the Reagan administration, was under investigation by a special prosecutor, Morrison. Under the Ethics in Government Act special prosecutors were chosen by the Special Division of the U.S. Court of Appeals for the District of Columbia. Olson attacked the constitutionality of the Act, in part, because the prosecutorial function is a purely executive function as described by the Court in *MYERS*. The *MORRISON* majority, however, disagreed. In an opinion written by Chief Justice William Rehnquist, the majority upheld the Act. The Appointments Clause of the Constitution provides for the appointment of "inferior officers" by persons other than the president. The Court ruled that a special prosecutor qualifies as an inferior officer whose appointment by the judges of the special division is constitutionally permissible.

One final case that illustrates an encroachment in violation of separation of powers is *IMMIGRATION AND NATURALIZATION SERVICE V. CHADHA* (1983). Under the Immigration and Nationality Act, the attorney general was empowered to permit persons scheduled for deportation to remain in the United States. Chadha, a native of Kenya, had been ordered deported, but his deportation was suspended by the attorney general. Section 244 (c)(2) of the Act permitted what is commonly called a legislative veto. Under the legislative veto, a simple resolution by either house of Congress could reverse the attorney general's suspension of deportation. The House of Representatives passed such a resolution, and Chadha challenged the constitutionality of the legislative veto. The Supreme Court held that § 244 (c)(2) violated the Presentments Clause of the Constitution. The Court found that the cancellation of the suspension of Chadha's deportation by the House was clearly a legislative action. Under the Presentments Clause legislative actions must be presented to the president for his signature or veto. The Court also held that because § 244 (c)(2) permitted only one house of Congress to cancel the attorney general's suspension, the principle of bicameralism was violated as well. CHADHA is significant because at the time there were some two hundred laws that contained similar legislative vetoes. The CHADHA decision cast a cloud over the constitutionality of each of these laws.

Conclusion

It would be easy to dismiss the doctrine of separation of powers as being of little interest to anyone except a few constitutional scholars and the justices of the Supreme Court. However, the framers of the Constitution created a system of government that established a delicate balance among the three branches of government. Separation of powers is fundamental to the maintenance of that balance. One premise of separation of powers is that each branch will try to expand its power at the expense of the other two. Another assumption is that each branch would be expected to resist such attempts. The role of the Supreme Court is to serve as an overseer to ensure that a proper balance is maintained. The Court's vigilance in preserving the separation of powers is responsible, at least in part, for the success of American constitutionalism for more than two hundred years.

LUTHER V. BORDEN
7 Howard 1 (1849)

BACKGROUND The events leading up to this case arose out of the so-called Dorr Rebellion, which occurred in Rhode Island during the early 1840s. Rhode Island, unlike many of the original states, did not write a new state constitution after the Revolution but continued to operate under its royal charter of 1663. Under that charter the right to vote was restricted to landowners and numerous attempts to broaden the franchise to include all adult males were unsuccessful. Finally, in 1841, a movement arose to write a new constitution for Rhode Island. Voluntary groups were formed, a new constitution was written, voted on, and approved by adult male citizens of the state. On May 3, 1842, Thomas Dorr was sworn in as governor under the new constitution. On June 24, the charter government declared martial law. On June 25, Dorr and his followers tried unsuccessfully to capture a public arsenal by force, and two days later Dorr fled the state. Subsequently, in 1844, Dorr was tried and convicted of treason.
  Martin Luther was a follower of Dorr. On June 29, 1842, Luther M. Borden and others arrived at Luther's home with an arrest warrant. Believing Luther to be hiding inside, Borden broke into and entered Luther's home. Luther later sued Borden for trespass. Borden's defense was his authority under the charter government to execute the arrest warrant. At the trial in a federal circuit court, Luther tried to introduce evidence to show that the Dorr government was the legitimate government of Rhode Island at the time, and therefore Borden's authority under the charter government was void. The circuit court refused to admit the evidence and found in favor of Borden. Luther then appealed to the U.S. Supreme Court.

CONSTITUTIONAL ISSUE

Whether federal courts have jurisdiction to determine which of two competing state governments is the legitimate government of the state under Article IV, § 4 (the republican form of government clause) of the Constitution? NO

MAJORITY OPINION   Chief Justice Roger B. Taney delivers the opinion of the Court. Chief Justice Taney begins the opinion by noting that the convention that met and established the Dorr constitution was not authorized under any existing state law. He also notes that the charter government later called its own convention in January 1842 and that a new state constitution, sanctioned by the charter government, went into effect in May 1843.

The key to this case, according to the chief justice, is a determination of the legitimate government of Rhode Island at the time Borden allegedly trespassed on Luther's property. That issue, the chief justice insists, is not a proper one for the courts to resolve. Luther sought to introduce evidence to prove that the Dorr constitution had been legally approved by the voters of Rhode Island. But neither the circuit court nor the Supreme Court is in a position to evaluate the accuracy of that evidence. How, Taney asks, could the circuit court determine if the persons who voted were qualified to vote or if they constituted a majority of the voters of the state? Taney declares that the Constitution treats interference with a state's domestic affairs as a political question, not a judicial one. It is true that Article IV, § 4 guarantees each state a "republican form of government," but the determination whether a particular state's government is republican is beyond judicial competence. Taney suggests that Congress could settle the issue by deciding whether or not to seat a state's congressional delegation. Taney admits that although Congress had no opportunity to make such a decision in this case, the power still rests with that body. Taney also suggests that the president could decide the issue. He notes that an act of Congress of February 28, 1795, authorizes the president to call out the militia in cases of insurrection. Although the charter government did request the president for help, the rebellion was over before it became necessary to provide federal troops. However, the president did express a willingness to support the charter government. Chief Justice Taney compares the Rhode Island situation to the president's right to recognize rival foreign governments. The government recognized by the president is always acknowledged by the courts as the legitimate government. In either case, however, the judiciary would be powerless to countermand the Congress or the president with its own independent determination.

Chief Justice Taney concludes the opinion by observing that a permanent military government could not be considered "republican" within the meaning of Article IV, § 4. However, in this case the charter government intended for martial law to be a temporary measure until the crisis was over. Therefore, the Court sustains the decision of the circuit court in favor of Borden.

OTHER OPINIONS   Justice Levi Woodbury delivers the only dissenting opinion. Justice Woodbury's approach to the case is not whether it raises a political question but whether the legislature of Rhode Island had the authority to declare martial law, under which Borden committed the trespass. This, Woodbury argues, is within the competence of courts to decide. Woodbury traces the history of martial law in Great Britain from which we derive most of our law. He notes that the British Parliament rarely imposes martial law and when it does so, martial law is carefully contained. Woodbury implies that Rhode Island is bound by the British tradition of using martial law only in extreme emergencies and under limited conditions. He observes that nothing in Rhode Island's royal charter, in effect at the time, even suggests that the legislature may impose martial law. He is also critical of the charter government for unnecessarily imposing martial law over the entire state. The crisis, he asserts, had not reached such a stage as to justify the imposition of martial law. Finally, he makes a strong case that martial law may only be imposed during wartime, and because only Congress may declare war, only Congress may declare martial law. Woodbury believes this is a simple case of illegal search and seizure, and that the decision favoring Borden should be reversed.

SIGNIFICANCE OF THE CASE   *Luther v. Borden* is usually cited as the definitive case for the origin of the "political question doctrine." This doctrine holds that a court may not ex-exercise jurisdiction in cases that raise political questions. In *Luther*, the Court concludes that the determination of the legitimate government of a state is left either to the Congress or the president. A political question, then, under the *Luther* precedent is a matter left to the discretion of one of the political branches of government. Although he claims otherwise, Chief Justice Taney in fact seems to support the charter government by refusing to reverse the circuit court's decision to disallow Luther's evidence. The political question doctrine is discussed more fully in Justice William Brennan's opinion in *Baker v. Carr*.

QUESTIONS FOR DISCUSSION

(1)   Did the Court, in fact, decide that the charter government was the legitimate government of Rhode Island? Why or why not?

(2)   Aren't most issues that come before the Supreme Court "political" questions? Why or why not?

(3)   Explain some of the problems the circuit court might have had with the truthfulness of Luther's evidence?

(4)   Has the Court definitively defined the meaning of "a republican form of government"?

RELATED CASES   *Colegrove v. Green*, 328 U.S. 549 (1946); *BAKER V. CARR*, 369 U.S. 186 (1962); *Wesberry v. Sanders*, 376 U.S. 1 (1964); *REYNOLDS V. SIMS*, 377 U.S. 533 (1964); *POWELL V. McCORMACK*, 395 U.S. 486 (1969); and *UNITED STATES V. NIXON*, 418 U.S. 683 (1974).

MISSISSIPPI V. JOHNSON
4 Wallace 475 (1867)

BACKGROUND   The state of Mississippi filed an original action in the Supreme Court requesting an injunction against the enforcement of the Reconstruction Acts by President Andrew Johnson.

CONSTITUTIONAL ISSUE

Whether the judicial branch may issue an injunction against the enforcement of a congressional act by the president? NO

MAJORITY OPINION   Chief Justice Salmon Chase writes the opinion of the Court. The Court cannot force the president to perform discretionary acts under mandamus nor can it restrain him from doing so. The constitutional requirement that the president shall see that the laws are faithfully carried out incorporates a wide latitude of judgment and "is purely executive and political." Government officials are subject to *mandamus* and injunctions only for ministerial duties, those to which "nothing is left to discretion." In the appropriate cases, activities of both Congress and the president are subject to review, but the Court will not restrain them if the activities are discretionary rather than ministerial.

SIGNIFICANCE OF THE CASE   This case is an intriguing discussion of the respective balancing of powers among the three branches of government. *Marbury v. Madison* established the principle that the Court would not examine the discretionary acts of government officials. Under *Mississippi v. Johnson*, discretionary acts of the president such as vetoing legislation or congressional decisions to appropriate funds are beyond review by the courts. These are political actions for which elected officials may be answerable through the election and impeachment processes. However, while making these important concessions to the authority of the other branches of government, the Court clearly reserves for itself the determination of whether an act is discretionary or ministerial and the determination of the effect of a finding that the act is a ministerial one.

QUESTIONS FOR DISCUSSION.

(1)   Do you agree that the president and Congress should be beyond the equitable powers of the Court for their discretionary acts? Why?

(2)   In your opinion, should the enforcement of an act of Congress be discretionary for the president? Why?

(3)   What policy or political reasons lead to this decision?

RELATED CASES   *MARBURY V. MADISON*, 1 Cranch 137 (1803); *LUTHER V. BORDEN*, 7 Howard 1 (1849); and *UNITED STATES V. NIXON*, 418 U.S. 683 (1974).

POWELL V. McCORMACK
395 U.S. 486 (1969)

BACKGROUND   During the Eighty-Ninth Congress (1965–66) a Special Subcommittee on Contracts of the Committee on House Administration concluded that Congressman Adam Clayton Powell and others had deceived the House of Representatives as to travel expenses. The Special Subcommittee indicated there was strong evidence that illegal salary payments had been made to Powell's wife. When the Ninetieth Congress convened in January 1967, Powell was asked to step aside while the other members were administered the oath of office. The House then immediately passed a resolution setting up a select committee to determine Powell's eligibility to serve in the House. The select committee recommended that Powell be seated, censured, fined $40,000 and stripped of his seniority.

The select committee's resolution was amended 248–176 to expel Powell and to declare his seat vacant. The select committee's resolution, HR 278, was then approved 307–116.

Powell and thirteen voters from his district filed suit in the District Court for the District of Columbia claiming that a member of Congress may only be excluded if he or she fails to meet the age, citizenship, and residency requirements of Article I, § 2, Clause 2 of the Constitution. The suit named Speaker of the House John McCormack, and the sergeant at arms, the clerk, and the doorkeeper of the House as defendants. It sought to restrain McCormack from enforcing HR 278 and to enjoin him from refusing to administer the oath of office to Powell. Powell also sought a declaratory judgment that his exclusion was unconstitutional. The district court dismissed "for want of jurisdiction in the subject matter," and the court of appeals affirmed. While the case was pending on the Supreme Court's docket, Powell was elected to the Ninety-First Congress, seated, and fined $25,000. The respondents filed a motion of mootness.

CONSTITUTIONAL ISSUES

(1)   Whether the subsequent seating of Powell in the Ninety-First Congress has rendered the case moot? NO

(2)   Whether the Speech and Debate Clause insulates McCormack's action from judicial review? NO

(3)   Whether the decision to *exclude* Powell is supported by the power granted by the House to *expel* a member? NO

(4)   Whether the Court has jurisdiction over the subject matter of this case? YES

(5)   Whether the case is nonjusticiable because it raises a political issue? NO

MAJORITY OPINION   Chief Justice Earl Warren delivers the opinion of the Court. The chief justice addresses the issues in order. McCormack claims that Powell's subsequent seating in the Ninety-First Congress renders the case moot. However, Powell claims that his salary for the Ninetieth Congress was withheld as a result of an allegedly unconstitutional resolution. The chief justice rules that the salary issue and alleged unconstitutionality of HR 278 are sufficient to create a "live" case or controversy.

Next, the chief justice addresses whether the Speech and Debate Clause bars this action. Powell claims that although McCormack, as a member of Congress, may be immune, the named House employees (the clerk, doorkeeper, and sergeant at arms) are not. The chief justice notes that even though the House employees are acting under orders of the House, it does not bar judicial review of the constitutionality of the underlying legislative action. In *Kilbourn v. Thompson*, Kilbourn recovered $20,000 for false imprisonment from Thompson even though Thompson, as sergeant at arms, was merely obeying the orders of the House. The judgment came after the Court ruled that Kilbourn's arrest for contempt was unconstitutional.

The third issue is whether Powell was excluded or expelled from the House. Chief Justice Warren notes that expulsion of a member requires a two-thirds majority. McCormack claims that HR 278, which passed 307–116, was in excess of the needed two-thirds majority. Because a member may be expelled from the House for any reason, Powell should be considered to have been expelled. The chief justice points out that Powell was never seated in the Ninetieth Congress having been prevented from taking the oath of office. In addition, when the Speaker was asked to make a ruling on the vote necessary on the amendment to exclude Powell, the Speaker ruled that only a majority vote was needed. Even though HR 278, as amended, was in excess of the needed two-thirds vote, the Court cannot assume that members would have voted for expulsion if they had been told by the Speaker that the vote was for expulsion instead of exclusion.

Chief Justice Warren then turns to the issue of jurisdiction. Federal courts may have jurisdiction over a case even if the issue involved is nonjusticiable. McCormack maintains that the House has exclusive judgment over the qualifications of its members. Therefore, cases of exclusion or expulsion are not cases "arising under the Constitution" within the meaning of Article III. But, the chief justice observes, Article III gives federal courts jurisdiction over "all cases arising under the Constitution." A case arises under the Constitution if one interpretation of the Constitution will sustain a plaintiff's claim while another one will defeat it. Powell's claim clearly meets this standard, and therefore it is within the jurisdiction of federal courts.

Finally, Chief Justice Warren addresses whether the case raises a nonjusticiable "political question." McCormack claims the present case clearly represents a "textually demonstrable constitutional commitment" to the House. In other words, the House and it alone can determine who is qualified to be a member and that determination is a political question. But, that, the chief justice contends, is precisely the issue raised by this case. The Court must first determine what power the Constitution confers on the House before it can decide to what extent that power is subject to judicial review. The chief justice then reviews the history of exclusion/expulsion before the writing of the Constitution, during the debates on the Constitution, and subsequent interpretations of Congress after the Constitution went into effect. The chief justice's analysis leads him to conclude that the only grounds for excluding a person otherwise duly elected were the three standing qualifications of age, citizenship, and residency. Because both parties agree Powell met all three qualifications, there is no need to remand the case on issue of whether he should have been seated. However, the Court does remand the case to resolve the issue of the amount of Powell's back pay.

OTHER OPINIONS Justice William O. Douglas writes a brief concurring opinion and Justice Potter Stewart writes a dissenting opinion. Justice Douglas agrees that Congress is the sole judge of the qualifications of its members but that judgment is limited to determining whether a duly elected representative has met the age, citizenship, and residency qualifications of the Constitution. Douglas notes that under McCormack's reasoning a person could be excluded because he or she is a Communist or a pacifist, or any number of other reasons. This, Douglas contends, is contrary to democratic government.

Justice Stewart dissents on the grounds that the case is moot. According to Stewart, Powell's request to be seated in the Ninetieth Congress became moot on January 3, 1969, when the Ninety-First Congress came into existence. In addition, the $25,000 fine and loss of seniority imposed by the Ninety-First Congress are unrelated to the issue of expulsion. The punishment was for Powell's misconduct in the Eighty-Ninth Congress. Justice Stewart then addresses the salary issue. First, he notes that because only the sergeant-at-arms pays congressmen, the suit is moot against the other officers of the House. Second, he notes that the office of sergeant-at-arms of the Ninetieth Congress no longer exists. Third, he doubts whether there is any money or power for the sergeant-at-arms for the Ninety-First Congress to pay a salary for the Ninetieth Congress. Finally, Stewart maintains that if Powell has a legitimate salary claim his case should be referred to the Court of Claims instead of remanded to the District Court. That would allow the Supreme Court to avoid unnecessarily making a constitutional ruling in this case.

SIGNIFICANCE OF THE CASE   *Powell* illustrates the enormous breadth of interpretation available to the Supreme Court under its power of judicial review. The phrase, "Each House shall be the Judge of the…Qualifications of its Members" would appear to preclude any judicial review. However, the antecedent question is whether the qualifications each House may judge can be expanded or are limited to those set forth in the Constitution. *Powell* makes it clear that the latter is the case. *Powell* is also significant because it raises the political question doctrine. At first blush it would seem that because the issue raised is an internal one for Congress, *Powell* clearly involves a political question. However, the Court reaffirms its role as the final arbiter of the Constitution even though the language of the Constitution is unequivocal.

QUESTIONS FOR DISCUSSION

(1)   Would it change anything if the Constitution read, "Each House shall be the *sole* judge of the…Qualifications of its Members"? Why or why not?

(2)   Do you think that the Court's holding that officers of the House can be sued but members of the House cannot is a fair one? Why or why not?

(3)   Suppose an avowed racist were elected to Congress. Should Congress be allowed to exclude him or her? Why or why not?

RELATED CASES   *Kilbourn v. Thompson*, 103 U.S. 168 (1881); *Tenney v. Brandhove*, 341 U.S. 367 (1951); *BAKER V. CARR*, 369 U.S. 186 (1962); *U.S. v. Johnson*, 383 U.S. 169 (1966); *Dombrowski v. Eastland*, 387 U.S. 82 (1967); and *Hutchinson v. Proxmire*, 443 U.S. 111 (1979).

THE PRIZE CASES
2 Black 635 (1863)

BACKGROUND   On April 19, 1861, President Abraham Lincoln announced a blockade of the ports of most of the southern states then in rebellion against the United States. On April 27 and 30 he extended the blockade to the rest of the Southern states. Ships belonging to neutrals had fifteen days in which to leave the blockaded ports. The ships in question, *The Brig Amy Warwick*, *The Hiawatha*, *The Brilliante*, and *The Crenshaw*, were seized by U.S. warships as they attempted to run the blockade. Each was seized as a prize of war and its cargo confiscated. (Only some tobacco owned by Northern citizens seized from *The Crenshaw* was returned to its owners.) These cases turn on the legality of the blockade under international law. The cases posed a problem because no formal declaration of war had been made by Congress. Congress did approve President Lincoln's blockade proclamation by law on July 13, 1861, but the ships in question were seized before that date. The owners also claimed that the law of July 13 was, in effect, an *ex post facto* law.

CONSTITUTIONAL ISSUE

Whether the president has a right to institute a blockade of ports in the possession of persons armed in rebellion against the United States? YES

MAJORITY OPINION Justice Robert C. Grier delivers the opinion of the Court. Justice Grier begins by stating that for a capture of a neutral vessel to be legitimate, the neutral must know that one of the belligerent parties plans to use the tactic of blockade against the ports of the other belligerent. That, in turn, depends on whether a state of war exists between the belligerent parties. War, he notes, does not require that both parties be sovereign nations. A civil war always begins by unlawful insurrection against the established government. When territory is taken and held, when the rebels have declared their independence, and have begun hostilities against the government "the world acknowledges them as belligerents and the contest a war." Normally the parties involved concede to each other belligerent rights. For example, captured rebels are treated as prisoners of war and not as traitors. So, although a civil war may not be publicly proclaimed, a *de facto* state of war can exist without a formal declaration by either party.

Justice Grier next notes that Congress has no constitutional power to declare war against a state or any group of states. Although the president has no power to declare war, the Congress in acts passed in 1795 and 1807 had previously authorized the president to call out the militia to repel foreign invasions and insurrections against either a state or the United States. The president is obligated to meet a threat "without waiting for Congress to baptize it with a name."

Justice Grier states that referring to the state of affairs as an "insurrection" cannot conceal the true nature of the conflict. He puts great store in the declarations of neutrality by the British and other foreign governments. These declarations and the president's proclamation gave notice to neutrals that hostilities had begun. As far as the charge that the seizures were tantamount to an *ex post facto* law, Justice Grier admits that it might be if this were a criminal indictment.

Justice Grier then turns to the issue whether the government had the right to seize the ships as "enemy" property. He says that the law of nations recognizes the right of a belligerent to capture the enemy's property on the high seas. Although some of the owners were foreigners and others claimed they remained loyal to the United States, their actions in attempting to run the blockade were illegal. Justice Grier then reviews the circumstances surrounding the capture of each ship and concludes that, with one lone exception, the seizures were all legal.

OTHER OPINIONS Justice Samuel Nelson writes the only dissenting opinion, although several justices dissented in the cases of some of the individual ships. Justice Nelson's first objection concerns the propriety of the seizures. He believes that before a seizure can occur lawfully there must be adequate warning, which he feels was not given in these cases. The majority believes that common knowledge of the insurrection and a reasonable assumption that all ships owners knew of the president's proclamation were sufficient warning. Justice Nelson does not.

Justice Nelson's major objection, however, is the legality of the blockade under international law. War, he asserts, cannot lawfully be commenced without a declaration of war by Congress. Justice Nelson distinguishes between a public war that involves two sovereign nations and a civil war that involves insurgents. In both cases our Constitution requires a formal declaration of war by Congress before the law of nations regarding war goes into effect. Justice Nelson admits that there existed a war in a "material sense" but denies a state of war existed in a legal sense. In an obvious reference to Shays's Rebellion, Justice Nelson asserts that the framers were hardly unaware of the possibility of insurrection when writing the Constitution, yet they vested the war power with Congress. Nor does Nelson believe that the Acts of 1795 and 1807 relied on by the majority confer on the president the power to declare war. The war power, he declares, cannot be delegated to the executive. The Act of July 13th recognized a state of civil war existed between the government and the Confederate states. However, because the ships were seized prior to that Act, no legal state of war existed and the seizures were illegal.

SIGNIFICANCE OF THE CASE   The war power is a prime example of the sharing of a constitutional power between the president and Congress. The Constitution clearly gives Congress the power to declare war, but it also gives the president, as commander-in-chief, the power to act in cases of invasion and insurrection. The question remains why President Lincoln did not seek a formal declaration of war after Fort Sumter. One explanation is that Lincoln, like many Americans, thought the war would be a short one. Another explanation is that Lincoln wanted to deal with the crisis with a free hand. Therefore, he delayed calling Congress into session to ensure greater flexibility. Yet a third explanation is that Lincoln believed a formal declaration of war would afford the South a status under international law he was unwilling to afford it. Some believe that in the era of nuclear weapons the question of who has the power to declare war is moot. However, as Korea, Vietnam, and the war with Iraq illustrate, the constitutional issue of war and peace may still be relevant today.

QUESTIONS FOR DISCUSSION

(1)   Did Lincoln "declare war" or merely acknowledge that a state of war existed?

(2)   Did the Act of July 13 constitute a formal declaration of war?

(3)   Why was Lincoln unwilling to afford the Confederate states the status of a sovereign nation?

(4)   Whose position, Grier's or Nelson's, are you more comfortable with and why?

RELATED CASES   *Hirabayashi v. United States*, 320 U.S. 81 (1943); *KOREMATSU V. UNITED STATES*, 323 U.S. 214 (1944); *Mitchell v. United States*, 369 F.2d. 323 (2nd Cir., 1966), *cert. denied*, 386 U.S. 942 (1967); *Mora v. McNamara*, 389 U.S. 934 (1967); *Massachusetts v. Laird*, 400 U.S. 886 (1970); and *Holtzman v. Schlesinger*, 414 U.S. 1304 (1973).

KOREMATSU V. UNITED STATES
323 U.S. 214 (1944)

BACKGROUND Korematsu was born in the United States of Japanese-born parents. On February 19, 1942, President Franklin Roosevelt issued an executive order authorizing military commanders to use their discretion to prohibit any and all persons from certain designated military areas. On March 2, Lt. General J. L. DeWitt, commander of the Western Defense Command, promulgated an order that stated that as a matter of military necessity certain persons would be excluded from Military Area No. 1. Korematsu lived in San Leandro, California, which was inside the designated area. On March 21, Congress passed a law declaring it a misdemeanor for persons or groups named by the military commander to remain in a military area. On March 24, General DeWitt issued a curfew order requiring Japanese-American citizens to stay in their homes between the hours of 8:00 P.M. and 6:00 A.M. This curfew was later upheld in *Hirabayashi v. United States*. On March 27, Japanese Americans and Japanese aliens were forbidden to leave the military area until further notice. On May 3, General DeWitt issued Civilian Exclusion Order No. 34. All persons of Japanese ancestry were to proceed to assembly centers for relocation outside the military area and were forbidden to be in the area after May 9. Korematsu was convicted of being in San Leandro on May 30 in violation of the March 21 Act of Congress and Civilian Exclusion Order No. 34. The maximum penalty on conviction was a $5000 fine and a year of imprisonment.

CONSTITUTIONAL ISSUE

Whether a military order that bars American citizens from certain designated areas solely on the basis of race is a constitutional use of the war power? YES

MAJORITY OPINION Justice Hugo L. Black delivers the opinion of the Court. Justice Black begins by stating that any law that excludes a racial group must be given the most rigid judicial scrutiny. He then notes that the Court had previously upheld General DeWitt's curfew order in the *Hirabayashi* case. Although exclusion from one's home is a greater deprivation of liberty than a mere curfew, Black maintains that there is a close and definite relationship between exclusion and the prevention of sabotage and espionage. The Court cannot deny that disloyal persons were among the admittedly mostly loyal Japanese. Nor can the Court deny that the president and Congress had adequate reason to believe that such persons posed a threat to our national security. The Court notes that 5000 American citizens of Japanese descent refused to take an unqualified oath of allegiance to the United States. The difficulty in segregating the loyal from the disloyal justified the curfew and now justifies the exclusion. The Court recognizes that this imposes a hardship on these citizens, but hardship is a part of war. Next, Justice Black turns to the issue of the contradictory orders. Korematsu essentially argued that General DeWitt's order of March 27 prohibited him from leaving the area (the curfew order), and his order of May 3 ordered him to leave. Justice Black argues that the March 27 order was valid until some future proclamation was made. The May 3 order superseded the March 27 order, and Korematsu was bound to obey it. Justice Black also argues that the provision that required the Japanese to leave via the assembly centers is also constitutional. Korematsu was not just ordered to leave San Leandro; he had to leave so that he could be placed in a relocation center in an interior state. The power to exclude, Black maintains, includes the power to exclude by force. Black ends the opinion by denying once again that racial prejudice is at the root of the exclusion.

OTHER OPINIONS   Justice Felix Frankfurter writes the only concurring opinion. Justice Frankfurter believes that the power to impose the curfew in *Hirabayashi* is the same as the power to exclude persons from military areas. Although such an action in peacetime would be unconstitutional, it is not necessarily unconstitutional in wartime. The war power, though subject to constitutional limitations, is nevertheless as broad as other powers of Congress, for example, the commerce power. He ends by noting that finding such measures constitutional does not mean individual members of the Court approve of them.

Justices Owen Roberts, Frank Murphy, and Robert Jackson write separate dissents. Justice Roberts says that in this case a citizen was convicted for not submitting to imprisonment in a concentration camp. That imprisonment is based solely on Korematsu's ancestry and without any evidence of disloyalty. Roberts traces the events in chronological order and concludes that the orders were designed to force Korematsu to appear at an assembly center so he could then be sent to a concentration camp. Roberts believes that Korematsu had the right to disregard what was essentially an unconstitutional order to begin with.

Justice Murphy notes that the order involved in this case was made in the absence of martial law. Because the order applied only to persons of Japanese descent, it denied Korematsu equal protection. Also, because no attempt was made to separate the loyal from disloyal, the order also denied him procedural due process of law. Murphy quotes at length some of the testimony of General DeWitt before the House Naval Affairs Subcommittee. That testimony reveals racial prejudice on his part. The Japanese people were accused of refusing to assimilate into American society like other immigrants, but Murphy attributes that to racial prejudice. In any event, a desire to preserve one's religious and social customs is not proof of disloyalty. Nor do cases of individual disloyalty prove group disloyalty. Murphy does not believe that time was a crucial factor for failure to hold individual hearings. It was four months after Pearl Harbor before the exclusion order was issued. The last "subversives" were not removed until eleven months after Pearl Harbor. Murphy believes there was adequate time to hold hearings for individual cases for the 70,000 persons who were American citizens, especially because many of these were women, children, and elderly men.

Justice Jackson wrote the final dissent. Jackson believes the removal had racial overtones. He notes that if a German enemy alien, an Italian enemy alien, and an American convicted of treason but on parole were also in the designated military area, only Korematsu would have been subject to the exclusion order. Justice Jackson dislikes the majority's upholding the order on the grounds of military expediency. If this order passes constitutional muster, then the Court might as well declare that any military order in wartime is constitutional and be done with it. The Court, Jackson argues, relies solely on General DeWitt's unchallenged statement that exclusion was a military necessity. Finally, Justice Jackson worries that the Court has set the dangerous precedent of permitting the transplanting of American citizens.

SIGNIFICANCE OF THE CASE   *Korematsu* is usually cited as the low point in the protection of civil liberties in this century. It presents the classic dilemma of whether the ends justify the means. Although we now know that the fear of a Japanese invasion was unfounded, the hysteria that seized the West Coast was real. When the nation's security is at risk, many people who might otherwise oppose such blatant violations of civil liberties are willing to tolerate them. *Korematsu* is complicated by the accusations of racial prejudice, a sensitive topic considering what the Nazis were doing to European Jews at the time. German and Italian aliens were not relocated but American citizens of Japanese descent were. Neither were the persons located given an opportunity to prove their loyalty nor was the government required to prove disloyalty. Korematsu's crime was that he had Japanese parents. On August 10, 1988, President Ronald Reagan signed a law awarding $20,000 in tax-free payments to the 60,000 survivors of the relocation centers that, it is hoped, puts an end to this dark chapter of American history.

QUESTIONS FOR DISCUSSION

(1)   Why do you think persons of German and Italian extraction were not excluded from the West or East Coast?

(2)   If we were at war today, would you support a similar relocation program? What changes would you make?

(3)   Do you agree with the decision to compensate the survivors? Why or why not?

(4)   Why do you think no real effort was made to give each Japanese American an individual hearing to determine loyalty? What problems could such hearings raise?

RELATED CASES   *EX PARTE MILLIGAN*, 4 Wallace 2 (1866); *EX PARTE McCARDLE*, 7 Wallace 506 (1869); *Hirabayashi v. United States*, 320 U.S. 81 (1943); and *Ex Parte Endo*, 323 U.S. 283 (1944).

YOUNGSTOWN SHEET AND TUBE CO. V. SAWYER
343 U.S. 579 (1952)

BACKGROUND   After contract negotiations between the nation's steel companies and the United Steelworkers of America failed to reach a labor agreement, the Union gave notice of its intent to strike beginning on December 31, 1951. After an unsuccessful attempt by the Federal Mediation and Conciliation Service to negotiate a settlement, President Harry S. Truman sent the dispute to the Federal Wage Stabilization Board on December 22, 1951. President Truman chose to use the Wage Stabilization Board rather than invoke the provisions of the Taft-Hartley Act. When the Board also failed to negotiate a settlement, the union announced it would strike at 12:01 A.M., April 9, 1952. On April 8, President Truman issued Executive Order 10340, which directed Secretary of Commerce Charles Sawyer to seize control of the steel companies and to prevent a work stoppage.

At the time of these events the United States was engaged in the Korean Conflict. In his Executive Order, President Truman asserted that a work stoppage in the steel industry would endanger our national defense. The president reported his actions to Congress in separate messages on April 9 and April 21, but Congress took no action. The steel companies sought preliminary and permanent injunctions against the enforcement of the Executive Order on the grounds that the president had usurped congressional law-making power. Lawyers for the president cited his inherent constitutional powers as chief executive and commander-in-chief as the basis for the seizure. The district court granted the injunction but the court of appeals stayed the injunction pending review by the Supreme Court. The Court heard oral arguments on May 12, 1952, and handed down its decision on June 2, 1952.

CONSTITUTIONAL ISSUE

Whether the seizure of the steel companies is within the constitutional powers of the president? NO

MAJORITY OPINION   Justice Hugo Black delivers the opinion of the Court. After reviewing the facts, Justice Black notes that any power the president has to seize the steel companies must come either from Congress or the Constitution. Although the Selective Service Act of 1948 and the Defense Production Act of 1950 permit seizures of this kind, the government failed to invoke them because such seizure provisions were "too cumbersome and time-consuming for the crisis at hand." In addition, Congress considered and rejected an amendment to the Taft-Hartley Act granting the president the power to seize private property in emergency labor disputes. As a result, Congress clearly intended to deny to the president the very power he is now attempting to exercise.

Next, Justice Black addresses the president's claim of constitutional authority for the seizures. Black observes that there is no express grant of power to seize private property given to the president in the Constitution. Justice Black rejects the notion that the president has an inherent power as commander-in-chief to seize private property to prevent a strike. Justice Black also rejects the president's claim that his action is justified by his oath to take care that the laws be faithfully executed because there is no congressional policy to execute. Indeed, as noted, Congress explicitly rejected giving the president the power he now seeks to exercise. Finally, Justice Black asserts that even if former presidents have exercised the seizure power, that fact does not deprive Congress of its exclusive authority to make laws regarding the seizure of private property for public use.

OTHER OPINIONS   There were five concurring and one dissenting opinions. Justice Felix Frankfurter's concurrence focuses on the denial of the seizure authority. He cites sixteen statutes in which Congress expressly authorized the seizure of private property under certain conditions. However, in labor disputes, Congress made it clear that it did not want the president to have the power to seize property to prevent a work stoppage. He also notes that a general governmental power to seize private property does not necessarily belong to the president. By rejecting the amendments to the Taft-Hartley Act that would have given the president seizure power, Congress made it clear it wanted the president to seek specific congressional authorization in cases he thought seizure was necessary.

Justice William O. Douglas files the second concurrence. Justice Douglas does not question that the emergency cited by President Truman is real. However, the seizure constitutes a "taking" in a legal sense. A "taking" is a form of sanction and as such is an exercise of legislative, not executive, power. A president's power to execute the law cannot begin until a law has been enacted. Douglas concludes by warning that a power exercised today by a kindly president may be abused by another, future president.

Justice Robert Jackson writes the major concurring opinion. Jackson notes that when the president acts with an express grant of power from Congress his authority is at its maximum. When the president acts in the absence of either a congressional grant or denial of power, he must rely solely on his independent powers to justify his action. Finally, when the president acts contrary to the clear will of Congress, his authority is at its lowest. If the president is to prevail he must show both that his action is clearly within his power as president and that the action is clearly beyond the authority of Congress. Jackson then examines the sources cited and relied on by the government and rejects them. He rejects the president's general executive power on the grounds that the framers' experience with George III taught them to limit, not encourage, the use of unrestricted executive power. Justice Jackson also rejects the president's power as commander-in-chief because the Constitution empowers Congress to raise and support the army. It is a legislative function to provide the necessary material for the military. Finally, Jackson rejects the idea that the president possesses some undefined emergency power. The framers, he asserts, were aware that the invocation of emergency power was often a pretext for the usurpation of power.

In the last two concurrences, Justice Harold Burton states that the decisive factor for him is Congress's clear rejection of seizure in favor of collective bargaining in labor disputes. Justice Tom Clark concedes the existence of presidential emergency power. However, the president may exercise emergency powers only in cases in which Congress has failed to act and never, as here, where there is a clear denial of congressional authority.

The sole dissenting opinion was written by Chief Justice Fred Vinson and joined by Justices Stanley Reed and Sherman Minton. Chief Justice Vinson chides the majority for closing its eyes to the threat of Communist aggression in Korea and in the world. The chief justice inventories the vast military, treaty, and political commitments of the United States throughout the world. The president, Vinson maintains, has a constitutional duty to execute these acts of Congress. Next, the chief justice cites numerous historical precedents from Washington to Franklin Roosevelt where presidents took action without specific authorization from Congress. The chief justice even quotes then Attorney General Robert Jackson's defense of President Franklin Roosevelt's seizure of an aviation plant in Inglewood, California, six months before Pearl Harbor. Finally, the chief justice argues that Congress had enacted military procurement and anti-inflation legislation. By seizing the steel companies while preventing inflationary price increases, the president was merely "taking care that the laws be faithfully executed." The seizure was merely an attempt to preserve the *status quo* until Congress had a chance to act and was not done in defiance of Congress.

SIGNIFICANCE OF THE CASE *Youngstown Sheet and Tube Co.* raises the difficult issue of the nature of presidential power in an emergency. Although, as Chief
Justice Vinson's dissent demonstrates, there are ample precedents for the use of
presidential emergency powers, the conflict is one of expediency versus limited
government. Our Constitution envisions a government of limited powers bestowed on
the national government within the framework of separation of powers. The system
was designed not to promote efficiency as much as to prevent tyranny. At the same
time, a government must be capable of protecting itself and the nation in times of real
emergencies. Unlike his predecessors who invoked emergency powers, President
Truman was unable to convince either the Court or the Congress that a work stoppage
posed a real danger to national security.

QUESTIONS FOR DISCUSSION

(1)   Why do you think Congress failed to respond to Truman's special messages about the
       crisis?
(2)   Did the government make a mistake in admitting that the provisions of the Defense Production
       Act were "too cumbersome and time-consuming"?
(3)   How real do you think the danger to national security was?
(4)   Discuss the existence of emergency powers in a constitutional system such as ours.

RELATED CASES *PRIZE CASES*, 2 Black 635 (1863); *Kohl v. United States*, 91 U.S.
367 (1876); *United States v. Midwest Oil Co.*, 236 U.S. 459 (1915); *MYERS V. UNITED
STATES*, 272 U.S. 52 (1926); *HOME BUILDING AND LOAN ASSOCIATION V.
BLAISDELL*, 290 U.S. 398 (1934); and *UNITED STATES V. CURTISS-WRIGHT EXPORT
CORP.*, 299 U.S. 304 (1936).

UNITED STATES V. CURTISS-WRIGHT CORPORATION
299 U.S. 304 (1936)

BACKGROUND   On May 28, 1934, Congress passed a joint resolution that authorized
President Franklin D. Roosevelt to prohibit the sale of military weapons to countries
engaged in armed conflict in an area known as the Chaco. The same day the president
issued a proclamation prohibiting the sale of munitions to either Bolivia or Paraguay.
On May 29 appellee Curtiss-Wright Corporation allegedly sold fifteen machine guns
to Bolivia. On November 14, 1935, the president revoked his earlier proclamation.
The indictment against Curtiss-Wright was handed down on January 27, 1936. The
corporation challenged the indictment on three grounds. First, that the joint resolution was an invalid delegation of legislative authority to the president. Second,
that the resolution never became effective because of the president's failure to make
certain findings of fact. Third, that the issuance of the second proclamation ended any
liability under the joint resolution. The district court ruled in favor of Curtiss-Wright on
the first issue and against it on the other two. Although the Supreme Court addresses
all three challenges, it is the first challenge that gives this case its constitutional
significance.

CONSTITUTIONAL ISSUE

Whether Congress may delegate to the president greater discretion in law-making authority in the area of foreign affairs than in domestic affairs? YES

MAJORITY OPINION Justice George Sutherland delivers the opinion of the Court. Justice Sutherland distinguishes between the powers of the national government in foreign relations as opposed to domestic relations. In domestic politics, the national government is limited to exercising its delegated powers and those powers that may be implied from the delegated powers. The states retain the powers not delegated to the national government. However, in the area of foreign relations the states, Sutherland maintains, never possessed any authority. The sovereignty of Great Britain in foreign affairs did not pass to the states individually but to the states collectively in their capacity as the United States. It was the national government under the Articles of Confederation that conducted foreign affairs on behalf of the United States. That sovereignty was then passed on to the current national government under the Constitution. The powers of external sovereignty, according to Sutherland, do not rest on an affirmative grant of power in the Constitution. The powers of external sovereignty are inherent in the concept of nationhood that the national government would possess even if they were not mentioned in the Constitution.

Justice Sutherland then turns to the paramount role of the president in the determination of foreign policy. The Constitution authorizes the president to make treaties with the advice and consent of the Senate, but it is the president who negotiates the treaty. Since the early days of the Republic Congress has recognized the preeminent role of the president in foreign affairs. Early Senates recognized that success in foreign policy "frequently depends on secrecy and dispatch." Justice Sutherland says that the president is often more knowledgeable of existing conditions in foreign countries. He notes the deference Congress shows the State Department. Although other executive departments are directed to furnish information to Congress, the State Department is merely requested to provide it, and a denial is seldom questioned.

Next, Justice Sutherland reviews the long history of similar delegations of legislative authority to the president in foreign affairs. Many of the laws Sutherland refers to allow the president, at his discretion, to impose or remove embargoes on trade with other countries. Although a long history of legislative precedents does not imply constitutionality, Sutherland argues that such precedents must be given great weight by the Court. Justice Sutherland concludes that both precedent and principle lend support to the broad delegation of authority to the president in foreign affairs. Sutherland ends the opinion by upholding the lower court on the second and third challenges by ruling, in effect, that President Roosevelt had made the necessary findings of fact to issue his proclamation and that the corporation could be held liable for violating it.

OTHER OPINIONS Justice James McReynolds merely notes that he does not agree with the Court's decision.

SIGNIFICANCE OF THE CASE *Curtiss-Wright Corporation* runs counter to a series of cases dealing with delegation theory that the Supreme Court handed down in the mid-1930s. The Court, in cases such as *Schechter Poultry Corp. v. United States*,

Carter v. Carter Coal Co., and *Panama Refining Co. v. Ryan* had ruled that excessive delegation of legislative power to the president was unconstitutional. In *Curtiss-Wright Corporation* the Court upholds the delegation by distinguishing between foreign and domestic politics. The case is often cited as the Court's definitive statement of presidential predominance in foreign policy making. It is also used to justify broad presidential discretion in the conduct of foreign relations.

QUESTIONS FOR DISCUSSION

(1) What is the delegation of law-making authority?

(2) Do you agree that foreign relations are different from domestic relations in terms of delegation theory?

(3) What other reasons can you think of to justify giving the president broad discretion in the conduct of foreign relations?

(4) What dangers do you see in giving the president broad discretion in the conduct of foreign relations?

RELATED CASES *PRIZE CASES*, 2 Black 635 (1863); *EX PARTE MILLIGAN*, 4 Wallace 2 (1866); *Panama Refining Co. v. Ryan*, 293 U.S. 388 (1935); *SCHECHTER POULTRY CORP. V. UNITED STATES*, 295 U.S. 495 (1936); and *Carter v. Carter Coal Co.*, 298 U.S. 238 (1936).

UNITED STATES V. NIXON
418 U.S. 683 (1974)

BACKGROUND As a result of the Watergate break-in seven persons, including former Attorney General John Mitchell, were indicted by a federal grand jury for conspiracy to defraud the United States and obstruction of justice. President Richard M. Nixon was named as an unindicted co-conspirator. On April 18, 1974, Judge John Sirica, at the request of Special Prosecutor Leon Jaworski, issued a third-party *subpoena duces tecum* to the president ordering him to produce certain tapes, memoranda, and papers related to conversations with the seven defendants. On May 1, 1974, Nixon filed a motion in Judge Sirica's court to quash the subpoena on the grounds that the dispute over the material was an "intrabranch dispute" and therefore a nonjusticiable political question. The president also maintained that the Supreme Court had no jurisdiction over the case because his claim of executive privilege precluded judicial review. On May 20, Judge Sirica denied the motion to quash, and the president filed an appeal with the court of appeals. However, before the appellate court could rule, both the president and the special prosecutor petitioned the Supreme Court for a writ of *certiorari* before judgment. Because of the importance of the case, the Supreme Court granted the petition.

CONSTITUTIONAL ISSUES

(1) Whether the dispute between the president and the special prosecutor is a nonjusticiable political question? NO

(2) Whether the president's claim of executive privilege affords him immunity from a *subpoena duces tecum*? NO

MAJORITY OPINION   Chief Justice Warren Burger delivers the opinion of the Court. The chief justice states that a threshold issue is whether the motion to quash a *subpoena duces tecum* is appealable and therefore properly before the Supreme Court. Normally such a motion is not appealable and leaves the person against whom the subpoena is directed in the position of either complying or risking contempt if his claims are later denied on appeal. However, exceptions do exist and this is such a case. To place the president in this position could lead to a dispute between the executive and judicial branches. Also, the issue whether a president may be cited for contempt would itself require adjudication resulting in further delay. For these reasons, the Court rules that the denial to quash the subpoena is properly before them.

The next issue is the claim that federal courts lack jurisdiction because the issue is nonjusticiable. The president posits two reasons for this claim. First, the president asserts that the dispute is an intrabranch dispute between himself and the special prosecutor, which makes it a "political question." The president declares that he alone decides what evidence is to be used in a criminal prosecution. However, the chief justice notes that in creating the office of special prosecutor, the attorney general delegated to Mr. Jaworski the authority to represent the United States in this case including the authority to challenge claims of executive privilege. Because the Attorney General has not revoked the authority, the Court is obliged to honor it.

The second reason is that the case fails to raise a "real case or controversy" required by Article III of the Constitution. The chief justice notes that a "controversy" is a dispute "that courts traditionally resolve." The controversy here is over the production or nonproduction of evidence needed for a criminal case. This, the chief justice asserts, is the kind of dispute that arises in the regular course of a criminal prosecution and the fact that both parties are officers of the executive branch cannot be viewed as a barrier to justiciability.

After discussing a procedural technicality, the chief justice turns to the president's claim of executive privilege. The president argues that it would be "inconsistent with the public interest" to force him to reveal confidential conversations with his close advisers. The president's argument is twofold: first, that the claim of executive privilege is absolute, and second, if the claim of absolute privilege should fail it should still prevail over a *subpoena duces tecum*.

The claim of absolute privilege is based on the contention that the president alone can define its use. The chief justice declares that *Marbury v. Madison* decided long ago that it is the duty of the courts to say what the law is. Because the Court has consistently ruled it has the power to delineate the express powers of the other two branches, it surely can delineate the scope of an implied power like executive privilege.

The president offers two justifications for absolute privilege. The first is the need to protect communications between the president and his advisers. The second is that the doctrine of separation of powers insulates the president from judicial subpoena. Although the chief justice recognizes the validity of both grounds, he rejects both. First, the need to protect confidential communications will not be jeopardized by *in camera* review of the documents by Judge Sirica. Second, a broad and general claim of privilege, without more, cannot be allowed to interfere with the administration of justice. If the president's claim were based on the need to protect sensitive military or diplomatic secrets, the claim might be valid. But a general assertion that disclosure is "inconsistent with the public interest" is insufficient to justify a claim of absolute privilege.

As to the assertion that the president's claim, if not absolute, should prevail over the subpoena, the chief justice states that Judge Sirica assumed that the president's refusal to produce the documents was "presumptively privileged," but Sirica also ruled that the special prosecutor had overcome the presumption. The Court must weigh the claims of both parties. Although constitutionally based, the doctrine of executive privilege is not explicitly mentioned in the Constitution. However, a criminal defendant's right "to have compulsory process for obtaining witnesses in his favor" and his right to due process of law are constitutionally based. Because the president's claim is general and the need for evidence specific, the president's claim cannot prevail over the need to ensure justice in a criminal case. The Court then affirms the order that the materials be transmitted to Judge Sirica.

SIGNIFICANCE OF THE CASE   *United States v. Nixon* was the final nail in Richard Nixon's political coffin. The disclosure of the Watergate tapes convinced all but his diehard supporters that he was involved the Watergate cover-up. Shortly after the Court's ruling, the House Judiciary Committee passed three articles of impeachment against the president, and he resigned in August 1974.

United States v. Nixon is a classic example of what political scientists David W. Rohde and Harold J. Spaeth call a "threat situation." Nixon's assertion that his claim of executive privilege was not reviewable by the Court posed a threat to the power of the Court. The Court's response, as it often is when its power and prestige are threatened, was to rule unanimously against the president.

QUESTIONS FOR DISCUSSION

(1)   Why didn't Nixon just claim the conversations did contain sensitive diplomatic or military secrets?
(2)   Is the president's fear that his advisers will not be totally candid if their conversations can be made public a real one?
(3)   Does the chief justice's opinion weaken or strengthen executive privilege?
(4)   Is Nixon's claim that he was only protecting executive privilege for future presidents credible?

RELATED CASES   *MARBURY V. MADISON*, 1 Cranch 137 (1803); *YOUNGSTOWN SHEET AND TUBE CO. V. SAWYER*, 343 U.S. 579 (1952); *BAKER V. CARR*, 369 U.S. 186 (1962); *POWELL V. McCORMACK*, 395 U.S. 486 (1969); *Gravel v. United States*, 408 U.S. 606 (1972); and *Nixon v. Fitzgerald*, 457 U.S. 731 (1982).

MYERS V. UNITED STATES
272 U.S. 52 (1926)

BACKGROUND   Frank S. Myers was appointed to a four-year term of office as a postmaster of the first class in Portland, Oregon, by President Wilson on July 21, 1917. Wilson demanded his resignation on January 20, 1920, but Myers refused to resign. The president removed him from office on February 2, 1920, and appointed a man named Jones to Myers's position. An 1876 Act of Congress provided that removal of postmasters required the consent of the Senate. On April 21, 1921, Myers brought a claim against the United States in the Court of Claims for $8,838.71, the salary he would have earned if he had been allowed to finish his four-year term. The Court of Claims ruled against Myers, and his case was appealed to the Supreme Court.

CONSTITUTIONAL ISSUE

Whether the 1876 Act that requires Senate consent for the removal of postmasters is an unconstitutional limitation on the president's executive power? YES

MAJORITY OPINION Chief Justice William Howard Taft delivers the opinion of the Court. Chief Justice Taft acknowledges that the Constitution is silent on the issue of the removal of the president's subordinates so he maintains that the Court must look to a decision of the First Congress for guidance. During the passage of the act creating the Department of State, a debate arose over the removal language in the act. The act made it clear that the secretary would be removable by the president. However, a few members of Congress, including James Madison, argued that placing the phrase "removable by the president" implied a congressional grant of power that might later be withheld. Madison contended that the removal power was inherent in the president's appointment power and need not be conferred by Congress. Madison further argued that the doctrine of separation of powers, as well as practical reasons, dictated removal by the president alone. Madison argued that the president needs subordinates he trusts, that his subordinates may act only in his name, that the president needs the "disciplinary influence" of removal, and that the president, not the Senate, knows the weaknesses of his subordinates. After a lengthy debate, the House passed the act without the phrase "removable by the president."

Chief Justice Taft argues that this decision of the First Congress should be given great weight for two reasons. First, the decision was made within two years of the framing of the Constitution and was therefore contemporaneous with it. Second, many of the members of the First Congress had been delegates to the Constitutional Convention and were well qualified to judge the intent of the framers. Taft also notes that between 1789 and 1863 no act of Congress or Supreme Court decision conflicted with the decision of the First Congress.

The chief justice rejects Myers's claims for other reasons. For example, he rejects Myers's contention that the decision of the First Congress should not apply to "inferior offices." However, Taft does acknowledge that in 1866 Congress forbade the president to remove military officers during peacetime without a court martial. He also acknowledges that the Tenure of Office Act of 1867 restricted the president's power to remove cabinet officers. These laws, Taft contends, were aberrations resulting from Congress's feud with President Andrew Johnson. Subsequent laws, like the 1876 law under review, were passed against the advice of several presidents. Taft attributes presidential acquiescence to a desire to enact other aspects of the legislation. In other words, presidents signed laws that limited their power to remove subordinates to secure passage of other, more vital legislation. Taft concludes that the Tenure of Office Act and others "of the same effect" are unconstitutional. Finally, Taft denies that the Court's decision signals a return to the spoils system as the dissenters claim.

OTHER OPINIONS   Justices James C. McReynolds, Louis Brandeis, and Oliver Wendell Holmes, Jr., write dissenting opinions. Justice McReynolds rejects the reasons for the majority's opinion as "forced and unsubstantial." First, McReynolds rejects the notion that the president has illimitable powers that are derived from his executive power. Such a position runs counter to the premise that our Constitution limits the power of government. All three branches, McReynolds contends, may exercise only those powers specifically granted by the Constitution and removal by the president alone, as the majority concedes, is not among the executive's powers. Second, McReynolds rejects the majority's reliance on the decision of the First Congress to strike "removable by the president" from an early law. The act in question dealt with a superior officer, that is, a cabinet-level position while postmasters are inferior officers. In addition, the same Congress passed two laws on August 7 and September 24, 1789, that ran directly counter to the majority's position. Third, McReynolds contends that because only Congress may or may not create such inferior offices it is difficult to see how such officers can be essential to the president's duty to see that the laws are faithfully executed. Fourth, in *Marbury v. Madison*, the Court ruled that Marbury's tenure as a justice of the peace was for a fixed term and not subject to the will of the president. Although not entirely relevant to the removal of *executive* officials, *Marbury* does demonstrate that Congress believes it may restrict the president's removal power. Finally, McReynolds demonstrates that from 1789 to 1836 postmasters were appointed and removed by the postmaster general, not the president. In conclusion, McReynolds notes that every judicial precedent and legislative enactment, including some of the First Congress, are contrary to the majority's finding.

Justice Brandeis claims that the only issue is whether a president, having acted under a statute to make an appointment, may ignore the provision under which a removal may occur. The usual practice, according to Brandeis, had been to assume the Senate gives its consent for removal on confirming a successor. Justice Brandeis also differentiates between removal and suspension noting that the president retains the power to suspend officials who are derelict in their duties. Brandeis notes that none of the original thirteen states gave its chief executive uncontrollable removal power at the time of the framing of the Constitution. He asserts that every president since 1861, except one, had given his consent to laws restricting presidential removal power. Brandeis believes a distinction should be made between high political officials and "inferior officers" such as postmasters. Brandeis also cites numerous laws where Congress placed limits on the president's appointment power. The implication is that if Congress may put limits on whom the president can nominate, it surely can limit the president's power to remove. Brandeis concludes his opinion by asserting that the doctrine of separation of powers was never intended to make a branch of government completely autonomous. He observes that the president's ability to "take care that the laws be faithfully executed" can be impeded by congressional failure to create the inferior offices needed to carry out the law, the failure to appropriate money to carry out the law, or the failure to confirm presidential nominees who will carry out the law. The failure of the law will lie with Congress, but the president will have done his constitutional duty.

In his brief opinion Justice Holmes states his agreement with McReynolds and Brandeis. In his opinion these inferior offices owe their existence to Congress, and it is difficult for him to understand how Congress can lack the power to limit removal from an office it can abolish at any time.

SIGNIFICANCE OF THE CASE   *Myers* illustrates that while something may make practical sense, it does not necessarily make constitutional sense. Chief Justice Taft, himself a former president, makes a strong case for why, as a practical matter, the president needs to be able to remove subordinates without undue Senate interference. But while Taft's logic may apply to cabinet-level positions, it is difficult to justify for inferior officers like postmasters. As the dissenters persuasively argue, there are equally powerful arguments why the president should not have uncontrollable removal power. Taft's victory, however, is brief. In 1935, in *Humphrey's Executor v. United States* the Court modifies *Myers* for persons appointed to independent regulatory commissions.

QUESTIONS FOR DISCUSSION

(1)   How important is an Oregon postmaster to the president's duty to see that the laws are faithfully executed?

(2)   Do you think Taft's status as a former president influenced others on the Court? In what ways?

(3)   Do you see any differences between cabinet-level officers and inferior officers from either a practical or constitutional standpoint?

(4)   What impact has the civil service system had on the president's removal powers?

RELATED CASES   *United States v. Perkins*, 116 U.S. 483 (1886); *McAllister v. United States*, 141 U.S. 174 (1891); *Parsons v. United States*, 167 U.S. 324 (1897); *Shurtleff v. United States*, 189 U.S. 311 (1903); *Humphrey's Executor v. United States*, 295 U.S. 602 (1935); and *Wiener v. United States*, 357 U.S. 349 (1958).

BUCKLEY V. VALEO
424 U.S. 1 (1976)

BACKGROUND   Congress passed the Federal Election Campaign Act of 1971 and amended it in 1974. The Act had a variety of features including the following: (1) limiting the amount of campaign contributions for federal officers to $1000 per individual and $5000 by political action committees and an overall $25,000 per year ceiling on individual contributors and (2) limiting expenditures by individuals or groups to $1000 per candidate as well as restricting the amount of personal or family funds a candidate could expend. In addition, political committees were required to keep detailed records of contributions and to disclose the source of those donations. An eight-member Federal Election Commission was set up with two members to be appointed by the president *pro tempore* of the Senate, two by the speaker of the House, and two by the president (all subject to confirmation by both the House and the Senate), and the secretary of the Senate and clerk of the House *ex officio*.

In companion legislation, the Internal Revenue Code was amended to provide for public financing of presidential nominating conventions as well as campaign financing for general and primary elections. The funds were to be distributed by formula according to the number of votes each candidate garnered. Candidates from "major" parties with 25 percent or more of the most recent vote were to be funded fully. Minor parties with between 5 percent and 25 percent of the most recent vote were to receive only a percentage of the funds, whereas "new" parties were limited to receiving postelection funds if the candidate received more than 5 percent of the vote. A coalition of federal officeholders and candidates, political organizations, and others brought suit challenging the various provisions.

CONSTITUTIONAL ISSUE

Whether campaign expenditures and contributions fall under the auspices of the First Amendment freedom of speech and freedom of association protections? YES

PER CURIAM OPINION During the course of a very lengthy opinion, the Court deals with several issues: (1) whether the matter constitutes an Article III "case or controversy" so as to give the Court jurisdiction; (2) whether the ceilings on expenditures and contributions violate the First Amendment; (3) whether the scheme of public financing as set forth in the Act invidiously discriminates against minor and new parties in violation of the Due Process Clause; (4) whether the appointment of the members of the Federal Election Commission by someone other than the president violates the Appointments Clause; and (5) whether the Commission's past acts are valid. The justices all agree that the complaint does demonstrate a "case or controversy" and that the litigants have "sufficient personal stake" in the matter to challenge the statute's validity. The power of Congress to pass legislation regulating federal elections is not challenged by the parties and is readily acknowledged by the Court, which then turns to other issues in the case.

Initially considered is the constitutionality of the limitations on campaign contributions and expenditures. The Court describes the public discussion of issues and candidates as an integral and critical aspect of our system of government and as one of the most fundamental of First Amendment rights. Political speech, like political association, is protected by the First Amendment. The Court recognizes that "virtually every means of communicating in today's mass society requires the expenditure of money" and that regulating the use of funds in federal election campaigns is an appropriate exercise of congressional power. However, that power must be balanced against the individual's or group's right to advance their candidates and ideas under the First Amendment.

The Court accepts the contribution limitations while rejecting the limitations on expenditures. Restrictions on expenditures for political communication reduces the "quantity of expression by restricting the number of issues discussed, the depth of their exploration, and the size of the audience reached," which is a severe and direct restraint on political speech under the First Amendment. The effect on the expenditure ceiling is not to equalize the ability of individuals and groups to influence elections but instead restricts the speech of some groups and individuals to enhance the relative voice of others. The Court finds that to be "wholly foreign to the First Amendment," which is designed to facilitate open and diverse discussions. The control of the quantity and depth of debates of public issues during campaigns should be left to the citizens, the Court declares.

The possibility of unlimited spending by candidates raises the specter of undue influence being exerted by large contributors who finance the expenditures, but the Court argues that the limitations on the amount of contributions (which they uphold) act to alleviate the corrupting influence of large contributions. Freedom of political association is a fundamental right, but it can be abridged if the government shows a sufficiently important interest and chooses means that are closely drawn so as to avoid any unnecessary infringement of those rights. In this instance, protecting the integrity of representative democracy by limiting the actuality and appearance of corruption resulting from large contributions is such an interest. The restrictions imposed by the statute do not directly or substantially impinge on the rights of candidates or citizens to engage in political discussion and debate. Despite the fact that limiting campaign contributions impairs freedom of association, the Court finds that the purpose of the limits is so significant as to overcome the small interference with citizens' rights and that the Act's provisions are sufficiently narrowly drawn to allow the statute to be upheld.

The Court also sustains the Act's provisions mandating disclosure of contributors and expenditures even while recognizing that "compelled disclosure, in itself, can seriously infringe on privacy of association and belief guaranteed by the First Amendment." There is a "relevant correlation" between the governmental interests—allowing voters to identify interests to which the candidate is likely to be responsive, deterring corruption and the appearance of corruption by disclosing large contributions, and gathering information of violations—and the information sought that outweighs individual and group rights to privacy. Minor parties and their members, although especially vulnerable to the effects of public disclosure, are free to seek additional protection from the judicial system if needed. The overall impact of the disclosure requirements is to open the system to public scrutiny and oversight, an admirable goal in the Court's eyes.

The Court also supports public financing of presidential campaigns even though access to the funds by new and minor parties was apparently unequal to that of the major parties. The Act is viewed as an effort to facilitate and expand public discussion and participation in the political process rather than to inhibit or censor speech. Minor and new parties are not prevented from being on the ballot, nor are they totally prohibited from receiving funds because they could receive postelection funds. Congress is commended for encouraging public discussion and political participation while at the same time safeguarding the public's funds from candidates without significant public support. The Constitution does not require Congress to treat all declared candidates the same, especially because those candidates who elected to decline public financing are released from the corollary obligation of limiting their expenditures.

Finally, the Court rejects the Act's provisions regarding the composition of the Federal Election Commission because four members are appointed by the Speaker of the House or by the president *pro tempore* of the Senate and the two *ex officio* members are employees of the House and Senate, respectively. This, the Court determined, violated the Appointments Clause (Article II, § 2, Clause 2) of the Constitution, which mandates that all lesser officers of the United States should be nominated by the president, by the heads of any department, or by the judiciary and approved by the Senate.

The past acts of the Commission are given *de facto* validity, but the Court requires that the Commission be reconstituted to carry out all the duties assigned to it by the Act.

OTHER OPINIONS   Chief Justice Warren Burger and Justices Byron White, Thurgood Marshall, Harry Blackmun, and William Rehnquist each write opinions concurring in part and dissenting in part. Chief Justice Burger first objects to considering the legislation in piecemeal fashion rather than as an integrated whole. He then turns to the major issues and discusses his disagreement with the Court's ruling upholding disclosure of small contributions on the basis that disclosure inhibits contributions because, for example, employees might be fearful of retribution for supporting candidates other than those favored by their employer. He also dissents with imposing limitations on contributions while not setting restraints on expenditures because contributors "spend money because they wish to communicate ideas and their constitutional interest in doing so is precisely the same whether they or someone else utters the words." In other words, there is no distinction between the goal and effect of contributions and expenditures in terms of political speech. He also disagrees with the provisions relating to public finance on two grounds. First, public financing is an unwarranted intrusion by government into the traditionally private political process. Second, the statutory scheme of financing invidiously discriminates against minor parties, and there is not any "justification for freezing the *status* quo of the present major parties at the expense of such future political movements."

His ideas find merit with two other justices. Justice Harry Blackmun agrees that there was "no principled constitutional distinction" between limiting expenditures and contributions; therefore, he does not join in the section upholding the limitations on contributions. Like the chief justice, Justice William Rehnquist opposes the formula for financing elections because it discriminates against minor parties in violation of both the First Amendment and the Fifth Amendment Equal Protection Clause.

Justice Byron White argues that limitations on expenditures do not significantly impact on the First Amendment rights of candidates when weighed against the government's interest in preventing corruption. The expenditure ceilings do not control the content of political speech, which means that First Amendment rights are not really affected. Congress recognizes that an imbalance of expenditures could also have a corruptive influence on the political process, and the Court should defer to congressional judgment regarding such matters.

Justice Thurgood Marshall also attacks the Court's ruling in allowing unlimited expenditures, although his focus is more narrow. He objects to the Court rejection of the provision limiting the candidates' expenditure of their private funds. The purpose of the expenditure limits is to equalize the relative financial resources of candidates, and without this ceiling the candidate with a substantial personal fortune not only has an initial head start but a possibly insurmountable advantage during the campaign in terms of being able to communicate his or her positions effectively.

SIGNIFICANCE OF THE CASE   The adoption of the Federal Election Campaign Act and its interpretation by the Court in *Buckley v. Valeo* reshaped political participation and elections in this country. The Court validated campaign contributions and expenditures as part and parcel of political expression and association under the First Amendment even while apparently restricting the influence that wealthier individuals or groups could exert on the political process. However, the proliferation of political action committees with various means of circumventing the prohibitions has proved the restriction to be somewhat illusory. The Federal Election Commission was restructured and with all members appointed by the president, it now carries out the duties assigned to it by the Act.

QUESTIONS FOR DISCUSSION

(1)   Do you believe that individuals or groups should be placed under limits as to the amount they may contribute to candidates? Why?

(2)   Are new or minor parties treated unfairly regarding the distribution of public monies for elections? Why?

(3)   Those who support new or minor party candidates, who often espouse somewhat unpopular ideas, could be subject to public animosity or unpopularity. Given that possibility, do the disclosure requirements hinder participation in the political process? Does the statute act to maintain the *status quo* of two major parties? Is this good or harmful?

RELATED CASES   *United States v. Germaine*, 9 Otto 508 (1879); *Burroughs v. United States*, 290 U.S. 534 (1934); *Sweezy v. New Hampshire*, 354 U.S. 234 (1957); *N.A.A.C.P. V. ALABAMA*, 357 U.S. 449 (1958); *NEW YORK TIMES CO. V. SULLIVAN*, 376 U.S. 254 (1964); and *Jenness v. Fortson*, 403 U.S. 431 (1971).

BOWSHER V. SYNAR
478 U.S. 714 (1986)

BACKGROUND In December 1985 President Ronald Reagan signed the Balanced Budget and Emergency Deficit Control Act, better known as the Gramm-Rudman-Hollings Act. The Act set maximum deficit ceilings for federal spending that were gradually reduced until the deficit reached zero in fiscal year 1991. If the projected deficit for any given year exceeded the maximum deficit ceiling, the Act called for across-the-board cuts to meet the target figure. Estimates of projected deficits were to be calculated by the directors of the Office of Management and Budget and the Congressional Budget Office acting independently. The Act required these two directors to submit their estimates in separate reports to the comptroller general who in turn was to recommend specific budget cuts to the president. The president was then required to issue a "sequestration" order mandating the reductions specified by the comptroller general. After the president had issued the order Congress could adjust the reductions, but if it failed to do so, the president's sequestration went into effect.

The constitutionality of the Gramm-Rudman-Hollings Act was challenged almost immediately. President Reagan expressed doubts about it as he signed it into law. Even Congress anticipated that the law might be declared invalid. It included a "fallback provision" that held that if the reporting provisions (§ 251 and § 252) of the Act were invalidated, Congress could implement the president's sequestration order by joint resolution. Representative Mike Synar and eleven other members of Congress challenged the constitutionality of the act within hours of its signing. A three-judge district court invalidated the reporting provisions on the grounds that they violated the doctrine of separation of powers.

CONSTITUTIONAL ISSUE

Whether the functions assigned to the comptroller general under the provisions of the Balanced Budget and Emergency Deficit Control Act of 1985 violate the doctrine of separation of powers? YES

MAJORITY OPINION   Chief Justice Warren Burger delivers the opinion of the Court. The chief justice begins the opinion by reviewing the doctrine of separation of powers. Persons designated as "officers of the United States" are nominated by the president and confirmed by the Senate. These executive officers possess executive powers and Congress may only remove them constitutionally by the impeachment process. However, the office of comptroller general, created by the Budget and Accounting Act of 1921, is an exception. The comptroller general is nominated by the president and confirmed by the Senate from a list of three names submitted to him by the Speaker of the House and the president *pro tempore* of the Senate. The comptroller general may be removed by a joint resolution of Congress for certain reasons, such as neglect of duty, specified in the 1921 Act. From this fact and from the legislative history of the Budget and Accounting Act of 1921, the chief justice concludes that the comptroller general is not an executive officer, but is an agent of the Congress created to be independent of the president except for his initial appointment.

The next issue is whether Congress may assign executive duties to one of its agents. The chief justice says no because to do so would permit Congress to control executive functions. Burger reasons that Congress's power to remove the comptroller general makes him subservient to the will of Congress. Congress could use the threat of removal to influence the decisions the comptroller general must make under the provisions of the Gramm-Rudman-Hollings Act. This, Burger asserts, would violate the doctrine of separation of powers.

Having established that the comptroller general is a legislative agent and that assignment of executive duties to him violates the doctrine of separation of powers, the chief justice turns to the issue of whether the reporting duties assigned to the comptroller general under § 251 and § 252 are "executive." The chief justice concludes that they are and therefore may not be assigned constitutionally to the comptroller general.

Finally, the chief justice turns to the issue of the proper remedy. Appellant Bowsher, the comptroller general, urges the Court to invalidate the removal provisions of the 1921 Act as unconstitutional and uphold § 251 and § 252. But to do so, Burger maintains, would require the Court to weigh the importance of the 1921 Act against that of the 1985 Act. This the chief justice declines to do. Such a choice is unnecessary because of the "fallback provision." The chief justice interprets this provision to mean that Congress prefers to retain both its control over the budget reductions and its power to remove the comptroller general. Therefore, the Court has no choice but to declare § 251 and § 252 unconstitutional.

OTHER OPINIONS   Justice John Paul Stevens writes the only concurring opinion. Justice Stevens agrees that § 251 and § 252 of Gramm-Rudman-Hollings are unconstitutional, but he disagrees with the majority's reasoning. Stevens concedes that the comptroller general is an agent of Congress; however, he does not believe that the comptroller general is subservient to Congress. Stevens agrees with Justice White who maintains that the comptroller general is remarkably independent of Congress. Nor does Stevens believe that characterizing the comptroller general's duties under Gramm-Rudman-Hollings as "executive" is helpful. Stevens notes that under the fallback provision (§ 274) Congress, through a joint resolution, may impose the same reductions as the comptroller general could have under § 251 and § 252. Because no one questions the power of Congress to impose the budget cuts in this manner, how can this function be "executive" when performed by the comptroller general but "legislative" when performed by Congress? For Justice Stevens the real issue is that Gramm-Rudman-Hollings has delegated the power to make public policy to the comptroller general, an agent of Congress. Public policies can be formulated only by delegating such power to executive officers, or by passage by both houses of Congress and presentment to the president as the Constitution requires. Because Congress may not delegate public policy making to a legislative officer, § 251 and § 252 are unconstitutional.

Justice Byron White writes the principal dissenting opinion. Justice White notes that the majority is not saying that only an executive official removable by the president may exercise the powers delegated in Gramm-Rudman-Hollings. If this were so, dozens of independent regulatory agencies of the federal government would be functioning unconstitutionally. What Justice White cannot see is why the duties in the Act may not be assigned to the comptroller general. Because Congress controls appropriations, delegating power to make budget cuts to the comptroller general encroaches on no constitutional power of the president. Nor does White agree that the comptroller general is subservient to Congress. He may only be removed for specified causes. His removal must pass both houses, and if vetoed by the president, must be overridden by two-thirds of both houses. This, White argues, makes removal potentially even more difficult than impeachment. Finally, White thinks it is ridiculous to use a sixty-five-year old provision of the Budget and Accounting Act of 1921 to invalidate a law the nation so desperately needs.

Justice Harry Blackmun also writes a dissenting opinion. Blackmun agrees that characterizing the comptroller general as subservient is unrealistic. Blackmun's major argument, however, is that the Court should have invalidated the removal provision of the Budget and Accounting Act rather than the Gramm-Rudman-Hollings Act. Blackmun contends that the Court's duty is to strike down the law less destructive of congressional objectives. Because the *amicus* briefs for both the House and Senate urged invalidation of the removal provision, that is the course the Court should have followed.

SIGNIFICANCE OF THE CASE   *Bowsher* is another in a series of cases that include *INS v. Chadha* and *Buckley v. Valeo* that indicate the Burger Court's concern for the doctrine of separation of powers. The majority in *Bowsher* avoids judging the merits of the Gramm-Rudman-Hollings Act, preferring instead to take what Justice White calls a "rigidly formalistic" approach to the Constitution. Historically, the Court has been caught in the dilemma of strict adherence to constitutional principles at the expense of a workable government and vice versa. *Bowsher* clearly indicates the Burger Court's unwillingness to sacrifice constitutional principles for expediency.

QUESTIONS FOR DISCUSSION

(1) Do you agree with the Court that the comptroller general is an agent of Congress? Why or why not?

(2) Could Congress have delegated the duties under Gramm-Rudman-Hollings to the secretary of the treasury? Would it have been constitutional?

(3) Who do you think is correct in this case, the majority or the dissenters? Why?

(4) Was the Court's decision a serious setback for deficit control? Why or why not?

RELATED CASES *MYERS V. UNITED STATES*, 272 U.S. 52 (1926); *Humphrey's Executor v. United States*, 295 U.S. 602 (1935); *Wiener v. United States*, 357 U.S. 349 (1958); *BUCKLEY V. VALEO*, 424 U.S. 1 (1976); and *IMMIGRATION AND NATURALIZATION SERVICE V. CHADHA*, 462 U.S. 919 (1983).

MORRISON V. OLSON
487 U.S. 654 (1988)

BACKGROUND Two subcommittees of the House of Representatives subpoenaed documents concerning the so-called Superfund from the Environmental Protection Agency (EPA). President Ronald Reagan, partly on the advice of Assistant Attorney General Theodore Olson, invoked executive privilege and ordered the administrator of the EPA to withhold the documents. The House of Representatives then voted to hold the administrator in contempt of Congress. A lawsuit was filed by the administrator against the House of Representatives, but a confrontation was avoided when the Reagan administration agreed to give the House limited access to the contested documents.

The next year the House Judiciary Committee began an investigation into the Justice Department's role in the EPA controversy. Olson testified before a House Subcommittee on March 10, 1983. A subsequent House report on the controversy suggested that Olson had given false or misleading information to the Subcommittee during his testimony. Pursuant to the Ethics in Government Act, the chair of the House Judiciary Committee asked the attorney general to appoint a special prosecutor to investigate the allegations against Olson and two others. James C. McKay was appointed special prosecutor and was later replaced by appellant Morrison. In 1987, Ms. Morrison caused a grand jury to issue subpoenas against the three appellees. Olson then asked a United States district court to quash the subpoenas on the grounds that the special prosecutor provisions of the Ethics in Government Act were unconstitutional. The district court upheld the constitutionality of the Act and denied a motion to quash the subpoenas. The court of appeals reversed, and Morrison appealed to the Supreme Court.

CONSTITUTIONAL ISSUES

(1) Whether the special prosecutor provisions of the Ethics in Government Act violate the Appointments Clause of Article II? NO

(2) Whether the provisions violate the limitations of Article III? NO

(3) Whether the provisions interfere with the president's authority in violation of the doctrine of separation of powers? NO

MAJORITY OPINION Chief Justice William Rehnquist delivers the opinion of the Court. The chief justice begins the opinion by reviewing the key provisions of the Ethics in Government Act. The Act provides that under certain circumstances and following a preliminary investigation, the attorney general may request the appointment of a special prosecutor. The actual appointment is made by the Special Division of the U.S. Court of Appeals for the District of Columbia. Also, as in the present case, certain designated members of Congress may ask the attorney general to seek the appointment of a special prosecutor. Once appointed, the special prosecutor may be removed only for good cause or on termination of the investigation.

After reviewing the background of the case, the chief justice addresses the issue whether the Act violates the Appointments Clause of Articl II. That Clause states that Congress may vest the appointment of "inferior" officers "in the Courts of Law, or in the Heads of Departments." The first question, then, is whether the special prosecutor is an inferior officer whose appointment can be made by the Special Division. The Court concludes that Morrison is an inferior officer for four reasons. First, the special prosecutor is subject to removal by a superior in the executive branch, either the attorney general or the president. Second, the special prosecutor may perform only limited duties and has no policy-making power. Third, the special prosecutor's jurisdiction is limited because only designated federal officials may be investigated for specified offenses. Finally, the position of special prosecutor is a limited one.

Appellee Olson argues that even if Morrison is an inferior officer, the Constitution prohibits officials in one branch (the judiciary) from appointing officers in another branch (the executive). The chief justice notes that the Appointments Clause gives Congress discretion "as they think proper" to place the appointment of executive officials in "Courts of Law." Neither the previous opinions of the Court, nor the history of the framing of the Constitution lends support to Olson's contention. Congress was obviously concerned with conflicts of interest caused by executive officials being called on to investigate other high-ranking executive officials including the president.

Chief Justice Rehnquist next turns to the question whether the Act violates Article III by imposing executive duties on the judiciary (Special Division). Rehnquist acknowledges that the Court has resisted past attempts to impose nonjudicial duties on the federal courts. However, once the power to appoint the special prosecutor is accepted, Congress may vest the Special Division with limited discretion to define the special prosecutor's jurisdiction. That jurisdiction is limited in the sense that it must concern the circumstances that caused the special prosecutor's appointment. Therefore, the chief justice rejects Olson's contention that the Special Division's power to appoint a special prosecutor is inconsistent with the judicial power.

Finally, the chief justice addresses whether the Act violates the doctrine of separation of power. The first issue to be decided is whether the Act impermissibly interferes with the president's exercise of his constitutional duties. Chief Justice Rehnquist notes that the Act is not an attempt by Congress to gain a role for itself in the removal of an executive official because only the attorney general can remove a special prosecutor. The chief justice admits that in the past the Court had distinguished between the removal of officials with "pure executive" functions (*Myers v. United States*) and those with quasi-legislative and quasi-judicial functions (*Humphrey's Executor v. United States*). Now, however, the Court prefers to examine whether Congress seeks to interfere with the president's exercise of his executive power. The chief justice concludes that subjecting the special prosecutor to removal for good cause does not unduly interfere with any central function of the executive branch.

The second issue to be decided is whether the Act reduces the president's ability to control prosecutorial powers. The chief justice notes that the Special Division may not appoint a special prosecutor on its own initiative but only after a request by the attorney general. Should the attorney general decide not to appoint one his decision is not reviewable. Nor does the Special Division exercise any supervision over the special prosecutor. Lastly, the special prosecutor is required to abide by existing Justice Department policies "when possible." From these facts the chief justice concludes that the president and the attorney general have sufficient control over the special prosecutor to avoid separation-of-powers problems.

OTHER OPINIONS   Justice Antonin Scalia writes the only dissenting opinion. Justice Scalia's major complaint is the majority's failure to make separation of powers the key issue in the case. Accordingly, he first addresses the issue whether the Ethics in Government Act violates the doctrine of separation of powers. Scalia dismisses the claim that the attorney general has unreviewable discretion to appoint a special prosecutor. In reality, the attorney general would dare not refuse for political reasons. Scalia implies that Congress might interpret the attorney general's refusal as grounds for impeachment. Next, Scalia admits that the Court normally seeks to avoid finding congressional acts unconstitutional. However, when the issue involves the doctrine of separation of powers, the usual deference afforded Congress is unnecessary.

Justice Scalia then turns his attention to the nature of the special prosecutor's function. The majority concedes that the prosecution of crimes is an executive function and that the Act deprives the president of exclusive control over the prosecutorial power. The majority, nevertheless, maintains that the attorney general's power to remove the special prosecutor with good cause provides enough control over the special prosecutor to save the Act. Justice Scalia, however, asserts that *Humphrey's Executor* made it clear that the good-cause-for-removal requirement was meant to limit, not enhance, presidential control over executive subordinates. Although it is true the attorney general exercises control in making the initial appointment, once it is made the special prosecutor exercises power independently of the president. Next, Justice Scalia discusses the legal, political, and practical consequences of a decision to prosecute. By removing the president's control over his subordinates the Act interferes with the "essence of prosecutorial discretion." The Act also reduces the president's ability to protect himself and his staff from political attacks.

Justice Scalia questions the majority's finding that the special prosecutor is an inferior officer. Because of the good-cause-for-removal restriction it is actually more difficult to remove a special prosecutor than the attorney general who serves merely at the pleasure of the president. Nor does the special prosecutor's limited jurisdiction contribute to the office's "inferior" status. Once appointed, the special prosecutor has the full powers of prosecution vested in the Justice Department. The majority's reliance on the special prosecutor's limited tenure is also misplaced according to Scalia. He notes that Morrison has already been in her position longer (two years) than the average cabinet member. Finally, the word "inferior" implies a "superior" in the sense of one who is subordinate. However, the stated purpose of the Act was to make the special prosecutor independent of, not subordinate to, the president and attorney general.

In the remainder of his opinion, Justice Scalia makes two final points. First, he accuses the majority of erasing the distinction between officials performing purely executive functions and those performing quasi-legislative and quasi-judicial functions (*Myers-Humphrey's Executor*). Although admitting the line has never been a clear one, Scalia says the majority's new rule is unacceptable. It permits Congress to limit the president's removal power unless it impairs the president's ability to accomplish his constitutional role. Justice Scalia considers such a vague standard suspect to say the least. The second point concerns abuse of power by the special prosecutor. Scalia concedes any prosecutor may abuse his or her power. The difference is that ordinary prosecutors answer to the president who is, in turn, accountable to the people. Scalia sees no realistic check on a special prosecutor who has a vendetta against the president or an official named in the Act. Justice Scalia concludes his opinion by voicing his faith in the system of separation of powers devised by the framers to check the abuse of power.

SIGNIFICANCE OF THE CASE *Morrison v. Olson* upholds the constitutionality of a device that increasingly has been used in our political system: the special prosecutor. Since the Watergate scandal of the 1970s virtually every political scandal, large or small, has been greeted with a demand for the appointment of a special prosecutor to investigate allegations. Some, like the Iran-Contra scandal of the Reagan administration, undoubtedly warrant a special investigation. However, Justice Scalia is probably right to be concerned about the potential for abuse of power by a special prosecutor. Conversely, it is difficult for the Justice Department to investigate political scandals without accusations of a cover-up should the attorney general decide no laws were violated. In light of this dilemma and the *Morrison* ruling, it seems likely that the special prosecutor will remain a part of the political landscape.

QUESTIONS FOR DISCUSSION

(1)   Identify the problems you see with leaving the prosecution of high government officials to the discretion of the Justice Department.

(2)   Even if they are constitutionally suspect, does public faith in the integrity of the political and legal systems justify having special prosecutors? Why or why not?

(3)   Whose opinion—Rehnquist's or Scalia's—do you personally find more convincing? Why?

(4)   What are the problems with the role played by the special division in the appointment of special prosecutors? Can you think of another way to select the special prosecutor without raising separation-of-powers questions?

RELATED CASES   *Ex parte Siebold*, 100 U.S. 371 (1880); *MYERS V. UNITED STATES*, 272 U.S. 52 (1926); *Humphrey's Executor v. United States*, 295 U.S. 602 (1935); *Wiener v. United States*, 357 U.S. 349 (1958); *UNITED STATES V. NIXON*, 418 U.S. 683 (1974); *BUCKLEY V. VALEO*, 424 U.S. 1 (1976); and *BOWSHER V. SYNAR*, 478 U.S. 714 (1986).

IMMIGRATION AND NATURALIZATION SERVICE V. CHADHA
462 U.S. 919 (1983)

BACKGROUND Jagdish Rai Chadha was a native of Kenya holding a British passport. He was admitted to the United States on a nonimmigrant student visa that expired on June 30, 1972. On October 11, 1973, he was ordered to appear before the Immigration and Naturalization Service (INS) to show cause why he should not be deported. A deportation hearing was held on January 11, 1974, and Chadha admitted that he was deportable. However, Chadha applied for a suspension of deportation under § 244 (a)(1) of the Immigration and Nationality Act. Section 244 (a)(1) permits the attorney general, at his discretion, to suspend deportation if deportation would cause the alien extreme hardship and if he is of good moral character. The attorney general granted Chadha's request and ordered his deportation suspended. Under § 244 (c)(1) of the same Act, the attorney general was required to report such suspensions to Congress.

Section 244 (c)(2) of the Immigration and Nationality Act contained a provision, commonly known as a legislative veto, which allowed either House of Congress to cancel the attorney general's suspension of deportation. Congressman Eilberg, chairman of the Judiciary Subcommittee on Immigration, Citizenship, and International Law, introduced a resolution opposing the attorney general's recommendation in the case of Chadha and five other aliens.Congressman Eilberg reported that he did not believe Chadha met the statutory definition of "extreme hardship." On December 16, 1975, the House of Representatives passed Eilberg's resolution. The INS began deportation proceedings against Chadha which he challenged on the grounds that § 244 (c)(2) was unconstitutional. The immigration judge ruled that he had no authority to rule § 244 (c)(2) unconstitutional, and Chadha was ordered deported. After an unsuccessful appeal to the Board of Immigration Appeals, Chadha appealed to the Ninth Circuit Court of Appeals, which declared § 244 (c)(2) unconstitutional. Interestingly, the INS agreed with Chadha's position that § 244 (c)(2) was unconstitutional. However, both the House and Senate intervened as parties to the case, thus meeting the Constitution's real case and controversy requirement.

CONSTITUTIONAL ISSUE

Whether § 244 (c)(2), which permits one House of Congress to exercise a legislative veto over executive decisions, violates the Presentment Clauses of Article I of the Constitution? YES

MAJORITY OPINION Chief Justice Warren E. Burger delivers the opinion of the Court. The chief justice's opinion is in four parts. Part I relates the events of Chadha's plight. In Part II, the chief justice disposes of several challenges to the Court's jurisdiction in the case. Congress alleged that: (1) the Supreme Court lacks appellate jurisdiction in the case; (2) § 244 (c)(2) cannot be severed from the rest of § 244; (3) Chadha lacks standing; (4) Chadha has alternative relief available that he must pursue before the constitutional question can be decided; (5) the court of appeals lacks jurisdiction; (6) the case is not a real case and controversy within the meaning of Article III; and (7) the case presents a nonjusticiable political question. The chief justice rejects, for various reasons, all of the challenges to the Court's jurisdiction, and he proceeds to address the question of the constitutionality of § 244 (c)(2) in Part III.

Chief Justice Burger begins Part III by citing several Article I clauses. Article I, § 1 states that the legislative power is vested in both Houses of Congress. Article I, § 7, Clause 2 requires every bill to be passed by both Houses and presented to the president for his action. Clause 3 of the same section says that every order, resolution, or vote shall be presented to the president. The chief justice concludes that these provisions constitute an integral part of the separation-of-powers doctrine. Presentment of bills to the president, along with his veto, was designed by the framers to protect the president from laws that encroached on his powers and to protect the nation from the enactment of bad laws. The chief justice also illustrates that the framers believed the requirement of passage by both Houses to be an essential safeguard against tyranny.

In Part IV, the chief justice addresses the particular actions of this case and the use of the legislative veto. He notes that not every action, for example, the approval of treaties, requires the approval of both Houses. However, he notes that all exceptions to the bicameral requirement are clearly spelled out in the Constitution. Chief Justice Burger asserts that the cancellation of the suspension of Chadha's deportation by the House is clearly a legislative action. Therefore, it must be passed by both Houses and sent to the president. He also notes that if Congress tried to pass a law ordering Chadha's deportation, such an action would clearly require passage by both Houses and presentment to the president. The chief justice recognizes that the legislative veto is more efficient than the old method of private bills to deal with immigration cases, but declares that the framers ranked other values higher than efficiency. The chief justice concludes the opinion by declaring § 244 (c)(2) unconstitutional.

OTHER OPINIONS   One concurring opinion by Justice Lewis Powell and two dissenting opinions by Justices Byron White and William Rehnquist are filed. Justice Powell agrees that § 244 (c)(2) is unconstitutional, but he fears that the Court's decision is far too sweeping in that its reliance on the Presentment Clauses seemingly invalidates all legislative vetoes. Powell prefers to decide the case on the narrower separation-of-powers ground. Powell believes that § 244 (c)(2) permits one House to determine if a deportable alien meets the statutory requirement of "extreme hardship" for suspension of deportation. This, Powell maintains, is a judicial function that Congress may not exercise.

Justice White writes the principal dissent. Justice White agrees with Powell that if § 244 (c)(2) is unconstitutional it should be ruled so on the narrower separation-of-powers ground. White believes that the use of the legislative veto in immigration cases is a narrow application that should not be used to invalidate its use in every instance. White points out that in almost every case in which the legislative veto has been employed, the president has consented to its use by signing it into law. Presidents, White asserts, can hardly question the constitutionality of the legislative veto after having consented to its enactment. Justice White denies that the legislative veto is a legislative action requiring joint action by the Congress and presentment to the president. White states that the legislative veto is no more law making than the president's use of his veto is law making. The law, in this case the Immigration and Nationality Act, has already been passed by both Houses and approved by the president. The legislative veto merely allows Congress to prevent the attorney general from using his power to suspend deportations in a way inconsistent with the will of Congress. White notes that Congress frequently delegates to administrative agencies the power to promulgate rules that have the force of law and that the Court has usually upheld the practice. If an administrative agency can make rules that have the force of law without meeting the bicameral and presentment requirements, surely Congress may ensure that agencies do not make decisions contrary to its will.

Justice Rehnquist's dissent centers on the issue of severability, one of the jurisdictional issues discussed in Part II of the majority opinion. Justice Rehnquist disagrees that § 244 (c)(2) can be severed from § 244. Rehnquist believes that if § 244 (c)(2) is unconstitutional, then § 244 must also be invalid.

SIGNIFICANCE OF THE CASE   As the opinions indicate, the increased use of the legislative veto is a fairly recent phenomenon. Congress finds it increasingly necessary to delegate much of its law-making power to administrative agencies. The problem is to avoid "excessive" delegation because Congress may not, without violating the doctrine of separation of powers, delegate away all of its law-making power. The legislative veto has been viewed by some as a way to guarantee that Congress, and not administrative agencies, possesses the ultimate power to make public policy in the United States. Chadha certainly casts a cloud over the future of the legislative veto. Although Congress continues to enact laws with legislative veto provisions, the validity of those laws and that of many of the two hundred other statutes with such provisions remains in a kind of constitutional limbo.

QUESTIONS FOR DISCUSSION

(1)   Why does Congress use the legislative veto?

(2)   Do you agree with the majority that use of the legislative veto constitutes "law making"? Why or why not?

(3)   In light of alleged administrative excesses, do you think the legislative veto should continue to be a part of the system of checks and balances? Why or why not?

RELATED CASES   *J. W. HAMPTON & CO. V. UNITED STATES*, 276 U.S. 394 (1928); *YOUNGSTOWN SHEET & TUBE CO. V. UNITED STATES*, 343 U.S. 579 (1952); *BUCKLEY V. VALEO*, 424 U.S. 1 (1976); and *Nixon v. Administrator of General Services*, 433 U.S. 425 (1977).

4

THE COMMERCE POWER

INTRODUCTION

At first blush, the power to regulate interstate and foreign commerce may not seem to raise the kinds of issues that stir people's passions. In reality, many great issues of American history—slavery, monopolies, racial discrimination—have centered on the commerce power. Today, the scope of the commerce power is far beyond what the framers could have imagined. Virtually everything, including people, that crosses state lines is within its scope. The commerce power, along with the taxing power, has been instrumental in increasing the power of the national government.

Trade problems were the major source of conflict among the states after the American Revolution. The states were heavily in debt because of the war and sought to raise revenue through taxation. Each state, as sovereign, set its own policies concerning trade relations. A state was free to place taxes on goods coming in from another state (import tax) and on goods leaving the state (export tax). States could charge fees for the use of its ports by ships of other states and foreign countries alike. The increased taxation increased the cost of consumer goods adding to other economic problems.

When the framers met in Philadelphia in the summer of 1787, there was a consensus that the national government would have to play a larger role in regulating commerce. When the Convention adjourned, just how large that role would be was still largely undefined. Like other constitutional powers, the commerce power has undergone change as the nation changed. As new methods of transportation, such as steamboats, railroads, automobiles, and airplanes, were invented, new questions about the commerce power followed.

An early source of conflict over the commerce power was the proper division of commerce regulation between the national government and the states. It was never suggested by most people that the states should surrender all of their power to regulate commerce. However, it was unclear where the state's right to regulate ended and the national government's began. Another source of conflict was over the scope of the power itself. Did the commerce power permit Congress to ban some items from interstate commerce? What is the meaning of the phrase "affecting commerce"? These and other questions were to be raised and answered as the meaning of the commerce power evolved.

In this chapter we focus on the previously mentioned aspects of the commerce power. First, we examine the role of the national government and the states in regulating commerce. Next, we look at the cases in which the Supreme Court sought to define what regulation is permissible under the Commerce Clause.

Federal-State Regulation of Commerce

By ratifying the Constitution, the states displayed a willingness to surrender some of their powers to the national government. However, the extent to which the states had to give up their control over commerce was unclear. Having experienced sovereignty, some states were unwilling to give up any more of their power than was absolutely necessary. Conflict arose when federal laws concerning commerce clashed with state laws.

The issue came to a head in *GIBBONS V. OGDEN* (1824). New York passed a law giving Robert Livingston and Robert Fulton a monopoly over the use of steamboats on New York waterways. Any steamboat navigating in New York waters had to have a license from Livingston and Fulton. Gibbons operated a steamboat under a license obtained under a law of Congress, the Coasting Act. Under the federal license, Gibbons ran a ferry between New York and New Jersey. Ogden, with a license from Livingston and Fulton, competed with Gibbons and sought to prevent Gibbons from using New York waters. Gibbons challenged the constitutionality of the New York monopoly law and the case reached the U.S. Supreme Court.

New York's position was that a state had exclusive power to control the waterways inside the state. Gibbons argued that because his steamboat traveled between two states, he was engaged in interstate commerce that only Congress can regulate. The problem with New York's position was that it would enable other states to grant similar monopolies to their citizens. This, in turn, would defeat the framers' goal of removing state barriers to interstate commerce by vesting the power over commerce in Congress. Only the government that represents the will of the whole nation can be trusted to regulate commerce fairly. States will always seek to place their own commerce at an advantage as the New York monopoly shows.

Chief Justice John Marshall wrote the majority opinion in *GIBBONS*, which has influenced the scope of the commerce power ever since. Chief Justice Marshall ruled that the Constitution recognizes both intrastate and interstate commerce. Commerce that is entirely within a single state may be regulated within the state's police power. Commerce among two or more states is within the power of Congress to regulate. Marshall asserted that it was not necessary in *GIBBONS* to decide if a state may pass a law affecting interstate commerce in the absence of a federal law. Congress has acted by passing the Coasting Act under which Gibbons was licensed. When a state law regulating interstate commerce clearly conflicts with a national law, under the Supremacy Clause, the state law must yield. The Court held the New York monopoly law to be unconstitutional.

GIBBONS left unanswered whether a state may regulate interstate commerce in the absence of federal law. In 1851, the Supreme Court addressed this question in COOLEY V. BOARD OF WARDENS. A Pennsylvania law required ships entering and leaving the port of Philadelphia to be piloted by an experienced local pilot. If a ship failed to hire a local pilot, a fee was imposed. Cooley challenged the law on the grounds that it was a regulation of interstate commerce by the state. The Supreme Court readily admitted that the law was a regulation of interstate commerce. However, in 1789 Congress had passed a law that, in effect, adopted the local laws of navigation as its own. That is, instead of trying to write a national law that would cover the vagaries of individual ports, Congress chose to defer to local regulation. Although the law challenged in COOLEY was not passed until 1803, Congress had still chosen not to exercise its right to regulate local harbor conditions. In the absence of federal regulation, the Court held that states could enact laws of a local nature even if they affect interstate commerce. There was an implicit understanding, however, that should Congress choose to act its law would preempt state law.

The next several cases will demonstrate the increasing complexity of the division of power over commerce between the national government and the states. In HOUSTON, EAST AND WEST TEXAS RAILWAY CO. V. UNITED STATES (THE SHREVEPORT RATE CASE) (1914), the Supreme Court had to decide if state regulation of intrastate commerce affected interstate commerce. Freight rates between points in Texas and Louisiana were set by the Interstate Commerce Commission. Rates between two points within Texas were set by the Texas Railroad Commission. Because there were two rate-making bodies, rates were different. As a result, it was cheaper to ship goods from Dallas to Longview, Texas, than from Shreveport to Longview even though Shreveport was closer. Because shipping costs add to the selling price of items, merchants in Shreveport were at a disadvantage compared to Dallas merchants.

The Supreme Court had to decide whether the difference in rates "affected interstate commerce." Because the transactions between Longview and Dallas were completely within Texas, it was certainly intrastate commerce. However, the Court ruled that when a particular activity has a "close and substantial relationship" to interstate commerce, only Congress may regulate that activity. The purpose of the Commerce Clause was to prevent a state from favoring its citizens by giving them an unfair advantage over people in other states. Texas had given the railroads engaged in intrastate commerce a competitive edge over those engaged in interstate commerce. Texas merchants also reaped the benefits of the lower freight rates.

In Stafford v. Wallace (1922), the Supreme Court ruled on the power of Congress to regulate "local" activities that affect interstate commerce. Congress passed a law regulating the practices of brokers in the meat-packing industry. Cattle were shipped to stockyards where they were bought, sold, and then shipped to buyers. Among other controls, the law regulated the commissions that brokers could charge. Stafford claimed that the sales were purely local and could only be regulated by the state. The Supreme Court noted that the stockyards were not the final destinations of the cattle but a mere resting place in the stream or flow of interstate commerce. The Court held that although the transactions were local, they were a part of the stream of interstate commerce and therefore could be regulated by Congress. The stream of commerce approach became important in *SCHECHTER POULTRY CORP. V. UNITED STATES* (1935). In striking down the New Deal's National Industrial Recovery Act, the Court held that poultry brought in from outside a state but sold entirely within a state was no longer in the stream of interstate commerce.

Finally, *SOUTHERN PACIFIC CO. V. ARIZONA* (1945) illustrates the difficulty of balancing state and federal power over interstate commerce. Arizona's Train Limit Law restricted the length of freight trains in the state to seventy cars and passenger trains to fourteen. The law was a safety measure designed to protect railroad workers from "slack action." Slack action is the movement between trains as they brake or start and is more dangerous in longer trains. Trains longer than the limit set by the law had to remove the extra cars on entering the state. Although Congress had the power to regulate the length of trains, it had chosen not to exercise its power. Under the *COOLEY* ruling states were free to regulate interstate commerce in the absence of federal legislation. However, in *SOUTHERN PACIFIC* the Court ruled states could not enact laws that placed an undue burden on interstate commerce even if Congress had failed to act.

The Scope of the Commerce Power

The scope of the commerce power has expanded and contracted throughout American history. Perhaps the most expansive view of the power is found in *GIBBONS*. In *GIBBONS* Chief Justice John Marshall asserted that only two limitations constrained the commerce power. The first limitation is the Constitution itself. For example, Article I, § 9, paragraph 6 reads, "No preference shall be given by any regulation of commerce or revenue to the ports of one State over those of another." The second limitation is a political one. Marshall contended that the identity the people have with their elected representatives in Congress is also a check on any abuse of the commerce power. Marshall argued, in effect, that the commerce power is as broad or narrow as the American people wish it to be. Presumably Congress will not exercise the commerce power in a way that is disapproved by a majority of the people.

When Chief Justice Marshall writes in *GIBBONS* that the Constitution serves to limit the commerce power, he probably did not have the Tenth Amendment in mind. The Tenth Amendment proclaims that the powers not delegated to the national government nor prohibited to the states by the Constitution are reserved to the states or to the people. The Tenth Amendment, then, is the source of the so-called reserved powers of the state. Throughout U.S. history, whenever the Supreme Court found a violation of the commerce power it often did so because Congress was attempting to exercise powers reserved to the states.

The Tenth Amendment was used, at least temporarily, to frustrate congressional efforts to control monopolies. The Sherman Antitrust Act made it illegal for companies to conspire to monopolize trade among the states. When the American Sugar Company gained control of 98 percent of the nation's sugar market, the federal government sought to break up its monopoly. Although conceding a monopoly existed, the Supreme Court held in *UNITED STATES V. E. C. KNIGHT CO.* (1893) that the manufacture of a commodity was a purely local concern. Therefore, only the states in the exercise of their police power could regulate monopolies. The fact that it was virtually impossible for one state to regulate the activities of a multistate corporation did not matter to the Court. The enforcement of the Sherman Act was reduced to those monopolies, such as railroads, that were directly related to the transportation of goods in interstate commerce.

Although the Supreme Court forbade the use of the commerce power to regulate monopolies, the question arose whether it could be used to ban products from interstate commerce. In 1895 Congress passed a law prohibiting the transportation of lottery tickets in interstate commerce. In *CHAMPION V. AMES* (1903), the Court upheld the law as a valid use of the commerce power. In language similar to that of Chief Justice Marshall, the Court ruled that it is for the elected representatives of the people to decide what items may be banned from interstate commerce. Based on the *CHAMPION* decision, Congress moved to ban prostitutes, certain impure food and drugs, and diseased animals from interstate commerce.

The extent to which the Supreme Court was willing to let Congress ban items in interstate commerce was soon tested again in *HAMMER V. DAGENHART* (1918). The Child Labor Act of 1916 banned products manufactured with child labor from interstate commerce. Specifically, a factory or mine was forbidden to employ children under the age of fourteen. Children under sixteen were not allowed to work more than eight hours a day. In North Carolina a child could begin to work at age twelve. Roland Dagenhart challenged the constitutionality of the Child Labor Act on behalf of his two minor sons. The Supreme Court struck down the Act for several reasons. The Court argued that the law was not an attempt to regulate commerce but labor conditions. Second, Congress was attempting to exercise a power reserved to the states. Finally, the power to ban products from interstate commerce applied only to things that were inherently bad, such as impure food and drugs. Only by prohibiting access to interstate commerce could Congress control the evil it wished to prevent.

HAMMER was merely the first of many attempts by Congress to use the commerce power to regulate the conditions of workers. State attempts to use the police power to improve working conditions were also frustrated by the Supreme Court. In *LOCHNER V. NEW YORK* (1905), for example, the Court struck down a state law limiting the number of hours bakers could work. Although passed by the state as a health measure, the Court held that the law violated the freedom of contract between workers and employers. Apparently the Court believed workers could negotiate their own favorable working conditions without interference from the state. Thus, states could not regulate working conditions under their police powers and the national government could not under the commerce power.

The coming of the New Deal brought renewed attempts to use the commerce power to regulate working conditions. The National Industrial Recovery Act (NIRA) was an early attempt to have industries set wages and hours in the guise of "codes of fair competition." The Supreme Court invalidated the NIRA in the *SCHECHTER POULTRY* case. However, in the aftermath of the 1937 Court-packing controversy, the Court began to alter its position. In *NATIONAL LABOR RELATIONS BOARD V. JONES & LAUGHLIN CORP.* (1937), the Court upheld the constitutionality of the National Labor Relations Act. Among other provisions, the Act protected the right of workers to join unions and to bargain collectively. The Jones & Laughlin Corporation was a massive operation employing tens of thousands of workers in twenty states. The Court said that it would be idle to argue that a work stoppage in the nation's fourth largest steel company would have only an indirect effect on interstate commerce. Congress is empowered to act to remove barriers that impede the flow of interstate commerce. Therefore, Congress may act to prevent labor strikes that disrupt the flow of commerce.

The *JONES & LAUGHLIN* case was just the beginning of congressional use of the commerce power to regulate labor conditions. In 1938 it passed the Fair Labor Standards Act. The Act forbade the shipment in interstate commerce of goods manufactured under substandard labor conditions. The Act set a minimum wage for workers, fixed the maximum number of hours in the work week at forty-four, and required payment of overtime wages for hours over forty-four. Substandard labor conditions were defined as those that failed to meet the Act's minimum requirements. The Court recognized that in light of its decision in *JONES & LAUGHLIN* its decision in *DARBY* appeared unnecessary. However, the Court thought it was necessary to overrule *HAMMER V. DAGENHART*. The *DARBY* Court abolished the distinction made in *HAMMER* between products that could and could not be banned from interstate commerce. *DARBY* left the decision about what could be prohibited from interstate commerce to the discretion of the Congress.

DARBY and *JONES & LAUGHLIN* involved congressional regulation of man- ufacturing. The question whether the commerce power included the regulation of agricultural production was raised in *WICKARD V. FILBURN* (1942). The Agricultural Adjustment Act of 1938 limited the amount of wheat a farmer could produce even for home consumption. Filburn grew more than his allotment and was fined for doing so. He argued that wheat consumed on his farm could not be construed to be a part of interstate commerce. The Supreme Court conceded that Filburn's wheat, if taken alone, had a minuscule effect on interstate commerce. However, if every farmer exceeded his or her allotment, the total effect on interstate commerce would be enormous. Congress was attempting to control the price of wheat by controlling production. That goal could not be reached if individual farmers exceeded the allotment. *WICKARD* demonstrated that even the amount of wheat grown on a single farm could "affect" interstate commerce.

Just how far the Supreme Court was willing to let Congress go in defining what affected interstate commerce was answered in *HEART OF ATLANTA MOTEL, INC. V. UNITED STATES* (1964) and *Katzenbach v. McClung* (1964). The Civil Rights Act of 1964 forbade racial discrimination in hotels, motels, restaurants, theaters, and other places of public accommodation. In *HEART OF ATLANTA MOTEL, INC.* the Court noted that the motel received 75 percent of its business from outside the state. In *McClung*, a small town barbecue received well over half its meat from out of state. The Court took notice of congressional hearings on the Civil Rights Act. Congress found that African Americans had trouble securing food and shelter while traveling. The Court reasoned that Congress could logically conclude that racial discrimination greatly affected the flow of interstate commerce. By discouraging African Americans from traveling, racial discrimination reduces the amount of goods moving in interstate commerce. The Court held it was within the commerce power to eliminate any barrier to interstate commerce.

One final area that deserves notice is whether Congress may use the commerce power to regulate the activities of states. Congress undoubtedly may regulate the activities of private enterprises engaged in interstate commerce. But should Congress be permitted to regulate a state-owned railroad, for example? The issue arose in *Maryland v. Wirtz* (1968) in which Congress imposed federal minimum wage standards on specified employees of public schools, state-owned hospitals, and other public institutions. The Supreme Court upheld Congress's action but reversed itself eight years later in *NATIONAL LEAGUE OF CITIES V. USERY* (1976). In *USERY*, the Court distinguished between activities in which a state competed with private enterprise and a state's "traditional governmental functions." Congress could not, the Court ruled, use its commerce power to regulate the latter. The issue was still not settled, however. Nine years after *USERY*, the Court reversed its position again in *GARCIA V. SAN ANTONIO MASS TRANSIT AUTHORITY* (1985). Justice Harry Blackmun, a member of the majority in *USERY*, changed his mind. Blackmun found the "traditional governmental functions" approach unworkable. He reasoned that members of Congress represent the states and therefore the Court should defer to Congress on the use of the commerce power to regulate the activities of states as states. The dissenters in *GARCIA*, probably thinking of *Wirtz* and *NATIONAL LEAGUE OF CITIES*, predicted that the debate was far from over.

Conclusion

Today the commerce power is virtually unlimited. As Chief Justice Marshall observed more than 170 years ago, the only real check on the commerce power is the restraint the people place on their elected representatives. The commerce power is as broad as the people are willing to let it be. Whether preventing monopolies, child labor, unfair working conditions, or discrimination, the commerce power is a reflection of how the people wish the national government to operate. Those who feared a strong national government cautioned against expanding the scope of the commerce power. They feared opening a Pandora's box. For better or worse, that box has been opened and the immense power of the commerce clause has forever been released.

GIBBONS V. OGDEN
9 Wheaton 1 (1824)

BACKGROUND   The New York Legislature passed a law granting a monopoly to Robert Livingston and Robert Fulton. The monopoly awarded Livingston and Fulton the exclusive right to the use of steamboats on the state's waterways. Livingston and Fulton transferred the right to John R. Livingston who in turn transferred it to Aaron Ogden. Under the monopoly Ogden was given exclusive authorization to navigate a steamboat between Elizabethtown, New Jersey, and New York City. Thomas Gibbons operated two steamboats between the same two cities under a license obtained under a 1793 act of Congress. The license authorized Gibbons to engage in the coasting trade. Ogden filed a bill of complaint in a New York Court of Chancery seeking an injunction against Gibbons prohibiting him from operating his two steamboats between Elizabethtown and New York. The court granted the injunction, which was later upheld by the Court of Impeachment and Correction of Errors, the highest court of equity in New York. Gibbons then appealed the case to the U.S. Supreme Court.

CONSTITUTIONAL ISSUE

Does a state law that grants an exclusive right of navigation on state waters in ships propelled by fire or steam interfere with the exclusive right of Congress to regulate commerce among the states? YES

MAJORITY OPINION   Chief Justice John Marshall delivers the opinion of the Court. Although Gibbons argues that the New York law violates the provision of the Constitution granting Congress the power to promote the progress of science and useful arts, Marshall limits the opinion to the issue of commerce. Ogden argues that the Constitution should always be interpreted narrowly, although Marshall notes that this position is not supported by the text of the Constitution. Ogden argues that the term "commerce" should be narrowly interpreted to mean the buying and selling of articles and should not include the rules of navigation. The chief justice answers that this would restrict a general term, commerce, to just one of its meanings. Commerce, Marshall asserts, must include navigation. He states that the mind can scarcely comprehend a system of commerce that excludes navigation. He also notes that from its very first session Congress has passed rules of navigation. Article I, § 9 forbids Congress to show preference to the ports of one state over the ports of another state. All America, Marshall claims, understands commerce to include navigation.

After ruling that commerce includes navigation, Marshall turns to the phrase "among the several states" as it applies to commerce. Marshall asserts that commerce among the states means "intermingled with" and therefore commerce cannot end at a state's borders. Marshall notes that interstate commerce is mentioned in the same sentence as foreign commerce which is also regulated by Congress. He points out that it would be impossible for nations to trade if the ships of one nation could not enter the ports of another. Likewise, it is impossible for states to trade if the ships of one state cannot travel on the waterways within another state's territory. Marshall concedes that commerce totally within a state is beyond the power of Congress but that commerce that crosses state lines is not.

In the next part of the opinion Marshall defines the commerce power as the power to prescribe the rule by which commerce is governed. That power, Marshall asserts, is plenary, or whole, and is limited only by specific provisions in the Constitution. Although such plenary power is subject to abuse, Marshall believes that the wisdom of Congress and its close identity with the American people will serve to check such abuse.

Ogden argues that the regulation of commerce, like the taxing power, is a concurrent power shared by the national government and the states. Marshall disagrees by observing that the taxing power can be exercised by each level of government with little or no interference with the other. The commerce power, however, cannot be exercised without interference as the present case demonstrates. The grant of a monopoly by New York directly conflicts with the coasting license granted by Congress. Nor is it necessary to settle the issue whether the states may regulate commerce in the absence of congressional regulation because in passing the coasting law Congress has acted. Marshall observes that the constitutional provision that forbids the placing of taxes on imports and exports is a limitation on the taxing power, not the commerce power.

Chief Justice Marshall ends the decision by tying up a few loose arguments. He states that Congress may adopt state regulations of commerce on subjects such as pilotage as its own if it chooses or Congress may write its own rules. State inspection laws are not a regulation of commerce because they control articles before they enter into interstate commerce. Finally, as to the issue of coasting, Marshall claims that the practice has always included the transportation of passengers. At any rate, Ogden's bill of complaint was against the means of propulsion, not Gibbons's cargo. Marshall's opinion makes clear that a state may not regulate interstate commerce while Congress is regulating it.

OTHER OPINIONS Justice William Johnson writes a separate concurring opinion. Justice Johnson states that the commerce power is the power that had previously existed in the individual states. He notes that one overriding object of the Constitutional Convention was to keep trade among the states free from "all invidious and partial restraints." Justice Johnson believes that the commerce power must be exclusive and that it may be exercised by only one sovereignty. Justice Johnson's major point of departure from the majority's opinion is that he believes Gibbons would have had the right to operate his steamboat even if he had not been licensed to do so by Congress.

SIGNIFICANCE OF THE CASE It would be difficult to overestimate the importance of *Gibbons v. Ogden*. At the time the decision was handed down several states, in addition to New York, were granting monopolies to steamboat operators. The exclusive right of one steamboat owner to navigate the waterways of a state would have had a detrimental effect on the growth of commercial activity. So, from the standpoint of commercial growth alone, *Gibbons* is significant. In addition, in *Gibbons* Chief Justice Marshall set the stage for the use of the commerce power as a means of expanding the power of the national government. The states were forbidden to enact laws that interfere with the national government's right to regulate commerce. The power is as broad as Congress wishes it to be. The only limitations on its use are those few restrictions (such as no showing of favoritism to the ports of one state over those of another), specifically mentioned in the Constitution and Congress's own sense of self-restraint. Although later Courts attempted to use the Tenth Amendment as a restraint on the commerce power, modern Courts have all but eliminated it as a barrier to the exercise of the commerce power. Thus, we have returned to the meaning of the power as originally interpreted by Chief Justice Marshall.

QUESTIONS FOR DISCUSSION

(1) What do you think might have happened if the Court had ruled in favor of Ogden?
(2) What are some of the ways Congress uses the commerce power today?
(3) What do you think was the reaction of the slave states to the *Gibbons* decision? Why?
(4) Do you think the transportation of people is "commerce"? Why or why not?

RELATED CASES *Passenger Cases*, 7 Howard 282 (1849); *COOLEY V. BOARD OF WARDENS OF THE PORT OF PHILADELPHIA*, 12 Howard 299 (1851); *CHAMPION V. AMES*, 188 U.S. 321 (1903); *HOUSTON, E. AND W. TEXAS RAILWAY CO. V.*

UNITED STATES (THE SHREVEPORT RATE CASE), 234 U.S. 342 (1914); *HAMMER V. DAGENHART*, 247 U.S. 251 (1918); *HEART OF ATLANTA MOTEL, INC. V. UNITED STATES*, 379 U.S. 241 (1964); and *Katzenbach v. McClung*, 379 U.S. 294 (1964).

COOLEY V. BOARD OF WARDENS OF THE PORT OF PHILADELPHIA
12 Howard 299 (1851)

BACKGROUND Although the Constitution gives Congress the power to regulate interstate and foreign commerce, in 1789 the first Congress passed a law declaring that local laws and customs governing the nation's ports should remain in effect until Congress passed further legislation. An 1803 Pennsylvania law required a ship entering and leaving the port of Philadelphia to take on board a local pilot, familiar with the port, to navigate the ship into or out of the port. Failure to comply with the law resulted in a fine equal to half of the pilotage fee. The proceeds of the fees and fines went to a fund for the widows and orphans of ship pilots. Cooley challenged the law on several grounds. First, he argued that the law was discriminatory because it did not apply to ships under 75 tons or to ships engaged in the coal trade. Second, the money was designated for a private, charitable organization. Third, Cooley maintained that the law violated the constitutional ban on states placing taxes, or imposts on imports and exports. Finally, Cooley argued that the state was exercising the power to regulate interstate and foreign commerce that belongs exclusively to the Congress.

CONSTITUTIONAL ISSUE

Whether a state law, in the absence of a conflicting federal law, that regulates navigation interferes with congressional power to regulate interstate commerce? NO

MAJORITY OPINION Justice Benjamin R. Curtis delivers the opinion of the Court. Justice Curtis dismisses the complaint that the law discriminates by exempting ships under 75 tons and ships engaged in the coal trade by simply pointing out that it is within the discretion of the legislature to make such exemptions. Justice Curtis also states that it is within the legislature's discretion to decide how to use the money that is raised. Finally, he observes that the common understanding at the time of the framing of the Constitution was that imposts and duties on imports and exports were distinct from fees or charges for pilotage.

Having disposed of the early objections to the law, Justice Curtis turns to the claim that Pennsylvania is regulating interstate and foreign commerce, a power that belongs exclusively to Congress. Justice Curtis concedes that the imposition of the requirement is in fact a regulation of interstate commerce. However, he notes that the first Congress, to avoid problems, specifically authorized local rules and customs to be followed until further legislation from Congress was forthcoming. Congress, in effect, adopts the rules of local ports as its own. Justice Curtis acknowledges that Congress may not return to the states a power that has been granted to it by the Constitution. That is, Congress may not return to the states the power to regulate interstate and foreign commerce when the Constitution vests that power in Congress. However, Curtis argues that the mere grant of a power to Congress does not preclude the exercise of that power by a state. It is only when Congress actually uses a power that states are forbidden to exercise that same power.

In this case, Congress has not sought to impose uniform rules of pilotage on the ports of the nation. Therefore, in the absence of a congressional exercise of its power, states are free to impose their own local regulations. The Act of 1789 declared that regulation could best be provided for by allowing the legislatures of the individual states to devise a system suited to the peculiarities of the ports within the state. Justice Curtis argues that to do otherwise would impose a rule of uniformity where uniformity makes no sense. Justice Curtis is careful to narrow the scope of the decision to the regulation of pilotage in ruling that the Pennsylvania law is constitutional.

OTHER OPINIONS Justice Peter V. Daniel delivers the only concurring opinion. Justice Daniel agrees that the Pennsylvania law is constitutional but for different reasons. He does not think that the regulation of pilots falls within the commerce power of Congress. Justice Daniel states that local regulation is needed to meet local conditions. Finally, he asserts that the real issue is which level of government is the more appropriate one to exercise local regulation.

Justice John McLean writes the only dissenting opinion. Justice McLean believes that the Act of 1789 intended for state laws to be in effect only until Congress passed further legislation. The implication of the Act is that Congress controls the whole field of regulation of pilotage. The decision by Congress to allow local laws to remain in effect was necessary; otherwise local rules would have been unenforceable. Justice McLean believes that Congress merely adopted the rules of the states as its own. But the first Congress adopted only the laws of the states then in existence. The Pennsylvania law in question was not passed until 1803. The Court's ruling, according to McLean, permits states to make changes in rules adopted by Congress in 1789. This results in states regulating interstate and foreign commerce in violation of the Constitution.

SIGNIFICANCE OF THE CASE Early cases, such as *Gibbons v. Ogden*, debated whether a state could regulate an aspect of interstate or foreign commerce in the absence of congressional regulation. In *Gibbons*, the Court ruled that it was unnecessary to decide the issue directly because Congress had indeed passed legislation. One school of thought was that the states could never intrude into the field whether Congress had acted or not. The other school of thought held that state regulation was permissible in the absence of congressional action. *Cooley* obviously supports the second view. At the time of its announcement, Cooley was seen as a commonsense approach that allowed local regulation of what was considered to be purely local port conditions.

QUESTIONS FOR DISCUSSION

(1) What, if any, is the significance of the fact that the Pennsylvania law in dispute was passed in 1803?

(2) Does the Court's decision make sense to you? Why or why not?

(3) What possible conflicts could arise trying to distinguish between "local" and "national" conditions?

(4) What, if any, is the significance of the penalty for not using a local pilot being equal to one half the pilotage fee?

RELATED CASES *GIBBONS V. OGDEN*, 9 Wheaton 1 (1824); *License Cases*, 5 Howard 504 (1847); *Passenger Cases*, 7 Howard 283 (1849); *South Carolina Highway Department v. Barnwell Brothers, Inc.*, 303 U.S. 177 (1938); and *SOUTHERN PACIFIC CO. V. ARIZONA*, 325 U.S. 761 (1945).

HOUSTON, EAST & WEST TEXAS RAILWAY COMPANY V. UNITED STATES (THE SHREVEPORT RATE CASE)
234 U.S 342 (1914)

BACKGROUND The Houston, East & West Texas Railway Company charged higher rates on goods shipped between Shreveport, Louisiana, and cities in Texas than on goods shipped between two cities entirely in Texas. For example, the rate on furniture shipped from Dallas to Longview, Texas, a distance of 124 miles, was $0.248 per 100 pounds. The rate for furniture shipped from Shreveport to Longview, a distance of 65.7 miles, was $0.35 per 100 pounds. Thus, it was cheaper to ship furniture from Dallas to Longview than to ship it from Shreveport to Longview even though the distance was almost double. The reason was that goods shipped from Dallas to Longview were *intrastate* commerce whose rates were set by the Texas Railroad Commission. Goods shipped from Shreveport to Longview were *interstate* commerce whose rates were set by the Interstate Commerce Commission (ICC). The ICC found that the rates unjustly discriminated in favor of traffic within Texas and ordered the railway to increase its intrastate rates to equal the interstate rates. The railway challenged the order on two grounds. First, the railway argued that Congress may not set rates on goods shipped in intrastate commerce. Second, if Congress does have such power it has not been exercised, and therefore the ICC has exceeded its authority in issuing the order. The railway also suggested that the ICC should lower the interstate rates to make them more competitive with the intrastate rates.

CONSTITUTIONAL ISSUE

> Whether Congress has the power under the Commerce Clause to set rates on intrastate carriers whose operations have a close and substantial relation to interstate commerce? YES

MAJORITY OPINION Justice (later Chief Justice) Charles Evans Hughes delivers the opinion of the Court. Justice Hughes first discusses the issue whether Congress has the power to set rates for intrastate carriers. He notes that the commerce power of Congress is paramount. The original purpose of the Commerce Clause was "to protect the national interest by securing the freedom of interstate commercial intercourse from local control." The commerce power gives Congress the right to control matters that have a close and substantial relation to interstate traffic. The fact that a carrier engages in both interstate and intrastate commerce does not diminish federal power to control the operations of those carriers when they harm interstate commerce. Congress, Justice Hughes writes, has the power to make the final and dominant rule; otherwise Congress would not be able to exercise its constitutional authority, and state, not federal, regulation would govern commerce.

Justice Hughes looks at previous Supreme Court decisions where interstate and intrastate commerce were so closely linked. In those cases the Court ruled that Congress could regulate the hours and safety of railroad workers when their intrastate activities could not be separated from their interstate activities. In this case, Congress undoubtedly has the power to prohibit the evil of discriminatory rates. It does not matter that the discrimination is caused by the Texas Railroad Commission and not by the railroad. A state railroad commission may not authorize a railroad to do something Congress has forbidden. Nor should the ICC be required to lower the interstate rate to make it competitive with the intrastate rate. To do so, says Justice Hughes, would require the ICC to sacrifice its independent judgment of what is a "reasonable" rate. Justice Hughes then concludes that the ICC's order is not invalid on the ground that it exceeded Congress's commerce power.

Justice Hughes turns to the scope of the ICC's power granted to it by Congress. The purpose of the Interstate Commerce Act was clearly to eliminate unjust discrimination among carriers. There is no basis to believe that Congress intended to exempt any kind of unjust discrimination that affects interstate commerce. Justice Hughes says that it is not true that the act applies only to purposeful discrimination on the part of the railroad. The railroad contends that any discrimination that results is due to its compliance with rates set by the Texas Railroad Commission. Justice Hughes merely repeats his earlier argument that local rules may not nullify the lawful exercise of federal authority. Justice Hughes concludes the opinion by announcing that the decision of the Commerce Court is affirmed.

OTHER OPINIONS   No other opinions are filed, but Justices Horace H. Lurton and Mahlon Pitney register their dissent.

SIGNIFICANCE OF THE OPINION   The *Shreveport Rate Case* does little to clarify the distinction between interstate and intrastate commerce. Although the shipment of goods between two cities within Texas (Dallas to Longview) is clearly intrastate, the Court formulates the "close and substantial relation" test for interstate commerce. If an intrastate activity has a close and substantial relation to interstate traffic, that activity is subject to congressional authority. This is significant because in subsequent cases it provides the basis for the rule that if interstate commerce is affected, it does not matter how "local" the operation. The *Shreveport Rate Case* established the principle that the acid test is the effect on interstate commerce, not whether a particular activity is local. As Congress, especially after 1937, expanded its authority over interstate commerce to include the regulation of labor conditions, farm production, oil production, and even racial discrimination, the key test becomes the impact those activities have on interstate commerce.

QUESTIONS FOR DISCUSSION

(1)   Because compliance with the ICC's order would result in a rate increase for hauls within Texas, why do you think the Houston, East & West Texas Railway Company challenged the order?

(2)   Does the Court give any clear indication of what constitutes a "close and substantial relation" to interstate commerce? Does that bother you?

(3)   Does the Court's ruling necessarily put the Texas Railroad Commission out of the business of setting rates for railroads in the state? Why or why not?

(4)   Re-read the Background section. Why do you think the intrastate rates were less when the distances traveled were longer? Does this make any sense?

RELATED CASES   *NATIONAL LABOR RELATIONS BOARD V. JONES & LAUGHLIN STEEL CORPORATION*, 301 U.S. 1 (1937); *UNITED STATES V. DARBY LUMBER CO.*, 312 U.S. 100 (1941); *WICKARD V. FILBURN*, 317 U.S. 111 (1942); *HEART OF ATLANTA MOTEL, INC. V. UNITED STATES*, 379 U.S. 241 (1964); and *Katzenbach v. McClung*, 379 U.S. 294 (1964).

SCHECHTER POULTRY CORPORATION V. UNITED STATES
295 U.S. 495 (1935)

BACKGROUND   Petitioners, owners of the Schechter Poultry Corporation, were convicted of eighteen counts for violating the Live Poultry Code, which was promulgated under § 3 of the National Industrial Recovery Act. The Act permitted representatives of an industry, with the president's approval, to create a "code of fair competition" for the industry. The Live Poultry Code in question was approved by representatives of 90 percent of the live poultry industry. The Code included provisions governing the minimum wages and maximum hours of workers. Petitioners were convicted of violating the wage and hour provisions, as well as provisions prohibiting "straight killing" and the butchering of unfit chickens. Violations of the Code carried a $500 fine for each offense. The Schechters challenged the constitutionality of the NIRA on the grounds that it is an unconstitutional delegation of Congressional power, that it unconstitutionally regulates intrastate commerce, and that it violates the due process clause of the Fifth Amendment. The Supreme Court found it necessary to address only the first two challenges.

CONSTITUTIONAL ISSUES

(1)   Whether § 3 of the NIRA which permits the president to establish codes of fair competition, is an unconstitutional delegation of congressional power? YES.

(2)   Whether the Schechter Poultry Corporation is engaged in interstate commerce subject to congressional regulation? NO.

MAJORITY OPINION   Chief Justice Charles Evans Hughes delivers the opinion of the Court. The chief justice first addresses the delegation issue. Chief Justice Hughes acknowledges that NIRA was passed by Congress to deal with the crisis brought on by the Great Depression. Nevertheless, he asserts that, "Extraordinary conditions do not create or enlarge constitutional power." The codes in question are not mere guidelines because once approved by the president they have the force of law. The NIRA has delegated to private associations the power to make laws binding on all parties whether or not they have agreed to those laws. The Constitution prohibits Congress from abdicating or transferring its essential legislative functions.

   Chief Justice Hughes admits that Congress must sometimes delegate its authority to executive agencies, but Congress must also establish the standards of legal obligation. For example, the term "fair competition" is not defined in the Act. Although at common law the term "unfair competition" is defined, fair competition is not the antithesis of unfair competition. Hughes notes, for example, that the Federal Trade Commission (FTC) was given authority by Congress to regulate "methods of unfair competition," but the definition of what constitutes unfair competition is subject to judicial interpretation. The codes of fair competition created by NIRA are much broader in scope. Congress has permitted private associations, albeit subject to presidential approval, to define what is fair competition in a particular industry. Once established, violations of the fair code are deemed unfair competition within the meaning of the FTC Act. The real purpose of the Act, according to Hughes, was not to deal with unfair competition but to formulate new prohibitions thought to be wise or beneficial by the people in the industry. The chief justice repeats that even the president cannot be given such "unfettered discretion." The only limit on the president's discretion is that the codes must be written by groups "truly representative" of the industry and that they may not be monopolistic. The president is even permitted to include additional conditions as he sees fit. Such sweeping delegation finds no support in the Constitution.

Chief Justice Hughes then turns to the interstate commerce issue. Earlier in the opinion Hughes noted that 96 percent of New York City's live poultry comes from other states. Although the Schechters received their poultry from outside the state, they sold it entirely in New York. Hughes observes that, "The mere fact that there may be a constant flow of commodities into a state does not mean that the flow continues after the property has arrived and has become commingled with the mass of property within the state and is there solely for local distribution and use." It is the effect on commerce, not the source of the injury, that gives Congress its power to regulate interstate commerce. The chief justice declares that to allow the use of the commerce power in this case would give Congress authority over "practically all activities of the people" and virtually eliminate state power over commerce. The chief justice maintains that the Schechters' employees are not engaged in interstate commerce, and therefore their wages and hours are not subject to congressional regulation. The chief justice concludes that given the majority's position on the delegation and commerce issues, it is unnecessary to address the due process issue.

OTHER OPINIONS   Justice Benjamin Cardozo, in an opinion joined by Justice Harlan Fiske Stone, concurs. Justice Cardozo says the problem is that the delegated power in this Act is not "canalized." Congress has created a "roving commission" free to seek out evils and then to correct them. The old approach, he says, was for Congress to identify unfair methods of competition and then prohibit them. The new approach is to give an ordinance power that allows the president and the industry to pass rules thought to be helpful to the industry. "This," Cardozo writes, "is delegation run riot." Even if Congress had passed the wage and hour provisions itself, Cardozo doubts they would be constitutional under the Commerce Clause. To find a "direct effect" here is to find it almost anywhere he concludes.

SIGNIFICANCE OF THE CASE   *Schechter*, as indicated by the majority opinion, concerns delegation theory and use of the commerce power. Delegation theory says that Congress may not redelegate its law-making authority to another branch and certainly not to private groups. However, as a practical matter, Congress frequently is forced to delegate broad rule-making authority to administrative agencies like the FTC. The issue in

Schechter is a question of degree; Congress merely went too far in delegating its law-making under the NIRA.

Schechter is also significant as one of the last attempts to limit congressional power under the Commerce Clause. With rare exceptions, the Court has been reluctant since *Schechter* to place limits on the commerce power of Congress. The Court has virtually eliminated the distinction between "direct" and "indirect" effects on interstate commerce leaving Congress to use its own discretion in using the commerce power.

QUESTIONS FOR DISCUSSION

(1) Why should Congress be forbidden to delegate its law-making authority to private parties?
(2) Does the president's role in the approval of the codes serve as sufficient check on private law-making? Why or why not?
(3) Do you agree that the "flow of interstate commerce" had ended when the Schechters bought and then sold the poultry? Why or why not?
(4) Do you see any practical limits to congressional power under the Commerce Clause? If so, what are those limits?

RELATED CASES   *Stafford v. Wallace*, 258 U.S. 495 (1922); *J. W. HAMPTON & CO. V. UNITED STATES*, 276 U.S. 394 (1928); *HOME BUILDING AND LOAN ASSOCIATION V. BLAISDELL*, 290 U.S. 398 (1934); *Panama Refining Co. v. Ryan*, 293 U.S. 388 (1935); *Carter v. Carter Coal Co.*, 298 U.S. 238 (1936); *NATIONAL LEAGUE OF CITIES V. USERY*, 426 U.S. 833 (1976); and *GARCIA V. SAN ANTONIO MASS TRANSIT AUTHORITY*, 469 U.S. 528 (1985).

SOUTHERN PACIFIC CO. V. ARIZONA
325 U.S. 761 (1945)

BACKGROUND   The Arizona Train Limit Law restricted the number of passenger cars to a maximum of fourteen and the number of freight cars to a maximum of seventy. The Southern Pacific Co. admitted operating trains in the state in excess of the limit but challenged the law as imposing an unconstitutional burden on interstate commerce. The trial court found for the railroad, but the Arizona supreme court reversed holding that state power to regulate the length of interstate trains had not been restricted by Congress. Furthermore, the Arizona supreme court found the law to be a valid safety measure well within the state's exercise of its police power.

CONSTITUTIONAL ISSUE

Whether a state law limiting the number of cars on freight and passenger trains places an undue burden on interstate commerce in violation of the Commerce Clause? YES

MAJORITY OPINION   Chief Justice Harlan Fiske Stone delivers the opinion of the Court. Chief Justice Stone begins his opinion by conceding that the Court has long held that, in the absence of congressional legislation, states may regulate local matters that touch on interstate commerce. Such state legislation is permitted as long as the subject of regulation is truly local and does not seriously interfere with interstate commerce. But, the Court has also held for more than a hundred years that the Commerce Clause, standing alone, affords some protection from state regulation that is harmful to interstate commerce and that it is the role of the Court to be the arbiter in such situations. Although the chief justice concedes that states should be given great latitude in these matters, the final determination is the nature and extent of the burden of state law on interstate commerce.

Turning to the facts of the present case, the chief justice notes that long trains are the norm across the United States with only two other states having limit laws similar to Arizona's. The Arizona law requires a long train, on entering the state, to be broken up and then reconstituted on leaving the state. If all the other states passed train-limit laws, the net effect would be that train length would be determined by the state with the most restrictive law, or trains would have to add or delete cars on entering each new state. Chief Justice Stone implies that the burden such a situation would place on interstate commerce is obvious.

Chief Justice Stone next discusses the effect of the Arizona law on railroad efficiency. Because more than 90 percent of Southern Pacific's passenger and freight traffic is interstate, to comply with the law the company had to operate 30 percent more trains in Arizona at a cost of an additional $1 million a year. He also notes that the inefficiency of short trains led the Interstate Commerce Commission (ICC) to suspend train-limit laws during World War II.

Finally, Chief Justice Stone addresses the law as a valid safety measure. The Arizona trial court found that the law had no reasonable relation to safety and actually made train operations more dangerous. The Arizona trial court found that the law was designed to reduce the "slack action," between railroad cars, a frequent source of injury to railroad workers. However, the trial court also found that the reduction in the length of trains increases the number of trains, which in turn increases the number of train accidents. The trial court found that in 1938 only three persons died as a result of slack action, whereas 1398 persons died in grade-crossing accidents (car-train accidents). Therefore, by increasing the number of trains operating in Arizona by 30 percent the train-limit law actually increased the possibility of grade-crossing deaths. Given the increased cost and inefficiency of the law coupled with almost negligible safety benefits, the chief justice concludes that the Arizona Train Limit Law places an unconstitutional burden on interstate commerce.

OTHER OPINIONS Justices Hugo L. Black and William O. Douglas write separate dissenting opinions. Justice Black begins by noting that the long train–short train controversy has been debated for a long time, but there is little doubt that longer trains increase the danger of injury resulting from slack action. He also notes that in 1937 the Senate Interstate Commerce Committee recommended a seventy-car limit for trains, but that the House took no action on the recommendation. However, Black's main point is that the issue is one of legislative policy. Black accuses both the Arizona trial court and the Court's majority of acting as a "superlegislature." The issue, according to Black, tried by the Arizona trial court was not whether Southern Pacific was guilty of violating the train-limit law but whether the Arizona legislature had erred in concluding that short trains were safer than long trains. Black maintains that the determination of the safety issue is a matter of public policy to be made by legislative bodies, not courts. The issue is not whether more deaths result from grade-crossing accidents or slack action accidents. The legislature's failure to address the problem of grade-crossing deaths does not mean it cannot address the problem of injuries caused by slack action because both are legitimate safety concerns within the state's police power. As to the problem of other states enacting train-limit laws, Black says that if that should indeed happen it is for Congress to determine the burden it places on interstate commerce and for Congress, not the courts, to prescribe the remedy. The issue, in Black's opinion, boils down to the fact that shorter trains cost the railroads more money. He does not believe the Constitution forbids a state to weigh the safety of railroad workers more heavily than increased costs and reduced efficiency.

In his short dissent Justice Douglas states that, in his opinion, the Court should not invalidate state legislation affecting interstate commerce unless it discriminates against interstate commerce or it is clearly contradictory to federal legislation. In this case, Douglas does not feel that the evidence of undue burden on interstate commerce produced by the railroad is sufficient to overcome the presumption of validity to which the Arizona law is entitled.

SIGNIFICANCE OF THE CASE   On one level *Southern Pacific* represents yet another victory for the forces of nationalism in the battle between the states and the national government. State power to regulate safety must give way to the national interest in maintaining the free flow of commerce. However, on another level the case can be viewed as a triumph of business interests over the interests of the "little man," which is clearly how Justice Black views the case. In the final analysis, efficiency and cost outweigh the safety of railroad workers. Ironically, if a state did take action to reduce grade-crossing deaths the Court might also find that its efforts place an undue burden on interstate commerce. The case resurrects the perennial debate over the proper role of the Court in our constitutional system. Clearly the Court finds that the Arizona legislature has made, in its opinion, a poor policy choice. Even assuming that policy choice was a poor one, Black argues it is not for the Court to substitute its policy choices for those of our elected representatives. Finally, *Southern Pacific* raises the "dormant" commerce clause question. This question asks to what extent the Court may use the commerce clause to invalidate state laws in the absence of any congressional action. Clearly, the majority is willing to take positive action to invalidate state laws it deems placing a burden on interstate commerce even if Congress is unwilling to do so.

QUESTIONS FOR DISCUSSION

(1) Is it proper for the Court to invalidate the Arizona Train Limit Law in the absence of any congressional law? Why or why not?

(2) Is the Court qualified to make judgments concerning railroad safety? Has it done so?

(3) Do you agree that the Arizona Train Limit Law places an undue burden on interstate commerce?

(4) Do you agree or disagree with Justice Black's charge that the Court is acting as a "superlegislature"? Why?

(5) Does the states' rights position of Justice Douglas surprise you given his usual willingness to overturn state laws that limit liberties under the Bill of Rights?

RELATED CASES *GIBBONS V. OGDEN*, 9 Wheaton 1 (1824); *Wilson v. Black Bird Creek Marsh Co.*, 2 Peters 245 (1829); *COOLEY V. BOARD OF WARDENS*, 12 Howard 299 (1851); *Atlantic Coast Line R. Co. v. Georgia*, 234 U.S. 280 (1914); *South Carolina Highway Department v. Barnwell Brothers, Inc.*, 303 U.S. 177 (1938); and *Kassel v. Consolidated Freightways Corp. Delaware*, 450 U.S. 662 (1981).

UNITED STATES V. E. C. KNIGHT CO.
156 U.S. 1 (1895)

BACKGROUND The Sherman Antitrust Act made it illegal "to monopolize, or combine or conspire with other persons to monopolize trade and commerce among the several states." The American Sugar Refining Company purchased the stock of the E. C. Knight Company and three other Pennsylvania refineries that gave the company control of 98 percent of the manufactured sugar in the United States. The government alleged that the contracts constituted combinations in restraint of trade in violation of the Sherman Act and sought cancellation of the agreements.

CONSTITUTIONAL ISSUE

Whether, conceding the existence of a monopoly of manufacture is established by the evidence, can that monopoly be suppressed under the act of Congress? NO

MAJORITY OPINION Chief Justice Melville W. Fuller delivers the opinion of the Court. Chief Justice Fuller is willing to concede that a monopoly has been established but maintains that the relief of the burden of monopoly falls within the police power of the state. While also conceding the supremacy of the national government in the regulation of commerce, Fuller, quoting *Gibbons v. Ogden*, asserts that whatever does not belong to commerce falls within the jurisdiction of the state's police power. Although the government argues that sugar is a "necessary of life," Fuller maintains that the government's argument must include all articles of general consumption, not just necessities.

Chief Justice Fuller also concedes that although a monopoly over the manufacture of an item necessarily gives control over its disposition, that control is secondary and the effect on commerce is only "indirect." "Commerce," Fuller asserts, "succeeds to manufacture, and is not part of it." The power to prescribe the rule of commerce is independent of the power to regulate or suppress monopolies. The former belongs to Congress but the latter, as previously noted, falls within the police power of the state. However perplexing it may be to keep the two activities separate, it is necessary to do so to maintain our dual system of government.

The chief justice then argues that the Sherman Act was directed at contracts to buy, sell, or exchange goods to be transported among the states. But the fact that an article is manufactured with the intent to export it to another state does not make it an article of interstate commerce. Manufacture, Fuller argues, is the transformation of raw materials into a finished product. In Fuller's view, the regulation of interstate commerce is limited to the transportation of goods. If it were otherwise, virtually nothing would be beyond the scope of the commerce power including agriculture, ranching, mining, "in short, every branch of human industry." Fuller repeats that any effect these combinations have on interstate commerce is indirect. The chief justice concludes the opinion by upholding the circuit court's decision to deny the government the relief it sought.

OTHER OPINIONS Justice John Marshall Harlan I delivers the lone dissenting opinion. That the acquisition of the four Pennsylvania companies by a New Jersey corporation constitutes a monopoly is too self-evident even for the majority to deny. Justice Harlan agrees that the powers of the states must be preserved but argues that the national government must be allowed to exercise its powers as well. Justice Harlan maintains that previous Court decisions have made three points very clear. First, one of the primary concerns of the framers was that the control over commerce would be vested in the national government. Second, it has been well settled since *Gibbons v. Ogden* that the commerce power is plenary and is limited only by the Constitution. Third, the power to regulate commerce "embraces something more than the mere physical transportation of articles of property."

After establishing the scope of the commerce power, Justice Harlan examines the case law regarding monopolies in the states. State courts have consistently struck down combinations in restraint of trade in the coal, salt, lumber, gas, and match industries. The state courts have consistently ruled that combinations such as that made by the American Sugar Refining Company are contrary to public policy and to the public interest.

Next, Harlan acknowledges that it is within the state's police power to punish monopolies. But, he argues, there is also trade among the states that is beyond the territorial control of a single state and that trade is under the control of Congress. Congress, Harlan asserts, may remove any unlawful obstruction to the free course of trade among states. This does not interfere with state autonomy because interstate commerce is expressly given to Congress. Therefore, any combination that obstructs the buying and selling of articles manufactured to be sold in other states directly affects all of the people of all of the states. Justice Harlan concedes that manufacture precedes commerce, but he maintains that it is equally true that when manufacture ends the product is a subject of commerce. He argues that whatever improperly obstructs interstate commerce may be reached by Congress under the commerce power.

Finally, Justice Harlan notes that if a suit were brought by the American Sugar Refining Company to enforce the monopolistic terms of the contract in question, under the principles of law the courts would have to deny the relief asked. How, then, can it be said that Congress is unable to enact a law forbidding the same practices a federal court would rule unenforceable? The Sherman Act, according to Harlan, is a legitimate means to a legitimate end that the Court ruled in *McCulloch v. Maryland* makes it constitutional. What power other than the national power is competent to protect the people from the evils of monopoly? The authority of the national government should not be weakened to prevent it from accomplishing the great objects it was intended to accomplish.

SIGNIFICANCE OF THE CASE   *United States v. E. C. Knight Co.* is credited with taking the "bite" out of the Sherman Antitrust Act. The Court did not, however, declare the Act unconstitutional. Instead, it interpreted the Act so narrowly that for all practical purposes enforcement was limited. In the finest tradition of "dual federalism," the Court determined that manufacturing, even the manufacturing of goods destined for interstate commerce, precedes the "flow" of interstate commerce and therefore falls within the police power of the states. The Sherman Act is limited to combinations that monopolize the transportation of goods in interstate commerce. By tying the hands of the national government, the Court left the job of curbing the tremendous economic power of monopolies in the inadequate hands of the states. *E. C. Knight Co.* is also notable for its early reference to the "direct-indirect effect" test in commerce cases. Only those activities that have a direct effect on interstate commerce can be regulated by Congress. It falls on the Court to decide which activities have a direct and which have an indirect effect on interstate commerce.

QUESTIONS FOR DISCUSSION

(1)   Is it realistic to leave the regulation of monopolies to the states? Why or why not?

(2)   Does the fact that the American Sugar Refining Company is a New Jersey corporation make a difference in terms of interstate commerce? Why or why not?

(3)   Would it make sense to limit congressional power to regulate monopolies to those items the Court calls a "necessary of life"? Why or why not?

RELATED CASES   *McCULLOCH V. MARYLAND,* 4 Wheaton 376 (1819); *GIBBONS V. OGDEN,* 9 Wheaton 1 (1824); *Kidd v. Pearson,* 128 U.S. 1 (1888); *UNITED STATES V. DARBY LUMBER CO.,* 312 U.S. 100 (1941); and *WICKARD V. FILBURN,* 317 U.S. 111 (1942).

CHAMPION V. AMES
188 U.S. 321 (1903)

BACKGROUND   In 1895 Congress passed a law prohibiting the transportation of lottery tickets in interstate commerce and through the mails. In 1899, Charles Champion was arrested and charged with shipping Paraguayan lottery tickets from Dallas, Texas, to Fresno, California, via the Wells Fargo Company. Champion sought a writ of *habeas corpus* against U.S. Marshal John Ames on the grounds that his arrest was illegal because the Act of 1895 was unconstitutional. Champion argued that the transportation of lottery tickets is not commerce within the meaning of the Commerce Clause. The government argued that Congress may make it an offense to carry lottery tickets from one state to another.

CONSTITUTIONAL ISSUE

Whether Congress may prohibit the transportation of lottery tickets in interstate commerce under its power to regulate commerce among the States? YES

MAJORITY OPINION Justice John Marshall Harlan I delivers the opinion of the Court. Justice Harlan states that the leading case is *Gibbons v. Ogden*. In *Gibbons* the Court ruled that the power of Congress to regulate commerce is plenary, whole, complete, and knows no restrictions other than those prescribed in the Constitution itself [Article I, § 9, Clause 6, for example, forbids Congress to favor the ports of one state over the ports of another state]. The power to regulate commerce, Harlan maintains, is that which is possessed by every sovereign state. He then cites cases to show that the regulation of commerce has been interpreted to include navigation, communication, the transportation of persons, and even the transmission of telegraph messages. Harlan rejects Champion's contention that the tickets in themselves are worthless and therefore cannot be commerce. The lottery prize had value, and each ticket had a face value from $0.25 to $2. Harlan also rejects Champion's contention that Congress may regulate but not prohibit lottery tickets from interstate commerce. Must Congress, Harlan asks, be required to tolerate an evil because it may only regulate it and not prohibit it? To Harlan the answer is obvious. Harlan finds no provision in the Constitution to prohibit the banning of lottery tickets from interstate commerce. He rejects the idea that the law interferes with Champion's liberty. Finally, he addresses the question of whether Congress may prohibit anything it wishes from interstate commerce. Harlan states that the Court's decision is limited to lottery tickets and that the extent of the use of the commerce power by Congress will have to await future cases. He acknowledges that Congress could abuse its commerce power but observes that the possible abuse of power is not an argument against its existence.

OTHER OPINIONS Chief Justice Melville Fuller delivers the only dissenting opinion, which was joined by Justices David Brewer, George Shiras, and Rufus Peckman. Fuller begins by asserting that the power to forbid the transportation of lottery tickets would be an appropriate means of suppressing lotteries if the power to suppress lotteries belonged to Congress. Fuller thinks that it does not. He believes that the power to suppress lotteries falls within the police power of the states and is therefore reserved to the states by the Tenth Amendment. In addition, Fuller argues that lottery tickets are not articles of commerce anyway. He cites a case in which the Court ruled that insurance policies issued in one state to persons living in another state were not commerce. Fuller also sees problems with the majority's opinion. If a state operated a lottery, could it sell tickets to people in other states if Congress so permitted? Would the receiving state be forced to admit the lottery tickets even if it had a law forbidding lotteries? Fuller also argues that virtually anything that crosses state lines becomes an article of commerce subject to congressional regulation under the majority's ruling. Such an interpretation destroys the distinction between interstate and intrastate commerce. Fuller asserts that it is no argument to say that state laws attempting to regulate lotteries have been ineffective. The powers of Congress cannot be enlarged merely because it is in the public interest to do a particular thing. Finally, Fuller disagrees with the majority's position that Congress's power to regulate interstate commerce is the same as its power to regulate foreign commerce and commerce with the Indian tribes. Power over interstate commerce was given to Congress to prevent state discrimination in trade not to prevent certain articles from moving from state to state. Although Fuller concedes that Congress may ban diseased animals from interstate commerce, it is because they are injurious to commerce.

SIGNIFICANCE OF THE CASE *Champion* is one of the commerce cases that gives an expansive view of the power of Congress to regulate interstate commerce. The Court allows Congress to ban lottery tickets that, unlike diseased cattle, are not harmful in themselves. Although later in *Hammer v. Dagenhart* the Court limits the articles Congress may ban from interstate commerce to things that are bad in themselves, like diseased animals, prostitutes, and explosives, the *Champion* case opens the door for a more expansive use of the commerce power. Ultimately, the commerce power provides Congress with a "quasi-police power." Congress later uses the commerce power to prevent the transportation of stolen automobiles, firearms, and even people (kidnapping) in interstate commerce. This permits federal agencies such as the FBI to become involved in fighting crime to a much greater extent. *Champion*, with *Gibbons v. Ogden*, opens the door for the broad interpretation of the commerce power prevalent today.

QUESTIONS FOR DISCUSSION

(1) Does this ruling actually *prohibit* a state from operating its own lottery? Why or why not?

(2) Do you agree with Chief Justice Fuller that lottery tickets, unlike diseased animals, are not harmful in themselves?

(3) Do you think a state should be allowed to prevent a person with AIDS from entering the state?

(4) Do you think that Congress should have the power to ban something if state efforts prove ineffective?

(5) Do you think it is correct to call prostitutes and kidnapped persons "commerce"? Why or why not?

RELATED CASES. *GIBBONS V. OGDEN*, 9 Wheaton 1 (1824); *HAMMER V. DAGENHART*, 247 U.S. 251 (1918); *HEART OF ATLANTA MOTEL, INC. V. UNITED STATES*, 379 U.S. 241 (1964); and *Katzenbach v. McClung*, 379 U.S. 294 (1964).

HAMMER V. DAGENHART
247 U.S. 251 (1918)

BACKGROUND In 1916 Congress passed the Child Labor Act, which prohibited the movement in interstate commerce for thirty days of any products of mines or factories employing children under the age of fourteen. The Act further prohibited the removal within thirty days of products made by children within the ages of fourteen and sixteen if such children worked before 6:00 A.M. or after 7:00 P.M. or if they worked more than eight hours a day or six days a week. Roland Dagenhart, on behalf of his two minor sons, Reuben and John, filed suit to enjoin U.S. Attorney W. C. Hammer from enforcing the Act. The two boys were employees of a cotton mill in Charlotte, North Carolina. The Dagenharts attacked the Child Labor Act on the grounds that it was not a regulation of commerce but an attempt to regulate labor conditions. They also alleged that the Act was contrary to the Fifth and Tenth Amendments. The U.S. District Court for the Western District of North Carolina declared the Act unconstitutional.

CONSTITUTIONAL ISSUE

Whether Congress may prohibit the transportation in interstate commerce of goods manufactured by factories or mines employing child labor? NO.

MAJORITY OPINION   Justice William R. Day delivers the opinion of the Court. Justice Day states that as a general rule the power to regulate interstate commerce does not include the power to prohibit certain items from interstate commerce entirely. Justice Day acknowledges that previous decisions of the Court may seem to indicate that ordinary products may be banned from interstate commerce if Congress should choose to do so. However, in those cases where the Court has upheld Congress's power to ban certain items from interstate commerce, the decisions rested on the character of the items Congress sought to ban. For example, Congress banned impure food and drugs, lottery tickets, prostitutes, and intoxicating liquors from interstate commerce, and these bans have been upheld by the Court. The difference, Justice Day asserts, is that congressional regulation could only be achieved by prohibiting the use of the facilities of interstate commerce to the items banned. The Child Labor Act does not seek to regulate the transportation of goods in interstate commerce. The real purpose of the Act is to standardize the age at which children can be employed in factories and mines. A second difference, according to Justice Day, is that the products previously banned from interstate commerce were either immoral or harmful in themselves. However, goods produced by child labor are not intrinsically harmful.

Justice Day lists additional reasons for declaring the Child Labor Act unconstitutional. First, he argues that if the law were upheld all products intended for interstate commerce would come under federal control, a result never intended by the framers. Second, Day addresses the argument that one state's lenient child labor laws gives that state a competitive advantage over states with stricter child labor laws. The nature of our federal system, Day claims, results in numerous occasions where one state could gain an economic advantage over her sister states. He notes state laws regulating the hours and wages of women as one example. However, the commerce power does not enable Congress to equalize economic conditions among the states especially in areas clearly reserved to the states. Finally, Justice Day admits that the use of child labor is universally condemned. North Carolina herself prohibits the employment of children under the age of twelve. But, the determination of child labor policy is a local matter reserved to the states under the Tenth Amendment. However desirable uniform child labor laws might be, the Constitution entrusts the power to regulate purely internal affairs to the states. Therefore, the judgment of the District Court must be affirmed.

OTHER OPINIONS   Justice Oliver Wendell Holmes, Jr., writes a dissenting opinion that was joined by Justices Joseph McKenna, Louis D. Brandeis, and John H. Clarke. Justice Holmes agrees that Congress has no direct power to meddle in the states' exclusive control over the regulation of the production of goods. However, he believes that any regulation within a power conferred on Congress by the Constitution is valid despite any indirect effects it may have on the powers of the states. The commerce power, he asserts, is given to Congress in unqualified terms, and even the majority admits that the power to regulate includes the power to prohibit. The Court's prior decisions, Holmes asserts, have made clear that a power of Congress cannot be reduced because it might interfere with the carrying out of a state's domestic policy.

Justice Holmes also chides the majority for questioning the motives of Congress in enacting the Child Labor Act. For example, in *McCray v. United States*, the Court upheld a tax on artificially colored oleomargarine, noting that the Court may not inquire into the motives of Congress as long as it is exercising a power conferred on it by the Constitution. Holmes also questions the argument that the law encroaches on the police power of the states. He argues that the regulation of impure food and drugs, lotteries, and prostitution all have "the character of police regulations." Holmes does not see the logic of the harmful-harmless effect distinction. Even so, he argues, there is more agreement among civilized nations on the evil of child labor than there is on the evil of alcohol, which Congress may ban from interstate commerce. Finally, Holmes denies that the Act interferes with any power of the state. If there were no Constitution and no Congress, the other states could ban goods manufactured in states employing child labor. Under our Constitution, Holmes maintains, that power is given to Congress. Congress determines the public welfare of the nation, and the national welfare may be different from the self-seeking interests of an individual state.

SIGNIFICANCE OF THE CASE   The Child Labor Act was passed during the Progressive Era in American history. The United States was beginning to develop a national economy that required national solutions to national problems like child labor. Under our federal system, businesses were free to locate in states with the most lenient labor laws. Because it was cheaper to use child labor, industries were naturally drawn to states like North Carolina that had the most permissive laws. This, in turn, put the states with stricter child labor laws at a competitive disadvantage. What Congress was seeking to do was to eliminate the competitive disadvantage of the lenient states by standardizing child labor requirements. The generally probusiness Supreme Courts of the time refused to allow this. It would take the Great Depression of the 1930s to drive home the point that the United States has a national economy and that the states, acting separately, cannot adequately solve difficult economic and social problems.

Hammer v. Dagenhart is significant for another reason. It is a part of the "dual federalism" tradition of the Supreme Court. In *Hammer* the Court maintains the belief that there is a line between interstate and intrastate commerce and that it is the duty of the Court to draw that line. *Hammer* is also another use of the Tenth Amendment as a restraint on the use of the commerce power. The *Hammer* majority clearly perceives that if the Child Labor Act is upheld, there may be virtually nothing beyond the scope of federal regulation. In the final analysis, *Hammer* merely postponed the inevitable elimination of the distinction between interstate and intrastate commerce.

QUESTIONS FOR DISCUSSION

(1)   Is the distinction between goods or activities that are harmful and those that are harmless a logical one? Why or why not?

(2)   Name some ways federalism could give one state economic advantages over other states.

(3)   Can Congress regulate child labor today? If so, under what authority?

(4)   Does Justice Holmes see any limits on the power of Congress to ban things from interstate commerce? If so, what are those limits?

(5)   If the Dagenharts were destitute enough to have their sons work, where do you think they got the money to take this case to the Supreme Court?

RELATED CASES *GIBBONS V. OGDEN*, 9 Wheaton 1 (1824); *CHAMPION V. AMES*, 188 U.S. 321 (1903); *MCCRAY V. UNITED STATES*, 195 U.S. 27 (1904); *Hipolite Egg Company v. United States*, 200 U.S. 45 (1911); *UNITED STATES V. DARBY LUMBER CO.*, 312 U.S. 100 (1941); and *Katzenbach v. McClung*, 379 U.S. 294 (1964).

NATIONAL LABOR RELATIONS BOARD
V. JONES & LAUGHLIN STEEL CORPORATION
301 U.S. 1 (1937)

BACKGROUND In 1935 Congress passed the National Labor Relations Act, which created the National Labor Relations Board. The Act gives employees the right to organize and to engage in collective bargaining. It also prohibits employers from engaging in unfair labor practices among which is discrimination against employees involved in union activities. The Jones & Laughlin Corporation discharged ten employees, several of whom were officers in the Iron, Steel and Tin Workers of America union. At a hearing before the National Labor Relations Board (NLRB), lawyers for the corporation appeared but solely for the purpose of challenging the validity of the National Labor Relations Act and the Board's jurisdiction. The corporation argued that the regulation of labor relations was a reserved power of the states and not within the scope of the commerce power of Congress. When the Board upheld both the validity of the Act and its own jurisdiction, the corporation's lawyers withdrew from the hearing. The Board proceeded to hear only the union's evidence and then ruled in favor of the discharged employees. The Board ordered Jones & Laughlin to reinstate the employees and to post notices for thirty days that it would not discharge or discriminate against workers wishing to join a union. When the corporation failed to comply with the Board's order, the Board petitioned the circuit court to enforce its decision.

However, the circuit court denied the Board's request and held that the order was beyond the range of the federal government's power. The Board then appealed to the Supreme Court.

CONSTITUTIONAL ISSUE

Whether Congress has the authority under the commerce power to regulate labor relations in companies engaged in manufacturing goods that are to be shipped in interstate commerce?
YES

MAJORITY OPINION Chief Justice Charles Evans Hughes delivers the opinion of the Court. After outlining the major provisions of the National Labor Relations Act, the chief justice lists the objections raised by Jones & Laughlin. The corporation maintains that the Act is an attempt to regulate labor relations disguised as a regulation of interstate commerce. Second, the federal government has no power to regulate relations with production employees, and, third, the Act violates Article III, § 2 (exercise of judicial power by a regulatory agency), as well as the Fifth (denial of property without due process of law) and Seventh (denial of jury trial in a civil case more than $20) Amendments.

In the next section of the opinion, Chief Justice Hughes outlines the magnitude of the Jones & Laughlin Corporation. The corporation is the nation's fourth largest producer of steel. It has nineteen subsidiaries. It controls mines, railroads, steamships, and factories for the manufacture and transportation of its steel. Approximately 75 percent of that steel is shipped out of Pennsylvania. The Aliquippa plant alone employs ten thousand workers. Next, the chief justice notes that the evidence supports the Board's conclusion that the ten employees were discharged for union activities and that the corporation did not take advantage of its opportunity to refute the charges against it before the Board. The chief justice then turns to the constitutional issues raised by the case.

First, the chief justice addresses the scope of the National Labor Relations Act. The corporation argues that the references to interstate commerce are merely a pretext for regulating labor relations. However, the chief justice believes that the Act is limited to those industries that affect commerce and those practices that affect the flow of commerce. Thus, the Board is not given unlimited and unchecked power by Congress. Next, the chief justice examines the unfair labor practices in question. Section 7 of the Act guarantees workers the right to join a labor union and defines interference with that right as an unfair labor practice. Congress has recognized and the Court has upheld the importance of the right to unionize in the railroad industry. Congress is free to safeguard the same right for other employees engaged in industries that affect interstate commerce. Third, the chief justice discusses the application of the law to persons engaged in manufacturing. Although manufacturing may be deemed a local activity, labor unrest may lead to a shutdown of a factory, that in turn would stop the flow or stream of interstate commerce. The Court previously held in *Stafford v. Wallace* that local activities that burden interstate commerce are subject to congressional regulation. Fourth, the chief justice observes that given the magnitude of the Jones & Laughlin operation, it would be absurd to describe the effect of a work stoppage on interstate commerce as remote or indirect. Experience has shown that the failure to recognize workers' rights to bargain collectively is a major cause of industrial strife. Finally, the chief justice addresses the due process and other constitutional issues. The Act sets forth procedures that the Board must follow. The Court is satisfied that those procedures meet the requirements of the due process clause. Nor does the Board's administrative proceedings violate the Seventh Amendment, which requires that suits at common law exceeding $20 in value must be by jury trial. The case in question is a statutory proceeding, not a case at common law. Therefore, the judgment of the circuit court is reversed and remanded for further proceedings consistent with the Court's opinion.

OTHER OPINIONS Justice James C. McReynolds, joined by Justices Willis Van Devanter, George Sutherland, and Pierce Butler, dissents. Justice McReynolds believes that the Court has departed from its own well-established principles set forth in *Schechter Poultry Corp. v. United States* and *Carter v. Carter Coal Co.* Those cases drew a distinction between the importation of raw materials into a state, the manufacture of those materials into finished goods, and the exportation of those goods to other states. Both the importation and exportation involve the transportation of the goods and fall within the commerce power. However, the manufacture of those goods is a purely local matter left to state regulation under the Tenth Amendment. The ten employees discharged were manufacturing employees and therefore not subject to federal regulation.

McReynolds criticizes the Court for departing from the direct-indirect test for interstate commerce. He notes that only ten employees out of ten-thousand were discharged. Even if discontent had followed and a strike had occurred, McReynolds argues that it is difficult to imagine a more remote effect on interstate commerce. McReynolds denies that the magnitude of the Jones & Laughlin operation is pertinent. If, McReynolds asserts, Congress may regulate any activity that may disrupt the flow or stream of interstate commerce, virtually nothing is free from congressional regulation. If a rancher ships his cattle in interstate commerce, he may not fire his ranch hands. Finally, McReynolds notes that it is somewhat ironic that the Act specifically protects the workers' right to strike. The employer is forbidden to engage in unfair labor practices because they may lead to a strike, but workers retain the right to strike, the very evil Congress is seeking to prevent.

SIGNIFICANCE OF THE CASE *Jones & Laughlin* is significant because the Court permits Congress to exercise broad powers under the Commerce Clause. In previous cases the Court had tried to draw fine distinctions between what was interstate commerce subject to federal regulation and what was intrastate commerce subject to state regulation. Perhaps in simpler times the interstate-intrastate distinction could be justified, but *Jones & Laughlin* recognizes the difficulty of separating interstate from intrastate commerce in a modern industrial nation. It also recognizes that activities seemingly local in nature can have a ripple effect throughout the nation. Finally, *Jones & Laughlin* is significant because it paved the way for an even more expansive interpretation of the commerce power in subsequent cases.

QUESTIONS FOR DISCUSSION

(1) Why do you think the Court reversed itself so soon after the *Schechter* and *Carter* decisions?

(2) Do you find the direct-indirect effect test helpful for determining whether something is intrastate or interstate commerce? Why or why not?

(3) Do you agree with Justice McReynolds that the firing of ten employees out of ten thousand has only a remote impact on interstate commerce? Why or why not?

(4) What, if any, are the limits to the commerce power?

RELATED CASES *GIBBONS V. OGDEN*, 9 Wheaton 1 (1824); *UNITED STATES V. E. C. KNIGHT CO.*, 156 U.S. 1 (1895); *Stafford v. Wallace*, 258 U.S. 495 (1922); *SCHECHTER POULTRY CORPORATION V. UNITED STATES*, 295 U.S. 495 (1935); *Carter v. Carter Coal Company*, 298 U.S. 238 (1936); *WICKARD V. FILBURN*, 317 U.S. 111 (1942); *HEART OF ATLANTA MOTEL, INC. V. UNITED STATES*, 379 U.S. 241 (1964); and *Katzenbach v. McClung*, 379 U.S. 294 (1964).

UNITED STATES V. DARBY LUMBER CO.
312 U.S. 100 (1941)

BACKGROUND In 1938 Congress passed the Fair Labor Standards Act, which prohibited from shipment in interstate commerce goods produced in violation of the Act's wage and hours provisions. The Act set the minimum wage at $0.25 an hour and set the maximum number of hours to be worked in one week at forty-four. Overtime hours were to be paid at a rate of one and a half times the regular rate. The purpose of the Act was to exclude from interstate commerce goods produced under conditions detrimental to minimum living standards. The Act was also designed to eliminate substandard labor conditions from among the states. Congress had concluded that substandard labor conditions burdened the free flow of interstate commerce. The Act required employers to keep records of the wages and hours of their employees and imposed a fine or imprisonment for violations. Darby, who owned a small lumber company in Statesboro, Georgia, was indicted for employing workers at less than the minimum wage and for failing to keep records of his employees' wages and hours. He was also charged with shipping goods manufactured under substandard labor conditions in interstate commerce. The federal district court quashed the indictment on the grounds that the Act was a regulation of manufacturing, not commerce, and consequently was not within the Commerce Power of Congress. The United States appealed the district court's ruling to the Supreme Court.

CONSTITUTIONAL ISSUE

Whether Congress has the power, under the Commerce Clause, to ban from interstate commerce goods manufactured by workers earning less than a minimum wage and working more than a maximum number of hours? YES

MAJORITY OPINION Justice Harlan Fiske Stone delivers the opinion of the Court. Justice Stone begins the opinion by conceding that although manufacturing itself is not commerce, the shipment of manufactured goods is. The power to regulate commerce includes the power to prohibit goods from interstate commerce. For example, the Court has upheld the prohibition of the transportation of lottery tickets, stolen goods, and kidnapped persons from interstate commerce. Justice Stone then discusses Darby's claim that the real motive and purpose of the Act is not to regulate commerce but to regulate wages and hours, which is a power Darby argues is reserved to the states under their police power. Stone notes that Congress is free to exercise its Commerce Power even if it is in an area where the state may also act. That is, Georgia's refusal to set minimum wages and maximum hours under its police power does not prevent Congress from doing so under its commerce power. Congress, Stone says, has determined that substandard labor conditions are injurious to interstate commerce and that interstate commerce should not be used to encourage such conditions. Stone concludes that the regulation of commerce is indeed the real motive and purpose of the Act. He says that unless Congress adopts means that are clearly prohibited by the Constitution, it is not the duty of the Court to question those means. In this case the prohibition of the shipment of goods manufactured under substandard labor conditions is a legitimate means of exercising the commerce power.

Justice Stone then discusses the *Hammer v. Dagenhart* decision in which the Court ruled that the prohibition from interstate commerce of goods manufactured by child labor was unconstitutional. In *Hammer* the Court had ruled that Congress could not ban goods from interstate commerce unless the goods, like lottery tickets, were inherently bad. Justice Stone says that *Hammer* was a departure from the Court's previous commerce decisions and is inconsistent with commerce cases that followed it. Consequently, Stone declares that *Hammer* is overruled.

Next, Justice Stone addresses the validity of the wage and hour requirements of the Fair Labor Standards Act. The question is whether the manufacture of goods is so closely related to commerce that Congress may regulate it under its commerce power. Stone says that it is clear Congress understood that when goods are being manufactured it is impossible to tell which ones will be sold in the state and which ones will be shipped to other states. Nevertheless, Congress may regulate intrastate activities that affect interstate commerce. For example, in *National Labor Relations Board v. Jones & Laughlin Corp.*, the Court ruled that Congress could regulate labor relations that might disrupt the flow of interstate commerce even though only manufacturing is involved.

Finally, Justice Stone discusses the claims that the Fair Labor Standards Act violates the Tenth and Fifth Amendments. Stone argues that the Tenth Amendment was added to the Constitution to prevent the national government from exercising powers not granted to it. However, the Amendment was never meant to prevent Congress from exercising its delegated powers to their fullest extent. Stone dismisses the Fifth Amendment claim on the basis of the Court's decisions in *Muller v. Oregon* and *Bunting v. Oregon* (regulation of hours) and *West Coast Hotel Co. v. Parrish* (regulation of wages). In those cases the Court had ruled that regulation of hours and wages was not a denial of property without due process of law.

SIGNIFICANCE OF THE CASE   *Darby*, along with several other cases, as *National Labor Relations Board v. Jones & Laughlin Corp.* and *Wickard v. Filburn* virtually removes the Tenth Amendment as a restraint on the commerce power. Although the Tenth Amendment is resurrected by the Court in *National League of Cities v. Usery*, *Darby* marks the end of any serious attempt to limit Congress's commerce power. In *Heart of Atlanta Motel, Inc. v. United States*, for example, the Court will uphold the Congress's use of the commerce power to ban racial discrimination in businesses engaged in interstate commerce on the grounds that racial discrimination "affects the flow of interstate commerce."

QUESTIONS FOR DISCUSSION

(1)   Do you agree with *Darby* that the regulation of commerce is just a pretext for regulating wages and hours? Why or why not?

(2)   Do you think each state should be free to set minimum wages, or is it better to let Congress set them? Why?

(3)   How do you think the existence of low wages hurts interstate commerce?

(4)   Why can't the problem of low wages and long hours be left to the individual states to handle?

RELATED CASES *HAMMER V. DAGENHART,* 247 U.S. 251 (1918); *CHAMPION V. AMES,* 188 U.S. 321 (1903); *Muller v. Oregon,* 208 U.S. 412 (1908); *Bunting v. Oregon,* 243 U.S. 426 (1917); *WICKARD V. FILBURN,* 317 U.S. 111 (1942); *WEST COAST HOTEL CO. V. PARRISH,* 300 U.S. 379 (1937); *HEART OF ATLANTA MOTEL, INC. V. UNITED STATES,* 379 U.S. 241 (1964); and *NATIONAL LEAGUE OF CITIES V. USERY,* 426 U.S. 833 (1976).

WICKARD V. FILBURN
317 U.S. 111 (1942)

BACKGROUND The Agricultural Adjustment Act (AAA) of 1938 allowed the secretary of agriculture to impose quotas on the production of wheat. A national quota was determined, and in turn the states, counties, and individual farms were given their allotments. The quotas could only be imposed after a referendum vote in which two-thirds of the wheat farmers agreed to them. The Act provided that excess wheat could be stored or delivered to the secretary of agriculture without penalty. The AAA was designed to raise wheat prices by curtailing excess production.

Filburn owned a small farm in Montgomery County, Ohio. His 1941 wheat allotment was 11.1 acres at 20.1 bushels per acre. However, Filburn sowed 23 acres and harvested 239 bushels in excess of his allotment. The AAA, as amended May 26, 1941, imposed a penalty of $0.49 per bushel on the excess wheat for a total of $117.11. Filburn filed suit against Secretary of Agriculture Wickard. He claimed that the excess wheat was totally for home consumption and therefore was not subject to regulation under the commerce power of Congress. He also claimed that the law violated the due process clause of the Fifth Amendment. A three-judge federal court ruled in favor of Filburn and Secretary Wickard appealed.

CONSTITUTIONAL ISSUE

Whether a law that limits the amount of wheat that can be grown for home consumption is a valid exercise of the commerce power? YES

MAJORITY OPINION Justice Robert Jackson delivers the opinion of the Court. Justice Jackson states that in light of the Court's decision in *United States v. Darby,* this case would normally merit little consideration. *Darby* held that the commerce clause does allow federal regulation of production of goods intended for interstate commerce. This case, however, involves regulation of the production of goods not intended for interstate commerce but wholly for consumption on the farm. The Agricultural Adjustment Act defines "market" to include wheat disposed by feeding to livestock or that which is sold, bartered, or exchanged.

Filburn's claim is basically that any effect his production of wheat used for home consumption has on interstate commerce is "indirect" and consequently beyond the scope of the commerce power. In response, Justice Jackson discusses the scope of the commerce clause. He acknowledges that previous Courts have used the terms "direct" effects and "indirect" effects to distinguish proper and improper uses of the commerce power, but notes that of late their use has been abandoned. Jackson states that whether the subject of regulation is called "production," "consumption," or "marketing" is really not relevant. Nor does it matter if an activity is deemed "local" if it has a substantial economic effect on interstate commerce. The production of wheat is heavily involved in interstate commerce. Thirty-two of the then forty-eight states had to import wheat from the sixteen surplus wheat-producing states. Wheat production, Jackson concludes, is a proper subject of congressional regulation.

Next, Jackson addresses Filburn's use of the wheat. The fact that Filburn's 239 excess bushels are a trivial part of the total wheat crop is irrelevant. His part, taken together with others like him, is far from trivial. His wheat could be held back until prices rise and then could be sold creating a surplus the Act seeks to reduce. Even if the wheat is never sold, "it supplies a need of the man who grew it which would otherwise be reflected by purchases in the open market." To the argument that the law gives unfair advantage to some, Jackson merely observes that unfairness is inherent in all regulation, but it is for the Congress, not the courts, to make those decisions. Finally, Justice Jackson notes that Filburn could have avoided the penalty by storing the wheat as the law provides and concludes that he has not been denied due process of law.

SIGNIFICANCE OF THE CASE *Wickard v. Filburn* was decided after the major battles over the New Deal had been fought. Although unsuccessful with his Court-packing scheme, through appointments President Roosevelt was able to change the philosophy of the Court to one that favored expansion of the power of the national government. *Darby* and *Wickard* bring full circle the process of broad interpretation of the Commerce Clause begun by Chief Justice John Marshall in *Gibbons v. Ogden*. The authority of Congress became so broad that by 1964 the Commerce Clause becomes the basis for outlawing racial discrimination in such local establishments as hotels, restaurants, and movie theaters. Today, it is becoming increasingly difficult to find any activity beyond the scope of the commerce power should Congress choose to exercise it.

QUESTIONS FOR DISCUSSION

(1) Do you think the Court has stretched the meaning of interstate commerce too far?

(2) What are your own feelings about the Court's decision? Do you think it is unfair that Filburn is not allowed to grow wheat for his own use without penalty?

(3) Does the referendum before the imposition of quotas affect your views of the fairness of the Act?

(4) Is the regulation of wheat production better left to the states? The free-market system?

RELATED CASES *GIBBONS V. OGDEN*, 9 Wheaton 1 (1824); *UNITED STATES V. E. C. KNIGHT CO.*, 156 U.S. 1 (1895); *UNITED STATES V. DARBY LUMBER CO.*, 312 U.S. 100 (1941); *HEART OF ATLANTA MOTEL, INC. V. UNITED STATES*, 379 U.S. 241 (1964); and *Katzenbach v. McClung*, 379 U.S. 294 (1964).

HEART OF ATLANTA MOTEL, INC. V. UNITED STATES
379 U.S. 241 (1964)

BACKGROUND Title II of the Civil Rights Act of 1964 guarantees that all persons shall be entitled to full and equal enjoyment of goods and services in places of public accommodation without regard to race, color, religion, or national origin. The legislative history of the Act indicates that Congress relied on its commerce power to enact the legislation. However, there was some evidence that Congress also relied on § 5 of the Fourteenth Amendment.

After the passage of the Act, the owners of the Heart of Atlanta Motel, Inc. sought declaratory relief attacking its constitutionality and an injunction against its enforcement. The record showed that the motel advertised nationally and that up to 75 percent of its guests were interstate travelers. The motel indicated that it intended to continue its policy of refusing to rent rooms to Negroes. The motel contended that Congress exceeded its authority under the Commerce Clause, that the Act constituted a taking of liberty and property in violation of the Fifth Amendment's due process clause, and that by forcing it to serve Negroes against its will Congress subjected it to involuntary servitude in violation of the Thirteenth Amendment.

CONSTITUTIONAL ISSUE

Whether Congress, under its commerce power, may prohibit racial discrimination in motels, hotels, and other places of public accommodation? YES

MAJORITY OPINION Justice Tom Clark delivers the opinion of the Court. Justice Clark first gives a brief history of civil rights legislation in general and the 1964 Act in particular. He then discusses the application of Title II of the Act to the Heart of Atlanta Motel, Inc. and concludes that the motel is sufficiently engaged in interstate commerce to be covered by the Act. Justice Clark then proceeds to discuss the grounds for the Court's decision to uphold the Act.

Justice Clark believes it is appropriate to discuss the application of the *Civil Rights Cases*. In those cases the Supreme Court declared a similar public accommodations section of the Civil Rights Act of 1875 unconstitutional. Several factors distinguish the 1964 Act from the 1875 Act. First, the 1875 Act sought to prohibit all discrimination in places of public accommodation without regard to the effect on interstate commerce. Second, the scope of interstate travel is greater today than in 1875, and its impact on interstate commerce is also much greater. Third, there is language in the opinion of the *Civil Rights Cases* that indicates the Court did not fully consider the commerce power as a basis for the law's enactment. These factors led the Court to conclude that the *Civil Rights Cases* are not relevant to the present case.

Justice Clark next explores whether Congress had a rational basis for concluding that racial discrimination has an adverse effect on interstate commerce. Hearings before congressional committees produced ample evidence that the difficulty in finding dining and lodging facilities affected both the quality and quantity of interstate travel for Negro citizens. Justice Clark then discusses the development of the commerce power. He states that commerce has been interpreted to include the interstate transportation of persons as well as articles. He cites a long list of activities, such as gambling, prostitution, and kidnapping that have been upheld as valid exercises of the commerce power. The fact that Congress was legislating against moral wrongs, as here with racial discrimination, does not make the legislation invalid. Finally, Justice Clark points out that previous Court decisions have held that local activities that have an impact on interstate commerce are not immune from the commerce power.

Justice Clark quickly disposes of both the Fifth and Thirteenth Amendment attacks on the Act. The motel owners have not been deprived of their liberty because they have no right to select their guests free of government regulation. Clark notes that thirty-two states have public accommodation laws that prohibit discrimination. Even the majority in the *Civil Rights Cases* observed that states could guarantee equal access to public accommodations through the exercise of their police power. Nor has there been a denial of property because economic losses do not bar legislation of a regulatory nature. Also, because thirty-two states have public accommodation laws, it is difficult for the Court to see how the Act imposes "involuntary servitude" on the appellants. Finally, the opinion concludes by observing that the Constitution leaves to Congress the discretion to choose the appropriate means for implementing its power to regulate interstate commerce. As long as there is a rational basis to conclude that the means chosen are appropriate to a legitimate end, the Court must defer to the judgment of the Congress.

OTHER OPINIONS   Justices Hugo L. Black, William O. Douglas, and Arthur Goldberg write concurring opinions. Justice Black's opinion repeats many of the same arguments set forth in the majority opinion with only a slight difference. Black emphasizes that the Civil Rights Act of 1964 is valid under the Commerce Clause *and* the Necessary and Proper Clause. Justice Black agrees that the Heart of Atlanta Motel, Inc. is sufficiently involved in interstate commerce to bring it under the Act. Consequently, he does not think it is necessary to decide whether the Act is also valid under § 5 of the Fourteenth Amendment.

In his opinion, Justice Douglas agrees that the Commerce Clause provides adequate grounds for upholding the Act, but he prefers reliance on the Fourteenth Amendment because he believes the furtherance of human dignity "occupies a more protected position in our constitutional system than does the movement of cattle, fruit, steel and coal across state lines." He believes that reliance on the Fourteenth Amendment would have a more settling effect because it would be unnecessary for lower courts to decide if a particular business were covered by the definitions of commerce contained in the Act. Douglas argues that any enforcement of a state's trespass laws against a Negro citizen attempting to patronize a public business would meet the requirement of state action under the Fourteenth Amendment. He compares the enforcement of state trespass laws with judicial enforcement of racially restrictive covenants which the Court ruled unconstitutional in *Shelley v. Kraemer*. Justice Goldberg's short opinion echoes Justice Douglas's. He too believes that both the Commerce Clause and § 5 of the Fourteenth Amendment should be considered adequate grounds for Congress to enact the Civil Rights Act of 1964.

SIGNIFICANCE OF THE CASE *Heart of Atlanta Motel, Inc.* of course, was a great victory for the civil rights movement in the United States. It put the Supreme Court's official stamp of approval to the policy of eliminating racial discrimination in places of public accommodation. The Act was an important step toward guaranteeing all citizens equal treatment and ending the badges of servitude to which black Americans had long been subjected. *Heart of Atlanta Motel, Inc.* was also a significant victory in the struggle over national power versus states' rights. Along with such cases as *United States v. Darby Lumber Co.* and *Wickard v. Filburn*, the Supreme Court continued its policy of upholding the increased expansion of congressional regulation under the Commerce Clause.

QUESTIONS FOR DISCUSSION

(1) Explain how racial discrimination could have an adverse effect on interstate commerce.

(2) Do you think the regulation of commerce is merely a pretext for legislating against a moral wrong? Why or why not?

(3) Why couldn't Congress leave the regulation of race relations to the states?

(4) Read § 5 of the Fourteenth Amendment. Does it, in your opinion, empower Congress to legislate against racial discrimination? Why or why not?

(5) As long as the Act is upheld, does it make any difference on what grounds it is held to be constitutional? Why?

RELATED CASES *GIBBONS V. OGDEN*, 9 Wheaton 1 (1824); *The Passenger Cases*, 7 Howard 283 (1849); *CIVIL RIGHTS CASES*, 109 U.S. 3 (1883); *PLESSY V. FERGUSON*, 163 U.S. 537 (1896); *Hoke v. United States*, 227 U.S. 308 (1913); *HOUSTON, EAST AND WEST TEXAS RAILWAY CO. V. UNITED STATES (THE SHREVEPORT RATE CASE)*, 234 U.S. 342 (1914); *UNITED STATES V. DARBY LUMBER CO.*, 312 U.S. 100 (1941); *WICKARD V. FILBURN*, 317 U.S. 111 (1942); and *Shelby v. Kramer*, 334 U.S. 1 (1948); *Katzenbach v. McClung*, 379 U.S. 294 (1964).

NATIONAL LEAGUE OF CITIES V. USERY
426 U.S. 833 (1976)

BACKGROUND In 1938 Congress passed the Fair Labor Standards Act, which imposed minimum wage and overtime provisions for industries engaged in interstate commerce. The 1938 Act specifically exempted the states and their political subdivisions from its provisions. In 1966 the Act was amended and its wage and overtime provisions were extended to include employees of state hospitals, institutions, and schools. In *Maryland v. Wirtz*, the Supreme Court upheld the 1966 amendments. In 1974 Congress again amended the Act to include virtually all public employees. The 1974 amendments did attempt to make provisions for activities, such as police and fire protection, that are without counterpart in the private sector. The National League of Cities, along with individual states and cities, challenged the constitutionality of the 1974 amendments. A three-judge federal court, relying on *Wirtz*, dismissed the suit.

CONSTITUTIONAL ISSUE

Whether Congress, under its commerce power, may extend the wage and overtime provisions of the Fair Labor Standards Act to employees of state and local governments engaged in "traditional governmental functions"? NO

MAJORITY OPINION Justice (later Chief Justice) William Rehnquist delivers the opinion of the Court. Justice Rehnquist declares at the outset that given the substantial implications of *Maryland v. Wirtz*, that case should be overruled. Justice Rehnquist asserts that the Constitution has set affirmative limitations on the exercise of the commerce power and that when Congress seeks to regulate the activities of the states directly, it transgresses that affirmative limitation. Justice Rehnquist notes that while the commerce power allows Congress to regulate private activities that the state may also regulate, it is a different situation when the commerce power is used to regulate the "states as states." Rehnquist believes that state sovereignty limits the exercise of the commerce power and that an undoubted attribute of state sovereignty is the power to determine the wages and hours of state employees.

Justice Rehnquist is also concerned about the financial burden that compliance with the 1974 amendments places on the states. The city of Nashville estimates it will cost $938,000 a year to comply with the amendments, and the state of California estimates the cost between $8 million to $16 million a year. The Act also removes policy choices from the states. For example, the state may wish to employ teenagers during the summer at less than the minimum wage. Rather than hire fewer teenagers at the higher wage, the state may simply cancel the program. The states are forced either to increase their revenue to comply with federal wage and overtime provisions or reduce the number of their employees. The Act also puts in doubt the status of volunteer fire fighters, on which small towns depend heavily.

Justice Rehnquist states that the Act "impermissibly interferes with the integral governmental functions of these bodies." He limits the holding to services and areas that the states have "traditionally afforded." Finally, he states that insofar as the challenged amendments interfere with the states' freedom to structure their integral operations, they are not within the authority of Congress. He repeats that in light of the Court's holding in this case, *Wirtz* must be overruled.

OTHER OPINIONS Justice Harry Blackmun writes a brief concurring opinion in which he admitted that he was troubled about some implications of the decision raised by Justice Brennan in his dissent. However, Blackmun said that he read the majority to take a balancing approach that would not always preclude the exercise of federal power in areas such as environmental protection, for example. With this understanding, Blackmun joined the majority.

Justice William Brennan writes the principal dissent in which he is joined by Justices Byron White and Thurgood Marshall. Justice Brennan accuses the majority of repudiating a doctrine that can be traced in an unbroken line back to *Gibbons v. Ogden*. That doctrine holds that the only restraint on the exercise of Congress's plenary power to regulate interstate commerce lies in the political process, not the judicial process. Chief Justice John Marshall, in *Gibbons*, said that the wisdom of Congress, the identity of members of Congress with the people, and the election process were the chief restraints on the exercise of the commerce power. Justice Brennan recognizes that there are constitutional limits on the commerce power such as the First, Fifth, and Sixth Amendments, but declares "there is no restraint based on state sovereignty." Brennan quotes *United States v. California* in which the Court said, "The sovereign power of the states is necessarily diminished to the extent of the grants of power to the federal government in the Constitution." In that case, the Court ruled that valid general regulations of commerce do not cease to be valid because a state is involved. Brennan accuses the majority of fashioning a rule merely because they disagree with Congress's policy decision.

Justice Brennan next attacks some of the majority's justifications. He asserts that any increased costs to the states to comply with the 1974 amendments is a policy question, not a judicial question. He also claims that the cost estimates are highly exaggerated. He then cites federal funding for the two areas specifically mentioned by the majority. Brennan notes that in fiscal year 1977 the federal government appropriated $716 million for local law enforcement and $400 million to finance youth employment programs that created 670,000 jobs. The estimated $1 billion in increased compliance costs, even if accurate, pales in comparison with the $60.5 billion states receive in aid from the federal government. The states, he assures the majority, are quite capable of protecting their own interests because members of Congress are elected from the states. Justice Brennan closes his dissent by calling the majority's characterization of "essential functions," "integral operations," and "traditional functions" as essentially unworkable.

Justice John Paul Stevens's brief dissent pokes fun at the majority's concern about the loss of state sovereignty. The state, he says, has an inherent right to pay the capitol janitor a substandard wage, but the federal government may require the state to hire the janitor on a nondiscriminatory basis, withhold federal taxes from his paycheck, forbid him to burn too much soft coal in the capitol furnace, or forbid him to drive the governor's limousine over 55 miles per hour. Even though he may doubt the wisdom of applying the wage and overtime provisions to the states, Stevens has no doubt about Congress's right to impose them.

SIGNIFICANCE OF THE CASE   *National League of Cities* raises the interesting question whether Congress may directly regulate the activities of a state by use of one of its delegated powers. The commerce power is one that has been given broad scope through Supreme Court interpretation but *National League of Cities* narrows that scope at least as the commerce power is applied to the activities of states. The majority seems to be limiting the ruling to areas of "traditional governmental functions" of the states. The problem, as the Court later concedes in *Garcia v. San Antonio Mass Transit Authority*, is defining what constitutes a "traditional governmental function." At any rate, the victory for states' rights is short-lived because just nine years later the Court uses *Garcia* to reverse *National League of Cities*.

QUESTIONS FOR DISCUSSION

(1) Do you accept the majority's contention that "state sovereignty" serves to limit Congress's exercise of the commerce power? Why or why not?

(2) Could Congress make the payment of a minimum wage to state employees a condition for receiving federal grant money? Why or why not?

(3) Why should Congress force states to pay their employees a minimum wage in the first place?

(4) If private businesses have to pay minimum wages and overtime pay, why shouldn't state and local governments?

RELATED CASES *GIBBONS V. OGDEN*, 9 Wheaton 1 (1824); *United States v. California*, 297 U.S. 175 (1936); *Maryland v. Wirtz*, 392 U.S. 183 (1968); *United Transportation Union v. Long Island R. Co.*, 455 U.S. 678 (1982); *E.E.O.C. v. Wyoming*, 460 U.S. 226 (1983) and *GARCIA V. SAN ANTONIO MASS TRANSIT AUTHORITY*, 469 U.S. 528 (1985).

GARCIA V. SAN ANTONIO MASS TRANSIT AUTHORITY
469 U.S. 528 (1985)

BACKGROUND In 1938, when Congress passed the Fair Labor Standards Act (FLSA), city and state employees were exempted from its minimum wage and overtime provisions. In 1966, Congress extended the provisions to state and local employees of public hospitals, schools, and mass transit carriers and the Supreme Court upheld the extension in *Maryland v. Wirtz*. In 1974, Congress removed all overtime exemptions for mass transit employees and brought virtually all state and local employees under the Act. In 1976, the Supreme Court overruled *Maryland v. Wirtz* in *National League of Cities v. Usery*. In *National League of Cities*, by a 5–4 decision, the Court ruled that the Fair Labor Standards Act "could not be constitutionally applied to the traditional governmental functions of state and local governments." In 1979, the Department of Labor ruled that the San Antonio Mass Transit Authority (SAMTA) was not entitled to an exemption under the *National League of Cities* ruling. SAMTA filed an action against secretary of labor, Robert Donovan, and Garcia and other SAMTA employees were allowed to join the suit. The U.S. District Court for the Western District of Texas ruled in favor of SAMTA, and Garcia appealed. The Supreme Court, noting conflict in the courts below in trying to define "traditional governmental functions" granted the appeal. Justice Harry Blackmun, author of the majority opinion, writes a concurring opinion in *National League of Cities*.

CONSTITUTIONAL ISSUE

Whether Congress, under its commerce power, may extend the wage and overtime provisions of the FLSA to employees of state and local governments engaged in "traditional governmental functions"? YES

MAJORITY OPINION Justice Harry Blackmun delivers the opinion of the Court. After tracing the history of this case, Justice Blackmun proceeds to explain the Court's reasons for overturning *National League of Cities*. Blackmun begins by noting that

SAMTA concedes that if it were a privately owned enterprise it would be subject to the wage and overtime provisions of FLSA. The key issue, according to Blackmun, is whether mass transit constitutes a traditional governmental function under the *National League of Cities* ruling. Blackmun outlines the Court's attempts to apply the traditional governmental function standard and concludes that its application has been irrational and without any organizing principles. Reliance on the historical performance of a given function has not been helpful. For example, in the present case the city of San Antonio assumed ownership of the city's mass transit company only in 1959. Justice Blackmun looks at alternative standards of identifying "traditional governmental functions" and also rejects them. Functions that are "necessarily" or "uniquely" performed by state and local governments are as elusively defined as those performed "historically." At any rate, Blackmun asserts, it is not for a nonelected judiciary to decide which functions are exempt from Congress's commerce power.

In the next part of the opinion, Justice Blackmun discusses the commerce power. He notes there is no specific constitutional language that limits Congress's use of its commerce power when a state's sovereignty is involved. Blackmun points out that the Constitution itself limits state sovereignty in at least three areas. First, Article I, § 10 forbids states to coin money, enter into treaties, and so forth. Second, by allowing the Supreme Court to invalidate state laws contrary to the supreme law of the land, Article III limits state sovereignty. Finally, the Fourteenth Amendment, which has made most of the provisions of the Bill of Rights applicable to the states, is a third limitation. The states, Blackmun asserts, have "a significant measure of sovereign authority," but the states may exercise that sovereign authority only insofar that it does not interfere with a power delegated to Congress or prohibited by the Constitution.

Justice Blackmun concludes his opinion by asserting that there are safeguards within our federal system of government to protect the interests of the states. He notes that federal financial assistance normally accompanies federal regulation. SAMTA itself is a recipient of subsidies under the Urban Mass Transit Act. Although he says that the law would be constitutional without federal aid, Blackmun maintains that members of Congress, elected from the states, will protect the states' interests. Blackmun also cites legislation in which Congress has expressly exempted the states from its provisions. The political dynamics of federalism will check any abuse of power by Congress in the use of its commerce power.

OTHER OPINIONS Justices Lewis Powell, William Rehnquist, and Sandra Day O'Connor write dissenting opinions. Justice Powell begins by observing that the Court has reaffirmed its ruling in *National League of Cities*, sometimes unanimously, many times since 1976. Then Powell attacks the majority for undermining the federal structure of our government. He accuses the majority of reducing the Tenth Amendment, the source of the states' reserved powers, to "meaningless rhetoric." He castigates the majority for virtually surrendering the Court's power of judicial review in cases involving the commerce power. Next, Powell denies that the Court has been unable to devise an "organizing principle" in the cases cited by the majority. The decisions, he claims, have balanced the seriousness of the problem Congress wishes to regulate against the effects of state compliance on its sovereignty. This balancing approach, he claims, is workable. Finally, Powell does not have faith that members of Congress will protect the interests of the states. Changes in the political system have increased the influence of special-interest groups and the news media while reducing members' responsiveness to local interests.

Justice O'Connor believes that the majority's decision ignores the checks-and-balances feature of our federal system. The states were intended to check abuses of the national government's power. States, O'Connor asserts, have rights that the national government is bound to respect even if the latter's laws are supreme. Quoting *McCulloch v. Maryland*, Justice O'Connor states that it is not enough that the ends be legitimate; they must be consistent with the spirit of the Constitution as well. In her opinion, this decision is inconsistent with the spirit of federalism. Like Justice Powell, O'Connor is not confident that Congress's own sense of self-restraint is sufficient to protect the interests of the states.

Justice Rehnquist writes a brief opinion in which he joined the opinions of Powell and O'Connor. Although he does not fully agree that their analysis is fully congruent with *National League of Cities*, he believes it should be followed.

SIGNIFICANCE OF THE CASE. Until 1937 the Supreme Court had often used the Tenth Amendment as grounds for limiting Congress's commerce power. After 1937, the Court has generally upheld broad use of the commerce power. The decision in *National League of Cities*, therefore, was an aberration, a return to the days of dual federalism. In a sense, then, *Garcia* is merely a return to the general trend of commerce cases of the post–1937 era. *Garcia* appears to be saying what the dissenters fear most: that the Court is unwilling to use its power of judicial review to strike down any use of the commerce power even if it impinges on a power reserved to the states. Although the majority does not say so outright, the implication is clear that the Court prefers to allow the political process to provide the necessary checks on congressional use of the commerce power. Whether the Court will again change its stance, as the dissenters are confident it will, remains to be seen.

QUESTIONS FOR DISCUSSION

(1)   Should Congress have the power to set wage and overtime requirements for state and local employees? Why or why not?

(2)   How do federal wage and hour requirements interfere with a state's right to perform its "traditional governmental functions"?

(3)   Do you agree with the majority that members of Congress, elected from the states, will adequately protect state interests? Why or why not?

(4)   Does the presence of federal subsidies make any difference to you in this case? Why or why not?

RELATED CASES *McCULLOCH V. MARYLAND*, 4 Wheaton 316 (1814); *Maryland v. Wirtz*, 392 U.S. 183 (1968); *Fry v. United States*, 421 U.S. 542 (1975); *NATIONAL LEAGUE OF CITIES V. USERY*, 426 U.S. 833 (1976); *United Transportation Union v. Long Island R. Co.*, 455 U.S. 678 (1982); and *E.E.O.C. v. Wyoming*, 460 U.S. 226 (1983).

5

THE TAXING POWER

INTRODUCTION

Along with the commerce power the power "to lay and collect taxes" is among the most potent Congress possesses. The taxing power allows Congress to favor certain groups by granting them tax exemptions. Congress may also use the taxing power to handicap other groups by singling them out for unfavorable treatment. It is easy to understand why interest groups spend so much time and energy on tax legislation.

In general, the major purpose of taxation is to enable government to raise the revenue it needs to operate. But, taxation has another purpose: Taxation can be used to regulate. Certain activities can be encouraged by use of the taxing power. For example, Congress encourages people to buy homes when it allows mortgage interest to be tax deductible. Similarly, Congress encourages contributions to churches and charitable organizations by making such contributions tax deductible. Congress may also discourage other activities by imposing heavy taxes on them. So-called sin taxes are placed on alcohol and cigarettes to discourage people from excessive use.

The power to tax is granted to Congress in Article I, § 8 of the Constitution. Like the commerce power, there are only a few constitutionally imposed limits on the taxing power. Article I, § 9 forbids Congress to lay a tax or duty on articles imported from any state. Like the commerce clause, the greatest control over the taxing power is the control the people have over their elected representatives. It is this political control that stays the hand of Congress and keeps it from imposing taxes in an arbitrary and capricious manner.

The cases in this chapter are of two types. The first type of case questions whether the Constitution empowers Congress to lay certain taxes. Included are cases that question the purpose for which the revenue is used. A second type of case concerns the use of the taxing power for regulation. The latter category assumes that Congress has a hidden motive behind a tax and that revenue raising is merely a pretext for using the taxing power to regulate. We begin with the cases that challenge the taxing and spending power.

Taxing and Revenue Raising

One of the first cases ever to reach the Supreme Court was a challenge to a tax. Article I, § 9 reads "No capitation, or other direct, tax shall be laid, unless in proportion to the census or enumeration herein before directed to be taken." This clause appears to create two kinds of taxes: direct and those that are not direct. When Congress imposed a tax on carriages, a man named Hylton challenged it. Hylton argued that a tax on carriages was a direct tax and had to be apportioned on the basis of population. The Supreme Court rejected his position in *Hylton v. United States* (1796). The justices expressed their views separately in *seriatim* opinions. The prevailing view was that only capitation taxes and property taxes were direct taxes within the meaning of the Constitution. All other taxes were either duties, imposts, taxes, or excises. As an aside, the *Hylton* Court first exercised its power of judicial review by sustaining the carriage tax against the charge it was unconstitutional.

A major question concerning the extent of the taxing power was whether a state could tax the national government and vice versa. In *McCULLOCH V. MARYLAND* (1819), the Supreme Court was asked to rule on the constitutionality of a tax Maryland had placed on the Second Bank of the United States. In his opinion, Chief Justice John Marshall coined the famous phrase, "The power to tax involves the power to destroy." Marshall ruled that Maryland could not tax the Bank that was an instrumentality of the national government. To allow Maryland to tax the Bank would allow it to interfere with and to disrupt the Bank's operation. Marshall held that the Bank was an institution created by Congress that represents all the American people. The tax was imposed by the Maryland legislature, which represents only the people of Maryland. The representatives of a part of the people cannot be permitted to tax (destroy) an instrumentality of the whole people.

McCULLOCH gave birth to the doctrine of intergovernmental tax immunity. If, it was argued, a state may not tax an instrumentality of the national government, then the national government may not tax an instrumentality of the state. This position was precisely the one rejected by Chief Justice Marshall in *McCULLOCH*. In Marshall's view, the government of the whole people could tax the governments of the parts. However, as explained in *McCULLOCH*, the parts could not tax the whole. Nevertheless, the doctrine of intergovernmental tax immunity found constitutional acceptance in *COLLECTOR V. DAY* (1871). Joseph Day, a Massachusetts judge, challenged the constitutionality of an income tax Congress had passed during the Civil War. In a prior case, *Dobbins v. Erie County* (1842), the Court had struck down a state tax on the salary of Dobbins, a federal officer. In *COLLECTOR*, the majority reasoned that if a state may not tax an officer of the national government, neither may the national government tax state officials. The Supreme Court virtually overruled *COLLECTOR* in *Helvering v. Gerhardt* (1938). The Court ruled that state employees were not exempt from federal income taxes. State employees, like other citizens, were subject to an otherwise neutral tax. The purpose of the income tax, unlike the tax on the Bank in *McCULLOCH*, was not to destroy state government.

COLLECTOR V. DAY was a challenge to a federal income tax as applied to a state judge. In *POLLOCK V. FARMERS' LOAN AND TRUST CO.* (1895), the Supreme Court ruled on the constitutionality of the income tax in general. Congress passed what was, by modern standards, a modest 2 percent tax on incomes more than $4000. Charles Pollock, a shareholder in Farmers' Loan and Trust Company, filed suit against the company to enjoin it from paying the tax. The Court had to decide whether a tax on income was a direct tax. In an opinion whose logic can only be described as tortured, Chief Justice Melville Fuller ignored *Hylton* and ruled that an income tax was a direct tax. Although the Constitution does not forbid direct taxes, it does require them to be apportioned by population. In other words, a state with 8 percent of the nation's population must pay 8 percent of the tax. Unfortunately, wealth is not necessarily distributed on the basis of population. A state with 5 percent of the population may possess 10 percent of the wealth. Similarly, a state with 10 percent of the population may have only 5 percent of the wealth. To apportion a tax on the basis of population is patently absurd.

POLLOCK proved to be only a temporary obstacle to a federal income tax. The Civil War income tax, challenged in *COLLECTOR*, was accepted as an expediency caused by war. The income tax had been resorted to when the nation's revenue-raising capabilities proved inadequate to meet the war's costs. Many Americans worried that another crisis might find the national government without the necessary resources to meet the emergency. In 1913 Congress and the states added the Sixteenth Amendment to the Constitution. That Amendment permits Congress to levy taxes on incomes "from whatever source derived without apportionment among the several States."

It is one thing to challenge how taxes are imposed and another to challenge how the revenue they produce is spent. In the 1920s a case reached the Supreme Court that raised the question whether a taxpayer could challenge the Congress's spending policies. In *FROTHINGHAM V. MELLON* (1923), the Supreme Court all but closed the door on taxpayers' suits. The Court held that an individual's share of the total tax burden was so minute that he or she lacked sufficient standing to sue. The Court's decision was important because had it ruled otherwise every spending program passed by Congress would be subject to challenge. This would put the Court in the position of having to decide the constitutionality of those programs. That was not a position the Court was anxious to be in.

The Supreme Court's ban against taxpayers' suits held firm for forty-five years. In 1968, in *FLAST V. COHEN*, the Court opened the door slightly to challenges to government spending. At issue was the constitutionality of the Elementary and Secondary Education Act of 1965. This Act provided federal aid to religious and sectarian schools. In *FLAST* the Court permitted the petitioner to challenge use of public funds for educational and instructional material for religious schools. The Court held that a taxpayer must first establish a link between his or her status as a taxpayer and the spending power of Congress. Second, the taxpayer must allege the law violates a specific part of the Constitution. In *FROTHINGHAM*, Mrs. Frothingham failed to specify what part of the Constitution the Maternity Act of 1921 violated. Here, petitioner Flast alleged the Elementary and Secondary Education Act violated the First Amendment's Establishment

Clause. *FLAST* merely gets the taxpayer in the courthouse door. The taxpayer must still prove that the use of funds actually violates the Constitution.

Taxing and Regulation

Congress may sometimes have an ulterior motive when exercising the taxing power. Congress may wish to encourage or discourage certain activities by using taxation as a regulatory device. The problem the use of taxation for regulation presents to the Supreme Court is whether it is a "proper" use of the taxing power. In other words, is Congress limited in its use of taxation to raising revenue? If the Court does take on itself the job of deciding the proper use of the taxing power, it leaves itself open to charges of acting like a superlegislature. Conversely, our Constitution seeks to limit governmental power, and to ignore the hidden motives behind a tax invites abuse of the taxing power.

McCRAY V. UNITED STATES (1904) is a good example of the use of taxation to regulate. In 1902, Congress amended an earlier law that placed a tax on oleomargarine colored to resemble butter. The 1902 law increased the tax from $0.02 to $0.10 per pound. Uncolored oleomargarine was taxed at the rate of only $0.0025 per pound. The tax rate on colored oleomargarine was therefore forty times the rate for uncolored oleomargarine. Obviously, the dairy industry had persuaded Congress to place the higher rate on colored oleomargarine because it was cheaper than real butter without the tax. With the tax oleomargarine was not the bargain it was without the extra $0.10 per pound tax added. McCray challenged the law as discriminatory.

The Supreme Court upheld the oleomargarine tax in *McCRAY*. There were several challenges to the law, but the Court focused on the constitutionality of the tax. The Court asserted that it was not its duty to rule on the wisdom of laws passed by Congress. If Congress abuses the taxing power, it is for the people, not the Court, to correct the abuse. Nor is it within the judicial power to question the motives of Congress. Although it may be true Congress caved in to the dairy lobby's pressure, it may equally be true that Congress was trying to prevent the public from purchasing oleomargarine disguised to look like butter. Because the latter explanation is just as plausible as the former, it is not for the Court to say Congress has abused its power.

McCRAY seemed to signal a hands-off policy toward the use of taxation to regulate. However, in *BAILEY V. DREXEL FURNITURE CO.* (1922), the Supreme Court violated its own policy announced in *McCRAY*. After the Supreme Court had invalidated Congress's use of the commerce power to regulate child labor in *HAMMER V. DAGEN-HART* (1918), Congress tried a different approach. In 1919 it passed the Child Labor Tax Act, which imposed a 10 percent tax on the net profits of any company employing child labor. Although *McCRAY* warned against questioning Congress's motives, the majority stated it would have to be blind to not see that the true purpose of the law was to regulate child labor and not to raise revenue. The law was explicit about the ages of children and the hours certain age groups could work. The tax was imposed only if the company knowingly used child labor. Under these circumstances, the Court could not help but conclude that the tax was a mere pretext for banning child labor.

Another area in which taxation has been heavily used to regulate is tariff protection. A tariff is a tax on goods imported into the United States from a foreign country. Congress may help American industries or protect them from foreign competition by imposing tariffs on imported goods. The prices of foreign goods are raised to equal or exceed comparable American goods. A high tariff makes foreign goods less attractive to consumers.

Because the dynamics of international trade cause prices to rise and fall quickly, Congress delegates to the president the authority to change tariffs to respond to market changes. The practice was challenged as an unconstitutional delegation of the taxing power to the president in *J. W. HAMPTON, JR. & CO. V. UNITED STATES* (1928). The use of the tariff to protect American industries was also challenged. Chief Justice William Howard Taft rejected both challenges. Using language reminiscent of *McCRAY*, the Court held that because the tax raised revenue, the Court will not question the other motives of Congress.

During the Great Depression Congress attempted to use the taxing power to regulate farm production. The Agricultural Adjustment Act (AAA) levied a tax on cotton processors. The tax revenue, in turn, was given to cotton farmers who voluntarily reduced their acreage of cotton. The idea was to increase the price of cotton by reducing the supply. The plan would only work if the farmer had a financial incentive to reduce production.

The Supreme Court invalidated the AAA in *UNITED STATES V. BUTLER* (1936). The Court emphasized that it was not trying to impose its economic views on the rest of the country. Nevertheless, the tax was not a general revenue-raising measure. The revenue was "earmarked" to benefit a particular class of citizens and not to promote the general welfare of all Americans. The Court also emphasized that the regulation of agriculture is "local" and that the tax was a thinly-veiled disguise to regulate an activity reserved to the states.

The final example of taxation as regulation centers on federal grants-in-aid. A grant-in-aid is money the federal government gives to a state to encourage it to participate in a federally-mandated program. Federal grants are also used to help the states fund programs, such as highway construction, for which the states are responsible. Federal taxes are collected from citizens of a state and part of the revenues is returned to the states as federal grants.

The issue is whether the national government can threaten to withhold federal funds to force state compliance with a federal mandate. Congress passed a law that reduced a state's federal highway funds by 5 percent if the state's legal drinking age was under twenty-one. The intent of the law was clearly to force states to raise the drinking age to twenty-one. In *SOUTH DAKOTA V. DOLE* (1986), the Supreme Court upheld the law. The Court found that the general welfare goal of saving lives was furthered. It also observed that the law violated no one's constitutional rights. Finally, the Court held that the 5 percent penalty was minor and therefore only mildly coercive.

Conclusion

Like the commerce power, the taxing power has been important to the expansion of the national government's power. Congress may use the taxing power to accomplish indirectly what it may not command directly. Whether Congress has abused the taxing power is, of course, debatable. We should recall, however, the words of Chief Justice John

Marshall in *GIBBONS V. OGDEN* (1824). Although Marshall was speaking of the commerce power, his words apply equally to the taxing power. Marshall observed that in our representative form of government, the wisdom and discretion of the Congress, its identity with the people, and the influence the people exercise over its members are the real restraints on the abuse of power. So it is with the taxing power as well.

COLLECTOR V. DAY
11 Wallace 113 (1871)

BACKGROUND Congress, to help pay the cost of the Civil War, briefly imposed an income tax. Joseph Day was a probate judge in Massachusetts who paid the tax in 1866 and 1867 under protest. He sued James Buffington, the collector of internal revenue, for $61.51 in back taxes and interest on the grounds that the tax, as applied to him, was unconstitutional. Day argued that as a state judge he was an "instrumentality" of the state, which cannot be impaired by taxation. This case raises the issue of intergovernmental tax immunity, which holds that neither government in our federal system may tax instrumentalities of the other. The issue had been raised previously in *McCulloch v. Maryland* when Maryland tried to impose a tax on the Second Bank of the United States.

CONSTITUTIONAL ISSUE

Whether Congress may impose an income tax on the salary of a state judge? NO

MAJORITY OPINION Justice Samuel Nelson delivers the opinion of the Court. Justice Nelson begins his opinion by citing *Dobbins v. Erie County*, an 1842 case, in which the Supreme Court ruled that a state could not tax the salary of a United States officer. Dobbins, the captain of a revenue cutter, was assessed a tax by Erie County, Pennsylvania. The Court ruled that Dobbins was an instrumentality of the national government employed to carry out a legitimate power of that government. Therefore, Dobbins could not be interfered with by taxation by the state. In *McCulloch v. Maryland*, Chief Justice John Marshall observed that, "The power to tax involves the power to destroy." Although there was no express provision in the Constitution forbidding Maryland from imposing a tax on the Second Bank of the United States, the Court ruled it was forbidden by implication. Justice Nelson then proceeds to argue that the principle set forth in *Dobbins* also works in reverse, that is, neither may the national government tax an instrumentality of state government. Justice Nelson asserts that when the national government is exercising its delegated powers under the Constitution, it must be free of interference from state taxation. Likewise, Nelson argues, when a state is exercising one of its reserved powers under the Constitution, it must be free from interference at the hands of the national government. Undoubtedly, one of the state's reserved powers is to establish a judicial department for the administration of justice. Justice Nelson claims that the national government and a state are equal sovereigns entitled to equal treatment from each other. Finally, Justice Nelson states that the limitation on the national government's power to tax the salaries of state judges, like the limitation on the state's power to tax federal officers, is not specifically provided for in the Constitution but is logically derived by implication.

OTHER OPINIONS   Justice Joseph Bradley files the only dissenting opinion. Justice Bradley observes that if it is within the power of the national government to tax its own officers, then surely it is within its power to tax state officers. Judge Day did not cease to be a citizen of the United States when he became an officer of the state. Justice Bradley believes that the implication of the decision is that the national government is somehow hostile or foreign to the states. He notes that when a state taxes an instrumentality of the national government it places a burden on the exercise of a governmental power in an area where citizens of other states may have an interest. Finally, he foresees numerous problems in exempting state instrumentalities from federal taxes. A state-owned railroad, for example, would be exempt, a result Bradley believes is not justified by the Constitution.

SIGNIFICANCE OF THE CASE   *Collector v. Day* is an extension of the doctrine of intergovernmental tax immunity. This doctrine, first announced in *McCulloch v. Maryland*, held that a state (Maryland) could not tax an instrumentality of the national government (the Second Bank of the United States). Although the Court indicated that the same principle did not restrict the national government's ability to tax state instrumentalities, *Collector* does just that. The decision in *Collector* forced the Supreme Court to decide if and when one level of government in our federal system could tax an instrumentality of the other. The Supreme Court began modifying the doctrine of intergovernmental tax immunity in cases such as *Helvering v. Gerhardt* and *Graves v. O'Keefe* so that the doctrine has been robbed of much of its vitality. Today, *Collector* remains but a relic of the theory of dual federalism that was popular with the pre–1937 Supreme Court.

QUESTIONS FOR DISCUSSION

(1)   Do you agree that a judge is an instrumentality of the state? Why or why not?

(2)   Does it follow that if a state may not tax an instrumentality of the national government, the reverse is also true? Why or why not?

(3)   Give some justification for exempting the states from federal taxation.

RELATED CASES   *McCULLOCH V. MARYLAND*, 4 Wheaton 316 (1819); *Panhandle Oil Company v. Mississippi*, 277 U.S. 218 (1928); *Helvering v. Gerhardt*, 304 U.S. 405 (1938); and *Graves v. O'Keefe*, 306 U.S. 466 (1939).

POLLOCK V. FARMERS' LOAN & TRUST COMPANY
158 U.S. 601 (1895)

BACKGROUND   The Constitution creates two classes of taxes: direct taxes and "duties, imposts, and excises." Direct taxes must be apportioned on the basis of population while "indirect" taxes need only be uniform throughout the United States. On August 15, 1894, Congress passed the Wilson Tariff Act imposing a 2 percent tax on income derived from wages, rents, interest on stocks and bonds, and other sources of income. Although income tax laws passed during the Civil War had previously been upheld by the Court, the 1894 law was labeled an attack on the wealthy by the poor. Charles Pollock, owner of ten shares of Farmers' Loan & Trust Company, instituted a class action suit on behalf of himself and other stockholders to enjoin the company from paying the tax. Among his charges, Pollock asserted that the tax was a direct tax as it applied to income derived from real property and municipal stocks and bonds, and therefore must be apportioned by population. Supporters of the income tax argued that the tax fell into the category of "duties, imposts, and excises," and met the test of uniformity.

In *Pollock I*, 157 U.S. 429 (1895), an eight-member Court agreed that the tax, as applied to income derived from real property, was a direct tax and therefore unconstitutional. The Court also agreed that income derived from municipal stocks and bonds could not be taxed by the national government. However, the Court was evenly divided on other aspects of the income tax law. In *Pollock II*, reported here, the full nine-member Court broadens the field of inquiry to include all aspects of the income tax law.

CONSTITUTIONAL ISSUE

Whether an income tax is a direct tax that must be apportioned among the states on the basis of population? YES

MAJORITY OPINION   Chief Justice Melville Fuller delivers the opinion of the Court. The chief justice reaffirms the holding of *Pollock I* that a tax on income from real estate is the same as a tax on land. A tax on land is a "direct" tax and must be apportioned on the basis of population. It was also decided in *Pollock I* that because the national government may not tax an instrumentality of the state, neither may it tax the income from state and municipal stocks and bonds.

Next, the chief justice turns his attention to the issue whether a tax on income derived from personal property is also a direct tax. If so, it would extend the Court's ruling to include income derived from nonmunicipal stocks and bonds including the investments in private corporations. The Court extends the ruling of *Pollock I* to include income from all personal property.

Chief Justice Fuller then tries to justify the Court's decision in light of *Hylton v. United States*. In *Hylton*, the Court ruled that a tax on carriages was an excise tax and not a direct tax. The *Hylton* Court found that only capitation or head taxes and taxes on property were direct taxes under the Constitution. But Fuller disputes the findings in *Hylton*. First, he argues that the opinions in *Hylton* were badly reported. Second, he argues that the statements in the opinions that would limit direct taxes to capitation and property taxes were mere *obiter dicta* and therefore not binding. Fuller then repeats the argument he made in *Pollock I* that a tax on the profits of property is the same as a tax on the property itself.

Chief Justice Fuller disputes the contention of the dissenters that a tax based on apportionment by population is inherently unfair. Congress, he asserts, could decide how much revenue it required and then apportion each state's share according to its population. The state, in turn, could raise its share by taxing property if necessary. If a state failed to produce its share, the national government could act directly to collect the tax. Fuller denies the Court is making any judgments about the desirability of the income tax as a matter of policy and suggests that if an income tax is needed the Constitution should be amended.

After ruling that a tax on income derived from personal property is unconstitutional, the chief justice observes that the only remaining portion of the income tax provisions of the Wilson Tariff Act are those that tax the salaries on professionals and workers. Fuller acknowledges that the general practice is to invalidate only the unconstitutional parts of a statute while leaving the remaining portions intact. However, in this case he asserts that Congress clearly did not intend for the burden of the income tax to fall exclusively on the shoulders of professional and working people. Therefore, the Chief Justice concludes that the remaining provisions must also be invalidated thus striking down all of the income tax provisions of the Act.

OTHER OPINIONS   Justices John Marshall Harlan I, Henry Brown, Howell Jackson, and Edward White all file dissenting opinions. Justice Harlan, author of the principal dissent, takes the majority to task on several points. First, numerous precedents of the Court have held, sometimes unanimously, that a tax on income derived on taxable subjects is not a direct tax. Justice Harlan reviews the *seriatim* decisions in the leading case, *Hylton v. United States*. Justices William Paterson and James Wilson, both of whom had been delegates to the Constitutional Convention, were of the opinion that only capitation taxes and taxes on land were direct taxes within the meaning of the Constitution. The *Hylton* Court found that the requirement of apportionment was placed in the Constitution to protect Southern states that had huge tracts of land and small populations. A federal tax on land in states with large areas would place an unfair burden on the small populations of those states. Harlan observes that all challenges to the income tax during the Civil War were upheld by the Court and castigates the Court for ignoring a century of precedents.

Next, Justice Harlan discusses the case from a policy perspective. He criticizes the majority for denying to the national government an important source of revenue. If the nation were at war, he asks, is it possible Congress could not tax incomes to protect the very survival of the nation? He also finds it ironic that income derived from capital (rents, dividends, etc.) are exempt, but income derived from labor is taxable. True, the entire law is invalidated but only the tax on capital gains for constitutional reasons. Justice Harlan then demonstrates the inherent unfairness of an apportioned tax. Finally, he declares that if the income tax is "socialism," it is a question of public policy for Congress, not the Court, to decide.

Justice Brown echoes many of Harlan's concerns. He asserts that the apportionment requirement was necessary to secure Southern ratification of the Constitution. He believes that no tax is a direct tax unless it is capable of fair apportionment. He also demonstrates how inherently unfair an apportioned tax would be. Finally, he disagrees with the majority's finding that a tax on the profits of land is a tax on the land.

Justice Jackson criticizes the majority for invalidating all the income tax provisions of the Act. He asserts that the income tax was virtually unknown to the framers so it is unlikely they intended to prohibit one. Like Justice Brown, he believes the test of a direct tax is whether it is capable of fair apportionment.

Justice White's dissent is relatively brief because he wrote the major dissent in *Pollock I*. He repeats his belief that the majority erroneously concludes that a tax on real property is a direct tax within the meaning of the Constitution.

SIGNIFICANCE OF THE CASE *Pollock II* is one of the most universally criticized decisions in Supreme Court history. Not only did the Court ignore a century of constitutional precedents holding only capitation and property taxes were direct taxes, but it clearly injected its own policy views into its decision. Although many Supreme Court decisions have economic repercussions and social class overtones, *Pollock II* is considered one of the most blatant examples of the Court substituting its economic views of public policy for that of the elected representatives in Congress. The decision, of course, was nullified eighteen years later with the passage of the Sixteenth Amendment, which permits Congress to levy a tax on income derived from any source.

QUESTIONS FOR DISCUSSION

(1)   Does it make sense to conclude that a tax on income derived from land is the same as a tax on the land itself?

(2)   Why does the Court also invalidate the income tax on salaries from laborers and professionals?

(3)   Explain why the dissenters believe an income tax can never be fairly apportioned on the basis of population.

(4)   How does the majority explain the constitutionality of the Civil War income taxes?

RELATED CASES *Hylton v. United States*, 3 Dallas 171 (1796); *Pollack v. Farmers' Loan and Trust Co.*, (Pollack I) 157 U.S. 429 (1895); *Pacific Insurance Co. v. Soule*, 7 Wallace 433 (1869); *Veazie Bank v. Fenno*, 8 Wallace 533 (1869); *COLLECTOR V. DAY*, 11 Wallace 113 (1871); *Merchant's National Bank of Little Rock v. United States*, 11 Otto 1 (1880); and *Springer v. United States*, 12 Otto 586 (1881).

FROTHINGHAM V. MELLON
and
MASSACHUSETTS V. MELLON
262 U.S. 447 (1923)

BACKGROUND In 1921 Congress passed the Maternity Act, which was a forerunner of modern federal grant-in-aid programs. The Act provided an initial appropriation and annual appropriations over a five-year period that was to be apportioned among the states. The purpose of the Act was to encourage states to develop their own programs to find ways to reduce infant and maternal deaths by providing financial assistance. The Act created guidelines with which the states had to comply and a federal bureau to ensure compliance with the Act's provisions. Participation was voluntary on the part of the states.

The Commonwealth of Massachusetts filed suit under the Supreme Court's original jurisdiction to enjoin the Secretary of the Treasury, Andrew Mellon, from enforcing the law. Massachusetts alleged that the appropriations provided for by the Act were for concerns that were of a local, not national, character. The state also alleged that the Act forced the states to surrender a portion of their sovereignty, that the burden of paying for the Act fell largely on the industrial states, like Massachusetts, and that Congress was attempting to exercise a power reserved to the states by the Tenth Amendment.

Mrs. Frothingham, a taxpayer, challenged the constitutionality of the Act on the grounds that it takes her property under the guise of taxation without due process of law in violation of the Fifth Amendment. The Supreme Court, without ruling on the constitutionality of the Act, focused on whether the Court had jurisdiction in the cases.

CONSTITUTIONAL ISSUES

(1)   Whether the Maternity Act of 1921 usurps powers reserved to the states under the Tenth Amendment? NO
(2)   Whether a federal taxpayer, based solely on her status as a taxpayer, has standing to challenge the constitutionality of an act of Congress? NO

MAJORITY OPINION   Justice George Sutherland delivers the opinion of the Court. Justice Sutherland separates the two cases and disposes of the State's claim first. Massachusetts argues that the Act usurps powers reserved to the states by the Tenth Amendment. However, the Maternity Act imposes no obligation on the state because participation is voluntary. Justice Sutherland notes that Article III of the Constitution does give the Court jurisdiction in cases in which a state is a party but only in cases that involve a true controversy. The Court is not obligated to hear a case that fails to raise a real controversy merely because a state is a party. A real controversy means that the plaintiff has suffered some injury, but Massachusetts has not been injured. The state makes a general complaint that its sovereignty has been usurped by the Act. Sutherland notes that the state may frustrate this attempt to usurp its power by refusing to participate in the program. Sutherland also points out that it is the inhabitants of Massachusetts as federal taxpayers who finance the program, not the State. The question, Sutherland asserts, is essentially a political one that the Court normally will not adjudicate. Nor may Massachusetts file suit on behalf of its citizens. Although the Court refuses to say a state may never intervene to protect its citizens, this is not a case in which it may. A state may not institute judicial proceedings to protect its citizens from the operation of a federal law.

Justice Sutherland then turns to Mrs. Frothingham's claim and acknowledges that the Court has never ruled on the right of a taxpayer to challenge a federal appropriation. Although the Court has upheld the right of a municipal taxpayer to enjoin the illegal use of public monies by a city, the situation of a federal taxpayer is different. The interest of the municipal taxpayer is direct and immediate, whereas the interest of the federal taxpayer is remote, minute, and indeterminate. The federal tax burden is shared with millions of other taxpayers, and each taxpayer's individual share is small. Justice Sutherland also alludes to the mischief that would result if every taxpayer had standing to challenge every use of public funds. Justice Sutherland concludes his opinion by observing that the Court has no general power to rule on the constitutionality of acts of Congress. It may only do so in cases that raise controversies in which a party has sustained a direct injury as the result of the enforcement of a law. To assume jurisdiction over these cases would give the Court a power over Congress the Constitution never intended the Court to have.

SIGNIFICANCE OF THE CASE   *Frothingham* virtually closed the door on so-called taxpayer's suits. If allowed, a taxpayer's suit would permit the average citizen to challenge the constitutionality of a law based merely on his or her status as a taxpayer. Because almost every law is opposed by someone, virtually every appropriation law passed by Congress could be challenged and subjected to judicial review. This would elevate the

Supreme Court to the status of a superlegislature and give the Court the last word in the spending of public money. The framers of the Constitution obviously did not intend for that to happen. Still, it is frustrating for citizens to be unable to challenge what they consider to be unconstitutional uses of public money. The Court modified the *Frothingham* decision somewhat in *Flast v. Cohen*, but overcoming the barrier created by *Frothingham* is formidable. *Massachusetts v. Mellon* is significant because it paved the way for expansion of the federal grant-in-aid concept. Such programs have significantly changed the character of our federal form of government. *Massachusetts v. Mellon* should also be recognized as an example of the discredited doctrine of interposition. Interposition was a pre–Civil War doctrine that held that a state may interpose its authority between its citizens and the national government. Southern states invoked the doctrine to protect slaveowners from the threat of real or imagined congressional antislavery legislation.

QUESTIONS FOR DISCUSSION

(1) Should a taxpayer, as a taxpayer, be allowed to challenge the constitutionality of acts of Congress? Why or why not?

(2) Do taxpayer's suits conflict with the ideal of representative government? Why or why not?

(3) What possible harms could result from taxpayer's suits?

RELATED CASES   *FLAST V. COHEN*, 392 U.S. 83 (1968); *United States v. Richardson*, 418 U.S. 166 (1974); *Schlesinger v. Reservists Committee to Stop the War*, 418 U.S. 208 (1974); and *Allen v. Wright*, 468 U.S. 737 (1984).

FLAST V. COHEN
392 U.S. 83 (1968)

BACKGROUND   In 1923 the Supreme Court handed down the decision of *Frothingham v. Mellon*, which held that a federal taxpayer has no standing to challenge the constitutionality of a statute. Mrs. Frothingham had filed suit challenging a grant program designed to reduce maternal and infant mortality on the grounds that Congress had acted improperly and invaded the prerogatives of the states under the Tenth Amendment and that her increased tax bill effectively deprived her of property without due process of law in violation of the Fifth Amendment. The Court held that Frothingham's injury was too remote and uncertain, and her interest in the Treasury's funds was "comparatively minute and indeterminable" to give her standing. The effect of the case was to bar taxpayers from suing to challenge statutes except regarding their own personal tax bill.

Plaintiffs in the present case are suing as taxpayers to prevent the public financing of instruction and educational materials in religious and sectarian schools under the Elementary and Secondary Education Act of 1965. They claim that use of federal revenue in this manner violates the Establishment and Free Exercise Clauses of the First Amendment. A specially-convened panel of three district judges considered only the threshold question of standing and did not reach the merits of the case. The denial of standing on the basis of *Frothingham* was appealed to the Supreme Court on direct appeal.

CONSTITUTIONAL ISSUE

Whether taxpayers—solely as taxpayers—have standing to challenge the constitutionality of federal statutes? YES

MAJORITY OPINION Chief Justice Earl Warren writes the majority opinion for the Court. There are two questions with which the Court must deal in this case. The first is the government's challenge to the lower court panel and to the method of appeal. The panel was properly convened under statutes governing court procedures because, although the relief sought (an injunction) would narrowly apply to New York City's Board of Education, it has broader implications to any such program in the nation. The statute regarding the invocation of such panels is designed to prevent a single judge from paralyzing entire programs, and the panel is appropriate in these circumstances. In addition, the plaintiffs are challenging the constitutionality of the Act and not merely its administration. The Court finds that the direct appeal is proper.

The second issue is the crux of the case, whether the plaintiffs who are asserting only their status as taxpayers have standing to maintain such a suit in federal court. Standing and the matter of justiciability are nebulous concepts and pose difficulties for courts and litigants alike. The primary focus of standing is on the person asking the court for redress of grievances; however, even if the court finds that the party has standing, the court may decline to hear the case on a variety of grounds—for instance, if the case involves a political question or if it is not a true case or controversy. The controlling precedent is *Frothingham v. Mellon*, which rejected such suits; however, there is confusion about the nature of *Frothingham*: Is it a constitutionally-mandated bar to taxpayer suits or merely a Court-imposed rule of self-restraint? The opinion could be read either way. It contains language indicating that such suits derogate the separation of powers by allowing the Court to invade the provinces of other branches of government, but it also contains language indicating that policy considerations, such as the prevention of a flood of litigation, were the determinative factors.

No constitutional bar to this type of litigation exists. But for taxpayers to have standing, they must show the necessary stake in the outcome of the litigation by meeting a two-pronged test. First, they must show a "logical link between that status [as taxpayer] and the type of legislative enactment attacked"—the taxing and spending power of Congress. "It will not be sufficient to allege an incidental expenditure of tax funds in the administration of an essentially regulatory statute." Second, the taxpayer must show the nexus between that status and the "precise nature of the constitutional infringement alleged," that is, that the law violates specific constitutional limitations on the congressional taxing and spending power. Here, the taxpayers are challenging congressional power to spend for the general welfare in violation of the Establishment and Free Exercise Clauses of the First Amendment. The basic concern is that the powers to raise and disburse revenue would be used to favor one religion over another or to support religion in general. The taxpayer in *Frothingham* did not make such specific allegations and was actually setting forward the states' complaint; therefore, *Frothingham* can be distinguished from the present case.

OTHER OPINIONS Justice Potter Stewart writes one of three concurring opinions. This challenge is to be maintained only because it involves the Establishment Clause of the First Amendment, and "every taxpayer can claim a personal constitutional right not to be taxed for the support of a religious institution." Taxpayer suits challenging legislation on any other ground should not be permitted, and the principle of *Frothingham* that courts should not become forums for taxpayers to air "generalized grievances" about the conduct of government should prevail.

Justice Abe Fortas also concurs in the opinion. Like Stewart, he favors an extremely narrow exception to *Frothingham* and does so only because the Establishment Clause is involved.

Justice William O. Douglas writes a concurring opinion. The bar to taxpayer lawsuits should be totally abolished. Taxpayers, acting as private attorneys general, can be vigilant in limiting the overreaching power of government, especially the bureaucracy. It is an abdication of judicial responsibility to shut the courthouse doors to those who have grievances, especially in a legislative and executive system dominated by special-interest groups where the courts are often the only avenue available to individuals for redress of those grievances. Abolishing the barrier would not necessarily lead to inundation of the courts because of various other standing requirements.

Justice John Marshall Harlan II writes the dissenting opinion. Taxpayers do have standing to contest individual tax obligations that affect their personal and proprietary interests, but this is not such a case. Taxpayers do not retain any special rights in their tax payments once they are paid into the Treasury, which holds its general funds as a surrogate for the population as a whole. The taxpayers here are "as litigants, indistinguishable from any group selected at random from among the general population, taxpayers and non-taxpayers alike." They have no personal, individual stake in the outcome of the suit. The interest that one has in a lawsuit does not vary according to the constitutional provision under which one states a claim. Historical analysis and prior court decisions have indicated that the intent of the framers in creating the Establishment Clause is not clear, and no grounds exist to allow the Court to distinguish it from other constitutional provisions or to contend that it weighs more heavily on the taxing and spending powers of Congress than other provisions. "[S]uits under the Establishment Clause are not in these circumstances meaningfully different from other public actions."

It is inappropriate for the court to interpose itself in this matter, which should be left to the other branches of government. Judicial power should be exercised prudently, and the other branches, no less than the Court, are responsible for protecting the liberties and welfare of the people. The Court should refrain from entering this thicket, which may alter the allocation of power among the branches of government if the Court begins to rule on every governmental expenditure.

SIGNIFICANCE OF THE CASE   *Flast v. Cohen* allows taxpayers to challenge in court the expenditures of the national government within certain parameters. The taxpayer must show sufficient interest in the litigation by establishing a logical link between taxpayer status and the legislation attacked *and* by alleging the violation of a specific constitutional limitation on the taxing and spending powers of Congress and not just a general dislike of the program or policy the expenditure supports. Within those limits, the case increases the power of the Court to review the wisdom of legislative and executive policies. Regarding the merits, the Court upheld the New York state law allowing textbooks purchased with public funds to be loaned to students attending parochial, other private, and public schools in the face of First Amendment claims during the same term it decided *Flast.*

QUESTIONS FOR DISCUSSION

(1)   Should taxpayers be "private attorneys general?" Why?

(2)   The justices express concern that litigation of this nature will further strain the limited resources of the courts. Is this an adequate reason to limit access to courts? Under what circumstances would you favor such limitations?

(3)   Going behind the face of the decision, does the majority invite or avoid confrontation with the other branches of government with its decision? How does this case affect the public's perception of its role in government as well as its perception of the Court.

RELATED CASES   *FROTHINGHAM V. MELLON*, 262 U.S. 447 (1923); *BAKER V. CARR*, 369 U.S. 186 (1962); *Board of Education v. Allen*, 392 U.S. 236 (1968); *Schlesinger v. Reservists Committee to Stop the War*, 418 U.S. 208 (1974); *United States v. Richardson*, 418 U.S. 166 (1974); *Valley Forge Christian College v. Americans United for Separation of Church and State, Inc.*, 454 U.S. 464 (1982); and *Allen v. Wright*, 468 U.S. 737 (1984).

McCRAY V. UNITED STATES
195 U.S. 27 (1904)

BACKGROUND   In 1886 Congress passed a law imposing a $0.02 per pound tax on oleomargarine artificially colored to look like butter. In 1902 the law was amended to increase the tax rate to $0.10 per pound for artificially colored oleo and $0.0025 per pound for uncolored oleo. Leo McCray was penalized $50 for purchasing a 50-pound package of colored oleo to which was affixed an internal revenue stamp at the lower rate. McCray argued that the oleo in question had been manufactured by using artificially colored real butter and therefore the lower rate should apply because no additional artificial coloring had been added. Second, McCray argued that Congress had exceeded its taxing power by imposing a tax that was excessive, discriminatory, and an exercise of a power reserved to the states under the Tenth Amendment.

CONSTITUTIONAL ISSUE

Whether Congress, by imposing different tax rates for colored and uncolored oleomargarine, has exceeded its power to tax under the constitution? NO

MAJORITY OPINION   Justice Edward D. White delivers the opinion of the Court. Justice White begins the opinion by presenting six propositions or allegations that McCray has made in challenging the constitutionality of the tax. First, McCray alleges that the real purpose of the tax is to suppress the manufacture of oleo. Second, the regulation and sale of oleo fall within the reserved powers of the states and are not subject to congressional statutes. Third, the tax rate imposed is so high that it is designed to suppress an otherwise lawful activity, and therefore the tax is not a legitimate means to a lawful end. Fourth, the tax discriminates against the oleomargarine industry in favor of the butter industry. Fifth, the tax violates the Fifth Amendment because it is so out of proportion to the value of the property taxed that it destroys that property. This, in turn, amounts to a taking of McCray's property without due process of law. Finally, the tax is so excessive it is confiscatory.

Before addressing the constitutionality of the tax law, Justice White discusses the application of the tax to McCray. Despite the fact that McCray's oleo was manufactured with artificially colored real butter, the clear intent of the 1902 Act was to tax artificially colored oleo at a higher rate regardless of the source of the coloring. Therefore, White concludes, McCray was correctly assessed the higher, $0.10 per pound, rate.

After ruling that the correct tax rate was imposed on McCray's oleo, Justice White turns to the issue of the constitutionality of the tax. White begins the discussion by describing the function of the Court in constitutional matters. Although the Court has a duty to uphold the Constitution, it is not the Court's duty to make judgments about the wisdom of laws of Congress or whether they are just or unjust. Any attempt to do so, White asserts, would be an abuse of judicial power. It is no argument, White maintains, that an alleged abuse of the taxing power by Congress somehow justifies an abuse of the judicial power by the Court. If Congress has abused its taxing power by passing an oppressive or discriminatory tax, it is for the people through the election process to correct that abuse. Next, White addresses the famous quote of Chief Justice John Marshall that, "The power to tax involves the power to destroy." Justice White asserts that this reference is only to items that Congress or a state has no authority to tax. In *McCulloch v. Maryland*, from which the quote was taken, Maryland was attempting to levy a burdensome tax on an instrumentality of the national government, the Second Bank of the United States, which Maryland could not do. Besides, White says, all taxes are oppressive to someone. It is not the function of the Court to inquire into the reasonableness of a tax if the object taxed is within the taxing power of Congress. Because in a previous case the Court had ruled that states may completely prohibit the sale of oleomargarine, it can hardly be argued that oleo is not taxable.

The issue of the violation of the Fifth Amendment is the next topic of discussion. McCray asserts that the tax is so excessive that it amounts to a taking of property without due process of law. Justice White notes that there are only three limitations on the taxing power of Congress: Congress may not tax exports, direct taxes must be apportioned on the basis of population, and all other taxes must be uniform throughout the United States. White consequently rejects the Fifth Amendment argument on the grounds that the Amendment, by itself, places no additional limits on the congressional taxing power.

Justice White concludes his opinion by conceding that under certain extraordinary circumstances there may be an instance in which the abuse of the taxing power is so clear that judicial intervention may be justified. An example would be the use of the taxing power to destroy a right so fundamental that no free government could exist without it. However, the right to manufacture and sell artificially colored oleomargarine is certainly not such a right.

SIGNIFICANCE OF THE CASE   Congress could have had at least four reasons for imposing such a high tax on artificially colored oleo. First, it could, as the Court suggests, be attempting to protect consumers from mistakenly purchasing oleo instead of real butter. Second, as McCray alleges, Congress could have been protecting the butter industry from the competition of oleo. Third, Congress could have been trying to destroy the oleo industry. Finally, Congress could have been raising revenue for the operation of the national government. The issue, of course, is that only the fourth reason, raising revenue, is a legitimate use of the taxing power even though the other three may be intended or unintended side effects. In *McCray*, the Supreme Court announced a significant expansion of the power of the national government by giving a broad interpretation to the use of the taxing power and allowing Congress to use its taxing power for regulatory purposes. Generally speaking, Congress lacks the so-called police power, that is, the power to regulate health, safety, and morals. Therefore, Congress could not pass a consumer protection law to prohibit oleo manufacturers from trying to masquerade artificially colored oleo as butter. However, by disguising its true intent by placing a high tax on artificially colored oleo only, Congress was able to achieve the same result. By refusing to inquire into the motives of Congress in enacting the different tax rates for colored and uncolored oleo, the Court opened the door for future and innovative uses of the taxing power as a means of regulating activities Congress is otherwise forbidden to regulate.

QUESTIONS FOR DISCUSSION

(1)   Do you think the Court ruled correctly in *McCray*? Why?

(2)   Do you think Congress was protecting a special-interest group by enacting this tax? Why or why not?

(3)   Suppose Congress placed a $5 per package tax on cigarettes. Would such a tax be constitutional? Why or why not?

(4)   Can you think of any other activities or circumstances in which Congress might use its taxing power for regulatory purposes?

(5)   Do you really think the purpose of the tax was to raise revenue for the national government? Why or why not?

RELATED CASES   *McCULLOCH V. MARYLAND*, 4 Wheaton 316 (1819); *CHAMPION V. AMES*, 188 U.S. 321 (1903); *United States v. Doremus*, 249 U.S. 86 (1919); *BAILEY V. DREXEL FURNITURE CO.*, 259 U.S. 20 (1922); *United States v. Constantine*, 296 U.S. 287 (1935); *United States v. Kahriger*, 345 U.S. 22 (1953); and *Marchetti v. United States*, 390 U.S. 39 (1968).

BAILEY V. DREXEL FURNITURE CO.
259 U.S. 20 (1922)

BACKGROUND   In 1919 Congress passed the Child Labor Tax Act. The Act prohibited the employment of persons under the age of sixteen in mines and quarries, and under the age of fourteen in mills, factories, and other manufacturing establishments. The Act also forbade the employment of persons between the ages of fourteen and sixteen for more than eight hours a day or six days a week or for employers to allow such persons to work before 6:00 A.M. or after 7:00 P.M.. Employers hiring children were subject to a 10 percent tax on their net profits for the tax year. Bailey, an Internal Revenue collector for the western district of North Carolina, assessed the Drexel Furniture Company a tax of $6,312.79 in 1919 for having employed a boy under the age of fourteen. The company paid the tax under protest, sought a refund, and when the refund was denied, brought suit against Bailey in federal court. The district court ruled in favor of the company, and Bailey appealed to the Supreme Court.

CONSTITUTIONAL ISSUE

Whether the Child Labor Act is an unconstitutional use of the taxing power to regulate an activity reserved to the states? YES

MAJORITY OPINION   Chief Justice William Howard Taft delivers the opinion of the Court. Chief Justice Taft notes at the outset that the law is attacked on the grounds that its purpose is to regulate child labor, which is a function of the states under the Constitution. The law is defended on the grounds that it is a mere excise tax, which may be levied by Congress under its broad taxing power. Chief Justice Taft acknowledges that it is ordinarily the custom of the Court to give Congress broad discretion in the exercise of its delegated powers. However, in this case the Court would have to be blind not to see that the purpose of this tax is to regulate the employment of children. First, the Act outlines numerous details not normally associated with taxation. For example, tax laws do not normally stipulate the number of hours a person between the ages of fourteen and sixteen may work each day, the number of days a week he or she may work, and the hours (6:00 A.M. to 7:00 P.M.) he or she may work. Second, the employer does not have to pay the tax if he or she unknowingly employs someone underage. Third, the tax is paid regardless whether the employer employed one minor or five hundred minors for 1 day or for 365 days. Finally, the chief justice notes that the secretary of labor is also empowered along with the commissioner of Internal Revenue to inspect factories for the presence of underage workers. All these provisions give the Act a regulatory character.

Chief Justice Taft states that despite the good intentions of the law, Congress has adopted a constitutional means (taxation) to achieve an unconstitutional end (the regulation of child labor). Taft asserts that it is for the states alone to regulate child labor. To permit Congress to get away with this misuse of the taxing power would open the door to congressional regulation of virtually anything under the guise of a tax. It would, Taft argues, remove all limits on the powers of Congress and "completely wipe out the sovereignty of the states." Chief Justice Taft states that this case is similar to *Hammer v. Dagenhart* in which Congress tried to use its commerce power to regulate child labor. Congress must not be permitted to use one of its delegated powers to regulate activities reserved to the states. To do so would undermine our federal form of government.

OTHER OPINIONS   There are no other opinions, but Justice John H. Clarke dissents.

SIGNIFICANCE OF THE CASE   *Bailey*, like *Hammer*, was an unsuccessful attempt by Congress to use one of its delegated powers to put an end to an admitted social evil:

the use of child labor. The Supreme Court continued to maintain the myth that it was possible to delineate clearly the powers of the national government and the powers of the states under the Constitution. By refusing to recognize that national problems, like the use of child labor, required national action, the Court retarded the development of a truly national economy.

QUESTIONS FOR DISCUSSION

(1)   Why can't the regulation of child labor be left to the individual states?

(2)   What, in your opinion, provides the greatest evidence for Taft's conclusion that the purpose of the Child Labor Tax Act was the regulation of child labor?

(3)   Should the Court have closed its eyes to the constitutionality of the Child Labor Tax Act because it had a noble purpose?

(4)   Why is the regulation of child labor by Congress "a constitutional means to an unconstitutional end"?

RELATED CASES   *Veazie Bank v. Fenno*, 8 Wallace 533 (1869); *McCRAY V. UNITED STATES*, 195 U.S. 27 (1904); *HAMMER V. DAGENHART*, 247 U.S. 251 (1918); and *United States v. Doremus*, 249 U.S. 86 (1919).

J. W. HAMPTON, JR. & CO. V. UNITED STATES
276 U.S. 394 (1928)

BACKGROUND   The Tariff Act of 1922 authorized the president to raise or lower duties on products imported into the United States. This so-called flexible tariff was designed to protect American industries from foreign competition. The president, after comparing manufacturing costs for foreign and domestic industries was permitted to raise tariffs on imported products to equalize their cost with American products. President Coolidge raised the duty on barium dioxide from $0.02 per pound to $0.06 per pound. The J. W. Hampton, Jr. & Co., as an importer of barium dioxide, protested the increase first to the United States Customs Court and then to the United States Court of Customs Appeals. The company alleged that the Tariff Act is unconstitutional because it is an unlawful delegation of law-making authority to the president. Second, because one of the purposes of the Act is to protect American industries, the Act is invalid because Congress's power to lay and collect taxes is limited to raising revenue only.

CONSTITUTIONAL ISSUES

(1)   Whether the Tariff Act of 1922 is an unconstitutional delegation of congressional taxing authority to the president? NO

(2)   Whether Congress may use its taxing power for purposes other than just raising revenue? YES

MAJORITY OPINION   Chief Justice William Howard Taft delivers the opinion of the Court. The chief justice states that the purpose of the Tariff Act is clear: Congress wanted to raise revenue while enabling domestic producers to compete with foreign producers. Because of the difficulty of determining with exactness the proper duty to be imposed, Congress authorized the president and his agents to make the initial investigation, and then to raise or lower the tariff as needed. The statute spells out what steps must be taken by the president and the Tariff Commission before the tax may be changed. For example, all interested parties must be notified of pending changes and rates go into effect after thirty days.

Chief Justice Taft then turns to the issue of delegation. Although it is true that Congress or any other branch may never surrender one of its constitutional powers to another branch, it is also true that one branch may enlist the aid of the other branches in the performance of the former's constitutional duties. Congress, in exercising its legislative power, may leave to the executive the determination when the power is to be used at some future date. Chief Justice Taft compares the flexible tariff with Congress's power to regulate interstate commerce. Congress created the Interstate Commerce Commission (ICC) to set "just and reasonable rates" for railroad service. Congress merely lays down the general rule and allows the ICC to make specific rates. Such commissions are constantly in session, are exclusively concerned with the subject matter, and can alter rates to suit ever-changing conditions. Chief Justice Taft dismisses the argument that the principle of delegation has never before been applied to the taxing power. Taft states that as long as Congress has passed a law that sets forth an "intelligible principle" to guide the actions of the president, "such legislative action is not a forbidden delegation of legislative power."

Chief Justice Taft then addresses the second challenge to the Tariff Act, which asserts that the taxing power may not be used for a purpose other than to raise revenue. The real purpose of the Act, according to the company, is to protect American industries from foreign competition. Taft states that regardless of the wisdom of protectionism, it has never been doubted that Congress may encourage the growth of American industries by protecting domestic production. The second act passed by the First Congress was the first tariff law. Section 1 of that act mentions "the encouragement and protection of manufactures" as one of its purposes. Because many of the members of the First Congress were also delegates to the Constitutional Convention, great weight must be given to their interpretations of the powers of Congress under the Constitution. Taft concludes that as long as one of the motives of the law is to secure revenue for the benefit of the general government, the existence of other motives does not make the law unconstitutional.

SIGNIFICANCE OF THE CASE Delegation of legislative authority has long been accepted in the regulation of interstate commerce. Congress enacts a law setting forth the general purposes and then authorizes an agency of the executive branch to "fill in the details" of the legislation. This principle is the foundation of modern administrative government, which has become increasingly important since the New Deal. Without delegation the national government would be unable to regulate railroads, securities, nuclear power, and telecommunications just to name a few activities. The significance of *J. W. Hampton, Jr. & Co.* is that it extends the delegation of legislative authority to the field of taxation.

J. W. Hampton, Jr. & Co. also reaffirmed the principle set forth in *McCray v. United States* that the Supreme Court will not question any ulterior motives Congress may have when enacting legislation. Congress has frequently used the commerce power as a pretext for regulating activities indirectly what it may not regulate directly. Likewise, Congress may use its taxing power as a pretext for regulating activities not generally within its delegated powers. For example, Congress may not directly regulate illegally-manufactured liquor. However, it may impose a tax on liquor. Then, failure to pay the tax is a federal offense enforceable by agents of the Internal Revenue Service. However, as a reading of some of the related cases indicates, the Court will not always be blind to hidden uses of the taxing power. Generally, the Court is ready to give the Congress the benefit of the doubt when exercising one of its delegated powers.

QUESTIONS FOR DISCUSSION

(1)   Do you think Chief Justice Taft's status as a former president had anything to do with his decision? How so?

(2)   Chief Justice Taft believes that delegation of law-making authority in such instances just makes good common sense. Do you agree or disagree? Why?

(3)   Think of some other examples of how the taxing power might be used as a pretext for some hidden purpose.

RELATED CASES   *McCRAY V. UNITED STATES*, 195 U.S. 27 (1904); *United States v. Doremus*, 249 U.S. 86 (1919); *BAILEY V. DREXEL FURNITURE CO.*, 259 U.S. 20 (1922); and *UNITED STATES V. BUTLER*, 297 U.S. 1 (1936).

UNITED STATES V. BUTLER
297 U.S. 1 (1936)

BACKGROUND   During the Great Depression farm prices were so low that farmers often could not sell their crops for what it cost to produce them. A major reason for this was that overproduction had created a greater supply than demand. In 1933 Congress passed the Agriculture Adjustment Act (AAA) which was designed to raise prices on farm commodities. The plan was to reduce production to drive up prices. A key feature of the AAA was a processing tax. The tax, as it applied to cotton, worked like this: The secretary of agriculture would determine the ideal price of cotton based on the price and purchasing power of farmers during the period 1909 to 1914, the "Golden Age" of agriculture. Then, the secretary would subtract the current market price of cotton from the ideal price and the difference was the tax levied on the first processor of the cotton. For example, if the ideal price was $0.12 per pound and the current market price was $0.08 per pound, the tax rate would be $0.04 per pound. The revenue raised by the tax was to be used to make rental and benefit payments to farmers who voluntarily agreed to reduce their production of cotton. In other words, the tax revenue was used to pay farmers not to grow cotton. The decline in production would cause the price of cotton to increase until it reached the ideal price of $0.12 per pound. To get the program started, Congress appropriated $100 million, which was to be repaid from the tax revenue collected. Butler, a receiver of the Hoosac Mills Corporation, refused to pay the tax on the grounds that it was unconstitutional. Another issue, not considered by the Supreme Court, involved the question whether the law was also an unconstitutional delegation of authority to the secretary of agriculture.

CONSTITUTIONAL ISSUE

Whether the processing tax in question is an unconstitutional attempt to regulate agricultural production, which is a power reserved to the states? YES

MAJORITY OPINION Justice Owen Roberts delivers the opinion of the Court. Justice Roberts first addresses the issue of Butler's standing to challenge the tax. In *Massachusetts v. Mellon*, the Supreme Court ruled that individual taxpayers lacked sufficient financial interest to challenge the constitutionality of programs supported by their tax dollars. However, in this case, the taxing scheme is an "indispensable part in the plan of regulation." In other words, because the tax is merely a means to implement a plan of regulation, the Court is willing to allow Butler to have standing.

In the next part of the opinion, Roberts discusses the "so-called tax." He denies that the Court is using its judicial power to impose its own economic views on the nation. The judicial duty, he maintains, is to place the Constitution next to the challenged law and then "to decide whether the latter squares with the former." In our system of government, he notes, the regulation of agricultural production is a reserved power of the states. The Court cannot allow the Congress to use its taxing power to invade the powers of the states.

Justice Roberts then turns to the question of the scope of the taxing power and notes that two theories have prevailed. The first theory, held by James Madison, limited the taxing power to exercising the enumerated powers of Congress. That is, taxes could only be imposed to implement a power Congress was delegated under the Constitution. The second theory, held by Alexander Hamilton and Justice Joseph Story, asserted that the taxing power was separate from the enumerated powers. Congress could tax to promote the general welfare, but it must be the national welfare. Although Roberts purports to take the Hamilton view, the regulation of agriculture, he declares, is a purely local matter. It is no defense to say that local conditions throughout the country have made agriculture a national concern because that position would allow Congress to invade the rights of the states each time there is a widespread similarity of local conditions.

Finally, Justice Roberts discusses the compulsory aspects of the taxing scheme. Farmers may refuse to limit their crop production, but then they would lose out on the cash benefits. The processors have no choice but to pay the tax. However, Roberts is most concerned with the precedent that would be set by upholding the law. If this tax were upheld, there would be no limit to what Congress could regulate merely by disguising the regulation as a tax. The framers placed a barrier on the powers of the national government, but approval of this tax would destroy that barrier.

OTHER OPINIONS Justice Harlan Fiske Stone delivers a dissenting opinion. Justice Stone begins his opinion with a lecture to the majority on judicial restraint. He states that the only real check on the abuse of judicial power is the Court's own sense of self-restraint. Justice Stone then proceeds to discuss the merits of the case.

First, he notes (and the majority does not deny) that the tax is within the power of Congress to levy. If Congress had levied the tax independently of the benefit payments to farmers, none would deny its constitutionality. Second, he points out that an exercise of the taxing power is no less an exercise of that power merely because Congress designates some part of the revenue earned to a particular program. Third, he denies that there is any coercion involved in the program because farmers stand to gain financially from their participation. As far as the processors are concerned, all taxes are coercive and therefore coercion is not an argument against imposing them. Finally, he scolds the majority for its logic. Farmers are asked to reduce production in return for the cash payments. But Congress often places conditions on the receipt of money. In the Morrill Act, for example, Congress gave states grants to establish land-grant colleges. Is it unreasonable, Stone asks, to require the state to use the grant for the purpose for which it was intended?

SIGNIFICANCE OF THE CASE   *United States v. Butler* was one in a series of cases, including *Schechter Poultry Corp. v. United States*, *Panama Refining Co. v. Ryan*, and *Carter v. Carter Coal Company*, in which the "nine old men" of the Supreme Court invalidated key parts of Franklin D. Roosevelt's New Deal program. The Court was accused by its critics of being obstructionists who were trying to frustrate the plans for economic recovery by clinging to outdated economic and political theories. The Court's reliance on the outmoded theory of "dual federalism" is such an example. The Court rather naively ignores the fact that falling agricultural prices were a worldwide, not local, problem. *Butler* is also famous for Justice Roberts's passage describing the judicial role. The Court merely places the Constitution and the challenged law side by side, and determines if one squares with the other. This position, called the mechanical school of jurisprudence, denies that a judge's personal views enter into his decisions. As noted, critics of the *Butler* decision charged the majority with doing exactly that.

QUESTIONS FOR DISCUSSION

(1)   Do you agree with the majority that farm production is purely a local concern? Why or why not?

(2)   Do you believe government should be involved in securing higher prices for farm products?

(3)   A program may be perfectly reasonable but still unconstitutional. How does *Butler* illustrate this statement?

(4)   Discuss some other ways Congress might use its taxing power to regulate areas reserved to the states. What are the checks on congressional abuse of the taxing power?

RELATED CASES   *McCULLOCH V. MARYLAND*, 4 Wheaton 316 (1819); *McCRAY V. UNITED STATES*, 195 U.S. 27 (1904); *United States v. Doremus*, 249 U.S. 86 (1919); *BAILEY V. DREXEL FURNITURE CO.*, 259 U.S. 20 (1922); *Panama Refining Co. v. Ryan*, 293 U.S. 388 (1935); *Schecter Poultry Corp. v. United States*, 295 U.S. 495 (1935); *United States v. Constantine*, 296 U.S. 287 (1935); and *Carter v. Carter Coal Company*, 298 U.S. 238 (1936).

SOUTH DAKOTA V. DOLE
483 U.S. 203 (1987)

BACKGROUND   South Dakota brought suit in federal court challenging the statute that allowed the secretary of transportation to withhold 5 percent of a state's federal highway funds if the state's drinking age was below twenty-one. South Dakota allowed the sale of 3.2 percent beer to those age nineteen or older.

CONSTITUTIONAL ISSUE

Whether Congress may, under the spending clause, condition receipt of national funds not on compliance with a federal statute or regulation but on modification of state laws in an area typically controlled by states? YES

MAJORITY OPINION   Chief Justice William Rehnquist delivers the opinion of the Court. Under the Spending Clause, Congress has the power to condition receipt of federal money on compliance with federal statutes or regulations. In prior decisions, the Court has established an analytical framework for examining questions about the spending power of Congress. First, the power must be exercised for "the general welfare," and substantial deference should be given to Congress in determining what qualifies to meet this standard. Second, any conditions imposed must be clear, both in expression and in consequences. Third, the conditions must further the federal interest in the project or program. Fourth, there must not be any other constitutional provisions that bar the grant.

In the instant case, the statutory provisions and the consequences are plainly stated and not open to any misinterpretation. The law is designed to serve the general welfare—save lives—and is directly related to the main purpose of highway fund expenditures—safe interstate travel. Although South Dakota contends that the fourth element prohibits the indirect achievement of goals that Congress cannot do directly, that is not an accurate interpretation. Instead, it means that Congress cannot compel states to engage in activities that are unconstitutional. Here, "Were South Dakota to succumb to the blandishments offered by Congress and raise its drinking age to 21, the State's action in so doing would not violate the constitutional rights of anyone." It is true that congressional power to impose conditions could be coercive under some conditions, but withholding only 5 percent of the funds does not qualify as compulsion because this is not a major penalty.

OTHER OPINIONS   Justice William Brennan dissents on the basis that establishing the minimum age for purchasing liquor is solely the prerogative of the states under the Twenty-First Amendment, and Congress cannot circumvent this or seek to abridge this by setting conditions on receipt of federal funds.

Justice Sandra Day O'Connor also dissents. Without question, Congress has a general right to attach conditions to the receipt of funds to further a federal interest, but the conditions must be reasonably related to the program's purpose. Congress is not entitled to insist on conditions that force a state to alter other areas of its social or economic life because of some attenuated or tangential relationship to the federal program.

The crux of the question is whether the spending requirement is a condition on a grant or a regulation. This supposed condition is, in fact, a regulation determining who shall be able to consume liquor. This is a regulation that falls squarely within the states' powers under the Twenty-First Amendment and is an unconstitutional exercise of governmental power. This is a government of enumerated powers, and Congress cannot act under the guise of the "general welfare clause" to do by guile what it cannot do directly and in the process invade the states' prerogatives.

SIGNIFICANCE OF THE CASE Grants-in-aid exemplify federalism in action and illustrate intergovernmental dependency and networking. Congress has frequently engaged in the carrot-stick approach to "persuade" states to follow its policy decisions. *South Dakota v. Dole* confirms that Congress may not only use this approach regarding compliance with federal statutes and regulations, but also to "encourage" states to bring their own statutes into compliance, even in areas generally regarded as primarily the province of the states.

QUESTIONS FOR DISCUSSION

(1) What should be the line between permissible and impermissible conditions on federal grants? Why?

(2) Does the Twenty-First Amendment state that matters relating to liquor sales and consumption are reserved to the states? What is the source of that interpretation?

(3) In trying to resolve the balancing line between national powers and the states' reserved powers, what factors should be considered? What tests has the Court established?

RELATED CASES *UNITED STATES V. BUTLER*, 297 U.S. 1 (1936); *Steward Machine Co. v. Davis*, 301 U.S. 548 (1937); *Oklahoma v. Civil Service Comm'n*, 330 U.S. 127 (1947); *California Retail Liquor Dealers Assn. v. Midcal Aluminum, Inc.*, 445 U.S. 97 (1980); *Fullilove v. Klutznick*, 448 U.S. 448 (1980).

6

FREEDOM
OF RELIGION

INTRODUCTION

The First Amendment contains two clauses that deal with religion: the Establishment Clause and the Free Exercise Clause. Although it is difficult to separate the two clauses, they have different purposes. The Establishment Clause was intended to maintain a separation of church and state, whereas the Free Exercise Clause was designed to prevent government interference with religious liberty.

The meaning of the establishment of religion has sparked considerable debate. One interpretation is that the Establishment Clause forbids the creation of an official or state-sponsored religion. Supporters of this view argue that if government treats all religions equally, no violation of the separation of church and state has occurred. Even a policy that benefits religion, such as tax exemptions, is constitutional because all religions receive the benefit. A second interpretation of the Establishment Clause holds that the First Amendment creates a "wall of separation" between church and state. This theory asserts that when religion and politics are mixed, both become corrupted. According to this view, the framers of the Constitution intended to minimize government involvement in religious affairs and vice versa. At various times in our nation's history each of the two theories has commanded a majority of the Supreme Court.

The Free Exercise Clause is the second guarantee of religious liberty. Most people accept that the purpose of the Clause is to prohibit government from interfering with a person's religious beliefs. A major problem has been differentiating between religious beliefs that are sacrosanct and religious practices that are not. Frequently the line where a belief ends and the right to act on that belief begins is not a clear one. A further complication occurs when the Free Exercise Clause conflicts with the Establishment Clause. Suppose, for example, the government chooses to exempt Quakers from military combat because of their pacifism. Some might argue that such an exemption is justified because forcing a person to violate his religious beliefs interferes with freedom of religion. Conversely, it could be argued that the government is showing favoritism to the Quaker religion by granting an exemption other religious adherents do not receive.

In the following essay we examine some problems associated with the Establishment and Free Exercise Clauses. It should come as no surprise that the two clauses have generated a considerable amount of litigation before the Supreme Court. As we survey the cases, the reader might want to consider how the two clauses are related and whether they are inherently contradictory.

The Establishment Clause

The United States is a nation whose people are predominantly Christian. Because of our democratic commitment to majority rule, many people believe that laws and customs should reflect the views and wishes of the majority. To that end, these people see nothing wrong in permitting religious practices acceptable to the majority. Although it is unfortunate if religious minorities are offended, in a democratic society it is the will of the majority that prevails.

Litigants who challenge practices alleged to be violations of the Establishment Clause tend to be atheists, members of non-Christian religions, or civil libertarians. Atheists, of course, want to eliminate completely any reference to God or support for religion. Atheists do not complain that one religion, for example Christianity, is receiving preferential treatment so much as they protest believers being preferred over nonbelievers. The second group, non-Christian religious members, does object to what it believes is preferential treatment of the Christian majority. Finally, civil libertarians oppose the establishment of religion on principle. The Constitution's framers, in their view, wisely concluded that differences over religious beliefs are highly divisive in a society. Therefore, government should follow a policy of strict neutrality to avoid the problems resulting from religious differences.

Two examples will illustrate the conflict between the will of the majority and rights of a minority. Many cities and towns erect displays with religious themes on public property at Christmas. Non-Christians argue that such displays, especially if at taxpayer expense, are violations of the Establishment Clause because they favor the Christian religion over other religions. However, in *Lynch v. Donnelly* (1984), the Supreme Court held a city could erect a creche as part of a Christmas display without violating the Establishment Clause. The second example involves the practice of many state legislatures of having a chaplain offer a prayer at the beginning of the legislative day. In *Marsh v. Chambers* (1983), the Court also ruled that this practice did not violate the Establishment Clause.

Although the erection of nativity scenes and legislative prayers have raised establishment questions, education is by far the most litigated area of the Establishment Clause. Religion and schools have raised two distinct establishment issues: the extent of public aid to religiously affiliated schools and religious practices, especially prayer, in the public schools. Therefore, the remainder of our discussion focuses on schools and religion under the Establishment Clause.

In the last two decades there has been a proliferation of religious-affiliated private schools in the United States. However, until this growth the Catholic Church operated the largest private school system in America. The danger, then, was that the issue of aid to parochial schools would become a Protestant-Catholic issue. Undoubtedly, the Supreme Court was aware of this situation when it first confronted the issue of aid to religious schools in *Everson v. Board of Education* (1947). A New Jersey statute provided reimbursement to parents who sent their children to school on city buses instead of on traditional school buses. The state reimbursed the parents of children attending parochial schools the same as parents whose children attended the public schools. Justice Hugo Black, in a decision that strongly affirmed the wall of separation between church and state nevertheless upheld the New Jersey statute. The Court ruled that the religious schools themselves benefited only indirectly from the reimbursement program. The primary recipients were the parents and their children. The state has an interest in seeing that children are transported to and from school safely. Parents of children in parochial schools are entitled to receive the same benefits as other parents whose taxes support the public schools. The Court found that when the benefit to the religious school is only indirect, there is no violation of the Establishment Clause.

After *Everson* the Supreme Court had to review numerous statutes involving state aid to religious schools. In *Lemon v. Kurtzman* (1971), the Court held that a state could not provide salary supplements for teachers and certain instructional materials without violating the Establishment Clause. In *Lemon* the Court also devised its famous "three-prong test" for establishment violations. To pass the test, a law must have a secular legislative purpose, it may neither advance nor inhibit religion, and it must avoid excessive entanglement between church and state. The Court found the laws challenged in *Lemon* to cause excessive entanglement between the state and the schools.

The Supreme Court has applied the *Lemon* test on numerous occasions sometimes approving and sometimes disapproving state aid to religious schools. In *Meek v. Pittenger* (1973) the Court held that states could provide textbooks that cover secular subjects, such as science and mathematics, to religious schools. State support for diagnostic tests was upheld in *Wolman v. Walter* (1977). In 1983, in *MUELLER V. ALLEN*, the Court upheld a Minnesota law that permitted parents to deduct expenses related to their children's elementary and secondary education on their state income tax returns. The Court upheld the statute, although the law clearly favored those parents who sent their children to sectarian, rather than public, schools. Finally, the Court has been careful to distinguish between elementary and secondary education and higher education. Generally the Court has been more supportive of aid to religiously-affiliated colleges because college students are less susceptible to the religious indoctrination associated with education in the primary and secondary schools.

State support for religion has not been limited to financial aid for sectarian schools. Even more controversial have been attempts by states to introduce religion into the schools. One such attempt was contested in *McCollum v. Board of Education* (1948). Public schools in Champaign, Illinois, permitted school children to receive religious instructions during school hours and on school premises. The instructors were chosen by the individual religions and were not paid by the state. The religious instruction required the permission of a student's parents. The Supreme Court ruled that the program violated the Establishment Clause primarily because state facilities were used to teach the classes. Four years later in *ZORACH V. CLAUSON* (1952) the Court distinguished *McCollum.* New York law permitted public school children to be released from school for one hour per week to receive religious instructions. Children were released from school if written permission from their parents was received. Unlike *McCollum*, the instruction occurred away from the schools and the Court found this to be sufficient to pass constitutional muster.

A more direct attempt to introduce religion into the public schools has centered on prayer in school. In *ENGEL V. VITALE* (1962), the Supreme Court was asked whether requiring school children to recite a prayer composed by the New York State Board of Regents violated the Establishment Clause. The Regents had composed a nonsectarian prayer that was to be recited in every class each day. Justice Hugo Black, writing for the majority, held that governmental bodies have no business composing official prayers to be recited. The Court found the prayer to be an unconstitutional endorsement of religion by government. The next year, in *ABINGTON SCHOOL DISTRICT V. SCHEMPP* (1963), the Court ruled that a Pennsylvania law that required the reading of ten verses of the Bible was also constitutionally infirm. In wording that foreshadowed the *Lemon* test, the majority observed that a law that promotes or inhibits religion violates the Establishment Clause.

Since *ENGEL* and *SCHEMPP*, there have been other attempts to introduce religion into public schools. A Kentucky law that required the posting of the Ten Commandments in the public school classrooms of the state was held unconstitutional in *Stone v. Graham* (1980). An Alabama law that authorized a one-minute period of silence for prayer or quiet meditation was struck down in *Wallace v. Jaffree* (1985). State attempts to include the study of creationism, the biblical account of creation, have been equally unsuccessful. When Arkansas attempted to ban the teaching of evolution, a theory contradictory to creationism, in the state's public schools the Supreme Court ruled the law unconstitutional in *Epperson v. Arkansas* (1968). More recently, in *EDWARDS V. AGUILLARD* (1987), the Court struck down a Louisiana law that required the teaching of creationism whenever the theory of evolution is taught.

Extensive coverage of every establishment question is beyond the scope of this introduction and this book. However, the cases covered, especially those dealing with prayer in public school, illustrate different facets of an extremely complex question. Undoubtedly, there will be even more difficult questions of what is an establishment of religion in the future.

The Free Exercise Clause

Throughout history governments have been guilty of persecuting religious minorities. Whether we are discussing Rome under Nero or modern Iran, people have used the power of the state to oppress religious minorities. Nor is religious persecution limited to tyrannical states. The framers of the Constitution were aware of the "tyranny of the majority" that may exist in a democratic society. It was to ensure that the government never became an instrument of religious oppression that the framers placed the Free Exercise Clause in the Constitution.

As previously noted, it is difficult to determine where the line between religious beliefs and actions based on those beliefs is drawn. In one sense it is worthless to say that a person may believe something if he or she is not permitted to act on those beliefs. Conversely, government cannot permit a person to do something in the name of religion that another person would be forbidden by law to do. The Supreme Court was faced with this dilemma in *Reynolds v. United States* (1879). Polygamy, the practice of having more than one wife at a time, was a tenet of the Mormon religion. The Court had to decide whether a ban on polygamy and punishment for its practice were permissible under the First Amendment. In upholding the ban on polygamy, the Court was careful to distinguish between action and belief. Although the First Amendment would not permit a person to be punished for believing in polygamy, when a person took action based on a belief, that action might be punished. The Court noted that if a religious group wished to practice human sacrifice as part of its religious service, the First Amendment would afford the group no defense against murder charges.

The *Reynolds* case poses the fundamental question of free exercise: When should a person or group be exempted from a general law that interferes with a religious belief? In *Minersville School District v. Gobitis* (1940), the constitutionality of Pennsylvania's flag salute law was challenged by members of the Jehovah's Witness religion. Members of this sect interpret the Bible's admonition about worshipping graven images literally. Therefore, its members refused to salute the flag as required by the law. The Supreme Court upheld the law 8–1 despite a biting dissent by Justice Harlan Fiske Stone. However, just three years later, in a surprisingly quick reversal, the Court ruled in *WEST VIRGINIA STATE BOARD OF EDUCATION V. BARNETTE* (1943) that an identical West Virginia law was unconstitutional. At issue was whether a state could force a person to attest to something that was not in his or her heart. Justice Robert Jackson, writing for the majority, stated, "If there is any fixed star in our constitutional constellation, it is that no official, high or petty, can prescribe what shall be orthodox in politics, nationalism, religion, or other matters of opinion or force citizens to confess by word or act their faith therein."

Although one might agree with the great principles of religious tolerance proclaimed in *BARNETTE*, the dilemma posed by its logic is troublesome. Never was it asserted that the flag salute law was enacted to persecute or even embarrass members of the Jehovah's Witness faith. Its primary purpose was to promote patriotism and instill nationalism in school children. That the law put Witnesses in an embarrassing dilemma was only an indirect effect of the law and not its motive for passage. A similar situation arose when a South Carolina law denied unemployment benefits to persons who were otherwise able, but refused to work because of religious reasons. Sherbert, a Seventh Day Adventist, was discharged from her job for refusing to work Saturdays, that religion's Sabbath. She refused to accept other jobs offered to her because they also required her to work Saturdays. The South Carolina Employment Security Commission held that she was otherwise able to work and denied unemployment benefits to her. In *SHERBERT V. VERNER* (1963), the Supreme Court held the state's interest was not compelling enough to overcome Sherbert's First Amendment claim of abridgement of the free exercise of religion.

The question whether a religious group should be exempt from a general law was also raised in *WISCONSIN V. YODER* (1972). Like all states, Wisconsin law requires children to attend school until a certain age or, in this case, tenth grade. Yoder, a member of the Old Order Amish, refused to send his children beyond the eighth grade and was fined under the law. The Supreme Court held that because of the life-style of the Amish the usually compelling reasons for compulsory school attendance were insufficient to overcome the religious liberty issue. The Court ruled that sincerely-held religious beliefs justified an exemption for the Amish in this case.

In *BARNETTE, SHERBERT*, and *YODER*, the Supreme Court confirmed that it is willing to grant a religious group an exemption from a general law when such an exemption is based on sincerely held religious beliefs. However, the Court leaves itself open to criticisms of favoritism when it applies its criteria for exemption unevenly. Two cases illustrate the problem. In *Goldman v. Weinberger* (1986) Goldman, a Jewish Air Force officer, was ordered not to wear a yarmulke while in uniform and on duty. Goldman challenged the regulation as an abridgement of his free exercise of religion. However, the Supreme Court ruled against him, stressing the military's need for uniformity and obedience to authority. In *Employment Division, Department of Human Resources of Oregon v. Smith* (1990), two members of the Native American Church were discharged from their positions for use of peyote. The two men, Alfred Smith and Galen Black, asserted that the peyote was used in religious ceremonies. When the two applied for unemployment benefits they were denied because their dismissals were due to misconduct. In upholding the state's denial of benefits the Court held that previous cases, such as *SHERBERT*, did not involve illegal activities. The Court found the state's interest in eliminating drug use in society sufficient to overcome Smith's and Black's claim to religious liberty.

Conclusion

Nothing touches the heart and soul of a person more deeply than sincerely held religious beliefs. The framers of the Constitution wished to create a nation in which every individual was free to believe or not believe, and worship or not worship as dictated by his or her own conscience. The framers also understood that throughout history millions of people have been killed in the name of religion. They feared a situation in which people in the majority would employ the power of government to promote their own religion, or worse, to persecute the religion of others. For these reasons the framers placed the Establishment and Free Exercise Clauses in the Constitution.

In *ZORACH V. CLAUSON*, Justice William O. Douglas, writing for the majority, stated, "We are a religious people whose institutions presuppose a Supreme Being." His observation illustrates the tension inherent in the religion clauses. We are a religious people, and many in our society wish our institutions to reflect religious values. However, government, in its effort to guarantee religious liberty, cannot become a weapon against religion. Maintaining governmental neutrality while avoiding governmental favoritism is the unenviable task faced by the Supreme Court each time it hears a freedom-of-religion case.

MUELLER V. ALLEN
463 U.S. 388 (1983)

BACKGROUND Minnesota taxpayers were allowed to deduct expenses incurred in providing "tuition, textbooks, and transportation" for their children attending sectarian elementary and secondary schools on their state income tax returns. A suit was brought in federal court challenging the statute on the grounds that it violated the Establishment Clause of the Constitution.

CONSTITUTIONAL ISSUE

Whether a state statute that permits tax deductions that primarily benefit the parents of students in sectarian schools is in violation of the Establishment Clause of the Constitution? NO

MAJORITY OPINION Justice William Rehnquist (later Chief Justice) writes the opinion for the 5–4 majority. Interpreting and applying the deceptively simple provisions of the Establishment Clause, "Congress shall make no law respecting the establishment of religion," presents difficult and troublesome problems for the Court. This provision has not been interpreted to mean that if any benefit, however tenuous, accrues to institutions with religious affiliation that the program must be rejected.

In *Lemon v. Kurtzman*, the Court established a three-prong test that is to be applied in such cases. First, the statute must have a "secular legislative purpose." Here, the state's purpose is to ensure the educated populace needed for political and economic health of the community through helping to defray educational costs. The Court should defer to the legislature and not "attribute unconstitutional motives to the states, particularly when a plausible secular purpose may be ascertained from the face of the statute." Second, the primary effect of the statute "must be one that neither advances nor inhibits religion." Legislatures have great latitude in creating tax statutes, and this deduction is only one of many including one for charitable contributions and is available to all parents, not just those whose children attend secular schools. Third, the statute must not foster "an excessive entanglement with religion." The state's involvement here is merely an administrative function of disallowing the deductions for instructional materials that are used to teach religious tenets. This is not an instance when the aid is flowing directly to the schools themselves but instead allows parents to offset the costs of education by reducing their tax payment.

OTHER OPINIONS Justice Thurgood Marshall—joined by Justices William Brennan, Harry Blackmun, and John Paul Stevens—enters a dissenting opinion. This statute subsidizes religion in violation of the Establishment Clause. Of the more than 900,000 students enrolled in all Minnesota elementary and secondary schools in 1978 to 1979, the parents of 815,000 were ineligible to receive the tax credit because their children were in public schools that did not charge tuition or money for textbooks, whereas 95 percent of the remaining 90,000 students were enrolled in sectarian schools that did charge tuition. The effect of the statute is to allow indirect assistance to sectarian schools. No steps were taken to guarantee the "separation between secular and religious educational functions" that the Court has demanded in prior cases. Even the deduction for textbooks covers books selected by the schools, not the state, and is likely to forward the school's religious teachings. "What is of controlling significance is not the form but the 'substantive impact' of the financial aid," and this statute is "little more than a subsidy of tuition masquerading as a subsidy of general educational expenses."

SIGNIFICANCE OF THE CASE *Mueller v. Allen* is an example of the Court's ongoing struggle to determine exactly what constitutes establishment of religion under the First Amendment. The question is how impermeable is the wall between church and state. It is a thorny question and has arisen in several contexts, separate and apart from public school issues, as for example, a crèche on municipal property at Christmas (*Lynch v. Donnelly*), polygamy as a religious tenet (*Reynolds v. United States*), and the availability of unemployment benefits to those whose religious beliefs cause either a voluntary or involuntary loss of job (*Hobbie v. Unemployment Appeals Commission*).

QUESTIONS FOR DISCUSSION

(1)   Do you agree with the majority or the dissenters about the effect of the statute? Why?

(2)   What constitutes a religion? Should the Court be in the position of determining what constitutes sincerely-held religious beliefs? If not the Court, then whom?

(3)   Substantial numbers of people in this country are not adherents of the mainstream Catholic, Jewish, or Protestant faiths. What is the role of government in guaranteeing that the tenets of the major religions are not favored over others? Where are the lines to be drawn?

RELATED CASES *Reynolds v. United States*, 8 Otto 145 (1878); *Everson v. Board of Education*, 330 U.S. 1 (1947); *Lemon v. Kurtzman*, 403 U.S. 602 (1971); *Committee for Public Education and Religious Liberty v. Nyquist*, 413 U.S. 756 (1973); *Meek v. Pittenger*, 421 U.S. 349 (1975); *Wolman v. Walter*, 433 U.S. 229 (1977); *Lynch v. Donnelly*, 465 U.S. 668 (1984); and *Hobbie v. Unemployment Appeals Comm'n of Florida*, 480 U.S. 136 (1987).

ZORACH V. CLAUSON
343 U.S. 306 (1952)

BACKGROUND New York law permitted public school students to leave school grounds one hour per week to attend religious instruction or devotional exercises. Students were released on the written request of their parents. The churches were required to make weekly reports of the students who were released but failed to attend the religious classes. However, there was no indication that nonattending students were punished for truancy. Appellant Zorach, whose children attended public school in New York City, challenged the constitutionality of this so-called released-time program on the grounds that it violated both the Free Exercise and Establishment Clauses of the First Amendment. Zorach argued that the weight and influence of the state are behind the program, that public school teachers police it, that regular school activity is suspended, and that without school support the program would fail.

CONSTITUTIONAL ISSUE

Whether a released-time program that allows students to attend off-premises religious instruction during regular school hours violates either the Free Exercise Clause or the Establishment Clause of the First Amendment? NO

MAJORITY OPINION Justice William O. Douglas delivers the opinion of the Court. Justice Douglas immediately distinguishes this case from *McCollum v. Board of Education*. In *McCollum*, the Court ruled that religious instruction held on the school grounds violated the Establishment Clause. In this case there is no instruction on the school premises, and there is no expenditure of public funds. Justice Douglas dismisses the notion that the law violates the Free Exercise Clause almost out of hand. He concedes, however, that if coercion could be shown, a wholly different case would be presented. But the trial court deemed the issue of coercion to be irrelevant to the question of constitutionality and precluded Zorach from producing evidence of coercion at trial.

Justice Douglas then turns to the question whether the program violates the Establishment Clause. He asserts that the First Amendment does not require a wall of separation in every and all respects. To do so would mean that churches would have to pay taxes, churches could not receive police and fire protection from the state, prayers at the opening of legislative sessions would be prohibited, and other manifestations of religious life would be forbidden. Our institutions and law, he writes, presuppose the existence of a Supreme Being. It is not unconstitutional for the state to cooperate with religious authorities by adjusting the schedule of public events to meet sectarian needs. Government must only remain neutral toward religion; it does not have to be hostile toward it. Otherwise, government would favor the nonbeliever over the believer. In *McCollum*, classrooms were being used, and the force of the public school was used to promote religious instruction. Such is not the case here.

OTHER OPINIONS Justices Hugo Black, Felix Frankfurter, and Robert Jackson write separate dissenting opinions.

Justice Black maintains there is no difference between this case and *McCollum*. The majority in *McCollum* made it clear that the use of classrooms was not the only factor that made the program unconstitutional. The *McCollum* Court held that the program aided sectarian groups by helping to provide them with students for their religious classes through the use of the state's compulsory school attendance laws. Black says that the real issue is whether the state can use its compulsory school attendance laws to "get students presumably too unenthusiastic to go unless moved by the pressure of this state machinery." In Black's opinion, any use of coercion to help or hinder any or all religions violates the First Amendment. Black believes that participation should be a matter of free choice and that the majority's opinion favors believers over nonbelievers.

Justice Frankfurter maintains that, contrary to the majority's contention, the schools are not just adjusting their schedules to accommodate religious groups. The schools do not suspend operation, and formalized religious instruction is substituted for some other school activity. Frankfurter criticizes the majority for dismissing the presence of coercion when the trial court refused to allow appellants to show it. Frankfurter notes that the unwillingness of advocates of released-time programs to support early dismissal from school for all children "betrays a surprising want of confidence in the inherent power of the various faiths to draw children to outside sectarian classes."

Justice Jackson states that the law forces the child to surrender part of his time for secular education and then "releases" it back to him on the condition that he use it only for religious instruction. Schooling is suspended so that the nonreleased children will not get ahead of the released ones. In Jackson's view, the school becomes a temporary jail for the child who won't go to church. Finally, Jackson accuses the majority of confusing objection to compulsion with objection to religion.

SIGNIFICANCE OF THE CASE   *McCollum* set off a fierce debate in the nation over the place of religion in the public schools that continues even today. Some constitutional scholars accuse the Court of buckling under to public pressure in *Zorach*. As the dissenters show, the fact that religious instruction occurred on school grounds in *McCollum* and off-campus in *Zorach* is a flimsy constitutional distinction.

Zorach is also important because it foreshadows some of the other issues of church and state, such as prayer in legislative assemblies, that will confront the Court in later cases.

QUESTIONS FOR DISCUSSION

(1)   Is the on-campus/off-campus distinction a significant difference between *McCollum* and *Zorach*?
(2)   If children were free to choose between early dismissal and religious instruction, which option would most children likely choose?
(3)   Are the churches using the public schools to recruit children for their religious classes?
(4)   What kind of coercion is possible to pressure children to attend these religious classes?

RELATED CASES   *Everson v. Board of Education*, 330 U.S. 1 (1947); *McCollum v. Board of Education*, 333 U.S. 203 (1948); *ZORACH V. CLAUSON*, 343 U.S. 306 (1952); *ENGEL V. VITALE*, 370 U.S. 421 (1962); *ABINGTON SCHOOL DISTRICT V. SCHEMPP*, 374 U.S. 203 (1963); *Widmar v. Vincent*, 454 U.S. 263 (1981); and *Marsh v. Chambers*, 463 U.S. 783 (1983).

ENGEL V. VITALE
370 U.S. 421 (1962)

BACKGROUND   The New York State Board of Regents drafted the following prayer: "Almighty God, we acknowledge our dependence upon Thee, and we beg Thy blessings upon us, our parents, our teachers, and our Country." The Board of Education of Union Free School District No. 9, New Hyde Park, New York, adopted the prayer, which was recited every day in class in the presence of a teacher. Those students who did not wish to participate could either remain silent or be excused from the classroom. Parents of ten students maintained that the prayer was contrary to the religious beliefs and practices of both themselves and their children.

CONSTITUTIONAL ISSUE

Whether mandating the use of a nondenominational prayer in public school classrooms violates the First Amendment Establishment Clause? YES

MAJORITY OPINION Justice Hugo Black delivers the majority opinion for the Court. The First Amendment's prohibition against enacting any law "respecting an establishment of religion" is applicable to the states through the Fourteenth Amendment. Indubitably, prayer is a religious activity. Involvement of the state is also clear as a government body (the Board of Regents) drafted the prayer and another government entity (the local Board of Education) mandated its use in a government-sponsored activity, compulsory education in public schools.

The early colonists and Founding Fathers knew from "bitter personal experience" the problems arising from a state-sponsored religion, the very thing that had prompted many of the immigrants to come to the New World. They had seen that government involvement with religion led to the degradation of both, to the "hatred, disrespect, and even contempt of those who held contrary beliefs," and to religious persecutions.

They were well aware of the danger posed to freedom when government was involved in the religious realm, and they drafted the First Amendment to preclude such activity. "Religion is too personal, too sacred, too holy, to permit its 'unhallowed perversion' by a civil magistrate." The First Amendment was not written to destroy religion but instead to ensure that it flourishes, unshackled by government. The Regent's Prayer, although not seeking to establish one religion over another, does endorse religious activity by government and therefore violates the First Amendment.

OTHER OPINIONS Justice William O. Douglas enters a concurring opinion in which he stated his opposition to government financing of any religious activities. Government cannot constitutionally finance religious activities in light of the First Amendment even though the system "is presently honeycombed with such financing." Prayers led by public officials in whatever capacity—military or congressional chaplains or public school teachers—involve a "captive audience" and are a divisive influence in communities. The First Amendment is designed to ensure government neutrality in religious matters. Neutrality is not tantamount to hostility to religion and, in fact, it encourages religious activity.

Justice Potter Stewart enters a dissenting opinion. Religion is, and has been, an integral aspect of American life; it motivated many of the colonists to flee from state-established religions to seek the right to follow their own religious practices. Governmental bodies often open their deliberations with invocations, and numerous presidents have invoked the protection and help of God. The actions of the public school officials in writing this prayer and mandating its use do not establish an "official religion" in violation of the Constitution but instead merely recognize and follow the "deeply entrenched and highly cherished spiritual traditions of our Nation."

SIGNIFICANCE OF THE CASE This decision set off a firestorm of criticism and calumny that has rarely been matched in the long history of the Court. It is one of the most misunderstood and most often deplored cases in the Court's annals. Although many have heard of the case, few have read it to understand that the Court is protecting the rights of all to practice religious freedom, free from government interference or restraint. Instead, critics have proclaimed it as antireligious and destructive of the nation's moral fiber. Mere mention of the case often raises people's hackles, and it is often invoked to generate hostility toward other religions, the Court, and liberals.

QUESTIONS FOR DISCUSSION

(1)   If you were a member of a denomination other than mainstream Protestant or Catholic, would you find requiring your children to participate in this prayer offensive? Why? What if the prayer was Hindu, Islamic or some other religion, and you were a fundamentalist Christian?

(2)   Do you agree that the nation should recognize the religious beliefs of its citizens? Why? What should be the proper balance in protecting the religious beliefs of the minority?

(3)   Why do you agree or disagree with Douglas's position that government should be absolutely neutral regarding all religious activity?

(4)   How do you think classmates would react to a student who refused to participate in the prayer or who asked to be excused? Do you think there would be adverse consequences for the child? If so, is there an element of informal or societal coercion to conform? Is that a problem? Why?

RELATED CASES   *McCollum v. Board of Education*, 333 U.S. 203 (1948); *ZORACH V. CLAUSON*, 343 U.S. 306 (1952); *ABINGTON SCHOOL DISTRICT V. SCHEMPP*, 374 U.S. 203 (1963); and *Wallace v. Jaffree*, 472 U.S. 38 (1985).

ABINGTON SCHOOL DISTRICT V. SCHEMPP
374 U.S. 203 (1963)

BACKGROUND   Pennsylvania law required that ten verses from the Bible be read at the beginning of each school day in the state's public schools. Each day at Abington Senior High the ten verses were read, without comment, by a student who selected both the verses and the version of the Bible to be used. Following the reading of the verses, the students recited, in unison, the Lord's Prayer. The exercises were broadcast into the classrooms over the school's intercom system. In schools in the district without an intercom system, the exercises were either led by the teacher or a student chosen by the teacher. Students could be excused from the exercise on the written request of their parents or guardians.

Edward L. Schempp, a Unitarian, sought an injunction on behalf of his children, Roger and Donna, to prohibit the enforcement of the Bible-reading law as a violation of the First and Fourteenth Amendments. At the trial, the two children testified that certain religious doctrines mentioned in the Bible readings were contrary to their religious beliefs. Edward Schempp testified that he considered having his children excused from the exercises but feared that they would be labeled "oddballs" or "atheists" or "Communists" by other students and teachers. He also noted that forcing his children to stand out in the hall during the exercises would appear as if they were being punished. In striking down the Pennsylvania law, the trial court noted that both school attendance and the Bible reading were required by law. The trial court also noted that the law required the use of the "Holy Bible," a Christian document. In a companion case, *Murray v. Curlett*, the petitioner, Madalyn Murray [O'Hair] challenged a similar practice in the Baltimore schools on behalf of her son, William. The Murrays were avowed atheists.

CONSTITUTIONAL ISSUE

Whether a state law requiring the reading of ten verses from the Bible at the beginning of the public school day violates the Establishment and Free Exercise Clauses of the First Amendment? YES

MAJORITY OPINION   Justice Tom Clark delivers the opinion of the Court. Justice Clark begins the opinion by acknowledging the importance of religion in our national life and in our history. He notes that many state legislatures open their sessions with a prayer and that there are opportunities for worship provided for those in the military. However, Justice Clark also points out that we are also a religiously diverse nation with many sects within the majority Christian religion. Because of our nation's religious diversity the First Amendment forbids Congress from passing laws "respecting an establishment of religion." Justice Clark reaffirms the Court's position that states are also forbidden to "establish" a religion by the Due Process Clause of the Fourteenth Amendment. Next, Clark rejects the view that the Establishment Clause only forbids government from favoring one religion over another. Citing other cases that have interpreted the Establishment Clause, Clark concludes that the purpose of the Clause is to separate church and state. The Establishment Clause requires the state to be neutral but not hostile toward religion. Its purpose is to avoid the fusing of religious and governmental functions.

Justice Clark restates a test employed by the Court in earlier cases involving the Establishment Clause. The "neutrality" required by the Clause means that when a state enacts a law with religious overtones there first must be a secular or nonreligious legislative purpose for the law. Second, if the primary effect of the law is either to advance or to inhibit religion, the law is forbidden by the Constitution. Applying these two principles to the Pennsylvania law, Justice Clark says that the Court agrees with the trial court that the morning exercise is a religious ceremony without any secular legislative purpose. Even if it could be argued that the Bible reading promoted secular legislative purposes, such as the study of the Bible's literary value, the Court found that argument to be inconsistent with the policy of excusing children from the exercise. Justice Clark rejects the idea that the Court's ruling, in effect, establishes a "religion of secularism." He also rejects the argument that the majority's right to "free exercise of religion" is abridged. Free exercise, Clark notes, does not mean that the majority can use the coercive power of the state to force its religious beliefs on a minority. Justice Clark concludes the majority opinion by reaffirming that the Court's decision does not forbid the study of the Bible in a class on comparative religions or in a literature class. But because the Pennsylvania law under challenge clearly has no secular legislative purpose and was clearly enacted to advance religion, the law is unconstitutional.

OTHER OPINIONS   Justice William Brennan writes the major concurring opinion. Brennan argues that the purpose of the Establishment Clause is to keep church and state from becoming interdependent. One school of thought says that the Establishment Clause was designed only to prevent the national government from creating an official state religion. Others, like Brennan, argue that the reach of the Clause is much broader. But

Brennan notes that the debate over what the framers intended the Clause to mean is irrelevant to the question of school prayer for several reasons. First, both sides can produce evidence to support their view so the historical evidence is largely inconclusive. Second, because public schools were nonexistent in the eighteenth century, it is impossible to tell if the framers intended the Establishment Clause to forbid public school prayer. Third, the United States is much more religiously diverse today than in the eighteenth century. Finally, the First Amendment guarantees that parents have the right to choose the nature and content of their children's religious instruction. Brennan concludes his opinion by giving examples of what the majority's decision does not forbid. It does not, in Brennan's opinion, prohibit prayer in legislative assemblies, tax exemptions for religious institutions, or activities that have ceased to have religious significance, such as the use of the phrase, "In God We Trust," on U.S. coins.

Justice Potter Stewart writes the only dissenting opinion. Stewart believes that the records in both cases are inadequate to support the majority's decision. For example, he says that the Court has no evidence to support the assertion that the Schempp children would have been branded "outcasts" or "oddballs" for their refusal to participate in the exercises. Nor does Stewart think that the minor role teachers play in the exercise constitutes state support for religion. Stewart believes that the majority opinion ignores what he sees as an inherent tension between the Establishment and Free Exercise Clauses. If the government, for example, provides chaplains for soldiers it is establishing a religion; if it refuses to provide chaplains the government is preventing soldiers from practicing their religion. Justice Stewart believes that the majority's decision infringes on the rights of those who do wish to pray in school. Decisions about how to accommodate the various religious groups in our society are best left to local school boards and not the Supreme Court.

SIGNIFICANCE OF THE CASE   *Abington School District* set off a storm of protest unlike any other case since *Brown v. Board of Education* in 1954. The Court was attacked as "godless and Communist," and was accused of taking God out of the public schools. However, all attempts to reverse the decision have failed. Efforts to overrule the decision by the constitutional amendment process have been unsuccessful. In 1985, the Court, in *Wallace v. Jaffree* struck down an Alabama law requiring students to observe a period of prayer or silent meditation.

QUESTIONS FOR DISCUSSION

(1)   Does the fact that teachers led the students in the exercises where there was no intercom system make a difference to you? Why or why not?

(2)   Do you think the Court's decision favors nonbelievers over believers?

(3)   Were the Schempp children's fears of becoming social outcasts real or imagined?

RELATED CASES   *Everson v. Board of Education*, 330 U.S. 1 (1947); *ENGEL V. VITALE*, 370 U.S. 421 (1962); *Murray v. Curlett*, 374 U.S. 203 (1963); *Stone v. Graham*, 449 U.S. 39 (1980); and *Wallace v. Jaffree*, 472 U.S. 38 (1985).

EDWARDS V. AGUILLARD
482 U.S. 578 (1987)

BACKGROUND The Louisiana Legislature passed a law, The Balanced Treatment for Creation-Science and Evolution-Science in Public School Instruction Act, that mandated that if evolution was taught as a scientific theory in public elementary and secondary schools, creation-science must also be taught. The law did not require that either be included in the school curriculum. Both the district court on a motion for summary judgment and the court of appeals held that the statute violated the Establishment Clause of the First Amendment.

CONSTITUTIONAL ISSUE

Whether the Establishment Clause of the First Amendment is violated by a statute that requires that creationism be taught in public schools whenever the theory of evolution is taught? YES

MAJORITY OPINION Justice William Brennan writes the opinion of the Court. The Establishment Clause of the First Amendment prohibits the enactment of any law "respecting an establishment of religion." In *Lemon v. Kurtzman* (1971), the Court created a three-pronged test to determine the validity of statutes involving the Establishment Clause. First, the legislature must have adopted the law with a secular purpose. Second, the principal effect of the law must not advance or inhibit religion. Third, it must not result in an excessive entanglement of government with religion. If a statute does not meet all of the three prongs, it must fall.

The Court has been particularly solicitous to ensure that public school class-rooms will not intentionally be used to advance religious views that may conflict with the private beliefs of students and their families. Because children in this age group are particularly impressionable and their attendance at school is compelled by state law, the Court has previously invalidated state laws or regulations that promoted religion in public schools.

Whenever the state enacts a law to serve a religious purpose, it is invalid under *Lemon* whether it advances a specific religious belief or it promotes religion in general, and there is no need to move to the second and third prongs of the test. Here, the stated secular purpose of the law is to promote academic freedom, but both the district court and the court of appeals rejected that stated purpose and found instead that the intended goal was to narrow the science curriculum by decreasing flexibility to supplement the theory of evolution with other theories about the origin of life. The courts based their decision on the legislative history of the act, which indicated that the legislature was clearly motivated by religion.

[T]he Creationism Act is designed either to promote the theory of creation science which embodies a particular religious tenet by requiring that creation science be taught whenever evolution is taught *or* to prohibit the teaching of a scientific theory disfavored by certain religious sects by forbidding the teaching of evolution when creation science is not also taught.

The Establishment Clause forbids either goal, and the statute is constitutionally infirm.

OTHER OPINIONS   Justice Lewis Powell, joined by Justice Sandra Day O'Connor, writes a concurring opinion. The Court should not interfere with the broad discretion given to local and state agencies in the selection of public school curriculum unless the purpose of such a law or regulation is clearly religious. An extensive review of the legislative history of this particular statute clearly indicates its religious purpose. This does not mean that there must be a complete absence of religion from schools but instead that school officials cannot promote one dogma or the interests of any one sect.

Justice Byron White also writes a concurring opinion stating his position that the Supreme Court should defer to the findings of the lower courts, which determined that there was a religious purpose to this statute.

Justice Antonin Scalia writes a dissenting opinion in which Chief Justice William Rehnquist joined. The Louisiana legislators who passed this bill were sworn to support the Constitution, and they very carefully considered the Establishment Clause problems in pondering the adoption of the legislation. The Louisiana supreme court has never considered the matter nor has there been a full evidentiary hearing on the matter (the district court had granted summary judgment). Therefore, "we can only guess at its meaning" and can only speculate as to the true motives of the legislators who proposed and supported the bill. It is impossible for legislators to be totally divorced from their religious beliefs in casting their votes, and the Establishment Clause does not demand that religiously active men and women be deprived of their right to participate in the political process.

In the past, the Court has typically found a secular purpose for questionable statutes, and the Court should deviate from that pattern only if the Louisiana law had *no* secular purpose. The mere fact that a law "happens to coincide or harmonize with the tenets of some or all religions" does not mean it is unconstitutional. The Court should defer to the states and not attribute unconstitutional motives to them. In this instance, creationism can be approached as a collection of scientific data that can be taught without religious content, and then students could receive all the evidence about the origins of life.

The Court's decisions "have made such a maze of the Establishment Clause that even the most conscientious government officials can only guess what motives will be held unconstitutional" and "determining the subjective intent of legislators is a perilous enterprise." The Court needs to strive for clarity and predictability and to that end, the *Lemon* purpose test should be abandoned.

SIGNIFICANCE OF THE CASE   Few matters raise such a frenzy among the general public as the issue of religion in public schools. The Court has drawn fire for trying to ensure neutrality toward religion in the public schools. The cases are based on the Court's recognition that this country is highly diverse in terms of religions and that school-age children are particularly vulnerable and impressionable. The Court, in trying to preserve the rights of all religious groups including smaller, less popular sects, has antagonized nearly everyone.

Since *Scopes v. State* (1927), the rhetoric over teaching evolution and creationism has been fiery and often intolerant, with zealots on both sides of the issue. The more recent battles have often been cast in terms of repression of religion by either Christian fundamentalists or by secular humanists. *EDWARDS V. AGUILLARD* temporarily stilled this particular argument, but it certainly does not close debate on the matter or preclude other Establishment Clause cases in the context of public schools.

QUESTIONS FOR DISCUSSION

(1)   What factors would you consider in resolving the issues relating to the Establishment Clause in the context of public schools?

(2)   Should the Court, in examining freedom-of-religion cases, be more concerned about the rights of the majority or of the minority?

(3)   Justice Scalia urged the abandonment of the *Lemon* three-pronged test. If that were done, what analytical framework would you recommend for cases involving the Establishment Clause?

RELATED CASES *Scopes v. State*, 154 Tenn. 105, 289 S.W. 363 (1927); *ABINGTON SCHOOL DISTRICT V. SCHEMPP*, 374 U.S. 203 (1963); *Epperson v. Arkansas*, 393 U.S. 97 (1968); *Lemon v. Kurtzman*, 403 U.S. 602 (1971); *Stone v. Graham*, 449 U.S. 39 (1980); and *Wallace v. Jaffree*, 472 U.S. 38 (1985).

WEST VIRGINIA STATE BOARD OF EDUCATION V. BARNETTE
319 U.S. 624 (1943)

BACKGROUND West Virginia enacted a law that required the teachers and pupils of the state's schools to salute the American flag. A student's refusal was deemed an act of insubordination punishable by expulsion. The expelled child was considered "unlawfully absent" from school, which could lead to delinquency charges and, ultimately, sentencing to a reformatory. Similarly, the child's parents were subject to a $50 fine and thirty days in jail for the child's absence.

Appellee Barnette, a Jehovah's Witness, successfully challenged the law before a three-judge federal district court. Barnette claimed that saluting the flag was tantamount to worshiping a "graven image," which the Bible expressly forbids. Barnette maintained that the law interfered with the freedom of religion guaranteed by the First Amendment. The lower court's ruling was unusual in that just three years before in *Minersville School District v. Gobitis*, the Supreme Court had upheld the Pennsylvania flag salute law. However, some of the justices in the *Gobitis* majority had indicated second thoughts about the ruling. Thus, the lower court's ruling in this case paved the way for reconsideration by the Supreme Court.

CONSTITUTIONAL ISSUE

Whether a state law requiring compulsory flag saluting violates the First Amendment's guarantee of religious liberty made applicable to the states through the Due Process Clause of the Fourteenth Amendment? YES

MAJORITY OPINION Justice Robert Jackson delivers the opinion of the Court. Justice Jackson starts by noting what the case does not involve. First, the freedom asserted in this case does not collide with the rights of anyone else. The conflict is purely between the state's authority and the rights of the individual. Second, the state does not claim that the pledge requirement has any legitimate educational value. Third, the state does not deny that appellee's behavior in refusing to salute the flag was peaceful and orderly. Finally, the state does not contend that refusal to salute the flag creates a clear and present danger that it has a right to prevent.

The purpose of the law, Jackson asserts, is clearly to compel students to declare a belief. The issue, then, is whether the Bill of Rights allows a state to compel a person to utter what is not in his or her mind. Although some might argue that the Pledge of Allegiance is inoffensive, Jackson demonstrates otherwise. For example, some might object to the use of the word "republic" instead of "democracy." Others might debate whether there is "liberty and justice for all" in the United States. Jackson also points out that numerous constitutional scholars, and not just the Witnesses, have criticized compulsory flag saluting and the *Gobitis* decision.

In light of the recentness of the *Gobitis* decision, Justice Jackson believes it is necessary to explain why the Court is reversing itself. *Gobitis* was based on the premise that the decision whether to require compulsory flag saluting should be left to legislative discretion. But, Jackson insists, the purpose of the Bill of Rights is to place certain subjects beyond the reach of legislative majorities. A second justification in *Gobitis* was the need to promote national unity. To this Jackson replies that coercion can never be the basis for patriotism and that mildly coercive measures become progressively harsher as opposition to them mounts. Finally, in a famous and often quoted passage, Justice Jackson asserts that, "If there is any fixed star in our constitutional constellation, it is that no official, high or petty, can prescribe what shall be orthodox in politics, nationalism, religion, or other matters of opinion or force citizens to confess by word or act their faith therein."

OTHER OPINIONS   Justice Hugo Black, writing for himself and Justice William O. Douglas, concurs. In light of their earlier agreement with the *Gobitis* decision, these justices thought it necessary to explain their position. In *Gobitis*, the issue was whether the Constitution should serve as a barrier to the legitimate exercise of legislative power. Although they reaffirm their position as sound, they maintain that its application in this case is wrong. Patriotism cannot be compelled at the expense of religious freedom. In any case, Black observes that "Love of country must spring from willing hearts and free minds."

Justice Frank Murphy also concurs. He maintains that flag saluting is not essential to the maintenance of an orderly society. In addition, he does not believe that the benefits obtained from compulsory flag saluting justify this invasion of religious liberty.

Justice Felix Frankfurter writes the only dissenting opinion. Frankfurter's primary concern is the majority's lack of judicial restraint. No one denies that instilling patriotism in children is a legitimate end of government nor that requiring recitation of the Pledge of Allegiance is an appropriate means to that end. The question of the wisdom of the policy or whether there should be exceptions to it on religious grounds are decisions to be made by legislators, not judges. Frankfurter claims that if his views alone controlled his decision, he would gladly join the majority's libertarian position. But, he maintains, a judge's duty is not to write his private notions of policy into the Constitution.

Frankfurter cannot accept the majority's conclusion that the law violates Barnette's religious freedom. Neither Jefferson, Madison, nor any of the other defenders of religious freedom argued that the First Amendment grants religious minorities exceptional immunity from general laws. To do so would permit religious minorities to veto general laws. "The validity of secular laws," writes Frankfurter, "cannot be measured by their conformity to religious beliefs." To value the religious beliefs of dissenters is to make the conscience of a minority more sacred than the conscience of the majority. Frankfurter insists that the Jehovah's Witnesses are free to send their children to schools of their own choosing, as have other religious minorities, if they object to the law. He also argues that no one has been punished because the action here is an injunction. He claims that the majority's use of the clear and present danger test is a distortion of that doctrine. Lastly, he contends that on the previous occasions when the question of compulsory flag salute laws came before the Court they were always upheld, sometimes unanimously.

SIGNIFICANCE OF THE CASE The *Barnette* case is considered a classic civil liberties case because, as Justice Jackson observes, it pits the authority of the government against the rights of the individual. Although the Court only briefly alludes to the Nazi-like salute that accompanied the recitation of the Pledge, the irony of fighting a war against totalitarianism while upholding the flag salute law could not have been lost on the justices. Jackson's opinion is considered the definitive defense of individual liberty against state encroachment. Frankfurter's eloquent plea for judicial restraint is also considered a classic interpretation of that doctrine.

QUESTIONS FOR DISCUSSION

(1) Would it have made any difference if Barnette had objected to the law on nonreligious grounds?
(2) Is Justice Frankfurter correct when he asserts Barnette can elude the law by sending his children to private school?
(3) Does the Court's ruling prohibit compulsory flag saluting in all instances?
(4) What, if any, influence do you think World War II had on the Court's decision?

RELATED CASES *Stromberg v. California*, 283 U.S. 359 (1931); *Hamilton v. Regents of the University of California*, 293 U.S. 245 (1934); *Minersville School District v. Gobitis*, 310 U.S. 586 (1940); *Jones v. Opelika*, 316 U.S. 584 (1942); and *TEXAS V. JOHNSON*, 491 U.S. 397 (1989).

SHERBERT V. VERNER
374 U.S. 398 (1963)

BACKGROUND Sherbert joined the Seventh Day Adventist Church in 1957. At the time she was employed as a textile mill worker in Spartanburg, South Carolina. In 1959 her employer changed from a five-day to a six-day work week. Because Seventh Day Adventists observe Saturday as the Sabbath, she refused to work on Saturdays and was discharged. She tried to find employment in other mills, but all had converted to the six-day work week. She also sought employment in other industries but was still unable to find a suitable position without Saturday work. She then applied for unemployment benefits, but they were denied because the South Carolina Employment Security Commission ruled that she had, without good cause, refused to accept available work when offered. The South Carolina supreme court upheld the Commission's ruling against Sherbert's claim that the denial of benefits abridged the Free Exercise Clause of the First Amendment.

CONSTITUTIONAL ISSUE

Whether a state law denying unemployment benefits to a person who refuses to work on Saturdays on religious grounds abridges the Free Exercise Clause of the First Amendment? YES

MAJORITY OPINION   Justice William Brennan delivers the opinion of the Court. Justice Brennan explains the test that is applied to Free Exercise claims. To prevail, South Carolina must show either that its unemployment law, as applied to Sherbert, does not abridge her freedom of religion, or that the state's interest is compelling enough to override any adverse effect on the free exercise of religion.

Justice Brennan concedes that the denial of unemployment benefits places only an indirect burden on Sherbert's free exercise of religion. He also concedes that there are no criminal penalties in this case that inhibit the free exercise of religion. Nevertheless, he claims that if the effect of a law impedes the observance of a religion or invidiously discriminates against a religion, the law may be invalid even though the effect is only indirect. In this case, the ruling of the Employment Security Commission forces Sherbert to choose between following her beliefs and forfeiting benefits, and abandoning her beliefs to accept work. The state has, in effect, conditioned the availability of unemployment benefits on Sherbert's willingness to violate a cardinal principle of her religion. Such a law penalizes the free exercise of religion. Justice Brennan also notes that under South Carolina law, no person, even in a state of national emergency, can be forced to work on Sundays if he or she is conscientiously opposed to Sunday work.

Justice Brennan then turns to the question whether the state's interests are compelling enough to overcome the adverse effect on freedom of religion. South Carolina asserts that unscrupulous claimants might fraudulently file claims based on refusal to work on Saturdays. Brennan replies that this point was never raised before the South Carolina supreme court, but even if it had been the state produced no evidence to support this contention. The second argument made by the state is that payment of these benefits would both dilute available funds for other unemployed persons and make it difficult to schedule Saturday work. Even if this is true, Brennan counters, the state would still have to show that it has chosen the means that pose the least interference with First Amendment rights. By contrast, in *Braunfeld v. Brown*, the Court upheld a Sunday Closing Law on the grounds that the state could achieve its goal of providing a uniform day of rest only by declaring Sunday to be that day.

In the remainder of the opinion Justice Brennan denies that the Court's ruling is fostering the establishment of the Seventh Day Adventist religion. The ruling, he says, merely reflects the traditional requirement of government neutrality in the treatment of religion. Brennan is also quick to point out that the Court is not declaring a general constitutional right to unemployment benefits to all persons whose religious beliefs are the source of their unemployment. The narrow ruling applies only to the facts of this case.

OTHER OPINIONS   Justices William O. Douglas and Potter Stewart write concurring opinions while Justice John Marshall Harlan II writes a dissent.

Justice Douglas's main objection is that the law, in his view, forces Sherbert to conform with the principles of the majority to obtain benefits. To Douglas, this invades an area of privacy the state is forbidden to enter.

Justice Stewart agrees with the decision but is unable to join the majority opinion. Stewart maintains that claims under the Free Exercise Clause invariably conflict with the Establishment Clause and that the majority has skirted this issue. He calls the Court's Establishment Clause jurisprudence "wooden" and therefore opposes it. For example, if the Court were to follow its Establishment, precedents South Carolina would actually be *required* to deny Sherbert benefits. Because her claim is based on religious grounds, an exemption based on religious reasons actually favors the Seventh Day Adventist religion. By its ruling, the majority is forcing South Carolina to violate the Establishment Clause. No one denies that the state could deny Sherbert benefits if she merely wanted to watch Saturday television. Yet, the Court's ruling forces South Carolina to accept a religious reason for not working on Saturdays but not a secular one.

Nor does Stewart believe the majority's opinion squares with *Braunfeld*. In *Braunfeld*, a Jewish merchant who operated his business on Sundays was subject to criminal penalties. This, Stewart asserts, is a much more direct effect on Braunfeld's freedom of religion than a denial of temporary benefits is to Sherbert.

Justice John Marshall Harlan II, in dissent, believes that close examination of the law sheds light on the Court's flawed reasoning. The purpose of the unemployment act is to provide benefits for periods of "involuntary unemployment" during periods when "work is unavailable." South Carolina has consistently held that benefits can be denied to persons who refuse work for personal reasons. The fact that Sherbert's reason stems from her religious beliefs is irrelevant. The majority is forcing South Carolina to make an exception to its general law for religious reasons. Harlan also maintains that the majority's statement notwithstanding, the Court has effectively overruled *Braunfeld*. The decision will also force the state, and eventually the courts, to scrutinize the sincerity of religious beliefs of individuals.

SIGNIFICANCE OF THE CASE   *Sherbert v. Verner* is a difficult case because both sides are partially correct. Justice Harlan may be right in arguing that all personal reasons, of which religion is but one, are unacceptable justifications for refusing Saturday work. Conversely, perhaps South Carolina should have been more sensitive to our nation's religious diversity in writing its unemployment law. *Sherbert* again raises the debate over what is a right and what is a privilege in our modern welfare society.

QUESTIONS FOR DISCUSSION

(1)   Could a state require recipients of unemployment benefits to refrain from using alcohol while receiving benefits?

(2)   Does the fact that South Carolina exempted people from forced work on Sundays affect your view of this case? Why or why not?

(3)   Sherbert and one other person were the only Seventh Day Adventists unable to find suitable work in the Spartanburg area. Does this affect your view of the case?

RELATED CASES   *Prince v. Massachusetts*, 321 U.S. 158 (1944); *Speiser v. Randall*, 357 U.S. 513 (1958); *Braunfeld v. Brown*, 366 U.S. 599 (1961); *WISCONSIN V. YODER*, 406 U.S. 205 (1972); and *Goldman v. Weinberger*, 475 U.S. 503 (1986).

WISCONSIN V. YODER
406 U.S. 205 (1972)

BACKGROUND   Wisconsin law requires children to attend school until age sixteen. Jonas Yoder, a member of the Old Order Amish religion, refused to send his children to public school beyond the eighth grade. Yoder maintained that the values taught in high school were at variance with Amish values. Yoder was fined $5 under the law, which carried a maximum fine of $50 and up to three months in jail. Yoder argued that compliance with the law could result in his censure by the Amish church community and endanger his and his children's chances for salvation. The state did not question the sincerity of his beliefs. The Wisconsin appellate court sustained Yoder's conviction, but the Wisconsin supreme court reversed on the grounds that the law, as applied to Yoder, violated the Free Exercise Clause of the First Amendment.

CONSTITUTIONAL ISSUE

Whether a compulsory school attendance law, as applied to members of the Old Order Amish religion, violates the Free Exercise Clause of the First Amendment? YES

MAJORITY OPINION   Chief Justice Warren Burger delivers the opinion of the Court. Chief Justice Burger briefly outlines some of the history and tenets of the Old Order Amish religion. He notes that church members de-emphasize material success, reject the competitive spirit, and generally insulate themselves from the modern world. They emphasize physical labor and a sense of community within the church. Although the Amish accept the need for education through the eighth grade so that they can read the Bible and deal with outsiders, they believe high school emphasizes values such as competitiveness, worldly success, and peer pressure. These values tend to draw children away from the Amish community, which in turn threatens the survival of the church.

The chief justice then turns to the appropriate analysis for resolving this case. The Court must balance the state's interests against the religious interests of the Amish. For the state to prevail, it must show either that its law does not interfere with the free exercise of religion or that the state's interest is important enough to overcome any effect on the free exercise of religion. As to the first question, Chief Justice Burger relies on expert witnesses who testified at trial that the values and programs of the modern secondary school are at variance with Amish values. The chief justice concludes that the compulsory school attendance law compels the Amish to perform acts at odds with the fundamental principles of their religion. Burger also notes that the expert witnesses testified that enforcement of the law would gravely endanger and maybe even destroy Amish religious beliefs.

Wisconsin argues that its interest in public education is sufficiently great to overcome any interference with religious freedom. The state concedes that beliefs are absolute, but actions may be regulated by nondiscriminatory general laws. The chief justice agrees that the Court has ruled that some religious activities, such as polygamy, may be regulated despite interference with sincerely held religious beliefs. Still, that does not mean that all action based on religious beliefs falls outside the protection of the First Amendment.

Wisconsin poses two arguments for its claim that its interests should prevail. First, quoting Thomas Jefferson, the state argues that education is needed to prepare children to participate in the political life of the community. However, the chief justice remarks that Jefferson did not necessarily have a particular age or level of education in mind. An eighth-grade education may very well be sufficient to accomplish this democratic goal. Indeed, six states require children to attend school only through the eighth grade.

The second argument is that education is needed to prepare children to be self-reliant so that they will not become a burden on society. The chief justice counters that additional education may be essential to function in modern society, but that is not necessarily true for Amish children living within the Amish community. Besides, Amish education does not end with the eighth grade. Amish children learn vocational skills, such as farming, which prepare them to be self-sufficient. There is little evidence to suggest that Amish children are likely to become wards of the state given their sense of community. Finally, the state offered no evidence that an additional two years of education would significantly reduce the risk of an Amish child later becoming a burden to society.

The chief justice concludes the majority opinion by observing that sincerely held religious beliefs coupled with the traditional right of parents to oversee the education of their children outweigh the two rationales offered by the state. The interrelationship between the Amish way of life and their religious beliefs is an additional factor in the decision. Finally, the threat posed by two additional years of formal education to the survival of the Old Order Amish religion is yet another factor in the Court's holding that the law, as applied to the Amish, violates the First Amendment.

OTHER OPINIONS   Justices Potter Stewart and Byron White write concurring opinions while Justice William O. Douglas dissents in part.

Justice Stewart writes to emphasize that it is the religious beliefs of the parents, not their children, at issue in this case. It was Jonas Yoder who was fined and his religious beliefs that were in question. The Court had no reason to believe that the children were being denied the right to attend high school against their wishes. The record shows that the wishes of the children and their parents were the same in this matter.

Justice White writes to underscore that neither this case nor *Pierce v. Society of Sisters* holds that parents may replace state educational requirements with their own personal views of knowledge. *Pierce* merely held that as long as religious schools comply with state education requirements, parents may not be denied the right to send their children to private religious schools. For White, the state fails to prove that Amish children who might leave their faith will be unable to function in the modern world.

Justice Douglas dissents because of what he views as the majority's failure to include the interests of the children. The majority's analysis balances the state's interests against the religious interests of the parents but not their children's. Douglas concedes that Frieda Yoder testified that high school attendance was against her religious beliefs, but the children of the other respondents did not. Douglas maintains that a fourteen-year-old is mature enough to participate in making decisions about his or her future. The Court's analysis precludes any consideration that the child's interests may conflict with the religious preference of the parent. Justice Douglas notes that the defection rate among Amish children is between 30 to 50 percent in some communities. To allow a child's life to be "stunted and deformed" because of his or her parents' religious beliefs alone denies the child the protection of the Bill of Rights.

SIGNIFICANCE OF THE CASE *Wisconsin v. Yoder* raises the difficult question of which actions grounded on religious beliefs should be exempt from general state laws. A nondiscriminatory law that adversely impacts the beliefs of a religious group does not necessarily violate the First Amendment. In the famous case of *Reynolds v. United States* the Court ruled that although Mormons are free to believe in polygamy, actions taken on that belief are punishable under general, nondiscriminatory laws. The classic example is that a religious group that practices human sacrifice is not exempt from laws against murder, even if the victim consents to be sacrificed. The state's interest in protecting human life outweighs the religious interests involved. The Court must engage in a "balancing of interests" analysis, and *Yoder* is an excellent example of such analysis.

QUESTIONS FOR DISCUSSION

(1)   How receptive do you think the majority would have been to a similar claim made by devil worshippers?

(2)   Does the Court's analysis require it to determine which religions are *bona fide* religions?

(3)   Do you agree with Justice Douglas's view that an unwilling Amish child may be "forever barred from entry into the new and amazing world of diversity that we have today"?

RELATED CASES *Reynolds v. United States*, 8 Otto 145 (1879); *Meyer v. Nebraska*, 262 U.S. 390 (1923); *Pierce v. Society of Sisters*, 268 U.S. 510 (1925); *WEST VIRGINIA STATE BOARD OF EDUCATION V. BARNETTE*, 319 U.S. 624 (1943); *Prince v. Massachusetts*, 321 U.S. 158 (1944); *SHERBERT V. VERNER*, 374 U.S. 398 (1963); and *Goldman v. Weinberger*, 475 U.S. 503 (1986).

7

FREEDOM
OF SPEECH, PRESS,
AND ASSOCIATION

INTRODUCTION

Certain liberties, such as freedom of religion, are in the Constitution because they are intrinsically the right thing to do. Despite one's personal feeling about a certain religion, most Americans would argue that it is simply wrong to interfere with another's religious beliefs. Consequently, government's guarantee of religious liberty is intrinsically right. However, the First Amendment freedoms discussed in this introduction—speech, press, and association—do not fall into this category. In other words, the protection of speech, press, and association is not defensible solely because it is intrinsically right for government to do so. Freedom of speech and the others are fundamental to a democratic society. It might be possible to have a democracy without religious liberty, but it is inconceivable to have one without freedom of speech, press, and association. Supporters of these freedoms maintain that they are the essential ingredients that make a political system democratic.

As fundamental as these freedoms are to a democratic government, they are not without controversy. It seems to be inherent in human nature to wish to silence those with whom we disagree even to the point of violence. Similarly, it seems to be inherent in the nature of a government to silence its critics. Nor is the desire to silence one's enemies and critics limited to dictatorships. Even democratic governments find it difficult to resist the temptation to suppress those guilty of wrongheadedness. Another truism is that those in power like to stay in power and will use the power of the state to do so.

The framers of the Constitution understood the need to silence one's critics and the use of governmental power to do it. Some of them had been listed as traitors by King

George III. They also understood that the best way to safeguard democracy was to safeguard the right of the citizens to criticize those in power. Only through criticism, discussion, and debate would the truth emerge from what Justice Oliver Wendell Holmes, Jr. called, "the marketplace of ideas."

In this introduction we examine aspects of free speech, press, and association. As with our other introductions, we caution the reader that an exhaustive treatment of these concepts is beyond the scope of this book. We hope that this introduction and the cases that follow provide a good foundation for some understanding of the most cherished freedoms Americans enjoy.

Freedom of Speech

The cases that have come before the Supreme Court dealing with free speech are among the most troublesome the Court hears. The Supreme Court has never held that speech is an absolute, that is, never subject to punishment. Consequently, the Court must decide when speech may or may not be punished. Another problem is that "pure speech" is hardly ever at issue. Usually speech is accompanied by action. Although the speech may be protected, the action may not. The Court must somehow separate the protected behavior from the unprotected behavior. Yet another problem is what to do about so-called symbolic speech. Symbolic speech is the use of means other than pure speech to get an idea across. Finally, free-speech cases tend to involve individuals or groups whose ideas or causes are unpopular with most Americans. This is only logical because people who espouse popular ideas rarely, if ever, need the protection of the First Amendment. In this section we examine all of the preceding themes as we discuss the cases dealing with free speech.

Many free-speech cases involve persons with radical ideas such as Communists or Socialists. These cases spotlight the classic dilemma for democratic governments: Should free speech be afforded to those who advocate violent overthrow of established government? How can a radical wrap himself or herself in the First Amendment while simultaneously advocating the destruction of the government that affords the protection? It is a position difficult to defend and yet, as we have seen, the framers considered the protection of free speech vital to democratic government.

One of the first cases to raise the issue of the radical and free speech was *SCHENCK V. UNITED STATES* (1919). Schenck, a Socialist, mailed leaflets to soldiers who were being drafted to fight in World War I. The leaflets argued that conscription amounted to "involuntary servitude" in violation of the Thirteenth Amendment and urged resistance. Justice Oliver Wendell Holmes, Jr., writing for the majority, sought to balance the individual's freedom with governmental power. Holmes articulated the "clear and present danger" test. Although he conceded that in peacetime Schenck's words would be protected by the First Amendment, speech must be judged in light of the circumstances. If the words bring about a clear and present danger of an evil Congress is empowered to prevent, the speech may be punished. This is so even if the speaker's efforts ultimately prove unsuccessful.

Although Holmes authored the "clear and present danger" test, he often broke with the majority over its application. In *Abrams v. United States*, decided the same year as

SCHENCK, Holmes dissents. Abrams was accused of advocating a general strike of workers in protest of U.S. policy toward Russia. The majority's application of the "bad tendency" test was a break with Holmes's clear and present danger standard. Holmes dissented again in *GITLOW V. NEW YORK* (1925). Benjamin Gitlow was prosecuted under New York's criminal anarchy law. Gitlow published the *Left Wing Manifesto*, which called for a Communist revolution and massive political strikes. Again the majority held that speech that created a "bad tendency" was punishable under the law. The majority held that a government does not have to wait until the revolution has begun to take action to protect itself from overthrow by violence.

Another breed of unpopular orators who have posed problems for the Supreme Court is the street corner orator. As noted earlier, there is a tendency among some to want to silence a person with whom he or she disagrees. A problem created by street corner orators is the heckler's veto. Often in street corner oratory the words of the speaker are upsetting to some in the crowd. To stir the passions of one's listeners is usually the goal of such orators. However, where impassioned speech-making ends and inciting to riot begins is never clear. Does the fact that some in the audience may find the words of the speaker offensive justify silencing the speaker? Should the heckler be permitted to veto the words of the speaker?

The Supreme Court has addressed the problem of audience reaction to a speaker in three landmark cases. In *Chaplinsky v. New Hampshire* (1942), the Court held that a person could be punished for uttering "fighting words," words that would reasonably be expected to provoke another to fight. In *Terminello v. Chicago* (1949), the Court overturned the conviction of a controversial speaker whose speech was causing a near riot outside a rented auditorium. Finally, in *Feiner v. New York* (1951), the Court upheld the conviction of Feiner who had made incendiary remarks about the president, thereby angering his listeners.

One final area of note regarding free speech is that of symbolic speech. Symbolic speech includes activities such as picketing, marching, and displaying symbols or banners to express an idea. The leading case on symbolic speech is *Tinker v. Des Moines Independent Community School District* (1969). Some students, to protest U.S. involvement in Vietnam, decided to wear black armbands to school. The principal, fearing trouble, ordered the students not to wear the armbands and suspended several when they did anyway. The Supreme Court recognized that symbolic speech, although not pure speech, nevertheless was protected under the First Amendment as freedom of expression.

Tinker was followed by numerous other cases that tested the boundaries of free expression. In *United States v. O'Brien* (1968), the Supreme Court rejected draft-card burning as a form of symbolic speech. The Court found the government's interest compelling enough to overcome the usually strict scrutiny afforded free-expression cases. In *Cohen v. California* (1971), the Court ruled that Cohen's right to wear a jacket that read, "Fuck the Draft" was protected under the First Amendment.

Undoubtedly the most controversial form of symbolic speech is flag burning. The Supreme Court was faced with the issue in a 1969 case entitled *Street v. New York*. Street, upset about hearing of the shooting of a black civil rights leader, took an American flag, burned it on the street, and said, "We don't need no damn flag." Street was prosecuted under a New York law that made it a crime to both desecrate and utter derogatory words about the flag. The Supreme Court was able to postpone the issue of flag burning by ruling that it was unclear whether Street had been convicted for the words he uttered or for the act of burning the flag. Because of the uncertainty, Street's conviction was reversed.

The issue of flag desecration continued to come before the Supreme Court during the Vietnam era. In cases such as *Smith v. Goguen* (1974) and *Spence v. Washington* (1974), the Court circumvented the constitutionality of flag burning per se by ruling on the narrowest grounds possible. Finally, the Court confronted the issue head on. In *TEXAS V. JOHNSON* (1989), the Court ruled 5–4 that flag burning is a form of freedom of expression protected by the First Amendment. After *JOHNSON* Congress enacted legislation to protect the flag, but it too was ruled unconstitutional by the Supreme Court. Attempts to protect the flag through the passage of a constitutional amendment have also been unsuccessful.

Freedom of Press

Censorship of the press involves several different facets. For example, one issue is whether government may take action to prevent the publication of certain information or material. This type of action is called prior restraint and has as its objective the prevention of a publication on grounds such as national security. A second form of censorship is the attempt to hold a publication accountable for something that has already been published. If, for example, a publication knowingly prints false and malicious information about a person, it can be punished for libel. Although libel suits are not censorship in the same sense as prior restraint, they can, nevertheless, have a "chilling effect" on freedom of the press. Finally, a special area of censorship deals with the question of obscenity and the First Amendment.

Fortunately, the occurrences of prior restraint have been few in the United States. This is, in part, because of a responsible press and, in part, to the reluctance of the Supreme Court to endorse prior restraint except under the most unusual circumstances. The issue of whether a state could impose prior restraint on a publication came before the Court in *NEAR V. STATE OF MINNESOTA* (1931). A Minnesota law permitted a judge to issue an injunction against publications found to be "malicious, scandalous, and defamatory." Near's publication, *The Saturday Press*, was found to be such a publication, and the trial judge issued a permanent injunction against it. In striking down the Minnesota law, the Supreme Court held that this was not an attempt to punish the newspaper for libelous articles, but a clear attempt to enforce prior government censorship. If *The Saturday Press* printed libelous material it could be sued under the state's existing libel laws. However, any attempt to prevent the publication of information is presumed to be forbidden by the Constitution.

As mentioned, one field in which the Supreme Court is more likely to permit prior restraint is national security. Yet even in cases that involve national security, the Court has ruled that the government bears the heavy burden of showing that national security interests are sufficiently compelling to override First Amendment concerns. In *NEW YORK TIMES CO. V. UNITED STATES* (1971), for example, the Nixon administration sought to enjoin the *Times* and the *Washington Post* from publishing the so-called Pentagon Papers. The Nixon administration argued that publication of the history of America's decision-making policy in Vietnam would, among other things, jeopardize our relations with the countries involved. The Supreme Court held, however, that a broad claim of injury to national security was insufficient to justify prior restraint in this case.

Prior restraint can sometimes be justified on grounds other than national security. One difficult area is when freedom of press conflicts with other constitutional rights. Perhaps the most litigated field is where freedom of press conflicts with the accused's right to a fair and impartial trial. The landmark case is *Sheppard v. Maxwell* (1966) involving the murder trial of a Cleveland physician named Sam Sheppard. In reversing Sheppard's conviction the Court took notice of the circuslike atmosphere that was permitted during the trial. Since *Sheppard*, the Court has ruled on the use of gag orders against the press (*Nebraska Press Association v. Stuart*, 1976), closed preliminary judicial proceedings (*Gannett Co. v. DePasquale*, 1979), and closed trials (*Richmond Newspapers, Inc. v. Virginia*, 1980). In 1981, the Court reversed an earlier case, *Estes v. Texas* (1965), and permitted television coverage of criminal trials in *Chandler v. Florida*. More recently, in *Cable News Network v. Noriega* (1990), the Supreme Court refused to hear a case of prior restraint involving the ousted dictator of Panama, Manuel Noriega. Cable News Network (CNN) had acquired tapes of an interview with Noriega and wished to broadcast them. The trial judge refused to allow the tapes to be shown on the grounds they might prejudice Noriega's impending trial.

Punishment for libel is another area of concern for advocates of a free press. Libel suits seek to penalize, by means of monetary damages, a publication for something it has printed or broadcast. A key issue in libel suits is whether the libeled individual is a public figure. One theory holds that a person who deliberately places himself or herself in the public eye is less entitled to privacy than someone who does not. In *Gertz v. Robert Welch, Inc.* (1974), for example, Gertz was a lawyer involved in a controversial Chicago case. A magazine characterized him as a Communist, and he sued for libel. The Supreme Court held that regardless of how controversial the case was, Gertz was not a public figure. In a similar vein, the Court held in *Time Inc. v. Firestone* (1976) that public interest in the details of a nasty divorce did not make Mrs. Firestone a public figure. More recently, in *Hustler Magazine v. Falwell* (1988), the Court held that a public figure could not sue for emotional distress suffered because of an allegedly libelous publication.

Because of the public figure theory, it is extremely difficult for a public official to win a libel suit. In the landmark decision, *NEW YORK TIMES CO. V. SULLIVAN* (1964), the Supreme Court held that merely false statements about a public official were insufficient to establish libel. The Court ruled that "actual malice" had to be proven to demonstrate libel against a public official. Justice William Brennan, writing for the majority, asserted that freedom of press is designed to ensure that there will be vigorous debate of public issues.

The third and final area in our discussion of free speech concerns obscenity. Although most people might agree that obscenity is not protected under the First Amendment, there is disagreement over defining obscenity. In a famous remark he later regretted making, Justice Potter Stewart succinctly summed up the dilemma. Referring to obscene material in *Jacobellis v. Ohio* (1964), Stewart writes, "But I do know it when I see it." Stewart's statement recognizes that obscenity is subjective and defies attempts to define it.

The difficulty of defining obscenity notwithstanding, the Supreme Court has devised various tests to apply to allegedly obscene material. In *ROTH V. UNITED STATES* (1957), the Court declared that obscenity is definitely not protected by the First Amendment. The Court proceeded to articulate the *ROTH* test. A work could be declared obscene if the average person, applying contemporary community standards, found the work, taken as a whole, appealed to prurient interests. The *ROTH* test immediately raised questions of who the average person was and how contemporary community standards were to be measured.

The Supreme Court made another attempt to devise a workable obscenity test in the celebrated *Fanny Hill Case* (1966). John Cleland's *Fanny Hill: Memoirs of a Woman of Pleasure* is undoubtedly highly erotic. However, it does not contain language that is normally considered vulgar and obscene. When the attorney general of Massachusetts sought to ban the distribution of the book in the state, its publisher challenged the action. The Supreme Court held that to be deemed obscene, a work had to be "utterly without redeeming social importance." Depending on one's viewpoint, *Fanny Hill* set a standard so high (or low) that getting a work declared obscene was virtually impossible.

Because under the *Fanny Hill* test virtually anything could be argued to have "redeeming social importance," the Supreme Court tried again. In 1973 the more conservative Burger Court announced yet another obscenity standard in *MILLER V. CALIFORNIA*. Instead of the "utterly without redeeming social importance" criterion of *Fanny Hill*, the work merely had to "lack serious literary, artistic, political, or scientific value." That this new test was no more workable than the old ones became apparent almost immediately. In *Jenkins v. Georgia* (1973) the Court had to reverse a local jury's finding that a highly acclaimed movie, *Carnal Knowledge*, was obscene. The jury found the nudity in the movie obscene. The Court held that the jury's finding notwithstanding, mere nudity did not make a work obscene.

The same day that *MILLER* was announced the Supreme Court handed down an important decision regulating adult theaters. In *PARIS ADULT THEATRE I V. SLATON* (1973), the Court ruled that a state could regulate the commercial exhibition of obscenity even when it is shown only to consenting adults. *PARIS ADULT THEATRE I* was later followed by *Young v. American Mini Theaters, Inc.* (1976) and *City of Renton v. Playtime Theaters, Inc.* (1986). These cases signaled the Supreme Court's willingness to accept the state's power to regulate the quality of life in the community as a legitimate means of regulating obscenity.

Freedom of Association

Americans believe a person has the right to choose his or her friends. They also believe that a person is known by the company he or she keeps. Therein lies the heart of freedom of association. Not only does a person have the right to choose his or her own friends, but who those friends are, at least for an adult, is no one else's business. Conversely, we are judged by the company we keep and that sometimes results in guilt by association.

Freedom of association is important because a person's associates play an important role in determining his or her personal happiness. Whom we wish to associate with says a great deal about who we are. Freedom of association is also important because it often involves questions of free speech. Just as some human beings wish to silence those with whom they disagree, so too they wish to destroy groups whose ideas, goals, or life-styles are different from their own. In the cases that follow, we examine the attempts by those in government to suppress freedom of association, especially among groups considered radical by many Americans.

In this century there have been two major "Red scares." After World War I and the Russian Revolution, many Americans feared that communism would spread to the United States. As we have already seen, *SCHENCK* and *GITLOW* were products of the first Red scare. Because of the Red scare, the national government and some states passed laws dealing with sedition, criminal syndicalism, and anarchy. In *WHITNEY V. CALIFORNIA* (1927), Charlotte Whitney was charged under California's syndicalism law for participating in a Communist Labor Party convention and attending several of the Party's executive committee meetings. Under this law mere advocacy of the use of violence to effect political change was a crime. The Supreme Court unanimously upheld Whitney's conviction, ruling that a legislative body may use its police powers to suppress potential danger to the existence of the state.

The second Red scare came after World War II. Although the former Soviet Union had been America's ally during the war, its actions in eastern Europe afterward alarmed many Americans. Communist world domination was seen by some as the goal of the former Soviet Union. Congress passed the Smith Act, which made it a federal offense to advocate, knowingly or willfully, the overthrow of government by force or violence. In *DENNIS V. UNITED STATES* (1951), the defendants were charged with conspiracy to organize the Communist Party in the United States. Although Dennis and his codefendants were guilty of no overt acts, the Supreme Court upheld their convictions. The Court disregarded the "clear and present danger" test in favor of the "gravity of the evil" approach to free speech. This theory holds that the more serious the evil—in this case, the overthrow of government—the less protection afforded by the First Amendment. Thus, a street corner orator who poses little threat to society receives more protection from the First Amendment than someone like Dennis. The mere advocacy of the use of violence to overthrow government could be punished by government. Although the Court couched its decision in free-speech terms, Dennis and his codefendants were punished for organizing and belonging to the Communist Party. Their punishment for organizing the Communist Party was a violation of freedom of association.

As mentioned, as a result of the Red scares both the national government and the states passed laws dealing with sedition during this period. *PENNSYLVANIA V. NELSON* (1956) raised the issue whether a federal law supersedes state sedition laws. Nelson, an avowed Communist, was prosecuted and convicted under federal law. He subsequently was prosecuted under Pennsylvania law for sedition against the United States. The Supreme Court ruled that the federal law preempted state laws in the area of sedition. As a result, states were precluded from prosecuting persons for sedition in most cases.

Six years after *DENNIS*, the Supreme Court modified its interpretation of the Smith Act in *Yates v. United States* (1957). A reaction to McCarthyism and a change in the Court's makeup resulted in a more libertarian approach to freedom of association. In *Yates*, the Court distinguished between advocacy of an abstract doctrine and advocacy of action. Mere discussion of the desirability of communism or the overthrow of government by force was different from advocating these actions. Advocacy of communism as an abstract doctrine permits individuals to associate with whom they please and to discuss theories of government. This approach is not as intrusive of freedom of association as was the approach taken in *DENNIS*. With the passage of time and the collapse of Soviet communism, the cases that emerged from the two Red scares seem like relics of the distant past. Yet intolerance of the viewpoints of others is not the product of a single generation or two. Supporters of the First Amendment realize there are still battles to be fought over freedom of speech.

The three remaining cases covered in this section raise the issue of freedom of association and the "witch hunt." After members of subversive organizations had been identified, some individuals were subpoenaed to testify before congressional committees such as the House Un-American Activities Committee (HUAC). A major goal of HUAC was to force known Communists to "name names," that is, to identify or to confirm the identity of other subversives. In *WATKINS V. UNITED STATES* (1957), for example, Watkins was cited for contempt of Congress for refusing to answer questions about other individuals active in the Communist Party. The Supreme Court overturned Watkins's conviction because HUAC had failed to make clear the purpose of its questions. The Court held that congressional committees have no power to "expose for the sake of exposure."

In *NATIONAL ASSOCIATION FOR THE ADVANCEMENT OF COLORED PEO-PLE V. ALABAMA* (1958), the Supreme Court was asked to rule on the constitutionality of Alabama's attempt to require the N.A.A.C.P. to produce its membership list. Among the issues raised was whether the N.A.A.C.P. could assert a right to privacy on behalf of its members. The Court, realizing that public exposure of the N.A.A.C.P.'s membership list would subject its members to reprisals, held that the state's request violated freedom of association.

In the section's last case, *BARENBLATT V. UNITED STATES* (1959), the Supreme Court adopted a balancing approach to freedom of association. Barenblatt refused to answer questions from a congressional committee investigating Communist infiltration into higher education. Instead of relying on the Fifth Amendment, however, Barenblatt invoked the First Amendment. The Court upheld Barenblatt's conviction relying in part on the "gravity of the evil" approach. The Court said that if the government's needs were "compelling" they may be sufficient to overcome an individual's First Amendment rights.

Freedom of association is not limited to Red scares and witch hunts. In recent years another issue has arisen: whether a person has a constitutionally-protected right *not* to associate with others. In 1984 the Supreme Court held in *Roberts v. United States Jaycees* that a state may prohibit an organization from excluding a person on the basis of sex. The Jaycees, a men's civic organization, excluded women from full membership violating a Minnesota antidiscrimination law. The Court's decision led to the removal of similar barriers in organizations like Kiwanis, International. However, the opening of other organizations, such as the Boy Scouts and Little League, has not been without controversy. It is almost certain that the issue of the freedom *not* to associate will appear again.

Conclusion

Freedom of speech, press, and association are vital to a democracy. Essential to democratic theory is the belief in the worth of each individual. It holds that each person is unique and has something to contribute to society. The freedom to express oneself is fundamental to the democratic process. A democracy must permit the free flow of ideas so that a consensus on what truth is can be reached. For a society to be democratic, there simply is no other way.

Freedom of speech, press, and association are part of a larger concept—freedom of expression. Whether it is political or artistic expression, people have a need to communicate their ideas and feelings. Personal expression leads to self-fulfillment. Although freedom of expression is not absolute, maximum freedom is necessary for democracy and personal happiness. The framers of the Bill of Rights understood how important freedom of expression is, and it seems that members of each generation of Americans must learn for themselves just how fundamental it is.

SCHENCK V. UNITED STATES
249 U.S. 47 (1919)

BACKGROUND   Schenck, as general secretary of the Socialist Party, acted on a directive from the Executive Committee to have certain leaflets printed and distributed. These pamphlets urged men being conscripted or drafted for military service during World War I to oppose the draft through such measures as working for the repeal of the Conscription Act, which they argued violated the Thirteenth Amendment, which forbids involuntary servitude. They also stated that every draftee was "little better than a 'convict.'" The leaflets were mailed through the Post Office to men who had been called and accepted for military service. Schenck and another member of the Executive Committee were indicted for violating the Espionage Act of 1917 by participating in a conspiracy "causing and attempting to cause insubordination in the military forces...and to obstruct the recruiting and enlistment service of the United States" and for conspiring to use and actually using the mails for unlawful purposes, that is, the mailing of the leaflets. The government did not argue that Schenck actually interfered with the war effort, which was clearly within congressional authority to prohibit; however, instead the question was whether the pamphlets were attempts to interfere with such efforts.

CONSTITUTIONAL ISSUE

Whether the extraordinary condition of war can convert speech normally protected by the First Amendment into speech that is unprotected? YES

MAJORITY OPINION   Justice Oliver Wendell Holmes authors the unanimous opinion of the Court. He recognizes that the arguments and statements contained in the pamphlet would have been constitutionally protected in other—peaceful—times; however, "the character of every act depends on the circumstances in which it is done." For example, the First Amendment protection of free speech would not give immunity to a person "falsely shouting fire in a theatre and causing a panic" nor would it protect someone "uttering words that may have the effect of force."

Holmes establishes the standard by which speech is to be measured as "whether the words used are used in such circumstances and of such a nature as to create a clear and present danger that they will bring about the substantive evils that Congress has a right to prevent." In the instant case, Congress had the right to protect the sovereignty of the nation through conscription in time of war, and that interest, during wartime, was superior to Schenck's First Amendment rights.

SIGNIFICANCE OF THE CASE   In matters involving the issue of when speech could be suppressed by government, the "clear and present" test became the touchstone for determining constitutionality. The test had three elements: (1) the danger must be clear and immediate; (2) the speaker must have specific intent, that is, the intent to achieve certain criminal effects; and (3) the gravity of evil must be such that there is probability of serious injury to the state. Thus, in balancing the individual's freedom of speech versus public interests, speech that was likely to incite violence or illegal activities could be quashed under the standard enunciated in this case; however, the context of the speech and the proximity of the danger were all important. It remained the landmark case in the area of government repression of speech until *Gitlow v. New York*, but the factors of context and proximity remain inextricable elements of First Amendment jurisprudence.

QUESTIONS FOR DISCUSSION

(1)   What limits would you impose on government suppression of speech in terms of social or internal political matters?

(2)   What limits would you impose on government repression of speech in peacetime on military matters or in foreign affairs? In wartime?

(3)   During the Vietnam conflict, bumper stickers proclaimed "America: Love It or Leave It." How would the people critical of the war have fared under the "clear and present danger?" Is it unpatriotic to criticize the government or its leaders? Even in time of war? Why?

RELATED CASES   *Abrams v. United States*, 250 U.S. 616 (1919); *GITLOW V. NEW YORK*, 268 U.S. 652 (1925); *WHITNEY V. CALIFORNIA*, 274 U.S. 357 (1927); *Chaplinsky v. New Hampshire*, 315 U.S. 568 (1942); *Terminiello v. Chicago*, 337 U.S. 1 (1949); *DENNIS V. UNITED STATES*, 341 U.S. 494 (1951); and *Cohen v. California*, 403 U.S. 15 (1971).

GITLOW V. PEOPLE OF THE STATE OF NEW YORK
268 U.S. 652 (1925)

BACKGROUND   Benjamin Gitlow, a member of the Left Wing Section of the Socialist Party, was indicted and convicted under a New York statute for criminal anarchy. The conviction was based on his role as business manager and member of the board of managers for the group's newsletter, *The Revolutionary Age*, and on his speaking activities on behalf of the Party. Among the publications of the group was *The Left Wing Manifesto*, which advocated the Communist Revolution by militant and revolutionary socialism including mass political strikes. The publication and circulation of the *Manifesto* were the basis of Gitlow's conviction.

CONSTITUTIONAL ISSUE

Whether a state, under its police powers, may enact criminal statutes limiting speech in its pure form, that is, without showing that it incited or was likely to incite subversive action? YES

MAJORITY OPINION   Justice Edward Sanford delivers the majority opinion of the Court. Freedom of speech and of the press, he writes, are fundamental liberties that are protected by the Due Process Clause of the Fourteenth Amendment from impairment by the states. However, they are not unlimited or absolute rights and may be limited by the states under their police powers when the speech is "inimical to the public welfare." Governments have the right of self-preservation, and speech which threatens the unlawful overthrow of government may be punished. Here, the jury found, and the Court agrees, that *The Manifesto* was not some abstract discussion of theory but involved the likelihood of "substantive evil," the use of force and violence to subvert the government.

The New York Legislature determined that such evil may exist even without action and thus passed the piece of legislation at issue here. In interpreting state statutes, there is a presumption of validity, particularly when the state's police power to regulate public safety is involved. That presumption, coupled with the Court's traditional deference to the elected representatives of the people, allows the Court to uphold the constitutionality of the statute. The case of *Schenck v. United States* that established the "clear and present danger" test may be distinguished from this case and the two reconciled, because *Schenck* concerns the immediate effects of speech as it led to action, whereas in *Gitlow* the legislature has already predetermined the danger of this particular type of speech and has acted to forbid it without regard of the likelihood of its leading to action.

OTHER OPINIONS   Justice Oliver Wendell Holmes, joined by Justice Louis Brandeis, enters a dissenting opinion. They state that the Fourteenth Amendment does protect freedom of speech and that there was nothing in the record that indicated that there was any immediate danger of violence (a point that the majority concedes.) Holmes writes that "every idea is an incitement," which may or may not come to fruition. If freedom of speech is to have meaning, ideas must be given the chance to flourish—even those ideas that might lead to a change in the form of government.

SIGNIFICANCE OF THE CASE   *Gitlow* is noteworthy because it is the incorporation case for freedom of speech and because the Court upheld a statute that made advocacy itself a crime without reference to any type of action or to the immediacy of the threat. The effect was to limit the freedom of speech regarding public criticism of government if that criticism took the form of advocating the overthrow of government in anything but the most theoretical of discussions. In *Dennis v. United States* (1951), a case dealing with communism, the Court accepted the "gravity of evil" test in which the gravity of evil, discounted by its improbability, justified the limitation of speech. Today, the two approaches have been merged into a two-prong test of advocacy: (1) Is the speech directed to inciting or producing imminent unlawful activity? and (2) Is the speech likely to incite or produce such action? To limit the speech, it must meet both prongs.

QUESTIONS FOR DISCUSSION

(1) What should be the role of government in limiting speech that expresses unpopular or minority viewpoints?

(2) If you were on the Court, what criteria would you establish for criminalizing speech?

(3) Is it somehow un-American or unpatriotic to be critical of the government or its policies, even in time of war?

RELATED CASES *SCHENCK V. UNITED STATES*, 249 U.S. 47 (1919); *Abrams v. United States*, 250 U.S. 616 (1919); *DENNIS V. UNITED STATES*, 341 U.S 494 (1951); and *Brandenburg v. Ohio*, 395 U.S. 444 (1969).

TEXAS V. JOHNSON
491 U.S. 397 (1989)

BACKGROUND During the 1984 Republican National Convention, Gregory Lee Johnson participated in a demonstration to protest the policies of President Ronald Reagan. Although vandalism occurred, Johnson himself was not involved. However, one protestor did steal an American flag that Johnson doused with kerosene and set on fire. Johnson was convicted under a Texas statute that made it unlawful to knowingly desecrate an American flag. The Texas Court of Criminal Appeals reversed the conviction on the grounds that the statute, as applied to Johnson, conflicted with the First Amendment.

CONSTITUTIONAL ISSUE

Whether a state law that makes it illegal to knowingly desecrate an American flag violates freedom of expression under the First Amendment? YES

MAJORITY OPINION Justice William Brennan delivers the opinion of the Court. Justice Brennan states that to decide this case it must first be determined whether Johnson's conduct "possesses sufficient communicative elements to bring the First Amendment into play." The Court ruled in *Tinker v. Des Moines Independent Community School District* that certain actions could be construed as "symbolic speech" or expression and therefore protected under the First Amendment. Even Texas, Brennan notes, concedes that Johnson's conduct was expressive conduct. The flag burning occurred at the end of a series of demonstrations surrounding the Republican party's national convention. The context, therefore, was political and sufficiently communicative to be called symbolic speech within the meaning of the First Amendment.

Having established that the flag burning was symbolic speech, Brennan next discusses the *O'Brien* test. In *United States v. O'Brien*, the Court ruled that symbolic speech (in this case, draft-card burning) could be punished if the government's interest in punishing the action was unrelated to freedom of expression. In other words, it must be shown that the state's interest in convicting Johnson is unrelated to the suppression of expression. Texas asserts two interests in enacting its flag desecration law. The first is to prevent breaches of the peace, and the second is to protect the flag as a symbol of national unity. Justice Brennan then discusses each of these two interests separately.

Justice Brennan says that Texas's claim to preventing breaches of the peace cannot be maintained. In the first place, no breach of the peace actually occurred or was even threatened as a result of the flag burning. Although some people testified at Johnson's trial that they were offended by the flag burning, no breach of the peace charges were filed. The Court has repeatedly held that government may not presume that every expression of a provocative idea will incite a riot. Nor could the flag burning fall within the category of "fighting words" because no reasonable onlooker would take Johnson's criticism of the Reagan administration's policies personally. Finally, because Texas already has a breach of the peace statute, it already has ample power to punish disruptive conduct without making flag desecration unlawful.

The second interest is that of preserving the flag as a symbol of national unity. However, as noted, under the *O'Brien* test the interest must be unrelated to the suppression of expression. In the majority's opinion Johnson was prosecuted for his expression of dissatisfaction with the nation's policies. Indeed, if Johnson had burned the flag because it was torn or dirty, he could not have been prosecuted because federal law designates burning as the preferred means of disposing of an unfit flag. It is clear, then, that the Texas law is not designed to protect the flag from burning in all instances but only when doing so gives offense to others. Therefore, it is the intention of the flag burner, not the act itself, that gives offense and warrants punishment. The Court has ruled consistently that government may not prohibit an expression merely because it disagrees with its message.

Justice Brennan concludes the opinion by asserting that the Court's decision would be approved by the framers who were "not noted for their reverence for the Union Jack." He also asserts that the opinion will strengthen the place of the flag as a reaffirmation of the principles of freedom it reflects.

OTHER OPINIONS Justice Anthony Kennedy writes the only concurring opinion. Justice Kennedy notes his agreement with the majority opinion but wished to add some personal remarks. It is a difficult fact, he states, that judges must sometimes make decisions they dislike. Such decisions must be made because there is, as in this case, "a pure command of the Constitution." As honored as the flag may be, the Constitution makes no exception to the First Amendment for it. "It is," he writes, "poignant but fundamental that the flag protects those who hold it in contempt."

Chief Justice William Rehnquist writes a dissenting opinion. In it he asserts that the flag is a unique symbol of our nation. He chronicles the history of the flag and concludes that it is not merely another "idea" competing with other viewpoints in the marketplace of ideas. Rehnquist claims that Johnson's act was not an essential part of any exchange of ideas. Nor was Johnson punished for anything he said or did until he burned the flag. In no way can it be said that Johnson was punished for the content of his message. The Texas law removed but one mode of expression—flag desecration—while leaving Johnson a whole range of other symbols and expressions to convey his disapproval of the nation's policies. The chief justice concludes by observing that if Johnson had defaced the Lincoln Memorial no one would doubt the government's power to punish him.

Justice John Paul Stevens writes the other dissenting opinion. Justice Stevens also emphasizes the flag's unique symbolism. He says that the burden on freedom of expression is trivial given the alternative modes of expression available to dissenters. Justice Stevens believes comparing this case to the Flag Salute Case is inappropriate because Johnson is not being forced to believe in something or display respect for the flag. Like Rehnquist, Justice Stevens believes that Johnson's punishment has nothing to do with his message. "The case," he asserts, "has nothing to do with disagreeable ideas." He believes the government has a legitimate interest in preserving an important national asset.

SIGNIFICANCE OF THE CASE   The decision in *Texas v. Johnson* immediately set off a storm of controversy. President George Bush called for a constitutional amendment to prohibit flag desecration. Congress was unwilling to go that far, but it did pass a federal flag protection statute. In early 1990 two lower federal courts declared the new law unconstitutional in light of *Johnson*. The debate is clearly not over. Should a constitutional amendment be passed, it would be the first constitutional restriction placed on the First Amendment in our nation's history.

QUESTIONS FOR DISCUSSION

(1)   The dissenters suggest Johnson had other ways to express his views. Does that make a difference? Why or why not?
(2)   Would it matter if Johnson had burned the flag during wartime?
(3)   Is there a difference between flag burning and defacing a national monument like the Lincoln Memorial?
(4)   Although Johnson's flag was stolen, would it make any difference if he had owned the flag?

RELATED CASES   *WEST VIRGINIA STATE BOARD OF EDUCATION V. BARNETTE*, 319 U.S. 624 (1943); *United States v. O'Brien*, 391 U.S. 367 (1968); *Tinker v. Des Moines Independent Community School District*, 393 U.S. 503 (1969); *Street v. New York*, 394 U.S. 576 (1969); *Schacht v. United States*, 398 U.S. 58 (1970); *Smith v. Goguen*, 415 U.S. 566 (1974); and *Spence v. Washington*, 418 U.S. 405 (1974).

NEAR V. STATE OF MINNESOTA
283 U.S. 697 (1931)

BACKGROUND   During the early part of the century, several newspapers that the Court characterized as scandal sheets were being published in Minnesota. There were allegations that one such newspaper sanctioned corrupt government and illegal gambling, and actually engaged in blackmail. In 1925, the Minnesota Legislature passed a civil statute classifying papers that were "malicious, scandalous, and defamatory" as a public nuisance and providing for suits of abatement and for damages to be assessed against those involved with publishing such a paper. In 1927, Near and his colleagues at *The Saturday*

Press published a series of articles employing colorful and inflammatory language alleging corruption, dereliction of duty, and ties to organized crime on the part of the mayor and the chief of police of Minneapolis, the county attorney, the grand jury, Jews, and other newspapers in Minneapolis. In a series of trials and appeals, Near did not present evidence to show that the allegations were true and were not published in bad faith but instead challenged the constitutionality of the statute. The trial court found the articles were scandalous and defamatory, and issued a permanent injunction against Near from possessing or publishing such articles. In addition, if Near wished to start another newspaper, he would have "to satisfy the court as to the character of a new publication" to avoid contempt of court for violating the injunction. The Supreme Court of Minnesota upheld the decision.

CONSTITUTIONAL ISSUE

Whether the First Amendment protection of freedom of the press bars government from engaging in censorship before articles are published when there is no issue of national security involved? YES

MAJORITY OPINION   Chief Justice Charles Evans Hughes delivers the 5–4 majority opinion of the Court. Freedom of the press is a fundamental right, one that is protected by the Fourteenth Amendment against improper action on the part of states, although it is not absolute. The state may engage in regulation of the press in such areas as obscenity and may punish the abuse of the right through civil and criminal libel laws under the state's police powers. However, the effect of this particular statute is not to punish those who engage in unlawful or irresponsible acts, but to allow prior censorship of the press by government.

Protection against prior government censorship is the chief purpose of the provision for freedom of the press. Historically, in England and under the Constitution, liberty of the press has meant immunity from antecedent government restrictions on what is published except for matters involving national security in time of war. It is a right well entrenched in the common law and statutes, but it must be balanced against the power of the state to enact laws to promote the health, safety, morals, and general welfare of its people. Certainly, allegations of misconduct by public officials are scandalous and likely to stir up controversy within the community. However, the greater evil than the resulting commotion and acrimony is the possibility that the public officers are actually engaging in wrongdoing that would otherwise go undiscovered and unknown to the public. Officials whose activities come under attack are not left without a remedy, because they can file libel suits. In testing the constitutionality of state statutes, the Court must look to the operation and effect of such laws; here, the effect is one of unconstitutional suppression and restraint and therefore the statute must fail.

OTHER OPINIONS   Justice Pierce Butler authors a dissenting opinion joined by Justices Willis Van Devanter, James C. Clark, and George Sutherland. There is no disagreement with the majority that freedom of the press is an important constitutional right and one that falls within the protection of the Fourteenth Amendment against arbitrary and capricious state action. The Minnesota Legislature in passing this statute was properly acting within the scope of its police powers to regulate flagrant abuses of the press in its state. The Court should defer to the state and its judgment about what is necessary for the preservation of peace and good order unless it is clearly shown that the state acted without just cause. In this instance, Near conceded that the articles were defamatory in nature and did not show any evidence that the articles were not published in bad faith. That formed the basis of the Minnesota court decisions and is not subject to review by the Supreme Court. If Near had shown the truth of the material and that it was published with good motives and justifiable ends, then the case would have been cast in totally different terms, because then freedom of the press is "an inestimable privilege in a free government" but without such protections, freedom of the press becomes "the scourge of the republic."

This statute does not act as a prior restraint on publication in that no government official controls in advance what is to be published but instead merely provides a remedy for abuse of the right of a free press. Publications that do not violate the statutory provisions are not barred. In balancing the freedom of scurrilous publications against the public good, the majority was wrong in allowing freedom of the press to weigh more heavily than the good of the community.

SIGNIFICANCE OF THE CASE *Near v. State of Minnesota* is noteworthy for two reasons. First, it is the incorporation case for freedom of the press. Second, it explicitly proclaimed the Court's bar on prior governmental restraint of communications and expression except in extraordinary circumstances. Today, these extraordinary circumstances include well-founded national security claims, not items that are merely potentially embarrassing, and a defendant's right to a fair trial vis-à-vis pretrial publicity. The Court has also upheld restraints before publication (circulation) of certain commercial advertisements and films as well as limiting the location of certain expressive activities such as passing out pamphlets, or speaking in malls or airports. The effect of the decision is to limit government censorship of the flow of information that is available to the public and to put public officials on notice that their actions are subject to public comment.

QUESTIONS FOR DISCUSSION

(1) As a justice, would you affirm prior censorship of commercial speech such as advertisements? Of record albums or films? Of radio programs?

(2) Do you think that libel suits that are filed after publication provide adequate remedies for those who are defamed or insulted? Why?

(3) Does it make a difference if the person is a public or elected official versus a private person—even one who has chosen to become well known as an entrepreneur, athlete, or entertainer?

(4) What rules would you enunciate for withholding information concerning the operation of government from the people? Should this be solely a matter for the executive or legislative branch, with their vested interests, to decide?

RELATED CASES *SCHENCK V. UNITED STATES*, 249 U.S. 47 (1919); *Times Film Corp. v. Chicago*, 365 U.S. 43 (1961); *Shuttlesworth v. Birmingham*, 394 U.S. 147 (1969); *NEW YORK TIMES CO. V. UNITED STATES*, 403 U.S. 713 (1971); *Nebraska Press Association v. Stuart*, 427 U.S. 539 (1976); and *Posadas de Puerto Rico Associates v. Tourism Co. of Puerto Rico*, 478 U.S. 328 (1986).

NEW YORK TIMES CO. V. UNITED STATES
403 U.S. 713 (1971)

BACKGROUND The U.S. government brought separate actions to enjoin publication in the *New York Times* and the *Washington Post* of the "History of U.S. Decision-Making Process on Viet Nam Policy," also known as The Pentagon Papers. *The New York Times* began publication of the series on Sunday, June 13, and the government filed suit on Tuesday, June 15, after the *Times* refused a telephone request on Monday to cease publication of the material.

The New York District Court initially granted and then denied the relief, and that denial was overturned by the Court of Appeals for the Second Circuit regarding the *New York Times*. The District of Columbia District Court also refused to issue the injunction, which was affirmed by the Court of Appeals for the District of Columbia regarding the *Washington Post*. The newspapers requested accelerated consideration on June 24 of the June 23 judgments of the courts of appeals. The Court set the hearing for June 26, and the briefs of the parties arrived less than two hours before argument on June 26.

CONSTITUTIONAL ISSUE

Whether prior restraints should be placed on newspapers to prevent them from publishing documents that the executive branch termed confidential and threatening to national security in derogation of the First Amendment right to freedom of press? NO

MAJORITY OPINION The Court issued a *per curiam* opinion that the government had not met its "heavy burden" to justify prior restraints of expression as required by earlier court decisions and refused to grant the injunctions.

OTHER OPINIONS Justice Hugo Black, with whom Justice William O. Douglas joined, enters a concurring opinion. The First Amendment, intended to be a limit on all branches of government, is explicit and absolute in its meaning. The invocation of national security ("a broad, vague generality") should not be allowed to "abrogate the fundamental law embodied in the First Amendment." It is not the role of any branch of government, including the judiciary, to make a law abridging freedom of the press. The press must be unimpaired in its duty to publish news, "whatever the source, without censorship, injunctions, or prior restraints," because only then can the press fulfill the role that the Founding Fathers envisioned, that of curtailing the government by exposing deception or deceit of the people.

Justice William O. Douglas, joined by Justice Hugo Black, also concurs. The First Amendment bars governmental restraint on the press. Moreover, there is no statute providing for injunctive relief in this matter; the appropriate remedies would be criminal prosecutions under the Espionage Act. Congress considered, but chose not to enact, provisions, allowing prior restraint when debating the Espionage Act. "Secrecy in government is fundamentally antidemocratic, perpetuating bureaucratic errors. Open debate and discussion of public issues are vital to our national health." The government has not met its "heavy burden" to justify prior restraint in this case.

Justice William Brennan also enters a concurring opinion. The First Amendment is an absolute bar to prior restraint on the publication based on conjecture or surmise that national security might be endangered unless the country is at war and then only if publication would "inevitably, directly, and immediately cause the occurrence of an event kindred to imperiling the safety of a transport already at sea." If the executive branch seeks to shelter materials, it must "submit the basis upon which that aid is sought to scrutiny by the judiciary," which was not done in the instant case.

Justice Potter Stewart, joined by Justice Byron White, also writes a concurring opinion. The president and the executive branch are endowed with "enormous power" in the fields of national defense and international relations, but it is not unfettered power. It is to be controlled both by an "enlightened citizenry—in an informed and critical public opinion which alone can here protect the values of democratic government," by the other branches of government, and by the executive branch itself. The executive has "awesome responsibility, requiring judgment and wisdom of a high order"; however, secrecy for its own sake should be avoided, and the hallmark of a truly effective internal security system would be "the maximum possible disclosure, recognizing that secrecy can best be preserved only when creditability is truly maintained." It is the responsibility of the executive, not the courts, to preserve government secrets under the Constitution. In balancing the interests here, no showing is made that "direct, immediate, irreparable damage to our Nation or its people" will result from disclosure and therefore the First Amendment demands that the relief sought be denied.

Justice Byron White, joined by Justice Stewart, concurs. The government did not meet its "heavy burden" against prior restraint in the instant case, especially because the security breakdown is already known, and the efficacy of equitable relief is doubtful. In addition, Congress has addressed the issue and has not approved the issuance of injunctions, choosing instead to rely on criminal penalties. Imposing criminal sanctions remains a viable possibility, and the Court is not giving a stamp of approval to the newspapers to publish the information with this case. Instead, the Court is holding that the government "has not satisfied the very heavy burden it must meet to warrant an injunction...in the absence of express and appropriately limited congressional authorization for prior restraints in circumstances such as these."

Justice Thurgood Marshall also enters a concurring opinion. The executive branch has the authority to classify information as secret, but it is has no authority to invoke the Court's equitable or contempt jurisdiction to prevent behavior that Congress has specifically declined to prohibit. It may be more convenient to ask the Court to act rather than to wait for Congress to pass a law as well as politically wise to "get a court to share the responsibility for arresting those who the Executive Branch" believes is violating the law, but "convenience and political considerations do not justify a basic departure" from the doctrine of separation of powers. The Court does not have authority to issue the requested relief.

Chief Justice Warren Burger authors a dissenting opinion. This is a case of great importance when "imperative of a free and unfettered press comes into collision with another imperative, the effective functioning of a complex modern government and specifically the effective exercise of certain constitutional powers of the Executive." The newspapers are at fault in two respects: (1) They failed to advise public officers that they possessed stolen property, the "basic and simple" duty of every citizen; and (2) they have demanded that the cases proceed at a frantic pace despite the fact that they have had the voluminous papers for several months—"[W]hy should the United States Government, from whom this information was illegally acquired by someone, along with all the counsel, trial judges, and appellate judges be placed under needless pressure?" The newspapers were certainly aware that the government would object to the release of this information and could have followed the traditional practice of working with the government to reach an agreement as to which documents should be suppressed and which should be released. The haste in which the cases were brought to the Court has prevented thorough development of the legal issues, and the cases should be remanded to allow for more complete unfolding of the issues.

Justice John Marshall Harlan II is joined by the chief justice and Justice Harry Blackmun in his dissent. These are very difficult questions of law with serious and far-reaching consequences if wrongly decided, and the Court has acted rashly in allowing a precipitous review in which many issues are not adequately addressed. In addition, the scope of the Court's powers in this area are limited to determining that the matter is actually within the president's foreign relations power and to insisting that the head of the executive department should personally review the material before deciding that disclosure would "irreparably impair the national security." The Court should not go beyond this and determine for itself that such injury would result as this is a political rather than judicial decision.

Justice Harry Blackmun also authors a dissenting opinion. The First Amendment is "only one part of an entire Constitution," and the provisions giving the executive branch responsibility for foreign affairs is equally valid. "What is needed here is a weighing upon properly developed standards, of the broad rights of the press to print and of the very narrow right of the government to prevent." The issues in this case have not been properly developed, and given the magnitude of the issues, they should be "tried as lawyers should try them and as courts should hear them, free of pressure and panic and sensationalism." Remand is proper for further development of the cases.

SIGNIFICANCE OF THE CASE   *New York Times v. United States* is important on two fronts. First, the Court has rarely acted to brake the burgeoning expansion of the powers of the president in the fields of foreign relations and national security. Both Congress and the judiciary have almost routinely deferred to the president in these matters. Second, the Court refused to issue the injunctions sought by the government on First Amendment grounds. Particularly noteworthy were the votes of Justices Stewart and White who clearly felt that the publication of the information was wrong and dangerous to American interests, but still came down on the side of the First Amendment.

QUESTIONS FOR DISCUSSION

(1)   What should be the parameters in release of information relevant to national security?

(2)   Do you think administrations at all levels of government are more likely to hide or to disclose politically damaging or embarrassing information? What limits would you set on the local investigative reporters in ferreting out and publishing that information?

(3)   What protections do "we, the people" truly have against deceptive or secretive government officials when we do not have access to information?

(4) Unfortunately, some government officials act in the public's name to create either political or financial power bases for themselves. What tools are available for the public protection?

RELATED CASES *EX PARTE MILLIGAN*, 4 Wallace 2 (1866); *NEAR V. STATE OF MINNESOTA*, 283 U.S. 697 (1931); *UNITED STATES V. CURTISS-WRIGHT EXPORT CORP.*, 299 U.S. 304 (1936); *YOUNGSTOWN SHEET & TUBE CO. V. SAWYER*, 343 U.S. 579 (1952); *Organization for a Better Austin v. Keefe*, 402 U.S. 415 (1971); and *Nebraska Press Association v. Stuart*, 427 U.S. 539 (1976).

NEW YORK TIMES CO. V. SULLIVAN
376 U.S. 254 (1964)

BACKGROUND Sullivan, a city commissioner who directed the police force in Montgomery, Alabama, brought a suit in state court alleging that he had been libeled by an advertisement published in the *New York Times*. He sued not only the New York Times Co. but also four individuals who were listed as endorsers of the statements in the advertisement. The individuals claimed that they had not authorized their names to be used. The advertisement concerned events in Montgomery during the civil rights movement, and all conceded that there were factual errors in it. Sullivan was not named in the advertisement nor were there any references to his office, although it did mention a couple of instances of police activity. An Alabama jury awarded Sullivan $500,000 in punitive damages, which was affirmed by the state supreme court.

CONSTITUTIONAL ISSUE

Whether newspapers that publish advertisements critical of public officials may be sued in state court for libel if there is no proof of malice? NO

MAJORITY OPINION Justice William Brennan writes the majority opinion for the Court. The case must be considered against "the background of a profound national commitment to the principle that debate on public issues should be uninhibited, robust and wide-open, and that it may well include vehement, caustic, and sometimes unpleasantly sharp attacks on government and public officials." Judges, although mindful of the dignity and reputation of the courts, accept criticism of themselves and their decisions, and so too must other government officials accept criticism. The ability to question the stewardship of public officials is an integral and very necessary aspect of democracy and representative government.

The Court would not permit prosecutions for libel of government itself although it has stated that the Constitution does not protect libelous statements in suits involving private individuals. An otherwise impersonal attack on governmental operations may not by some legal alchemy be converted into libel of an official responsible for those operations. Factual error or content defamatory of the person's official reputation does not mandate an award of damages unless the official protests that the statement was made with "'actual malice'—that is, with knowledge that it was false or with reckless disregard of whether it was false or not." In the instant case, the evidence does not support a finding of malice or defamation, especially because neither the respondent nor his office were named. The fact that the statements appear in a paid advertisement does not move it outside the freedom of expression protected by the First Amendment.

The First Amendment, through incorporation, does apply to the states, and the application of a rule of law that allows the awarding of a judgment in a civil action is "state action" under the Fourteenth Amendment. States cannot chill the exercise of First Amendment rights directly through criminal statutes or indirectly through civil statutes without coming under the Court's review.

OTHER OPINIONS   Justice Hugo Black, joined by Justice William O. Douglas, enters a concurring opinion. The First and Fourteenth Amendments provide an absolute bar against a government officer's suing private citizens or the news media for criticism of official conduct. "The requirement that malice be proved provides at best an evanescent protection for the right critically to discuss public affairs and certainly does not measure up to the sturdy safeguard embodied in the First Amendment." These state libel laws are nothing more than tools of harassment and punishment with the intent to chill criticism by allowing substantial judgments against the media. "This nation, I suspect, can live in peace without libel suits based on public discussions of public affairs and public officials. But I doubt that a country can live in freedom where its people can be made to suffer physically or financially for criticizing their government, its actions, or its officials."

Justice Arthur Goldberg is also joined in his concurring opinion by Justice Douglas. The Court today provides citizens and the media a "'conditional privilege' immunizing non-malicious misstatements of fact regarding the official conduct of a government official." Protection under the First Amendment does not depend on the motivation of the citizen or the press. Those who assume governmental offices in whatever capacity must expect that official acts will be commented on and criticized. These officials are not left without recourse as they have equal, if not greater, access to the media to correct and educate the electorate.

SIGNIFICANCE OF THE CASE   This First Amendment case is important because it clearly reiterates the principle that criticism of American officials in the performance of their official duties is constitutionally protected in the absence of malice. The effect is to liberate citizens and the media to scrutinize and monitor the performance of their officials while also providing an avenue for public officials who are maliciously attacked to have their day in court. Those in public office frequently argue that neither the standard set in *New York Times Co. v. Sullivan* nor journalistic ethics provide sufficient recourse for overzealousness on the part of the press.

Today, those who are so well known as to be public figures must also show malice or intentional publication of information knowing it to be false to recover in libel, whereas private individuals must only prove negligence.

QUESTIONS FOR DISCUSSION

(1)   Where does the public's "right to know" end and the official's right to privacy in his or her personal life begin? What about the activities of the official's family members?

(2)   What lines should be drawn if the person is not an elected official but instead is a public figure whose fame comes from success as an athlete, entertainer, or entrepreneur?

(3) Is criticism of government unpatriotic, and should it be protected even when the sentiments are not generally shared by the public?

RELATED CASES *Bridges v. California*, 314 U.S. 252 (1941); *Beauharnais v. Illinois*, 343 U.S. 250 (1952); *National Association for the Advancement of Colored People v. Button*, 371 U.S. 415 (1963); *Curtis Publishing Co. v. Butts*, 388 U.S. 130 (1967); *Gertz v. Robert Welch, Inc.*, 418 U.S. 323 (1974); and *Hustler Mag. v. Falwell*, 485 U.S. 46 (1988).

ROTH V. UNITED STATES
354 U.S. 476 (1957)

BACKGROUND This decision encompasses two cases. In the first, Roth was convicted of mailing an obscene book, circulars, and advertising in violation of federal law. In the second, Alberts was convicted of keeping for sale obscene materials as well as for advertising them in an obscene fashion under violation of California law.

CONSTITUTIONAL ISSUE

Whether distribution of obscene materials is protected as freedom of speech or of press either under the First Amendment against the federal government or under the Due Process Clause of the Fourteenth Amendment against state action? NO

MAJORITY OPINION Justice William Brennan delivers the opinion of the Court. The First Amendment does not protect all utterances, but instead is designed to facilitate the exchange of ideas, even those that are unorthodox, controversial, or hateful to the prevailing climate of opinion, but that may bring about political and social changes desired by the people. The free exchange of ideas lies at the heart of democracy and representative government.

Obscenity is not protected by the First Amendment, but the difficulty is in determining what is obscene and therefore not protected by the First Amendment. The early approach was to judge the work, not in its entirety, but by its effect on particularly susceptible persons. The current test is whether "to the average person, applying contemporary community standards, the dominant theme of the material taken as a whole appeals to prurient interest." Sexual content and obscenity are not synonymous; obscene material deals with sex in a manner appealing to prurient interest. The focus of the test shifts from what is offensive to an individual to what is offensive to the community, which will vary from locale to locale.

Brennan agrees that the standard is not very precise but denies that it violates the fair-notice requirement of due process, that is, the requirement that criminal statutes provide adequate notice and clear standards for defining criminal conduct before a person may be imprisoned for engaging in such activities. "[L]ack of precision is not itself offensive to the requirements of due process" in that the language does convey a clear warning of the prohibited activity. Upholding the federal law barring the use of the mails to distribute obscenity unshielded by the First Amendment does not preempt the state's activity under its police powers to protect the public welfare.

OTHER OPINIONS Chief Justice Earl Warren concurs in the result. He would limit the case holding to the particular statutes before the Court. Each statute involved an intentional and knowing or calculated act on the part of the defendant, and because each was involved in the commercial distribution of such prurient materials, Warren does not have any difficulty in affirming their convictions. He does exhibit great concern that the test adopted by the Court is too broad and could be used to limit communication improperly. He stresses that in the instant case it is the individuals who are on trial, and the proceedings here are not to determine the obscenity of the work itself. The recognized existence of a social problem does not mandate that the Court uphold all statutes dealing with the issue.

Justice John Marshall Harlan II concurs with the decision regarding Alberts but disagrees regarding Roth. He objects to the failure of the Court to determine for itself if the materials are, in fact, obscene and utterly without social redeeming value. "Every communication has an individuality and 'value' of its own," and it is the responsibility of the reviewing court to make an individual decision as to whether the material should be suppressed within constitutional standards. It is not sufficient to merely accept the fact finder's label of obscenity because this is "not really an issue of fact but a question of constitutional *judgment* of the most sensitive and delicate kind."

Harlan is concerned because one law is federal, and the other is a state law. The standard of review for state law is different from that for federal legislation. The Court's role in reviewing state statutes is narrow, and the Court is to defer to the state legislatures unless there is an invasion of a fundamental liberty and no rational basis to sustain such invasion. Here, the California legislature has acted on the basis of the belief that the printed word can incite one to antisocial or immoral behavior, although there is a great deal of disagreement and controversy over that belief. The "domain of sexual morality is preeminently a matter of state concern" and one in which the Court should hesitate to intervene. In regulating such matters, the state is bound by court decisions including the test that the work must be judged as a whole and in relation to the normal adult reader.

Different issues are involved regarding the federal statute because federal censorship imposes one standard across the nation in a total suppression of the material where if one state bans a work, it may be acceptable just a few miles away across the state boundary. It may be constitutional (although undesirable) for the states to engage in censorship in the name of sexual morality, but Congress has no such substantive right. The strength of the nation is that the states are free to experiment with policies and ideas, but when the national government imposes a blanket ban on the work, it is "intolerable and violative of both the letter and spirit of the First Amendment." The test enunciated by the majority is overly broad and encompasses materials that could fall under protected speech and the "Federal Government has no business, under the postal or commerce power, to bar the sale of books because they might lead to any kind of 'thoughts.'"

Justice William O. Douglas, joined by Justice Hugo Black, dissents. The focus of their dissent is censorship based on the judge's or jury's belief that the work has an "undesirable" impact on thoughts. Punishment is imposed, not for overt acts or antisocial behavior, but for thoughts. There is no certainty that impure thoughts lead to improper or illegal activity. The effect of the decision is to curtail the First Amendment drastically on the basis of subjective beliefs about the "purity of thought which a book or tract instills in the mind of the reader." Statutes infringing on the First Amendment should be scrutinized most carefully and should be narrowly drawn to avoid the dangers of suppressing freedom of ideas as expressed in literature. Speech and communication occupy a preferred position, and should be suppressed only if and when it is an inseparable part of illegal action, and there has been no such showing here.

SIGNIFICANCE OF THE CASE   *Roth v. United States* is the first of a series of cases attempting to balance freedom of speech and communication against the government's interest in regulating public health and welfare. In this case, the Court identified the factors to be considered in an obscenity case: (1) that the work would be judged in its entirety and not on selected portions; (2) that it would be examined in terms of community standards and not on its effect on one person; and (3) that the focus would be whether it appealed to "prurient interests" rather than immorality. Later cases such as *A Book Named "John Cleland's Memoirs of a Woman of Pleasure" v. Attorney General of Massachusetts* and *Miller v. California* further refined the test by which the Court defined obscenity. The Court, in holding that obscenity is not protected, made it incumbent on the Court to define obscenity—a task yet undone.

QUESTIONS FOR DISCUSSION

(1)   In legal terms, how would you define obscenity? What interests do you think are at stake?

(2)   Do you agree with Justice Harlan that there is a major distinction between national and state regulation of obscenity?

(3)   Are you more persuaded by the dissent, or by the majority? Why?

(4)   Should only those who distribute obscenity be punished or should those who merely possess it also be punished?

RELATED CASES   *A Book Named "John Cleland's Memoirs of a Woman of Pleasure" v. Attorney General of Massachusetts*, 383 U.S. 413 (1966); *Stanley v. Georgia*, 394 U.S. 557 (1969); *MILLER V. CALIFORNIA*, 413 U.S. 15 (1973); *New York v. Ferber*, 458 U.S. 747 (1982); and *Osborne v. Ohio*, 495 U.S. 103 (1990).

MILLER V. CALIFORNIA
413 U.S. 15 (1973)

BACKGROUND   Miller was convicted of mailing sexually explicit material — advertisements for certain books and film — in violation of a California statute. The recipients of the material had not solicited it.

CONSTITUTIONAL ISSUE

Whether the states may regulate obscenity in derogation of the First Amendment right of speech and press? YES

MAJORITY OPINION   Chief Justice Warren Burger writes the majority opinion of the Court. Obscenity is not protected by the First Amendment, and the states' authority to regulate pornographic material under its police powers is accepted by the courts. However, the Court "must always remain sensitive to any infringement on genuinely serious literary, artistic, political, or scientific expression."

The Court has struggled to balance the competing interests of expression and the state's police power for several years, and has never mustered a full and complete accord of its members about the subject. That lack of accord has created confusion for state legislatures and spawned numerous lawsuits in both state and federal courts that have clogged the docket. Yet, a majority of the Court is not willing to adopt an absolutist view of the First Amendment and thereby abdicate its responsibilities. Instead, the Court is opting for a new test by which the work is to be tested: (1) "whether 'the average person, applying contemporary community standards' would find that the work, taken as a whole, appeals to the prurient interest"; (2) "whether the work depicts or describes in a patently offensive way, sexual conduct specifically defined by the applicable state law"; and (3) "whether the work, taken as a whole, lacks serious literary, artistic, political, or scientific value."

The Court recognizes that a test that applies "contemporary community standards" will create a hodgepodge of different rules within various states and communities. This is nothing more than is done regarding other criminal statutes, and the Court places great confidence in the jurors to apply the standard correctly. The Court rejects the idea of a national standard in favor of diversity and acceptance of each community's values and morals. Moreover, the test set out in this opinion provides adequate guidance for state legislatures to draft constitutionally acceptable criminal statutes regarding the distribution of obscenity.

OTHER OPINIONS   Justice William O. Douglas enters a dissenting opinion. He points out that by remanding the case to be decided in accordance with the First Amendment standards decided in this case the Court is sanctioning imprisonment of Miller "under freshly written standards defining obscenity that until today's decision were never the part of any law" or, in effect, punishing him for acts for which he had no "fair notice," an integral requirement of criminal law. If people are to be punished for distribution of obscenity, then the process should take place in two stages: The materials should be determined obscene in a civil proceeding, and only then should the person be tried for distribution. Otherwise, the criminal law becomes a trap.

In addition, he diverges from the majority to again iterate his absolutist position on the First Amendment, that is, the provision about freedom of speech and press should be read literally and no exception for regulation of obscenity should be created. People are not being "compelled to look or to listen" to that which they find objectionable. They may leave the location, or turn off the radio or television. Although it is true that the materials "may be garbage...so is much of what is said in political campaigns, in the daily press, on TV, or over the radio."

The effect of decisions such as this is to impose government censorship, and for the government to dictate our tastes and standards in literature, art, and entertainment. If the American people want government censorship, then the appropriate vehicle would be a constitutional amendment adopted after full debate by the people.

Justice William Brennan, joined by Justices Potter Stewart and Thurgood Marshall, also enters a dissenting opinion. Justice Brennan, in his lengthy dissent in *Paris Adult Theatre I v. Slaton*, which was decided at the same time as *Miller*, abandoned his earlier stance that states could regulate obscenity and moved toward the absolutist position of Black and Douglas. The chaos created by this series of opinions does not provide "fair notice" to potential wrongdoers; therefore, a clearer line should be drawn. "In the absence of distribution to juveniles or obtrusive exposure to unconsenting adults, the First and Fourteenth Amendments prohibit the state and federal governments from attempting wholly to suppress sexually oriented materials on the basis of their allegedly 'obscene' contents."

SIGNIFICANCE OF THE CASE   The Court struggled for several years with the issue of obscenity in a number of cases. Here, in *Miller v. California*, they set out the latest version of the test by which freedom of expression under the First Amendment is to be limited. The standard set out in *Memoirs* that had allowed the work to be classified as obscene only if it was "utterly without" redeeming merit was altered. The Court has agreed that this form of speech may be regulated in interests of young children, unwilling viewers, and neighborhoods.

Public furor and outcry withered for several years, although in recent years there has been a resurgence of interest in censorship in terms of removing "objectionable" books from libraries and in public funding of works of art, but more particularly regarding the lyrics of popular music and child pornography. The traditional focus was the publication and distribution of obscenity rather than the possession of such; however, in 1990, the Court reversed its long-standing decision in *Stanley v. Georgia* and allowed states to criminalize the private possession of pornography in a case involving child pornography.

QUESTIONS FOR DISCUSSION

(1)   Do you agree with Justice Douglas that Miller was effectively being subjected to an *ex post facto* law?

(2)   If you were on the Court, would you adopt the absolutist position? If not, what limits would you as a judge impose?

(3)   Do you favor laws requiring truth in advertising? Laws requiring truth in political campaigns? Laws requiring truth in commercial transactions such as credit? Are each of these forms of government censorship?

RELATED CASES   *ROTH V. UNITED STATES*, 354 U.S. 476 (1957); *A Book Named "John Cleland's Memoirs of a Woman of Pleasure" v. Attorney General of Massachusetts*, 383 U.S. 413 (1966); *Ginsberg v. New York*, 390 U.S. 629 (1968); *Stanley v. Georgia*, 394 U.S. 557 (1969); *PARIS ADULT THEATRE I V. SLATON*, 413 U.S. 49 (1973); *Jenkins v. Georgia*, 418 U.S. 153 (1974); *New York v. Ferber*, 458 U.S. 747 (1982); and *Osborne v. Ohio*, 495 U.S. 103 (1990).

PARIS ADULT THEATRE I V. SLATON
413 U.S. 49 (1973)

BACKGROUND Civil complaints were filed by local prosecutors against two Atlanta, Georgia, adult movie theaters and their owners and managers. The basis of the complaint was that the two theaters were showing films (*Magic Mirror* and *It All Comes Out in the End*), which depicted sexual conduct described by the Georgia Supreme Court as "hard core pornography." The advertising for the theater specified that it was adult entertainment and that no minors were permitted. No pictures were posted outside the theater. The trial court dismissed the complaint, even though "obscenity was established," on the basis that such shows were constitutionally protected under the First Amendment because no minors were admitted and because there was sufficient warning to the public about the contents. The Georgia Supreme Court reversed on the grounds that the state could regulate the commercial exhibition of obscenity under its police powers.

CONSTITUTIONAL ISSUE

Whether the state has the right to regulate the commercial exhibition of obscenity when the audience is composed solely of consenting adults in light of the First Amendment? YES

MAJORITY OPINION Chief Justice Warren Burger delivers the opinion of the Court. He casts the decision in terms of states' rights and the prerogative of the states, under their police powers, to regulate morality. Burger writes that

we do not undertake to tell the states what they must do, but rather to define the area in which they may chart their own course in dealing with obscene material. This Court has consistently held the obscene material is not protected by the First Amendment as a limitation on the state police power under the Fourteenth Amendment.

In the companion case of *Miller v. California*, the Court establishes the newest constitutional test for obscenity that contains the following elements: (1) whether the "average person, applying contemporary community standards" finds that the work, taken as a whole, appeals to prurient interest; (2) whether the work depicts or describes in a patently offensive way, sexual conduct specifically defined by state law; and (3) whether the work, taken as a whole, lacks serious literary, artistic, political, or scientific value. If the work fails the Miller test (as these films do), it is within the power of the states to regulate the exhibition of such.

The mere fact that the materials were shown only to consenting adults and not to minors or nonconsenting adults does not give the theaters immunity. The Constitution does not include the notion that all conduct involving consenting adults is always beyond state regulation. This case is distinguished from *Stanley v. Georgia* where the Court ruled that viewing obscenity in the privacy of one's own home fell under the First Amendment and the right to privacy, but the zone of privacy does not encompass the right to view obscenity in a public arena. A commercial theater cannot be equated with a private home; a theater falls within the definition of public accommodation. The power of the states to regulate commerce and the public environment is well established, and the exhibition of obscenity falls squarely within that regulatory power.

Burger argues that it is a "well nigh universal belief" that good books, plays, and art exert a positive influence on people, and despite a lack of empirical data, state legislatures may act on the corollary assumption that obscenity exerts a negative or "corrupting and debasing impact on people," and may therefore prohibit commercial exhibition of obscenity. In addition, barring the public exhibition of obscenity is not tantamount to controlling the moral content of a person's thoughts. The Court's decision is directed at the "depiction and description of specifically defined sexual conduct" and not at thoughts or speech.

OTHER OPINIONS Justice William O. Douglas enters a dissenting opinion that adhered to his often-stated position that government should not be involved in censorship. His argument here focuses on the individual. "[M]atters of taste, like matters of belief, turn on the personal idiosyncrasies of individuals." Although Supreme Court justices, like others, may find works to be personally offensive, the First Amendment precludes them from acting as censors. This society "makes the individual, not government, the keeper of his tastes, beliefs, and ideas," and it is the responsibility of the individual adult, not the government, to avoid that which he or she finds offensive.

Justices William Brennan, Potter Stewart, and Thurgood Marshall also dissent. Brennan begins the dissenting opinion by describing the issue as the "vexing problem of reconciling state efforts to suppress sexually oriented material with the protections of the First Amendment, as applied to the states through the Fourteenth Amendment" and decries the disharmony the issue generates as well as the amount of resources consumed by the cases.

The "outright suppression of obscenity cannot be reconciled with the fundamental principles" of the Constitution, and despite its best efforts, the Court has not been able to structure adequate guidelines for the states. The necessary vagueness of the standards creates several problems. First, a vague statute fails to give adequate notice of potential wrongdoing to people. There is a lack of predictability that compels people to guess whether they are acting illegally and that also leads to arbitrary and erratic enforcement. This violates a basic premise of American jurisprudence that criminal laws must give fair notice of what they forbid. Second, statutes that have the potential for chilling protected speech (such as obscenity statutes) must be drawn narrowly to be upheld according to prior court cases. Third, the vague guidelines create institutional stress in that the Court is required to consider scores of obscenity cases because "one cannot say with certainty that material is obscene until at least five members of this Court, applying inevitably obscure standards, have pronounced it so." This process not only creates tension between state and federal courts, but consumes the Court's limited resources. The standards enunciated in *Miller* do not solve the vagueness issue because the ultimate responsibility still lies with the Supreme Court.

The state's police power does include the regulation of morals, but that interest is not clearly delineated and does not justify interference with the First Amendment. Attempts to limit speech not protected by the First Amendment necessarily spill over to speech protected by the First Amendment.

While I cannot say that the interests of the state—apart from the question of juveniles and unconsenting adults—are trivial or nonexistent...these interests cannot justify the substantial damage to constitutional rights and to this Nation's judicial machinery that inevitably results from state efforts to bar the distribution even of unprotected material to consenting adults.

The problems generated by the case-by-case approach should force the Court to abandon the process and to adopt the position that neither the state or national government can wholly suppress sexually-oriented materials in the absence of distribution to minors or "obtrusive exposure" to unconsenting adults.

SIGNIFICANCE OF THE CASE   In this case, the Court returned to a concept that scholars have referred to as "constant obscenity," that is, what is obscene is obscene under all circumstances and for all people—the doctrine established in *Roth*. During the interim from *Roth* to *Paris Adult Theatre I*, the Court had followed the "variable obscenity" approach, which noted constitutional scholars Ducat and Chase describe as having a "chameleonlike quality and differs according to time and place."

QUESTIONS FOR DISCUSSION

(1)   Today, issues of obscenity in films and books are not on the "hit parade" of court issues. Why do you think the topic has become less heated?

(2)   More recent discussions of obscenity focused on works financed by government. Do you think that the National Endowment for the Arts or other government agencies should sponsor controversial works that some argue are obscene? Would you reach a different decision as a member of the Court charged with protecting the First Amendment? Would you rule differently if no public funds were involved in the production of the work? Why?

(3)   If one accepts Burger's premise that good books, plays, and arts uplift the human spirit and obscenity degrades it, can the state compel adults, on pain of imprisonment, to read Shakespeare or other great authors?

RELATED CASES   *ROTH V. UNITED STATES*, 354 U.S. 476 (1957); *A Book Named "John Cleland's Memoirs of a Woman of Pleasure" v. Attorney General of Massachusetts*, 383 U.S. 413 (1966); *Ginzburg v. United States*, 383 U.S. 463 (1966); *Stanley v. Georgia*, 394 U.S. 557 (1969); *Miller v. California*, 413 U.S. 15 (1973); *Jenkins v. Georgia*, 418 U.S. 153 (1974); *Federal Communications Commission v. Pacifica Foundation*, 438 U.S. 726 (1978); and *Osborne v. Ohio*, 495 U.S. 103 (1990).

WHITNEY V. PEOPLE OF STATE OF CALIFORNIA
274 U.S. 357 (1927)

BACKGROUND   Charlotte Whitney was convicted of assisting to organize and being a member of an organization with the goal of advocating, teaching, or aiding criminal syndicalism—the doctrine of advocating, teaching, or aiding the commission of crime, sabotage, force and violence, or terrorism as "a means of accomplishing a change in industrial ownership or control, or effecting any political change"—under California law.

The basis of her conviction was membership in the Communist Labor Party, participation in its initial convention, and attending a couple of meetings of the State Executive Committee as an alternate.

CONSTITUTIONAL ISSUE

Whether statutes that prohibit advocacy (without action) of criminal anarchy and criminal syndicalism may be upheld under the First Amendment protection of freedom of speech? YES

MAJORITY OPINION Justice Edward Sanford delivers the opinion for the majority. The Court will not review whether the defendant's mere presence in the convention and later Executive Committee meetings is sufficient basis for the conviction. That is a factual determination made by the jury and affirmed by the court of appeals, and the Court declines to consider the issue because it does not involve a constitutional question.

The Criminal Syndicalism Act is sufficiently explicit to advise of the prohibited conduct, and people of "common intelligence" would not have to "guess at its meaning" or "differ as to its application." It is not void for vagueness under the Due Process Clauses of the Fifth and Fourteenth Amendments.

The equal protection arguments advanced by Whitney are also rejected. Freedom of speech, assembly, and association are not absolute rights. States have wide discretion to legislate under their police powers, and the Court will defer to the judgment of the legislature as to the extent of the danger of activities such as Whitney's. The Court will not intervene unless the state acts in an arbitrary or unreasonable manner.

OTHER OPINIONS Justice Louis Brandeis, joined by Justice Oliver Wendell Holmes, enters a concurring opinion. Fundamental rights such as freedom of speech and assembly are included in the protection of the Fourteenth Amendment, but they are not absolute rights. They may be restricted if there is a "clear and imminent danger of some substantive evil." It is the prerogative of the legislature to decide when those conditions exist within the parameters established by the Court. The danger must go beyond fear of serious injury as that alone will not sustain suppression of free speech. Although denunciation of existing laws tends to increase the possibility that there will be a violation, mere advocacy is not the same as incitement or preparation for violating the law. It must be an immediate danger, one "so imminent that it may befall before there is an opportunity for full discussion." Suppression of speech should not be undertaken lightly and should be employed in only the most grave situations.

Assembly of a political party, formed to advocate change at some future date, is within the protection of the Fourteenth Amendment, but the Court has the right to examine the particular facts of the case to determine whether the "clear and present danger test" has been applied appropriately. Here, the California statute provides a rebuttable presumption that such conditions exist, and Whitney failed to meet her burden to defeat the presumption. Her mere presence at the assembly is not sufficient to sustain the conviction, but other evidence indicates a conspiracy of the members to commit serious crimes that can be, and are, prohibited.

SIGNIFICANCE OF THE CASE *Whitney* is one of a series of cases dealing with suppression of the rights of speech, association, and assembly of members of the Socialist and Communist Parties during this time. It is noted more for the Brandeis-Holmes concurrence and the explication of the "clear and present danger test," with the requirement that the Court examine the application of the test to the facts before them, instead of examining the constitutionality of the statute than the majority's holding. Brandeis said the following about speech and its role:

> [T]hat it is hazardous to discourage thought, hope, and imagination; that fear breeds repression; that repression breeds hate; that hate menaces stable government; that the path of safety lies in the opportunity to discuss freely supposed grievances and proposed remedies....Men feared witches and burned women. It is the function of speech to free men from the bondage of irrational fears.

QUESTIONS FOR DISCUSSION

(1) Do you think that the Court should have examined the adequacy of the grounds for conviction? Why would the Court make such a flat statement about not considering the sufficiency of evidence on which the conviction was based?

(2) Brandeis stated that the Founding Fathers "did not exalt order at the cost of liberty." Which do you favor, liberty or order? Why?

(3) If the content of speech is threatening such as statements of racial superiority (from any race), should the government act to suppress such language? What if there is an intent to inflame emotions as when Neo-Nazis march through predominantly Jewish neighborhoods? What if violence seems likely but is not assured? As a justice, what factors would you consider in such cases?

RELATED CASES *SCHENCK V. UNITED STATES*, 249 U.S. 47 (1919); *GITLOW V. NEW YORK*, 268 U.S. 652 (1925); *DENNIS V. UNITED STATES*, 341 U.S. 494 (1951); and *Brandenburg v. Ohio*, 395 U.S. 444 (1969).

DENNIS V. UNITED STATES
341 U.S. 494 (1951)

BACKGROUND Dennis and others were indicted under the Smith Act, which made it a crime for any person to advocate knowingly or willfully the overthrow or destruction of the government by force or violence. They were charged with conspiring willfully and knowingly to organize the Communist Party, a group that taught and advocated the violent overthrow of the government, and with actually teaching and advocating such position. The trial lasted over nine months, and the defendants were found guilty. The court of appeals affirmed the conviction.

CONSTITUTIONAL ISSUE

Whether Congress exceeded its constitutional power in passing a statute that criminalized speech? NO

PLURALITY OPINION   Chief Justice Fredric Vinson delivers the plurality opinion. He is joined by Justices Stanley F. Reed, Harold Burton, and Sherman Minton. He begins by iterating that Congress certainly has the power, indeed the duty, to protect the government from violent overthrow and passing statutes to that end, such as the Smith Act, is well within its recognized authority.

The statute, however, criminalizes advocation and teaching that contain elements of speech that are protected under the First Amendment and therefore requires close and careful scrutiny by the Court. The Constitution, and the Court, recognizes "the inherent value of free discourse," but it is not an unlimited or absolute right. The defendants in this case were convicted for espousing the overthrow of the government and not merely teaching about the precepts of different theories in an abstract discussion. The former is not protected speech, whereas the latter falls within the right of citizens to discuss and evaluate political questions freely. It is the prerogative of citizens under the First Amendment to advocate what they wish unless "there is a clear and present danger that a substantial public evil will result therefrom," the standard established in earlier court cases.

Here the "clear and present danger" is the organizing and recruiting of people to overthrow the U.S. government by force. The government need not wait to act until everything is in place for the revolution but may act to prevent such activity even when its failure is assured because of "inadequate numbers or power of the revolutionists." Preservation of the state is its ultimate value, and its possible demise is of sufficient evil for Congress to limit freedom of speech.

It was appropriate for the trial court judge to reserve the question of the existence of the danger for himself as it is a matter of law and not a question of fact for the jury. In another procedural matter, the judge was also correct in instructing jury members that they must find that the defendants actually had the "intent" to overthrow the government "as speedily as circumstances would permit" to convict them. That intent could be shown by the stated goals of the organization and the recruitment of members by defendants as well as the defendants' own advocation of the goals. The parties charged under the statute were given adequate notice by the provisions of the Act that "there is a line beyond which they may not go" under the First Amendment.

OTHER OPINIONS   Justice Felix Frankfurter concurs in the judgment. He perceives the issue to be one of balancing competing interests. On one side of the scales is the government's right to maintain its existence—"the most pervasive aspect of sovereignty"—whereas, on the other side, is the First Amendment's very specific limitation on governmental power to infringe on a person's right to "think what he pleases, to write what he thinks, and to have his thoughts made available for others to hear or read." However, "not every type of speech occupies the same position on the scale of values." Speech that advocates the violent overthrow of government, like speech that advocates criminal activity, ranks low on the scale.

It is the responsibility of Congress as the elected, representative body to adjust the competing interests. "[T]he independence of the judiciary is jeopardized when courts become embroiled in the passions of the day and assume primary responsibility in choosing between competing political, economic and social pressures." It is the role of the Court to ensure procedural fairness and the impact on the individuals but not to act as a superlegislature. To that end, the Court must consider the context of the speech and various precedents where it weighed competing interests versus speech and must not allow distortion of judgment merely because of inflammatory attitudes or events. However, the Court cannot overturn a legislative judgment merely because it would have made a different choice regarding the competing interests if making the initial judgment. Frankfurter cautions that "Preoccupation by our people with the constitutionality, instead of the wisdom, of legislative or of executive action is preoccupation with a false value" and that "without open minds there can be no open society. And if society be not open the spirit of man is mutilated and becomes enslaved."

Justice Robert Jackson also concurs in the judgment but he bases his assent on a different legal principle—the law of conspiracy. In his view, the basis for his conviction is a conspiracy to teach about and to advocate the overthrow of the government by force and violence in violation of the statute. A conspiracy may be "evil in itself, independently of any other evil it seeks to accomplish." The present Communist Party, an organization that eschews violence in favor of stealth, is such an evil. Given that perspective, the application of the "clear and present danger" test in cases such as this would require that the government could not take action in the preparatory stages which is extremely shortsighted. By using instead the law of conspiracy, the government could act immediately as it has here.

Justice Hugo Black enters a dissenting opinion. His emphasis is the First Amendment and the freedom of speech. He characterizes "what the crime is not." The defendants were not charged with attempting to overthrow the government, nor with committing overt acts to that end, nor were they charged with actually writing or saying anything to overthrow the government. Instead they were charged with organizing the Party and with using speech and the press in the future to teach and advocate. This conviction is a "virulent form of prior censorship of speech and press, which I believe the First Amendment forbids." It is the First Amendment and the free society it reflects that will ensure the defeat of communism.

Justice William O. Douglas also dissents. He defines these defendants' activity as teaching themselves and others about communism with the "hope that some day it would be acted upon." Teaching about communism in other settings such as classrooms is not criminal; thus "the crime then depends on not what is taught but who teaches it" and the intent of the teacher. That path is dangerous because examining people's motives leads to criminalizing not people's acts but their thoughts. Free speech and its protection are "essential to the very existence of a democracy." The government can justify limiting it only when there is a very real likelihood of an immediate danger to society. In the instant case, the Court is dealing with speech alone—without overt acts—and there is no evidence of clear and present danger in the record before the Court. The issue, if the supporting evidence had been introduced at trial, should have been submitted to the jury rather than decided by the judge.

SIGNIFICANCE OF THE CASE   This case is part of the Court's continuing struggle to determine the proper standard by which to measure governmental actions designed to limit citizens' First Amendment right of speech. The Court is concerned with balancing national security versus that constitutional right. Here the Court adopted a "gravity of evil" test or as formulated by Chief Judge Learned Hand at the court of appeals level and adopted by the Court, "[W]hether the gravity of the 'evil,' discounted by its improbability, justifies such invasion of free speech as is necessary to avoid the danger." Supposedly this test, which downplays the immediacy of threat, was more suited to deal with large-scale conspiracies than the "clear and present danger" test. The latter seemed more appropriate for testing the constitutionality of the isolated speech of individuals and small groups.

QUESTIONS FOR DISCUSSION

(1) The Court's view of the Communist Party was obviously a reflection of the passions and traumas of the time. Should the Court mirror such societal concerns or should the Court be more detached? Why?

(2) In considering major issues of this period such as abortion, acquired immunodeficiency syndrome (AIDS), and drugs, what role would you advocate for the Court? Observer or participant?

(3) Do you agree with the dissenters that the Court should exert especially close scrutiny of First Amendment rights when the ideas or the groups espousing them are especially unpopular, or appear to be outside the mainstream of political thought?

(4) Is there any one standard that can be used to measure the constitutionality of free speech in all circumstances, or do you agree that the speech must be taken in context including the situation? Why?

RELATED CASES *SCHENCK V. UNITED STATES*, 249 U.S. 47 (1919); *GITLOW V. NEW YORK*, 268 U.S. 652 (1925); *Yates v. United States*, 354 U.S. 298 (1957); *Scales v. United States*, 367 U.S. 203 (1961); and *Brandenburg v. Ohio*, 395 U.S. 444 (1969).

PENNSYLVANIA V. NELSON
350 U.S. 497 (1956)

BACKGROUND The Pennsylvania Sedition Act made it a crime to advocate knowingly the use of force or violence to overthrow the government of Pennsylvania or the government of the United States. Steve Nelson, an acknowledged member of the Communist party, was convicted under the Act and sentenced to twenty years in prison and fined $10,000 plus assessed $13,000 for costs of prosecution. Nelson was found guilty of sedition against the United States but not against the state of Pennsylvania. The Pennsylvania Supreme Court reversed Nelson's conviction solely on the issue of *supersession*. That is, the Pennsylvania Supreme Court held that federal laws prohibiting sedition superseded the enforceability of the state law. It should be noted that at the time of his state conviction, Nelson had been prosecuted and convicted under federal law.

CONSTITUTIONAL ISSUE

Whether federal sedition laws supersede state sedition laws, thereby precluding their enforcement? YES

MAJORITY OPINION   Chief Justice Earl Warren delivers the opinion of the Court. Chief Justice Warren is careful to state at the outset of the opinion what the Court's decision does not do. It does not prevent a state from punishing a crime in an area unless the federal government has "occupied the field." For example, although counterfeiting is a federal offense, state law may still punish the passing of counterfeit money. The key question, then, is whether Congress intended to supersede state sedition laws with the passage of federal sedition laws. If Congress intended to occupy the field of sedition enforcement, states may not punish offenders.

Chief Justice Warren sets forth three criteria that help the Court determine if Congress intended to occupy the field of sedition enforcement. The first criterion is whether federal regulation is so pervasive that it is reasonable to conclude that Congress left no room for supplemental state enforcement. The chief justice examines the provisions of the Smith Act, which makes it unlawful to advocate the use of force or violence to overthrow *any* government in the United States. The Internal Security Act of 1950 and the Communist Control Act of 1954 imposed heavy fines and prison sentences on conviction. This leads the chief justice to conclude that Congress did intend to occupy the field of sedition enforcement.

The second criterion is whether the activity touches a field where the federal interest is so dominant that the federal system assumes preclusion of enforcement of similar state laws. Chief Justice Warren asserts that Congress treated the enforcement of sedition laws as a matter of vital *national* concern. Prosecution of sedition is an issue of national importance and national, not local, enforcement.

The third criterion applied by Chief Justice Warren is whether enforcement of state sedition laws would present a serious danger of conflict with the administration of federal sedition laws. The chief justice quotes a statement made by President Roosevelt in 1939 in which the President requested all local authorities to turn over information about espionage to the Federal Bureau of Investigation (FBI). The chief justice also quotes FBI director J. Edgar Hoover, who in a speech stated that a centralized, coordinated effort was needed to battle seditious conduct. Hoover also feared "amateur handling" of such a vital matter. To echo this problem, the chief justice notes that the Pennsylvania Sedition Act permits an indictment to be initiated on an information by a private citizen. The chief justice concludes by observing that there has never been a successful prosecution against an attempt to destroy a state or local government. The Court then holds that the decision of the Pennsylvania Supreme Court is affirmed.

OTHER OPINIONS   Justice Stanley Reed, joined by Justices Harold Burton and Sherman Minton, dissent. Justice Reed begins by noting that Congress has not specifically barred the state's right to punish sedition under its police power. In the absence of a specific bar, Reed asserts, the Court should not infer that Congress intended to do so. The cases the majority relies on to illustrate areas where Congress meant to occupy the field of legislation are all commerce cases. In those cases the Court believed that enforcement of state laws would interfere with the regulatory plan of Congress. But in this case, criminal actions are involved, and no such interference is likely. Also, Justice Reed notes that Congress was undoubtedly aware of existing state sedition laws when it passed the Smith Act, the Internal Security Act, and the Communist Control Act. He believes that if Congress intended to occupy the field of legislation it would have said so when it passed those laws. As far as state interference with federal sedition enforcement, Justice Reed quotes the Justice Department's *amicus curiae* brief in which the Department denies that state sedition laws have interfered with federal enforcement. Finally, Reed observes that Title 18, § 3231 of the U.S. Code, which codifies federal criminal law, states that nothing in Title 18 shall take away or impair the jurisdiction of state courts under state laws.

SIGNIFICANCE OF THE CASE *Pennsylvania v. Nelson* is a controversial case not so much because it precludes state prosecutions for sedition, but because it impinges on states' rights. In this sense, the case is really a dispute over federalism. It raises the issue whether a person can be prosecuted by a state for advocating the use of force or violence to overthrow the *national* government. On the one hand, the national government is quite capable of protecting itself from violent overthrow without state assistance. Conversely, a state may punish certain kinds of behavior under its police power. Many states were simply resentful that the Supreme Court held that federal sedition laws superseded the enforcement of their own sedition laws.

QUESTIONS FOR DISCUSSION

(1) Should a state be allowed to prosecute a person for sedition against the state itself?

(2) Should a state be allowed to prosecute a person for sedition against the United States?

(3) Does Nelson's prosecution by Pennsylvania at a time he was being prosecuted under federal laws constitute double jeopardy? Why or why not?

RELATED CASES *Allen-Bradley Local v. Wisconsin Employment Relations Board*, 315 U.S. 740 (1942); *Hill v. Florida*, 325 U.S. 538 (1945); and *Railroad Transfer Service v. Chicago*, 386 U.S. 351 (1967).

WATKINS V. UNITED STATES
354 U.S. 178 (1957)

BACKGROUND Watkins was convicted of a misdemeanor for his failure to answer questions when he appeared as a witness before a Subcommittee of the House of Representatives Committee on Un-American Activities. During his appearance, he readily answered questions about his own involvement with the Communist movement and even identified other individuals currently involved with the Communist Party; however, he balked at naming those "who to my best knowledge and belief have long since removed themselves" from the Communist movement. Watkins was prosecuted by the U.S. Attorney's Office and was found to be in "contempt of Congress," and he appealed the conviction on the grounds that questions concerning prior associations of others were outside the scope of the congressional inquiry, and his refusal to answer was therefore correct.

CONSTITUTIONAL ISSUE

Whether separation of powers between Congress and the Court precludes the Supreme Court from requiring legislative subcommittees to meet minimal procedural guarantees such as providing adequate notice of the topic and such as explaining the pertinency of questions when compelling testimony from witnesses? NO

MAJORITY OPINION   Chief Justice Earl Warren delivers the majority opinion of the Court. He begins by recognizing that the power to conduct investigations is inherent in the legislative process because the lawmakers must gather information to pass laws and to act as a check on the other branches of government. This power is not unlimited, however; all such investigations must be tied to a legitimate task of Congress, and the power to conduct them is not to be construed as general authority to inquire into the exercise of an individual's constitutional rights.

Warren then proceeds to a historical analysis of the evolution of the power to punish for "contempt of Congress" from its beginnings in Parliament to its adaptation to Congress. He notes that the Congress rarely exercised the contempt power until the 1950s when the House Un-American Activities Committee began investigating subversive activities. Although the earlier cases such as *Kilbourn* and *McGrain* emphasized the limited nature of congressional inquiries, recent cases focus on accommodating government interests with the rights and privileges of individuals. Oddly enough, the increase in congressional use of the contempt power was accompanied by an almost total abandonment of the power in Parliament.

One major distinction between Parliament and Congress is that Congress's use of the contempt power is subject to judicial review, whereas that of Parliament is not. It is appropriate for the Court to consider the balancing of public interest and individual's rights, and if the Court did not do so, it would "abdicate the responsibility placed by the Constitution on the judiciary to insure that Congress does not unjustifiably encroach upon" individual's rights. Congress is constrained by the Bill of Rights even when it is pursuing a legitimate legislative task of investigation.

Summoning a witness to testify about his or her activities, beliefs, or associations is governmental interference and has an inhibiting effect in and of itself, not only for the witness but for others who are aware of the situation. This is particularly true, Warren says, when the cause or belief is unpopular or unorthodox, and may hold the advocate up for public shame or embarrassment and economic harm such as loss of employment. Or, as Warren succinctly stated, "Abuses of the investigative process may imperceptibly lead to abridgment of protected rights."

The Court has previously set the prerequisite for holding a person in contempt of Congress for exercise of First Amendment rights. The Court requires that the delegation of power to the committee must be clear. Here, Warren declares, Congress has not met that responsibility, and the Committee's charter is both overly broad and vague. Furthermore, the House has exercised little or no oversight over the Committee that, Warren says, has greatly exceeded its charge and conducted "ruthless exposure of private lives in order to gather data that is neither desired by the Congress nor useful to it."

Congress has no legitimate authority to seek information that is not pertinent to the legislative matters before it. "[T]here is no congressional power to expose for the sake of exposure." Warren, on an ironic note, states that because the courts, after trial and appeal, do not understand the subject of the inquiry and the pertinency of the questions, it is unreasonable to expect the witness to do so contemporaneously. It is the responsibility of Congress to explain the subject of the inquiry and how the questions are related to it rather than to make the witness guess as to each. In this case, neither the charge nor related matters provide adequate notice to Watkins; therefore, the conviction should not stand.

OTHER OPINIONS   Justice Felix Frankfurter, in his concurring opinion, reiterates the importance of the witness's having adequate notice of the topic being investigated and of the witness clearly understanding the pertinency of the questions as prerequisites before a witness may be held in contempt of Congress.

Justice Tom Clark files a dissenting opinion. He is chiefly concerned that the Court is unnecessarily curbing the power of Congress and its committees to investigate in order to legislate. This information-gathering function of Congress is generally done by the committees, and several standing committees are given broad and vague responsibilities. He cites as an example that the Committees on Armed Services are given jurisdiction over "Common defense generally." If the Court limits the investigative scope of the House Committee on Un-American Activities because of overbreadth, then the Court should limit all committees. Clark finds this to be an unacceptable inhibition of Congress in carrying out its responsibilities. In addition, the facts of this case indicate that Watkins clearly understood the topic under investigation and the pertinency of the questions as is indicated by Watkins's prepared statement. Therefore, the Court should not find that the charge was overly broad nor should it determine that Watkins was improperly held in contempt because he did not understand the pertinency of the questions.

Clark points out that Watkins testified as to his own activities and that actually what Watkins was attempting to do was to protect the constitutional rights of others. "It is settled that one cannot invoke the constitutional rights of another." Also, Watkins and the others are free to believe as they wish, but the committee was investigating their affirmative actions in support of those beliefs. Clark states that refusal to testify about past activities is not protected by the freedom of expression provisions of the First Amendment.

SIGNIFICANCE OF THE CASE   The congressional power to investigate, although broad, is not unlimited, and the actions of congressional committees are subject to judicial review. Here, the Supreme Court imposes important procedural safeguards regarding compelled testimony. These include the requirement that Congress must clearly state the scope of the committee's authority and the subject matter of the inquiry. It is the committee's responsibility to make the pertinency of the questions clear to the witness before charging him or her with contempt.

QUESTIONS FOR DISCUSSION

(1)   What are the appropriate parameters for congressional committees in investigating matters concerning people's private lives and beliefs?

(2)   Do you agree with Clark's position that Watkins was actually claiming other people's constitutional rights? Why or why not?

(3)   Do you think the facts supported the majority's position that Watkins did not clearly understand the purpose of the inquiry or the pertinency of the questions?

(4)   Why do you feel that this is an example of either judicial restraint or judicial activism?

RELATED CASES *Kilbourn v. Thompson*, 13 Otto 168 (1881); *McGRAIN V. DAUGHERTY*, 273 U.S. 135 (1927); *Sinclair v. United States*, 279 U.S. 263 (1929); *BARENBLATT V. UNITED STATES*, 360 U.S. 109 (1959); and *Eastland v. United States Servicemen's Fund*, 421 U.S. 491 (1975).

NATIONAL ASSOCIATION FOR THE ADVANCEMENT OF COLORED PEOPLE V. ALABAMA
357 U.S. 449 (1958)

BACKGROUND The N.A.A.C.P., a nonprofit membership corporation chartered in New York, had established independent, unincorporated branches in Alabama as early as 1918 and had opened, in 1951, a regional office staffed by three people in the state. The organization failed to comply with the state law requiring foreign (out-of-state) corporations to file their charters with the state and to designate a place of business and agent to receive service of process. In 1956, Alabama brought a suit in equity against the N.A.A.C.P. seeking to enjoin it from conducting further activities in the state and to force its ouster from the state on the premise that its activities were causing irreparable injury to the state's citizens. During the course of the litigation, the organization refused to produce its membership lists although it did provide other information as ordered by the trial judge. It was adjudged in contempt of court and fined $100,000. The state Supreme Court denied *certiorari* to review the contempt judgment.

CONSTITUTIONAL ISSUE

Whether organization membership lists are protected from disclosure to state governments under the First and Fourteenth Amendments unless the state shows a sufficiently compelling interest? YES

MAJORITY OPINION Justice John Marshall Harlan II writes the opinion of the Court. He first recognizes the Association's standing to assert, on behalf of its members, their individual rights to associate freely under the First Amendment and to have that freedom protected against disclosure. Requiring the members to claim those rights personally would nullify the "right at the very moment of its assertion" and, in addition, the N.A.A.C.P. and its members were "in every practical sense identical."

The nexus of the rights of speech, association, and assembly in the advancement of beliefs and ideas is an integral and entrenched aspect of liberty protected by the Fourteenth Amendment from state action. Privacy in group associations, particularly when the group advocates unpopular ideas, is an indispensable ingredient in the survival of these associations. For example, in the instant case, the N.A.A.C.P. has shown uncontroverted proof that prior disclosures of its membership lists has resulted in economic and other reprisals against its members. The Court recognizes the vulnerability of such groups and their members to public hostility and the resultant chilling of the exercise of First Amendment rights if the members' names were made public. Merely to claim, as Alabama did, that the repressive effects stems from private rather than state action is not sufficiently convincing to the Court because such private actions could occur only after the state's exertion of its power to force release of the membership lists.

The participation of the state as a party and the participation of its judicial officials is considered to be state action that triggers the applicability of the Fourteenth Amendment. Even though Alabama has not taken any direct action to restrict association, its actions are to be subjected to the closest scrutiny because "abridgment of such rights, even though unintended, may inevitably follow from varied forms of governmental action." Alabama does not, in this instance, meet the Court's requirement of showing a compelling state interest sufficient to overcome the fundamental association and privacy rights of the members of the N.A.A.C.P.

SIGNIFICANCE OF THE CASE   This case marked the inclusion of the First Amendment freedom of association among the rights protected by the Fourteenth Amendment against state action. It also furthered the pattern of protecting privacy of one's associations from public scrutiny and therefore from reprisals from whatever source, private or public.

QUESTIONS FOR DISCUSSION

(1)   Under what circumstances do you believe that the government, state or national, should be able to force organizations to disclose their membership lists?

(2)   Should candidates, political parties, and political action committees be required to disclose their contributors? Why or why not?

(3)   What parameters, if any, would you set on the right of association?

(4)   Should groups be allowed to exclude certain people or groups from membership? If so, what are acceptable guidelines?

RELATED CASES   *American Communications Ass'n. v. Douds*, 339 U.S. 382 (1950); *BUCKLEY V. VALEO*, 424 U.S. 1 (1976); and *Roberts v. United States Jaycees*, 468 U.S. 609 (1984).

BARENBLATT V. UNITED STATES
360 U.S. 109 (1959)

BACKGROUND   Barenblatt was summoned in 1954 to testify before a Subcommittee of the U.S. House of Representatives Committee on Un-American Activities, which was investigating alleged Communist infiltration into the field of education. The Subcommittee was primarily interested in Barenblatt's activities during the time that he was a graduate student and teaching fellow at the University of Michigan, some four years before his Subcommittee appearance. After providing some initial background information, Barenblatt refused to answer further questions about his political and religious beliefs or his associational activities. He based his refusal on the First, Ninth, and Tenth Amendments rather than on the Fifth Amendment's protection against self-incrimination. He was convicted of a misdemeanor for refusing to answer the questions of the Subcommittee and was sentenced to six months' imprisonment and was given a fine.

CONSTITUTIONAL ISSUE

Whether a congressional subcommittee has the authority to compel testimony and to force disclosure of one's associational relationships? YES

MAJORITY OPINION   Justice John Marshall Harlan II delivers the opinion of the Court. He structures the opinion around two issues: (1) the right of an individual to resist the exercise of congressional power; and (2) the protection of an individual's First Amendment rights including freedom of association balanced against the protection of society in meeting the threat of communism.

Justice Harlan first focuses on Congress and its use of investigative committees. He initially examines the legitimacy of the congressional power of inquiry and then examines the legitimacy of this committee. A brief review of the history of congressional investigative power shows that from the nation's beginning Congress has conducted inquiries into matters about which it might legislate, and its power to do so is well established and almost unquestionable. The repeated renewal and extension of this particular committee's life and appropriations indicate continued congressional commitment to its purpose and functions. Because of this history and legislative precedent, Harlan determines that both the congressional power of inquiry and the role of this committee are virtually unassailable.

Having established the legitimacy of the inquiry, Harlan then turns to Barenblatt's claim that the committee's charge was unconstitutionally vague, both generally and as specifically applied to him, and that it did not authorize the probe into communism in education. Harlan states that the meaning of the congressional authorization is not to be interpreted by the charge alone but also by the "legislative gloss" that is derived from the legislative reports, administrative interpretation, and long usage. Here he determines that the extensions of the committee's life and Congress's failure to limit the scope of the inquiry are indicative that the inquiry into Communist influences in education is appropriate. It is clearly the prerogative of the House to determine the scope of the investigations. In addition, Harlan states that Barenblatt clearly understood the Subcommittee's purpose in investigating him as is shown by Barenblatt's prepared memorandum that he presented to the Subcommittee.

Harlan then turns to the First Amendment question of freedom of association. The Court determines that the protection against disclosing one's associational relationships is not absolute. The interests of society are to be weighed against the constitutional rights of the individual in determining whether the associations must be revealed. To overcome the individual's rights, the state's interest "must be compelling." In this case, the nation's interest in self-preservation and the "widely-accepted view that the tenets of the Communist Party included the ultimate overthrow of the government of the United States by force and violence" are sufficiently "compelling" to infringe on Barenblatt's associational rights. The Court notes that the inquiry is not aimed at theoretical classroom discussions of communism which would be an inappropriate exercise of congressional power but instead is focused on the affirmative actions of Barenblatt and others similarly situated.

Harlan ends the opinion with a somewhat lackluster defense of the Committee and its motives. He states that the Court cannot intervene in congressional business simply because of questionable motives on the part of legislators when Congress is exercising a constitutional legislative purpose. The remedy for such action lies "not in the abuse by the judicial authority of its functions, but in the people."

OTHER OPINIONS Justice Hugo Black, Chief Justice Earl Warren, and Justice William O. Douglas dissent. First, they find that rule under which Barenblatt was punished was impermissibly vague in that it does not provide clear guidelines for citizens to follow in terms of First Amendment rights. They disagreed with establishing a balancing test for such rights and making a person "guess—at the penalty of imprisonment" whether a court will later find the state's interest to be so compelling as to overcome the individual's rights. The basic requirement for holding a person in contempt is that the person must have a clear understanding of his or her duties and responsibilities, and that the person has violated those duties. Here, that is missing because Barenblatt could not have the requisite certainty of either the pertinency of the question or the legitimacy of the inquiry.

Second, the dissenters argue that the Constitution unequivocally states that there shall be no abridgement of the First Amendment rights. Black argues "that the Bill of Rights means what it says," and the Court should enforce it or the Constitution will "be more honored in the breach than in the observance." For him, the strength of the nation is the power of the people to think, speak, and associate politically without government reprisal. The fact that a minority political party, even an unpopular one, can be treated in such a fashion sets a dangerous precedent.

Third, Black scathingly attacks the role of the committee and describes its purpose as trying witnesses and punishing them by public humiliation, shame, and the accompanying loss of economic benefits. He charges that the House Un-American Activities Committee is exceeding its powers and assuming the role of the judiciary in trying and punishing people for exercising their First Amendment rights. The dissenters' views are summarized in the following:

> Ultimately all the questions in this case really boil down to one—whether we as a people will try fearfully and futilely to preserve democracy by adopting totalitarian methods, or whether in accordance with our traditions and our Constitution we will have the confidence and courage to be free.

Justice William Brennan also dissents. He states that there is no purpose of investigating Barenblatt except "exposure, purely for the sake of exposure," which is "outside the pale of congressional inquiry."

SIGNIFICANCE OF THE CASE This case deals with the scope of governmental power, specifically that of congressional inquiries into constitutionally protected areas of speech and belief. The majority in *Barenblatt* implements a balancing test—that is, the rights of the individual may be overcome by a "compelling state interest"—as the appropriate standard for court review. In contrast to *Watkins v. United States*, this decision upholds the grant of power to the House of Un-American Activities Committee despite challenges of vagueness. The Court reiterates the scope of statutory interpretation by employing the "legislative gloss" of the charge, the reports, the administrative interpretations, and custom and usage in finding the law was not too vague. Black's dissent in *Barenblatt* is particularly noted because of his strong (and quotable) defense of the First Amendment and his attack on the House Un-American Activities Committee.

QUESTIONS FOR DISCUSSION

(1) If you had been on the Court, would you have agreed with Harlan or Black? Why?

(2) Do you feel that Black's argument that suspected Communists were "singled out and, as a class, are subjected to inquisitions which the Court suggests would be unconstitutional but for the fact of communism" are relevant to any issues now? Do you see any application to either drug users or AIDS patients today in terms of "witch hunts"? Why?

RELATED CASES *McGRAIN V. DAUGHERTY*, 273 U.S. 135 (1927); *DENNIS V. UNITED STATES*, 341 U.S. 494 (1951); *Sweezey v. New Hampshire*, 354 U.S. 234 (1957); *WATKINS V. UNITED STATES*, 354 U.S. 178 (1957); and *Gibson v. Florida Legislative Committee*, 372 U.S. 539 (1963).

8

RIGHTS
OF THE ACCUSED

INTRODUCTION

Americans exhibit great ambivalence about the rights of those accused of criminal activity. On the one hand are those who agree with Edwin Meese, then attorney general of the United States, who said, "If a person is innocent of a crime, then he is not a suspect" with the corollary that those guilty of wrongdoing are less deserving of consideration from government. Conversely, there are those who believe that all, even miscreants, are entitled to claim protection under the Constitution. In today's world there prevails a "get-tough-on-crime" attitude with the accompanying view that society is too easy on those accused of crime unless, of course, you are the one who is the focus of the attention of law-enforcement officers and prosecutors. Then the "technicalities" suddenly convert to constitutional rights to which you are absolutely and unequivocally entitled.

The major bulwarks of protection from an overzealous government in the field of criminal justice are located in the Bill of Rights. The Bill of Rights, on its face, applies only to the national government and not to the states. Chief Justice John Marshall reiterated that principle in *BARRON V. BALTIMORE* (1833), a case involving the eminent domain provision of the Fifth Amendment. He stated that the national Constitution was established by the people to constrain the national government and that the states enacted their own individual constitutions to restrain unwarranted government actions on that level.

The adoption of the Fourteenth Amendment in 1868 with its Due Process Clause, which specifically limits state action, provided a new avenue of attack for those seeking application of the Bill of Rights to state governments. In *HURTADO V. CALIFORNIA* (1884), the narrow question before the Court was whether the right to indictment by grand jury provided in the Fifth Amendment was mandated in state courts. The Court answered negatively, responding that each state had the right to control criminal procedure inside its boundaries but that the states cannot act in an arbitrary and capricious manner. The Due Process Clause of the Fourteenth Amendment does protect "[t]hose fundamental principles of liberty and justice which lie at the base of all our civil and political institutions."

The difficulty is in determining exactly which principles are deemed to be so fundamental as to be included. The Court tried to clarify the matter in *PALKO V. CONNECTICUT* (1937) when it established the new standard that rights "implicit in the concept of ordered liberty" were encompassed within the Fourteenth Amendment and therefore applicable to state governments, although the same problem of identifying those rights lingered. *PALKO* involved yet another Fifth Amendment right—protection against double jeopardy. The Court recognized that there was differential treatment in that a second prosecution would be barred if Palko was in federal court but declined to apply the principle to state courts. It was not until *Benton v. Maryland* was decided in 1969 that the double-jeopardy clause was finally applied to the states.

The Court's struggle to define which rights are basic or fundamental or essential to a fair trial continued in *DUNCAN V. LOUISIANA* (1968). In the one hundred years since the adoption of the Fourteenth Amendment, the arguments of those favoring selective incorporation or piecemeal adoption and of those favoring total incorporation had crystallized. While accepting that the right to trial by jury in serious criminal cases was fundamental, the Court declined to impose juries for petty crimes or mandate unanimity in jury verdicts. Justices Hugo Black and William O. Douglas, longtime advocates of total incorporation, rejoined that all provisions of the Bill of Rights must apply to the states; otherwise, the promise of due process is empty in that it changes with the membership of the Court, and each time one crosses the border into another state.

Other theorists argue that due process is an independent right and may encompass rights not specifically enumerated in the Bill of Rights, such as the right of privacy, or may be violated when the government acts in a manner so as to "shock the conscience." In *ROCHIN V. CALIFORNIA* (1952), deputies went into the defendant's home, broke into the room where Rochin and his wife were, and saw two capsules lying on the bedside table. Rochin grabbed the tablets and swallowed them. He was then taken to the hospital where his stomach was pumped without his consent. The Court was not quite willing at that point to further limit the powers of the states by using the Due Process Clause to incorporate certain rights further. However, clearly appalled at the acts, the Court accepted the premise that government acts that "shock the conscience" could violate the Due Process without reference to an underlying provision of the Bill of Rights.

An excellent summary of the Court's endeavors to define the content and parameters of due process is found in *ADAMSON V. CALIFORNIA* (1947). Although *ADAMSON* was later overruled by *Malloy v. Hogan* (1964), which incorporated the privilege against self-incrimination, its analysis of due process remains invaluable.

Search and Seizure

The Fourth Amendment shelters the "right of the people to be secure in their persons, houses, papers, and effects against unreasonable searches and seizures." In *Olmstead v. United States* (1928), which involved tapping Olmstead's telephone without a physical trespass onto his property, the Court unequivocally defined the scope of the Fourth Amendment as covering only the search of the person and his or her material possessions, not conversations. However, the focus expanded when the Supreme Court, in *KATZ V. UNITED STATES* (1967), stated that "the Fourth Amendment protects people, not places...what he seeks to preserve as private, even in an area accessible to the public, may be constitutionally protected." The revamped standard calls the Fourth Amendment into play whenever a person has a reasonable expectation of privacy. In some ways this is a more difficult standard to enforce than the earlier one because it is subjective rather than objective and is not nearly as definite as the old emphasis on material objects.

There is also the requirement that the search be reasonable and that it be founded on a warrant supported by probable cause. For various reasons, the Court has allowed warrantless searches in limited conditions such as exigent circumstances where evidence might be destroyed before a warrant could be obtained or because of the mobility of vehicles, but the requirement of probable cause remains intact. Courts have also exempted certain administrative searches from these stringent provisions. Those enforcing building or fire codes, inspecting restaurants for health departments, or determining a corporation's compliance with tax or other regulatory measures are not required to obtain a warrant or to have probable cause. However, in the field of criminal justice where the penalty is loss of liberty, the Court has been more rigorous in applying the Fourth Amendment, but even there exceptions have been developed.

One such exception is the practice of stop and frisk, validated by the Court in the landmark decision of *TERRY V. OHIO* (1968). Any time that a police officer interferes with a person's movements or frisks a person it carries Fourth Amendment implications. The question for the Court then becomes whether the government invasion is reasonable under all the circumstances. Stop and frisk is a procedure designed to protect the safety of the officer and nearby bystanders. In weighing the competing interests of the person's right to move about freely without being stopped or searched and the concerns for the officer's safety, the Court finds such minimal intrusions to be acceptable within certain limits. The officer must be able to articulate specific, objective facts about why there is reasonable suspicion to detain someone, and the search is to be limited to a patdown of outer clothing to determine if the person is carrying a hidden weapon.

The Burger-Rehnquist Courts have altered the equilibrium between government and citizens by more frequent application of the nebulous balancing test rather than strict adherence to the requirement of probable cause as the basis of search. An example is *NEW JERSEY V. T. L. O.* (1985) wherein the purse of a high school freshman was searched by school officials after she was caught smoking in the school lavatory. The search of the purse revealed it contained marijuana, money, and documents that appeared to indicate that the student might be engaged in the commerce of selling marijuana to her fellow students, a fact that was not suspected by officials until after the search. The student was reported to the juvenile authorities. The Court applied the balancing test and decided that the need to maintain order and discipline in public schools overcame the student's privacy interests in her purse, and the search was reasonable in the context of public schools. The case exemplifies the trend away from rigid compliance with probable cause as the standard for search and the new focus on reasonableness in searches.

Violations of the Fourth Amendment result in the exclusion of evidence at trial. The decentralized structure of our system of policing does not lend itself to litigation against individual officers for search-and-seizure violations (although it may lead to individual reprimands). Instead, the remedy that has been developed is the exclusionary rule, which is designed to protect the integrity of the judicial system. To paraphrase *People v. Defoe* (1926), it is better that the criminal go free when the constable blunders than to condone the illegal activities of the government. Applied as early as 1914 in federal courts in *Weeks v. United States*, the exclusionary rule was only made applicable to the states in 1961 in *MAPP V. OHIO.*

Just as the Court has continued to carve out exceptions to the requirement for a warrant before conducting a search, so too has the Court proceeded to create exemptions from the Exclusionary Rule. In *UNITED STATES V. LEON* (1984), officers received a warrant from a state-court judge to conduct a search for drugs; federal charges resulted from the location of the drugs. The U.S. District Court excluded the drugs from evidence on the basis that the affidavits underlying the warrant did not provide adequate probable cause. The Supreme Court held that evidence seized by officers acting on a facially-valid warrant can be admitted at trial even though the warrant is ultimately invalid. The effect is to insulate officers and magistrates from appellate review and to move away from the Fourth Amendment's mandate that warrants be issued and arrests be made only on probable cause.

Right to Counsel and Self-Incrimination

The Fifth Amendment protection against self-incrimination and the Sixth Amendment right to counsel are closely connected and frequently inseparable. The protection against self-incrimination encompasses more than the right to not testify in one's own criminal trial; it also includes statements taken in custodial interrogation or involuntary seizure of other incriminating evidence such as blood samples. The key to admissibility at trial is lack of coercion in gathering the inculpatory evidence—whether it is a voluntary oral statement or a noninvasive harvesting of physical evidence such as snipping a lock of hair. The Court in *Chambers v. Florida* (1940) plainly stated that the adversarial process demands that the government must provide the evidence "by its own independent labors, rather than by the cruel, simple expedient of compelling it from his own mouth" (or body in an invasive procedure).

Although the Court has frequently stated its unwillingness to condone coerced confessions, the problem has been in identifying exactly what constitutes "coercion." Actions such as beating a suspect, or denial of food and water are clearly unacceptable. But what about conditions that raise the specter of psychological coercion during interrogation? It was those concerns that led the Court to *Escobedo v. Illinois* (1964) and to *MIRANDA V. ARIZONA* (1966) which emphasized the presence of counsel as the major counterweight in the imbalance of power between the state and the defendant. These and other cases have established the right to counsel at critical stages of the investigatory process and not just at trial.

The assistance of counsel in navigating the arcane world of courts and trial procedures is thought to be one of the most basic of rights, but that guarantee was slow to be applied to indigents in state courts. The process began in 1932 with *POWELL V. ALABAMA*, more commonly known as *The Scottsboro Boys Case*. Defendants—all black and all young—were accused of raping two white girls on a freight train on March 25, 1931. They were indicted six days later and went to trial on April 6. The trial judge complied with Alabama law, which provided for counsel to be appointed in capital cases (a possible penalty for rape at that time) but instead of appointing specific attorneys, the judge appointed "all the members of the bar." An out-of-state attorney and one rather reluctant local attorney did offer to help with representation on the morning of the trial. The young men, not surprisingly, were assessed the death penalty.

The Court applied the test discussed in the first portion of this introduction and determined that denial of counsel in these circumstances ("ignorance and illiteracy of defendants, their youth, the circumstances of public hostility," isolation from friends and family, and the possibility of the death penalty) violated the "fundamental principles of liberty and justice which lie at the base of all our civil and political institutions." The refusal to provide counsel here was tantamount to a denial of due process.

Following *POWELL*, the Court required appointed counsel for indigent defendants in noncapital cases when "special circumstances" existed. States were not required to routinely provide attorneys for indigents until *GIDEON V. WAINWRIGHT* (1963). In that case, a man with an eighth-grade education submitted a handwritten petition to the Supreme Court and changed forever the complexion of the criminal justice system. Clarence Earl Gideon was convicted in a Florida court on a felony charge after being denied right to counsel by the trial judge. The Court recognized the imbalance in an indigent defendant representing himself or herself against a professional prosecutor backed by the immense investigatory power of the police apparatus and offset that imbalance by requiring that an attorney be appointed to represent indigents in felony cases. *Argersinger v. Hamlin* (1972) extended the rule to cover those misdemeanors, which involved the possibility of incarceration.

Cruel and Unusual Punishment

The Court has also been called on to interpret the meaning of the Eighth Amendment prohibition against cruel and unusual punishment. In *Robinson v. California* (1962), the Court applied the Eighth Amendment to the states. Robinson was convicted of being "addicted to the use of narcotics" under a California statute. The Court accepted that narcotic addiction is a disease and ruled that to imprison one for a disease is cruel and unusual punishment. However, in *Powell v. Texas* (1968), the Court declined to find that a chronic alcoholic who was intoxicated in public was protected under *Robinson* because Powell, unlike Robinson, had committed an affirmative act—being intoxicated in public—rather than being locked up solely for his alcoholism.

The bulk of the cases involving the Eighth Amendment has focused on two areas—rights of prisoners and capital punishment. The Court has examined the constitutionality of physical punishment—for example, the use of corporal punishment on inmates or the method of execution—under the Eighth Amendment. The test used is the one enunciated in *Trop v. Dulles* (1958), that is, whether the punishment meets "the evolving standards of decency that mark the progress of a maturing society." In applying the standard, the Court has forbidden the use of physical force on prisoners except in limited circumstances such as quelling a riot or subduing a violent prisoner. The Court even abandoned its "hands-off policy" regarding prison management and has examined the conditions of incarceration to determine if they come up to the "standards of decency" demanded by society, and has required that basic living and sanitary conditions be improved for both the general prison population and those in administrative or punitive segregation.

The other primary focus of the Court has been the issue of capital punishment. The Court has never ruled that the death penalty is cruel and unusual or in violation of the Constitution. However, the Court has examined the imposition of the death penalty under various statutes to determine if the penalty was being assessed fairly in a procedural sense. In *Furman v. Georgia* (1972), the Court found that the Georgia scheme was flawed because it allowed jurors unfettered discretion and allowed them to act in a wholly arbitrary and capricious manner. The result of the decision was a hiatus in executions across the nation as states reevaluated their own sentencing procedures and the ensuing revision of several capital punishment statutes in an attempt to make them acceptable to the Court.

Among those states that drafted new statutes were Georgia and North Carolina. Georgia's statute, which included new features of a bifurcated trial, jury consideration of statutorily identified aggravating factors as well as nonidentified mitigating factors, a limited number of crimes for which the death penalty could be given, and mandated expedited review by the state Supreme Court passed constitutional muster in *GREGG V. GEORGIA* (1976). The key to acceptance by the Court was that the jury had to weigh aggravating and mitigating circumstances in giving the penalty, thereby assuring that the individual circumstances of the crime and of the defendant were considered. The lack of the particularized examination of the case and the defendant was the downfall of North Carolina's statute in the companion case of *WOODSON V. NORTH CAROLINA* (1976). North Carolina's law mandated an automatic death penalty for certain types of homicide without any consideration of aggravating and mitigating circumstances and without automatic appellate review. The Court found that mandatory death penalties had been repudiated in this country in favor of discretionary jury sentencing and that the statute violated the "evolving standards of decency."

One of the concerns frequently voiced is that capital punishment is assessed in a racially discriminatory manner. In *McCLESKEY V. KEMP* (1987), McCleskey, who is black, introduced a sophisticated statistical study showing that blacks are more likely to be given the death penalty and that those who murder white victims are also more likely to face execution. The Court did not dispute the validity of the numbers but ruled that a defendant seeking to overturn a death sentence on the basis of racial discrimination has a double burden of proof—to show discrimination generally and to show it actually affected the outcome of his or her trial.

Issues arising in the context of capital punishment appear to be a morass from which the Court is unable to extricate itself. For example, where is society willing to draw the line for executing those who are under the age of eighteen at the time of commission of the crime? In the 1989 case of *STANFORD V. KENTUCKY*, the Court said that under contemporary standards, the age is sixteen. Do those "standards of decency" permit the execution of those who are insane or mentally retarded? The Court replied no to the first, but yes to the second in *Penry v. Lynaugh* (1989). The Court has recognized the difficulty in being the arbiter of society's standards and, more and more, under Chief Justices Burger and Rehnquist, has deferred such questions to the legislative bodies, the elected representatives of the people.

Conclusion

The contours of constitutional protections in the field of criminal justice appear to be much more fluid than in many other areas of constitutional law. The overarching concept is due process and the right to a fair trial, but the application of the concepts is a most arduous task for the Court. The Court continues to hone the balance between a person's right to be free from government intrusion into his or her life and belongings against society's need for order.

HURTADO V. CALIFORNIA
110 U.S. 516 (1884)

BACKGROUND The Constitution of California, adopted in 1879, provided that formal charges could be filed against a criminal defendant either through indictment by grand jury or by information, after examination and commitment by a magistrate. Hurtado was tried on the basis of an information, was convicted, and was sentenced to die. His appeal was based, in part, on the fact that he was not indicted by a grand jury which he claimed was part of due process protected by the Fourteenth Amendment.

CONSTITUTIONAL ISSUE

Whether a defendant's right to indictment by grand jury as provided in the Fifth Amendment is applicable to the states through the Fourteenth Amendment? NO

MAJORITY OPINION Justice Stanley Matthews writes the opinion of the Court. He deems the question of whether the right to indictment by grand jury is covered by the Due Process Clause of the Fourteenth Amendment to be one of great magnitude. It is important because a finding that the Fourteenth Amendment is applicable will limit the rights of state legislatures to write laws and to determine procedures within their own boundaries.

The crux of the question is the nature of due process and what it entails. Justice Matthews extensively reviews the history of the Magna Charta, interpretations of its provision relating to indictment, common law, and current English law to ascertain the meaning of due process. He determines that it is the right to trial and the substance of the trial that is critical and not the form of the initial charge—indictment or information. Due process is to be defined by reference to the Constitution and to the common and statutory law of England at the time of the adoption of the Constitution. However, the common law is not the only source of law and justice, and other systems of jurisprudence also provide justice; the advantage to the common law is its flexibility and adaptability including the willingness to borrow from other systems of law. As society changes, law, its forms, and its processes evolve also. The Court is not bound by the rigid rules of the past in defining due process but instead by "the spirit of personal liberty and individual right" in devising new forms and processes to meet "modern ideas of self-government."

"[T]hose fundamental principles of liberty and justice which lie at the base of all our civil and political institutions" are those that are protected against state action through the Fourteenth Amendment. Each state may prescribe its own modes of judicial proceedings as long as the procedures do not violate those fundamental principles of liberty and justice. Thus, it is the substance, and not the form, of legal proceedings that is important under the Due Process Clause of the Fourteenth Amendment. Given the fact that grand jury proceedings are preliminary matters and do not result in final convictions, the Court does not find that indictment by grand jury is such a fundamental principle of justice that it is required under the Fourteenth Amendment.

SIGNIFICANCE OF THE CASE   In *Hurtado*, the Court begins the process of determining whether all the protections of the Bill of Rights apply against state governments by reason of the adoption of the Fourteenth Amendment. The Court answers negatively, thus sparking the debate over selective incorporation, and total incorporation, which has continued to the present time. The Court notes the states' right to control criminal procedure within their own boundaries while posting a clear warning that "Arbitrary power, enforcing its edicts to the injury of the persons and property of its subjects, is not law" and is "subject to enforcement of these limitations by judicial process." The case establishes the test the Court will employ in such cases, whether the matter is within the "fundamental principles of liberty and justice which lie at the base of all our civil and political institutions."

QUESTIONS FOR DISCUSSION

(1)   As an advocate of selective incorporation, which of the provisions of the Bill of Rights would you not apply to the states?

(2)   Do you think that the Fourteenth Amendment has been expanded too far—to incorporate too much? Why?

(3)   *Hurtado* clearly indicates that differences in criminal procedure because of federalism are acceptable to the Court. Do you agree that you should be treated differently if you are arrested in New Mexico rather than New York? Why?

RELATED CASES   *Twining v. New Jersey*, 211 U.S. 78 (1908); *PALKO V. CONNECTICUT*, 302 U.S. 319 (1937); *ADAMSON V. CALIFORNIA*, 332 U.S. 46 (1947) (dissent); and *DUNCAN V. LOUISIANA*, 391 U.S. 145 (1968).

PALKO V. CONNECTICUT
302 U.S. 319 (1937)

BACKGROUND Palko was convicted of second-degree murder and was sentenced to life imprisonment. The state appealed and won a retrial on grounds that testimony was improperly excluded and that the instructions to the jury did not adequately inform them of the difference between first-and second-degree murder. Palko was retried, convicted of first-degree murder, and sentenced to die. Palko appealed his timely objection to the new trial on the grounds that he was protected from double jeopardy by the Fourteenth Amendment.

CONSTITUTIONAL ISSUE

Whether the protection against double jeopardy provided by the Fifth Amendment is applicable to state prosecutions under the Fourteenth Amendment? NO

MAJORITY OPINION Justice Benjamin Cardozo writes the majority opinion for the Court. The Bill of Rights on its face applies only to the national government and does not offer protection from state governments even though the national government could not take such action. The Court has never established a general shield covering the entire Bill of Rights from state governments but instead has selectively guarded certain rights.

The test for determining which rights fall under this protection is whether the right "is implicit in the concept of ordered liberty." If the right is "of the very essence of ordered liberty," then it is covered under the provision of the Fourteenth Amendment barring the deprivation of "life, liberty, or property without due process of law" by states. Liberty means more than freedom from physical restraint; it includes freedom of mind and action as well. Because the First Amendment rights of freedom of speech, press, religion, and assembly are basic to liberty ("indispensable condition of nearly every other form of freedom"), the Court has sheltered them from oppressive and arbitrary action of state governments. However, most of the protections offered to criminal defendants such as the right to jury trial and right to indictment do not have such a character as justice and fair trials may prevail without them.

It is true that if this were a federal prosecution that Palko would be protected from double jeopardy in this situation by the Bill of Rights. The Court, by a narrow margin, has established in prior cases that jeopardy does preclude a new trial if the appeal is by the national government and not the defendant. The goal of the state here is "a trial free from the corrosion of substantial legal error" and not to harass the defendant with a multitude of lawsuits. The Court does not reach the question of whether a new trial would have been improper if there were an error-free trial. The Court is merely extending the same right to the state as the defendant has in seeking reversal of error adverse to him.

SIGNIFICANCE OF THE CASE This case is noteworthy in the ongoing discussion of selective versus total incorporation of the Bill of Rights by the Fourteenth Amendment. It establishes the test for incorporation as to whether the right is basic to "ordered liberty."

If it is, then it is protected from arbitrary and capricious state action by the Fourteenth Amendment. To make such a determination the Court will examine the history and legal precedent relevant to the right and will consider the importance of the right and whether it is a "principle of justice so rooted in the traditions and conscience of our people as to be ranked as fundamental." The protection against double jeopardy was one of the last major provisions of the Bill of Rights to be applied to the states and that did not occur until 1969 when the Court decided *Benton v. Maryland.*

QUESTIONS FOR DISCUSSION

(1) The effect of selective incorporation is to create a hodgepodge of rights, some protected from the state government and some not. Is this an effective means of justice? Why or why not?

(2) Which provisions of the Bill of Rights do you consider important enough to be protected from government at all levels? What is your reasoning for your decision?

(3) Do you think the Court's selection is internally consistent? Why?

(4) Is the Court providing clear guidance to the states and to the people of the rights that are protected and those that are not? What standards would you create?

RELATED CASES *HURTADO V. CALIFORNIA,* 110 U.S. 516 (1884); *Kepner v. United States*, 195 U.S. 100 (1904); *Twining v. New Jersey*, 211 U.S. 78 (1908); *POWELL V. ALABAMA,* 287 U.S. 45 (1932); *ADAMSON V. CALIFORNIA,* 332 U.S. 46 (1947) (dissent); *Poe v. Ullman*, 367 U.S. 497 (1961) (dissent); *DUNCAN V. LOUISIANA,* 391 U.S. 145 (1968); and *Benton v. Maryland*, 395 U.S. 784 (1969).

DUNCAN V. LOUISIANA
391 U.S. 145 (1968)

BACKGROUND Gary Duncan was charged with simple battery, a misdemeanor punishable by a maximum of two years imprisonment and a fine of $300 in Louisiana. Duncan's timely request for a jury trial was turned down by the judge because the state constitution provided for jury trials only in cases in which imprisonment at hard labor or the death penalty could be imposed. Duncan was convicted and filed an appeal.

CONSTITUTIONAL ISSUE

Whether the state must provide the opportunity for trial by jury in serious criminal cases under the Sixth and Fourteenth Amendments? YES

MAJORITY OPINION Justice Byron White authors the majority opinion of the Court. The Fourteenth Amendment provides that the states may not "deprive any person of life, liberty, or property without due process of law." The Court, in deciding the meaning of these words, has looked to the Bill of Rights for guidance. In determining which provisions should be applied to the states, the Court has applied the test of whether the right is "basic to our system of jurisprudence" or whether it is "a fundamental right, essential to a fair trial."

The right to trial by jury in criminal cases, stemming from the Magna Carta, was well entrenched when the Sixth Amendment was written. Its purpose was protection from arbitrary and capricious action on the part of government; it protects the criminal defendant "against the corrupt or overzealous prosecutor and against the compliant, biased, or eccentric judge." It is a fundamental right to have trial by jury in serious criminal cases, and states must provide an opportunity to have jury trials in those cases that, if tried in federal court, would come within the Sixth Amendment. Cases such as *Palko v. Connecticut*, which contained dicta that the provisions relating to jury trials were not applicable to the states, are specifically rejected by Justice White.

Justice White finds strong support for the jury trials in that every state provided the opportunity for jury trials in serious criminal cases. He cautions that the Court's ruling does not mandate jury trials in all cases, nor does it cast doubt on the integrity of bench trials. Juries are not required when the defendant waived the right in serious criminal cases, and they are not required in petty offenses. Justice White avoids the question of what is a petty crime and what is a serious crime—"We need not, however, settle in this case the exact location of the line between petty offenses and serious crimes"; however, a crime that is punishable by two years, as this is, is deemed to be a serious crime under both past and contemporary standards, and Duncan should have been given a jury.

OTHER OPINIONS   Justice Abe Fortas concurs in the decision that the right to jury trial in major prosecutions is an integral part of due process, but he emphasizes that this decision does not impose all federal requirements about juries such as unanimous verdicts or juries of twelve on the states.

Justice Hugo Black—joined by Justice William O. Douglas—writes a concurring opinion. They argue that the Fourteenth Amendment made the entire Bill of Rights applicable to the states, that is, they advocate the theory of total, rather than selective, incorporation. They interpret the Due Process Clause of the Fourteenth Amendment as extending every protection of the Bill of Rights to citizens and argue against the theory that "due process is an evolving concept." They reject the theory that tests such as "fundamental fairness" and "shocking the conscience of the Court" should be the measure of the Fourteenth Amendment because they rely too much on the particular makeup of the Court and each "judge's idea of ethics and morals" rather than on the "written words of the Constitution." They also reject any notion that "under the guise of federalism the states should be able to experiment with the protections afforded our citizens through the Bill of Rights." Black and Douglas interpret the language of the Fourteenth Amendment that "No State shall make or enforce any law" abridging due process as an absolute guarantee of citizens' rights against state action.

Justice John Marshall Harlan II—joined by Justice Potter Stewart—dissents. Justice Harlan casts the case in terms of federalism and the right of the states to set their own procedures. He begins by recognizing the antiquity and importance of jury trials and the need for fundamentally fair criminal proceedings. He notes that the states "have always borne primary responsibility for operating the machinery of criminal justice," that he has always resisted any efforts to impose "federal notions of criminal justice" on the states, and that he opposed uniformity merely for uniformity's sake regarding criminal procedure.

Using the legislative history of the Fourteenth Amendment and other sources as the basis, he argues that the meaning of due process is evolutionary in nature. The determining factor in deciding the content of due process is not that a certain right is contained in the Bill of Rights, but, instead, that the right is fundamental. Citizens have other rights and protections beyond those found within the first ten amendments to the Constitution; the origin of the right is not critical but its fundamental nature is. Whether a defendant has a jury trial is not critical, but whether the trial is fundamentally fair is critical. Harlan argues that the issue of trial fairness should be the target of the Court's inquiry and not whether there was a jury involved. As even the majority recognized, jury trials are not the only fair means of conducting a trial and are "not demonstrably better than the alternatives states might devise."

SIGNIFICANCE OF THE CASE   The Court extended the Sixth Amendment right of trial by jury to state prosecutions for serious crimes (without clearly defining what constitutes a serious versus petty crime). The case is also noted for the continuing discussion of selective and total incorporation approaches of applying the Bill of Rights to the states.

===

QUESTIONS FOR DISCUSSION

(1)   Scholars, judges, and others (including presidents) now debate over strict interpretation and "original intent" of the Constitution. In light of that debate, what is your reaction to Black's and Douglas's reading of the Fourteenth Amendment?

(2)   Do you think that Black and Douglas are arguing for both a literal interpretation of the words of the Constitution and a reduction of states' powers? Is that consistent with most advocates of strict interpretation?

(3)   Do you agree with Justice Powell that the need for a jury as protector against arbitrary and capricious governmental action has disappeared? Why or why not?

RELATED CASES   *BARRON V. BALTIMORE*, 7 Peters 243 (1833); *PALKO V. CONNECTICUT*, 302 U.S. 319 (1937); *United States v. Carolene Products Co.*, 304 U.S. 144 (1938); and *Moore v. East Cleveland*, 431 U.S. 494 (1977).

===

ROCHIN V. CALIFORNIA
342 U.S. 165 (1952)

BACKGROUND   Three deputy sheriffs who had "some information" that Rochin was selling narcotics went to his home where he lived with several family members. The deputies found the front door open, entered, forced open the door of the bedroom where Rochin and his wife were, and saw two capsules lying on the bedside table. They asked, "Whose stuff is this?" Rochin then seized the tablets and put them in his mouth. Although the deputies tried to force him to spit the tablets out, he swallowed them. The deputies then took the handcuffed Rochin to the hospital where his stomach was pumped against his will. The two capsules were found to contain morphine and were the basis of his conviction.

CONSTITUTIONAL ISSUE

Whether a violation of the Due Process Clause of the Fourteenth Amendment without reference to an underlying provision of the Bill of Rights can, in and of itself, cause reversal of a criminal conviction? YES

MAJORITY OPINION   Justice Felix Frankfurter writes the majority opinion for the Court. The opinion focuses on the meaning of the Due Process Clause of the Fourteenth Amendment and the protection it offers against arbitrary and capricious state action in criminal cases. The administration of criminal justice is primarily an arena of state power and activity, especially regarding the enactment of criminal statutes. The Supreme Court admittedly defers to states in this matter, but the states are limited in the scope of their authority by the Constitution, particularly regarding procedure. It is the duty of the Supreme Court to ensure that such procedures are in accordance with rights described as "fundamental," "implicit in the concept of ordered liberty," or the "canons of decency and fairness which express the notions of justice of English-speaking peoples."

Due process of law is an evolving concept, one that is not frozen at same fixed stage of time, but instead is to be defined not by "inanimate machines" but by judges whose independence is safeguarded by the Constitution. These judges are guided by history, concepts of justice and fairness, and legal precedent. Due process is not a matter of judicial caprice, drafted by judges relying solely on their private notions of fairness. Judges are restrained by their judicial function as well as by their habits of self-discipline and self-criticism.

Due process does consider the method by which evidence is gathered, and just as coerced confessions are not accepted, neither should this type of activity, which is so "close to the rack and the screw" be permitted. "This is conduct that shocks the conscience" in violation of the principles of due process.

OTHER OPINIONS   Justice Hugo Black concurs in the decision. He bases the result on the self-incrimination clause of the Fifth Amendment. When incriminating evidence is forcibly taken from one, one is being compelled to testify against one's self in violation of the Fifth Amendment. "[F]aithful adherence to the specific guarantees in the Bill of Rights insures a more permanent protection of individual liberty than that which can be afforded by the nebulous standards stated by the majority."

Black states that relying on such vague standards as "conduct that shocks the conscience" invites unacceptable expansion of the Due Process Clause as well as vesting too much discretion with judges who can expand and contract due process at will. "I long ago concluded that the accordion-like qualities of this philosophy must inevitably imperil all the individual safeguards specifically enumerated in the Bill of Rights."

Justice William O. Douglas also concurs. He too focuses on the specific guarantee of the Fifth Amendment. The issue is not whether the protection against self-incrimination serves justice because the founders incorporated it in the Constitution, but whether it is applicable to the states as well as the national government. A right important enough to be guaranteed in federal trials is equally as important in state trials and should be protected in state courthouses as well as federal ones. It is wrong to refuse to apply the Fifth Amendment to the states as the Court recently did in *Adamson v. California* and then to criticize the states for violating the Due Process Clause on the basis of the "decencies of civilized conduct." "That is to make the rule turn not on the Constitution but on the idiosyncrasies of the judges who sit here."

SIGNIFICANCE OF THE CASE   *Rochin v. California* has two interesting aspects: the narrow one of removing evidence from a criminal defendant's body involuntarily and the overarching one of due process. In 1952, when this case was decided, the Court had not yet guaranteed many of the Bill of Rights provisions against the states. It is obvious that the Court is appalled at the acts of the officers, but it is unwilling to explicitly limit the powers of the states by using the Due Process Clause to further incorporate certain rights. Instead it establishes the test of whether the activity is "one that shocks the conscience," a test that in future cases would be applied across a broad spectrum of economic and social policies.

The issue of self-incrimination and physical evidence taken from one's body has proven to be a fertile source of lawsuits in both civil and criminal cases. In the criminal area, the Court has allowed the use of blood, breath, urine samples, fingerprints, voice samplers, and bitemarks even if taken involuntarily. It also has important implications for the current issue of drug testing to obtain or retain a job or benefits such as a college scholarship. If one must participate in such testing or suffer certain detriments (possibly even imprisonment), can the test truly said to be voluntary? The area remains open.

QUESTIONS FOR DISCUSSION

(1)   Black and Douglas advocate total incorporation of the Bill of Rights. Why do you agree or disagree with their arguments in this case?

(2)   The statements of Black and Douglas regarding the role of judges in interpreting the Constitution sound as though they were written by Rehnquist and Scalia, noted judicial conservatives, but Douglas is usually considered as a very liberal judge. What conclusions and observations can you draw from this?

(3)   Frankfurter outlines the parameters of judicial discretion. Do you think these are effective? Why?

(4)   Are the actions of the law-enforcement officials here particularly repugnant? What parallels may you draw regarding today's issues of AIDS, drugs, and driving while intoxicated? What limits would you set on government action in these matters?

RELATED CASES   *PALKO V. CONNECTICUT*, 302 U.S. 319 (1937); *Malinski v. New York*, 324 U.S. 401 (1945); *ADAMSON V. CALIFORNIA*, 332 U.S. 46 (1947); *Schmerber v. California*, 384 U.S. 757 (1966); *Skinner v. Railway Labor Executives Association*, 489 U.S. 602 (1989); and *NATIONAL TREASURY EMPLOYEES UNION V. VON RAAB*, 489 U.S. 656 (1989).

ADAMSON V. CALIFORNIA
332 U.S. 46 (1947)

BACKGROUND Adamson was charged with first-degree murder. He had previously been convicted of burglary, larceny, and robbery. Under California law, convictions for previous offenses could not be mentioned at a defendant's trial unless he took the stand in his own defense. If the defendant did take the stand, evidence of his previous crimes could be revealed to the jury on cross-examination to impeach his testimony. In addition, California law permitted the prosecutor to comment on the defendant's failure to deny or explain away the evidence against him, and the jury was free to draw negative inferences from a defendant's failure to testify. Adamson chose not to testify and was convicted. Adamson argued that California forced him to choose between the risk of having his prior convictions revealed to the jury or of having the jury draw harmful inferences from evidence only he could deny or explain away. Second, he argued that the law, in effect, compelled him to be a witness against himself in violation of the Fifth Amendment. Third, Adamson argued that the Fifth Amendment's privilege against self-incrimination was a privilege or immunity of national citizenship that the states are forbidden from abridging by the Fourteenth Amendment. Fourth, he maintained that the law violated the Due Process Clause of the Fourteenth Amendment by abridging the privilege against self-incrimination. Finally, he argued that the law had the effect of shifting the burden of proof to the defendant, who was forced to prove his innocence.

CONSTITUTIONAL ISSUES

(1) Whether the Fifth Amendment's privilege against self-incrimination is a privilege or immunity of national citizenship that may not be abridged by the states under the Fourteenth Amendment? NO

(2) Whether the privilege against self-incrimination is binding on the states by virtue of the Due Process Clause of the Fourteenth Amendment? NO

MAJORITY OPINION Justice Stanley Reed delivers the opinion of the Court. Justice Reed begins his analysis by conceding that any law permitting the prosecutor to comment on the defendant's failure to testify in his own defense would be a violation of the Fifth Amendment in a federal court. However, that fact does not determine Adamson's rights in a state court. In *Barron v. Baltimore* the Court ruled that the purpose of the Bill of Rights was to protect individuals against violations of their fundamental rights by the national government and not against similar violations by state governments. In *Twining v. New Jersey*, the Court specifically addressed this issue and ruled that the privilege against self-incrimination was not a privilege or immunity of national citizenship but a privilege of state citizenship that could be granted or denied by the individual states.

Justice Reed then addresses the question of whether the California law violated the Due Process Clause of the Fourteenth Amendment. Adamson contended that due process embodies the fundamental rights of citizens and that the privilege against self-incrimination is one of those rights. The Court, however, disagrees. The Due Process Clause of the Fourteenth Amendment does not draw all of the provisions of the Bill of Rights under its protection. The requirement that a defendant testify does not, by itself, violate his right to a fair trial. Although due process prohibits testimony gained "by fear of hurt, torture, or exhaustion," it does not necessarily prohibit a state from forcing a defendant to choose between testifying and having his previous crimes revealed to the jury, and remaining silent and having the jury make harmful inferences from his silence. Justice Reed concludes by stating that if there is evidence that only the defendant can explain away, it is quite natural that a prosecutor would call the defendant's failure to do so to the attention of the jury. Justice Reed notes that, "The purpose of due process is not to protect an accused against a proper conviction but against an unfair conviction."

OTHER OPINIONS   Justice Felix Frankfurter writes a concurring opinion. Frankfurter begins his opinion by stating his belief that *Twining* was decided correctly and that it should be upheld. He sees nothing wrong in allowing the prosecutor to draw harmful inferences from a defendant's refusal to testify in his own defense. He believes a jury will understand that past convictions do not mean that the defendant is guilty of the current charge. Frankfurter then addresses the question whether the protection against self-incrimination is a fundamental part of due process that the states are forbidden to abridge by the Fourteenth Amendment. Frankfurter concludes that it is not. He flatly rejects the idea of total incorporation of the Bill of Rights into the Due Process Clause and rejects the doctrine of selective incorporation because judges are left in the dark about which provisions are included and which are not. Frankfurter believes that only those rights deemed "fundamental" should be incorporated into the Due Process Clause of the Fourteenth Amendment.

Justice Hugo Black writes the principal dissent. First, Black believes that the California law compels a person to testify against himself. Second, Black joins the debate over whether the authors of the Fourteenth Amendment intended to make the protection of the Bill of Rights applicable to the states. Black's dissent contains a lengthy appendix that outlines his historical analysis of the passage of the Fourteenth Amendment. Black concludes from his analysis that the authors of the Amendment intended to overturn the *Barron* decision. Black argues that previous cases holding that the Bill of Rights does not apply to the states, such as the *Slaughterhouse Cases*, did not have the benefit of his analysis. Black states that he favors total incorporation of the Bill of Rights into the Due Process Clause of the Fourteenth Amendment. However, he notes that if he must choose between selective incorporation or no incorporation, he prefers the former. Finally, he notes that federal prosecutors have not been unduly burdened by forbidding them to comment on the defendant's failure to testify.

Justice Frank Murphy joins Black's dissent and writes a brief separate dissent. Murphy believes that the California law is a violation of the privilege against self-incrimination and therefore violates due process. However, unlike Black, he would not limit the concept of due process to just the provisions of the Bill of Rights, but would have due process also include safeguards not necessarily stated in the Bill of Rights.

SIGNIFICANCE OF THE CASE   *Adamson* is significant for two reasons. First, it contains a thoughtful discussion of the political and historical reasons for extending the privilege against self-incrimination to those accused of crimes. Second, *Adamson* presents the various positions on the incorporation of the Bill of Rights into the Due Process Clause of the Fourteenth Amendment. One theory totally rejects any attempt to make the provisions of the Bill of Rights applicable to the states. Under our federal form of government states should be free to grant or deny rights to criminal defendants as they choose. The second theory argues that only those rights that are deemed "fundamental" are binding on the states. Provisions that guarantee freedom of speech, press, and religion would be included, but others such as grand jury indictment would not. This theory is called selective incorporation. The third theory, supported by Justice Black, calls for total incorporation of the Bill of Rights. Finally, a fourth theory argues that due process may also include rights not specifically mentioned in the Bill of Rights, such as the right to privacy. The justices continued the debate in cases that followed *Adamson* including *Malloy v. Hogan,* which overruled *Adamson.* However, *Adamson* remains one of the best cases for understanding the debate over the incorporation of the Bill of Rights into the Fourteenth Amendment.

QUESTIONS FOR DISCUSSION

(1)   What is the exact nature of the dilemma in which the California law placed Adamson?

(2)   Do you agree with Justice Black that it is unfair to comment on a defendant's prior convictions? Why or why not?

(3)   Do you think that the privilege against self-incrimination should be granted to persons tried in state courts? Why or why not?

(4)   What, if any, provisions of the Bill of Rights would impose an unreasonable burden on the states? Why do you think so?

RELATED CASES   *BARRON V. BALTIMORE,* 7 Peters 243 (1833); *SLAUGHTER-HOUSE CASES,* 16 Wallace 36 (1873); *Twining v. New Jersey,* 211 U.S. 78 (1908); *PALKO V. CONNECTICUT,* 302 U.S. 319 (1937); and *Malloy v. Hogan,* 378 U.S. 1 (1964).

KATZ V. UNITED STATES
389 U.S. 347 (1967)

BACKGROUND   Katz was convicted of transmitting illegal bets by telephone from Los Angeles to Miami and Boston in violation of federal law. FBI agents placed an electronic listening device to the outside of a public phone booth used by Katz and then recorded his conversations. At his trial, Katz challenged the admission of the conversations into evidence on Fourth Amendment grounds, but the court of appeals rejected the challenge because there was no physical penetration of the phone booth. In his appeal to the Supreme Court, Katz urged it to hold that a public telephone booth is a constitutionally protected area and that physical penetration of a constitutionally-protected area is not necessary to constitute a violation of the Fourth Amendment.

CONSTITUTIONAL ISSUE

Whether the listening to and taping of a conversation made in a public telephone booth without a warrant constitute an unreasonable search and seizure within the meaning of the Fourth Amendment? YES

MAJORITY OPINION Justice Potter Stewart delivers the opinion of the Court. Justice Stewart starts by rejecting Katz's request to rule that a public telephone booth is a constitutionally-protected area. That, Stewart maintains, would require the Court to recognize a general right of privacy or impute a general right of privacy in the Fourth Amendment where none exists. Justice Stewart asserts that the protection of the general right to privacy, like one's life and property, is left to the individual states. Besides, deciding if a particular place is a "constitutionally protected area" is misdirected because "the Fourth Amendment protects people, not places." Nor does Justice Stewart give any credence to the government's argument that the phone booth was largely made of glass. It was the uninvited ear, not eye, that Katz sought to exclude.

Justice Stewart next addresses the issue of physical penetration assumed to be required for a search and seizure. He acknowledges that at one time *Olmstead v. United States* foreclosed further Fourth Amendment inquiry in wiretapping cases. But, he maintains that subsequent cases have eroded *Olmstead*. In *Silverman v. United States* the Court ruled that the Fourth Amendment governs the seizure of oral recordings as well as tangible objects. The requirement that some sort of trespass must occur is no longer controlling.

Having ruled that wiretapping is covered by the Fourth Amendment, Justice Stewart turns to the issue of the reasonableness of the wiretap. The government argues that the agents placed the wiretap after an initial investigation led them to suspect that Katz was a bookmaker. The agents made sure that only Katz's conversations were heard and recorded. Given that the agents understood *Olmstead* to be the rule governing wiretapping, the government claims the wiretap was reasonable. But Justice Stewart points out that with the probable cause they already had, any magistrate would have issued a warrant making the wiretap legal. The existence of adequate probable cause cannot be used as an after-the-event justification except under limited circumstances. This was not a search of an automobile, a search incident to a lawful arrest, or a search where consent has been given. The fact that the agents acted with restraint is irrelevant because the Fourth Amendment requires the interposition of a judicial officer between the police and a citizen. The agents ignored the procedure of antecedent justification, which Stewart says is central to the Fourth Amendment.

OTHER OPINIONS Justices Byron White, William O. Douglas, and John Marshall Harlan II file separate concurring opinions and Justice Hugo L. Black writes the only dissenting opinion. Justice White concurs with the result but is concerned about the warrant requirement in cases involving national security. He believes that the president or the attorney general should be able to authorize a wiretap without a warrant in national security cases and that such wiretaps are not unreasonable under the Fourth Amendment.

Justice Douglas disagrees with White that a warrant is unnecessary in national security cases for two reasons. First, the president and the attorney general are not judicial officers nor are they "neutral and detached." In most cases, the president and attorney general would be vigorous prosecutors of someone endangering our national security. Therefore, Douglas believes that to allow them to place a wiretap without a warrant violates the doctrine of separation of powers. Douglas's second reason is that the Fourth Amendment makes no exception to its warrant requirement based on the substantive nature of the crime. There is no reason to distinguish between national security crimes and other crimes simply because we may believe the former to be more heinous.

Justice Harlan joins the Court's opinion in so far as it holds that: (1) a phone booth is a place where a person has a constitutionally-protected reasonable expectation of privacy; (2) an electronic intrusion may violate the Fourth Amendment; and (3) the invasion of a constitutionally-protected area is presumed unreasonable in the absence of a search warrant. Justice Harlan believes that the Court's decision effectively overturns *Olmstead.* Finally, he does not read the Court's decision to preclude exceptions to warrantless wiretaps of public telephone booths.

Justice Black's dissent is based on two objections. First, he does not believe that the language of the Fourth Amendment supports the decision. Second, he does not believe that the Court should rewrite the Constitution "to bring it into harmony with the times." The literal language of the Fourth Amendment refers to "persons, houses, papers, and effects." This clearly indicates that the framers intended to cover tangible objects under the Amendment. The Amendment also requires that the "things" to be searched and seized be "particularly described." Justice Black argues that a conversation cannot be seized, nor is it possible to ask an FBI agent to describe a conversation that will occur some indefinite time in the future. Black concedes that electronic eavesdropping was unknown to the framers, but ordinary eavesdropping was known to them. If they had wanted to prohibit evidence secured by eavesdropping they easily could have done so. Black's understanding of the Fourth Amendment is that it was designed to prevent physical break-ins by the police. Justice Black disagrees that the *Olmstead* decision has been eroded by subsequent Court decisions. One case, *Warden v. Hayden,* cited by the majority as eroding *Olmstead,* involved the seizure of clothes, not wiretapping. For these reasons, Justice Black dissents.

SIGNIFICANCE OF THE CASE   Although the majority refuses to discuss whether the Fourth Amendment protects a general right of privacy, its pronouncement that the Fourth Amendment "protects people not places" assumes that privacy is the value that underlies the Amendment. Despite Justice Stewart's protestation that the protection of the right of privacy, like the protection of life and property rights, is left to the states, much of the Court's analysis centers around the concept of a reasonable expectation of privacy. The Court mentions that when a person enters a phone booth and deposits his money there is the assumption that his words will be heard only by the person called.

Another interesting aspect of *Katz* is the apparent jockeying going on between Justices White and Douglas. Note that even though *Katz* has nothing to do with national security, White, Douglas, and, to some extent, Harlan debated when a wiretap could be placed without a warrant in national security cases. The justices are apparently trying to lay groundwork for future cases where national security might be an issue.

QUESTIONS FOR DISCUSSION

(1)   Look up *Olmstead v. United States.* Is there any reason to believe that it is not overruled by *Katz*? Why?

(2)   Would you make an exception for requiring a warrant for a wiretap in national security cases? Why or why not?

(3)   Do you agree with Justice Black that conversations are not "things" that can be seized? Why or why not?

(4)   Because the FBI agents believed they were acting legally under the *Olmstead* ruling, should Katz's conviction be upheld and the *Katz* ruling apply only to future cases? Why or why not?

RELATED CASES   *Olmstead v. United States*, 277 U.S. 438 (1928); *Goldman v. United States*, 316 U.S. 129 (1942); *Silverman v. United States*, 365 U.S. 505 (1961); *GRISWOLD V. CONNECTICUT*, 381 U.S. 479 (1965); and *Warden v. Hayden*, 387 U.S. 294 (1967).

TERRY V. OHIO
392 U.S. 1 (1968)

BACKGROUND   Detective Martin McFadden, who had nearly forty years experience in police work, observed three men on a street and noted that they repeatedly walked an identical path, stopping each time to stare into the same store window. McFadden believed they were "casing a job, a stick-up," so he approached them and identified himself as a police officer. In the course of the transaction, McFadden patted down Terry's outside clothing and found in his overcoat pocket a revolver that McFadden was unable to remove. He ordered the trio into the store, removed Terry's coat and the gun. He patted down the outer clothing of the other two men and seized a revolver from the overcoat pocket of one. The two men were charged with carrying concealed weapons. The trial court admitted the guns into evidence at trial.

CONSTITUTIONAL ISSUE

Whether it is always unreasonable, under the Fourth Amendment, for a police officer to seize a person and subject him to a limited search unless there is probable cause? NO

MAJORITY OPINION   Chief Justice Earl Warren writes the majority opinion for the Court. The Fourth Amendment imposes the requirement of probable cause before officers may search or seize a person. People have the liberty to move about freely and to be free from searches on the streets just as much as in their own homes. "[W]henever a police officer accosts an individual and restrains his freedom to walk away, he has 'seized' that person," and it is "nothing less than sheer torture of the English language" to describe a frisk as something less than a search. Both the stop and the frisk are governed by the Fourth Amendment, and the governing question is the "reasonableness in all the circumstances of the particular governmental invasion of a citizen's personal security."

Although the Court always prefers that officers obtain warrants for searches and seizures, that is not always possible because of the exigencies of the situation. One such exigency is the safety of the officer and nearby bystanders and the critical need to determine if the suspect is carrying a weapon. This is a paramount governmental interest, and tied to the need for effective law enforcement, will justify the limited intrusion of the citizen's rights against search and seizure.

However, ratification of stop-and-frisk procedures does not free the police from certain requirements. First, the officer's activities will be tested by the standard of whether a person of reasonable caution is warranted in believing that the action taken was appropriate. The officer must be able to articulate objective and specific facts to support the intrusion. Second, the search must be strictly circumscribed by the exigencies of the circumstances, and it is to be no more extensive than necessary to search for hidden weapons. Third, the search and seizure must be reasonable both at the time of inception and as conducted. The Fourth Amendment continues to limit police activity in this area just as the Court will continue to monitor the reasonableness of police action in invading citizen's rights.

OTHER OPINIONS Justice John Marshall Harlan II concurs in the opinion. Stop-and-frisk procedures fall within the Fourth Amendment and must be reasonable in nature. For the officer to conduct a frisk, he or she must first have constitutional grounds to make a forcible stop to investigate a suspected crime.

Justice Byron White also concurs. A brief stop to interrogate the person is also appropriate, although "absent special circumstances, the person approached may not be detained or frisked but may refuse to cooperate and go on his way." In the appropriate circumstances, however, it is acceptable to detain the person and ask questions, and it is the temporary detention that chiefly justifies the protective frisk for weapons.

Justice William O. Douglas enters a dissenting opinion. The majority clearly states that stop-and-frisk procedures are searches and seizures. Given that, how can such procedures be permitted unless the officers meet the Fourth Amendment mandate of probable cause? Here, the men were charged with carrying concealed weapons, and the officer himself did not allege that he had probable cause to believe they were carrying concealed weapons—the crime with which they were charged. If the officer had sought a warrant, a magistrate would not have been authorized to issue one because of the lack of probable cause. This decision gives police "a greater authority to make a 'seizure' and conduct a 'search' than a judge has to authorize such action." The effect is to impair the Fourth Amendment severely through the abrogation of the requirement for probable cause. That action should be taken by the people through constitutional amendment and should not be undertaken by the Court.

SIGNIFICANCE OF THE CASE This Fourth Amendment case is important for two reasons. First, it creates another recognized exception to the requirement for a warrant and legitimizes the stop-and-frisk procedure. Second, the standard for conducting such searches and seizures is reduced from probable cause to reasonable suspicion, a much less onerous burden on the police, although they are still required to base the intrusions on objective, articulable facts and not mere hunches.

QUESTIONS FOR DISCUSSION

(1) Citizens have the right to move about freely, uninterrupted by police interference; yet, there is a need for effective law enforcement. How would you balance these competing interests?

(2) These brief investigatory stops can be used as tools of harassment. Do you think that this case adequately guards against such? Why?

(3) Why do you agree or disagree with Douglas that the majority is vesting the police with more authority than a magistrate?

(4) The Court has approved the use of roadblocks through which all drivers must pass for the interception of those driving while intoxicated. What policy and legal arguments can you make for and against such a practice?

RELATED CASES *KATZ V. UNITED STATES*, 389 U.S. 347 (1967); *Adams v. Williams*, 407 U.S. 143 (1972); *Pennsylvania v. Mimms*, 434 U.S. 106 (1977); *United States v. Sokolow*, 490 U.S. 1 (1989); and *Michigan Dept. of Police v. Sitz*, 496 U.S. 444 (1990).

NEW JERSEY V. T. L. O.
469 U.S. 325 (1985)

BACKGROUND T. L. O., a fourteen-year-old high school freshman, and her companion were discovered smoking in the school lavatory by a teacher. Smoking in that location was prohibited by school rules, although the school provided smoking areas elsewhere. The two were taken before the school's assistant vice-principal. When T. L. O. denied smoking, the assistant vice-principal demanded to see her purse. He opened it, found a package of cigarettes and a package of cigarette rolling papers commonly used with marijuana. He then proceeded to search the purse thoroughly, including a zippered compartment, and found some marijuana, a pipe, plastic bags, and a fairly substantial sum of money as well as two letters and an index card containing the names of students who owed the student money, all of which he read. He then notified the student's mother and turned the material over to the juvenile authorities. The state then brought delinquency charges against T. L. O. on the basis of her confession that she was selling marijuana at school and on the evidence seized by school officials; she sought to have the materials suppressed during the criminal proceedings.

CONSTITUTIONAL ISSUE

Whether the full panoply of protection under the Fourth Amendment search-and-seizure provisions extends to students in public schools? NO

MAJORITY OPINION Justice Byron White writes for the majority of the Court. Abandoning the Court's initial question of whether the exclusionary rule applied to searches carried out by public school officials, Justice White focused instead on the issue of the proper application of the Fourth Amendment to public schools. The inquiry requires balancing the privacy interests, if any, of the students against the need to maintain order and discipline in the schools. There is no doubt that the Fourth Amendment does extend to students enrolled in public schools, albeit in a limited fashion. School officials are agents of the state, not parents' surrogates, in carrying out searches and other functions pursuant to disciplinary policies mandated by state statutes and are therefore constrained by the Fourteenth Amendment.

The analytical framework for examining Fourth Amendment questions is to determine the reasonableness of the search in the context in which the search occurs. Such a test allows school officials the flexibility needed to maintain order in the schools and yet does not authorize unrestrained intrusions on the privacy of schoolchildren. Requiring school officials to obtain a warrant or even to meet the probable cause standard is too stringent given the unique environment of the school setting. Reasonableness, for this purpose, involves two questions: (1) Was the search initially justified? and (2) Was the scope of the search appropriate? Searches of students' property are justified at their inception when there are "reasonable grounds" to believe the student is violating either the law or school rules. The scope of the search should be limited in nature and "not excessively intrusive in light of the age and sex of the student and the nature of the infraction." In this instance, the search was not unreasonable.

OTHER OPINIONS   Justice Lewis Powell, joined by Justice Sandra Day O'Connor, concurs in the decision. Students, although protected under the Fourth Amendment, do have lesser expectations of privacy in the school setting than do members of the population generally. The reasons for the lesser expectation of privacy include the very close association with classmates and teachers for long periods, and the openness of the public school because of community supervision because the students return home at night. Also, the relationship between teachers and students is generally nonadversarial, which contrasts with the relationship between law-enforcement personnel and criminal suspects.

Justice Harry A. Blackmun also concurs in the judgment. The traditional criterion for determining the constitutionality of governmental searches is whether probable cause existed. That should be abandoned in favor of a balancing test only in "exceptional circumstances in which special needs...make the warrant and probable cause requirement impracticable." The government's heightened obligation to safeguard students whom it compels to attend school meets those exceptional circumstances, but the Court should not frequently deviate from the traditional rule nor should it routinely substitute the balancing test as the measure in dealing with the Fourth Amendment.

Justice William Brennan, joined by Justice Thurgood Marshall, concurs in part and dissents in part. The Court has clearly established the parameters of search and seizure in prior cases. First, warrantless searches are unreasonable *per se* unless they fall into one of the narrow, recognized exceptions. Second, searches must be based on probable cause that a crime has been committed and that evidence of the crime will be found in a specific location. Third, less intrusive searches, such as a *Terry v. Ohio* patdown search, may be justified by a balancing test but only if the test gives sufficient weight to the privacy interests that will be infringed and only when the governmental stakes are very high.

Abandoning the probable cause requirement creates substantial costs for society and renders useless Fourth Amendment protections. "Moved by whatever momentary evil has aroused their fears, officials—perhaps even supported by a majority of citizens—may be tempted to conduct searches that sacrifice the liberty of each citizen to assuage the perceived evil." The majority, by altering the tests, is engaged in an "unanalyzed exercise of judicial will" according to "its momentary vision of the social good."

The Court itself has described the probable cause standard as "nontechnical" and "easily applied." Compliance with such a standard is not too arduous for administrators and would not inhibit the flexibility of officials to deal decisively with emergencies. The "amorphous 'reasonableness under all the circumstances'" test favored by the majority will merely generate more uncertainty and more litigation. In addition, there is no need to create a single standard to govern all school searches; precedent in criminal cases allows for variations in searches, such as limited searches for weapons versus more comprehensive searches, which are controlled by different rules.

Justice John Paul Stevens is joined by Justice Thurgood Marshall and, in part, by Justice William Brennan. The Court has overstepped its bounds by "unnecessarily and inappropriately" reaching out to decide a constitutional question—the scope of the Fourth Amendment as applied to school officials—on a rather picayune violation of school rules where a student smoked. In addition, the Court had heard twice oral arguments on the issue of the exclusionary rule and therefore should decide the merits of that matter. This case does not involve the use of the seized evidence in disciplinary hearings but in a juvenile matter in the courts. The exclusionary rule should apply if the evidence is improperly seized by school officials.

This search is a serious invasion of the student's privacy and stems from a minor infraction of school rules, not some violent, unlawful, or seriously disruptive conduct when the warrantless search of a student by an administrator would be reasonable. The standard adopted by the majority will encourage arbitrary, capricious action on the part of school officials for petty violations of guidelines for student behavior. "[T]he nature of the infraction should be the matter of first importance in deciding whether *any* invasion of privacy is permissible." Finding of more serious violations through "unexpected discovery" does not justify the initial invasion.

Perhaps more important is the message that is sent to students by allowing such governmental action. Values learned in the schoolroom are taken into life, and one of those cherished values is that government may not intrude into personal privacy without a warrant or compelling circumstances. This case is an important statement to young people about whether we really mean it when we say "our society attaches serious consequences to a violation of constitutional rights."

SIGNIFICANCE OF THE CASE   *New Jersey v. T. L. O.* exemplifies the shift in Fourth Amendment jurisprudence from strict adherence to probable cause as an absolute requisite for searches to the amorphous balancing test. Such a change carries important implications for the equilibrium between government and citizens and their right to be free from unwanted government intrusion into their privacy. The balancing test seems to be skewed in favor of the government and away from individual citizen's interests. The case is also interesting because those judges often thought of as the liberal wing of the Rehnquist Court and who are most frequently deemed judicial activists by conservatives—Stevens, Marshall, and Brennan—describe the majority's action as a "characteristic disregard of the doctrine of judicial restraint." It perpetuates the trend of shrinking the protections of the Fourth Amendment by creating more and more exceptions to the requirements of probable cause as an absolute mandate for search and seizure.

The case limits even further the protections extended by the Constitution to public school students. The case strengthens the power of school administrators over students, not just in trivial school disciplinary proceedings but also regarding involvement with the courts. It certainly encourages arbitrary and capricious actions on the part of unscrupulous teachers and administrators who may be more concerned about school order than safeguarding the rights of students.

QUESTIONS FOR DISCUSSION

(1) What problems do you see with the scope of the search and the issue of the student's privacy? Would you have upheld the validity of the search under *Katz* and related cases?

(2) Do you agree with the jettisoning of the probable cause standard for searches? Why?

(3) Do you agree with the statement that American schools are among the most oppressive institutions regarding constitutional rights? What court decisions would you cite to support your position? Are schools hypocritical in the messages they send—teaching one thing but practicing another?

RELATED COURT CASES *WEST VIRGINIA STATE BOARD OF EDUCATION V. BARNETTE*, 319 U.S. 624 (1943); *Camara v. Municipal Court of San Francisco*, 387 U.S. 523 (1967); *KATZ V. UNITED STATES*, 389 U.S. 347 (1967); *TERRY V. OHIO*, 392 U.S. 1 (1968); and *Goss v. Lopez*, 419 U.S. 565 (1975).

MAPP V. OHIO
367 U.S. 643 (1961)

BACKGROUND Three police officers went to Mapp's home pursuant to information that a person connected with a bombing was there and also that there was a large amount of policy material there. They requested entry into the two-family home, telling Mapp only that they wanted to question her. After calling her attorney whom she had engaged for a civil matter, Mapp refused to allow them to enter without a search warrant. The house was placed under surveillance, and approximately three hours later, seven or more officers forcibly entered the home when Mapp did not immediately come to the door. Mapp was halfway down the stairs from the upper floor when the officers broke in, and she demanded to see the warrant. An officer held up a piece of paper that he claimed was the warrant. Mapp grabbed the paper and "placed it in her bosom." During the ensuing struggle, the paper was recovered by the police, and Mapp was handcuffed and taken forcibly upstairs where the officers searched the apartment as well as the basement. Meanwhile, her attorney arrived and was denied the opportunity to see her and even to enter the house. Allegedly obscene materials—"four pamphlets, a couple of photos, and a little pencil doodle"—were found during the search, and Mapp was convicted of knowingly having in her possession and control certain lewd and lascivious books, pictures, and photographs in violation of Ohio law. During the trial, no warrant was produced nor was there any explanation offered by the state as to its absence. Mapp's conviction was upheld by the Ohio Supreme Court even though it admitted that the conviction was based on an illegal search and seizure.

CONSTITUTIONAL ISSUE

Whether the exclusionary rule, which bars the introduction at trial of evidence that is the product of improper searches and seizures, is applicable in state criminal trials under the Fourteenth Amendment? YES

MAJORITY OPINION Justice Tom Clark delivers the opinion of the Court. The opinion initially notes the nexus between the Fourth Amendment prohibition against unreasonable search and seizures and the Fifth Amendment prohibition against self-incrimination. As noted in the landmark case of *Boyd v. United States*, "[b]ut any forcible and compulsory extortion of a man's own testimony or of his private papers to be used as evidence to convict him of crime or to forfeit his goods" is unacceptable. This connection between the two is the basis of the exclusionary rule, which prevents the introduction of improperly seized evidence at trial. Justice Clark points out that without such an interpretation, the Fourth Amendment is merely empty words, and he stresses that it is the Court's role, as defined by the writers of the Constitution, to protect the integrity of individual rights.

Having established the general constitutional background, Clark attacks the controlling precedent, *Wolf v. Colorado*, which declared that the Fourteenth Amendment did not bar the use of improperly-seized evidence in state prosecutions for state crimes. His arguments against *Wolf* fall into three general categories: (1) factual grounds on which *Wolf* was based; (2) failure of alternative means to secure compliance with constitutional requirements; and (3) subsequent cases that essentially abandoned *Wolf*. First, Clark distinguishes the factual differences between the cases as well as the general acceptance of the exclusionary rule. Before *Wolf*, two-thirds of the states opposed the rule, but now more than one-half of the states had adopted it either by court or legislative decision. Second, *Wolf* included the argument that there were other means to secure compliance such as disciplinary action within the police department, but Clark states that there is an acknowledged failure of the alternatives and notes continued widespread abuse by law enforcement officials. Third, the Court has discarded the "silver platter doctrine," which allowed federal judicial use of evidence if the state authorities seized it and subsequently barred the use in state court of evidence wrongly seized by federal officials. Clark therefore argues that *Wolf's* rationale is so eroded that the case should be overturned.

The next portion of the opinion deals with the application of the doctrine to the states. Clark writes that there is "no war between the Constitution and common sense," and that it is counterproductive to apply the Fourth Amendment's right to privacy against the states without also applying the exclusionary rule as well; otherwise, the Fourth Amendment protection is "valueless." To illustrate, he uses the example of federal prosecutors who could not use the evidence, whereas the state's attorney across the street could use the evidence even though both operate under the enforcement provisions of the same Amendment. The result is that the state encourages disobedience to the very Constitution that it is bound to uphold. He concludes with an argument about judicial and governmental integrity summarized by his quote of a statement from *People v. Defoe*, "Nothing can destroy a government more quickly than its failure to observe its own laws, or worse, its disregard of the charter of its own existence."

OTHER OPINIONS Justice Hugo Black writes the chief concurring opinion in which he rejects the "shock-the-conscience" test that the Court had previously applied in such cases; that test stated the evidence was to be excluded if the method of search and seizure shocked the conscience. However, he argues that only when the Fourth and Fifth Amendments are combined is it sufficient to bar the evidence, and the Fourth Amendment standing alone would not be enough.

Justices John Marshall Harlan II, Felix Frankfurter, and Charles Whittaker join in the dissenting opinion. They vehemently argue that the Court was overreaching itself to overturn *Wolf*, particularly in light of the fact that the pivotal issue in the case (and the one argued to the Court) was the interpretation of the First Amendment and whether criminalization of mere possession, albeit knowing possession, of obscene material was consistent with rights of free thought and expression. In addition, they argue that the exclusionary rule is primarily aimed at deterrence of future misconduct, and that the application of federal substantive standards of search and seizure is an inappropriate intrusion into an area of state power.

SIGNIFICANCE OF THE CASE *Mapp* altered state criminal trial procedures and investigatory procedures by requiring local officials to follow constitutional standards of search and seizure by mandating exclusion of improperly seized evidence. This, not unnaturally, set off an outcry by local police who felt they were beleaguered by this Court, which was drastically changing the old rules in such other cases as *Gideon v. Wainwright* and *Miranda v. Arizona*. The exclusionary rule has continued to come under attack, and the judicial trend is to carve out exceptions to such rule.

QUESTIONS FOR DISCUSSION

(1) Do you agree with the premise that it is better for the criminal to go free if the constable has blundered and not followed the constitutional precepts? Why?

(2) What arguments for and against the exclusionary rule can you suggest? Why do you think former Chief Justice Warren Burger and others so adamantly oppose the exclusionary rule?

(3) Do you think that criminal procedure should be uniform across the nation, or should the states be allowed to structure their own procedures? Why?

RELATED CASES *Boyd v. United States*, 116 U.S. 616 (1886); *People v. Defoe*, 242 N.Y. 13, 150 N.E. 585 (1926); *Weeks v. United States*, 232 U.S. 383 (1914); *Wolf v. Colorado*, 338 U.S. 25 (1949); *Rea v. United States*, 350 U.S. 214 (1956); *Elkins v. United States*, 364 U.S. 206 (1960); *GIDEON V. WAINWRIGHT*, 372 U.S. 335 (1963); *MIRANDA V. ARIZONA*, 384 U.S. 436 (1966); *Warden v. Hayden*, 387 U.S. 294 (1967); and *UNITED STATES V. LEON*, 468 U.S. 897 (1984).

UNITED STATES V. LEON
468 U.S. 897 (1984)

BACKGROUND The Burbank Police Department, acting on information from an informant of unproven reliability, began a drug-trafficking investigation involving surveillance of the defendants' activities. The officers sought and received a search warrant from a state-court judge to search the residences and automobiles of defendants. The searches did turn up drugs, and federal charges were filed against the defendants. The district court, in ruling on motions to suppress evidence, determined that the underlying affidavits did not provide adequate probable cause for the issuance of the warrant and therefore excluded the evidence. The court of appeals affirmed.

CONSTITUTIONAL ISSUE

Whether evidence seized by officers under a facially-valid search warrant may be included at trial even though the warrant is ultimately found to be invalid? YES

MAJORITY OPINION   Justice Byron White writes the majority opinion of the Court. The exclusion of improperly-seized evidence at trial is not explicitly provided by the Fourth Amendment, and the exclusionary rule is merely "a judicially created remedy designed to safeguard Fourth Amendment rights generally." Exclusion does not automatically follow when police violate Fourth Amendment rights.

Determining the proper balance between the rights of persons under the Fourth Amendment and the needs of society for effective law enforcement is not an easy task. The exclusionary rule exacts a substantial toll by impeding the truth-finding functions of judge and jury and may allow some guilty defendants to go free. The Court has not extended the exclusionary rule to every aspect of criminal proceedings as, for example, grand jury proceedings and federal *habeas corpus* proceedings.

The Court has always expressed its preference for searches conducted under warrants issued by neutral and detached magistrates. In the instant case, the officers did seek and obtain a warrant, thereby substituting the objectivity of the uninvolved magistrate for the officers' own judgment. The intent of the exclusionary rule is deterrence of police misconduct and not deterrence of judicial error, and there is no basis to believe that the exclusion of evidence seized under a warrant will have a significant deterrent effect on judges and magistrates who are "not adjuncts to the law enforcement team" and who have "no stake in the outcome of particular criminal prosecutions."

An officer who seeks a warrant "cannot be expected to question the magistrates's probable-cause determination or his judgment that the form of the warrant is technically sufficient." Penalizing the officer for the magistrate's error does not contribute to the deterrence of Fourth Amendment violations. This lack of benefit means that the substantial costs of exclusion cannot be justified.

Officers and magistrates are not totally freed from restraints, however. The officer's reliance must be objectively reasonable. Suppression of the evidence is still appropriate when the officer misled the magistrate in the underlying affidavit, when the issuing magistrate acted merely "as a rubber stamp" and failed to make a neutral evaluation in violation of his or her duty to do so, and when the officer could not have reasonably believed that there was probable cause. If the officer acted in good faith under the warrant, then the evidence should be admitted.

OTHER OPINIONS   Justice Harry Blackmun enters a concurring opinion. This decision advances the legitimate interests of law enforcement without sacrificing the individual rights protected by the Fourth Amendment. Notice is nonetheless given to law-enforcement officials that the good-faith exception to the exclusionary rule is provisional and may be reversed if there is a "material change in police compliance with the Fourth Amendment" as a result of the opinion.

Justice William Brennan, joined by Justice Thurgood Marshall, dissents. The Court in recent years has steadily eroded Fourth Amendment protections, and today's decision abrogating the exclusionary rule completes the "Court's victory over the Fourth Amendment." The majority employs a cost-benefit approach to constitutional law that is inappropriate; the Court, in answering "the seductive call of expediency," reduces the Fourth Amendment protections to a meaningless form of words.

The Bill of Rights restrains government as a whole. The judiciary is an integral part of the criminal justice system, and its actions cannot be divorced from those of the police as the two are inextricably linked. Admission of unlawfully-seized evidence incorporates the judiciary in governmental action barred by the Amendment. The exclusionary rule is more than a judicially fashioned remedy; it is compelled by direct constitutional command to protect citizens from encroachments of individual liberties. The heart of the exclusionary rule is the protection of the individual's privacy from government intrusion and not deterrence of police misconduct as stated by the majority. The loss of evidence is the price that society pays for "enjoying the freedom and privacy safeguarded by the Fourth Amendment." Empirical studies show that less than one-half of 1 percent of all dismissals result from the exclusionary rule.

The Fourth Amendment clearly commands that no search shall be undertaken without probable cause. Here there was no probable cause, the warrant should not have been issued, and stripped of the authority of the warrant, the officers' acts are clearly unconstitutional. How can the interposition of the warrant convert a clearly unconstitutional act to a constitutional one? The effect of this decision is to destroy the institutional deterrence against improper searches, to put a premium on police ignorance of the law, to encourage police to provide only the bare information in their affidavits and to proceed in doubtful situations rather than seeking more evidence, and to insulate magistrates' decisions to issue warrants from judicial review.

Justice John Paul Stevens also dissents. An official search cannot be both "reasonable" and "unreasonable" at the same time. Searches undertaken without probable cause are constitutionally unsound, and police officers are aware of their obligation to provide the magistrate with sufficient facts for a determination of probable cause and that a failure to do so will invalidate the warrant. However, that deterrent is now gone, and police will be likely to submit questionable evidence to the magistrate "on the chance that he may take the bait." The courts become the actual motivating force in a unconstitutional chain of events. Expediency would be served by totally ignoring the mandates of the Fourth Amendment, but the very purpose of the Bill of Rights is to "identify values that may not be sacrificed to expediency." This decision "tarnishes the role of the judiciary in enforcing the Constitution."

SIGNIFICANCE OF THE CASE In *Leon*, the Court follows its pattern of increasing the number of exceptions to principles governing criminal procedure that were established under the Warren Court. Many perceive the exclusionary rule as one of those technicalities that encourages criminal activity, whereas others view it as one of the valued safeguards against overreaching by the government. The effect of the decision is to carve out an exception to the exclusionary rule, which insulates officers and magistrates from appellate review.

QUESTIONS FOR DISCUSSION

(1) Why do you support either the majority's or dissenters' position? Which has the most validity?
(2) Is this an example of judicial activism or judicial restraint? Why?

(3)   Do you agree that judges and magistrates are "not adjuncts of the criminal justice team" and that they do not have "a stake in the outcome"? What about elected judges when the case is extremely well publicized or controversial?

(4)   Do you think that magistrates usually conduct careful evaluation of affidavits presented to them by police officers, or do they frequently act as "rubber stamps"?

RELATED CASES   *Weeks v. United States*, 232 U.S. 383 (1914); *MAPP V. OHIO*, 367 U.S. 643 (1961); *United States v. Calandra*, 414 U.S. 338 (1974); *Stone v. Powell*, 428 U.S. 465 (1976); *Illinois v. Gates*, 462 U.S. 213 (1983); and *Massachusetts v. Sheppard*, 468 U.S. 981 (1984).

MIRANDA V. ARIZONA
384 U.S. 436 (1966)

BACKGROUND   Ernesto Miranda, age twenty-three, was an indigent who had completed one-half of the ninth grade. He was arrested at his home and taken to the Phoenix police station on charges of kidnapping and rape. After being identified by the eighteen-year-old victim, he was questioned by two officers who did not advise him of his right to have counsel, nor was counsel present. Miranda orally confessed to the crime and then signed the written confession, which contained a printed statement that he understood his rights and that the confession was entered voluntarily. At trial, the confession was used against him and he was convicted. After exhausting his state remedies, he appealed to the Supreme Court.

CONSTITUTIONAL ISSUE

(1)   Whether the Fifth Amendment protection against self-incrimination and the Sixth Amendment right to counsel extends to custodial police interrogation in state proceedings? YES

(2)   Whether statements taken in violation of the Fifth and Sixth Amendments in such circumstances are to be excluded at trial? YES

MAJORITY OPINION   Chief Justice Earl Warren delivers the opinion of the Court. Warren identifies the issue as one that goes "to the roots of our concepts of American criminal justice: the restraints society must observe consistent with the Federal Constitution in prosecuting individuals for crimes." It is the Court's obligation to prevent the Constitution from becoming merely "a form of words," and the case of *Escobedo v. Illinois* is used as an example. In *Escobedo*, the defendant's request to speak with his attorney who was in the police station had been denied by officers, and his subsequent confession was held to be inadmissible. Warren cites *Escobedo* as an illustration of the Court explicating basic rights that had long been recognized and traces the historical development of the right against self-incrimination.

Warren then turns to police interrogations and the impact of such interrogations on the individual. He acknowledges that today's interrogation is more psychological than physical, although he comments that brutality and police violence in questioning suspects are both well documented and widespread in all areas of the country, and that coercion may be mental as well as physical. Present police practices can be determined from texts and manuals concerning interrogation methods, although there is some difficulty in determining exactly what occurs because of the secrecy involved in interrogations. He characterizes the environment as one created solely to subjugate the person to the will of his captor and as one that "exacts a heavy toll on individual liberty and trades on the weakness of individuals." All of this, he says, is at odds with the Constitution and the privilege against self-incrimination. The presence of counsel would mitigate the legal and mental effects of such an atmosphere, he argues.

Warren then expounds on the Fifth Amendment, first tracing its historical development and then identifying it as a basic right. The Court traditionally examines confessions in light of the "voluntariness" of the confession; if there is coercion, then the confession should be excluded at trial. Warren argues that unless the defendant is fully aware of his constitutional rights, including the right against self-incrimination and the right to counsel, then the confession is not truly voluntary.

Therefore, officers are mandated to advise the accused of the following rights until the Court is shown other procedures that are at least as effective in informing the accused of their rights. First, the accused is to be advised of the right to remain silent in clear and unequivocal terms. Second, the accused is to be told that any statements he or she makes may be used as evidence at court. Third, the accused has the right to consult with an attorney, and if indigent, an attorney will be appointed. Issuing these warnings eliminates the need to speculate whether the suspect knows of his or her constitutional rights. These warnings are a prerequisite for admissibility of any statement by defendants at trial.

Warren responds to arguments that the decision precluded the use of all confessions and that it was a "constitutional straitjacket" on law enforcement personnel. He reminds officers that they have other tools of investigation including evidence gathered in the field and statements from witnesses. Volunteered confessions and confessions taken after meeting these prerequisites would still be admissible. He cites the FBI practice of using a similar warning. In addition, he points out that the accused may waive the right to have counsel present during the interrogation so long as it is an intelligent and knowing waiver after being informed of the right to have the attorney present. Although society's interest in controlling crime is recognized, Warren argues that giving these warnings is not too onerous for police. He concludes by again pointing out that the issues are of constitutional dimensions and therefore it is appropriate, if not obligatory, for the Court to deal with them.

OTHER OPINIONS   Justice John Marshall Harlan II, joined by Justices Potter Stewart and Byron White, writes the major dissent. The primary thrust of his argument is that the Court is really relying on the Sixth Amendment right to counsel rather than the Fifth Amendment right against self-incrimination. Other stages of the criminal justice proceedings, such as grand jury investigations and filing of *certiorari* petitions which are equally critical, are conducted without counsel. In addition, they argue that this case does nothing to deter officers who are prepared to lie about the voluntariness of the confession and, in fact, is designed only to impair and frustrate the investigation process. Also, the United States government and thirty states have indicated their opposition against new restrictions on police questioning, and no state has chosen to go so far on its own.

Justice White, joined by Justices Harlan and Stewart, opposes the decision because he argues that there is no historical support for it and because the Court is making new law and new policy. He claims that it is irrational to admit confessions if the accused volunteers or blurts out the statement, while at the same time excluding them if the accused responds to a general question such as, "Do you have anything to say?" The Fifth Amendment seeks to prevent *compelled* statements that are given when the free will of the accused is taken away, but here the Court is substituting the will of counsel for the will of the accused when it provides that counsel be present during interrogation. He weighs the rule's perceived consequences of making convictions of criminals more difficult against the community values and finds that society's interests lose.

Justice Tom Clark pens a separate dissenting opinion. He argues in favor of continuing the "totality of circumstances" test regarding the voluntariness and confessions, and would base such decisions on the Due Process Clause of the Fifth and Fourteenth Amendments. He would, however, support the requirement that police advise the suspect of the right to counsel including appointed counsel if indigent.

SIGNIFICANCE OF THE CASE   This case was loudly derided by police and public alike. The dissenters' position that police were being unduly handicapped in the pursuit of criminals was widely accepted. However, subsequent events have shown that the requirement of advising people of their constitutional rights has not substantially hindered police in their investigations as relatively few cases turn solely on confessions, and confessions are commonly used in criminal cases either as bargaining chips in plea bargains or at trial.

QUESTIONS FOR DISCUSSION

(1)   How do you think the presence of counsel during interrogations affects the outcome of the questioning? Why?

(2)   Do you think the familiarity of the *Miranda* warnings has blunted their effectiveness? Why?

RELATED CASES   *Bram v. United States*, 168 U.S. 532 (1897); *Mallory v. United States*, 354 U.S. 449 (1957); *Malloy v. Hogan*, 378 U.S. 1 (1964); *Escobedo v. Illinois*, 378 U.S. 478 (1964); and *Michigan v. Mosley*, 423 U.S. 96 (1975).

POWELL V. ALABAMA
287 U.S. 45 (1932)

BACKGROUND   Defendants—all black and all young—were accused of raping two white girls on a freight train on March 25, 1931. They were taken off the train and transported to Scottsboro, Alabama, where they were met by a large, hostile crowd; the military was called in to assist the sheriff in protecting them. They were indicted in state court on March 31, 1931, and the defendants were tried in three groups. At that time, conviction for rape carried a possible punishment ranging from ten years imprisonment to the death penalty.

On April 6, the three trials were started, and each completed in one day. Alabama law provided for the appointment of counsel in capital cases; however, rather than appointing specific attorneys, the trial judge named "all the members of the bar" to assist with the arraignments, and no further arrangements were made. On the morning of the trial, no attorney had been specifically named to represent any of the defendants. At trial, an out-of-state attorney did offer to assist with representing the defendants along with a rather reluctant local attorney. After summary trials, the jury convicted the defendants and assessed the death penalty.

CONSTITUTIONAL ISSUE

Whether the Due Process Clause of the Fourteenth Amendment requires the states to appoint counsel in capital murder cases in special circumstances? YES

MAJORITY OPINION Justice George Sutherland renders the opinion of the Court. He first notes the deference that should be given to state judicial proceedings if justice is not administered in either an arbitrary or capricious manner. Alabama law provided for the appointment of counsel in capital cases. The right to counsel, although originally limited to misdemeanors and civil cases in England, was provided in the colonies even before the adoption of the present Constitution and the Sixth Amendment provision regarding counsel. It is such an important right that it cannot be denied without "violating those 'fundamental principles of liberty and justice which lie at the base of all our civil and political institutions.'" The state court decisions in point support this position.

It is the responsibility of the judge to ensure a fair trial, and this judge effectively denied the defendants right to counsel, an essential component of due process, during the very critical period of the proceedings, from the time of arraignment until trial, when thorough investigation and preparation is imperative. Few laypersons, even educated and intelligent, have the skill and training to represent themselves adequately, and those who are ignorant, illiterate, or have poor intelligence are even more severely handicapped in proving their innocence. The characteristics of these capital defendants and their situation—youth, ignorance and illiteracy, the public hostility, isolation from family and friends, imprisonment and guarding by the military—made the trial court's failure to appoint counsel a clear violation of due process.

OTHER OPINIONS Justice Pierce Butler, joined by Justice James C. McReynolds, enters a dissenting opinion. Butler argues that the defendants were given adequate due process with the separate trials, the appearance of the sole local counsel who cross-examined the witnesses, and the state appeals in which several justices found the procedures to be adequate under state law. The application of the Fourteenth Amendment in this case is both intrusive into areas previously reserved for the states and too broad in that it goes beyond merely resolving the matter for these particular defendants.

SIGNIFICANCE OF THE CASE This case is a very important in the development of the Sixth Amendment even though its application is narrow in scope—a capital offense and indigent defendants unable to defend themselves because of low intelligence, illiteracy, or some other handicap. Six years later, the Court extended the right to counsel to all federal defendants, but the Court was slow to extend the right to state defendants unless there were "special" or "exceptional" circumstances. Later cases, *Gideon v. Wainwright* and *Argersinger v. Hamlin,* provided that indigent defendants in state trials who are charged with felonies or misdemeanors that carry imprisonment as punishment must be provided counsel. That same right has been extended to other phases of the criminal justice process such as indictment, interrogation, and postindictment lineups as well as the first appeal of a conviction.

QUESTIONS FOR DISCUSSION

(1)   Assume that the defendant is charged with a misdemeanor that carries the possibility of incarceration. Is the judge already deciding punishment before hearing the case when he or she makes a decision as to whether to appoint counsel? If the judge does not appoint counsel before trial is the range of punishment limited to a fine?

(2)   What stages of the criminal process would you deem to be so critical that the right to counsel should accrue?

(3)   Those accused of driving under the influence of alcohol or drugs are often videotaped. Is this such a critical stage of the proceedings that the right to counsel should apply?

RELATED CASES   *Johnson v. Zerbst*, 304 U.S. 458 (1938); *Betts v. Brady*, 316 U.S. 455 (1942); *GIDEON V. WAINWRIGHT*, 372 U.S. 335 (1963); *Argersinger v. Hamlin*, 407 U.S. 25 (1972); *Scott v. Illinois*, 440 U.S. 367 (1979); and *Pennsylvania v. Muniz*, 496 U.S. 582 (1990).

GIDEON V. WAINWRIGHT
372 U.S. 335 (1963)

BACKGROUND   Clarence Earl Gideon was charged with breaking and entering a pool-room with intent to commit a misdemeanor, a felony charge under Florida law. At trial, Gideon, an indigent, requested that the judge appoint an attorney for him. The judge declined and explained that Florida law permitted counsel to be appointed only in capital cases. Gideon responded, "The United States Supreme Court says I am entitled to be represented by counsel." Nevertheless, the trial proceeded without court-appointed counsel for Gideon, who was found guilty and sentenced to five years in the state penitentiary. Gideon continued to represent himself from prison and filed writs of *habeas corpus* to the state courts and then to the Supreme Court. The state courts denied all relief, but the Supreme Court accepted his writ and appointed counsel to represent Gideon at this highest appellate level. Three states filed *amici curiae* briefs in support of Florida's position, and twenty-two states filed briefs against upholding Gideon's conviction. The Supreme Court reversed and remanded the case whereupon Gideon was retried with the aid of counsel and acquitted.

CONSTITUTIONAL ISSUE

Whether the Sixth Amendment provisions that the "accused shall enjoy the right to...Assistance of Counsel for his defence" requires the appointment of counsel for indigents in state felony proceedings? YES

MAJORITY OPINION   Justice Hugo Black delivers the unanimous opinion of the Court. He begins by noting that "Put to trial before a jury, Gideon conducted his defense as well as could be expected from a layman." However, that is not the focus of the opinion, instead it is framed in terms of whether the assistance of counsel is a fundamental part of due process, and, as such, is essential to a fair trial. If the answer to the query is yes, then neither federal nor state governments may abridge such a right, and appointment of counsel is obligatory. To arrive at an answer to this question, the Court must deal with its own somewhat contradictory precedents.

In *Powell v. Alabama* (1932), the Court determined that the assistance of counsel was a fundamental right but limited the holding to the particular facts (ignorance and illiteracy of youthful defendants, circumstances of public hostility, and deadly peril of their lives), thereby creating the "special circumstances test." The Court found that capital cases, for instance, met that test and required the appointment of counsel in such cases. In addition, the Court ensured the right to counsel in federal trials in a 1938 case. However, in *Betts v. Brady*, the Court specifically held that refusal to appoint counsel for a defendant charged with a state felony did not violate due process.

Betts was a break with precedent, and the Court should return to the spirit of the earlier cases. The indigent, often illiterate, defendant is at a great disadvantage in an adversarial system against the state, which has many resources as well as trained prosecutors to present its arguments. This imbalance skews the system in favor of the state unless the defendant is represented by counsel. Therefore, *Betts* is overruled, and assistance of counsel in a criminal proceeding is determined to be a "fundamental safeguard of liberty immune from" invasion by both state and national governments.

OTHER OPINIONS   Justice John Marshall Harlan II writes the main concurring opinion. He agrees that the special circumstances test should be abandoned, but he does not view this precedent as applicable to all criminal cases, nor does he accept this as total incorporation of the Sixth Amendment.

Justice William O. Douglas, also concurring, targets Harlan's denial of total incorporation and seeks to defeat it by citing precedents.

Justice Tom Clark, in his concurring opinion, stresses that the distinction in the right to counsel cases between capital and noncapital felonies is abolished.

SIGNIFICANCE OF THE CASE   *Gideon* not only altered trial proceedings with the insistence on appointed counsel for indigent defendants, but also affected investigation procedures as the right to counsel was later expanded to cover pretrial procedures as well. However, *Gideon* did not mandate counsel in *all* court procedures nor even in all criminal trials. Other cases such as *Argersinger v. Hamlin* have delineated the scope of that right.

QUESTIONS FOR DISCUSSION

(1)   Why, do you think, did twenty-two states file *amici curiae* briefs supporting the appointment of counsel for indigent defendants in state proceedings?

(2)   At what stage should the right to counsel in criminal proceedings attach?

(3)   What is the significance of a person with an eighth-grade education successfully challenging the procedures of the criminal justice system?

RELATED CASES *POWELL V. ALABAMA*, 287 U.S. 45 (1932); *Johnson v. Zerbst*, 304 U.S. 458 (1938); *Betts v. Brady*, 316 U.S. 455 (1942); *Hamilton v. Alabama*, 368 U.S. 52 (1961); *United States v. Wade*, 388 U.S. 218 (1967); *Argersinger v. Hamlin*, 407 U.S. 25 (1972); and *Murray v. Giarranto*, 492 U.S. 1 (1989).

ROBINSON V. CALIFORNIA
370 U.S. 660 (1962)

BACKGROUND Robinson was convicted under a California statute that made it a misdemeanor offense "to be addicted to the use of narcotics." At the time of his arrest, Robinson was not under the influence of drugs; nevertheless, he was taken into custody because the officer observed scars, scales, and needle marks on Robinson's arms. Under questioning, Robinson admitted to the occasional use of narcotics. His conviction was upheld by the state appellate court.

CONSTITUTIONAL ISSUE

Whether the Eighth Amendment, which prohibits cruel and unusual punishment, is applicable to the states through the Fourteenth Amendment? YES

MAJORITY OPINION Justice Potter Stewart delivers the opinion of the Court. The statute is not one that punishes possession or sale of a banned substance, but instead is one that punishes the "status" of narcotic addiction as a criminal offense. The Court accepts California's position that narcotic addiction is a disease like leprosy or mental illness and declares that imprisoning someone merely for being diseased is a violation of the Eighth Amendment's provision against cruel and unusual punishment. The Court recognizes the "vicious evils of the narcotics traffic" and the government's right to regulate the sale and possession of narcotics, but does not accept that addiction itself should be treated as a crime.

OTHER OPINIONS Justice William O. Douglas, in his concurring opinion, employs a historical analysis in examining the issue; he compares the treatment of narcotic addiction with the treatment of the mentally ill, with the unequivocal conclusion that "each has a disease and each must be treated as a sick person." As with those who are mentally ill, the state has the alternative of civil commitment for treatment and as a means of protecting society; the civil commitment does not carry the same stigma or damage to a reputation as does a criminal conviction. The Eighth Amendment prevents overly severe punishments in such cases in which the penalty is excessive in relation to the act as, for example, the imposition of the death penalty for petty crimes or, as here, in punishing someone who is ill.

Justice John Marshall Harlan II also concurs on the basis that because the state could and does punish the sale and possession of narcotics, this statute is authorizing criminal punishment for "a base desire to commit a criminal act" that is not permissible under the Constitution.

Justice Tom Clark enters a dissenting opinion. He construed the statute as one that provides treatment rather than one that imposes punishment. He would defer to the judgment of the California legislature, which had studied the issue and would declare that "the overriding purpose of the statute is to cure the less seriously addicted person by preventing further use." Hospitalization, in his view, is not the sole or even preferred treatment for narcotics addiction, and therefore the Eighth Amendment is not applicable in this case.

Other status offenses, such as drunkenness, are recognized by the criminal law. In addition, the state's civil commitment law mandates that the person must have lost self-control, which based on the evidence presented at trial, Robinson had not. Therefore, the state's selection of criminal prosecution and incarceration is the only treatment method available.

Justice Byron White also dissents because he thinks that the majority is departing from two of its guiding principles—to avoid deciding constitutional questions except where necessary and to construe state statutes in such a way as to save their constitutionality. He agrees with Clark that the Court should defer to the state legislature, which has more expertise, in deciding the appropriate remedy for narcotics addiction. He, like Clark, discounts civil commitment because Robinson was a "redeemable user," and it was arguably better to sentence him to jail than to allow him to go forward with his destructive behavior pattern. White thinks that the Court is improperly "imposing its own philosophical predilections" and would eschew the application of the Eighth Amendment in the present case.

SIGNIFICANCE OF THE CASE   This case continues the process of "selective incorporation" of the Bill of Rights and makes the Eighth Amendment prohibition against cruel and unusual punishment applicable to the states. In *Powell v. Texas*, the Court declined to rule that a "chronic alcoholic" who was arrested for public intoxication fell within the gambit of *Robinson* because Powell, unlike Robinson, did engage in an affirmative act—being intoxicated in public—rather than being incarcerated for merely being a "chronic alcoholic."

QUESTIONS FOR DISCUSSION

(1)   It is widely accepted that this country has a pervasive drug problem. What ramifications do you see in terms of civil liberties and civil rights in this most current edition of the War on Drugs?

(2)   What parallels, if any, would you draw between the attitudes toward drugs and drug users and the attitudes shown to those suspected of communism in the early 1950s?

(3)   Do you agree with Justice Douglas and the majority, or with Justices Clark and White? Why?

RELATED CASES   *O'Neil v. Vermont*, 144 U.S. 323 (1892); *Francis v. Resweber*, 329 U.S. 459 (1947); *Whipple v. Martinson*, 256 U.S. 41 (1921); *Powell v. Texas*, 392 U.S. 514 (1968); and *Furman v. Georgia*, 408 U.S. 238 (1972).

GREGG V. GEORGIA
428 U.S. 153 (1976)

BACKGROUND This case arises under the statutory scheme in Georgia for assessing capital punishment. In the 1972 case of *Furman v. Georgia*, the Supreme Court rejected Georgia's prior procedure because it left juries with "untrammeled discretion to impose or withhold the death penalty." The Georgia legislature responded by adopting a new statute that incorporated the following features: (1) a bifurcated trial; (2) jury consideration of mitigating or aggravating factors including, but not limited to, the ten aggravated circumstances contained in the statute; (3) establishment of the death penalty as punishment for only six crimes; and (4) mandatory expedited review by the state Supreme Court.

Troy Gregg was tried for committing armed robbery and murder. He was sentenced to death by the jury, and the Georgia Supreme Court affirmed.

The Supreme Court agreed to hear Gregg's appeal along with challenges to the new capital punishment statutes of other states. This opinion is accompanied by four others concerning the death penalty—*Proffit v. Florida, Jurek v. Texas, Woodson v. North Carolina,* and *Roberts v. Louisiana.*

CONSTITUTIONAL ISSUE

Whether the imposition of the death penalty is unconstitutional *per se* under the Eighth and Fourteenth Amendments? NO

PLURALITY OPINION Justice Potter Stewart, joined by Justices Lewis Powell and John Paul Stevens, issues the judgment of the Court that punishment by death is not, under all the circumstances, always unconstitutional. Stewart initially conducts a historical analysis of the meaning of the Eighth Amendment's prohibition against cruel and unusual punishment. He describes it as a flexible, evolving doctrine; a concept that is borrowed from *Trop v. Dulles*, which described the Eighth Amendment as drawing "its meaning from the evolving standards of decency that mark the progress of a maturing society." It bars excessive punishment or punishment that involves the unnecessary and wanton infliction of pain or is grossly disproportionate to the crime. He then turns to the role of the court versus that of elected bodies, here the state legislatures. Great weight is to be given to the acts of the legislators who are elected as the representatives of the people and who are aware of and responsive to the contemporary standards of their constituents regarding punishment. For the reasons that the elected representatives in Georgia, in thirty-four other states, and in Congress enacted new death penalty statutes in light of *Furman*, and that it is not excessive punishment under the Eighth Amendment, Stewart upholds the constitutionality of capital punishment.

He then addresses the question of whether the specific Georgia statute adequately addresses the concerns of *Furman*, that is, minimizing the risk of wholly arbitrary and capricious action on the part of those assessing the death penalty. He examines the procedures of the new statute that provide consideration of mitigating and aggravating circumstances and for automatic review by the appellate court, which he determines adequately meets these concerns. He rejects the defendant's arguments that the scheme vests too much discretion in prosecutors regarding the decision about charging a particular defendant with the death penalty and that the statutory aggravating circumstances are too vague.

OTHER OPINIONS   In the concurring opinion, Justice Byron White, Chief Justice Warren Burger, and Justice William Rehnquist stress that the new statute provides the sentencing guidance that *Furman* lacked. Justice Harry Blackmun files a statement concurring in the judgment. Justices William Brennan and Thurgood Marshall both file dissenting opinions.

Brennan's dissent questions the moral and ethical aspects of the question, "The country has debated whether a society for which the dignity of the individual is the supreme value can, without a fundamental inconsistency, follow the practice of deliberately putting some of its members to death." He accuses the majority of focusing on the procedures rather than the "essence" of the death penalty. He finds that the death penalty is always cruel and unusual punishment because the state, in carrying out the death penalty, fails to recognize the intrinsic worth of the prisoner as a human being.

Marshall, in his dissent, essentially argues that the death penalty is excessive punishment and that the American people, if truly informed, would reject it.

SIGNIFICANCE OF THE CASE   *Gregg* and the accompanying cases ended the hiatus of executions that had followed *Furman*. However, the cases did not resolve the issue either for the Court or the American people as the debate rages on about the efficacy and the morality of the death penalty. Procedural questions concerning the application of the various state statutes continue to trouble the Court.

QUESTIONS FOR DISCUSSION

(1)   What arguments are used to support and oppose the imposition of the death penalty? What is your position? Why?

(2)   For what crimes should the death penalty be imposed?

(3)   Should executions be shown on television?

RELATED CASES   *Trop v. Dulles*, 356 U.S. 86 (1958); *Furman v. Georgia*, 408 U.S. 238 (1972); *Jurek v. Texas*, 428 U.S. 262 (1976); *Proffit v. Florida*, 428 U.S. 242 (1976); *Roberts v. Louisiana*, 428 U.S. 325 (1976); *WOODSON V. NORTH CAROLINA*, 428 U.S. 280 (1976); *Enmund v. Florida*, 458 U.S. 782 (1982); *Penry v. Lynaugh*, 492 U.S. 302 (1989); and *STANFORD V. KENTUCKY*, 492 U.S. 361 (1989).

WOODSON V. NORTH CAROLINA
428 U.S. 280 (1976)

BACKGROUND   This case arises under the statutory scheme in North Carolina for assessing capital punishment. In 1972, the Supreme Court handed down *Furman v. Georgia*, which found Georgia's capital punishment statute unconstitutional because it left juries with "untrammeled discretion to impose or withhold the death penalty." The North Carolina General Assembly responded to *Furman* by adopting a new statute that incorporated the following features: specifying certain types of homicide including murder while committing a felony (arson, rape, robbery, kidnapping, burglary, or others) as murder in the first degree, and establishing the punishment for first-degree murder as a mandatory death penalty.

This was the statute in place when James Tyrone Woodson was tried, convicted, and sentenced to death for his participation in an armed robbery of a convenience store in which the clerk was killed. This appeal was heard along with challenges to the newly enacted capital punishment statutes of other states. This opinion is accompanied by four others concerning the death penalty—*Gregg v. Georgia*, *Proffit v. Florida*, *Jurek v. Texas*, and *Roberts v. Louisiana*.

CONSTITUTIONAL ISSUE

Whether the imposition of a mandatory death penalty is unconstitutional under the Eighth and Fourteenth Amendments? YES

PLURALITY OPINION   Justice Potter Stewart, joined by Justices Lewis Powell and John Paul Stevens, writes the plurality opinion. The Eighth Amendment is to ensure that punishment is "exercised within the limits of civilized standards," which include requirements that the punishment is not excessive in its brutality and that it is not disproportionate to the crime. History reveals that in colonial times there were automatic death penalties, but such punishment has been repudiated through legislative enactments and jury determinations in favor of discretionary jury sentencing. In addition to society's aversion to mandatory death penalties, the Court's own precedents indicate a dislike of such sentences. Stewart recognizes that following *Furman* several states enacted mandatory death penalties, but he attributes that to misreading the Court's multi-opinioned decision in that case and determines that these mandatory sentences are constitutionally impermissible departures from contemporary standards.

Having established the historical context for rejecting automatic capital punishment, Stewart turned to the specific procedures for assessing the death penalty under the North Carolina statute. He faults the enactment's response to the complaint in *Furman* of unfettered jury discretion because this statute does not provide standards to guide the jury, does not allow for mitigating or aggravating circumstances, and does not provide for an automatic review of the decision. These are fatal flaws, and the statute is determined to be unconstitutional.

OTHER OPINIONS   Justices William Brennan and Thurgood Marshall concur because they oppose the death penalty. Justice William Rehnquist writes the major dissenting opinion. He states that it is "by no means clear" that the prohibition against cruel and unusual punishment is not limited to those punishments so deemed at the time of the adoption of the Bill of Rights. He further rejects the historical arguments of the plurality and argues that the society never turned away from the death penalty for such aggravated murders as this. In addition, he argues that the requirement of considering individual circumstances in each case is not supported by case authority or reason. He therefore agrees that the death penalty is not unconstitutional *per se* and opposes the expansion of the Due Process Clause of the Fourteenth Amendment to impose these procedures on states regarding assessing capital punishment.

SIGNIFICANCE OF THE CASE *Woodson* and the accompanying cases ended the hiatus of executions that had followed *Furman*. Procedural questions concerning the application of the various state statutes continue to trouble the Court, although the Court has continued to require consideration of aggravating and mitigating circumstances in death penalty cases.

QUESTIONS FOR DISCUSSION

(1) What arguments are used to support and oppose the imposition of the death penalty? How do you feel about them?
(2) For what crimes should the death penalty be imposed?
(3) Assume that the defendant is mentally retarded—a condition unlikely to change in the future. Should that factor be considered? Is it an aggravating circumstance or a mitigating one?

RELATED CASES *Trop v. Dulles*, 356 U.S. 86 (1958); *Furman v. Georgia*, 408 U.S. 238 (1972); *GREGG V. GEORGIA*, 428 U.S. 153 (1976); *Jurek v. Texas*, 428 U.S. 262 (1976); *Proffit v. Florida*, 428 U.S. 242 (1976); *Roberts v. Louisiana*, 428 U.S. 325 (1976); *Enmund v. Florida*, 458 U.S. 782 (1982); *McCLESKEY V. KEMP*, 481 U.S. 279 (1987); *Penry v. Lynaugh*, 492 U.S. 302 (1989); and *STANFORD V. KENTUCKY*, 492 U.S. 361 (1989).

McCLESKEY V. KEMP
481 U.S. 279 (1987)

BACKGROUND Warren McCleskey, a black man, was convicted of murdering a white police officer during the course of a store robbery in Fulton County, Georgia. The jury recommended the death penalty after considering the evidence of aggravating and mitigating circumstances as required by the state's death penalty statute. The conviction was affirmed by the Georgia Supreme Court, and McCleskey then challenged his conviction by means of a *habeas corpus* petition in federal district court which, among other things, included a claim that the Georgia death penalty statute was administered in a racially discriminatory manner in violation of the Eighth and Fourteenth Amendments.

To support his claim, McCleskey presented the Baldus study, a sophisticated statistical study of more than two thousand Georgia murder cases during the 1970s. The statistical tool was a multiple regression model with 230 variables, which allowed researchers to correlate race and the assessment of the death penalty. Defendants charged with murdering whites received the death penalty in 11 percent of the cases, whereas those killing blacks received the same penalty in only 1 percent of the cases. Baldus and his colleagues also examined the combination of the race of the defendant and the race of the victim, and the assessment of the death penalty: (1) black defendant and white victim, assessed in 22 percent of the cases; (2) white defendant and white victim, assessed in 8 percent of the cases; (3) white defendant and black victim, assessed in 3 percent of the cases; and (4) black defendant and black victim, assessed in 1 percent of the cases. Prosecutors chose to pursue the death penalty in 70 percent of the cases involving black defendant and white victim, in 32 percent of the cases involving white defendant and white victim, in 19 percent of the cases involving white defendant and black victim, and in 15 percent of the cases involving black defendant and black victim. The researchers concluded that those charged with killing white victims were 4.3 times as likely to receive a death sentence as those charged with killing blacks and that those blacks charged were 1.1 times as likely to receive a death sentence as other defendants. The study indicated that black defendants, such as McCleskey, who killed white victims are most likely to receive the death penalty.

The trial court held an extensive evidentiary hearing but did not grant any relief based on the Baldus study. The court of appeals accepted the validity of the study but again rejected McCleskey's claim. The Supreme Court declined to enter the morass of statistics by commenting (in a footnote) that the Court assumed the study to be statistically valid, and then by continuing on to focus on the chief issues of racial discrimination in sentencing and the proper weight to be given to such statistical studies.

CONSTITUTIONAL ISSUE

Whether a defendant has the burden of proof to prove racial bias influenced the decision in his or her particular capital trial even when proving bias in the general application of the statute, a violation of the Eighth and Fourteenth Amendments? YES

MAJORITY OPINION   Justice Lewis Powell writes the majority opinion for the Court. The first claim addressed is the equal protection argument arising from the showing that blacks are more likely to be given the death penalty and so are those who murder white victims. This claim encompasses discriminatory activity on the part of the prosecutors who make decisions as to which cases should be filed as capital cases, the jurors who assess the punishment, and the state that created the statute and allows it to remain in place.

Defendants who allege equal protection claims have the burden of proving "the existence of purposeful discrimination" generally and specifically on him. Here, McCleskey did not offer any evidence of specific racial considerations that affected the outcome in his case but instead relied solely on the Baldus study. The Court has, in other situations, accepted statistics (including multiple regression) as proof of intent to discriminate when "a stark pattern" was shown, but the unique nature of a capital murder case distinguishes this case. The jury in a death penalty case must examine a variety of factors that vary according to the particular case and defendant. Therefore, the application of an inference drawn from general statistics to a specific decision is not appropriate, especially because the jurors cannot be questioned as to the motives behind their votes.

Those within the criminal justice system, especially prosecutors and jurors, are vested with a great deal of discretion, an essential of the process, and the Court will demand "exceptionally clear proof before we would infer that the discretion has been abused." Although some discretion does remain with the jury in assessing the death penalty under *Gregg*, that discretion is controlled by clear and objective standards that focus on the individualized nature of the crime and the characteristics of the defendant.

The Court is very concerned that racial considerations may affect a decision and has "engaged in 'unceasing efforts' to eradicate racial prejudice from our criminal justice system" such as requiring that the jury be representative of the defendant's community. Statistics merely indicate the likelihood that a particular factor entered into a decision, and even the study's authors do not state that the study proves racial discrimination in the statute's application generally nor in McCleskey's case specifically. The Court declines to find a constitutionally significant risk of racial bias in the Georgia scheme in light of the safeguards designed to minimize bias, the value of the jury trial, and the benefits (such as a refusal to prosecute or a reduction in charge) that discretion provides to criminal defendants.

If McCleskey succeeds in his claims, it would call into question all sentences and punishments. The Court is not willing to demand that states extinguish all possible factors other than factual guilt to operate a constitutional sentencing scheme. It is for the legislatures to determine the punishment for crimes; it is the legislatures that are better able to weigh and evaluate the results of such statistical studies; and it is the legislature that is the proper venue to seek redress, not the courts.

OTHER OPINIONS Justice William Brennan, joined by Justice Thurgood Marshall, writes a dissenting opinion that restated their belief that the Eighth Amendment forbids the death penalty. They were joined by Justice Harry Blackmun and Justice John Paul Stevens in the remainder of the dissent.

Beginning with *Furman*, the Court has focused on the risk of an arbitrary and capricious sentence being imposed in a death penalty case rather than the proven fact of one. McCleskey shows, by empirical evidence, that the risk of race influencing his sentence was "intolerable by any imaginable standard." The findings of the Baldus study should be given great weight because of the very sophisticated multiple-regression analysis used that controls for other permissible factors, and it "relentlessly" documents the risk that race did influence this sentence.

Also, the conclusion suggested by the numbers is "consonant with our understanding of history and human experience" in that Georgia at one time did have a dual system of crime and justice—one for whites and one for blacks. Although that is no longer in effect, there may be lingering, "subtle, less consciously held racial attitudes" that could come into play. "Sentencing data, history and experience all counsel that Georgia has provided insufficient assurance of the heightened rationality we have required in order to take a human life."

The majority's reasons for rejecting McCleskey's claims—the need for discretion, the existence of statutory safeguards against abuse of discretion, and the possibility of challenges to the sentencing process—can all be discounted. Although there is a presumption that those in the criminal justice system act wisely and responsibly in exercising their discretion, that is not always the case; the Court has acted to remedy those situations in the past. Even statutory safeguards can be circumvented, and it is the role of the Court to ensure the quality of the process just as it is the role of the Court to prevent the arbitrary administration of sentencing and punishment.

Justice Harry Blackmun, joined by Justices Thurgood Marshall and John Paul Stevens, and, in part, by Justice William Brennan also enters a dissent. The focus is on the Fourteenth Amendment Equal Protection Clause. The proper standard for examining death penalty cases is that of heightened scrutiny because of the gravity of the punishment, and the majority incorrectly adopts a lesser standard here by concluding that "legitimate" explanations outweigh the defendant's claim of the constitutionally impermissible risk of racial discrimination.

To succeed, the defendant must prove the existence of purposeful discrimination by showing three factors: (1) He is the member of a recognizable, distinct class which is singled out for different treatment; (2) He must show substantial degree of differential treatment; and (3) He must show that the allegedly discriminatory procedure is susceptible to abuse or is not racially neutral. McCleskey has indisputedly done all three, and the state has failed to meet its burden of explaining the racial selections. "[R]acial discrimination within the criminal justice system is particularly abhorrent." The proper remedy for violation of the Equal Protection Clause in this context is to set aside the conviction.

Justice John Paul Stevens is joined by Justice Harry Blackmun in his dissent. There is a strong probability that the jury in this case was influenced by the race of the defendant and the race of the victim. If so, that is constitutionally intolerable. However, before overturning McCleskey's conviction on the record before the Court, there are two procedural matters that should be resolved: the Court of Appeals must decide whether the Baldus study is valid, and the District Court must determine whether the particular facts of this crime and this defendant's background bring him within the group that faced an unacceptable risk that race played a decisive role in the sentence.

SIGNIFICANCE OF THE CASE   Courts are often reluctant to accept new or unusual forms of knowledge as the basis for convictions. They have been slow to accept DNA tests, for example, and have been even more hesitant to accept social science's statistical studies. That hesitancy has rarely been more apparent than in this case where a very sophisticated study presents rather compelling evidence, but even here the Court does allow the test into evidence and does treat it as credible.

Not only does the case portend more willingness on the part of the Court to accept this type of evidence, it also illustrates the Court's growing reluctance to consider and to overturn capital punishment sentences.

QUESTIONS FOR DISCUSSION

(1)   Is it possible to limit racial bias in affecting the decisions of juries? If so, how would you do it?

(2)   Is it be appropriate to question jurors on the issue of racial bias? Before accepting a juror on the jury? After the return of the sentence?

(3)   How would you have voted if you had been on the Court? Why?

(4)   Is the majority's fear of being inundated with challenges to sentences a reasonable one? Is that sufficient reason to reject McCleskey's claim?

RELATED CASES   Gomillion v. Lightfoot, 364 U.S. 339 (1960); Furman v. Georgia, 408 U.S. 238 (1972); GREGG V. GEORGIA, 428 U.S. 153 (1976); WOODSON V. NORTH CAROLINA, 428 U.S. 280 (1976); Castaneda v. Partida, 430 U.S. 482 (1977); and Batson v. Kentucky, 476 U.S. 79 (1986).

STANFORD V. KENTUCKY
492 U.S. 361 (1989)

BACKGROUND   Stanford was seventeen years old when he committed murder during the course of a robbery. A Kentucky juvenile court transferred him to stand trial as an adult wherein he was tried and given the death penalty. Wilkins was sixteen years old when he, too, committed murder during the course of a robbery, and he was convicted and given the death penalty following certification and transfer as an adult.

CONSTITUTIONAL ISSUE

Whether the Eighth Amendment prohibition against cruel and unusual punishment precludes the assessment of the death penalty for those who commit capital crimes at age sixteen or seventeen? NO

PLURALITY OPINION   Justice Antonin Scalia writes the plurality opinion. Punishment may be found to violate the Eighth Amendment if the punishment was thought to be cruel and unusual at the time of the adoption of the Bill of Rights or if the punishment fails the standard enunciated in *Trop v. Dulles* (1958), that is, it is contrary to "evolving standards of decency that mark the progress of a maturing society." Common law, at the time of the adoption of the Eighth Amendment, contained a rebuttable presumption of maturity at age fourteen regarding the commission of felonies and theoretically allowed the execution of those older than the age of seven. Therefore, Stanford and Wilkins must rely on the latter if they are to challenge their convictions successfully.

The difficulty lies in discerning the content of those "evolved" standards of decency. To do so, the Court traditionally has looked to society as a whole for guidance rather than to the justices' subjective feelings. To that end, the Court examines the statutes enacted by the elected representatives. Fifteen of the thirty-seven states that impose capital punishment do not allow it for sixteen year olds, and twelve preclude it for those under seventeen. A majority of those states sanctioning capital punishment authorize it for crimes committed by offenders age sixteen or older. Congress has authorized sixteen and seventeen year olds to be tried as adults for all federal offenses "including those bearing a capital penalty that is not limited to eighteen-year-olds." Other indicia of an alleged national consensus such as public opinion polls, views of interest groups, or professional associations are not sufficient proof. "We decline the invitation to rest constitutional law on such uncertain foundations."

The claim that the small number of death penalties assessed to juveniles indicates a consensus that prosecutors and juries are reluctant to assess the punishment, but the fact that it is given may mean that juries and prosecutors believe that it should be used sparingly, not that society thinks it should never be imposed on juveniles. In addition, there are relatively fewer juveniles who commit the type of crime deserving of the death penalty.

Laws that set age eighteen or more as the legal age for such activities as voting or driving are irrelevant. One does not have to be mature enough to vote or drive to recognize that killing someone is "profoundly wrong." Laws setting these standards do so for the population as a whole, but those youthful offenders facing capital punishment receive very particularized consideration in proceedings to certify him or her as an adult as well as during the trial and in the punishment phase particularly.

It is the Court's role to decide whether punishment is cruel and unusual, "to *identify* the 'evolving standards of decency,' to determine, not what they *should* be, but what they are." That finding is to be based on objective indicators and not on the justices' own judgments. To do otherwise is to replace "judges of the law with a committee of philosopher-kings." Here, the young offenders have failed to meet their "heavy burden" to prove a national consensus against the death penalty under these circumstances.

OTHER OPINIONS   Justice Sandra Day O'Connor concurs in the judgment and in part of the opinion. In examining the minimum ages expressly set by the legislatures, each one has set the limit at age sixteen or older, which indicates that there is no national consensus against establishing sixteen as the minimum age. However, those who would be tried as juveniles except for certification as an adult may be executed only if the capital punishment statute specifies a minimum age, and the defendant had reached that age at the time that the crime was committed.

It is the province and responsibility of the Court to go beyond the specific punishment statutes to determine if the crime itself is deserving of such punishment as well as the blameworthiness of each defendant, that is, to judge the proportionality issue.

Justice William Brennan is joined by Justices Thurgood Marshall, Harry Blackmun, and John Paul Stevens in dissent. In considering Eighth Amendment cases, the Court's analytical framework has two parts: The first is to decide if the punishment does fit within the "evolving standards of decency," and the second is to decide if the punishment is constitutionally excessive either because it is disproportionate given the blameworthiness of the offender or because it meets no legitimate penal goal.

Determining whether society approves a punishment is done by considering attitudes of state legislatures and juries certainly, but also by those with expertise in the field and the public generally. In tallying the figures, twenty-seven states would not allow the execution of seventeen year olds and thirty would not allow the execution of eighteen-year-olds; nineteen states have not squarely addressed the issue; and only a few of the remaining jurisdictions have explicitly set an age below eighteen at which a person may be executed. The latest death penalty statute emerging from Congress also excluded those below age eighteen. There is strong opposition to a lower age from experts in the field and from around the world.

Juvenile offenders are significantly less likely to receive the death penalty than adults; from January 1982 through June 1988, 1.8 percent of adults arrested for homicide received the death penalty, whereas only 0.5 percent of juveniles did so. It is "perfectly proper to conclude a sentence so rarely imposed is 'unusual.'" Given all these factors, it is clear that the death penalty should not be assessed against anyone younger than the age of 18 at the time of the commission of the crime.

Justice Scalia would terminate the analysis of Eighth Amendment cases after determining whether the punishment is cruel and unusual based on the examination of the legislation and jury verdicts. The Court has an obligation to determine the appropriateness of the death penalty in light of the precedents; otherwise, it abandons its "proven and proper role" to protect the people from the political majorities as the Bill of Rights intended. Encompassed in that obligation in Eighth Amendment cases is the need to examine proportionality including blameworthiness. It is easy to see that society, which does not trust juveniles with certain privileges and responsibilities, may not consider juveniles as morally reprehensible as adults and therefore should not receive the death penalty.

SIGNIFICANCE OF THE CASE Juveniles and the death penalty have posed troubling and recurring questions for the Court. The term before, the Court in *Thompson v. Oklahoma* rejected the death penalty for those younger than the age of sixteen when committing the offense.

Tension and disagreement among the members of the Court seep from this opinion. The justices in the majority decry the substitution of judicial opinion for that of the legislature and frame a narrow analytical framework and acceptable forms of proof, whereas those in the minority argue that their colleagues, in automatically deferring to legislatures, are abandoning the Court's assigned role of protecting the citizens from the tyranny of majorities. Each side chides the other about working "its statistical magic." The acrimony about the role of the Court and its various approaches to testing the constitutionality of matters may be expressed obliquely but nevertheless is very apparent.

QUESTIONS FOR DISCUSSION

(1) What is your position on the execution of those younger than the age of eighteen? Why?

(2) Do you agree with Justice Scalia or Justice Blackmun about the judge's role in interpreting the Constitution? Why?

(3) What is the proper analytical framework for Eighth Amendment cases?

RELATED CASES *Furman v. Georgia*, 408 U.S. 238 (1972); *Coker v. Georgia*, 433 U.S. 584 (1977); *Whitley v. Albers*, 475 U.S. 312 (1986); *Tison v. Arizona*, 481 U.S. 137 (1987); *McCLESKEY V. KEMP*, 481 U.S. 279 (1987); and *Thompson v. Oklahoma*, 487 U.S. 815 (1988).

9

CONSTITUTIONAL RIGHTS

INTRODUCTION

Americans have always jealously guarded their rights as individuals. Indeed, the rhetoric of the American Revolution framed the controversy between the colonies and Great Britain as a conflict over the rights of Englishmen. It is not surprising, therefore, that the defense of individual rights is a persistent theme of American law and politics. The history of American liberty has also been the struggle of specific groups—African Americans, women, gays—to win acceptance and equal treatment in society. In a sense, the struggle for liberty has been both an individual and a group effort. In this introduction we examine the development of constitutional rights in the United States. Specifically, we examine the impact of federalism on constitutional rights and then we discuss some major problem areas of discrimination under the Constitution.

Rights in a Federal System

To understand the struggle for constitutional rights in the United States, it is necessary to understand the influence of federalism. When the framers of the Constitution created our federal form of government, they created two distinct levels of government. Each level is capable of protecting liberty or destroying it. In addition, rights secured by one level of government may not be protected by the other. What is more, the violation of a person's rights by one level may not be safeguarded by the other. Federalism, without a doubt, has greatly affected the development of our concept of rights in America.

BARRON V. CITY OF BALTIMORE (1833) illustrates the problems created by federalism regarding constitutional rights. When the city of Baltimore made civic improvements to rechannel the city's waterways, the changes made Barron's wharf virtually worthless. Barron claimed this constituted a taking of private property for public purposes and sued the city. When he failed to receive compensation, he appealed his case to the U.S. Supreme Court. Barron argued that the city's action had denied him his property without just compensation violating the Fifth Amendment. However, in his ruling, Chief Justice John Marshall held that the first ten amendments to the Constitution, better known as the Bill of Rights, were intended to restrain the powers of the national government only. Because no action or policy of the national government had been involved, the Fifth Amendment did not apply, and federal courts had no jurisdiction over Barron's claim. The effect of the *BARRON* ruling was that the Bill of Rights could not be used as a shield to protect a person from an alleged injustice received at the hands of the state.

Although a blow for civil liberties, the *BARRON* decision was not fatal. After all, each state possessed its own constitution with its own bill of rights. State bills of rights typically included virtually the same guarantees of personal and religious liberties as the national bill of rights. The real concern of civil libertarians was that after *BARRON* the national government could not be relied on to protect the citizen from *state* violations of basic rights. In other words, *BARRON* did not provide a shield to protect persons from injustices at the hands of the states.

The adoption of the Fourteenth Amendment in 1868 added a new wrinkle to the problem of rights in a federal system. The Amendment reads, in part, that "No State shall make or enforce any law which shall abridge the privileges or immunities of citizens of the United States." Some constitutional scholars argued that this clause was designed to protect U.S. citizens, especially the newly freed slaves, from discrimination at the hands of state governments. Under the *DRED SCOTT V. SANDFORD* (1857) decision, the Supreme Court had distinguished between state and national citizenship. The Fourteenth Amendment made all persons born in the United States citizens of the United States as well as citizens of the state where they lived. The wording of the Amendment makes it clear that the rights of *national* citizenship may not be abridged.

The issue of what protection the national government could provide for abridgement of national privileges or immunities turned on what was a privilege or immunity of U.S. citizenship. The answer came quickly in the *SLAUGHTERHOUSE CASES* (1873). When the Louisiana legislature granted what amounted to a monopoly to a slaughterhouse in New Orleans, about one thousand small butcher shops were put out of business. One issue presented to the Supreme Court was whether the right to pursue a lawful occupation was a privilege or immunity of national citizenship. The Court held that it was not. It held that if the right to pursue a lawful occupation were a privilege or immunity, it was one of state, not national, citizenship. The Court reached a similar conclusion in *Bradwell v. Illinois* (1873) in which it ruled that a state could deny women the right to practice law. To support its *SLAUGHTERHOUSE* decision the Court cited *Corfield v. Coryell* (1823) in which Justice Bushrod Washington listed the privileges and immunities of national citizenship. The issue in *Corfield* was whether New Jersey could deny a noncitizen the right to gather oysters. The Supreme Court suggested that the privileges and immunities of national citizenship were limited to those listed by Justice Washington. Privileges and immunities of national citizenship, according to Justice Washington, included the right to interstate travel, to possess property, and to seek the protection of the government. Justice Washington did not mention the provisions of the Bill of Rights among the privileges and immunities of national citizenship. The Court's *SLAUGHTERHOUSE* decision made it clear that the guarantees contained in the national bill of rights were not to be considered privileges or immunities of national citizenship. As was true after the *BARRON* decision, a citizen could not turn to the federal courts for protection of his rights against violations by the state.

Although the *SLAUGHTERHOUSE CASES* foreclosed use of the Privileges and Immunities Clause of the Fourteenth Amendment to protect rights of U.S. citizens abridged by a state, the Equal Protection and Due Process Clauses of the same Amendment provided some hope. Although the Due Process Clause became extremely important in extending the protection of most of the Bill of Rights to the states, especially the rights of the accused, our coverage here is limited to the issues of discrimination and equal protection. We begin our analysis with racial discrimination.

Racial Discrimination

Early efforts to secure federal protection of the rights of former slaves met with resistance from the Supreme Court. In 1875, Congress passed a law making it illegal to deny anyone public accommodations in hotels, restaurants, and theaters on the basis of race. Congress based this law on its power to enforce the Fourteenth Amendment. Cases from four states were consolidated into the *CIVIL RIGHTS CASES* (1883). The issue in the cases was whether Congress could prohibit racial discrimination in privately-owned businesses. The Court ruled Congress could not. The Court noted that the law prohibited state-sponsored, not private, discrimination. The Fourteenth Amendment says that "No State" may deny a U.S. citizen the equal protection of the law. Because there was not any state action or support for the discrimination, Congress had no power to act.

The issue of state-supported discrimination came directly before in the Court in 1896 in *PLESSY V. FERGUSON*. Louisiana law required black and white passengers to ride in separate railroad cars. Because the enforced segregation was mandated by state law, there was no question of state action being present. However, the Supreme Court was able to uphold the Louisiana law by formulating the "separate but equal" doctrine. The Court ruled that as long as the law required equal facilities for members of both races, it could also require that the facilities be separate. For fifty-eight years, the doctrine of separate but equal permitted states to pass so-called Jim Crow laws, which sanctioned state-enforced segregation in schools, hospitals, parks, and other public facilities.

The death blow to the separate but equal doctrine came in 1954 with the case of *BROWN V. BOARD OF EDUCATION OF TOPEKA, KANSAS*. However, even before the *BROWN* decision the Court had been moving away from the doctrine of segregation. For example, in *SHELLEY V. KRAEMER* (1948), the Supreme Court ruled that racially-restrictive covenants of real property could not be enforced in state courts. The Court found that judicial enforcement of these racially-restrictive covenants was state action forbidden by the Fourteenth Amendment. In several significant cases preceding *BROWN*, such as *Missouri ex rel. Gaines v. Canada* (1938), *Sweatt v. Painter* (1950), and *McLaurin v. Oklahoma State Regents* (1950), the Court began chipping away at the separate but equal doctrine. In *Gaines*, the Court relied on the fact that a state had failed to provide equal facilities for its black citizens. In *Sweatt*, although separate facilities were provided, the ones for black citizens were patently inferior to those provided by the state for its white citizens. Finally, in *BROWN*, the Court officially ended state sanctioned discrimination in the field of public education by declaring the laws requiring racial segregation of public school children to be unconstitutional under all circumstances. Though *BROWN* was limited to public education, it soon became the precedent for eliminating racial discrimination in other areas of public policy as well.

Of course, a mere declaration by the Court that public school segregation was unconstitutional was inadequate. For years battles were waged in federal courts over the process of desegregating the schools. The Court settled the issue in *SWANN V. CHARLOTTE-MECKLENBURG BOARD OF EDUCATION* (1971) when it ruled that busing was a constitutionally permissible means of achieving school desegregation. More recently, however, in *Board of Education of Oklahoma City v. Dowell* (1991), the Court has signaled a retreat from its earlier commitment to school desegregation.

An unexpected source of support for civil rights turned out to be the Commerce Clause. In 1964, Congress passed a Civil Rights Act, which prohibited racial discrimination in hotels, motels, theaters, and other places of public accommodation. Unlike the law struck down in the *CIVIL RIGHTS CASES*, the 1964 law was based on Congress's power to regulate interstate commerce rather than on the Fourteenth Amendment. By using the Commerce Clause instead of the Fourteenth Amendment, Congress did not have to show that state action was involved. It merely had to conclude that racial discrimination had adverse effects on interstate commerce. In *HEART OF ATLANTA MOTEL, INC. V. UNITED STATES* (1964) and its companion case *Katzenbach v. McClung* (1964), the Supreme Court upheld the 1964 Civil Rights Act. The *HEART OF ATLANTA* decision was in harmony with an earlier case, *MUNN V. ILLINOIS* (1877), in which the Court ruled that when private property, such as a business, takes on a public character, it may be regulated by the state.

The end to legal discrimination against African Americans spawned another debate over discrimination—reverse discrimination. Reverse discrimination often involves affirmative action programs. In their attempt to eliminate the vestiges of racial discrimination some reformers have insisted that government take positive steps or "affirmative action" to bring disadvantaged groups into the mainstream of American society. To accomplish this, previously deprived minorities were to be given preferential treatment by the government. Minorities, especially women and African Americans, were most notably underrepresented in the professions, and it was here that the early battles over reverse discrimination were waged.

In *DeFunis v. Odegaard* (1974), the Supreme Court skirted the issue of reverse discrimination. A white applicant, Marco DeFunis, was denied admission to law school though minority applicants with lower Law School Admission Test scores and lower grade-point averages were admitted. A lower state court ordered DeFunis admitted pending the appeal of the case. By the time the case reached the U.S. Supreme Court, DeFunis was in his last quarter of law school. Consequently, the Court ruled the case moot despite the dissent of some members who believed the issue of reverse discrimination should be addressed.

The opportunity to address the question of reverse discrimination presented itself again in *REGENTS OF THE UNIVERSITY OF CALIFORNIA AT DAVIS V. BAKKE* (1978). Alan Bakke had applied to the University's medical school in 1973 and 1974. He was rejected both times, although minority applicants with lower Medical College Admission Test scores were admitted under the University's special admission program. In six separate opinions, the Court ruled that the Davis program, as applied, was unconstitutional but held that race could be included as a factor in the admissions process. Bakke won the case, but the opponents of affirmative action did not receive the definitive ruling against reverse discrimination they had hoped to win.

Far from clarifying the issue of affirmative action, *BAKKE* has required the Court to make additional rulings on its constitutionality in a variety of areas of public policy. For example, in *Fullilove v. Klutznick* (1980), the Court upheld a congressional law setting aside a certain percentage of public contract funds for minority business enterprises. However, the changes in the Court's membership brought on by the Reagan administration caused a shift in the Court's affirmative action pronouncements. In *Wygant v. Jackson Board of Education* (1986), the Court struck down a collective bargaining agreement in which white teachers with more seniority were to be laid off before minority teachers. More recently, in *CITY OF RICHMOND V. J. A. CROSON* (1989), the Court struck down a policy that required 30 percent of all city-awarded projects to be subcontracted to minority business enterprises. For the first time, the Court applied strict scrutiny to an affirmative action program and found it to violate the Equal Protection Clause. Evidently affirmative action will continue to be an issue coming before the Court.

Gender-Based Discrimination

Racial discrimination, of course, is not the only area of discrimination with which the Supreme Court has had to deal. Another heavily litigated field has been sex discrimination. We have already noted that in *Bradwell v. Illinois* the Court upheld a state law prohibiting women from practicing law. Nor was the discrimination always adverse to women's interests. Some laws were designed to treat women in a preferential, albeit patronizing, manner. Early labor laws, like the one challenged in *Muller v. Oregon* (1908), which sought to regulate the hours and working conditions of the "weaker sex" were often upheld by the courts.

Increasingly, laws discriminating against women are being challenged. In *Reed v. Reed* (1971), the Supreme Court unanimously struck down an Idaho law that automatically gave preference to the father over the mother in cases involving a dead child's estate. Although the Court often struck down gender-based laws that had no rational basis, such as *Reed*, proponents of women's rights wanted more. They wanted sex, like race, to be designated a suspect classification, thereby triggering strict scrutiny by the Court. The opportunity to do just that arose in *FRONTIERO V. RICHARDSON* (1973). An Air Force regulation automatically granted a housing allowance to married male officers but required a female officer to show that her husband was more than 50 percent dependent on her for support. Justice William Brennan, author of the Court's plurality opinion, failed to muster the necessary majority to have sex declared a suspect classification. Some justices believed that ratification battle over the then pending Equal Rights Amendment should settle the issue rather than the Court.

Sex discrimination in the private sector has also been a continuing problem. Title VII of the Civil Rights Act of 1964 prohibits sex discrimination but questions still arise. In *General Electric Co. v. Gilbert* (1976), the Supreme Court held that a company's health insurance program that excluded pregnancy coverage did not violate Title VII. Congress later reversed the *Gilbert* decision by passing the Pregnancy Discrimination Act. In *International Union, American Workers, Aerospace, Agricultural Implement Workers of America, UAW v. Johnson Controls, Inc.* (1991), the Court unanimously invalidated a company's fetal-protection policy. The company banned all fertile women from jobs that involved exposure to high levels of lead. The Court held that such policies violate the Pregnancy Discrimination Act.

Just as racial classifications have provoked charges of reverse discrimination, so too have gender-based laws. In *Schlesinger v. Ballard* (1975), the Court upheld a law requiring mandatory discharge of males who had failed to be promoted within nine years, although female officers were given thirteen years to become promoted. In *CRAIG V. BOREN* (1976), the Court struck down an Oklahoma law that permitted females to buy 3.2 percent beer at age eighteen but required males to be twenty-one years of age. In *Michael M. v. Superior Court of Sonoma County* (1981), the Court upheld a law permitting a male, but not a female, to be prosecuted for statutory rape. Michael M., a minor, had consensual sex with a minor female, and only he was subject to criminal prosecution. Finally, in *Rostker v. Goldberg* (1981), the Court upheld the practice of drafting only males into the military.

Eradicating sex discrimination in employment practices is not easy as *JOHNSON V. TRANSPORTATION AGENCY, SANTA CLARA COUNTY, CALIFORNIA* (1987) demonstrates. Efforts by public and private employers to provide equal employment opportunities create the risk of lawsuits by disadvantaged males. In *JOHNSON*, the Santa Clara County Transportation Agency voluntarily adopted an affirmation action plan. The plan provided that the sex of a qualified applicant would be considered for promotions in positions where women were significantly underrepresented. Johnson, a male, challenged a decision to promote a woman named Joyce whose score on at least one interview was lower than his. It should be noted that there were no women in the 238 positions and that neither Johnson nor Joyce had the highest score among all applicants. In sustaining the plan, the Supreme Court held that it did not bar males from promotion nor set a quota. The Court held that gender was not the determining factor in Joyce's selection. In *BAKKE*, the Court had previously ruled that race is a legitimate factor in medical school admissions. Here the Court finds that gender is one of several constitutionally permissible factors that may be considered.

Political and Economic Discrimination

Although race and sex discrimination are based on distinct physical characteristics, other forms of discrimination, among which are political and economic discrimination, have a subtler basis. For example, political gerrymandering, the practice of drawing legislative districts for partisan advantage, is as old as the nation. Similarly, malapportionment, the uneven distribution of constituents among elected representatives, raises questions of equal protection. The disadvantaged parties argue that such practices discriminate against them by weakening their ability to influence their elected officials. At first the Supreme Court refused to enter the reapportionment controversy ruling in *Colegrove v. Green* (1946) that reapportionment raised a political question beyond the Court's authority. The Court reversed itself, however, in 1962, holding in *BAKER V. CARR* that federal courts could assume jurisdiction over reapportionment cases. Since then the Court has extended its ruling to include congressional districts in *Wesberry v. Sanders* (1964) and both houses of a state legislature in *REYNOLDS V. SIMS* (1964). The Court has ruled that county-level districts must be apportioned on the basis of population in *Avery v. Midland County* (1968). Finally, in *Hadley v. Junior College District of Metropolitan Kansas City* (1970), the Court held that even municipal and special districts are required to follow the "one person, one vote" rule.

Perhaps one of the most blatant forms of political discrimination concerned voting. States imposed poll taxes, literacy tests, and difficult residency requirements for discouraging certain groups, such as the poor and African Americans, from voting. In 1965 Congress passed the Voting Rights Act, which empowered the national government to intervene in states where a pattern of voting discrimination prevailed. When challenged in *SOUTH CAROLINA V. KATZENBACH* (1966), the Supreme Court upheld the law. Subsequent revisions of the original 1965 Act have virtually eliminated voting discrimination and the Act is truly one of the success stories of the civil rights movement.

Another kind of discrimination difficult to prove is discrimination based on wealth. When California made it a crime to bring indigent people into the state, the Supreme Court ruled it unconstitutional. In *EDWARDS V. CALIFORNIA* (1941), a divided Court split on the constitutional basis of the decision. Some justices saw the law as an infringement on congressional power to regulate interstate commerce. In the *Passenger Cases* (1849), the Court had ruled that people were part of interstate commerce. Other justices in the majority favored using the right to travel on the ground that it is a privilege and immunity of national citizenship. In either case, the Court made it clear that a state may not ban people because of their lack of wealth.

The right to travel and discrimination based on wealth were at issue again in *SHAPIRO V. THOMPSON* (1969). Connecticut and Pennsylvania had laws that required one year of residency before a person could qualify for welfare benefits. The Court held that the law restricted a person's constitutional right to travel on the basis of wealth and denied such a person the equal protection of the law.

Like gender-based classifications, some people believe that classifications based on wealth should be suspect. However, as with gender-based classifications, the Court refused to elevate wealth to the suspect classification category. In *SAN ANTONIO INDEPENDENT SCHOOL DISTRICT V. RODRIGUEZ* (1973), the Court was asked to rule on the constitutionality of the Texas method of funding public schools. Texas's reliance on property taxes resulted in poor and wealthy school districts. This, in turn, resulted in inequitable amounts being spent per student in poor and wealthy districts. Not only did the Court refuse to recognize wealth as a suspect classification, but it also refused to designate the right to a public education as a "fundamental right." Given these developments, it is doubtful the Court will create any new suspect classifications in the near future.

Privacy and Personal Autonomy

Most Americans would assert that privacy is a fundamental right. Privacy is often characterized as the "right to be left alone." Certainly most Americans favor government leaving them alone at least most of the time. Strangely, however, there is no explicit guarantee of privacy in the Constitution. Instead, the Supreme Court has recognized an implied right to privacy by relying on other constitutional provisions. Freedom of association, recognized by the Court in *N.A.A.C.P. V. ALABAMA* (1958), is a source of privacy secured by the First Amendment. The Fourth Amendment's protection against unreasonable searches and seizures is based on the sanctity of the home and privacy interests.

Interestingly, many landmark cases have involved sexuality and reproductive freedom. In an early case, *Skinner v. Oklahoma* (1942), the Court invalidated a law that required forced sterilization of repeat criminal offenders. The major breakthrough came, however, in 1965 with the *GRISWOLD V. CONNECTICUT* case. Connecticut law forbade its citizens, even married ones, from using contraceptives. The majority opinion, written by Justice William O. Douglas, acknowledged there was no explicit constitutional right to privacy. Privacy was found to be within the "penumbras" of other constitutional guarantees. Justice Arthur Goldberg, in a separate opinion, argued that the Ninth Amendment provided an independent basis for the right to privacy. *GRISWOLD* opened the door for consideration of other privacy issues. In *Loving v. Virginia* (1967), the Court invalidated a state law prohibiting marriage between people of different races. In *Eisenstadt v. Baird* (1972), it struck down a law forbidding the use of contraceptives by unmarried couples.

The most highly charged privacy issue in recent years has been over reproductive privacy. As noted earlier, the *Skinner* case recognized that the right to control one's reproductive ability is fundamental. The landmark case on reproductive freedom is, of course, *ROE V. WADE* (1973). Although the Court did not hold that a woman's right to an abortion is absolute, it did rule that her privacy interests during the first trimester of her pregnancy defeated any interests the state might have in protecting the unborn fetus. *ROE* set off a debate over abortion that remains unresolved. Changes in the personnel of the Court and politics have been key elements of the ongoing debate. State legislatures have enacted laws that require parental or spousal notification of an abortion, restrict the funding of abortions, and require abortions to be performed in hospitals instead of clinics among other restrictions. In *WEBSTER V. REPRODUCTIVE HEALTH SERVICES* (1989), the Court upheld a Missouri law prohibiting public expenditures for abortions in public hospitals. The Court upheld other provisions of the law such as one requiring viability tests on the fetus if a woman is twenty or more weeks into her pregnancy. Undoubtedly, as states test the limits of the *WEBSTER* decision the Court will again be faced with new questions on the constitutionality of abortion.

A final case involving privacy and sexuality is *BOWERS V. HARDWICK* (1986). At issue was the constitutionality of Georgia's sodomy law. Hardwick alleged that the law punished consensual sexual behavior between adults and that its enforcement violated the right to privacy. In upholding the law, the Court distinguished between previous cases such as *GRISWOLD*, *ROE*, and *Loving*. In those cases the Court has stressed the marital and procreative aspects of the intimate relations. Because homosexual activity cannot further family, marital, or procreative interests, previous privacy cases are not controlling. Under the circumstances, the Court believed the law was within the police power of the state.

Finally, we turn to privacy and personal autonomy. Personal autonomy is the right of self-determination. The right to determine control over one's body is grounded in common law. As we have seen, the cases dealing with reproductive freedom often raise this same point. Issues may be as "trivial" as the right to decide the length of one's hair or as important as the right to die.

In *Kelley v. Johnson* (1976), a male police officer contested a departmental policy concerning the length of an officer's hair. The Supreme Court upheld the policy on the grounds that the state's interest in promoting uniformity of appearance among its officers outweighed the issue of personal autonomy. Other cases have raised Fourth Amendment and due process issues. In *ROCHIN V. CALIFORNIA* (1952), a suspect's stomach was forcibly pumped to produce evidence of narcotics possession. The Court found that such a practice "shocks the conscience" and ruled it violated due process of law. In other cases, such as *Schmerber v. California* (1966), the Court upheld the forcible taking of blood samples as a routine medical procedure. The Court did not find this to be a violation of the Fourth Amendment. More recently, in *NATIONAL TREASURY UNION V. VON RAAB* (1989) and *Skinner v. Railway Labor Executive Association* (1989), the Court has upheld mandatory drug testing under certain circumstances.

Perhaps the ultimate issue of personal autonomy is the right to refuse medical treatment. Such cases often involve persons opposed to medical treatment for religious reasons, thereby triggering First Amendment questions. Although conceding a competent person's right to refuse medical treatment, the Court, nevertheless, ruled in *Jacobson v. Massachusetts* (1905) that public health concerns, such as the need for smallpox vaccinations, outweigh individual religious beliefs. A related issue involves the right to end life-sustaining medical treatment, that is, the right to die. In *CRUZAN BY CRUZAN V. DIRECTOR, MISSOURI DEPARTMENT OF HEALTH* (1990), the Supreme Court refused to allow the parents of Nancy Cruzan to order the removal of her life-support system. The Missouri law required "clear and convincing evidence" that a patient would choose to end life-sustaining methods if she were competent to do so. The Court held that Missouri's interest in preserving human life justified such a high standard of proof.

Conclusion

This introduction has been designed to acquaint the reader with some key issues of constitutional rights both past and present. It was also designed to whet the reader's appetite for more information about the Supreme Court's role in safeguarding constitutional rights. Finally, it was designed to serve as a road map for the case summaries that follow. It is our hope that these case summaries will generate further study of the constitutional rights of individuals.

BARRON V. BALTIMORE
7 Peters 243 (1833)

BACKGROUND John Barron and John Craig owned a wharf in the City of Baltimore. From 1815 to 1821 the city embarked on a series of civic improvements that involved paving streets, and bending the natural course of the rivers and streams in the city. During heavy rainstorms these streams carried soil from the hills and deposited them in the area of Barron's wharf. During a period of years the buildup rendered the wharf useless because the water became too shallow for ships. Barron sued the city in 1822 and won a judgment of $4500 in the Baltimore County Court. However, the Maryland Court of Appeals reversed the judgment so Barron appealed to the U.S. Supreme Court. Barron declared that the Fifth Amendment to the U.S. Constitution prohibits the taking of private property for public use without just compensation. Barron argued that the use of his wharf had been taken from him without compensation. Most important, however, Barron claimed that the Fifth Amendment provision was binding on the states as well as the national government. That is, the Fifth Amendment prohibits both the national government and the states from taking private property for public use without just compensation.

CONSTITUTIONAL ISSUE

Whether the Fifth Amendment's prohibition against the taking of private property for public use without just compensation is applicable to the states? NO

MAJORITY OPINION Chief Justice John Marshall delivers the opinion of the Court. The key question, Marshall states, is whether the Supreme Court has appellate jurisdiction in this case. Marshall rules that the Court does not have jurisdiction. The Constitution, he states, was ordained by the people of the United States to place limitations on the powers of the national government. Each state already had its own constitution for the protection of the rights of the people. The limitations on the powers of state governments were to be determined by the people of each state acting separately. Barron argues that the Bill of Rights was intended to protect citizens from abuse at the hands of state governments as well as the national government. Barron cites Article I, § 10 as evidence that the Constitution was intended to restrict state power. Article I, § 10 forbids states to pass a bill of attainder or an *ex post facto* law. Barron cites this as proof the framers intended the Constitution to serve as protection against state government as well as the national government.

Marshall rejects Barron's position for two reasons. First, the restrictions in Article I, § 10 were placed on the states because they would interfere with powers that were either to be exercised exclusively by the national government or that were also forbidden to the national government. Second, the history of the passage of the Bill of Rights makes it clear that the purpose of the first ten amendments was to provide additional safeguards against the exercise of power by the national government. If the framers of the Bill of Rights had intended them to be restrictions on the states as well, they would have made that intention clear. Article I, § 10 shows that the framers knew how to make their intentions clear as to which level of government was being restricted. If the people of the states need additional safeguards for their liberty, it makes more sense for them to secure those safeguards by amending their state constitutions rather than securing them by the tedious process of amending the federal constitution. The Court rules that the provision declaring that private property may not be taken for public use without just compensation is not applicable to state legislation. The provision is binding on the national government only and because the national government had nothing to do with Barron's injury, federal courts have no jurisdiction in this case.

SIGNIFICANCE OF THE CASE   In *Barron v. Baltimore* John Marshall ruled that the provisions of the Bill of Rights were not intended to be binding on the states. The significance of this ruling was profound. It meant that a citizen of the United States could not look to the federal Constitution for protection if a state abridged one of his or her rights. For example, if a state constitution did not guarantee religious freedom, then the state was theoretically free to pass laws abridging freedom of religion. The effect of *Barron* is that the First Amendment and the rest of the Bill of Rights prohibit only Congress from passing laws abridging the freedoms listed. The Bill of Rights, then, did not apply to state legislation restricting a person's liberty. Similarly, if the state's constitution does not prohibit double jeopardy, a person subjected to double jeopardy cannot, under the ruling in *Barron*, seek the protection of federal courts or the Bill of Rights.

QUESTIONS FOR DISCUSSION

(1)   Does it make any sense to say that the national government is forbidden to take private property for public use without just compensation but a state is not?

(2)   Does it make any sense to say that the national government may not punish a person for exercising his freedom of speech, but a state may?

(3)   Most prosecutions for crimes are made by the states. How does *Barron* affect the rights of persons accused of crimes in state courts?

(4)   Has *Barron* ever been overruled?

RELATED CASES   *SLAUGHTERHOUSE CASES*, 16 Wallace 36 (1873); *Twining v. New Jersey*, 211 U.S. 78 (1908); *GITLOW V. NEW YORK*, 268 U.S. 652 (1925); *Hamilton v. Board of Regents*, 293 U.S. 245 (1934); and *ADAMSON V. CALIFORNIA*, 332 U.S. 46 (1947).

DRED SCOTT V. SANDFORD
19 Howard 393 (1857)

BACKGROUND   Dred Scott was a slave belonging to an army doctor named Emerson. In 1834 Dr. Emerson took Scott from Missouri, a slave state, to Illinois, a free state and kept him there as a slave until 1835. That year Dr. Emerson took Scott to Fort Snelling, in the Wisconsin Territory (part of the Louisiana Purchase), an area where slavery was forbidden under the terms of the Missouri Compromise Act. Scott met his wife, Harriet, at

Fort Snelling and the marriage produced two daughters. In 1838 Dr. Emerson returned to Missouri with Scott and his family as his slaves. Dr. Emerson then sold the Scotts to John Sandford. Scott sued Sandford for his and his family's freedom on the grounds that they had been emancipated on entering free territory. Scott won in a Missouri lower court, but the decision was reversed by the Missouri Supreme Court. Scott then filed suit in the U.S. Circuit Court for Missouri. Scott claimed the federal court had jurisdiction because he was a citizen of Missouri, and Sandford was a citizen of New York. Sandford claimed that Scott, as a Negro, was not a citizen of Missouri; therefore, the circuit court did not have jurisdiction. The circuit court ruled it had jurisdiction but on the merits the judgment was for Sandford. Scott then appealed the circuit court's decision to the U.S. Supreme Court.

CONSTITUTIONAL ISSUES

(1)   Whether Dred Scott is a citizen of the United States entitled to sue a citizen of another state in federal court? NO

(2)   Whether the Missouri Compromise Act, which prohibits slavery in the Louisiana Territory, is a constitutional use of Congress's power to make "needful rules and regulations" regarding U.S. territories? NO

MAJORITY OPINION   Chief Justice Roger B. Taney delivers the opinion of the Court. The chief justice first focuses on the jurisdiction of the circuit court. Scott had asserted that he was a citizen of Missouri and that Sandford was a citizen of New York. Sandford, in his plea in abatement, denied that Scott was a citizen of Missouri solely on the basis of his Negro ancestry. The circuit court ruled in Scott's favor and proceeded to try the case on the merits, eventually ruling that Scott remained a slave. Taney says that the Court must first settle the issue of Scott's citizenship because if he is not a citizen, the circuit court never had jurisdiction. Taney rejects that Scott is a U.S. citizen regardless of his Missouri status. States may confer state citizenship on whomever they please, but only Congress may confer U.S. citizenship. Taney says that Negroes were never intended to be a part of the "body politic" that ordained and established the Constitution. Even the signers of the Declaration of Independence did not include Negroes when that document proclaimed that "all men are created equal." Taney proceeds to show that even in Northern states Negroes were treated unequally. In Massachusetts, Rhode Island, and Connecticut, Negroes were forbidden to marry whites. In New Hampshire, only whites could join the militia. Congress itself had limited naturalization "to aliens being free white persons." All of this leads Taney to conclude that Scott is not a U.S. citizen, and therefore he is not entitled to the privileges and immunities of U.S. citizenship, one of which is the use of federal courts. The circuit court erred in deciding it had jurisdiction in the case.

Taney then proceeds to examine Scott's claim to freedom. He asserts that the Court must correct any error in the court below and Scott's claim to be free as a result of his living in Illinois and the Wisconsin Territory is clearly erroneous. Taney states that Congress's power to prohibit slavery in parts of the Louisiana Territory is allegedly based on Article IV, § 3, which authorizes Congress to make "needful rules and regulations respecting the territory or other property belonging to the United States." However, Taney asserts that this provision applies only to territories held by the U.S. at the time of the ratification of the Constitution and does not include territories subsequently acquired from foreign countries through treaties. Taney claims the provision was a reference to certain lands then claimed by some of the states under the Northwest Ordinance of 1787. This special provision was not intended to give Congress plenary power to govern all U.S. territories. Citizens of the United States who migrate to U.S. territories are not "mere colonists" dependent on the will of the national government for their rights. Under our Constitution, Congress may not deprive a citizen of basic rights including property rights. The Missouri Compromise Act of 1820 deprives a master of his property by the mere act of taking them into a free territory. Taney concludes that the law is a violation of the Fifth Amendment's prohibition against taking property without due process of law and is therefore unconstitutional.

Finally, Taney turns to the issue of whether Scott's residence in Illinois made him free. In a previous case, *Strader v. Graham*, the Court ruled that the status of a slave is dependent on the state of his origin, not the state of his presence. Thus, Scott's status depended on the laws of Missouri, not Illinois. The opinion concludes by ruling the judgment for the defendant (Sandford) must be reversed and the suit dismissed for want of jurisdiction.

OTHER OPINIONS   There were six concurring and two dissenting opinions. In his short concurrence, Justice James Wayne merely asserts his belief that the Court properly addressed the issue of the constitutionality of the Missouri Compromise Act. Justice Samuel Nelson, in his concurrence, claims that it is unnecessary to address the constitutionality of the Act. In his opinion, a state has supreme power over slavery within its territory. Therefore, regardless of Scott's status in either Illinois or Wisconsin Territory, his status on his return to Missouri is governed by Missouri law. Missouri has no obligation to enforce the laws of Illinois that freed Scott. Likewise, the Act of Congress, which prohibits slavery in the Louisiana Territory, has no force of law in Missouri. Finally, Nelson asserts that Dr. Emerson never intended to make his residences at the forts permanent and that he had not established domicile in either place. Justice Robert Grier writes a brief concurrence agreeing with Justice Nelson in part but also agreeing that the Missouri Compromise is unconstitutional.

The next two concurrences are by Justices Peter Daniel and John Campbell. Justice Daniel merely repeats many of Taney's arguments. He believes that a citizen must be born of another citizen. Justice Daniel discusses the status of slaves throughout history and concludes that a slave does not become a citizen on receiving his freedom. Otherwise, this would empower the master to confer citizenship, a right belonging exclusively to the state. Finally, Daniel discusses the parts of the Constitution that protect the rights of slave holders. It is illogical, he maintains, for the Constitution to empower Congress to strip a master of ownership of his slaves when other parts of that document protect his rights of ownership.

Justice Campbell's position is that Congress has no power to abolish slavery in the territories. Insofar as Article IV, § 3 gives Congress the power to make "needful rules and regulations," that power is limited to administrative procedures necessary to prepare territories for statehood. Justice Campbell does not believe the power permits Congress to dissolve the master-slave relationship.

Justice John Catron writes the final concurrence. In it he concedes that Congress has a general power to make needful rules and regulations for the territories because to deny such power would call into question the enforcement of laws in the territories for the last sixty years. However, he still denies Congress may prohibit slavery in the Louisiana Territory. According to the terms of the Treaty of 1803 with France, inhabitants of the territory were to retain their right to own slaves, and Congress may not alter that right. Catron agrees with Taney that the Missouri Compromise Act violates the Due Process Clause of the Fifth Amendment.

Justices John McLean and Benjamin Curtis write dissenting opinions. Justice McLean rebuts most of the majority's major premises. The majority equates citizenship with the right to vote, but women and children are citizens who may not vote, yet may sue in federal court. Neither is Scott's status as a citizen dependent on the status of his ancestors. McLean also disputes whether Scott must be "naturalized." Naturalization applies to aliens, not persons born in the United States. McLean rebuts Taney's assertion that blacks were not a part of the "body politic" that framed the Constitution. Blacks, he notes, were citizens of several New England states. Finally, McLean turns to the issue of Scott's freedom. He does not believe as *Strader* held that the master carries the law of the slave state with him into free territory. He also wonders why the free state of Illinois must respect the Missouri law that made Scott a slave, but Missouri must not respect the Illinois law that made him free.

Justice Curtis's dissent covers many of McLean's arguments. Curtis believes Sandford should have applied for a writ of error when his plea in abatement was denied. Curtis, like McLean, demonstrates that blacks were citizens in at least five states when the Constitution was ratified. Curtis believes that citizenship is acquired by birth because in Article II, § 1 the Constitution speaks of "natural born citizens" when discussing the qualifications for president.

Curtis believes it is improper to rule on the constitutionality of the Missouri Compromise once the Court held that the circuit court lacked jurisdiction. However, because it did, he feels obliged to as well. Curtis argues that Scott's domicile in Illinois and Wisconsin Territory changed his status to that of a free man. Under the common law and international law, Missouri must accept Scott's status unless changed by positive law, something Missouri has not done.

Finally, Curtis discusses the denial of property without due process argument. Curtis asserts that slavery can exist only in the presence of positive law, which was lacking in Illinois. To make his point Curtis draws an analogy. No one denies that Congress may prohibit the importation of slaves. Suppose a U.S. citizen owns a slave in Cuba and tries to bring him into the country. It is not a denial of due process for Congress to enforce its laws against the importation of slaves. Therefore, the Missouri Compromise Act is not a violation of the Fifth Amendment.

SIGNIFICANCE OF THE CASE   Some historians maintain that the *Dred Scott* decision accelerated the nation's move toward civil war. For at least a generation compromises over slavery in the territories and in new states had succeeded in postponing armed conflict over the issue. *Dred Scott* precluded congressional compromise over the slavery issue and implied that the slavery issue could only be decided by the inhabitants of the territories under the doctrine of popular sovereignty. That led to bloody confrontations between proslavery and antislavery factions in the Kansas and Nebraska territories. The case also undermined the authority of Congress to legislate for U.S. territories. Like the rest of *Dred Scott*, the position that Congress is limited in its power to govern territories has been discredited.

Dred Scott also exacerbated the debate over state and national citizenship. The holding that Negroes could not be citizens was contrary to both history and logic. However, the Court's ruling was rendered moot by the passage of the Fourteenth Amendment, which states, "All persons born or naturalized in the United States, and subject to the jurisdiction thereof, are citizens of the United States and of the State wherein they reside."

Finally, *Dred Scott* is significant because not since 1803 in *Marbury v. Madison* had the Court struck down an act of Congress. Ordinarily, the ruling that the circuit court had erroneously granted jurisdiction would have precluded any further pressing of Scott's claim. However, Taney seems almost to go out of his way to declare the Missouri Compromise Act unconstitutional. The immediate result was to bring down abolitionist wrath on the Court and, as we have seen, draw the nation closer to civil war.

QUESTIONS FOR DISCUSSION

(1) Does it make sense to require that a person be a citizen to use the federal courts? Why or why not?

(2) Why do you think Chief Justice Taney equates citizenship with one's right to vote? Are they the same?

(3) Suppose a state banned handguns within its jurisdiction. Could the state confiscate handguns brought into the state by a citizen of another state?

(4) Why does Chief Justice Taney seem to go out of his way to invalidate the Missouri Compromise?

RELATED CASES *Hylton v. United States*, 3 Dallas 171 (1796); *MARBURY V. MADISON*, 1 Cranch 137 (1803); *Corfield v. Coryell*, 6 Fed. Cases 3230 (1823); *Strader v. Graham*, 10 Howard 82 (1850); and *SLAUGHTERHOUSE CASES*, 16 Wallace 36 (1873).

SLAUGHTERHOUSE CASES
16 Wallace 36 (1873)

BACKGROUND In 1869 the Louisiana Legislature passed a law granting a twenty-five-year monopoly over the slaughterhouse business in New Orleans to the Crescent City Livestock Landing and Slaughterhouse Company. The law was justified as a health measure because it removed the small butcher shops and slaughterhouses scattered throughout the city and concentrated the slaughterhouse business in one section of the city as a modern zoning law might do. However, the law also required butchers to use the facilities of the Crescent City Company and to pay the company a fee for use of its facilities. A fine of $100 was imposed for each violation of the law. The law effectively put the owners of about one thousand small butcher shops out of business so they challenged the constitutionality of the law.

CONSTITUTIONAL ISSUES

(1)   Whether the law denies the nonfavored butchers the right to pursue a lawful occupation, which is a privilege and immunity of U.S. citizenship? NO

(2)   Whether the law takes away the butchers' property without due process of law? NO

(3)   Whether the law denies the butchers the equal protection of the law? NO

(4)   Whether the law constitutes involuntary servitude in violation of the Thirteenth Amendment? NO

MAJORITY OPINION Justice Samuel Miller delivers the Court's opinion. Justice Miller begins by observing that it is within the state's police power to protect the health and comfort of the community by requiring the concentration of the slaughterhouse business in one section of New Orleans. Miller notes that the Legislature could have given the monopoly to the city itself and argues that there is nothing unconstitutional in conferring the same monopoly to a private corporation.

Justice Miller first addresses the question of the Thirteenth Amendment. He admits that the wording of the Amendment is neutral on issue of race and that the purpose of the Amendment was to abolish all slavery in the United States. It could, Miller concedes, be used to forbid Mexican peonage and the use of Chinese coolie labor. However, he argues that the Amendment was passed so recently that it is clear that the evil it was designed to remedy was Negro slavery. Miller implies that the white butchers cannot claim the protection of the Amendment.

Justice Miller then turns to the Fourteenth Amendment issues raised. He relates some of the background leading to the passage of the Amendment and states that although Negroes were not the only ones protected by the Amendment, any interpretation of it must be done in light of its primary purpose, which was to secure the rights of Negroes. Miller then begins a discussion of the citizenship conferred by the Amendment. Persons born or naturalized in the United States "are citizens of the United States and of the state wherein they reside." Thus, Americans enjoy dual citizenship—state citizenship and U.S. citizenship. The Fourteenth Amendment prohibits a state from making or enforcing any law that abridges the privileges and immunities of *a U.S. citizen*. That is, there are privileges and immunities of *state* citizenship and privileges and immunities of U.S. citizenship and the Fourteenth Amendment only forbids the states from abridging the latter. Some of the privileges and immunities of state citizenship include the right to acquire property subject to reasonable restraints that are necessary for the good of all. Similarly, the right to pursue a lawful occupation is a privilege and immunity of state citizenship, but it, too, is subject to reasonable regulation. However, the right to pursue a lawful occupation is not necessarily a privilege and immunity of U.S. citizenship. The privileges and immunities of U.S. citizenship include the right to go to the seat of the national government, the right of access to U.S. seaports, protection of the United States on the high seas, and several other guarantees outlined in the Constitution. Any other interpretation of the Fourteenth Amendment would remove from the states their historic power to be the primary protector of privileges and immunities of citizens. Such an interpretation would also alter our entire federal system of government.

Justice Miller acknowledges that Article IV of the Constitution states that, "The citizens of each state shall be entitled to all privileges and immunities of citizens in the several states." However, that clause merely prohibits a state from adopting laws that unduly discriminate against citizens of other states in matters of "fundamental rights." The law in question does not discriminate against citizens of other states because it affects all butchers in the city of New Orleans regardless whether they are citizens of Louisiana or not.

Justice Miller dismisses the rest of the charges out of hand. He states that under no judicial interpretation existing can this law be called a deprivation of property without due process of law. The power to grant the monopoly clearly belongs to the state, and the law was duly passed by the legislature. As for equal protection, Miller states that in light of the fact that the Fourteenth Amendment was intended to secure the rights of Negroes, he doubts that any discrimination not directed at Negroes "will ever be held to come within the purview of this provision." The judgments of the Louisiana Supreme Court are affirmed.

OTHER OPINIONS   Justice Stephen Field delivers the major dissenting opinion. Field concedes that it may be valid to confine the slaughtering business to a particular part of the city but argues that the grant of a monopoly to a single corporation cannot be justified as a health measure. He also notes that if this monopoly is valid, then any monopoly that state wishes to grant is valid. Field also discusses the Thirteenth Amendment. He notes that the Amendment forbids all slavery, not just "African slavery." Congress, in passing the Civil Rights Act of 1866, listed the rights of U.S. citizens. Since the Act was of doubtful constitutionality, the Fourteenth Amendment was adopted, and the Civil Rights Act was reenacted by Congress. Field argues that the rights that belong to a person as a free human being and a free citizen now are a result of U.S. citizenship and not dependent on the citizenship of any state. Among those rights "must be placed the right to pursue a lawful employment in a lawful manner." Finally, Field discusses the Privileges and Immunities Clause of Article IV of the Constitution. That Clause was designed to prevent a state from passing hostile and discriminating legislation against nonresidents. Field argues that a state could not grant its own citizens the exclusive right to manufacture and sell shoes in the state. Just as the Privileges and Immunities Clause of Article IV was designed to protect nonresidents from state legislation encroaching on their natural rights, the Fourteenth Amendment was designed to protect all U.S. citizens from hostile and discriminating state legislation.

Justice Joseph P. Bradley also writes a dissenting opinion. He states that the issues in this case are simple. First, is the right to pursue a lawful occupation a privilege and immunity of U.S. citizenship? Second, is the granting of a monopoly over the slaughter-house business a reasonable regulation of a lawful occupation? Relying on English common law and traditions, Justice Bradley concludes that every free man is entitled to pursue lawful occupations with such reasonable restrictions as government may impose. Therefore, he believes that the right is a privilege and immunity of U.S. citizenship. Next, Bradley argues that the granting of a monopoly and the requirement that butchers pay a fee to the Crescent City Livestock Company are not reasonable restraints on a lawful occupation. Justice Bradley says that the law is "onerous, unreasonable, arbitrary and unjust." Although a state may grant a monopoly for certain public enterprises, never has a monopoly been granted for private occupations.

Justice Noah H. Swayne also files a separate dissent.

SIGNIFICANCE OF THE CASE The *Slaughterhouse Cases* virtually eliminated the use of the Privileges and Immunities Clause of the Fourteenth Amendment as a means of protecting the rights of U.S. citizenship from abridgement at the hands of the states. None of the Bill of Rights, for example, could be claimed as a "privilege and immunity" of national citizenship. Although the Bill of Rights continued to protect persons from abridgement by the national government, states were free to abridge First Amendment and other freedoms. This was especially significant in terms of the newly freed slaves who had many of their rights restricted by hostile State legislatures.

QUESTIONS FOR DISCUSSION

(1) Does it make any sense to have rights that are protected from abridgement by the national government but not by state government?

(2) If the Fourteenth Amendment offers no real protection for the rights of U.S. citizens, why was the Amendment added to the Constitution in the first place?

(3) Do you understand the difference between privileges and immunities of state citizenship and privileges and immunities of national citizenship?

(4) Does federalism help or hurt the protection of basic rights?

RELATED CASES *Corfield v. Coryell*, 6 Fed. Cases 3230 (1823); *Bradwell v. Illinois*, 16 Wallace 130 (1873); *CIVIL RIGHTS CASES*, 109 U.S. 3 (1883); and *PLESSY V. FERGUSON*, 163 U.S. 537 (1896).

THE CIVIL RIGHTS CASES
109 U.S. 3 (1883)

BACKGROUND In March 1875 Congress passed the Civil Rights Act. Section 1 of the Act entitles all persons in the United States to the full and equal enjoyment of public accommodations in hotels, inns, theaters, public conveyances, and places of amusement without regard to race, color, or previous condition of servitude. Section 2 of the Act makes it illegal to deny such accommodations to any person on the basis of race and imposes a fine from $500 to $1000 and imprisonment from thirty days to one year on conviction. These are five cases involving violations of the Act. Two of the cases involved denial of hotel or inn accommodations, two involved denial of access to theaters, and the fifth case involved denial of equal access to a railroad car. Interestingly, four of the cases came from non-Southern states: Kansas, California, New York, and Missouri. Only the railroad case came from a southern state, Tennessee.

CONSTITUTIONAL ISSUE

Whether Congress is empowered by either the Thirteenth or Fourteenth Amendment to prohibit discrimination on the basis of race, color, or previous condition of servitude against persons in privately owned places of public accommodation? NO

MAJORITY OPINION Justice Joseph P. Bradley delivers the opinion of the Court. Justice Bradley briefly recounts the background of each of the five cases. He then proceeds to examine the wording of the Fourteenth Amendment noting that it says "no state" shall make or enforce any law that abridges the privileges and immunities of citizens of the United States, deprives a citizen of life, liberty, or property, or denies a citizen the equal protection of the law. Bradley asserts that it is state action of a discriminatory nature that the law seeks to prohibit, not private discrimination. The purpose of the Fourteenth Amendment, he asserts, is corrective; that is, Congress may correct or nullify any state law that discriminates against citizens on the basis of race. That does not mean, Bradley insists, that Congress may enact legislation to regulate private rights. To allow such, Bradley maintains, would allow Congress to legislate in areas within the reserved powers of the states. Bradley compares the Fourteenth Amendment to the Impairment of Contract Clause in Article I, § 10 of the Constitution. Although states are forbidden to pass laws that impair the obligation of contracts, Congress's power is limited to taking measures to correct state laws that do. Article I, § 10 does not mean that Congress may legislate in the whole field of contracts. Until a state law has been passed, no federal legislation can provide a remedy. The Act of 1875 does not profess to be corrective of any state legislation, but seeks to redress private discrimination. It is direct legislation that supersedes and displaces state laws. Bradley concedes that in certain areas (the regulation of interstate commerce, for example) Congress has plenary power that allows it to take direct action, but the Fourteenth Amendment confers no such plenary power.

Bradley then turns to the question whether the Thirteenth Amendment authorizes Congress to enact the Civil Rights Act. Bradley concedes that the amendment is a primary and direct grant of power to Congress; however, the subject is limited to slavery. One argument is that race discrimination constitutes a "badge of slavery" that Congress under the Thirteenth Amendment may prohibit. Bradley notes that the Civil Rights Act of 1866 removed discrimination against former slaves in several areas including the right to enter into contracts, to inherit property, and to serve on juries. These topics, according to Bradley, appertain to the "essence of citizenship." They dealt with discriminatory practices that were holdovers from the days of slavery. But denial of public accommodations on the basis of race does not, in Bradley's view, constitute a "badge of slavery" because even free blacks who enjoyed all the privileges of citizenship before the passage of the Thirteenth Amendment were denied access to white establishments. If any injury occurs as a result of private discrimination, it is for the laws of the state to provide a remedy. In closing, Bradley maintains that it is time for the former slave to assume the rank of "mere citizen" and to cease being a special favorite of the law. It is time, he asserts, for the former slave to use remedies available to other citizens whose rights have been violated. Therefore, he concludes, § 1 and § 2 of the Civil Rights Act of 1875 are unconstitutional.

OTHER OPINIONS Justice John Marshall Harlan I delivers the only dissenting opinion. Justice Harlan believes that the majority's opinion undermines the spirit of the Thirteenth and Fourteenth Amendments. The Civil Rights Act was designed merely to make unlawful the denial of access to places of public accommodation on the basis of race. He also rejects the majority's view that the Thirteenth Amendment does not empower Congress to outlaw the badges of slavery. To illustrate his point Harlan notes that Article

IV, § 2, Clause 3 (persons held to service or labor) of the Constitution was the basis for the Fugitive Slave Acts of 1793 and 1850. Article IV, § 2, Clause 3, as interpreted, guaranteed slave owners the right to have fugitive slaves returned. Although the Constitution did not specifically empower Congress to enact fugitive slave laws, the power to do so was implied. Harlan argues that any right or privilege granted in the Constitution may be protected by congressional legislation. Race discrimination, he asserts, constitutes "a badge of slavery" that Congress may prohibit by direct legislation.

Next, Harlan asserts that private enterprises may acquire a public character. In *Munn v. Illinois*, the Court ruled that grain elevators, although privately owned, take on a public character that the state may regulate in the public interest. Harlan then proceeds to demonstrate the public character of inns, railroads, and places of public amusement.

Harlan also rejects the majority's comparison of the Fourteenth Amendment with the Impairment of Contract Clause. The Impairment of Contract Clause has no direct grant of legislative power to enforce its provision. Traditionally, the Clause has been enforced by the courts and not through legislation passed by Congress. Both the Thirteenth and Fourteenth Amendments have sections authorizing Congress to enact legislation to enforce its provisions. Harlan also reproaches the majority for narrowly limiting § 5 of the Fourteenth Amendment to provisions mentioning state action. Section 5 gives Congress the authority to enforce all provisions of the Amendment, not just those that deal with state action. Next, Harlan denies that black citizens have been the special favorites of the law. The Act merely affords blacks the same rights enjoyed by any other citizen. Finally, Harlan notes that it is ironic that before the Civil War the Congress was able to pass laws to protect the rights of slave owners but is unable now to pass laws to protect the rights of freed slaves.

SIGNIFICANCE OF THE CASE   In a sense, the *Civil Rights Cases* mark an end to post–Civil War attempts to guarantee the rights of freed slaves. Private discrimination, according to the Supreme Court, cannot be prohibited by Congress under the Thirteenth and Fourteenth Amendments. Coupled with the *Slaughterhouse Cases* and *Plessy v. Ferguson*, the *Civil Rights Cases* virtually derail the legislative movement for civil rights for blacks until 1957. Justice Bradley's remark that former slaves need to cease being the special favorites of the law and become "mere citizens" apparently echoed the sentiment of many Americans who wanted to close the Civil War chapter in American history.

QUESTIONS FOR DISCUSSION

(1)   Why does the majority fail to find any state action in these cases?

(2)   How would Justice Harlan argue that there is state action?

(3)   What kind of state action would be needed to enable Congress to act under the Fourteenth Amendment?

(4)   How have the *Civil Rights Cases* been modified as a result of recent Supreme Court decisions and congressional legislation?

(5)   In light of today's emphasis on affirmative action programs, do you agree with Bradley that it is time to remove special protections for African Americans? Why or why not?

RELATED CASES   *SLAUGHTERHOUSE CASES*, 16 Wallace 36 (1873); *MUNN V. ILLINOIS*, 4 Otto 113 (1877); *PLESSY V. FERGUSON*, 163 U.S. 537 (1896); *HEART OF ATLANTA MOTEL, INC. V. UNITED STATES*, 379 U.S. 241 (1964); *Runyon v. McCrary*, 427 U.S. 160 (1976); *REGENTS OF THE UNIVERSITY OF CALIFORNIA V. BAKKE*, 438 U.S. 265 (1978); and *Fullilove v. Klutznick*, 448 U.S. 448 (1980).

PLESSY V. FERGUSON
163 U.S. 537 (1896)

BACKGROUND   Plessy, a citizen of "seventh-eighths Caucasian and one-eighth African blood," boarded a car for whites only for his train trip between two Louisiana cities. When he refused the conductor's request to switch cars, Plessy was forcibly removed from the train and charged with a violation of Louisiana's criminal laws. The statute in question required railroad companies to provide separate but equal accommodations for the two races and assessed a penalty of $25 or twenty days in the parish prison for those passengers who insisted on going into "the coach of the race to which he does not belong." The Louisiana Supreme Court upheld the validity of the law.

CONSTITUTIONAL ISSUE

Whether the Equal Protection Clause of the Fourteenth Amendment bars states from enacting legislation that discriminates against persons on the basis of race? NO

MAJORITY OPINION   Justice Henry Billings Brown writes the majority opinion of the Court. The case turns on the Court's interpretation of the Thirteenth and Fourteenth Amendments and the Louisiana statute. Justice Brown quickly dismisses Plessy's claim that the Thirteenth Amendment—which abolished slavery—applied in the instant case. Brown flatly states that it "is too clear for argument" that the Thirteenth Amendment deals only with involuntary servitude and not with acts of discrimination and therefore did not enter into these deliberations.

The Fourteenth Amendment becomes the crux of the case. The Court views the Equal Protection Clause as ensuring "absolute equality of the two races before the law" but not as abolishing distinctions based on race or enforcing social, as opposed to political, equality. Equality results from equal civil and political rights. Separation of the races did not "necessarily imply the inferiority of either race" and any interpretation of enforced segregation in equal facilities as placing a badge of inferiority comes solely because "the colored race chooses to put that construction on it." Prejudice can only be overcome by voluntary consent of individuals and not by "enforced commingling" or by legislation, Brown writes.

The Court's test for measuring whether a statute violated the Fourteenth Amendment is whether the regulations were reasonable and enacted in good faith for the promotion of the public good and not for the oppression of a particular group or race. Great deference is to be given to the laws and regulations of the states. On occasion, the

Court has interpreted state laws that forbade exclusion based on race, whereas here they are interpreting a state law that required separate but equal facilities. In both cases, the Court defers to state legislatures that are "at liberty to act with reference to the established usages, customs, and traditions of the people." That Plessy intended to travel solely within the state's borders negated any effect of the Interstate Commerce Clause and bolstered Louisiana's claim of superiority in regulating travel within its boundaries. The Court finds that Louisiana's statute was reasonable in light of the circumstances and because it mandated "equal" accommodations.

OTHER OPINIONS Justice John Marshall Harlan I writes the lone dissent. Harlan declares the decision of the Court to be "pernicious," to be inconsistent with the personal liberties of citizens, and to be "hostile to both the spirit and letter of the constitution of the United States." He finds the statute to be nothing but a charade to continue the trappings of racism and racial subjugation—a goal he finds unacceptable in light of the Civil Rights Amendments and accompanying legislation. "But in view of the constitution, in the eye of the law, there is in this country no superior, dominant, ruling class of citizens.... Our constitution is color-blind.... In respect of civil rights, all citizens are equal before the law." Included in those personal liberties was the right to sit in a public coach on a public highway and not to be denied such right because of race.

Harlan also speaks of the division of powers among the branches and levels of government, but he emphasizes the role of the Court as the ultimate enforcer of the Constitution and the rights it grants. He states that it was wrong for the Court to allow the states to "regulate the enjoyment of citizens of their civil rights solely on the basis of race." Furthermore, it plants the "seeds of race hate" in the law. For him, "The sure guaranty of the peace and security of each race is the clear, distinct, unconditional recognition by our governments, national and state, of every right that inheres in civil freedom, and of the equality before the law of all citizens of the United States, without regard to race."

SIGNIFICANCE OF THE CASE *Plessy v. Ferguson* entrenched the separate but equal doctrine in the law and ensured enforced segregation of the races. *Plessy* was overturned by the landmark decision of *Brown v. Board of Education of Topeka* (1954).

QUESTIONS FOR DISCUSSION

(1) Do you agree with the majority that "separate but equal" does not imply inferiority or second-class citizenship? Why?

(2) Would you have voted with the majority or with Harlan?

(3) What if Plessy had been of Arab or Cambodian descent? Would this have affected your vote?

(4) If Plessy had not been a citizen but instead a resident alien or a visitor, would that make a difference either legally or morally?

RELATED CASES *DRED SCOTT V. SANDFORD*, 19 Howard 393 (1857); and *BROWN V. BOARD OF EDUCATION OF TOPEKA*, 347 U.S. 483 (1954).

BROWN V. BOARD OF EDUCATION OF TOPEKA
347 U.S. 483 (1954)

BACKGROUND Plaintiffs, "minors of the Negro race," challenged the constitutionality of statutes in Kansas, South Carolina, Virginia, and Delaware, which required or permitted segregation in public schools according to race. They urged the overturning of *Plessy v. Ferguson* with its "separate but equal" doctrine, arguing the segregated public schools were not equal and could not be made equal, which deprived them of equal protection of the laws. The Supreme Court first heard the case in 1952, and reargument that primarily centered on the events surrounding the adoption of the Fourteenth Amendment in 1868 was held the next year. The Court's opinion was issued in 1954.

CONSTITUTIONAL ISSUE

Whether the "separate but equal" doctrine in public schools violates the Equal Protection Clause of the Fourteenth Amendment? YES

MAJORITY OPINION Chief Justice Earl Warren writes the unanimous opinion of the Court. The crux of the case is interpretation of the Fourteenth Amendment. Warren notes that the extensive discussion during reargument and the Court's own analysis of the intent of Congress and state legislatures did not resolve the questions concerning the proposed scope of the Amendment. Because of the "inconclusive nature of the Amendment's history" and because the Court could not turn the clock back, the Court would consider the question of public education "in the light of its full development and its present place in American life." The Court's position on the significance of education, "perhaps the most important function of state and local governments," is plainly indicated.

Even more unequivocal are the blunt statements regarding segregation in public schools, "[I]n the field of public education the doctrine of 'separate but equal' has no place. Separate educational facilities are inherently unequal." The Court determines that segregation by race in public schools generated feelings of inferiority in the minority race and affected "their hearts and minds in a way unlikely ever to be undone." Language is included that expressly rejected *Plessy v. Ferguson* regarding public education.

SIGNIFICANCE OF THE CASE Seldom has such a brief and straightforward opinion set off such a firestorm of public opinion. Some school administrators, state officials, and others adamantly opposed desegregation of public schools, and vigorous opposition in such places as Little Rock led to the intervention of federal troops to ensure compliance with the court order. This landmark decision saw the demise of the "separate but equal" doctrine in education and foresaw its eventual abolition in all areas of government activity.

In *Brown v. Board of Education of Topeka (Brown II)*, the Court considered the issue of implementation of *Brown I*. Although the primary responsibility for desegregating schools rested with local school officials, federal district courts were assigned an active role in monitoring local plans and in fashioning remedies for failure to comply with the precepts laid out in *Brown*.

QUESTIONS FOR DISCUSSION

(1)   Why was there such entrenched opposition to *Brown v. Board of Education*?

(2)   Do you think that school desegregation was an issue which should have been left to Congress and the legislatures as the elected representatives of the people, or do you think that it was appropriate for the unelected justices of the Supreme Court to render an opinion so drastically changing public policy?

(3)   Should the Court follow public opinion in its decisions, or should it act independently in interpreting the Constitution on such emotional issues as homosexuality, abortion, or school desegregation?

RELATED CASES   *PLESSY V. FERGUSON*, 163 U.S. 537 (1896); *Sweatt v. Painter*, 339 U.S. 629 (1950); *McLaurin v. Oklahoma State Regents*, 339 U.S. 637 (1950); *Brown v. Board of Education of Topeka, Brown II*, 349 U.S. 294 (1955); and *SWANN V. CHARLOTTE-MECKLENBURG BOARD OF EDUCATION*, 402 U.S. 1 (1971).

SHELLEY V. KRAEMER
334 U.S. 1 (1948)

BACKGROUND   Two cases, one from Missouri and one from Michigan, were consolidated for hearing before the Supreme Court. Thirty of thirty-nine landowners of lots in a certain tract in St. Louis agreed that future land sales in this district would carry a condition prohibiting the use or occupancy of the land "by people of the Negro or Mongolian Race." At the time the covenant was signed, five of the parcels in the tract were owned by Negroes and had been so occupied from twenty-three to sixty-three years. The Shelleys, who were Negroes and who had no knowledge of the agreement, bought one of lots and were sued by the signatory landowners for the purpose of divesting the Shelleys of ownership. In Detroit, the Fergusons entered into a similar covenant that the occupants of their property must be of the Caucasian race. However, Negroes acquired title to the property and were sued by other landowners to force their removal from the property. In both Missouri and Michigan, the litigation was filed in the state court system and was appealed to the courts of last resort, which upheld the covenants.

CONSTITUTIONAL ISSUE

Whether the Equal Protection Clause of the Fourteenth Amendment prevents judicial enforcement by state courts of restrictive covenants based on race or color? YES

MAJORITY OPINION   Chief Justice Fredric Vinson delivers the opinion of the Court. He uses a three-pronged approach to the issue: (1) whether the restrictive covenants were, in and of themselves, unconstitutional; (2) whether enforcement by state courts constituted state action and brought into play the provisions of the Equal Protection Clause of the Fourteenth Amendment; and (3) whether the infringement of property rights based on race or color violated the Equal Protection Clause.

First, restrictive covenants based on race or color are not unconstitutional *per se*. These agreements between private individuals, standing alone, do not violate the Fourteenth Amendment: That Amendment erects no shield against merely private conduct, however discriminatory or wrongful.

Then the chief justice turns to the issue of whether the mere enforcement of the covenants by state courts was sufficient state action to trigger the provisions of the Fourteenth Amendment. He unequivocally states that "the actions of state courts and judicial officers in their official capacities are to be regarded as action of the State within the meaning of the Fourteenth Amendment." This shifts the restrictive covenant from the realm of private matters into state action and makes the state an active party in discriminating against the enjoyment of property rights.

The Fourteenth Amendment, its companion Civil Rights Act of 1866, and various court interpretations of the two clearly established the right to acquire, enjoy, own and dispose of property without discriminatory state action. "Equality in the enjoyment of property rights was regarded as an essential precondition to the realization of other basic civil rights and liberties." Discrimination by state action—whether created by state statute, city ordinance, or judicial enforcement—is not to be permitted under the Constitution.

The protections of the Fourteenth Amendment are personal rights, and the fact that restrictive covenants could be used against the white majority does not justify denial of equal protection to these individuals. The Court also rejects the argument that closing the courts for enforcement by the property owners denied equal protection. "The Constitution confers upon no individual the right to demand action by the State which results in the denial of equal protection of the laws to other individuals." The Court is obligated by the Constitution to prevent unconstitutional acts on the part of states.

SIGNIFICANCE OF THE CASE   The Court in this case reiterated that the state courts could not be used to enforce racially discriminatory private contracts or activities. The case forecast the Court's later interpretation of the Civil Rights Act as prohibiting private as well as public discrimination.

QUESTIONS FOR DISCUSSION

(1)   Americans generally have very strong convictions regarding their rights to use and deal with the property they own. Do you think that the Court is unwarranted in limiting your right to deal with your property in any way that you see fit?

(2)   What significance, if any, did this case have for governmental regulations regarding the use of property such as zoning laws?

RELATED CASES   *Buchanan v. Warley*, 245 U.S. 60 (1917); *Oyama v. California*, 332 U.S. 633 (1948); *Reitman v. Mulkey*, 387 U.S. 369 (1967); *Jones v. Alfred H. Mayer Co.*, 392 U.S. 409 (1968); and *Runyon v. McCrary*, 427 U.S. 160 (1976).

SWANN V. CHARLOTTE-MECKLENBURG BOARD OF EDUCATION
402 U.S. 1 (1971)

BACKGROUND   The Charlotte-Mecklenburg School District had more than 84,000 students in 107 schools during the 1968–69 school year. Approximately 29 percent (24,000) students were black; of these students, some 14,000 students attended 21 schools that were at least 99 percent black even though the District was operating under a 1965 court-approved desegregation plan. In 1968, Swann petitioned for immediate revision of the plan to provide a more racially balanced system.

CONSTITUTIONAL ISSUE

Whether the imposition of busing and other remedial measures to eliminate state-imposed segregation in schools is within the scope of the powers of federal district courts? YES

MAJORITY OPINION Chief Justice Warren Burger delivers the unanimous opinion of the Court. In the 1954 case of *Brown v. Board of Education*, the Court provided that state-imposed segregation by race in public schools denied equal protection under the Constitution. From that date forward, Burger notes, school boards and administrators frequently opted for noncompliance with the Court's mandate, but the Court had not wavered from its position and in *Green v. County School Board* (1968), the Court bluntly demanded that school boards produce plans that promise "realistically to work...*now*" to end such segregation.

When a constitutional right and a violation of that right have been shown, it is appropriate for courts to intervene. It is the task of the Court to "correct, by a balancing of the individual and collective interests, the condition that offends the Constitution." The failure of some local school boards to comply with the principles set forth in *Brown* triggered the courts' involvement in school desegregation; "judicial authority enters only when local authority defaults." Once involved, the courts have broad equitable powers to remedy past wrongs and to fashion a plan to assure a unitary school system. The Court construes Title IV of the 1964 Civil Rights Act, which contained language that some might consider as prohibiting busing as a means of achieving racial balance—"Nothing...shall empower any official or court to issue any order seeking to achieve a racial balance in any school by requiring the transportation of pupils or students from one school to another to achieve such racial balance, or otherwise enlarge the existing power of the court"—as merely preventing the expansion of existing powers and not as limiting the courts' present powers (including using busing as a remedial measure).

Burger admits that school boards, like courts, cannot control neighborhood residential patterns and notes that minorities frequently settled in one section of the community. However, the school board does control the opening and closing of schools, and such decisions do have an effect on the system in terms of racial balance, faculty, staff, transportation, extracurricular activities, and facilities. For example, the decision to close an older school in a racially mixed neighborhood and to open another in a suburban white area could contribute to further imbalance. The location of schools, along with the method of student assignment, determines the racial composition of the student body within each school. If a proposed desegregation plan contains provisions for schools that were all or predominantly one race, then the school district bears the burden of showing that student assignments were "genuinely nondiscriminatory."

Burger indicates that sending children to schools located close to their homes "might be desirable" but given a "system that has been deliberately constructed and maintained to enforce racial segregation," remedial measures are necessary. That courts employ such measures as busing of students to schools further away from their homes is an appropriate tool for correcting past wrongs. Busing of students to schools in town is the norm in the rural areas of the nation and is an accepted educational practice. Courts may consider such factors as the distance, time spent in transit, and ages of the students when fashioning remedial plans, and busing programs should not risk "the health of the children or significantly impinge on the educational process."

School desegregation does not mandate that each school must reflect the racial composition of the entire system, and any absolute quotas or formulas will not be sustained, although the courts could set acceptable ranges as guides for the schools.

SIGNIFICANCE OF THE CASE *Swann v. Charlotte-Mecklenburg Board of Education* confirmed the Court's continued opposition to state-imposed racially segregated schools and affirmed the practice of busing as one tool used to offset racial imbalances in schools. It also ratified the very active, almost daily, involvement of the judiciary in setting up and monitoring school desegregation plans.

RELATED CASES *BROWN V. BOARD OF EDUCATION*, 347 U.S. 483 (1954) (Brown I); *Brown v. Board of Education*, 349 U.S. 294 (1955) (Brown II); *Green v. County School Board*, 391 U.S. 430 (1968); *United States v. Montgomery County Board of Education*, 395 U.S. 225 (1969); and *Board of Education of Oklahoma City Public Schools v. Dowell*, 59 U.S.L.W. 4061 (1991).

REGENTS OF THE UNIVERSITY OF CALIFORNIA V. BAKKE
438 U.S. 265 (1978)

BACKGROUND The University of California at Davis (Davis) had two admissions programs—the regular admissions program and the special admissions program—for its entering class of one hundred students. Under the regular admissions program, students with undergraduate grade-point averages below 2.5 on a 4.0-point scale were automatically rejected. However, each applicant had the choice of being considered as either "economically and/or educationally disadvantaged" or members of a "minority group" (blacks, Chicanos, Asians, and Native Americans); if a candidate indicated on the application that he or she was disadvantaged or was a member of a minority group, then the applicant was considered for special admission. Special admission applicants did not have to meet the 2.5-grade-point-average requirement and were not rated against the candidates in the regular admission program. Candidates within the two groups were ranked, and selected candidates were then invited for interviews by the two committees. During a four-year period, no disadvantaged whites were admitted, but sixty-three minority students were admitted under the regular program and forty-four under the special program.

Bakke, a white male, applied in 1973 and 1974 for admission to the Medical School. He applied late in 1973 and was rejected because his test scores on the Medical College Admissions Test were lower than those being accepted at that point, although there were still four special admission slots unfilled. In 1974, he had raised his scores and filed early. Nevertheless, he was once again rejected. In both years special applicants were admitted with scores lower than his. He filed a lawsuit claiming that he had been excluded on the basis of his race in violation of the Equal Protection Clause of the Fourteenth Amendment, a provision of the California Constitution, and Title VI of the Civil Rights Act of 1964, which provides that no person shall be excluded on the grounds of race or color from any program receiving federal financial assistance. On appeal, the California Supreme Court ordered that Bakke be admitted and also held that Davis violated the state and national constitutions by taking race into account in making admission decisions.

CONSTITUTIONAL ISSUE

Whether state governments may use race-conscious—affirmative action—programs in various types of benefit programs under the Equal Protection Clause of the Fourteenth Amendment? YES

PLURALITY OPINION In announcing the decision of the Court, Justice Lewis Powell notes that there was a "notable lack of unanimity." The justices issue six different opinions, partially concurring with each other and partially disagreeing with each other. In part, the disagreement of the justices turns on the role and interpretation of Title VI of the Civil Rights Act of 1964, and, in part, on the proper standard of court review of racial classifications under the Equal Protection Clause of the Fourteenth Amendment. Justice Powell's opinion becomes the plurality opinion because he is the swing vote on some of the issues of the case; the issues include the following: (1) Bakke's admission; (2) the constitutionality of the Davis program; (3) the application of Title VI; and (4) the use of race as an admissions factor.

Justice Powell determines that Bakke should be admitted and that the special admissions program, as constructed, was unlawful; Chief Justice Warren Burger and Justices Potter Stewart, William Rehnquist, and John Paul Stevens concur in this result but not in the reasoning. Regarding Title VI, Powell adroitly sidesteps the question of whether private parties have a cause of action under Title VI by stating that it had not been argued or decided by lower courts, and therefore the Court does not have to address the issue and that he assumes that Bakke did have a right of action. He relies heavily on the legislative history of Title VI in his interpretation that the statute only proscribes racial classifications that would violate the Fourteenth Amendment's Equal Protection Clause if employed by a state or its agencies.

For Powell, classifications based on race are inherently suspect and subject to strict scrutiny by the Court. "The guarantee of equal protection cannot mean one thing when applied to one individual and something else when applied to a person of another color. If both are not accorded the same protection, then it is not equal." If a state seeks to establish racial classifications, it must show a compelling state interest. Such compelling state interest had been shown in prior cases, but Powell distinguishes those cases that approved remedial preferential classifications when there was proven constitutional or statutory violations. There is no such determination involved here.

Powell examines the purposes of the Davis program to determine if any established a compelling state interest sufficient to uphold the racial classification scheme. First, he deals with Davis's claim that the program would offset the lack of minorities in medical school and in the profession, and would counter the effects of societal discrimination. He agrees that is a legitimate interest of the state, but it did not justify a classification that disadvantaged persons such as Bakke who bore no responsibility for the traditional discrimination. Second, there is no evidence in the record that minority doctors would, in fact, return to disadvantaged communities to practice as Davis claimed; therefore, that could not be of compelling interest.

However, Powell finds validity in Davis's goal of attaining a diverse student body that he views as a constitutionally permissible goal based on the First Amendment and academic freedom and one that would provide a compelling state interest to set up racial classifications, but Powell will *not* accept as constitutional a program such as Davis's that focuses "*solely* on ethnic diversity." Thus, Powell determines that race could be considered as a factor in the admission process; Brennan, White, Marshall, and Blackmun concur in this result. Powell emphasizes that applicants should be judged as individuals, although race can be considered as a "plus" factor. With such a scheme, the applicant who was not selected "will not have been foreclosed from all consideration...simply because he was not the right color or had the wrong surname," and equal protection would be extended to both candidates.

OTHER OPINIONS Justices William Brennan, Byron White, Thurgood Marshall, and Harry Blackmun concur with Powell that government can use race-conscious programs to redress the continuing effects of past discrimination. They agree that both Title VI and the Equal Protection Clause proscribe the same types of discrimination; for these judges, however, the merger of Title VI and the Equal Protection Clause means that the remedial use of race as authorized by the Fourteenth Amendment is also authorized under Title VI. Both Title VI and the Fourteenth Amendment allow broad remedial use of such classifications to correct the long-lingering effects of prior discrimination, and Title VI would not bar the preferential treatment of racial minorities.

For these four justices, racial classifications are not invalid *per se*, and there could be benign or compensatory schemes that would be acceptable. Race could be considered only when it "acts not to demean or insult any racial group" and only "to remedy disadvantages cast on minorities by past racial prejudice." [Powell had rejected this argument with his assertions that equal protection means equal protection for all regardless of the color of one's skin. However, his agreement that race could be a factor was the fifth vote that permitted the use of affirmative action programs.] They rely on the legislative history of Title VI and the federal regulations of such agencies as the [then] Department of Health, Education, and Welfare, which either mandated such programs or authorized voluntary affirmative action programs as support for their position.

This group advocates an intermediate review standard for cases involving racial classifications; "the classification must serve important governmental objectives and must be substantially related to the achievement of those objectives" to be constitutional. In applying the test to the instant case, the objective is to remedy "past societal discrimination," a goal that the Court finds sufficiently important and worthy, and the means chosen to meet the goal does not stigmatize any group or attribute racial or personal inferiority to any applicant.

Justice Byron White writes an opinion stating that there was no private cause of action under Title VI.

Justice Thurgood Marshall authors an impassioned opinion, tracing the history of legal discrimination in this nation, and ending on the warning that "I fear that we have come full circle" by stepping in to halt such affirmative action programs such as the one used in Davis. "It is more than a little ironic that, after several hundred years of class-based discrimination against Negroes, the Court is unwilling to hold that a class-based remedy for discrimination is permissible."

In a separate opinion, Justice Harry Blackmun adds, "In order to get beyond racism, we must first take account of race....And in order to treat some persons equally, we must treat them differently. We cannot—we dare not—let the Equal Protection Clause perpetuate racial supremacy." His support for affirmative action is based on the need to remedy the effects of discrimination and also on the need for a diverse student body at universities to enhance academic freedom and exchange of ideas.

Justice John Paul Stevens—joined by Burger, Stewart, and Rehnquist—agrees that Bakke should be admitted to the medical school, but they take a much more narrow approach to the case. They argue that the provisions of Title VI alone mandate Bakke's admission because Davis had excluded him because of his race. Adhering to the Court's general practice of avoiding constitutional or broader questions, they do not reach the Fourteenth Amendment issues and decide the matter on the narrower statutory grounds. In effect, they deal with Bakke without providing general guidance as to whether the use of race as a remedy is permissible under the Equal Protection Clause.

SIGNIFICANCE OF THE CASE   The case, even with its multiple opinions, signaled the Court's approval for so-called reverse discrimination programs, that is, those programs employing race as a preferential factor.

QUESTIONS FOR DISCUSSION

(1)   Do you agree that there can be "benign" discrimination or do you agree with Justice Powell that equal protection is absolute? Why?

(2)   Given a changing society and attitudes, what do you foresee as the future for affirmative action programs?

RELATED CASES   *PLESSY V. FERGUSON*, 163 U.S. 537 (1896); *KOREMATSU V. UNITED STATES*, 323 U.S. 214 (1944); *BROWN V. BOARD OF EDUCATION OF TOPEKA*, 347 U.S. 483 (1954); *Fullilove v. Klutznick*, 448 U.S. 448 (1980); *Wygant v. Jackson Board of Education*, 476 U.S. 267 (1986); and *CITY OF RICHMOND, VIRGINIA V. J. A. CROSON CO.*, 488 U.S. 469 (1989).

CITY OF RICHMOND, VIRGINIA V. J. A. CROSON CO.
488 U.S. 469 (1989)

BACKGROUND   The City of Richmond, Virginia, adopted a plan that required that contractors receiving city construction contracts award at least 30 percent of the dollar amount of each contract to minority business enterprises. The "minority business enterprises" were defined as companies in which black, Spanish-speaking, Oriental, American Indians, Eskimo, or Aleut citizens had a 51 percent or higher ownership interest; the companies could be located anywhere within the nation.

The plan was adopted at a public hearing following presentation of evidence that included a statistical study showing that only 0.67 percent of its prime construction contracts had been awarded to minority businesses even though the population of the city was 50 percent black, that the local contractors' associations had virtually no black members, and that the proposed plan was constitutional under *Fullilove v. Klutznick* (the Supreme Court case upholding a similar set-aside scheme for minority businesses on the national level). J. A. Croson Co. lost a city contract on which it was the sole bidder when it could not obtain a waiver by showing that qualified minority businesses were either unavailable or unwilling to participate; the company brought suit alleging that the plan was unconstitutional under the Equal Protection Clause of the Fourteenth Amendment.

CONSTITUTIONAL ISSUE

Whether affirmative action remedial measures against race discrimination must meet the more stringent "strict scrutiny" test to be acceptable under the Equal Protection Clause of the Fourteenth Amendment? YES

PLURALITY OPINION   Justice Sandra Day O'Connor delivers the plurality opinion of the Court. First addressed is the power of the city to pass such remedial legislation. Although Congress has the power to redress the effects of society-wide discrimination, the states and their political subdivisions do not automatically share that power. Only if the city shows that it has become a "passive participant" in the system of discrimination practiced by local construction industry could it act to dismantle such a system; however, such evidence is lacking here in that no direct evidence of specific instances of discrimination by the city in letting contracts or by its prime contractors was introduced at the public hearing. "[S]imple legislative assurances of good intention cannot suffice" to support racial classifications; therefore, the regulation must fall in that no compelling interest in apportioning public contracts on the basis of race has been shown.

Racial classifications are naturally harmful, and the Court must be particularly vigilant in determining whether such classifications are "benign," "remedial," or illegitimate uses of political power. Because of the nature of these classifications, the Court must adopt the standard of review that examines most closely the use of "highly suspect classifications" by the state to ensure pure motives in the use of such categorizations.

Even if the state established its good intentions, it must also show that the remedial measure is "narrowly tailored" to correct the past wrong. This regulation encompasses many groups other than blacks as well as businesses from other locations and is not limited merely to Richmond-based businesses and is therefore too broad in scope. There are other race-neutral devices to improve the accessibility of the bidding process to entrepreneurs of all races, and this scheme encompasses too much. The state and its subdivisions are not powerless to rectify established patterns of racial discrimination, but there must be a compelling interest with a narrowly designed plan for doing so, and the plan must be in reaction to specific, demonstrated instances of discrimination.

OTHER OPINIONS   Justice John Paul Stevens concurs in the judgment and with part of the opinion. Those examining racial classifications to determine the constitutionality should focus primarily on the future impact of such decisions rather than on past wrongs. It should be the purview of the legislature, not the courts, to create policies that govern future behavior, whereas the courts are best suited to deal with past demonstrated wrongdoings. Therefore, when the Court looks at equal protection cases such as this, the emphasis should be on the shared characteristics of the advantaged or disadvantaged class that justifies the disparate treatment, and here the class of persons benefited is not limited to those previously wronged by the city of Richmond but encompasses many more including those who have never done business in the city, and it penalizes not only wrongdoers but those who have never engaged in discriminatory practices. The statute cannot be justified as a remedy for past discrimination.

Justice Anthony Kennedy concurs in the judgment and part of the opinion. The Fourteenth Amendment mandates that states must act to remedy racial discrimination when caused deliberately by the state and does not preclude state action to remedy either private or public discrimination unless such remedy contradicts federal law or violates the Constitution (which this regulation does).

Justice Antonin Scalia concurs in the judgment. Racial discrimination is "illegal, immoral, unconstitutional, inherently wrong, and destructive of democratic society," but states and local governments are powerless to discriminate to "ameliorate the effects of past discrimination" unless the state itself has acted to maintain the discriminatory system (such as school systems). Only the national government may create valid racial classifications as remedial measures even though racial discrimination is more likely at the state and local government level. The states and their subdivisions have alternative methods of correcting the wrongs. Racial quotas, even those that appear to "even the score," are discriminatory, and such blanket discrimination is not within the letter and spirit of the Constitution.

Justice Thurgood Marshall, joined by William Brennan and Harry Blackmun, enters a dissenting opinion. "[T]oday's decision marks a deliberate and giant step backward in this Court's affirmative-action jurisprudence." This broad attack on race-conscious remedies will chill any type of remedial action.

The appropriate standard of review for these cases examining remedial measures should be that the statute must serve important governmental objectives and must be substantially related to the achievement of those goals. The Richmond regulation does both. Its objective is to eradicate the effects of past racial discrimination and to prevent government from reflecting any prior private discrimination. Richmond certainly has provided sufficient proof of past discrimination, especially in light of *Fullilove v. Klutznick*, which also dealt with discrimination within the construction industry, even though the majority perfunctorily dismissed the evidence. The means selected are clearly appropriate to the goal of not perpetuating discrimination and are prospective only. The majority apparently believes that the days of racial discrimination are over, but "the battle against pernicious racial discrimination or its effects is nowhere near won," and this decision has the perverse effect of inhibiting those states and localities with the worst records from seeking corrective action.

Justice Harry Blackmun, with Justice William Brennan joining, also writes a dissenting opinion indicating "the Court today regresses," but that one day it "again will do its best to fulfill the great promises" of the Constitution.

SIGNIFICANCE OF THE CASE   The case of *CITY OF RICHMOND, VIRGINIA V. J. A. CROSON CO.* underlines the Court's recent deference to legislative bodies and its efforts to avoid even the appearance of creating policy. It also indicates a shift away from race-conscious remedial legislation on the part of the majority.

QUESTIONS FOR DISCUSSION

(1) If you were a member of a local city council, would you support a quota system to remedy past discrimination? Does it make a difference if you were considering the issue only from the point of ethics, that is, without the legal considerations? Should that make a difference?

(2) Do you agree with Justices Marshall, Blackmun, and Brennan that this decision casts a blight on affirmative action programs—if not actually ending them?

(3) What types of proof would you require to sustain this statute?

(4) Why do you agree or disagree that the Fourteenth Amendment allows the national government but not the states to redress societal discrimination?

RELATED CASES *REGENTS OF THE UNIVERSITY OF CALIFORNIA V. BAKKE,* 438 U.S. 265 (1978); *Fullilove v. Klutznick,* 448 U.S. 448 (1980); and *Wygant v. Jackson Board of Education,* 476 U.S. 267 (1986).

FRONTIERO V. RICHARDSON
411 U.S. 677 (1973)

BACKGROUND Federal statutes provided that spouses of male members of the armed services were automatically deemed "dependents" for purposes of obtaining medical and dental benefits and receiving allowances for living quarters, but spouses of female members had to show that they were in fact dependent for more than one-half of their support to receive the same benefits. Frontiero, a married woman Air Force officer, sought increased benefits for her husband as a "dependent" and was denied. The couple then filed suit on the basis that the statutes deprived service women of due process under the Fifth Amendment.

CONSTITUTIONAL ISSUE

Whether gender-based classifications are inherently suspect and therefore subject to close judicial scrutiny? YES

PLURALITY OPINION Justice William Brennan writes the opinion for the plurality. He sets the background by stating

There can be no doubt that our Nation has had a long and unfortunate history of sex discrimination...which, in practical effect, put women, not on a pedestal, but in a cage...throughout much of the 19th century the position of women in our society was, in many respects, comparable to that of blacks under the pre–Civil War slave codes.

However, both Congress in recent legislation and the Court in recent cases have determined that classifications based on sex are inherently invidiously discriminatory, violative of the Constitution. The case of *Reed v. Reed,* an equal protection case decided the prior term, which invalidated a statutory preference for males as administrators of estates controls here.

Brennan finds that pervasive and subtle discrimination, even in the face of congressional and judicial reforms, still exists in "educational institutions, in the job market, and perhaps, most conspicuously, in the political arena." Sex, like race and national origin, is an immutable characteristic determined solely by the accident of birth and has no relation to an individual's ability to perform or to contribute to society. Classifications based on sex, race, alienage, and national origin "are inherently suspect and must therefore be subjected to close judicial scrutiny." In the instant case, the government itself concedes that the sole purpose of the distinction is "administrative convenience" based on the premise that while wives were frequently dependent on their husbands, husbands are rarely dependent on their wives; therefore, it is more "convenient" to deem all wives as dependents automatically for purposes of receiving benefits rather than to consider each family's situation individually as to actual dependence. However, the record reflects "substantial evidence" that many wives would fail to qualify for benefits under the test employed for husbands. The Court fails to accept mere convenience as sufficient grounds to uphold this discriminatory scheme stating that "'administrative convenience' is not a shibboleth, the mere recitation of which dictates constitutionality."

OTHER OPINIONS Justice William Powell, joined by Chief Justice Warren Burger and Justice Harry Blackmun, concurs in the judgment. They agree with the others that the statutes constituted unconstitutional discrimination; however, they disagree with classifying gender as a suspect classification. *Reed v. Reed* "did not add sex to the narrowly limited group of classifications which are inherently suspect." Instead, they would avoid the constitutional question and defer to the elected representatives who had approved the Equal Rights Amendment and submitted it for ratification to the states. "[B]ut democratic institutions are weakened, and confidence in the restraint of the Court is impaired, when we appear unnecessarily to decide sensitive issues of broad social and political importance at the very time they are under consideration within the prescribed constitutional processes."

SIGNIFICANCE OF THE CASE The Court has shown considerable ambivalence in determining the proper standard for measuring the constitutionality of gender-based classification schemes. Initially, the Court, in *Reed v. Reed*, employed the less stringent "rational-basis test" and rejected that gender-based classification as lacking a rational relationship to the state objective that was being advanced and as being arbitrary. Then, in *Frontiero*, a plurality declared classifications based on sex were inherently suspect and subject to strict judicial scrutiny. For several years, the Court vacillated between the two without a majority ever declaring that gender-based distinctions actually were "suspect" and therefore subject to the more stringent, "compelling state interest test." Then in *Craig v. Boren*, the Court opted for an intermediate test that would uphold the classification if it served an important government objective and was substantially related to the achievement of those objectives. Despite the Court's vagaries in arriving at a proper test, *Frontiero* and like cases signaled the Court's heightened scrutiny and awareness of gender-based classifications and the tightened constitutional standards for such classifications.

QUESTIONS FOR DISCUSSION

(1)   Why do you think the Court had such a difficult time in choosing a proper standard for testing gender-based classification schemes?

(2)   What factors influenced the Court to choose an intermediate level of scrutiny?

RELATED CASES   *Reed v. Reed*, 404 U.S. 71 (1971); *CRAIG V. BOREN*, 429 U.S. 190 (1976); and *International Union, United Automobile, Aerospace & Agricultural Implement Workers of America, U.A.W. v. Johnson Controls, Inc.*, 111 S.Ct. 1196 (1991).

CRAIG V. BOREN
429 U.S. 190 (1976)

BACKGROUND   Like many other states, Oklahoma had recently changed its law regarding the age of majority to a single age of eighteen for both men and women from a system that established the age of majority for females at eighteen and for males at twenty-one. But, the state concurrently adopted a law stating that "nonintoxicating" 3.2 percent beer could not be sold to females under the age of eighteen or to males under the age of twenty-one. Craig, a male who was between the ages of eighteen and twenty-one, and Whitener, a licensed vendor of 3.2 percent beer, brought suit challenging the statute on the basis of gender-based discrimination against males between the age of eighteen and twenty-one in violation of the Equal Protection Clause.

CONSTITUTIONAL ISSUE

Whether gender-based discrimination is a "suspect classification," which is to be measured by the "strict scrutiny" test by the Court in applying the Equal Protection Clause of the Fourteenth Amendment? NO

MAJORITY OPINION   Justice William Brennan writes the Court's opinion. The first issue to be addressed is that of standing. Craig had attained the age of twenty-one by the time the case reached the Supreme Court, and the controversy is moot as to him. However, Whitener, as a licensed vendor, is entitled to assert the claims and advocate the rights of third parties who would seek access to her merchandise. The Court's reasoning is that the impact of this litigation on the third-party interests was apparent in that the rights of males within the specified age group would be affected by the outcome of the lawsuit as would the rights of other vendors because the statute forbids sale, not use, of the beer.

Having resolved the standing issue, Brennan turns to the question of gender-based discrimination and the proper test for the Court to employ in considering such questions. To be sustained, statutes that have "classifications by gender must serve important governmental objectives and must be substantially related to the achievement of these objectives." Here, the alleged state interest was to preserve public safety on highways. The state's use of studies showing that substantially more males were arrested for "driving under the influence" (DUI) and "drunkenness" than were females in the affected age group is not persuasive. Brennan not only challenges the statistics themselves but also questions the use of such statistics in deciding constitutional questions, because "proving broad sociological propositions by statistics is a dubious business, and one that inevitably is in tension with the normative philosophy that underlies the Equal Protection Clause." He, like the majority of the Court, does not find the gender-based statute in question— barring the *purchase* and not the use of 3.2 percent beer to males between 18 and 21—to be "substantially related" to the perceived goal of highway safety.

Brennan also addresses the interplay between the Twenty-First Amendment, which repealed prohibition and strengthened the state's police powers with respect to regulating alcohol and the Fourteenth Amendment Equal Protection Clause. The principle that invidious discrimination in violation of the Equal Protection Clause could not be justified under the Twenty-First Amendment is a well-established Court doctrine. Thus, although the state had significant powers reserved to it under the Twenty-First Amendment to regulate liquor sales, the individual's rights under the Equal Protection Clause are dominant.

OTHER OPINIONS   Justice Lewis Powell concurs in the result, although he would have employed the older "rational basis" test in determining the constitutionality of the statute. While agreeing that review of gender-based discrimination should be more sharply than that the "relatively deferential 'rational basis' standard," he does not agree that a new intermediate standard should be created to deal with these types of cases.

Justice John Paul Stevens in his concurring opinion states his belief that the two-tier approach is really one standard but explained in different ways. He questions whether the purpose of the statute is really traffic safety because it had only minimal effect on access to the 3.2 percent beer, and he also doubts that the law had a deterrent effect on consumption. He also describes the statute as visiting the sins of the 2 percent who had broken the law regarding DUI and drunkenness on the law-abiding 98 percent. For those reasons, he supports the decision of the Court but not its reasoning.

Justice Potter Stewart also concurs in the judgment. He believes that the disparity in age group according to gender created by the statute "amounts to total irrationality," and no state, even under the Twenty-First Amendment, is empowered to act with total irrationality or to invidiously discriminate against its residents.

Chief Justice Warren Burger, in his dissenting opinion, argues that the vendor, Whitener, lacked standing to pursue the case. One of the Court's threshold requirements, he states, was that a litigant could assert only his or her own constitutional rights; therefore, expanding standing to allow vendors to assert the constitutional rights of purchasers is not acceptable to him. In addition, he does not support elevating gender to a specially-protected classification for purposes of court review because there is no "independent constitutional basis" for doing so.

Justice William Rehnquist (later Chief Justice) dissents on two grounds. First, he objects to applying the same rules to all gender discrimination cases, whether applicable to men or to women. He declares that there was no history of past discrimination against males in this age group nor were they particularly disadvantaged or "in need of special solicitude from the Courts." Gender classifications standing alone should not automatically be a "talisman—which without regard to the rights involved or the persons affected—calls into effect a heavier burden of judicial review."

Second, he thinks that the appropriate standard of review in this case is the "rational basis test," and he sees no need to insert an intermediate level of scrutiny for gender-based discrimination. He also objects to the wording of the new standard, which requires "important" objectives and "substantial" relationship between the statute and the objectives that he describes as being so "diaphanous and elastic as to invite subjective judicial preferences." It would have been more appropriate for the Court to defer to the legislative branch's decision on what goals are "important" rather than intervening itself. In the instant case, the statistics used by Oklahoma were sufficient to show differences in driving habits of young men and women, and for the state to conclude reasonably that young men are more likely to pose a "drunk-driving hazard." Therefore, the differential treatment is justified under the "rational basis" test.

SIGNIFICANCE OF THE CASE   In cases involving discrimination and the Equal Protection Clause of the Constitution, two standards of review had been created by the Court. The first—involving categories known as "suspect classes" or involving "fundamental rights"—required "strict scrutiny" by the Court. The state's burden to justify any questioned statute was very difficult to meet. The second—involving nonsuspect classes or nonfundamental rights—required the state to show only a reasonable relationship between the classification and the legislation's objective, a much easier burden to meet.

Here, the Court created a third, intermediate tier for dealing with gender-based discrimination, called "heightened scrutiny," that is, the state must show that the statute serves "important governmental objectives and must be substantially related to the achievement of those objectives" to save a gender-based classification. In doing so, the Court declined to recognize gender as a "suspect class" for purposes of the Equal Protection Clause.

QUESTIONS FOR DISCUSSION

(1)   Which standard do you think is appropriate for testing the constitutionality of gender-based discrimination? Why?

(2)   What if the subject of the discrimination here was a woman, would that have affected your decision? What if the case had involved college scholarships, employment, or retirement benefits instead of sale of beer and the opposite gender had been the subject of the discriminatory practice? Would this affect your decision?

(3)   Under what conditions do you think that gender-based discrimination is constitutionally acceptable? Why?

RELATED CASES   *Reed v. Reed*, 404 U.S. 71 (1971); *Wisconsin v. Constantineau*, 400 U.S. 433 (1971); *FRONTIERO V. RICHARDSON*, 411 U.S. 677 (1973); *Rostker v. Goldberg*, 453 U.S. 57 (1981); *Mississippi University for Women v. Hogan*, 458 U.S. 718 (1982); and *International Union, Automobile, Aerospace & Agricultural Implement Workers of America, U.A.W. v. Johnson Controls, Inc.*, 111 S.Ct. 1196 (1991).

JOHNSON V. TRANSPORTATION AGENCY, SANTA CLARA COUNTY, CALIFORNIA
480 U.S. 616 (1987)

BACKGROUND The Transportation Agency of Santa Clara County voluntarily adopted an Affirmative Action Plan under Title VII of the Civil Rights Act of 1964 relating to the hiring and promoting of minorities and women. The plan provided, in part, that the sex of a qualified applicant would be considered in promotion decisions for positions in which women were significantly underrepresented. The stated long-term goal of the plan was to have a work force that mirrored the proportion of women and minorities in the area work force; however, there was no quota included within the plan.

The Agency had an opening for the position of dispatcher, which was classified as a skilled craft worker position. Of the 238 positions in that classification, none were held by women. Among the twelve applicants were Johnson and Diane Joyce, both of whom were rated as well qualified for the job. Johnson scored slightly higher (two points) after the first interview than Joyce (but neither had the highest score), and a three-member panel recommended that Johnson receive the position. In the interim, Joyce had contacted the Agency's affirmative action coordinator because she was concerned that her application might not receive disinterested review because of prior problems with two members of the interview panel, and the coordinator recommended her selection. The agency director, authorized to select among the seven finalists, thus considered the recommendations of the second interview panel and the coordinator, and then chose Joyce. At trial, the agency director testified that "I tried to look at the whole picture," which included qualifications, test scores, expertise, background, affirmative action, and "things like that." The trial court found that Joyce's gender was the "*determining* factor in her selection."

CONSTITUTIONAL ISSUE

Whether, in reverse discrimination cases, an affirmative action plan that does not impose quotas but that does allow gender or race to be a factor in hiring and promotion decisions is constitutional? YES

MAJORITY OPINION Justice William Brennan writes the majority opinion of the Court. He begins by outlining the analytical framework for employment discrimination cases. Once the plaintiff has established a *prima facie* case that race or sex has been a factor in the decision, then the burden shifts to the employer to show a nondiscriminatory reason for its decision. The existence of an affirmative action plan is an accepted reason, and the plaintiff has the burden of establishing that the plan is invalid.

To justify an affirmative action plan, an employer does not have to prove its own prior discriminatory practices but must merely show a "conspicuous" or "manifest" imbalance in "traditionally segregated job categories" under *Steelworkers v. Weber*. That imbalance may be measured against the general work population in the area or, if it is a skilled position, against those in the labor force with the requisite skills. There clearly was such an imbalance here because none of the 238 positions was held by a woman.

The Court must also consider the effect of the plan on the nonadvantaged class, here males. The plan imposes no absolute bar to their promotion and does not set aside several jobs to be filled only by women. There was no absolute entitlement on the part of Johnson to the position as all seven of the candidates deemed qualified were subject to promotion.

"*No* persons are automatically excluded from consideration; *all* are able to have their qualifications weighed against those of other applicants." If Joyce's gender had been *the* determining factor in her selection instead of one of several matters considered, or if the plan had set aside several jobs to be filled only by women or if it had ignored qualifications, then the plan would run afoul of the Constitution.

OTHER OPINIONS Justice John Paul Stevens writes a concurring opinion encouraging employers to engage in voluntary remedial plans and stressing that an employer does not have to admit to prior wrongdoing on its part. The plan approved by the Court here is not the only approach to this issue, and employers should not be discouraged from other voluntary approaches.

Justice Sandra Day O'Connor also concurs. The doctrine of *stare decisis* and prior decisions dictate that this plan be upheld. However, affirmative action plans are acceptable only as remedial devices to eliminate actual or apparent discrimination or the lingering effects thereof; determination of the legality of a public employer's plan should turn on whether there is a statistical disparity sufficient to support a *prima facie* claim of discrimination by the beneficiary employees under Title VII.

Justice Antonin Scalia—joined by Chief Justice William Rehnquist and, in part, by Justice Byron White—dissents. This decision signifies Court endorsement of racial or sexual discrimination in hiring and promotion practices if the employer purportedly does so to remedy prior discrimination, not just of itself but of society as a whole. Certain positions have traditionally been held by few women because women themselves viewed the jobs as less than desirable and did not seek to hold them. Here, the Court justifies state-enforced discrimination on the basis of societal attitudes rather than specific instances of individuals being denied employment or promotion on the basis of gender or race.

In addition, *Weber*, cited by the majority as controlling, applied only to private employers and should not be extended to state agencies that are subject to the Fourteenth Amendment. The overall effect of this decision is to convert Title VII from a statute guaranteeing that race or sex will not be the basis for employment decisions in either the private or public sector to a law that guarantees that it often will be.

Justice Byron White also dissents on the basis that *Weber* dealt with the intentional and systematic exclusion of blacks from certain job categories, that the majority here is unacceptedly broadening the meaning of "traditionally segregated jobs," and that he would overturn *Weber* based on this interpretation, which perverts Title VII.

SIGNIFICANCE OF THE CASE As noted by Justice Stevens in his concurring opinion, the Court's approach to antidiscriminatory statutes such as the Civil Rights Act has changed. Before *Regents of University of California v. Bakke* in 1978, the Court interpreted the Civil Rights of 1964 as an absolute prohibition against discrimination, but with *Bakke*, the Court hued to another line and accepted preferential and discriminatory practices if done voluntarily and done to benefit members of minority groups that the statute was designed to protect.

Johnson v. Transportation Agency extends that principle to gender discrimination cases and to public as well as private entities. There is no requirement that the employer must have actually discriminated to sustain the validity of an affirmative action plan. Plans that contain quotas or that ignore qualifications as a factor are not acceptable.

QUESTIONS FOR DISCUSSION

(1)   As corporate counsel, you are aware that employers who do not take affirmative action to remedy discrimination are liable to minorities, and those who do take action are liable to nonminorities. What course of action would you recommend?

(2)   What should be the Court's role in balancing the conflicting interests of rooting out discrimination against any person and of eliminating the lasting effects of discrimination against minorities? From society's perspective? In terms of equal protection jurisprudence?

(3)   What analytical framework would you set up for the Court to follow in such cases?

RELATED CASES   *REGENTS OF UNIVERSITY OF CALIFORNIA V. BAKKE*, 438 U.S. 265 (1978); *McDonnell Douglas Corp. v. Green*, 411 U.S. 792 (1973); *Steelworkers v. Weber*, 443 U.S. 193 (1979); *Wygant v. Jackson Board of Education*, 476 U.S. 267 (1986); *Sheet Metal Workers v. EEOC*, 478 U.S. 421 (1986); and *Firefighters v. Cleveland*, 478 U.S. 501 (1986).

BAKER V. CARR
369 U.S. 186 (1962)

BACKGROUND   In 1961 the Tennessee General Assembly was composed of thirty-three senators and ninety-nine representatives. The Tennessee Constitution required the general assembly to reapportion its seats by population after each federal decennial census but the general assembly had not done so since 1901. Between 1901 and 1961 the population of Tennessee grew from just over 2 million persons to almost 3.6 million. Population growth in Tennessee's urban counties without a similar increase in representation meant that urban representatives represented more and more people compared with rural representatives. Baker, a resident of an urban district, brought suit under 42 U.S.C. § 1983 claiming that this situation debased the value of his vote as an urban resident and denied him equal protection of the law guaranteed by the Fourteenth Amendment. The federal district court dismissed the suit without a hearing on the merits for lack of jurisdiction over the subject matter and for failure to state a claim on which relief can be granted. The Supreme Court noted probable jurisdiction.

CONSTITUTIONAL ISSUES

(1)   Whether federal courts have jurisdiction in cases involving the apportionment of state legislative districts? YES

(2)   Whether the issue of legislative apportionment presents a justiciable question on which relief can be granted? YES

MAJORITY OPINION   Justice William Brennan delivers the opinion of the Court. Justice Brennan divides his opinion into four parts. In the first part, Brennan seeks to clarify exactly what the Court is deciding in this case. The federal district court in

Tennessee dismissed Baker's suit for lack of jurisdiction over the subject matter and for failure to state a claim on which relief can be granted. The Court, Brennan asserts, is limiting its ruling to those questions and makes no judgment about the merits of Baker's claims because the case never got that far. The Supreme Court holds that federal courts do have jurisdiction in apportionment cases and that the issue presented is not a nonjusticiable political question. The Court sends the case back to the lower court for a decision on the merits of Baker's claims.

Part II of the opinion focuses on issue of jurisdiction. Federal courts have jurisdiction over cases "arising under" the Constitution. In this case the Tennessee federal district court relied on an earlier apportionment case, *Colegrove v. Green*, as the basis for dismissing Baker's suit. Justice Brennan states, however, that the district court misread *Colegrove*. Close reading of the opinions in that case shows that at least four of the seven participating justices either implicitly or explicitly assumed that the Court had jurisdiction over the subject matter. Citing other cases to support his view, Brennan rules that federal courts do indeed have jurisdiction in legislative apportionment cases.

Part III of the opinion addresses the issue of standing. Courts require parties to a case to have standing, which means that the party has "a personal stake in the outcome of the controversy to assure concrete adversariness." Baker claims that the 1901 apportionment statute constitutes an arbitrary and capricious action in that it debases the value of his vote and denies him equal protection of the law. Without making any judgment as to the merit of Baker's claim, Brennan rules that Baker at least has met the standard necessary to present his claim before a court.

Finally, in Part IV Brennan addresses the question whether Baker presents a claim on which relief can be granted. This question centers around whether or not apportionment cases raise a "political question." Historically, the Court has refused to hear cases that raise political questions by declaring them to be "nonjusticiable." Brennan gives a brief history of the political question doctrine and identifies common threads in the cases in which the doctrine has been invoked. Categories of political questions include those that involve issues that the Constitution clearly gives to the political branches to handle. Brennan, after identifying the relevant criteria, finds none of those criteria present in Baker's suit. Previously the Court had refused to hear cases that invoked the Guaranty Clause (Article IV, § 4) because such cases invariably raised political questions. Baker's claim, however, rests on the Equal Protection Clause of the Fourteenth Amendment and not on the claim that Tennessee's malapportioned system is not a "republican form of government."

In summary, the Court holds that Baker's claim presents a justiciable constitutional cause of action, that Baker has standing to sue, and that federal courts have jurisdiction over apportionment cases. The Court then remands the case to the Tennessee federal district court for further proceedings on the merits.

OTHER OPINIONS There are three concurring opinions by Justices William O. Douglas, Tom Clark, and Potter Stewart. Justice Douglas states that in his opinion most of the political question cases cited in the majority opinion were wrongly decided. Douglas argues that federal courts have always assumed jurisdiction over the protection of voting rights. He cites cases in which votes were not counted and cases of racial discrimination as evidence of his position.

Justice Clark writes the principal concurring opinion. Clark notes that the Tennessee Constitution's apportionment policy is not the problem: the problem is that the general assembly has not followed the Constitution's policy since 1901. Clark characterizes Tennessee's apportionment plan as a "crazy quilt without any rational basis." Not only are Tennessee's urban counties heavily underrepresented, but some counties have twice as many representatives as counties with about the same population. Although Clark is reluctant to allow federal courts to intervene in this case, he supports the majority's decision on the grounds that the people of Tennessee have no alternative way to change their malapportioned legislature. Tennessee has no initiative or referendum, and any call for a constitutional convention to change the system must come from the general assembly itself—an unlikely occurrence. Attempts to seek relief from state courts have also failed. Clark disagrees that the case should be remanded to the district court on the merits. Tennessee did not dispute the statistical evidence of discrimination nor did the state provide a rational basis for its existing apportionment plan. Therefore, Clark argues, the Court should enter a judgment in favor of Baker.

Justice Potter Stewart writes the final concurrence. Stewart wants to clarify exactly what the Court did and did not rule. The Court ruled that federal courts do have jurisdiction in apportionment cases, that the case presents a justiciable cause of action, and that the appellants have standing to sue. The Court did not rule, as both Justices Douglas and Harlan suggest, that states must apportion their legislatures with exact mathematical equality or that a state may never weight the votes of some of its political subdivisions.

Justice Felix Frankfurter writes the principal dissent. Justice Frankfurter attacks the Court's decision on several fronts. First, he criticizes the Court for remanding the case to the district court without providing any guidelines for resolving the case. One of Frankfurter's persistent themes is that there are no judicial standards for making decisions in apportionment cases. Frankfurter argues that ultimately the solution for malapportioned legislatures rests with "an aroused popular conscience that sears the consciences of the people's representatives," a position Justice Clark strongly rejects in his concurrence. Second, Frankfurter admonishes the Court for engaging in judicial policy making. Not only does the Court's involvement in political questions tarnish its image, but the Court is without means to provide relief. Could the Court, Frankfurter asks, order representatives to be chosen at-large instead of by districts? Frankfurter also argues that historically the Court has avoided intervening in cases concerning the structure and organization of the institutions of state government. He accuses the case of being a Guaranty Clause case masquerading as an Equal Protection Clause case. Third, Frankfurter makes a strong case for the position that population alone has never been the sole basis for representation in Anglo-American political systems. He traces Great Britain's experience, the American colonial experience, and the experience of almost every state to demonstrate that the representation of geographical units has been prominent in our concept of representation. Fourth, Frankfurter claims that this case is essentially asking the Court to make a judgment about the correctness of competing theories of representation which, in his opinion, the Court should not do. Finally, Frankfurter chides the Court for ignoring what he calls an "impressive body of rulings" on the question of federal jurisdiction in apportionment cases.

Justice John M. Harlan II writes the only other dissenting opinion. Harlan's position is the Equal Protection Clause of the Fourteenth Amendment does not support Baker's claim that one person's vote should weigh the same as another's. In other words, Harlan does not believe that a person has a federal constitutional right to have his or her vote count equally to that of another's. Harlan states that unless the state's scheme of representation is totally irrational (which he argues it is not), federal courts must uphold it. Finally, Harlan argues that a state is free to choose its method of representation just as it is free to choose its method of taxation. If a state chooses a less-than-perfect method, it does not mean that its choice is unconstitutional.

SIGNIFICANCE OF THE CASE *Baker v. Carr* opened the door for a rash of cases involving malapportioned state legislatures that ultimately resulted in the reapportionment of every state in the Union. Previously state legislatures had heavily favored voters in rural, more conservative parts of the state. *Baker* paved the way for the famous "one man, one vote" standard, which increased the political power of urban voters. *Baker*, along with the Voting Rights Act of 1965, also increased the power of black voters who often constituted majorities in large urban areas. Whether or not the reapportionment brought on by *Baker* has had any significant impact on public policy is debatable. However, *Baker* unquestionably is one of the most significant and far-reaching decisions of the Court in this century.

QUESTIONS FOR DISCUSSION

(1) Explain in your own words just what difference it makes that one person's vote counts more or less than another's.

(2) Do you think that the one person, one vote principle should apply to *judicial* districts as well as *legislative* districts?

(3) Is there any real difference between urban and rural voters in terms of their positions on issues of public policy?

(4) Do you agree with Justice Frankfurter that any change in Tennessee's system of representation ultimately rests with the people? Why or why not?

RELATED CASES *LUTHER V. BORDEN*, 7 Howard 1 (1849); *Colegrove v. Green*, 328 U.S. 549 (1946); *Wesberry v. Sanders*, 376 U.S. 1 (1964); *REYNOLDS V. SIMS*, 377 U.S. 533 (1964); and *Avery v. Midland County*, 390 U.S. 474 (1968); Clark v. Roemer, 59 U.S. Law. 4583 (1991).

REYNOLDS V. SIMS
377 U.S. 533 (1964)

BACKGROUND The 1901 Alabama Constitution required, with some restrictions, that the 106-member Alabama House and 35-member Senate be reapportioned after each federal census on the basis of population. However, the legislature had failed to do so for sixty years. Under the existing apportionment plan, 25.1 percent of the state's residents could elect a majority of the Senate and 25.7 percent could elect a majority of the House members. For example, Jefferson County, with 634,864 people and Lowndes County with just 15,417 people each had one state senator because the Alabama Constitution forbade any county from having more than one senator.

Sims and other voters, residents, and taxpayers of Jefferson County filed suit in federal court in an attempt to prevent the 1962 primary and general elections on the grounds that the malapportioned legislature violated both the Alabama Constitution and the Equal Protection Clause of the Fourteenth Amendment. Subsequently, the Alabama legislature proposed two alternative plans known as the 67-Senator Amendment and the Crawford-Webb Act. However, a three-judge federal court found all three schemes constitutionally unacceptable. The district court did allow parts of the two alternative plans to be used as a temporary reapportionment plan until a new legislature could pass a constitutionally acceptable plan. When the 1963 legislature failed to act, both parties challenged aspects of the district court's decision and the Supreme Court noted probable jurisdiction.

CONSTITUTIONAL ISSUE

Whether the failure of a state legislature to reapportion both houses on the basis of population violates the Equal Protection Clause of the Fourteenth Amendment? YES

MAJORITY OPINION Chief Justice Earl Warren delivers the opinion of the Court. Chief Justice Warren asserts from the start that the right to vote is undeniably protected by the Constitution. Similarly, the right to vote cannot be denied by debasing or diluting the weight of a citizen's vote. Previous decisions support the view that the Equal Protection Clause does apply to voting rights. The appropriate judicial focus, according to the chief justice, is whether there has been any discrimination that impairs a citizen's constitutional right to vote.

Chief Justice Warren asserts that protection of the voting right is fundamental because voting is necessary to preserve a citizen's other rights. In addition, the chief justice observes that legislators represent people, not trees, geographical, or economic interests. Chief Justice Warren notes that any scheme that would double or triple the weight of one person's vote would be unconstitutional on its face. Likewise, any similar scheme to increase the weight of one citizen's vote by devaluing another's is unconstitutional. Nor is there any logical reason for weighting a person's vote on the basis of where he lives.

The chief justice continues the opinion by holding that both houses of the Alabama legislature must meet the one person, one vote standard. In doing so, he agrees with the District Court in rejecting the so-called federal analogy. Alabama had argued that guaranteeing each of its counties at least one representative was analogous to guaranteeing each state at least one seat in the U.S. House of Representatives. But, the chief justice notes, "the political subdivisions of states never were and never have been considered sovereign entities." However, the chief justice asserts that a state may maintain the integrity of its political subdivisions as long as it does not depart too far from the one person, one vote standard. Nor is the chief justice willing to impose the frequency of reapportionment on the states, although he strongly hints any period longer than ten years may be unconstitutional.

In conclusion, the chief justice observes that congressional approval of the constitutions of new states admitted to the Union with similar apportionment schemes to Alabama's carries no constitutional weight. Nor does the fact that Alabama's apportionment plan is based on its constitution. The chief justice concludes that the District Court acted with restraint and upholds its decision.

OTHER OPINIONS   Justices Tom Clark and Potter Stewart write very brief concurring opinions. Justice John Marshall Harlan II writes the only dissenting opinion. Justice Harlan accuses the majority of ignoring the language and history of the Fourteenth Amendment as well as the Court's own precedents. Section 2 of the Fourteenth Amendment permits Congress to reduce a state's congressional representation for denying or abridging the right of its citizens to vote. This, Harlan argues, is implicit recognition that states retained the right under the Fourteenth Amendment to deny their citizens voting privileges. In addition, the history of the ratification of the Amendment shows that members of Congress did not believe the Amendment would alter states' control over the franchise. Also, many of the states that ratified the Amendment had malapportioned legislatures themselves. Finally, several previous attempts to rely on the Equal Protection Clause to support apportionment cases were all rejected by the Court.

Justice Harlan concludes his opinion by arguing that courts have no judicially manageable standards to decide apportionment cases. In addition, the Court's decision will draw federal courts into sensitive partisan political battles. Finally, Harlan chides the Court for overstepping its authority by amending the Constitution by judicial fiat.

SIGNIFICANCE OF THE CASE   *Reynolds v. Sims* and its companion cases struck down apportionment schemes in six states. Because all of the other states had similar schemes, *Reynolds* virtually assured that they too would be subject to judicial scrutiny, which in fact occurred. Justice Harlan's fear that the federal courts would become embroiled in the politics of reapportionment has proven to be the case. After each decennial census, federal courts in at least some of the states have become major political battlegrounds. Whether federal courts will ever be able to extricate themselves from the political thicket of reapportionment remains to be seen.

QUESTIONS FOR DISCUSSION

(1)   Why had the Alabama legislature failed to reapportion itself as required by the state constitution?

(2)   Should a county be afforded the same status in a state political system as the state enjoys in our federal system? Why or why not?

(3)   Would you consider a malapportioned state to have a "republican form of government"? Why or why not?

(4)   Do you think the dilution of one person's vote is a denial of equal protection? Why or why not?

(5)   Assume that the latest census shows a loss of population and that your state senatorial district is to be merged with another. What arguments would you make against such an action?

RELATED CASES   *Colegrove v. Green*, 328 U.S. 549 (1946); *BAKER V. CARR*, 369 U.S. 186 (1962); *Gray v. Sanders*, 372 U.S. 386 (1963); *Wesberry v. Sanders*, 376 U.S. 1 (1964); and *Avery v. Midland County*, 390 U.S. 474 (1968).

EDWARDS V. CALIFORNIA
314 U.S. 160 (1941)

BACKGROUND In 1940, Edwards brought his indigent brother-in-law, Duncan, from Texas to California. Edwards was convicted under a California statute that made it a misdemeanor to bring an indigent into the state.

CONSTITUTIONAL ISSUE

Whether a state statute that bars movement of indigents into the state violates the Privileges and Immunities Clause of the Constitution? YES

MAJORITY OPINION Justice James Byrnes writes the opinion of the Court. The Constitution grants to Congress the authority to regulate interstate commerce, and the transportation of persons is commerce within the meaning of the provision. The Court is not unmindful of the economic dislocation caused by the Great Depression and of the subsequent migration into California, which created problems of staggering proportions for the state. Also, the Court has repeatedly indicated that it will defer to the legislature's attempts to solve a state's problems; however, the state's powers are constrained by the Constitution.

In this case, California alone does not bear the burden of providing for the poor but instead "relief of the needy has become the common responsibility and concern of the whole nation" with the new welfare legislation. Such a statute is an open invitation to retaliatory measures, and if all states pass such legislation, the movement of these persons becomes impossible. In addition, they are left without a remedy because as nonresidents, they are deprived of the opportunity to exert political pressure on the legislatures to effect a change in the policy. This statute is not a valid exercise of the police power of California, and it imposes an unconstitutional burden on interstate travel. For these reasons, the statute cannot be sustained.

OTHER OPINIONS Justice William Douglas, joined by Justices Hugo Black and Frank Murphy, enters a concurring opinion. The right of citizens to move freely about the country "occupies a more protected position in our constitutional system than does the movement of cattle, fruit, steel and coal across state lines." It is an attribute of national citizenship, and states cannot regulate those stigmatized as poor or vagabonds to an inferior class of citizenship, thereby preventing them from entering into the state.

Justice Robert H. Jackson also concurs. Duncan is a citizen of the United States, and under the Fourteenth Amendment, states are not permitted to abridge his privileges and immunities. Movement into any state of the Union, either temporarily or permanently, is given to aliens and certainly should be recognized as a privilege of citizenship. "If national citizenship means less than this, it means nothing."

States must not be allowed to use poverty to "test, qualify, or limit his rights as a citizen of the United States." Duncan's poverty would not release him from his obligation as a citizen to render military service and to protect California. The statute must fall because it violates the Privileges and Immunities Clause of the Constitution.

SIGNIFICANCE OF THE CASE   *Edwards v. California* is an interesting case on several levels. First, the notion that transportation of people falls under the Commerce Clause has important ramifications in the regulation of various carriers and public accommodations across a spectrum of issues including civil rights and economic issues. Second, the insistence of Douglas and others that interstate travel is an attribute of national citizenship and of a fundamental nature portends the Court's decisions in such cases as *Shapiro v. Thompson.* Third, the Court reiterates national unity and expansion of national powers even if it does mean curtailment of the powers of the states. Fourth, the state is indirectly approving welfare as an intergovernmental program, although dominated by the national government.

QUESTIONS FOR DISCUSSION

(1)   Under what circumstances do you envision states being able to exclude U.S. citizens from entering the state? What about resident aliens? On what constitutional grounds would you justify the exclusion?

(2)   Do you think that the powers of the national government have eclipsed those of the states in terms of such programs as welfare and education? If so, why? How would you redress the balance of power if you perceive it to be unbalanced?

RELATED CASES   *City of New York v. Miln*, 11 Peters 102 (1837); *The Passenger Cases*, 7 Howard 283 (1849); *Truax v. Raich*, 239 U.S. 33 (1915); *Caminetti v. United States*, 242 U.S. 470 (1917); *Baldwin v. Seelig, Inc.*, 294 U.S. 511 (1935); and *SHAPIRO V. THOMPSON*, 394 U.S. 618 (1969).

SHAPIRO V. THOMPSON
394 U.S. 618 (1969)

BACKGROUND   Statutes in the District of Columbia and two states—Connecticut and Pennsylvania—imposed a one-year residency requirement before otherwise qualified persons could receive welfare assistance.

CONSTITUTIONAL ISSUE

Whether a one-year residency requirement for receiving welfare assistance impermissibly chills the right to travel? YES

MAJORITY OPINION   Justice William Brennan delivers the opinion of the Court. The effect of the statutory waiting period is to "create two classes of needy resident families indistinguishable from each other except that one is composed of residents who have resided a year or more, and the second of residents who resided less than a year, in the jurisdiction."

The constitutional right involved here is the liberty interest of citizens to be free to travel throughout the nation "uninhibited by statutes, rules, or regulations which unreasonably burden or restrict this movement." The right to travel is not explicitly found in the provisions of the Constitution, but the Court has, in earlier cases, found it to be a fundamental right. Because it is a fundamental right, the states of Pennsylvania and Connecticut and the national government regarding the District of Columbia must show a compelling state interest to infringe on that right.

The arguments advanced by the state and national governments in support of the legislation are not persuasive. Administrative arguments such as facilitation of budget planning, minimization of fraud, or encouragement of early entry into the work force are not sufficient reasons for interference with constitutional rights. Nor are the state's arguments that a waiting period discourages an influx of people seeking higher rates of assistance and that it allows states to distinguish between old and new residents on the basis of their prior tax contributions tenable. Although the Social Security Act governing the Aid to Families with Dependent Children program does provide for a one-year waiting period, the legislative history of the Act indicates that the purpose was to curb hardships resulting from excessive residence requirements and not to approve or prescribe any waiting period. In this case, the states have failed to show a compelling state interest to invade a fundamental right in violation of the Equal Protection Clause, and although the Fifth Amendment does not contain an Equal Protection Clause, the Due Process Clause forbids discrimination, and the District of Columbia provision also must fall.

OTHER OPINIONS Justice Potter Stewart enters a concurring opinion focusing on the designation of travel as a fundamental right. This is not an improper or capricious exercise of judicial power. "The Court simply recognizes, as it must, an established constitutional right, and gives that right no less protection than the Constitution itself demands....The Court...is not 'contriving constitutional principles.'...It is deciding these cases under the aegis of established constitutional law."

Chief Justice Earl Warren and Justice Hugo Black enter a dissenting opinion. There are three major points of disagreement with the majority. First, the question should be cast in terms of whether Congress, under its enumerated powers, may set minimum nationwide residency requirements or may authorize the states to do so. The answer quite clearly is yes. Numerous statutes and regulations that discriminate on the basis of residency have been upheld as valid exercises of the Interstate Commerce and the General Welfare Clauses of Article I. The regulations at question here do not create a flat prohibition against travel in that indigents may still move from state to state as they wish, albeit without receiving financial assistance in their new home. Second, the legislative history of the Social Security Act was misinterpreted by the majority. The Act clearly endorses a one-year waiting period, the intent of which is reinforced by congressional enactment of a similar law for the District of Columbia. Third, the right to interstate travel can be, and is, restricted for a variety of purposes such as safety regulations on interstate carriers and prohibition of crossing state lines to carry out criminal activity. The majority applied the incorrect test. If the states show a rational basis for the limitations, the statutes should be upheld and the reasons advanced by the states and by the national government are adequate to show why the residency requirements should be upheld.

Justice John Marshall Harlan II also enters a dissenting opinion. The comparatively new equal protection test that state statutes are unconstitutional if they create a suspect class or violate a fundamental right unless justified by a compelling governmental interest is not appropriate in this case. The test is correctly applied to cases involving racial discrimination, but not to cases involving matters of wealth, political allegiance, interstate travel, or other constitutional rights. The correct tool in seeking recourse in these matters is the Fourteenth Amendment's Due Process Clause against state government and the Fifth Amendment's Due Process Clause against the national government. "If a statute affects only matters not mentioned in the Federal Constitution and is not arbitrary or irrational…I know of nothing which entitles this Court to pick out particular human activities, characterize them as 'fundamental,' and give them added protection under an unusually stringent equal protection test."

The right to travel interstate is a fundamental right that stems from the Fifth Amendment; however, the governmental interests served here outweigh any burden imposed on the right to travel. This opinion reflects the Court's belief that it has a "peculiar wisdom all its own" and can, with "judicial ingenuity in contriving new constitutional principles," resolve the nation's problems. The essential function of the Court is to maintain the separation of powers among the branches of government and the constitutional divisions between state and national authority. Here, the Court goes far beyond that role, and it is "a step in the wrong direction."

SIGNIFICANCE OF THE CASE   *Shapiro v. Thompson* is an important equal protection case. The Court has created a three-tier approach to equal protection cases: (1) in the upper tier, the Court will apply the strict scrutiny test if suspect classifications or fundamental rights are involved; (2) in the middle tier, the Court applies intermediate scrutiny if a "near suspect" classification is involved; and (3) in the lower tier, the Court will employ the test of reasonableness or rational basis if there are nonfundamental rights or nonsuspect classifications. In *Shapiro*, the Court indicated that interstate travel falls into the upper tier as a fundamental right and states must show a compelling state interest to infringe on that right.

QUESTIONS FOR DISCUSSION

(1)   Do you think that the Court is straining in this case to overturn the regulations?

(2)   If you had been applying the rational basis test as advocated by the dissenters, would you have upheld or overturned the regulations? Why?

(3)   The plaintiffs in this case changed their residence because of health reasons, either their own or a family member's. It seems likely that the charitable feelings of the judges as individuals were raised by the plights. Could you have divorced these feelings from the legal issues? Should judges be influenced by the individuals and injustices in the case, or decide the matter solely on the objective legal questions in the case?

RELATED CASES   *SLAUGHTERHOUSE CASES*, 16 Wallace 36 (1873) (dissent); *EDWARDS V. CALIFORNIA*, 314 U.S. 160 (1941); *Kent v. Dulles*, 357 U.S. 116 (1958); *Aptheker v. Secretary of State*, 378 U.S. 500 (1964); *REYNOLDS V. SIMS*, 377 U.S. 533

(1964); *Zemel v. Rusk*, 381 U.S. 1 (1965); *United States v. Guest*, 383 U.S. 745 (1966); *CRAIG V. BOREN*, 429 U.S. 190 (1976); and *City of Cleburne, Texas v. Cleburne Living Center*, 473 U.S. 432 (1985).

SAN ANTONIO INDEPENDENT SCHOOL DISTRICT V. RODRIGUEZ
411 U.S. 1 (1973)

BACKGROUND Texas, like most states, financed public elementary and secondary education through both state and local financing. The state provided about half of the funding for local schools through a formula-driven program designed to provide minimum educational opportunities throughout the state. Each school district then supplemented state aid through *ad valorem* taxes on property within the district. Plaintiffs filed this class action lawsuit on behalf of children residing in school districts that had a low property tax base. They claimed that Texas's reliance on property tax resulted in substantial interdistrict disparities in per-pupil expenditures and in the quality of education because of the differences in the value of assessable property within the district, favoring wealthier school districts in violation of equal protection. A three-judge panel in the district court found that education was a fundamental right and that Texas had failed to show either a compelling state interest or even a reasonable or rational basis to justify the discrimination against poorer students and districts.

CONSTITUTIONAL ISSUE

Whether discriminatory practices in education based on wealth mandate the use of the "strict scrutiny" standard in the Court's review of the state statute under the Equal Protection Clause of the Fourteenth Amendment? NO

MAJORITY OPINION Justice Lewis Powell writes the majority opinion of the Court. He begins the discussion by reviewing the constitutional and legal history of public school financing in Texas. The Court notes that disparities in school expenditures did indeed exist and were primarily the product of the *ad valorem* tax system. For example, the Edgewood District (a poor district) had a tax rate of $1.05 per $100 valuation, which generated $26 per pupil, which was combined with $222 per pupil from the state and $108 in federal funds for a total of $356 per pupil. In contrast, the wealthier Alamo Heights District had a tax rate of $0.85 per $100 valuation which produced $333 per pupil which was added to the state's contribution of $225 and $36 federal money to allow an expenditure of $594 per pupil.

In dealing with the question of the appropriate standard of review, Powell first considers whether Texas's system of public school finance operated to infringe on a fundamental right "explicitly or implicitly" protected by the Constitution or to disadvantage a suspect class. He sets up two threshold questions to deal with the issue of the poor as a suspect class: (1) whether the "poor" here can be defined in traditional equal protection terms; and (2) whether equal protection applies when there is only a "relative" or partial deprivation of rights or benefits instead of a total or absolute deprivation. He determines that neither question could be answered affirmatively. First, he finds that the lower court record was devoid of necessary proof that the poorest people were concentrated in the poorest districts, and therefore they did not constitute a discrete and insular minority class such as is traditionally required in equal protection cases. Second, school children in less wealthy districts may have been receiving poorer quality education but they were not being totally deprived of education. In addition, Powell denies that a higher per-pupil expenditure automatically meant a better education; this further bolstered his arguments against extending the Court's "most exacting scrutiny to review a system that allegedly discriminates against a large, diverse, amorphous class...there is none of the traditional indicia of suspectness."

Powell then turns to the question of whether education is a fundamental right under the Constitution. While stressing the "historical dedication [of the Court] to public education," he nevertheless refuses to acknowledge public education to be a fundamental right. He declares the measure of a fundamental right to be whether it is "explicitly or implicitly" guaranteed in the Constitution and not in the "relative societal significance" of the questioned right even while conceding the importance of education. Even tying education to the exercise of First Amendment freedoms and the right to vote fails to persuade Powell of its fundamental nature; he agrees that education assists in exercising those rights but declaims that the Court had never guaranteed the "citizenry the most *effective* speech or the most *informed* electoral choice." Besides, Texas did provide its children the opportunity to acquire basic minimal skills for participation in government and for the exercise of First Amendment rights.

Finding neither the fundamental right nor suspect class needed to employ the strict scrutiny standard of review, Powell turns to the question of whether Texas's system of school finance showed a rational relationship to legitimate state purposes. The Court believes that the purpose of the Texas's finance scheme was to maintain local control of schools while assuring a basic education. This, the Court holds, is a legitimate state purpose with entrenched historical precedents in all fifty states. The fact that some inequality results from the state's actions is acceptable, and the entire system should not be overturned "simply because it imperfectly effectuates the state's goals." Otherwise, all taxation schemes that involve the drawing of jurisdictional lines, such as cities or states, would be subject to attack on the same grounds because there is inherent inequality and arbitrariness in drawing lines. The disparities found here are not so "irrational as to be invidiously discriminatory."

Powell emphasizes the Court's traditional deference to the states in matters that the Court lacks expertise and specialized knowledge. The Texas system of public school finance resembled that of the other states and to overturn it would cause considerable upheaval. The system, although discriminatory in nature, furthered a legitimate state purpose and therefore the majority sustained Texas's scheme of taxation and public school finance.

OTHER OPINIONS   Justice Potter Stewart writes a concurring opinion to explain his view of the Equal Protection Clause. For him, the Clause creates neither substantive rights nor liberties; instead it is merely "to measure the validity of classifications created by state laws." State laws are presumed to be valid unless they create a "suspect class" which, as the majority held, Texas did not do. He agrees that the state's system of public school finance does further a legitimate state goal.

Justice William Brennan dissents primarily because of his feeling that education is a fundamental right. He states that education was "inextricably linked" to participation in the electoral process and to the exercise of First Amendment rights. "'Fundamentality' is, in large measure, a function of the right's importance in terms of the effectuation of the rights which are in fact constitutionally guaranteed."

Justice Byron White—joined by Justices William O. Douglas and William Brennan—dissents. Although agreeing that local control and local decision-making policy are admirable and legitimate state goals, White argues that the Court should examine the means of achieving the goals as well as the ends. Only if there is a method whereby such districts as Edgewood could increase their per-pupil expenditures would such a system be rational. But, the poor school districts are precluded by law—for example, property-tax ceilings—as well as by fact, from yielding the same amount of money as wealthy districts. "We would blink at reality to ignore the fact that school districts, and students in the end, are differentially affected" by the disparity in their capabilities to supplement the state monies. White finds this denial of equality to be "invidious discrimination violative of the Equal Protection Clause."

Justice Thurgood Marshall—joined by Justice Douglas—also writes a dissent. He begins with the statement that "The Court today decides, in effect, that a state may constitutionally vary the quality of education which it offers its children in accordance with the amount of taxable wealth located in the school districts within which they reside," a position with which Marshall passionately disagrees. Equality of educational opportunity is the foundation that allows children to reach their full potential as citizens. The inability of district residents, "regardless of the enthusiasm" for public education, to change the taxable property wealth of the district and the lack of state compensatory funding requires that a new funding system that allows equitable per-pupil funding be established to end the discriminatory practices. It is self-apparent that schools with less money will have poorer physical plants, less experienced teachers, and a narrower range of classes than wealthier school districts, and that some children overcome those problems is to the children's credit and not the state's. For Marshall, the nexus between the First Amendment and education is clear, and he rejects the majority's position that the Equal Protection Clause applies only to rights "explicitly or implicitly" found in the Constitution. In addition, he, like White, Brennan, and Douglas, determines that the class discriminated against is discrete and easily identifiable, and that such suspect classification and infringement of a fundamental right merits the application of the strict scrutiny test.

Marshall also attacks the majority's position that either the strict scrutiny test or the rational basis test is the appropriate standard for review of equal protection cases. He cites other Supreme Court decisions that employed other measures and says that it is "inescapably clear that this Court has consistently adjusted the care with which it will review state discrimination in light of the constitutional significance of the interests affected and the invidiousness of the particular classification." Discrimination based on wealth can create a classification of a suspect character, and the classification created here on the basis of wealth is suspect and deprives children of equal opportunity to learn even though Texas does provide minimal educational skills. State regulations controlled many aspects of education in Texas such as curriculum, length of school days, and textbooks. In light of that, justifying discrimination on the basis of local control is a mockery. So too is the

Court's referral of the poor districts to seek redress from the state legislature where the vested interests of the wealthy districts would likely lead to defeat, but that referral is also an abdication of the Court's responsibility under the Constitution to eliminate unjustified state discrimination such as was found here.

SIGNIFICANCE OF THE CASE   This case indicated the refusal of the Court to mark wealth (or the lack thereof) as an automatically suspect classification under the Equal Protection Clause. In other Equal Protection cases, the Court had previously considered poverty as a factor in criminal cases involving indigents who could not pay for transcripts (*Griffin v. Illinois*) or for appellate counsel (*Douglas v. California*), denial of welfare assistance based on one-year residency requirements (*Shapiro v. Thompson*), and others. The Court also rejected the concept of education as a fundamental right.

QUESTIONS FOR DISCUSSION

(1)   Do you think that education should be considered as a fundamental right guaranteed by the Constitution? Why?

(2)   Many states are now requiring students to pass minimal-skills tests before graduating from high school. Is that appropriate? What does that mean for equality of education and for funding for schools?

(3)   Would you favor a school system completely funded by the state? Why or why not?

(4)   How would you achieve equality of educational opportunity if you even feel that is a desirable goal?

RELATED CASES   *Griffin v. Illinois*, 351 U.S. 12 (1956); *Douglas v. California*, 372 U.S. 353 (1963); *SHAPIRO V. THOMPSON*, 394 U.S. 618 (1969); and *Plyler v. Doe*, 457 U.S. 202 (1982).

GRISWOLD V. CONNECTICUT
381 U.S. 479 (1965)

BACKGROUND   The executive director of Planned Parenthood League and its medical director, a licensed physician, were convicted under a Connecticut statute which made it a crime for any person to use any drug or article to prevent conception. They were charged and convicted for giving married couples information about preventing contraception and then, following physical examinations, prescribing contraceptive devices for the wife.

CONSTITUTIONAL ISSUE

Whether there is a constitutionally-protected right to privacy? YES

MAJORITY OPINION   Justice William O. Douglas delivers the opinion of the Court. At the heart of his opinion is the concept of privacy. He argues that while privacy is not specifically mentioned in the Constitution, it is nevertheless a "right" that accrues to the

American people and that is entitled to the Court's protection against unwarranted government intrusion.

The "right" stems from a variety of constitutional provisions including, but not limited to, the First, Third, Fourth, Fifth, and Ninth Amendments. The specific guarantees that limit government intrusion into one's life have "penumbras, formed by the emanations from those guarantees that help give them life and substance....Various guarantees create zones of privacy."

In the instant case, the familial relationship is one that has been accorded special recognition by the law and is an area into which courts are unusually reluctant to enter. Government intrusion into aspects of the marital relationship that Douglas describes as "intimate to the degree of being sacred" and as "lying within the zone of privacy created by several fundamental constitutional guarantees" is particularly repugnant. One problem with the statute is enforcement, or as Douglas pungently questions, "Would we allow the police to search the sacred precincts of marital bedrooms for telltale signs of the use of contraceptives?"

OTHER OPINIONS Justice Arthur Goldberg is joined by Chief Justice Earl Warren and Justice William Brennan in his concurring opinion. The nucleus of this opinion is the interpretation of the Ninth Amendment. Goldberg begins with the premise that fundamental rights are protected against state intervention under the "liberty" provisions of the Fourteenth Amendment and that such fundamental right "embraces the right of marital privacy."

The Ninth Amendment provides that "The enumeration in the Constitution, of certain rights, shall not be construed to deny or disparage others retained by the people." The inclusion of this Amendment shows that the enumerated list of rights is not all inclusive. Such a finding does not expand the role of the Court but instead allows the Court to continue its practice of protecting fundamental rights. It does not give judges unfettered discretion to decide what are or are not fundamental rights because the judges must find the source of these rights in "the traditions and [collective] conscience of our people." Based on those, there can be no doubt that the right to marital privacy is of a "similar order and magnitude as the fundamental rights specifically protected."

In any case, the Connecticut statute cannot survive under the traditional tests of constitutionality. First, because a fundamental right is involved, the less-stringent "rational basis test" is inapplicable. Second, the state did not show a "compelling state interest" to justify infringing on a fundamental right.

Justice John Marshall Harlan II also enters a concurring opinion. He focuses on the concept of "ordered liberty" and the Due Process Clause of the Fourteenth Amendment. Harlan finds this statute violates the basic values that are part of "ordered liberty." He too expresses concern about the role of judges and their individual values being inserted into the Constitution and advocates judicial restraint—restraint that will come about only through reliance on history and basic values, and by continually emphasizing federalism and separation of powers in interpreting the Constitution.

Justice Byron White also enters a concurring opinion. He states that the right to marry and to raise a family are among "the basic civil rights." This statute discriminates against the poor who cannot afford "private counseling, access to medical assistance and up-to-date information" on birth control. The state fails to meet its burden of showing a compelling state interest for sustaining this sweeping statute under the Due Process Clause of the Fourteenth Amendment. The state's argument that such ban discourages illicit sexual relationships is spurious and wholly without merit.

Justice Hugo Black, joined by Justice Potter Stewart, enters a dissenting opinion. They emphasize their agreement with the other justices that the law and policy it embodies are unwise and offensive; however, they view the other justices as being too creative and stretching too much in their efforts to find grounds to overturn the statute. Black argues that it is not the role of the justices, but instead it is the prerogative of the legislative branch, to create new constitutional rights. He rejects both the notion that the Court must continually interpret the Constitution in such a way as to keep it current and the idea that the justices may concoct new rights that are not explicitly listed in the Constitution even by such ruses as claiming that laws violate the "collective conscience of the people." He argues that this places far too much power in the hands of the justices and threatens the balance of power among the branches of government as well as jeopardizing the role of the states to govern themselves.

Justice Potter Stewart, joined by Justice Hugo Black, also enters a dissenting opinion in which he terms the statute in question "uncommonly silly." He argues that the Due Process Clause of the Fourteenth Amendment is not applicable and that the Court has abandoned the policy of using it to determine "the wisdom, need, and propriety of state laws." The novel approach of applying the Ninth Amendment to limit the powers of state governments skews its original intent of limiting the powers of the federal government. It is the privilege of the legislatures to create laws, even asinine ones, and the justices must not substitute their own personal views for those of the duly elected representatives.

SIGNIFICANCE OF THE CASE *Griswold v. Connecticut* is a landmark decision because it gives privacy the status of a constitutional right. It is the precursor of such cases as *Katz v. United States* dealing with search and seizure and *Roe v. Wade* dealing with abortion in which the right to privacy becomes the touchstone of constitutionality. It heralded an emphasis on individual rights and more limited power for the government in dealing with people. In addition to creating a new substantive right under the Constitution, the case is also noteworthy because of the emphasis on the Ninth Amendment in the expansion of citizen's protections against government.

QUESTIONS FOR DISCUSSION

(1) In 1986, the Supreme Court focused on the issue of homosexual conduct in the Georgia sodomy case of *Bowers v. Hardwick* rather than on privacy despite the police intrusion into the privacy of a bedroom. What message did that send regarding the Court's future treatment of privacy matters?

(2) The Court, under Chief Justices Burger and Rehnquist, has carved out more exceptions to the exclusionary rule and made evidence that would previously have been inadmissible available to courts. Do you think that this reflects hostility toward the right to privacy? Why or why not? If so, what are your projections about the right to privacy in the war on drugs?

RELATED CASES *KATZ V. UNITED STATES*, 389 U.S. 347 (1967); *Eisenstadt v. Baird*, 405 U.S. 438 (1972); *ROE V. WADE*, 410 U.S. 113 (1973); and *BOWERS V. HARDWICK*, 478 U.S. 186 (1986).

ROE V. WADE
410 U.S. 113 (1973)

BACKGROUND Jane Roe, an unmarried pregnant woman, filed a class action suit seeking a declaratory judgment and injunction against Texas criminal statutes that barred abortion except for the purpose of saving the mother's life. Other parties also joined the litigation: Hallford, a licensed physician who was under indictment for performing abortions and the Does, a childless couple concerned about future injury if the wife accidentally became pregnant because of her health problems, although her pregnancy would not be life threatening. A specially-convened panel of three district judges found standing on the part of Roe and Hallford and issued the declaratory, but not injunctive, relief. The Supreme Court accepted the case on direct appeal from denial of the injunction and considered both forms of remedies because the arguments for injunctive and declaratory relief were identical.

CONSTITUTIONAL ISSUE

Whether the state may forbid abortions in all cases except when the mother's life is threatened?
NO

MAJORITY OPINION Justice Harry Blackmun writes the majority opinion. The preliminary issues in the case are the procedural aspects of the parties' standing to bring the lawsuit and of mootness. Courts do not hear cases in which the parties lack standing or that are moot. In this case, the Court finds that Roe has standing as a person affected by the operation of the statute, whereas the Does' interest is too speculative to maintain their intervention, especially in light of the fact that their claims are essentially the same as Roe's. Dr. Hallford will not be permitted to challenge the constitutionality of the state statute in federal court at the same time that he is under indictment when he makes no allegations of federal rights that cannot be asserted in his state trial. Technically, the case is moot and should be dismissed as none of the class members who were pregnant in 1970 would be pregnant with the same child in 1973. But, the Court notes that pregnancy litigation is unique because the human gestation period is so short that the usual appellate process would not be complete within the time framework, and the topic would evade review. Therefore, the Court approves an exception of mootness for this type of litigation.

Having dealt with the procedural questions, Justice Blackmun turns to the question of abortion itself, treating it as a medical rather than moral, religious, or ethical question. He traces attitudes toward abortion from ancient times when the Greeks and Romans freely practiced abortion to its treatment under English common law when abortion performed before "quickening" or the first discernible movements of the fetus was not subject to criminal penalty, whereas abortion after quickening led to criminal punishment. The common-law rule was generally accepted in this country until the mid-nineteenth century when the quickening distinction disappeared from the statutes. At the end of the 1950s, most states banned abortion unless done to save the mother's life.

He identifies three reasons for the criminalization of abortion laws: (1) to discourage illicit sexual conduct (although Texas does not employ that as justification here); (2) to protect the women's lives because historically abortion mortality was high (but advances in medical technology have made abortion, at least in the first trimester, relatively safe if performed in clinical conditions); and (3) to protect prenatal life. He notes the current division among members of the health community regarding abortion but noted that all agreed that it was a clinical medical procedure that should occur with proper safeguards if it is to occur at all.

Blackmun defines the interests to be weighed as the woman's right to privacy from governmental intrusion into personal matters and the state's interest, under its police powers, in protecting the health of the woman and its limited interest in the fetus. The right to privacy on the part of an individual vis-à-vis the government, although not explicitly mentioned in the Constitution, has been found in the Constitution in several contexts. Only personal rights are deemed to be "fundamental" or "implicit in the concept of ordered liberty," and surely no rights are more personal than those of marriage, procreation, and health. However, even with fundamental rights, the state's interest may be so compelling as to override the individual's rights. A woman's right to abortion is not absolute, and the state's interests in "safeguarding health, maintaining medical standards, and in protecting potential life" may override the woman's interest. Statutes that infringe on fundamental rights must show a compelling state interest and must be narrowly drawn to express only the legitimate state interests at stake.

The difficulty is in assigning the appropriate weight to each interest—the woman's and the state's. Blackmun avoids the religious and moral question of when life begins, by noting that "When those trained in respective disciplines of medicine, philosophy, and theology are unable to arrive at any consensus, the judiciary, at this point in the development of man's knowledge, is not in a position to speculate as to the answer." Instead, he relies on legal history and lower court decisions for guidance in balancing the respective interests. The unborn have never been recognized as persons in the whole sense by the law, and the Constitution itself does not explicitly define "person" but no phrase indicates that it has prenatal meaning.

Given the lack of agreement about when life begins and prior legal history, Texas cannot totally override the rights of the woman by adopting one theory of life, although the state's interest may become more compelling, as the pregnancy nears term. In weighing the competing interests, the Court adopts a trimester approach. In the first trimester of the pregnancy, the woman's interest is maximized, and the state may regulate abortion only for the purposes of protection of her health and shall leave the abortion decision to the woman and her doctor, free from state interference. At the beginning of the second trimester during which time the fetus becomes viable, the state's interest becomes more compelling, and the state may proscribe abortion except when necessary to preserve the life or health of the mother. The Texas statute as written is too broad in its application. The holding of the Court leaves the state free to impose more restrictions as the pregnancy advances while recognizing the woman's right to privacy and to medical treatment.

OTHER OPINIONS Justice Potter Stewart enters a concurring opinion. The liberty interest protected by the Fourteenth Amendment encompasses more than the freedoms enumerated in the Bill of Rights including matters of marriage and family life. It is the right of the individual to be free from unwarranted government intrusion into matters as personal as the decision of whether or not to have children. The Texas statute is impermissibly broad in asserting the state's interest and is therefore constitutionally infirm.

Chief Justice Warren Burger also concurs in the decision. He notes that, as admitted in oral argument by Texas, the statute is not uniformly enforced by prosecutors, and exceptions are sometimes allowed for nonconsensual pregnancies resulting from rape or incest. "In the face of a rigid and narrow statute, such as that of Texas, no one in these circumstances should be placed in a posture of dependence on a prosecutorial policy or prosecutorial decision." Although agreeing that the Texas law must fall, Burger would prefer a system requiring certification by two physicians before an abortion could be carried out. He maintains that a check on abortion will be maintained by physicians who will use only deliberate medical judgment in performing such procedures.

Justice William O. Douglas concurs also. The liberty interests are protected by the Fourteenth Amendment, some of which are absolute and totally protected from government intrusion while some are subject to limited government regulation and are protected under the Ninth Amendment's protection of unenumerated rights retained by the people. Among the totally protected liberty interests is "autonomous control over the development and expression of one's intellect, interests, tastes, and personality."

Among those rights over which the state may exert some control is the freedom of choice in basic decisions of one's life including marriage and procreation. These rights are fundamental, and to infringe on them the state must show a compelling interest and the statute must be narrowly drawn. The state may also exercise some control over the fundamental rights to care for one's health and person, to be free from physical restraint, and freedom to roam about. The right to privacy "has no more conspicuous place" than in the physician-patient relationship except in the priest-penitent relationship, and government should not intrude into this relationship without a compelling interest. That interest does include health of the woman and the fetus after quickening, but it is a limited interest.

Justice William Rehnquist files a dissenting opinion. He casts the dissent in terms of disagreement with the methodological approach taken by the majority. First, he states there is no indication of how far Roe's pregnancy had advanced at the time of the filing of the lawsuit. She might have been within the last trimester of pregnancy when the Court admitted that the state had a legitimate interest in proscribing abortion. The Court is thus dealing with a possibly hypothetical lawsuit in allowing abortion during the first trimester in violation of the Court's well-established policy against formulating a rule broader than is required by the precise facts.

Second, he disputes that the concept of privacy is appropriately applied in that privacy, as the majority interprets it here, is far removed from the traditional concept of privacy from government that exists in search and seizure law. Although agreeing that the liberty interest protected by the Fourteenth Amendment does embrace more than the rights enumerated in the Bill of Rights, he argues that the majority applied the wrong test to the case. He would substitute the test of whether the statute has a "rational relation to a valid state objective." The Due Process Clause of the Fourteenth Amendment does limit state authority, and if the statute totally barred abortion even when the mother's life is at stake, then the state would have exceeded its authority.

Third, Rehnquist exhibits his usual deference to legislatures and states. The majority is substituting its judgment of what is a compelling state interest for that of state legislatures, and in this case, the majority of state legislatures has enacted legislation restricting abortions. Fourth, the Court in striking down the entire statute swept with too broad a brush and should have limited the holding only to the facts before the Court.

Justice Byron White is joined by Justice Rehnquist in his dissent. He describes the decision as "an exercise of raw judicial power" and an usurpation of the perogatives of the legislative branch of government. Such a heated and emotional issue "should be left with the people and to the political processes the people have devised to govern their own affairs."

SIGNIFICANCE OF THE CASE   *Roe v. Wade* is one of the most important cases of this century and is the center of a firestorm of controversy and discussion. Few subjects raise the emotional furor that abortion does. The case has been heralded as a case protecting individual rights from government intrusion and decried as a case sanctioning murder. During recent administrations, attitudes toward abortion have been a litmus test for those being nominated for judicial positions, particularly the Supreme Court.

QUESTIONS FOR DISCUSSION

(1)   Setting aside your personal opinions as to the morality of abortion, would you agree with Rehnquist and White that this is a topic best left to state legislatures or with the majority that it is the Court's responsibility to deal with such matters in the appropriate case?

(2)   Blackmun essentially avoided entanglement in the religious and ethical issues surrounding abortion. Do you think that the Court should do so?

(3)   As the author of majority opinion, Blackmun has personally been the subject of much vituperation and vilification including shots fired into his home. Do you think that this is an appropriate or effective method of protesting court decisions? Why?

(4)   If you had been given the assignment of writing the majority opinion, would you have adopted Blackmun's tack of casting it in medical terms, Stewart and Douglas' Fourteenth Amendment approach, or some other tactic? Why? What justification would you offer?

RELATED CASES   *GRISWOLD V. CONNECTICUT*, 381 U.S. 479 (1960); *Eisenstadt v. Baird*, 405 U.S. 438 (1972); *BOWERS V. HARDWICK*, 478 U.S. 186 (1986); *WEBSTER V. REPRODUCTIVE HEALTH SERVICES*, 492 U.S. 490 (1989); *Hodgson v. Minnesota*, 497 U.S. 417 (1990) *Ohio v. Akron Center for Reproductive Health*, 497 U.S. 502 (1990); *and Planned Parenthood of Southeastern Pennsylvania v. Casey*, 60 U.S.L.W. 4795 (1992).

WEBSTER V. REPRODUCTIVE HEALTH SERVICES
492 U.S. 490 (1989)

BACKGROUND Missouri passed a statute with the following elements: (1) In § 1.205.1(1)9 the preamble states that "the life of each human being begins at conception" and requires that all state laws be interpreted to provide unborn children with the same legal rights enjoyed by other persons; (2) in § 188.029, it requires that physicians, before performing an abortion on a woman whom he or she believes to be twenty or more weeks pregnant, must conduct tests to determine whether the fetus is viable by determining gestational age, weight, and lung maturity; (3) in § 188.210, it bars the use of public employees or public facilities to perform or assist in any abortion that is not necessary to save the mother's life; and (4) in § 188.205, it makes unlawful any encouragement or counseling of women to have an abortion if any public funds are used or if done by public employees or if carried out in public facilities. Five health care professionals and two health care nonprofit corporations challenged the validity of the statute. The district court struck down each of the preceding provisions and the Court of Appeals for the Eighth Circuit confirmed the decision. The Supreme Court reversed.

CONSTITUTIONAL ISSUE

Whether the states may pass legislation that significantly limits the right of abortion established under *Roe v. Wade*? YES

PLURALITY OPINION Chief Justice William Rehnquist writes the plurality opinion for the Court. The fragmented Court agrees on only two portions of the opinion: (1) the statement of facts; and (2) that there was no case or controversy regarding § 188.205. The latter came about when Missouri appealed only the portion relating to the use of public funds for counseling, and the plaintiffs agreed that they were not adversely affected by such provision which effectively made the issue moot.

The chief justice moves sequentially through the statutory scheme in organizing the opinion. He thus begins with the questions concerning the preamble. Five of the justices (Rehnquist, Byron White, Anthony Kennedy, Sandra Day O'Conner, and Antonin Scalia) agree with the state that the preamble is merely precatory and imposes no substantive restrictions on abortions, although they recognize it is the statement of a value judgment. Because it is essentially ineffective in the instant case, the Court should refrain from dealing with its constitutionality.

The chief justice then turns his attention to the clause preventing the expenditure of public funds for performing abortions in public hospitals. Speaking for the same five justices, he upholds the prohibition. Government has no affirmative duty to provide aid in certain situations even if government could not deprive the individual of such interest without due process of law. A state's decision to "encourage childbirth over abortion" by providing public hospitals and other assistance to pregnant women and declining to provide public funds for abortion is not a governmental obstacle to women seeking to terminate pregnancies. These women are left with the same choices as if the state had chosen not to operate any public hospitals; they may choose physicians not affiliated with public hospitals. If indigent, they continue to be dependent on private sources. The state can allocate its resources in accordance with its value judgments and "nothing in the

Constitution requires states to enter or, remain in the business of performing abortions." If, as alleged in the case, the state recoups its costs in performing abortions and no state subsidies, either direct or indirect, are accessible, then it is even more apparent that Missouri's statute does not impair, or burden, procreational choices.

Rehnquist, joined by White and Kennedy in this portion of the opinion, upholds the requirement of determining fetus viability if the woman is twenty or more weeks pregnant before performing an abortion. Here there is a question of statutory construction because of the wording of the statute. The first sentence states that the physician "shall" determine viability by "using and exercising that degree of care, skill, and proficiency commonly exercised by the ordinarily skillful, careful and prudent physician," whereas the second sentence states that the physician "shall perform or cause to be performed" the examinations and tests necessary to determine viability. The two sentences apparently set up two different standards that could conflict. If the second sentence is read as to mandate the testing procedure despite the requirement that a physician apply reasonable professional skill and judgment, a conflict could arise if the physician determines that the test is irrelevant or even dangerous. Rehnquist construes the provisions to mean that the physician's determination is the primary factor, and the tests are to be subsidiary. The effect of this provision, according to the chief justice, is to create a presumption of viability at twenty weeks that the physician must rebut with tests before performing an abortion. The interest to be advanced is the state's interest in human life rather than maternal health. It is at the point of viability when the state's interest in potential human life becomes so compelling as to override the woman's rights. The statute "undoubtedly does superimpose state regulation on the medical determination of whether a particular fetus is viable."

Rehnquist declines to flatly overrule *Roe v. Wade* stating that the facts are different in the instant case and "therefore affords us no occasion to revisit the holding of *Roe*," even while downplaying the role of *stare decisis* in constitutional law. He criticizes *Roe* on several grounds. First, he criticizes the "rigid" framework of *Roe* being inconsistent with the notion of a Constitution cast in general terms because *Roe* with its trimester analysis more closely resembles a regulatory code. Second, neither of the key elements of the *Roe* framework—viability and trimesters—are found in the Constitution. The Court in *Roe* arbitrarily chose to emphasize the state's interest as beginning after viability and imposing regulations after that time, but for Rehnquist, the state's interest, "if compelling after viability, is equally compelling before viability."

As stated by the chief justice, "there is no doubt that our holding today will allow some governmental regulation of abortion which would have been previously prohibited." The issue will be shifted to the state legislatures where elected officials will deal with the matter.

OTHER OPINIONS   Justice Sandra Day O'Connor, concurs with part of the Rehnquist opinion and with the judgment. She initially addresses the effect of the language of the preamble that life begins at conception in terms of contraceptive choices because certain contraceptive devices act after fertilization. Although agreeing that postfertilization contraceptive devices may be protected under *Griswold v. Connecticut*, that is not the issue before the Court in this case. She agrees with that states may withhold public monies and prevent the use of public facilities for abortions under prior court rulings.

She disagrees with the plurality that Missouri's requirement of measuring viability at twenty weeks somehow conflicts with "any of the Court's past decisions concerning state regulation of abortion." The Court upheld all provisions of the Missouri statute properly before it and exercised judicial restraint in not straining to overturn *Roe*. Both *Roe* and *Webster* follow the same framework of recognizing the government's compelling interest in protecting life after viability and for her, the examinations and tests that Missouri might require to determine fetal viability "do not impose an undue burden on a woman's abortion decision."

Justice Scalia concurs in the judgment and in part with the plurality opinion. Scalia strongly denounces the decision of the Court not to overrule *Roe v. Wade*, the goal he advocates. He presents arguments as to why the Court should reject *Roe* and to "go beyond the most stingy possible holding today." First, although a narrow ruling normally avoids throwing settled law into confusion, here it merely "preserves" chaos. Second, the Court's continued involvement in a political issue demeans the stature of the Court in the public's eyes. In addition, the Court will continue to be deluged with requests to follow the popular will even though the Court is composed of "unelected and life-tenured judges who have been awarded those extraordinary undemocratic characteristics precisely that we might follow the law despite the popular will." For him, the Court's decision to avoid the fundamental question of *Roe v. Wade* is the least responsible of its options—to reaffirm *Roe*, to overrule it either explicitly or silently, or to avoid it.

Justice Harry Blackmun, joined by Justices William Brennan and Thurgood Marshall, enters a stinging dissent. He castigates the majority with the statement, "Never in my memory has a plurality announced a judgment of this Court that so foments disregard for the law and for our standing decisions....Nor, in my memory has a plurality gone about its fashion in such a deceptive fashion." Blackmun charges that, despite the disclaimer that the majority leaves *Roe* undisturbed, the plurality opinion is an open invitation for further limitations on abortion. It encourages the states to enact ever more restrictive abortion laws. It essentially overturns an established precedent, "a rare and grave undertaking," but when it involves fundamental liberties such as the right to privacy and procreational choices it is "unprecedented in our 200 years of constitutional history."

He argues that the statute is unconstitutional because there is not sufficient state interest even under a rational basis test for the viability testing because physicians are mandated to perform the tests even though they "have no medical justification, impose significant additional health risks on both the pregnant woman and the fetus, and bear no rational relation to the state's interest in protecting fetal life." Had the Court followed its own settled doctrine of deferring to the lower courts' understanding of such statutes, then the provision would fail. In fact, this section furthers "no discernible interest except to make the procurement of an abortion as arduous and difficult as possible."

Blackmun and the others agree that the state can regulate and even proscribe nontherapeutic abortions once the fetus is viable. If the tests are merely to determine viability, then that is not contradictory to *Roe*, and there is no need for the plurality to so harshly criticize *Roe* and to label its analytical core as being unsound. However the plurality's statement that the state's interest in potential life is paramount before and after viability is not justified nor supported by the precedents and *Roe's* trimester analysis serves to "fairly, sensibly, and effectively" safeguard the rights of women and to accommodate the state's interest in potential human life.

"The plurality opinion is far more remarkable for the arguments that it does not advance" because it does not address or even mention the right to privacy, which is the basis of such cases as *Griswold* and *Roe*. *Roe* "simply defines and limits that right to privacy in the abortion context to accommodate, not destroy, a state's legitimate interest in protecting the health of pregnant women and in preserving potential human life."

Justice John Paul Stevens also concurs in part and dissents in part. He is very critical of the plurality's acceptance of the Missouri statute as constitutional. The primary thrust of his opinion is the statement in the preamble that life begins at conception, and the effect of that statement on the other provisions violates constitutional principles under the Establishment Clause. The theory that life begins at conception is a theological argument and one that is not universally accepted even by mainstream denominations. The Missouri legislature cannot incorporate particular religious traditions into law without running afoul of the Constitution. Missouri must show a secular purpose for such legislation if it is to be sustained, and it has not done so here. The state does not have the same interest in protecting a freshly fertilized egg as it does a fully sentient fetus from physical pain or mental anguish.

By adopting the theological tenet as its basis, the state interferes with conception choices in that postfertilization birth control methods would be barred. Second, it conflicts with the constitutional principle that freedom of personal choice in matters of marriage and family life, including reproductive choices, is protected by the Due Process Clause of the Fourteenth Amendment and should be free from unwarranted government intrusion.

SIGNIFICANCE OF THE CASE   This case is significant for a variety of reasons. First it clearly shifted the matter of abortion into the hands of the state legislatures and sent a clear signal that a plurality of the Court is receptive to very restrictive legislation enacted by the states. Second, the case, like others decided by this Court, denigrated the role of *stare decisis*, the mainstay of American jurisprudence, in constitutional cases, which indicates the willingness to abandon decisions made by other courts. Third, the case is noted for the tenor of the opinions and acrimony among the judges. Seldom do the Court's opinions exhibit the disharmony and discord that is displayed here.

QUESTIONS FOR DISCUSSION

(1)   What does the case portend in terms of American jurisprudence regarding the role of *stare decisis*? What are the arguments in favor of *stare decisis*?

(2)   Is the Court assuming an activist stance or exhibiting judicial restraint in this case? Why?

(3)   Do you agree that the Court should not be involved in the "great debates" of our time? What about when individual rights are at stake?

(4)   Do you agree that the case is "remarkable" for what it does not say? In what ways?

RELATED CASES   *GRISWOLD V. CONNECTICUT*, 381 U.S. 479 (1965); *Eisenstadt v. Baird*, 405 U.S. 438 (1972); *ROE V. WADE*, 410 U.S. 113 (1973); *Maher v. Roe*, 432 U.S. 464 (1977); *City of Akron v. Akron Center for Reproductive Health, Inc.*, 462 U.S.

416 (1983); *Thornburgh v. American College of Obstetricians and Gynecologists*, 476 U.S. 747 (1986); *Hodgson v. Minnesota*, 497 U.S. 417 (1990); *Ohio v. Akron Center for Reproductive Health*, 497 U.S. 502 (1990); and *Planned Parenthood of Southeastern Pennsylvania v. Casey*, 60 U.S.L.W. 4795 (1992).

BOWERS V. HARDWICK
478 U.S. 186 (1986)

BACKGROUND　A police officer came to respondent Michael Hardwick's home to arrest him for a traffic violation. On lawfully entering Hardwick's bedroom, the officer observed Hardwick engaged in a homosexual act with another young man. Hardwick was arrested and charged under a Georgia law that makes sodomy a criminal offense. Although the district attorney chose not to prosecute the case, Hardwick nevertheless filed suit in a federal court seeking a declaratory judgment that the Georgia sodomy law was unconstitutional. The district court dismissed the suit, but it was later reversed by the court of appeals. The court of appeals held that the Georgia law violated Hardwick's fundamental rights. Georgia appealed and the Supreme Court granted *certiorari*.

CONSTITUTIONAL ISSUE

Whether the Ninth Amendment and the Due Process Clause guarantee a fundamental right to engage in consensual homosexual activities in the privacy of one's home? NO

MAJORITY OPINION　Justice Byron White delivers the opinion of the Court. Justice White begins by asserting that respondent Hardwick does not find support in the Court's previous decisions for his position that he has a fundamental right to engage in consensual homosexual activity. Justice White concedes that the Court established a constitutional right to privacy in *Griswold v. Connecticut* (1965). However, *Griswold* and similar cases were concerned with relationships within the family, within marriage, and within the realm of procreation. Because homosexual activity does not have any connection with any of these purposes, the *Griswold* line of cases provides no support for respondent's position. Nor does *Stanley v. Georgia* (1969) provide any support. In *Stanley*, the Court struck down a Georgia law making it a crime to possess obscene material in the privacy of one's own home. The difference, Justice White observes, is that *Stanley* had a basis in the First Amendment. The right to privacy, although recognized in *Griswold*, has no similar explicit basis in the Constitution.

Justice White also refuses to recognize as fundamental the right to engage in homosexual sodomy. Although he admits the Supreme Court has created substantive rights in the past, those rights have always been defined as "implicit in the concept of ordered liberty." Previously judge-made rights were such that "neither liberty nor justice would exist if they were sacrificed." The fact that homosexual sodomy was illegal in all thirteen original states argues against its status as a fundamental right. Twenty-five states, White observes, still have laws against homosexual sodomy.

Finally, the Court rejects the argument that just because an activity is committed between consenting adults in the privacy of the home it cannot be criminalized. Use of illegal drugs, incest, and adultery are not exempt from criminal prosecution merely because they are committed in the home. To have the Court grant special exemption to one form of illicit sexual behavior and not others would create problems. Justice White states that is a road the majority does not wish to travel.

OTHER OPINIONS   There were two concurring and two dissenting opinions. Chief Justice Warren Burger joins the majority opinion but simply wants to emphasize this view that there is no fundamental right to engage in homosexual sodomy. In his concurring opinion, Justice Lewis Powell wants to stress that the Court had reached no opinion on whether the Georgia sodomy law violates the Eighth Amendment's prohibition against cruel and unusual punishment. Justice Powell observes that the twenty-year maximum sentence allowed under the law might be viewed by some as excessive.

Justice Harry Blackmun writes the first dissenting opinion. Justice Blackmun accuses the majority of misstating the issue raised by this case. It is not, he asserts, about the right to engage in homosexual activities; it is about privacy. He compares *Bowers* to *Katz v. United States* (1967) where the Court overturned a gambling conviction based on the illegal wiretap of a public telephone booth. The Court, Blackmun argues, was protecting Katz's right to privacy, not his right to make illegal bets. Justice Blackmun also criticizes the majority for concentrating on the homosexual activity in the case. The Georgia law makes heterosexual sodomy punishable as well. Therefore, the majority's contention notwithstanding, the *Griswold* line of cases is controlling. The state's attorney who argued the case admitted that the state has no desire to prosecute heterosexuals under the law. This admission raised questions in Justice Blackmun's mind about whether this policy violates the Equal Protection Clause.

Justice Blackmun asserts that the Court's previous privacy cases have followed two lines of thinking. The first centers on the decisions that individuals may make free of government interference. In *Loving v. Virginia* (1967), the Court invalidated a law forbidding interracial marriages because it interfered with a person's right to choose a marriage partner. The second line of thinking centers on places. The Fourth Amendment recognizes that one's home is special and should be reasonably free from unnecessary governmental intrusions. This case involves both the types of personal relations a person may decide to engage in and the sanctity of the home.

Justice Blackmun contends that each individual has the right to decide his or her own emotional and physical needs free from government interference. The fact that a majority may disapprove of particular behavior is irrelevant. Justice Blackmun also asserts that the state's purported reasons—public health and public morality—for enforcing the law against homosexuals only would not even pass the rational basis test. Finally, Justice Blackmun argues that comparing Hardwick's behavior with adultery and incest is illogical. Adultery and incest involve innocent third parties that the state may seek to protect.

Justice John Paul Stevens writes the other dissenting opinion. Justice Stevens says that the case raises two questions. The first is whether the state may prohibit this conduct for everyone within its jurisdiction. The second is whether the state may selectively enforce the law against homosexuals only. Justice Stevens contends that a described activity cannot be banned solely because a majority finds it morally repugnant. Also citing *Loving*, he observes that laws against miscegenation are unconstitutional whatever the majority's view. He says that the state has no more right to regulate nonreproductive sexual activities than it has to regulate reproductive sexual activities. As to the second question, Justice Stevens argues that Georgia cannot provide a rational basis for enforcing the law against homosexuals but not heterosexuals.

SIGNIFICANCE OF THE CASE   *Bowers v. Hardwick* was definitely a setback for gay rights advocates who have long advocated the decriminalization of homosexual activities. Although homosexual activities have been decriminalized in about half the states, they are still illegal in the rest. *Bowers* was also a setback for supporters of the right to privacy. In *Griswold*, Justice William O. Douglas asked, "Would we allow the police to search the sacred precincts of marital bedrooms for telltale signs of the use of contraceptives?" The specter of the police invading bedrooms for evidence of either homosexual or heterosexual sodomy is appalling to most Americans, even those opposed to gay rights. Finally, *Bowers* puts in jeopardy other cases, like *Stanley* and *Roe v. Wade* (1973) that were largely decided on the presumed constitutional right to privacy.

QUESTIONS FOR DISCUSSION

(1)   Do you think a maximum of twenty years in prison for sodomy is cruel and unusual punishment? Why or why not?

(2)   Is it reasonable for the state to prosecute homosexual sodomy but not heterosexual sodomy? Why or why not?

(3)   Do you agree that homosexual activity between adults is comparable with adultery and incest? Why or why not?

(4)   Is Georgia's law enforceable? If not, why should it remain on the books?

RELATED CASES   *GRISWOLD V. CONNECTICUT*, 381 U.S. 479 (1965); *Loving v. Virginia*, 388 U.S. 1 (1967); *KATZ V. UNITED STATES*, 389 U.S. 347 (1967); *Stanley v. Georgia*, 394 U.S. 557 (1969); *Eisenstadt v. Baird*, 405 U.S. 438 (1972); *ROE V. WADE*, 410 U.S. 113 (1973); *Carey v. Population Services International*, 431 U.S. 678 (1977); and *Thornburgh v. American College of Obstetricians and Gynecologists*, 476 U.S. 747 (1986).

CRUZAN BY CRUZAN V. DIRECTOR, MISSOURI DEPARTMENT OF HEALTH
497 U.S. 261 (1990)

BACKGROUND   As a result of an automobile accident, Nancy Cruzan was hospitalized in a Missouri state hospital in a persistent vegetative state (one in which the person exhibits motor reflexes but has no indications of significant cognitive function). She was receiving artificial nutrition and hydration, a treatment plan to which her then husband had consented. Based on the physicians' advice that Cruzan would not ever recover, Cruzans' parents requested that such treatment be terminated. The hospital refused to do so without a court order.

A *guardian ad litem* was appointed to represent Cruzan's interests during the trial. Evidence was introduced at trial that Cruzan had made statements to a housemate and others that, if sick or injured, she would not wish to live unless she could do "at least halfway normally," that the relationship among the Cruzans was that of a very close and loving family, and that her parents were acting in good faith. The trial court authorized the termination of the life-sustaining procedures. The *guardian ad litem* agreed with the court but nevertheless felt compelled to appeal the decision. The Missouri Supreme Court reversed the decision.

CONSTITUTIONAL ISSUE

Whether a person's oral expression of wishes regarding the refusal of life-sustaining medical treatment, a protected liberty interest, may be overcome by the state's interest in the preservation of life? YES

MAJORITY OPINION   Chief Justice William Rehnquist delivers the majority (5–4) opinion. The opinion essentially eschews social, theological, and constitutional arguments in favor of narrow legal questions, that is, could the State of Missouri impose an unusually stringent standard of proof—"clear and convincing evidence"—rather than that usually imposed in civil cases—"preponderance of evidence"—and is the Missouri's Supreme Court decision on the sufficiency of the evidence under that standard constitutional?

One of the most basic liberties is the individual's right to the possession and control of his or her own person and that "notion of bodily integrity has been embodied" in the requirement of informed consent as a prerequisite for medical treatment. Numerous state decisions have held that the corollary, the right to refuse medical treatment, stems from the common-law right of informed consent, or on both that right and the constitutional right of privacy. A competent person has a liberty interest in refusing unwanted medical treatment, and for the purposes of this case, the Court assumes that the Constitution would protect the right of a competent person to reject life-sustaining treatment.

Cruzan, however, is not competent, and the decision must be made by surrogates. Missouri's statutes permit such a decision to be made by others, but only after meeting the procedural safeguard of showing that such withdrawal would confirm to the expressed wishes of the patient when competent and by making that showing by "clear and convincing evidence." The standard of proof is a reflection of society's view "about how the risk of error should be distributed among the litigants" as well as the importance of the issue. Here, the legislature's intent is to maintain the state's interest in the protection and preservation of human life and to guard against unscrupulous surrogates which the Cruzans patently are not. Missouri's elected representatives may establish the higher burden of proof to sustain the state's interest given the magnitude of this in that the effects of the withdrawal are irreversible.

Requiring a higher standard of proof does not violate the Due Process Clause, and it is the prerogative of the Missouri courts, not the Supreme Court, to decide on the weight to be given to the evidence. That the Missouri Supreme Court chose to discount evidence relating to the not-clearly expressed wishes of Cruzan does not amount to constitutional error. There are many situations in which the states may refuse to give effect to a person's intentions such as refusing to allow real property to be passed under an oral will or refusing to allow the terms of an written contract to be altered by oral communications.

OTHER OPINIONS Justice Sandra O'Connor writes a concurring opinion agreeing that refusing unwanted medical treatment is a protected liberty interest and emphasizing that this decision would not preclude the surrogate's decisions from being carried out under a different statutory scheme, especially if there is a written expression of the patient's wishes in a document such as a "living will" or durable power of attorney for health purposes.

Justice Antonin Scalia also concurs. It is absolutely the prerogative of the legislature as the elected representatives of Missouri residents to determine whether life-sustaining treatment should be maintained—even to the point of overriding or ignoring a competent patient's express wishes regarding this type of treatment. This is tantamount to suicide, and states have long prohibited suicide. However sympathetic to the Cruzans' plight judges may be, they should not be involved, especially at the national level, but should instead defer to the legislative branch.

Justice William Brennan is joined by Justice Thurgood Marshall and Justice Harry Blackmun in his dissent. The majority recognizes that people have a liberty interest in being free of unwanted medical treatment. That interest is a fundamental right, and one does not lose fundamental constitutional rights merely by becoming incompetent. To overcome the exercise of a fundamental right, the state must show a compelling state interest. Here the state's only asserted interest is the preservation of life, but the state has no general interest in someone's life—"In these unfortunate situations, the bodies and preferences and memories of the victims do not escheat to the state; nor does our Constitution permit the state or any other government to commandeer them."

However, the state does have a *parens patriae* interest in the procedures that are used to determine the wishes of the incompetent. Here a neutral *guardian ad litem* was appointed, and there was an adversarial proceeding in an open forum. The heightened evidentiary standard is skewed in Missouri's interest rather than being neutral; the effect is that the best evidence of Cruzan's wishes—statements made to family and friends—was deliberately excluded in "disdain for Nancy Cruzan's own right to choose." It allows the state to do indirectly (by imposing a procedural rule) that which it could not do directly—supersede Cruzan's wishes, as expressed to and by others, regarding the termination of unwanted medical treatment.

Justice John Paul Stevens also writes a dissenting opinion. A person does have a liberty interest in refusing life-sustaining medical treatment, and qualified guardians may make that choice for incompetents when procedural safeguards—the appointment of a *guardian ad litem;* an open, adversarial hearing; and even a higher standard of proof—are met. The Missouri Supreme Court's interpretation is an effort by the state to define the meaning of life and ignores that "life" encompasses more than the merely physical but is "an activity which is at once the matrix for, and an integration of, a person's interests" and relationships.

Here, the state is usurping the patient's rights, as expressed by her and by those closest to her, only to preserve what it defines as life, that is, "equating her life with the biological persistence of her bodily functions." It is the role of judges to deal with the case as "illuminated by the facts of the controversy before us" and that appropriate standard should be the best interest of the person which includes consideration of the quality of the person's existence. Here, Cruzan's rights and interests greatly outweigh the state's meager interest in mandating an empty physical existence for an individual who had indicated her desire to avoid such.

SIGNIFICANCE OF THE CASE   This case is noteworthy on two fronts. First, it exhibits the chief jurisprudential characteristics of the Rehnquist Court. Broader constitutional issues are dodged by focusing on narrow, technical grounds of statutory interpretation. There is great deference given to the legislature as the elected representatives of the people, and the splintering of policy by declaring it to be the states' prerogative rather than adopting a national standard for enforcement of constitutional rights. As in other cases, the Court discounts the right to privacy through its casual mention of the right and the failure to incorporate it as part of the Court's rationale.

Second, the case is important because of the substantive issue of an individual's right of self-determination in the matter of unwanted medical treatment. The advancement of medical technology that allows the prolonging of physical existence has created difficult questions for society as well as for individuals and their families. Quality of life and the dignity of one's existence are matters of great concern to many people. This case is thought to encourage unwarranted and very obtrusive government intrusion into matters traditionally outside the scope of government's interest. Many find the decision particularly intolerable because the appellate courts ignored the express wishes of the person as presented by the testimony and accepted in its place the judgment of strangers who were totally and absolutely separated from the trauma of seeing a loved one in this position and from the distress of making such a decision. However, that is offset by the agreement of eight justices (Scalia excluded) that the clear expression of one's wishes in the form of a living will or other documentary evidence are protected under the Fourteenth Amendment's liberty interest and should be given effect.

QUESTIONS FOR DISCUSSION

(1)   Is there an anomaly between the majority's concern here that an erroneous decision will be made because of the irreversibility of the withdrawal of life-sustaining treatment and the closure of the federal courts to a second round of appeals based on a condemned prisoner's claim that new evidence has been found that would prove the inmate's innocence? Why?

(2)   Why does the majority avoid the broader theological and moral implications of the question? How does the approach in this case compare with that of the abortion cases on these points?

(3)   Should it make a difference in such cases if the state is forcing the family to exhaust all its financial resources in caring for a person who, all medical experts agree, will not recover but can linger indefinitely?

(4)   Analysis of court decisions indicates informal statements of men that they would not wish to be kept alive in these circumstances are much more likely to be given effect than those of women. Why? What are the implications?

RELATED CASES *Jacobson v. Massachusetts*, 197 U.S. 11 (1905); *ROE V. WADE*, 410 U.S 113 (1973); *In re Quinlan*, 70 N.J. 10, 355 A.2d 647, cert. denied *sub nom. Garger v. New Jersey*, 429 U.S. 922 (1976); *BOWERS V. HARDWICK*, 478 U.S. 186 (1986); and *Washington v. Harper*, 494 U.S. 210 (1990).

NATIONAL TREASURY EMPLOYEES UNION V. VON RAAB
489 U.S. 656 (1989)

BACKGROUND One of the primary responsibilities of the United States Custom Service is the interdiction and seizure of contraband, including drugs, coming into this nation. The Service implemented a drug-screening program requiring urinalysis for all employees seeking transfer or promotion to positions in three categories—those having direct involvement in drug interdiction, those carrying a gun, and those handling "classified" materials. Employees considering transfer or promotion were notified in advance that such a change in status was contingent on successful completion of the drug-screening test. Results of the test could not be given to any other agency, including criminal prosecutors, without the employee's written consent, although a positive test could result in dismissal. The program included elements designed to prevent the adulteration or substitution of specimens while maintaining some degree of privacy for the person providing the specimen.

CONSTITUTIONAL ISSUE

Whether the Fourth Amendment permits employers to require employees to submit to bodily searches, specifically drug testing, without probable cause or individualized suspicion of wrongdoing? YES

MAJORITY OPINION Justice Anthony Kennedy writes the majority opinion for the Court. Searches generally must be supported by warrants and by probable cause under the Fourth Amendment, but neither the warrant or probable cause, or even individualized suspicion, is "an indispensable element" in every case. The Court has allowed routine administrative searches and searches of belongings in the public school context without imposing the more stringent standards found in criminal cases.

The Court must balance the individual's liberty and privacy interests against the interests of the state in deciding whether these searches are reasonable. The special physical and ethical demands of certain types of employment may diminish one's expectations of privacy even with respect to such personal searches, and Service employees are forewarned that such tests are a prerequisite for transfer or promotion within these three categories. The Service has a "compelling interest" for its employees to have "unimpeachable integrity and judgment" as well as for its need to protect citizens from agents with impaired judgment who might inappropriately use deadly force. Those with addictions might be more vulnerable to taking bribes or to exercising poor judgment in the use of force.

The nexus between the category of those with access to classified information and those actually tested (including messenger, animal caretaker, co-op student and others) is ambiguous, and the Service has defined the category more broadly than is necessary to meet the goals of the program. There must be a showing that people actually have access to sensitive materials before being subjected to such tests. However, the "suspicionless testing" of employees in the other two classifications is "reasonable."

OTHER OPINIONS   Justice Thurgood Marshall, joined by Justice William Brennan, enters a succinct dissenting opinion. The Fourth Amendment's protections against such searches are not susceptible to this balancing analysis, and the "Court's abandonment of the Fourth Amendment's express requirement that searches of the person rest on probable cause is unprincipled and unjustifiable."

Justice Antonin Scalia, joined by Justice John Paul Stevens, also dissents. Whether a particular search is reasonable depends largely on the social necessity that prompts the search. Here, the searches are primarily symbolic—designed to "set an important example in our country's struggle with this most serious threat to our national health and security" as described by the Director in his memo establishing the program. The Service did not provide any examples where drug use was shown to contribute to bribery, to skewed law enforcement, or to release of classified information unlike the situation in *Skinner v. Railway Labor Executives' Ass'n.* in which the connection between drug use and train accidents was well documented.

The Service certainly may subject employees who engage in unlawful activity, either at home or at work, to adverse employment decisions, even dismissal. But that is not the issue here where the focus is on the steps that constitutionally can be taken to detect such activity. The Court is departing from its precedent requiring particularized suspicion for body searches to allow this "immolation of privacy and human dignity in symbolic opposition to drug use."

SIGNIFICANCE OF THE CASE   In this case and in *Skinner v. Railway Labor Executives' Ass'n.*, which was handed down the same day, the Court further eroded protections under the Fourth Amendment. This opens the way for employers, both private and public, to demand that employees undergo drug testing as a condition of employment, although the Court does limit each case to its unique situation.

QUESTIONS FOR DISCUSSION

(1)   Is the scourge of drugs so terrible in this nation that it should invalidate the Bill of Rights? Why? Under what other circumstances would you allow this to happen?

(2)   Do you agree with Justice Scalia that symbolism is an inadequate justification for this shift in jurisprudence?

(3)   Is Justice Marshall correct in saying that the balancing analysis by the Court here is inappropriate? Why?

(4)   Should all university students or all government employees be required to submit to urinalysis even when there is no suspicion of wrongdoing?

RELATED CASES   *ROCHIN V. CALIFORNIA*, 342 U.S. 165 (1952); *Camara v. Municipal Court of San Francisco*, 387 U.S. 523 (1967); *NEW JERSEY v. T. L. O.*, 469 U.S. 325 (1985); *O'Connor v. Ortega*, 480 U.S. 709 (1987); and *Skinner v. Railway Labor Executives' Ass'n.*, 489 U.S. 616 (1989).

APPENDIX

The Constitution of the United States of America

THE PREAMBLE

We the People of the United States, in Order to form a more perfect Union, establish Justice, insure domestic Tranquility, provide for the common defence, promote the general Welfare, and secure the Blessings of Liberty to ourselves and our Posterity, do ordain and establish this Constitution for the United States of America.

ARTICLE I–THE LEGISLATIVE ARTICLE

Legislative Power

Section 1 All legislative Powers herein granted shall be vested in a Congress of the United States, which shall consist of a Senate and House of Representatives.

House of Representatives: Composition; Qualifications; Apportionment; Impeachment Power

Section 2 The House of Representatives shall be composed of Members chosen every second Year by the People of the several States, and the Electors in each State shall have the Qualifications requisite for Electors of the most numerous Branch of the State Legislature.

No person shall be a Representative who shall not have attained to the Age of twenty five Years, and been seven Years a Citizen of the United States, and who shall not, when elected, be an Inhabitant of that State in which he shall be chosen.

Representatives and direct Taxes[1] shall be apportioned among the several States which may be included within this Union, according to their respective Numbers, *which shall be determined by adding to the whole Number of free Persons, including those bound to Service for a Term of Years and excluding Indians not taxed, three fifths of all other Persons.*[2] The actual Enumeration shall be made within three Years after the first Meeting of the Congress of the United States, and within every subsequent Term of ten Years, in such Manner as they shall by Law direct. The Number of Representatives shall not exceed one for every thirty Thousand, but each State shall have at least one Representative; and until each enumeration shall be made, the State of New Hampshire shall be entitled to chuse three, Massachusetts

[1]Modified by the 16th Amendment
[2]"Other Persons" refers to black slaves. Replaced by Section 2. 14th Amendment

351

eight, Rhode-Island and Providence Plantations one, Connecticut five, New-York six, New Jersey four, Pennsylvania eight, Delaware one, Maryland six, Virginia ten, North Carolina five, South Carolina five, and Georgia three.

When vacancies happen in the Representation from any State, the Executive Authority thereof shall issue Writs of Election to fill such Vacancies.

The House of Representatives shall chuse their Speaker and other Officers; and shall have the sole Power of Impeachment.

Senate Composition: Qualifications, Impeachment Trials

Section 3 The Senate of the United States shall be composed of two Senators from each State, *chosen by the Legislature thereof,*[3] for six Years; and each Senator shall have one Vote.

Immediately after they shall be assembled in Consequence of the first Election, they shall be divided as equally as may be into three Classes. The Seats of the Senators of the first Class shall be vacated at the Expiration of the second Year, of the second Class at the Expiration of the fourth Year, and of the third Class at the Expiration of the sixth Year, so that one third may be chosen every second Year; *and if Vacancies happen by Resignation, or otherwise, during the Recess of the Legislature of any State, the Executive thereof may make temporary Appointments until the next Meeting of the Legislature, which shall then fill such Vacancies.*[4]

No person shall be a Senator who shall not have attained to the Age of thirty Years, and been nine Years a Citizen of the United States, and who shall not, when elected, be an inhabitant of that State for which he shall be chosen.

The Vice President of the United States shall be President of the Senate, but shall have no Vote, unless they be equally divided.

The Senate shall chuse their other Officers, and also a President pro tempore, in the Absence of the Vice President, or when he shall exercise the Office of President of the United States.

The Senate shall have the sole Power to try all Impeachments. When sitting for that Purpose, they shall be on Oath of Affirmation. When the President of the United States is tried, the Chief Justice shall preside: And no Person shall be convicted without the Concurrence of two thirds of the Members present.

[3]Repealed by the 17th Amendment
[4]Modified by the 17th Amendment

Judgment in Cases of Impeachment shall not extend further than to removal from Office, and disqualification to hold and enjoy any Office of honor, Trust or Profit under the United States; but the Party convicted shall nevertheless be liable and subject to Indictment, Trial, Judgment and Punishment, according to law.

Congressional Elections: Times, Places, Manner

Section 4 The Times, Places and Manner of holding Elections for Senators and Representatives, shall be prescribed in each State by the Legislature thereof; but the Congress may at any time by Law make or alter such Regulations, except as to the Places of chusing Senators.

The Congress shall assemble at least once in every Year, *and such Meeting shall be on the first Monday in December, unless they shall by Law appoint a different Day.*[5]

Powers and Duties of the Houses

Section 5 Each House shall be the Judge of the Elections, Returns and Qualifications of its own Members, and a Majority of each shall constitute a Quorum to do Business; but a smaller Number may adjourn from day to day, and may be authorized to compel the Attendance of absent Members, in such Manner, and under the Penalties as each House may provide.

Each House may determine the Rules of its Proceedings, punish its Members for disorderly Behaviour, and, with the Concurrence of two thirds, expel a Member.

Each House shall keep a Journal of its Proceedings, and from time to time publish the same, excepting such Parts as may in their Judgment require Secrecy; and the yeas and Nays of the Members of either House on any question shall, at the Desire of one fifth of those Present, be entered on the Journal.

Neither House, during the Session of Congress shall, without the Consent of the other, adjourn for more than three days, nor to any other place than that in which the two Houses shall be sitting.

Rights of Members

Section 6 The Senators and Representatives shall receive a Compensation for their Services, to be

[5]Changed by the 20th Amendment

ascertained by Law, and paid out of the Treasury of the United States. They shall in all Cases, except Treason, Felony, and Breach of Peace, be privileged from Arrest during their Attendance at the Session of their respective Houses, and in going to and returning from the same; and for any Speech or Debate in either House, they shall not be questioned in any other Place.

No Senator or Representative, shall, during the time for which he was elected, be appointed to any civil Office under the authority of the United States, which shall have been created, or the Emoluments whereof shall have been encreased during such time; and no Person holding any Office under the United States, shall be a Member of either House during his Continuance in Office.

Legislative Powers: Bills and Resolutions

Section 7 All Bills for raising Revenue shall originate in the House of Representatives; but the Senate may propose or concur with Amendments as on other Bills.

Every Bill which shall have passed the House of Representatives and the Senate, shall, before it become a Law, be presented to the President of the United States; if he approve he shall sign it, but if not he shall return it, with his Objections to that House in which it shall have originated, who shall enter the Objections at large on their Journal, and proceed to reconsider it. If after such Reconsideration two thirds of that House shall agree to pass the Bill, it shall be sent, together with the Objections, to the other House, by which it shall likewise be reconsidered, and if approved by two thirds of that House, it shall become a Law. But in all such Cases the Votes of both Houses shall be determined by yeas and Nays, and the Names of the Persons voting for and against the Bill shall be entered on the Journal of each House respectively. If any Bill shall not be returned by the President within ten Days (Sundays excepted) after it shall have been presented to him, the Same shall be a Law, in like Manner as if he had signed it, unless the Congress by their Adjournment prevent its Return, in which Case it shall not be a Law.

Every Order, Resolution, or Vote to which the Concurrence of the Senate and House of Representatives may be necessary (except on a question of Adjournment) shall be presented to the President of the United States; and before the Same shall take Effect, shall be approved by him, or being disapproved by him, shall be repassed by two thirds of the Senate and House of Representatives, according to the Rules and Limitations prescribed in the Case of a Bill.

Powers of Congress

Section 8 The Congress shall have Power To lay and collect Taxes, Duties, Imposts and Excise, to pay the Debts and provide for the common Defence and general Welfare of the United States; but all Duties, Imposts, and Excises shall be uniform throughout the United States;

To borrow Money on the Credit of the United States;

To regulate Commerce with foreign Nations, and among the several States, and with the Indian Tribes;

To establish an uniform Rule of Naturalization, and uniform Laws on the subject of Bankruptcies throughout the United States;

To coin Money, regulate the Value thereof, and of foreign Coin, and fix the Standard of Weights and Measures;

To provide for the Punishment of counterfeiting the Securities and current Coin of the United States;

To establish Post Offices and post Roads;

To promote the Progress of Science and useful Arts, by securing for limited Times to Authors and Inventors the exclusive Right to their respective Writings and Discoveries,

To constitute Tribunals inferior to the supreme Court,

To define and punish Piracies and Felonies committed on the high Seas, and Offences against the Law of Nations;

To declare War, grant Letters of Marque and Reprisal, and make Rules concerning Captures on Land and Water;

To raise and support Armies, but no Appropriation of Money to that Use shall be for a longer Term than two Years;

To provide and maintain a Navy;

To make Rules for the Government and Regulation of the land and naval Forces;

To provide for calling for the Militia to execute the Laws of the Union, suppress Insurrections and repel Invasions;

To provide for organizing, arming, and disciplining, the Militia, and for governing such Part of them as may be employed in the Service of the United States, reserving to the States respectively, the Appointment of the Officers, and the Authority of training the Militia according to the discipline prescribed by Congress;

To exercise exclusive Legislation in all Cases whatsoever, over such District (not exceeding ten Miles square) as may, by Cession of particular States, and the Acceptance of Congress, become the Seat of Government of the United States, and to exercise like Authority over all Places purchased by the Consent of the Legislature of the State in which the Same shall be, for the Erection of Forts, Magazines, Arsenals, dock-Yards, and other needful Buildings;—And

To make all Laws which shall be necessary and proper for carrying into Execution the foregoing Powers, and all other Powers vested by this Constitution in the Government of the United States, or in any Department or Officer thereof.

Powers Denied to Congress

Section 9 The Migration of Importation of such Persons as any of the States now existing shall think proper to admit, shall not be prohibited by the Congress prior to the Year one thousand eight hundred and eight, but a Tax or Duty may be imposed on such Importation, not exceeding ten dollars for each Person.

The privilege of the Writ of Habeas Corpus shall not be suspended, unless when in Cases of Rebellion or Invasion the public Safety may require it.

No Bill of Attainder or ex post facto Laws shall be passed.

No Capitation, or other direct, Tax shall be laid, unless in Proportion to the Census or Enumeration herein before directed to be taken.[6]

No Tax or Duty shall be laid on Articles exported from any State.

No Preference shall be given by any Regulation of Commerce or Revenue to the Ports of one State over those of another; nor shall Vessels bound to, or from, one State, be obliged to enter, clear, or pay Duties in another.

No Money shall be drawn from the Treasury, but in Consequence of Appropriations made by Law; and a regular Statement and Account of the Receipts and Expenditures of all public Money shall be published from time to time.

No Title of Nobility shall be granted by the United States; And no Person holding any Office of Profit or Trust under them, shall, without the Consent of the Congress, accept of any present, Emolument Office, or Title, of any kind whatever, from any King, Prince, or foreign State.

[6]Modified by the 16th Amendment

Powers Denied to the States

Section 10 No State shall enter into any Treaty, Alliance, or Confederation; grant Letters of Marque and Reprisal; coin Money; emit Bills of Credit; make any Thing but gold and silver Coin a Tender in Payment of Debts; pass any Bill of Attainder, ex post facto Law, or Law impairing the Obligation of Contracts, or grant any Title of Nobility.

No State shall, without the Consent of Congress, lay any Imposts or Duties on Imports or Exports, except what may be absolutely necessary for executing its inspection Laws; and the net Produce of all Duties and Imposts, laid by any State on Imports or Exports, shall be for the Use of the Treasury of the United States; and all such Laws shall be subject to the Revision and Controul of the Congress.

No State shall, without the Consent of Congress, lay any Duty of Tonnage, keep Troops, or Ships of War in time of Peace, enter into any Agreement or Compact with another State, or with a foreign Power, or engage in War, unless actually invaded, or in such imminent Danger as will not admit of Delay.

ARTICLE II—THE EXECUTIVE ARTICLE

Nature and Scope of Presidential Power

Section 1 The executive Power shall be vested in a President of the United States of America. He shall hold his Office during the Term of four Years and, together with the Vice President, chosen for the same Term, be elected as follows

Each state shall appoint, in such Manner as the Legislature thereof may direct, a Number of Electors, equal to the whole Number of Senators and Representatives to which the State may be entitled in the Congress: but no Senator or Representative, or Person holding an Office of Trust or Profit under the United States, shall be appointed an Elector.

The Electors shall meet in their respective States, and vote by Ballot for two Persons, of whom one at least shall not be an Inhabitant of the same State with themselves. And they shall make a List of all the Persons voted for, and of the Number of Votes for each; which List they shall sign and certify, and transmit sealed to the Seat of the Government of the United States, directed to the President of the Senate. The President of the Senate shall, in the Presence of the Senate and House of Representatives, open all Certificates, and the Votes shall then be counted. The

Person having the greatest Number of Votes shall be the President, if such Number be a Majority of the whole Number of Electors appointed; and if there be more than one who have such a Majority, and have an equal Number of Votes, then the House of Representatives shall immediately chuse by Ballot one of them for President; and if no person have a Majority, then from the five highest on the List the said House shall in like Manner chuse the President. But in chusing the President, the Votes shall be taken by States, the Representation from each State having one Vote; A quorum for this Purpose shall consist of a Member or Members from two thirds of the States, and a Majority of all the States shall be necessary to a Choice. In every Case, after the Choice of the President, the person having the greatest Number of Votes of the Electors shall be the Vice President. But if there should remain two or more who have equal Vote, the Senate shall chuse from them by Ballot the Vice President.[7]

The Congress may determine the Time of chusing the Electors, and the Day on which they shall give their Votes; which Day shall be the same throughout the United States.

No Person except a natural born Citizen, or a Citizen of the United States, at the time of the Adoption of the Constitution, shall be eligible to the Office of President; neither shall any Person be eligible to that Office who shall not have attained to the Age of thirty five Years, and been fourteen Years a Resident of the United States.

In Case of the Removal of the President from Office, or of his Death, Resignation, or Inability to discharge the Powers and Duties of the said Office, the same shall devolve on the Vice President, and the Congress may by Law provide for the Case of Removal, Death, Resignation, or Inability, both of the President and Vice President, declaring what Officer shall then act as President, and such Officer shall act accordingly, until the Disability be removed, or a President shall be elected.[8]

The President shall, at stated Times, receive for his Services, a Compensation, which shall neither be encreased nor diminished during the Period of which he shall have been elected, and he shall not receive within that Period any other Emolument from the United States, or any of them.

Before he enter on the Execution of his Office, he shall take the following Oath or Affirmation:—"I do solemnly swear (or affirm) that I will faithfully execute the Office of President of the United States, and will to the best of my Ability, preserve, protect and defend the Constitution of the United States."

Powers and Duties of the President

Section 2 The President shall be the Commander in Chief of the Army and Navy of the United States, and of the Militia of the several States, when called into the actual Service of the United States, he may require the Opinion, in writing, of the principal Officer in each of the executive Departments, upon any Subject relating to the Duties of their respective Offices, and he shall have the Power to grant Reprieves and Pardons for Offences against the United States, except in Cases of Impeachment.

He shall have Power, by and with the Advice and Consent of the Senate to make Treaties, provided two thirds of the Senators present concur; and he shall nominate, and by and with Advice and Consent of the Senate, shall appoint Ambassadors, other public Ministers and Consuls, Judges of the supreme Court, and all other Officers of the United States whose Appointments are not herein otherwise provided for, and which shall be established by Law: but the Congress may by Law vest the Appointment of such inferior Officers, as they think proper, in the President alone, in the Courts of Law, or in the Heads of Departments.

The President shall have Power to fill up all Vacancies that may happen during the Recess of the Senate, by granting Commissions which shall expire at the End of their next Session.

Section 3 He shall from time to time give to the Congress Information of the State of the Union, and recommend to their Consideration such Measures as he shall judge necessary and expedient; he may, on extraordinary Occasions, convene both Houses, or either of them, and in Case of Disagreement between them, with Respect to the Time of Adjournment, he may adjourn them to such Time as he shall think proper; he shall receive Ambassadors and other public Ministers; he shall take Care that the Laws be faithfully executed, and shall Commission all the Officers of the United States.

Section 4 The President, Vice President and all civil Officers of the United States, shall be removed from Office on Impeachment for, and Conviction of, Treason, Bribery, or other High Crimes and Misdemeanors,

[7]Changed by the 12th and 20th Amendments
[8]Modified by the 25th Amendment

ARTICLE III—THE JUDICIAL ARTICLE

Judicial Power, Courts, Judges

Section 1 The judicial Power of the United States, shall be vested in one supreme Court, and in such inferior Courts as the Congress may from time to time ordain and establish. The Judges, both of the supreme and inferior Courts shall hold their Offices during good Behaviour, and shall, at stated Times, receive for their Services, a Compensation, which shall not be diminished during their Continuance in Office.

Jurisdiction

Section 2 The judicial Power shall extend to all Cases, in Law and Equity, arising under this Constitution, the Laws of the United States, and Treaties made, or which shall be made, under their Authority;—to all Cases affecting Ambassadors, other public Ministers and Consuls;—to all Cases of admiralty and maritime Jurisdiction;—to Controversies to which the United States shall be a Party;—to Controversies between two or more States; *between a State and Citizens of another State;*[9]—between Citizens of different States;—between Citizens of the same State claiming Lands under Grants of different States, and between a State, or the Citizens thereof, and foreign States, Citizens, or Subjects.

In all Cases affecting Ambassadors, other public Ministers and Consuls, and those in which a State shall be Party, the supreme Court shall have original Jurisdiction. In all the other Cases before mentioned, the supreme Court shall have appellate Jurisdiction, both as to Law and Fact, with such Exceptions, and under such Regulations as Congress shall make.

The Trial of all Crimes, except in Cases of Impeachment, shall be by Jury; and such Trial shall be held in the State where the said Crimes shall have been committed; but when not committed within any State, the Trial shall be at such Place or Places as the Congress may by Law have directed.

Treason

Section 3 Treason against the United States, shall consist only in levying War against them, or in adhering to their Enemies, giving them Aid and Comfort. No Person shall be convicted of Treason unless on the Testimony of two Witnesses to the same overt Act, or on Confession in open Court,

The Congress shall have Power to declare the Punishment of Treason, but no Attainder of Treason shall work Corruption of Blood, or Forfeiture except during the Life of the Person attainted.

ARTICLE IV—INTERSTATE RELATIONS

Full Faith and Credit Clause

Section 1—Full Faith and Credit shall be given in each State to the public Acts, Records, and judicial Proceedings of every other State. And the Congresss may by general Laws prescribe the Manner in which such Acts, Records, and Proceedings shall be proved, and the Effect thereof.

Privileges and Immunities; Interstate Extradition

Section 2—The Citizens of each State shall be entitled to all Privileges and Immunities of Citizens in the several States.

A person charged in any State with Treason, Felony or other Crime, who shall flee from Justice, and be found in another State, shall on Demand of the executive Authority of the State from which he fled, be delivered up to be removed to the State having jurisdiction of the Crime.

No person held to Service or Labour in one State, under the Laws thereof, escaping into another, shall, in Consequence of any Law or Regulation therein, be discharged from such Service or Labour, but shall be delivered up on Claim of the Party to whom such Service or Labour may be due.[10]

Admission of States

Section 3 New States may be admitted by the Congress into this Union; but no new State shall be formed or erected within the Jurisdiction of any other State; nor any State be formed by the Junction of two or more States, or Parts of States, without the Consent of the Legislatures of the States concerned as well as of the Congress.

The Congress shall have Power to dispose of and make all needful Rules and Regulations respecting the Territory or other Property belonging to the

---

[9]Modified by the 11th Amendment

[10]Repealed by the 13th Amendment

United States; and nothing in this Constitution shall be so construed as to Prejudice any Claims of the United States, or of any particular State.

Republican Form of Government

Section 4 The United States shall guarantee to every State in this Union a Republican Form of Government, and shall protect each of them against Invasion; and on Application of the Legislature, or of the Executive (when the Legislature cannot be convened) against domestic Violence.

ARTICLE V—THE AMENDING POWER

The Compress, whenever two thirds of both Houses shall deem it necessary, shall propose Amendments to this Constitution, or, on the Application of the Legislatures of two thirds of several States, shall call a Convention for proposing Amendments, which, in either Case, shall be valid to all Intents and Purposes, as Part of this Constitution, when ratified by the Legislatures of three fourths of the several States, or by Conventions in three fourths thereof, as the one or the other Mode of Ratification may be proposed by the Congress; Provided that no Amendment which may be made prior to the Year One thousand eight hundred and eight shall in any Manner affect the first and fourth Clauses in the Ninth Section of the first Article; and that no State, without its Consent, shall be deprived of its equal Suffrage in the Senate.

ARTICLE VI—THE SUPREMACY ACT

All Debts contracted and Engagements entered into, before the Adoption of this Constitution, shall be as valid against the United States under the Constitution, as under the Confederation.

This Constitution, and the Laws of the United States which shall be made in Pursuance thereof; and all Treaties made, or which shall be made, under the Authority of the United States, shall be the supreme Law of the Land; and the Judges in every State shall be bound thereby, any Thing in the Constitution or Laws of any State to the Contrary notwithstanding.

The Senators and Representatives before mentioned, and the Members of the several State Legislatures, and all executive and judicial Officers, both of the United States and of the several States, shall be bound by Oath or Affirmation, to support this Constitution; but no religious Test shall ever be required as a Qualification to any Office or public Trust under the United States.

ARTICLE VII—RATIFICATION

The Ratification of the Conventions of nine States, shall be sufficient for the Establishment of this Constitution between the States so ratifying the Same.

done in Convention by the Unanimous Consent of the States present the Seventeenth Day of September in the Year of our Lord one thousand seven hundred and Eighty seven and of the Independence of the United States of America the Twelfth. *In Witness whereof We have hereunto subscribed our Names.*

THE BILL OF RIGHTS

[The first ten amendments were ratified on December 15, 1791, and form what is known as the "Bill of Rights"].

AMENDMENT 1—RELIGION, SPEECH, ASSEMBLY, AND POLITICS

Congress shall make no law respecting an establishment of religion, or prohibiting the free exercise thereof; or abridging the freedom of speech, or of the press; or the right of the people peaceably to assemble, and to petition the Government for a redress of grievances.

AMENDMENT 2—MILITIA AND THE RIGHT TO BEAR ARMS

A well regulated Militia, being necessary to the security of a free State, the right of the people to keep and bear Arms, shall not be infringed.

AMENDMENT 3—QUARTERING OF SOLDIERS

No Soldier shall, in time of peace be quartered in any house, without the consent of the Owner, nor in time of war, but in manner to be prescribed by law.

AMENDMENT 4—SEARCHES AND SEIZURES

The right of the people to be secure in their persons, houses, papers, and effects, against unreasonable searches and seizures, shall not be violated, and no Warrants shall issue, but upon probable cause, supported by Oath or affirmation, and particularly describing the place to be searched, and the persons or things to be seized.

AMENDMENT 5—GRAND JURIES, SELF-INCRIMINATION, DOUBLE JEOPARDY, DUE PROCESS, AND EMINENT DOMAIN

No person shall be held to answer for a capital, or otherwise infamous crime, unless on a presentment or indictment of a Grand jury, except in cases arising in the land or naval forces, or in the Militia, when in actual service in time of War or public danger; nor shall any person be subject for the same offence to be twice put in jeopardy of life and limb; nor shall be compelled in any criminal case to be a witness against himself, nor be deprived of life, liberty, or property, without due process of law; nor shall private property be taken for public use, without just compensation.

AMENDMENT 6—CRIMINAL COURT PROCEDURES

In all criminal prosecutions, the accused shall enjoy the right to a speedy and public trial, by an impartial jury of the State and district wherein the crime shall have been committed, which district shall have been previously ascertained by law, and to be informed of the nature and cause of the accusation; to be confronted with the witnesses against him; to have compulsory process for obtaining Witnesses in his favor, and to have the Assistance of Counsel for his defence.

AMENDMENT 7—TRIAL BY JURY IN COMMON LAW CASES

In Suits at common law, where the value in controversy shall exceed twenty dollars, the right of trial by jury shall be preserved, and no fact tried by a jury shall be otherwise re-examined in any Court of the United States, than according to the rules of the common law.

AMENDMENT 8—BAIL, CRUEL AND UNUSUAL PUNISHMENT

Excessive bail shall not be required, nor excessive fines imposed, nor cruel and unusual punishment inflicted.

AMENDMENT 9—RIGHTS RETAINED BY THE PEOPLE

The enumeration in the Constitution, of certain rights, shall not be construed to deny or disparage others retained by the people.

AMENDMENT 10—RESERVED POWERS OF THE STATES

The powers not delegated to the United States by the Constitution, nor prohibited by it to the States, are reserved to the States respectively, or to the people.

PRE-CIVIL WAR AMENDMENTS

AMENDMENT 11—SUITS AGAINST THE STATES

[Ratified February 7, 1795]

The Judicial power of the United States shall not be construed to extend to any suit in law or equity, commenced or prosecuted against one of the United States by Citizens of another State, or by Citizens or Subjects of any Foreign State.

AMENDMENT 12—ELECTION OF THE PRESIDENT

[Ratified July 27, 1804]

The Electors shall meet in their respective states, and vote by ballot for President and Vice President, one of whom, at least, shall not be an inhabitant of the same state with themselves; they shall name in their ballots the person voted for as President, and in distinct ballots the person voted for as Vice President, and they shall make distinct lists of all persons voted for as President, and of all persons voted for as Vice President, and of the number of votes for each, which lists they shall sign and certify, and transmit sealed to the seat of the government of the United States, directed to the President of the Senate;—The President of the Senate shall, in presence of the Senate and House of Representatives, open all the certificates and the votes shall then be counted;—The person having the greatest number of votes for President, shall be the President, if such number be a majority of the whole number of Electors appointed; and if no person have such majority, then from the persons having the highest numbers notexceeding three on the list of those voted for as President, the House of Representatives shall choose immediately, by ballot, the President. But in choosing the President, the votes shall be taken by states, the representation from each state having one vote; a quorum for this purpose shall consist of a member or members from two-thirds of the states, and a majority of all states shall be necessary to a choice. And if the House of Representatives shall not choose a President whenever the right of choice shall devolve upon them, *before the fourth day of March next following,* then the Vice President shall act as President, as in the case of the death or other constitutional disability of the President.[11] The person having the greatest number of votes as Vice President, shall be the Vice President, if such a number be a majority of the whole numbers of Electors appointed, and if no person have a majority, then from the two highest numbers on the list, the Senate shall choose the Vice President; a quorum for the purpose shall consist of two-thirds of the whole number of Senators, and a majority of the whole number shall be necessary to a choice. But no person constitutionally ineligible to the office of President shall be eligible to that of Vice President of the United States.

CIVIL WAR AMENDMENTS

AMENDMENT 13—PROHIBITION OF SLAVERY

[Ratified December 6, 1865]

Section 1 Neither slavery nor involuntary servitude, except as a punishment for crime whereof the party shall have been duly convicted, shall exist within the United States, or any place subject to their jurisdiction.

Section 2—Congress shall have power to enforce this article by appropriate legislation.

AMENDMENT 14—CITIZENSHIP, DUE PROCESS, AND EQUAL PROTECTION OF THE LAWS

[Ratified July 9, 1868]

Section 1 All persons born or naturalized in the United States, and subject to the jurisdiction thereof, are citizens of the United States and of the State wherein they reside. No State shall make or enforce any law which shall abridge the privileges or immunities of citizens of the United States; nor shall any State deprive any person of life, liberty, or property, without due process of law; nor deny to any person within its jurisdiction the equal protection of the laws.

Section 2 Representatives shall be apportioned among the several States according to their respective numbers, counting the whole number of persons in each State, excluding Indians not taxed. But when the right to vote at any election for the choice of electors for President and Vice President of the United States, Representatives in Congress, the Executive and Judicial officers of a State, or the members of the Legislature thereof, is denied to any of the male inhabitants of such State, being twenty-one[12] years of age, and citizens of the United States, or in any way abridged, except for participation in rebellion, or other crime, the basis of representation therein shall be reduced in the proportion which the number of such male citizens shall bear to the whole number of male citizens twenty-one years of age in such State.

Section 3—No person shall be a Senator or Representative of Congress, or elector of President or Vice President, or hold any office, civil or military, under the United States, or under any State, who, having previously taken an oath, as a member of Congress, or as an officer of the United States, or as a member of any State legislature, or as an executive or judicial officer of any State, to support the Constitution of the United States, shall have engaged in insurrection or rebellion against the same, or given aid or comfort to the enemies thereof. But Congress may by a vote of two-thirds of each House, remove such disability.

Section 4—The validity of the public debt of the United States, authorized by law, including debts incurred for payment of pensions and bounties for services in suppressing insurrection or rebellion, shall not be questioned. But neither the United States nor any State shall assume or pay any debt or obligation incurred in aid of insurrection or rebellion against the United States, or any claim for the loss or emancipation of any slave; but all such debts, obligations and claims shall be held illegal and void.

Section 5—The Congress shall have power to enforce, by appropriate legislation, the provisions of this article.

---

[11]Changed by the 20th Amendment

[12]Changed by the 26th Amendment

AMENDMENT 15—THE RIGHT TO VOTE

[Ratified February 3, 1870]

Section 1—The right of citizens of the United States to vote shall not be denied or abridged by the United States or by any State on account of race, color, or previous condition of servitude.

Section 2—The Congress shall have power to enforce this article by appropriate legislation.

AMENDMENT 16—INCOME TAXES

[Ratified February 3, 1913]

The Congress shall have power to lay and collect taxes on incomes, from whatever source derived, without apportionment among the several States, and without regard to any census or enumeration.

AMENDMENT 17—DIRECT ELECTION OF SENATORS

[Ratified April 8, 1913]

The Senate of the United States shall be composed of two Senators from each State, elected by the people thereof, for six years; and each Senator shall have one vote. The electors in each State shall have the qualifications requisite for electors of the most numerous branch of the Senate legislatures.

When vacancies happen in the representation of any State in the Senate, the executive authority of such State shall issue writs of election to fill such vacancies: *Provided*, That the Legislature of any State may empower the executive thereof to make temporary appointment until the people fill the vacancies by election as the legislature may direct.

This amendment shall not be so construed as to affect the election or term of any Senator chosen before it becomes valid as part of the Constitution.

AMENDMENT 18—PROHIBITION

[Ratified January 16, 1919; Repealed December 5, 1933 by Amendment 21]

Section 1 After one year from the ratification of this article the manufacture, sale, or transportation of intoxicating liquors within, the importation thereof into, or the exportation thereof from the United States and all territory subject to the jurisdiction thereof for beverage purposes is hereby prohibited.

Section 2 The Congress and the several states shall have concurrent power to enforce this article by appropriate legislation.

Section 3 This article shall be inoperative unless it shall have been ratified as an amendment to the Constitution by the legislatures of several states, as provided in the Constitution, within seven years from the date of the submission hereof to the States by the Congress. [13]

AMENDMENT 19—FOR WOMEN'S SUFFRAGE

[Ratified August 18, 1920]

The right of the citizens of the United States to vote shall not be denied or abridged by the United States or by any State on account of sex.

Congress shall have power, by appropriate legislation, to enforce the provision of this article.

AMENDMENT 20—THE LAME DUCK AMENDMENT

[Ratified January 23, 1933]

Section 1 The terms of the President and Vice-President shall end at noon on the 20th day of January, and the terms of the Senators and Representatives at noon on the 3rd day of January, of the years in which such terms would have ended if this article had not been ratified; and the terms of their successors shall then begin.

Section 2 The Congress shall assemble at least once in every year, and such meeting shall begin at noon on the 3rd day of January, unless they shall by law appoint a different day.

Section 3 If, at the time fixed for the beginning of the term of the President, the President elect shall have died, the Vice President elect shall become President. If a President shall not have been chosen before the time fixed for the beginning of his term, or if the President elect shall have failed to qualify, then the Vice President elect shall act as President until a President shall have qualified; and the Congress may by law provide for the case wherein neither a President elect nor a Vice President elect shall have qualified, declaring who shall then act as President, or the manner in which one who is to act

[13]Repealed by the 21st Amendment

shall be selected, and such person shall act accordingly until a President or Vice President shall have qualified.

Section 4 The Congress may by law provide for the case of the death of any of the persons from whom the House of Representatives may choose a President whenever the right of choice shall have developed upon them and for the case of the death of any of the persons from whom the Senate may choose a Vice President whenever the right of choice shall have devolved upon them.

Section 5 Sections 1 and 2 shall take effect on the 15th day of October following the ratification of this article.

Section 6 This article shall be inoperative unless it shall have been ratified as an amendment to the Constitution by the legislatures of three-fourths of the several States within seven years from the date of its submission.

AMENDMENT 21—REPEAL OF PROHIBITION

[Ratified December 5, 1933]

Section 1 The eighteenth article of amendment to the Constitution of the United Sates is hereby repealed.

Section 2 The transportation or importation into any State, Territory, or Possession of the United States for delivery or use therein of intoxicating liquors, in violation of the laws thereof, is hereby prohibited.

Section 3 This article shall be inoperative unless it shall have been ratified as an amendment to the Constitution by conventions in the several States, as provided in the Constitution, within seven years from the date of the submission hereof to the States by the Congress.

AMENDMENT 22—NUMBER OF PRESIDENTIAL TERMS

[Ratified February 27, 1951]

Section 1 No person shall be elected to the office of the President more than twice, and no person who has held the office of President, or acted as President, for more than two years of a term to which some other person was elected President shall be elected to the Office of the President more than once. But this Article shall not apply to any person holding the office of President when this article was proposed by the Congress, and shall not prevent any person who may be holding the office of President, or acting as President, during the term within which this Article becomes operative from holding the office of President or acting as President during the remainder of such term.

Section 2 This Article shall be inoperative unless it shall have been ratified as an amendment to the Constitution by the legislatures of three-fourths of the several states within seven years from the date of its submission to the States by the Congress.

AMENDMENT 23—PRESIDENTIAL ELECTORS FOR THE DISTRICT OF COLUMBIA

[Ratified March 29, 1961]

Section 1 The District constituting the seat of Government of the United States shall appoint in such manner as the Congress may direct.

A number of electors of President and Vice President equal to the whole number of Senators and Representatives in Congress to which the District would be entitled if it were a State, but in no event more than the least populous State; they shall be in addition to those appointed by the States, but they shall be considered, for the purposes of the election of President and Vice President, to be electors appointed by a State; and they shall meet in the District and perform such duties as provided by the twelfth article of amendment.

Section 2 The Congress shall have power to enforce this article by appropriate legislation.

AMENDMENT 24—THE ANTI-POLL TAX AMENDMENT

[Ratified January 23, 1964]

Section 1 The right of citizens of the United States to vote in any primary or other election for President or Vice President, for electors for President or Vice President, or for Senator or Representative in Congress, shall not be denied or abridged by the United States or any State by reason of failure to pay any poll tax or other tax.

Section 2 The Congress shall have power to enforce this article by appropriate legislation.

AMENDMENT 25—PRESIDENTIAL DISABILITY, VICE PRESIDENTIAL VACANCIES

[Ratified February 10, 1967]

Section 1 In case of the removal of the President from office or his death or resignation, the Vice President shall become President.

Section 2 Whenever there is a vacancy in the office of the Vice President, the President shall nominate a Vice President who shall take the office upon confirmation by a majority vote of both houses of Congress.

Section 3 Whenever the President transmits to the President pro tempore of the Senate and the Speaker of the House of Representatives has written declaration that he is unable to discharge the powers and duties of his office, and until he transmits to them a written declaration to the contrary, such powers and duties shall be discharged by the Vice President as Acting President.

Section 4 Whenever the Vice President and a majority of either the principal officers of the executive departments, or of such other body as Congress may by law provide, transmit to the President pro tempore of the Senate and the Speaker of the House of Representatives their written declaration that the President is unable to discharge the powers and duties of his office, the Vice President shall immediately assume the powers and duties of the office as Acting President.

Thereafter, when the President transmits to the President pro tempore of the Senate and the Speaker of the House of Representatives his written declaration that no inability exists, he shall resume the powers and duties of his office unless the Vice President and a majority of either the principle offi-cers of the executive departments, or of such other body as Congress may by law provide, transmit within four days to the President pro tempore of the Senate and the Speaker of the House of Representatives their written declaration that the President is unable to discharge the powers and duties of his office. Thereupon Congress shall decided the issue, assembling within 48 hours for that purpose if not in session. If the Congress, within 21 days after receipt of the latter written declaration, or, if Congress is not in session, within 21 days after Congress is required to assemble, determines by two-thirds vote of both houses that the President is unable to discharge the powers and duties of his office, the Vice President shall continue to discharge the same as Acting President; otherwise, the President shall resume the powers and duties of his office.

AMENDMENT 26—EIGHTEEN-YEAR-OLD VOTE

[Ratified July 1, 1971]

Section 1 The right of citizens of the United States, who are eighteen years of age, or older, to vote shall not be denied or abridged by the United States or by any State on account of age.

Section 2 The Congress shall have power to enforce this article by appropriate legislation.

AMENDMENT 27—CONGRESSIONAL SALARIES

[Ratified May 7, 1992]

No law, varying the compensation for the services of the Senators and Representatives, shall take effect, until an election of Representative shall have intervened.

TABLE OF CASES[*]

A Book Named "John Cleland's Memoirs of a Woman of Pleasure" v. Attorney General of Massachusetts, 383 U.S. 413 (1966), 195, 213, 215, 218

Abington School District v. Schempp, 374 U.S. 203 (1963), 169, 175, **177–79**, 182

Abrams v. United States, 250 U.S. 616 (1919), 191, 199, 201

Adams v. Williams, 407 U.S. 143 (1972), 254

Adamson v. California, 332 U.S. 46 (1947), 234, 240, 242, 246, **247–49**, 290

Adkins v. Children's Hospital of the District of Columbia, 261 U.S. 525 (1923), 29, 40, 43–45, 47, **53–56**

Adkins v. Lyons, 261 U.S. 525 (1923), 53, 56

Akron, City of v. Akron Center for Reproductive Health, Inc., 462 U.S. 416 (1983), 342

Allen v. Wright, 468 U.S. 737 (1984), 16, 152, 155

Allen-Bradley Local v. Wisconsin Employment Relations Board, 315 U.S. 740 (1942), 225

Allgeyer v. Louisiana, 165 U.S. 578 (1897), 39–40

Allied Structural Steel Co. v. Spannaus, 438 U.S. 234 (1978), 38

American Communications Assn. v. Douds, 339 U.S. 382 (1950), 229

Aptheker v. Secretary of State, 378 U.S. 500 (1964), 328

Argersinger v. Hamlin, 407 U.S. 25 (1972), 237, 265–68

Atlantic Coast Line Railroad Co. v. Georgia, 234 U.S. 280 (1914), 119

Avery v. Midland County, 390 U.S. 474 (1968), 286, 322, 324

[*]Cases in boldface are summarized in text.

Bailey v. Drexel Furniture Co., 259 U.S. 20 (1922), 144, **157–59**, 161, 163

Baker v. Carr, 369 U.S. 186 (1962), 3, 68, 72, 84, 155, 286, **319–22**, 324

Baldwin v. Seelig, Inc., 294 U.S. 511 (1935), 326

Barenblatt v. United States, 360 U.S. 109 (1959), 53, 197, 228, **229–32**

Barron v. Baltimore, 7 Peters 243 (1833), 233, 244, 247–49, 281–282, **289–90**

Batson v. Kentucky, 476 U.S. 79 (1986), 276

Beauharnais v. Illinois, 343 U.S. 250 (1952), 211

Benton v. Maryland, 395 U.S. 784 (1969), 234, 242

Betts v. Brady, 316 U.S. 455 (1942), 266–68

Board of Education v. Allen, 392 U.S. 236 (1968), 155

Board of Education of Oklahoma City Public Schools v. Dowell, 59 U.S.L.W. 4061 (1991), 283, 306

Bowers v. Hardwick, 478 U.S. 186 (1986), 287, 334–35, 338, **343–45**, 349

Bowsher v. Synar, 478 U.S. 714 (1986), 65, **91–94**, 97

Boyd v. United States, 116 U.S. 616 (1886), 258–59

Bradwell v. Illinois, 16 Wallace 130 (1873), 281, 284, 297

Bram v. United States, 168 U.S. 532 (1897), 264

Brandenburg v. Ohio, 395 U.S. 444 (1969), 201, 220, 223

Braunfeld v. Brown, 366 U.S. 599 (1961), 185–87

Bridges v. California, 314 U.S. 252 (1941), 211

Bronson v. Kinzie, 1 Howard 311 (1843), 43

Brown v. Board of Education of Topeka, 347 U.S. 483 (1954), 5, 179, 282–83, 301, **302–3**, 305–6, 309

Brown v. Board of Education of Topeka, 349 U.S. 294 (1955), 302–3, 306

Buchanan v. Warley, 245 U.S. 60 (1917), 304

Buckley v. Valeo, 424 U.S. 1 (1976), 64, **87–91**, 93–94, 97, 100, 229

Bunting v. Oregon, 243 U.S. 426 (1917), 45, 56, 130–31

Burroughs v. United States, 290 U.S. 534 (1934), 91

Cable News Network v. Noriega, 111 S. Ct. 451 (1990), 194

Calder v. Bull, 3 Dallas 386 (1798), 20, 28, **32–33**

California Retail Liquor Dealers Assn. v. Midcal Aluminum, Inc., 445 U.S. 97 (1980), 165

Camara v. Municipal Court of San Francisco, 387 U.S. 523 (1967), 257, 350

Caminetti v. United States, 242 U.S. 470 (1917), 326

Carey v. Population Services International, 431 U.S. 678 (1977), 345

Carter v. Carter Coal Company, 298 U.S. 238 (1936), 82, 116, 127–28, 163

Castaneda v. Partida, 430 U.S. 482 (1977), 276

Chambers v. Florida, 309 U.S. 227 (1940), 236

Champion v. Ames, 188 U.S. 321 (1903), 105, 109, **121–23**, 126, 131, 157

Chandler v. Florida, 449 U.S. 560 (1981), 194

Chaplinsky v. New Hampshire, 315 U.S. 568 (1942), 192, 199

Charles River Bridge v. Warren Bridge, 11 Peters 420 (1837), 20, 43

Chisholm v. Georgia, 2 Dallas 419 (1793), 5, 6, **16–18,** 25, 27

City of Akron v. Akron Center for Reproductive Health, Inc., 462 U.S. 416 (1983), **342**

City of Cleburne, Texas v. Cleburne Living Center, 473 U.S. 432 (1985), 329

City of Mobile, Alabama v. Bolden, 446 U.S. 55 (1980), 58

City of New York v. Miln, 11 Peters 102 (1837), 326

City of Renton v. Playtime Theatres, Inc., 475 U.S. 41 (1986), 186

City of Richmond, Virginia v. J. A. Croson Co., 488 U.S. 469 (1989), 284, **309–12**

City of Richmond, Virginia v. United States, 422 U.S. 358 (1975), 58

Civil Rights Cases, 109 U.S. 3 (1883), 133–35, 282–83, **297–300**

Clark v. Roemer, 59 U.S.L.W. 4583 (1991), 322

Cleburne, Texas, City of, v. Cleburne Living Center, 473 U.S. 432 (1985), 329

Cohen v. California, 403 U.S. 15 (1971), 192, 199

Cohens v. Virginia, 6 Wheaton 264 (1821), 6, 18, **23–25**

Coker v. Georgia, 433 U.S. 584 (1977), 279

Colegrove v. Green, 328 U.S. 549 (1946), 68, 286, 320, 322, 324

Collector v. Day, 11 Wallace 113 (1871), 142–43, **146–47,** 150

Committee for Public Education and Religious Liberty v. Nyquist, 413 U.S. 756 (1973), **173**

Cooley v. Board of Wardens of the Port of Philadelphia, 12 Howard 299 (1851), 103–4,
    109, **110-12,** 119

Cooper v. Aaron, 358 U.S. 1 (1958), 10

Corfield v. Coryell, 6 Fed. Cases 3230 (1823), 281, 294, 297

Craig v. Boren, 429 U.S. 190 (1976), 285, 313, **314–16,** 329

Cruzan by Cruzan v. Director, Missouri Dept. of Health, 497 U.S. 261 (1990), 288,
    345–49

Curtis Publishing Co. v. Butts, 388 U.S. 130 (1967), 211

DeFunis v. Odegaard, 416 U.S. 312 (1974), 4, 283

DeGeofroy v. Riggs, 133 U.S. 258 (1890), 51

Dennis v. United States, 341 U.S. 494 (1951), 196–97, 199–201, **220–23,** 232

Dobbins v. Erie County, 16 Peters 435 (1842), 142, 146

Dombrowski v. Eastland, 387 U.S. 82 (1967), 72

Douglas v. California, 372 U.S. 353 (1963), 332

Dred Scott v. Sandford, 19 Howard 393 (1857), 3, 9–10, 281, **290–94,** 301

Duncan v. Louisiana, 391 U.S. 145 (1968), 234, 240, **242–44**

Eastland v. United States Servicemen's Fund, 421 U.S. 491 (1975), 228

Edwards v. Aguillard, 482 U.S. 578 (1987), 169, **180–82**

Edwards v. California, 314 U.S. 160 (1941), 286, **325–26,** 328

Edwards v. Kearzey, 6 Otto 595 (1877), 43

E.E.O.C. v. Wyoming, 460 U.S. 226 (1983), 138, 140

Eisenstadt v. Baird, 405 U.S. 438 (1972), 287, 335, 338, 342, 345

Elkins v. United States, 364 U.S. 206 (1960), 259

Employment Division, Department of Human Resources of Oregon v. Smith, 494 U.S. 872 (1990), 171

Endo, Ex parte, 323 U.S. 283 (1944), 14, 77

Engel v. Vitale, 370 U.S. 421 (1962), 169, **175–77**, 179

Enmund v. Florida, 458 U.S. 782 (1982), 271, 273

Epperson v. Arkansas, 393 U.S. 97 (1968), 169, 182

Escobedo v. Illinois, 378 U.S. 478 (1964), 236, 262, 264

Estes v. Texas, 381 U.S. 532 (1965), 194

Everson v. Board of Education, 330 U.S. 1 (1947), 168, 173, 175, 179

Ex parte (See name of party)

Fairfax Devisee v. Hunter's Lessee, 7 Cranch 603 (1813), 21–22

Federal Communication Commission v. Pacifica Foundation, 438 U.S. 726 (1978), 218

Feiner v. New York 340 U.S. 315 (1951), 192

Firefighters v. Cleveland, 478 U.S. 501 (1986), 319

Flast v. Cohen, 392 U.S. 83 (1968), 15–16, 143–44, **152–55**

Fletcher v. Peck, 6 Cranch 87 (1810), 6, **19–20**, 23, 25, 28, 33, 38

Francis v. Resweber, 329 U.S. 459 (1947), 269

Frontiero v. Richardson, 411 U.S. 677 (1973), 284, **312–14**, 316

Frothingham v. Mellon, 262 U.S. 447 (1923), 4, 14–16, 143, **150–52**, 153–55

Fry v. United States, 421 U.S. 542 (1975), 140

Fullilove v. Klutznick, 448 U.S. 448 (1980), 165, 284, 300, 309–12

Furman v. Georgia, 408 U.S. 238 (1972), 238, 269–73, 275–76, 279

Gannett v. De Pasquale, 443 U.S. 368 (1979), 194

Garcia v. San Antonio Mass Transit Authority, 469 U.S. 528 (1985), 107, 116, 137, **138–40**

General Electric Co. v. Gilbert, 429 U.S. 125 (1976), 285

Gertz v. Robert Welch, Inc., 418 U.S. 323 (1974), 194, 211

Gibbons v. Ogden, 9 Wheaton 1 (1824), 102–4, **107–10**, 111–12, 119–23, 126, 128, 132, 135–38, 146

Gibson v. Florida Legislative Investigation Committee, 372 U.S. 539 (1963), 232

Gideon v. Wainwright, 372 U.S. 335 (1963), 237, 259, 265, **266–68**

Ginsberg v. New York, 390 U.S. 629 (1968), 215

Ginzburg v. United States, 383 U.S. 463 (1966), 218

Gitlow v. New York, 268 U.S. 652 (1925), 192, 196, **199–201**, 220, 223, 290

Gold Clause Cases, 294 U.S. 240 (1935), 50

Goldman v. United States, 316 U.S. 129 (1942), 252

Goldman v. Weinberger, 475 U.S. 503 (1986), 171, 187, 189

Gomillion v. Lightfoot, 364 U.S. 339 (1960), 276

Goss v. Lopez, 419 U.S. 565 (1975), 257

Gravel v. United States, 408 U.S. 606 (1972), 84

Graves v. O'Keefe, 306 U.S. 466 (1939), 147

Gray v. Sanders, 372 U.S. 368 (1963), 324

Green v. County School Board, 391 U.S. 430 (1968), 305–6

Gregg v. Georgia, 428 U.S. 153 (1976), 238, **270–71**, 272–74, 276

Griffin v. Illinois, 351 U.S. 12 (1956), 332

Griswold v. Connecticut, 381 U.S. 479 (1965), 252, 287–88, **332–35**, 338, 340, 342–45

Hadley v. Junior College District of Metropolitan Kansas City, 397 U.S. 50 (1970), 286

Hamilton v. Alabama, 368 U.S. 53 (1961), 268

Hamilton v. Regents of the University of California, 293 U.S. 245 (1934), 184, 290

Hammer v. Dagenhart, 247 U.S. 251 (1918), 35, 105–6, 110, **123–26**, 129–31, 144, 158–59

Hampton, J. W. Jr., & Co. v. United States, 276 U.S. 394 (1928), 100, 116, 145, **159–61**

Heart of Atlanta Motel, Inc. v. United States, 379 U.S. 241 (1964), 35, 106, 110, 114, 123, 128, 130–32, **133–35**, 283, 300

Helvering v. Gerhardt, 304 U.S. 405 (1938), 142, 147

Hepburn v. Griswold, 8 Wallace 603 (1870), 30, 48–50

Hill v. Florida, 325 U.S. 538 (1945), 225

Hipolite Egg Company v. United States, 220 U.S. 45 (1911), 126

Hirabayashi v. United States, 320 U.S. 81 (1943), 12, 74–77

Hobbie v. Unemployment Appeals Comm'n of Florida, 480 U.S. 136 (1987), 173

Hodgson v. Minnesota, 497 U.S. 417 (1990), 338, 343

Hoke v. United States, 227 U.S. 308 (1913), 135

Holden v. Hardy, 169 U.S. 366 (1898), 38, 40, 45, 54, 56

Holtzman v. Schlesinger, 414 U.S. 1304 (1973), 74

Home Building and Loan Ass'n v. Blaisdell, 290 U.S. 398 (1934), 29, 38, **40–43**, 80, 116

Houston, E. and W. Texas Railway Co. v. United States (The Shreveport Rate Case), 234 U.S. 342 (1914), 103, 109, **112–14**, 135

Humphrey's Executor v. United States, 295 U.S. 602 (1935), 64, 87, 94–97

Hurtado v. California, 110 U.S. 516 (1884), 234, **239–40**, 242

Hustler Mag. v. Falwell, 485 U.S. 46 (1988), 194, 211

Hutchinson v. Proxmire, 443 U.S. 111 (1979), 72

Hylton v. United States, 3 Dallas 171 (1796), 2, 10, 142–43, 148–50, 294

Illinois v. Gates, 462 U.S. 213 (1983), 262

Immigration and Naturalization Service v. Chadha, 462 U.S. 919 (1983), 65–66, 93–94, **98–100**

In re Chapman, 166 U.S. 661 (1897), 53

In re Quinlan, 70 N.J. 10, 355 A.2d 647, **cert. denied** *sub nom.* Garger v. New Jersey, 429 U.S. 922 (1976), 349

International Union, United Automobile, Aerospace & Agricultural Implement Workers of America, U.A.W. v. Johnson Controls, Inc., 111 S.Ct. 1196 (1991), 285, 314–16, **317–19**

Jacobellis v. Ohio, 378 U.S. 184 (1964), 194

Jacobson v. Massachusetts, 197 U.S. 11 (1905), 288, 349

Jenkins v. Georgia, 418 U.S. 153 (1974), 195, 215, 218

Jenness v. Fortson, 403 U.S. 431 (1971), 91

Johnson v. Transportation Agency, Santa Clara County, California, 480 U.S. 616 (1987), 285, **317–19**

Johnson v. Zerbst, 304 U.S. 458 (1938), 266, 268

Jones v. Alfred H. Mayer Co., 392 U.S. 409 (1968), 304

Jones v. Opelika, 316 U.S. 584 (1942), 184

Jurek v. Texas, 428 U.S. 262 (1976), 270–73

Kassel v. Consolidated Freightways Corp. of Delaware, 450 U.S. 662 (1981), 119

Katz v. United States, 389 U.S. 347 (1967), 235, **249–52**, 254, 257, 334–35, 344–45

Katzenbach v. McClung, 379 U.S. 294 (1964), 106, 110, 114, 123, 126, 128, 132, 135, 283

Kelley v. Johnson, 425 U.S. 238 (1976), 288

Kent v. Dulles, 357 U.S. 116 (1958), 328

Kepner v. United States, 195 U.S. 100 (1904), 242

Kidd v. Pearson, 128 U.S. 1 (1888), 121

Kilbourn v. Thompson, 13 Otto 168 (1881), 52–53, 70, 72, 226, 228

Knox v. Lee (The Legal Tender Cases), 12 Wallace 457 (1871), 30, **47–50**

Kohl v. United States, 1 Otto 367 (1876), 80

Korematsu v. United States, 323 U.S. 214 (1944), 12, 62, 74, **75–77**, 309

Legal Tender Cases, 12 Wallace 457 (1871), 30, **47–50**

Lemon v. Kurtzman, 403 U.S. 602 (1971), 168, 172–73, 180–82

License Cases, 5 Howard 504 (1847), 112

Lochner v. New York, 198 U.S. 45 (1905), 20, 29, **38–40**, 45, 47, 54–56, 105

Loving v. Virginia, 388 U.S. 1 (1967), 287–88, 344–45

Luther v. Borden, 7 Howard 1 (1849), 3, 60, 66–69, 322

Lynch v. Donnelly, 465 U.S. 668 (1984), 167, 173

McAllister v. United States, 141 U.S. 174 (1891), 87

McCardle, Ex parte, 7 Wallace 506 (1869), **12–14**, 61–62, 77

McClesky v. Kemp, 481 U.S. 279 (1987), 238, **273–76**, 279

McCollum v. Board of Education, 333 U.S. 203 (1948), 168–69, 174–75, 177

McCray v. United States, 195 U.S. 27 (1904), 35, 125–26, 144–45, **155–57**, 159, 161, 163

McCulloch v. Maryland, 4 Wheaton 316 (1819), 28, **33–35**, 48, 50, 56, 58, 120, 140, 142–44, 146–47, 156–57, 163

McDonnell Douglas Corp. v. Green, 411 U.S. 792 (1973), 319

McGrain v. Daugherty, 273 U.S. 135 (1927), 31, **52–53**, 226, 228, 232

McLaurin v. Oklahoma State Regents, 339 U.S. 637 (1950), 283, 303

Maher v. Roe, 432 U.S. 464 (1977), 342

Malinski v. New York, 324 U.S. 401 (1945), 246

Mallory v. United States, 354 U.S. 449 (1957), 264

Malloy v. Hogan, 378 U.S. 1 (1964), 234, 249, 264

Mapp v. Ohio, 367 U.S. 643 (1961), 236, **257–59**, 262

Marbury v. Madison, 1 Cranch 137 (1803), 3, 6, **7–10**, 23, 32–33, 35, 60, 69, 83–84, 86, 294

Marchetti v. United States, 390 U.S. 39 (1968), 157

Marsh v. Chambers, 463 U.S. 783 (1983), 167, 175

Martin v. Hunter's Lessee, 1 Wheaton 304 (1816), 6, **20–23**, 24–25

Maryland v. Wirtz, 392 U.S. 183 (1968), 107, 135–36, 138, 140

Massachusetts v. Laird, 400 U.S. 886 (1970), 63, 74

Massachusetts v. Mellon, 262 U.S. 447 (1923), 4, **14–16, 150–52**, 162

Massachusetts v. Sheppard, 468 U.S. 981 (1984), 262

Meek v. Pittenger, 421 U.S. 349 (1975), 168, 173

Merchant's National Bank of Little Rock v. United States, 11 Otto 1 (1880), 150

Meyer v. Nebraska, 262 U.S. 390 (1923), 189

Michael M. v. Superior Court of Sonoma County, 450 U.S. 464 (1981), 285

Michigan Dept. of Police v. Sitz, 496 U.S. 444 (1990), 254

Michigan v. Mosley, 423 U.S. 96 (1975), 264

Miller v. California, 413 U.S. 15 (1973), 195, **213–15**, 216–18

Milligan, Ex parte, 4 Wallace 2 (1866), 4, **10–12**, 14, 43, 61, 77, 82, 209

Minersville School District v. Gobitis, 310 U.S. 586 (1940), 170, 182–84

Miranda v. Arizona, 384 U.S. 436 (1966), 5, 236, 259, **262–64**

Mississippi v. Johnson, 4 Wallace 475 (1867), 61, **68–69**

Mississippi University for Women v. Hogan, 458 U.S. 718 (1982), 316

Missouri ex Rel. Gaines v. Canada, 305 U.S. 337 (1938), 283

Missouri v. Holland, 252 U.S. 416 (1920), 30–31, **50–51**

Missouri v. Jenkins, 110 S. Ct. 1651 (1990), 5

Mitchell v. United States, 369 F.2d 323 (2nd Cir. 1966), *cert. denied*, 386 U.S. 942 (1967), 63, 74

Mobile, City of, Alabama v. Bolden, 446 U.S. 55 (1980), 58

Moore v. East Cleveland, 431 U.S. 494 (1977), 244

Mora v. McNamara, 389 U.S. 934 (1967), 63, 74

Morrison v. Olson, 487 U.S. 654 (1988), 65, **94–97**

Mueller v. Allen, 463 U.S. 388 (1983), 168, **172–73**

Mugler v. Kansas, 123 U.S. 623 (1887), 40

Muller v. Oregon, 208 U.S. 412 (1908), 45, 54–56, 130–31, 284

Munn v. Illinois, 4 Otto 113 (1877), 30, **45–47**, 54, 56, 283, 299–300

Murray v. Curlett, 374 U.S. 203 (1963), 177

Murray v. Giarranto, 492 U.S. 1 (1989), 268

Muskrat v. United States, 219 U.S. 346 (1911), 4

Myers v. United States, 272 U.S. 52 (1926), 64–65, 80, **84–87**, 94–95, 97

N.A.A.C.P. v. Alabama, 357 U.S. 449 (1958), 91, 197, **228–29**, 287

N.A.A.C.P. v. Button, 371 U.S. 415 (1963), 211

National Labor Relations Board v. Jones & Laughlin Steel Corporation, 301 U.S. 1 (1937), 105–6, 114, **126–28**, 130

National League of Cities v. Usery, 426 U.S. 833 (1976), 107, 116, 130–31, **135–38**, 139–40

National Treasury Employees Union v. Von Raab, 489 U.S. 656 (1989), 246, 288, **349–50**

Near v. Minnesota, 283 U.S. 697 (1931), 193, **203–5**, 209

Nebbia v. New York, 291 U.S. 502 (1934), 47

Nebraska Press Association v. Stuart, 427 U.S. 539 (1976), 194, 205, 209

New Jersey v. T. L. O., 469 U.S. 325 (1985), 235, **254–57**, 350

New York v. Ferber, 458 U.S. 747 (1982), 213, 215

New York, City of, v. Miln, 11 Peters 102 (1837), 326

New York Times Co. v. Sullivan, 376 U.S. 254 (1964), 91, 194, **209–11**

New York Times Co. v. United States, 403 U.S. 713 (1971), 193, 205, **206–9**

Nixon v. Administrator of General Services, 433 U.S. 425 (1977), 100

Nixon v. Fitzgerald, 457 U.S. 731 (1982), 84

O'Connor v. Ortega, 480 U.S. 709 (1987), 350

Ogden v. Saunders, 12 Wheaton 213 (1827), 43

Ohio v. Akron Center for Reproductive Health, 497 U.S. 502 (1990), 338, 343

Oklahoma v. Civil Service Comm'n, 330 U.S. 127 (1947), 165

Olmstead v. United States, 277 U.S. 438 (1928), 235, 250–52

O'Neil v. Vermont, 144 U.S. 323 (1892), 269

Organization for a Better Austin v. Keefe, 402 U.S. 415 (1971), 209

Osborne v. Ohio, 495 U.S. 103 (1990), 213, 215, 218

Oyama v. California, 332 U.S. 633 (1948), 304

Pacific Insurance Co. v. Soule, 7 Wallace 433 (1869), 150

Palko v. Connecticut, 302 U.S. 319 (1937), 234, 240, **241–42**, 243–44, 246, 249

Panama Refining Co. v. Ryan and Amazon Petroleum Corp. v. Ryan, 293 U.S. 388 (1935), 81–82, 116, 163

Panhandle Oil Co. v. Mississippi, 277 U.S. 218 (1928), 147

Paris Adult Theatre I v. Slaton, 413 U.S. 49 (1973), 195, 215, **216–18**

Parker v. Davis (Legal Tender Cases), 12 Wallace 457 (1871), 30, **47–50**

Parsons v. United States, 167 U.S. 324 (1897), 87

Passenger Cases (The), 7 Howard 283 (1849), 109, 112, 135, 286, 326

Pennsylvania v. Mimms, 434 U.S. 106 (1977), 254

Pennsylvania v. Muniz, 496 U.S. 582 (1990), 266

Pennsylvania v. Nelson, 350 U.S. 497 (1956), 196, **223–25**

Penry v. Lynaugh, 492 U.S. 302 (1989), 239, 271, 273

People v. Defoe, 242 N.Y. 13, 150 N.E. 585 (1926), 236, 258–59

Pierce v. Society of the Sisters, 268 U.S. 510 (1925), 188

Planned Parenthood of Southeastern Pennsylvania v. Casey, 60 U.S.L.W. 4795 (1992), 338, 343

Plessy v. Ferguson, 163 U.S. 537 (1896), 135, 282, 297, 299, **300–301**, 302–3, 309

Plyler v. Doe, 457 U.S. 202 (1982), 332

Poe v. Ullman, 367 U.S. 497 (1961), 242

Pollock v. Farmers' Loan and Trust Co., 157 U.S. 429 (1895), 148–50

Pollock v. Farmers' Loan and Trust Co., 158 U.S. 601 (1895), 143, **147–50**

Posadas de Puerto Rico Associates v. Tourism Co. of Puerto Rico, 478 U.S. 328 (1986), 205

Powell v. Alabama, 287 U.S. 45 (1932), 237, 242, **264–66**, 267–68

Powell v. McCormack, 395 U.S. 486 (1969), 61–62, 68, **69–72**, 84

Powell v. Texas, 392 U.S. 514 (1968), 237, 269

Prince v. Massachusetts, 321 U.S. 158 (1944), 187, 189

Prize Cases, 2 Black 635 (1863), 62, **72–74**, 80, 82

Proffit v. Florida, 428 U.S. 242 (1976), 270–73

Railroad Transfer Service v. Chicago, 386 U.S. 351 (1967), 225

Rea v. United States, 350 U.S. 214 (1956), 259

Reed v. Reed, 404 U.S. 71 (1971), 284, 312–14, 316

Regents of the University of California v. Bakke, 438 U.S. 265 (1978), 284–85, 300, **306–9**, 312, 318, 319

Reid v. Covert, 354 U.S. 1 (1957), 51

Reitman v. Mulkey, 387 U.S. 369 (1967), 304

Renton, City of, v. Playtime Theatres, Inc., 475 U.S. 41 (1986), 186

Reynolds v. Sims, 377 U.S. 533 (1964), 68, 286, **322–24**, 328

Reynolds v. United States, 8 Otto 145 (1878), 170, 173, 189

Richmond, City of, Virginia v. J. A. Croson Co., 488 U.S. 469 (1989), 284, **309–12**

Richmond, City of, Virginia v. United States, 422 U.S. 358 (1975), 58

Richmond Newspapers, Inc. v. Virginia, 448 U.S. 555 (1980), 194

Roberts v. Louisiana, 428 U.S. 325 (1976), 270–73

Roberts v. United States Jaycees, 468 U.S. 609 (1984), 197, 229

Robinson v. California, 370 U.S. 660 (1962), 237, **268–69**

Rochin v. California, 342 U.S. 165 (1952), 234, **244–46**, 288, 350

Roe v. Wade, 410 U.S. 113 (1973), 287–88, 334, **335–38**, 339–42, 345, 349

Rostker v. Goldberg, 453 U.S. 57 (1981), 285, 316

Roth v. United States, 354 U.S. 476 (1957), 195, **211–13**, 215, 218

Runyon v. McCrary, 427 U.S. 160 (1976), 300, 304

San Antonio Independent School District v. Rodriguez, 411 U.S. 1 (1973), 286, **329–32**

Scales v. United States, 367 U.S. 203 (1961), 223

Schacht v. United States, 398 U.S. 58 (1970), 203

Schechter Poultry Corporation v. United States, 295 U.S. 495 (1935), 81–82, 104–5, **114–16**, 126–28, 163

Schenck v. United States, 249 U.S. 47 (1919), 191–92, 196, **198–99**, 200–201, 205, 220, 223

Schlesinger v. Ballard, 419 U.S. 498 (1975), 285

Schlesinger v. Reservists Committee to Stop the War, 418 U.S. 208 (1974), 16, 152, 155

Schmerber v. California, 384 U.S. 757 (1966), 246, 288

Scopes v. State, 154 Tenn. 105, 289 S.W. 363 (1927), 181, 182

Scott v. Illinois, 440 U.S. 367 (1979), 266

Shapiro v. Thompson, 394 U.S. 618 (1969), 286, **326–29**, 332

Sheet Metal Workers v. EEOC, 478 U.S. 421 (1986), 319

Shelley v. Kraemer, 334 U.S. 1 (1948), 134, 282, **303–4**

Sheppard v. Maxwell, 384 U.S. 333 (1961), 194

Sherbert v. Verner, 374 U.S. 398 (1963), 170–71, **184–87**, 189

Shreveport Rate Case (Houston, E. and W. Texas Railway Co. v. United States), 234 U.S. 342 (1914), 103, 109, **112–14**, 135

Shurtleff v. United States, 189 U.S. 311 (1903), 87

Shuttlesworth v. Birmingham, 394 U.S. 147 (1969), 205

Siebold, Ex Parte, 100 U.S. 371 (1880), 97

Silverman v. United States, 365 U.S. 505 (1961), 250, 252

Sinclair v. United States, 279 U.S. 263 (1929), 53, 228

Skinner v. Oklahoma, 316 U.S. 535 (1942), 287

Skinner v. Railway Labor Executives Association, 489 U.S. 602 (1989), 246, 288, 350

Slaughterhouse Cases, 16 Wallace 36 (1873), 248–49, 281–82, 290, 294–97, 299–300, **328**

Smith v. Goguen, 415 U.S. 566 (1974), 193, 203

South Carolina Highway Department v. Barnwell Brothers, Inc., 303 U.S. 177 (1938), 112, 119

South Carolina v. Katzenbach, 383 U.S. 301 (1966), 31, **56–58**, 286

South Dakota v. Dole, 483 U.S. 203 (1987), 145, **164–65**

Southern Pacific Co. v. Arizona, 325 U.S. 761 (1945), 104, 112, **116–19**

Speiser v. Randall, 357 U.S. 513 (1958), 187

Spence v. Washington, 418 U.S. 405 (1974), 193, 203

Springer v. United States, 12 Otto 586 (1881), 150

Stafford v. Wallace, 258 U.S. 495 (1922), 103, 116, 127–28

Stanford v. Kentucky, 492 U.S. 361 (1989), 239, 271, 273, **277–79**

Stanley v. Georgia, 394 U.S. 557 (1969), 213, 215–16, 218, 343, 345

Steelworkers v. Weber, 443 U.S. 193 (1979), 317–19

Steward Machine Co. v. Davis, 301 U.S. 548 (1937), 165

Stone v. Graham, 449 U.S. 39 (1980), 169, 179, 182

Stone v. Powell, 428 U.S. 465 (1976), 262

Strader v. Graham, 10 Howard 82 (1850), 292–94

Street v. New York, 394 U.S. 576 (1969), 192, 203

Stromberg v. California, 283 U.S. 359 (1931), 184

Sturges v. Crowninshield, 4 Wheaton 122 (1819), 41, 43

Swann v. Charlotte-Mecklenburg Board of Education, 402 U.S. 1 (1971), 283, 303, **304–6**

Sweatt v. Painter, 339 U.S. 629 (1950), 283, 303

Sweezy v. New Hampshire, 354 U.S. 234 (1957), 91, 232

Tenney v. Brandhove, 341 U.S. 367 (1951), 72

Terminiello v. Chicago, 337 U.S. 1 (1949), 192, 199

Terry v. Ohio, 392 U.S. 1 (1968), 235, **252–54**, 255, 257

Texas v. Johnson, 491 U.S. 397 (1989), 184, 193, **201–3**

Texas v. White, 7 Wallace 700 (1869), 18

Thompson v. Oklahoma, 487 U.S. 815 (1988), 279

Thornburg v. American College of Obstetricians and Gynecologists, 476 U.S. 747 (1986), 343, 345

Thornburg v. Gingles, 478 U.S. 30 (1986), 58

Time, Inc. v. Firestone, 424 U.S. 448 (1976), 194

Times Film Corp. v. Chicago, 365 U.S. 43 (1961), 205

Tinker v. Des Moines Independent Community School District, 393 U.S. 503 (1969), 192, 201, 203

Tison v. Arizona, 481 U.S. 137 (1987), 279

Trop v. Dulles, 356 U.S. 86 (1958), 238, 270–71, 273, 277

Truax v. Raich, 239 U.S. 33 (1915), 326

The Trustees of Dartmouth College v. Woodward, 4 Wheaton 518 (1819), 20, 28, **36–38**, 56

Twining v. New Jersey, 211 U.S. 78 (1908), 240, 242, 247–49, 290

United States v. Butler, 297 U.S. 1 (1936), 145, **161–63**, 165

United States v. Calandra, 414 U.S. 338 (1974), 262

United States v. California, 297 U.S. 175 (1936), 137

United States v. Carolene Products Co., 304 U.S. 144 (1938), 244

United States v. Constantine, 296 U.S. 287 (1935), 157, 163

United States v. Curtiss-Wright Export Corporation, 299 U.S. 304 (1936), 63, **80–82**, 209

United States v. Darby, 312 U.S. 100 (1941), 106, 114, 121, 126, **129–31**, 132, 135

United States v. Doremus, 249 U.S. 86 (1919), 157, 159, 161, 163

United States v. E. C. Knight Co., 156 U.S. 1 (1895), 105, **119–21**, 128, 132

United States v. Germaine, 9 Otto 508 (1879), 91

United States v. Guest, 383 U.S. 745 (1966), 329

United States v. Johnson, 383 U.S. 169 (1966), 72

United States v. Kahriger, 345 U.S. 22 (1953), 157

United States v. Leon, 468 U.S. 897 (1984), 236, **259–62**

United States v. Marigold, 9 Howard 565 (1850), 50

United States v. Midwest Oil Co., 236 U.S. 459 (1915), 80

United States v. Montgomery County Board of Education, 395 U.S. 225 (1969), 306

United States v. Nixon, 418 U.S. 683 (1974), 10, 60, 63, 68–69, **82–84**, 97

United States v. O'Brien, 391 U.S. 367 (1968), 192, 201–3

United States v. Perkins, 116 U.S. 483 (1886), 87

United States v. Richardson, 418 U.S. 166 (1974), 16, 152, 155

United States v. Sokolow, 490 U.S. 1 (1989), 254

United States v. Wade, 388 U.S. 218 (1967), 268

United Transportation Union v. Long Island R. Co., 455 U.S. 678 (1982), 138, 140

Valley Forge Christian College v. Americans United for Separation of Church and State, Inc., 454 U.S. 464 (1982), 155

Veazie Bank v. Fenno, 8 Wallace 533 (1869), 50, 150, 159

Wallace v. Jaffree, 472 U.S. 38 (1985), 169, 177, 179, 182

Warden v. Hayden, 387 U.S. 294 (1967), 251–52, 259

Washington v. Harper, 494 U.S. 210 (1990), 349

Watkins v. United States, 354 U.S. 178 (1957), 31, 53, 197, **225–28**, 231–32

Webster v. Reproductive Health Services, 492 U.S. 490 (1989), 287, 338, **339–43**

Weeks v. United States, 232 U.S. 383 (1914), 236, 259, 262

Wesberry v. Sanders, 376 U.S. 1 (1964), 68, 286, 322, 324

West Coast Hotel Company v. Parrish, 300 U.S. 379 (1937), 20, 29, 31, 38, 40, **43–45**, 55, 56, 130–31

West Virginia State Board of Education v. Barnette, 319 U.S. 624 (1943), 170–71, **182–84**, 189, 203, 257

Whipple v. Martinson, 256 U.S. 41 (1921), 269

Whitley v. Albers, 475 U.S. 312 (1986), 279

Whitney v. California, 274 U.S. 357 (1927), 196, 199, **218–20**

Wickard v. Filburn, 317 U.S. 111 (1942), 106, 114, 121, 128, 130, 131–32, 135

Widmar v. Vincent, 454 U.S. 263 (1981), 175

Wiener v. United States, 357 U.S. 349 (1958), 64, 87, 94, 97

Williamson v. Lee Optical, 348 U.S. 483 (1955), 29

Wilson v. Black Bird Creek Marsh Co., 2 Peters 245 (1829), 119

Wisconsin v. Constantineau, 400 U.S. 433 (1971), 316

Wisconsin v. Yoder, 406 U.S. 205 (1972), 171, **187–89**

Wolf v. Colorado, 338 U.S. 25 (1949), 258–59

Wolman v. Walter, 433 U.S. 229 (1977), 168, 173

Woodson v. North Carolina, 428 U.S. 280 (1976), 238, 270, **271–73**, 276

Wygant v. Jackson Board of Education, 476 U.S. 267 (1986), 284, 309, 312, 319

Yates v. United States, 354 U.S. 298 (1957), 196, 223

Young v. American Mini Theatres, Inc., 427 U.S. 50 (1976), 195

Youngstown Sheet and Tube Co. v. Sawyer, 343 U.S. 579 (1952), 12, 62–63, **77–80**, 84, 100, 209

Zemel v. Rusk, 381 U.S. 1 (1965), 329

Zorach v. Clauson, 343 U.S. 306 (1952), 169, 171, **173–75**, 177